The Role of the Religious Sector in the Economy of Late Bronze Age Mycenaean Greece

Susan M. Lupack

BAR International Series 1858
2008

Published in 2016 by
BAR Publishing, Oxford

BAR International Series 1858

The Role of the Religious Sector in the Economy of Late Bronze Age Mycenaean Greece

ISBN 978 1 4073 0341 3

BAR Publishing is the trading name of British Archaeological Reports (Oxford) Ltd. British Archaeological Reports was first incorporated in 1974 to publish the BAR Series, International and British. In 1992 Hadrian Books Ltd became part of the BAR group. This volume was originally published by Archaeopress in conjunction with British Archaeological Reports (Oxford) Ltd / Hadrian Books Ltd, the Series principal publisher, in 2008. This present volume is published by BAR Publishing, 2016.

Printed in England

BAR
PUBLISHING

BAR titles are available from:

BAR Publishing
122 Banbury Rd, Oxford, OX2 7BP, UK
EMAIL info@barpublishing.com
PHONE +44 (0)1865 310431
FAX +44 (0)1865 316916
www.barpublishing.com

Table of Contents

Acknowledgments

This book is a revised version (rather heavily revised in some places, less so in others) of my doctoral thesis. For that reason I think it is fitting for the acknowledgments that accompanied the thesis to be included here. Nonetheless, I do have several people to thank who have helped in various ways in the production of this fuller version. First I want to express my overwhelming respect and admiration for John Killen, whose incredibly wide-ranging and always sensible work has been the foundation of many of my theories (even the ones that he may not agree with), and whose kindness and ever gracious nature marks him out as a true gentleman. I also want to give particular thanks to John Bennet and Lisa French, who have both always been unfailingly generous with their knowledge, material and constructive criticism, despite the busy nature of their own lives. To Francoise Rougemont, Marie Louise Nosch and Massimo Perna I want to express my thanks both for their professional help and for the warmth of their friendship. I also want to thank my EBAP co-directors, Bryan Burns and Brendan Burke, and our EBAP person who can do anything and everything, Camilla Mackay, for our happy and supportive collaboration. I would also like to thank Chris Carey, Amanda Cater and the rest of the Greek and Latin Department at University College London for the way they welcomed me into their community, and made it possible for me to pursue my research. My gratitude also goes to Jessica Trelogan who not only read through the entire manuscript, but also solved many technical problems that were totally beyond my ability to deal with. I must also thank INSTAP for their crucial support at various stages of this project.

The two newest additions to my life, my children Jude and Rose, must be mentioned here, although I cannot exactly thank them for helping with this book since they were actually the source of many delays in its publication! But I can thank them for helping me to find in myself the ability to focus on the work at hand and be extremely productive whenever I did get a few precious hours to work. (And for being so cute and loving.) Finally, my greatest feeling of gratitude and thanks goes to my husband of five years now, Terrence Moloney, for all the ways in which he supports me and my work, and for how he manages to make our life together such a happy one. My thesis was dedicated to my grandmother, Gertrude Gardner, in acknowledgement of her gentle wit and the loving foundation she gave me in my early years, but this present work can only be dedicated to Terrence. Thank you.

London, 2008

Dissertation Acknowledgments, November 2002:

Many individuals and institutions have helped me during the course of this project, and grateful thanks are due to them all. First I would like to thank the Fulbright Institute, the University of Texas at Austin, the American School of Classical Studies at Athens and the Program in Aegean Scripts and Prehistory at UT Austin for the financial support that made the pursuit of my work possible. The latter two of these also assisted me greatly through their wonderful libraries and research facilities.

My greatest thanks are due to Cynthia Shelmerdine, the chair of my committee, who was able to pull from me, through a combination of encouragement and aptly applied criticism, a work that I am now proud of. Particular thanks are also due to Tom Palaima, not only for contributing greatly to my dissertation, but also for encouraging me early on in my academic aspirations. I thank him for the supportive and friendly role that he has continued to play in my career. To the rest of my committee members, Paula Perlman, Jack Kroll, John Bennet, and Michael White, I give thanks for the guidance they've given me throughout my graduate career, as well as the time they took to read what turned out to be a rather lengthy text. Their astute comments have substantially improved this dissertation and will doubtless serve to improve my subsequent work.

Besides those on my committee, thanks should also go to Emmett Bennett, Jr., Pierre Carlier, Lisa French, Jack Davis, Vassilis Aravantinos, Sarah Morris, Stefan Hiller, Sigrid Deger-Jalkotzy, Joseph and Maria Shaw, Fred Cooper, Olga Krzyszkowska, Iphigenia Tournavitou, Eleni Konsolaki-Yannopoulou, John Camp, Ione Shear and Willie Coulson, both for academic assistance and personal kindnesses along the way.

I have been very fortunate to have been part of several academic communities while working on my dissertation, and there are many, many people who deserve my thanks. Here I am only able to mention a few of those. At my home institution of the University of Texas, I would like to thank my friends Susanne Hofstra, Trish Parker, Kathy Hall, Joann Gulizio, Kevin Pluta, Dimitri Nakassis, Stephie Nikoloudis, John Erler, Brice Ericson, Ken Mayer and Kris and Paul(!) Munoz-Vetter, both for the fun we had together and the emotional support they often gave me. Dimitri Nakassis also gets my undying gratitude for his bibliographic assistance, and Constanze Witt and Albert Prieto for their essential technical expertise. Special thanks also go to Andrew Riggsby for some very fine repasts. I have also been lucky to have made many friends in Athens who have helped me in various ways in my work: Brendan Burke, Bryan Burns, Wendy Closterman, Yannis Lolos, Camilla MacKay, Nick Popielski, Tristan Carter, Michael Boyd, and Amalia Kakissis. My warm gratitude also goes to several people at Brooklyn College: Donna Wilson and Christopher Barnes for their ever encouraging words, Roger Dunkle, Ed Harris, Hardy Hansen, and Ellen Koven for being so welcoming, and to the many Brooklyn College students who helped to make my time there so stimulating and just plain fun. In Tokyo I received help from Megumi Naoi, who not only gave me access to Keio University's resources, but also introduced me to a wide variety of different Japanese food types (and helped to decipher the menus!). And finally, to my friends of the PRAP project, Susanne Hofstra (again), Amanda Sutphin, Rob Schon, Bill and Betsy Parkinson, Mike Galaty and Joanne Murphy what else can I say but, "To all Mike's friends!"

I owe special thanks to my friend Karen Stamm for listening both in Greece and in New York to the details of my trials and travails, and to my family who, as in all my endeavors, has supported me and buoyed me up through the process of producing this work. My loving thanks go to my sister Joyce for all her phone calls and e-mails that kept me sane, my brother David for "Run to Dagoba, run to Dagoba!" and lunches at Pret-a-Manger, my mother Mary Gardner, who gave me the courage to go out and explore, and my father Stephen Lupack and my step-mother Kathy Lupack, who between them instilled in me a love of intellectual investigation. Thanks also go to my newest mother, Inara Moloney, and the rest of the Canadian crew for their caring interest in my work. And, finally, my especial gratitude goes to my very dear soon-to-be husband Terrence Moloney for his loving support and stalwart endurance during this project that seemed to go on forever. Without his dreams and plans for our future together, and his penchant for setting up adventures for us, the work would have been much heavier by far.

Thanks to you all!!!

List of Figures

CHAPTER I

Introduction

Linear B Literature Review and Discussion of the Mycenaean Economy

There is a great deal of evidence within the Linear B tablets that the administrations of the Mycenaean palaces took an interest in the religious aspect of their communities. Many tablets record the offerings that the palace sent to various deities and their shrines, and it is clear that there were numerous religious festivals in which the communities of the Mycenaean palaces, presumably with the *wanax* at their head, took part. However, the exact nature of the relationship between the palace and the religious sector is more difficult to discern, and has recently become a matter for debate among some Mycenologists. One of the key questions that has been raised is, how independent from the palatial administration were the sanctuaries? Were they governed entirely by the palace, and did the religious sphere amount to nothing more than a subsidiary branch of the palatial administration to be used and directed as the *wanax* saw fit? Or, were they run more autonomously by the religious personnel of each sanctuary? The answers to these questions depend to a large extent on whether we see the shrines as financially independent. For this reason I have been examining both the Linear B and the archaeological evidence to see what can be deduced concerning the role of the religious sector, meaning the sanctuaries and the personnel that made up the communities of those sanctuaries, played in the Late Bronze Age Mycenaean economy.[1] This investigation has also shed light on the social standing that religious personnel might have held within their communities as well as on the relative amounts of power, both economic and political, that the palatial and religious sectors wielded in respect to each other.

One of the most visible pieces of evidence concerning the economics of the religious sphere is found in the tablets that record the offerings that the palace sent to various gods and goddesses at their sanctuaries. The fact that the palaces made these offerings indicates, on the one hand, the value that they attached to fulfilling their ritual obligations. But the offerings also entailed an economic investment on the part of the palace, and from the point of view of the religious sphere, these offerings constituted a source of support (although the significance of this support is open to question). It seems that on occasion the palace sent somewhat costly, or at least showy, offerings. Tn 316, for instance, records the offering of several gold cups and human servants to several different deities at their respective sanctuaries.[2] The more typical offerings consist of perfumed oil (PY Fr and KN Fp, Fh), honey (KN Gg), and spices (KN Ga), all of which could have been used in cultic contexts. Several tablets, such as PY Un 2, Un 6, Un 718, and Un 853 record livestock, wine, cheese, and other foodstuffs that seem to have been destined for use in ritual sacrifices and communal ceremonial banquets, which themselves seem to have had a religious element.[3] Still other tablets, in particular the Pylos Fn series, show the palace sending what looks more like ordinary rations to the religious sphere (and perhaps also to secular recipients). Grain and figs are found on Fn 187 and grain on its own is recorded on Fn 50. The variety of goods that were sent to the sanctuaries has caused some speculation as to the purpose of the offerings.[4] Chadwick for instance asked, "Are they used for cult purposes or to support a priestly establishment?" The answer, as he proposed, is that the offerings were probably used both for the specific worship of the deities and for the support of the religious personnel who were attached to the sanctuaries.[5] But that support may not have actually amounted to much on a day-to-day basis. The goods listed on the Un tablets were designated to be used during specific festivals, and were probably consumed by the entire community, thereby diminishing the benefit for the religious personnel. Also, Killen has recently proposed that the allocations of grain sent to the religious sector in the Fn series was most likely meant to be used during specific festival periods, which could run for three or five days.[6] Thus it seems

[1] I do not mean by this that I am interested in investigating the ritualistic aspects of crafts and industries. On this topic see S. Blakely Westover, "Smelting and Sacrifice: Comparative Analysis of Greek and Near Eastern Cult Sites from the Late Bronze through the Classical Periods," in *Metals in Antiquity* (BAR International Series 792), S. Young, ed., Oxford University Press 1999, pp. 86-90.

[2] T.G. Palaima, "Kn02 – Tn 316," in *Floreant Studia Mycenaea, Acts of the 10th International Mycenological Colloquium held at the University of Salzburg*, S. Deger-Jalkotzy, S. Hiller, and O. Panagl, eds., Wien 1999, pp. 437-461; also see *idem*, "The Last Days of the Pylos Polity," in *Politeia: Society and State in the Aegean Bronze Age* (*Aegaeum* 12), R. Laffineur and W.-D. Niemeier, eds., Liège and Austin 1995, pp. 623-634.

[3] For discussions of these tablets and feasting see J.T. Killen, "Observations on the Thebes Sealings," in *Mykenaïka* (*BCH* Suppl. 25), J.-P. Olivier, ed., Athens 1992, pp. 365-380; *idem*, "Thebes Sealings, Knossos Tablets and Mycenaean State Banquets," *BICS* 39 (1994) 67-84; *idem*, "Thebes Sealings and Knossos Tablets," in *Atti e Memorie del Secondo Congresso Internazionale de Micenologia* (*Incunabula Graeca* 98), E. De Miro, L. Godart, and A. Sacconi, eds., Rome 1996, pp. 71-82. Also see Isaakidou, Halstead, Davis, and Stocker ("Burnt Animal Sacrifice at the Mycenaean 'Palace of Nestor', Pylos," *Antiquity* 76 (2002) 86-92) for a discussion of the faunal evidence of Pylos which shows that "feasting and sacrifice were integrally related in a manner similar to the ritual dining at historical Greek sanctuaries."

[4] J. Chadwick, "What Do We Know about Mycenaean Religion?" *Linear B: A 1984 Survey* (*BCILL* 26), A. Morpurgo Davies and Y. Duhoux, eds., Louvain-la-Neuve 1985, pp. 191-202; see p. 205. Also see R. Hägg "Mycenaean Religion: The Helladic and the Minoan Components" also in *Linear B: A 1984 Survey*, pp. 203-225; see p. 205.

[5] V. Aravantinos also recognized this fact in "Old and New Evidence for the Palatial Society of Mycenaean Thebes: An Outline," in *Politeia, Society and State in the Aegean Bronze Age*, Vol. II (*Aegaeum* 12), eds., R. Laffineur and W.-D. Niemeier, Liège and Austin 1995, pp. 613-622.

[6] J.T. Killen, "Religion at Pylos: The Evidence of the Fn Tablets," in *Potnia: Deities and Religion in the Aegean Bronze Age* (*Aegaeum* 22), R. Laffineur and R. Hägg, eds., Liège and Austin 2001, pp. 435-443.

unlikely that the sanctuaries could have derived a very significant portion of their support from the offerings sent to them by the palace. Bendall, who looked at this issue from the palace's point of view, has shown that the offerings did not actually constitute a very large part of the palace's economic budget.[7] She estimates that only 10% of the palace's economic resources were allocated to the religious sphere.[8] Thus it seems that while the palaces were interested in fulfilling their ritual obligations and in financing high-profile festivals (which probably served to enhance their own reputations), nevertheless they were probably not so concerned about providing the sanctuaries' personnel with their daily sustenance.

This is significant because some scholars have taken the fact that the palace sent offerings to the sanctuaries to indicate that the sanctuaries were under the direct control of the palaces. Hiller for example states,

> [The fact that the palace sends offerings] shows us that the power of the palatial administration, which controlled a vast part of the economy, also extended to the cultic sector. Besides the cult personnel of certain sacral institutions, a number of sanctuaries therefore were also subject to the palace and thus to the central organs of the state's administration.[9]

This reasoning, however, is somewhat faulty. It does not automatically follow that the provision of offerings to a religious institution means that the agent making the offering was necessarily in control of the recipient. And if we remove from the argument the assumption that is behind Hiller's statement that the offerings provided for the maintenance of the religious personnel, the argument is on even shakier ground. Rather, we may instead propose that the regularity of the palatial offerings implies that there was an ongoing relationship between the religious and secular spheres, one that probably held responsibilities and obligations on both sides.

The possibility that such a relationship existed between the two spheres will be important as we turn to the main focus of this work. My main interest lies in the more active role that the religious sector seems to take on in the Mycenaean economic system. Specifically I am interested in discussing the instances seen on the tablets where either deities or religious personnel (who are very often unambiguously identified by titles such as *i-je-re-ja*: 'priestess', *i-je-re-u*: 'priest', and *te-o-jo do-e-ro/-ra*: 'servant of the god') are shown to be associated with economically productive resources. I will therefore discuss the religious personnel who are associated with tracts of land in the Pylos Ep/Eb and En/Eo series, and the deities who hold flocks of sheep and fleeces in the Knossos D, Dl and Dp series. I will also discuss the involvement of the religious sector in industrial concerns, as represented by the Potnian bronzesmiths of the Pylos Jn bronze-working series, the religious textile workers of the Thebes Of tablets, and the Potnian unguent boiler of PY Un 267.1. The involvement of religious personnel in industrial activities also seems to be demonstrated by tablets found within the Northeast Building at Pylos, such as An 1281 and Ub 1318, and perhaps the Oi series found at Mycenae. These tablets seem to constitute evidence that the religious sanctuaries and their personnel played an active role within the Mycenaean economy, and that they were probably able not only to support themselves through their economic activities, but that they were also able to maintain some amount of financial independence from the palace. The financial independence may also have brought with it political influence both in relation to the palace and within their particular communities.

This is not the view of the religious sector that has always been held by Linear B scholars, although several have noticed and tried to explain the apparent association of the religious sector with economic activities. Ventris and Chadwick, for instance, mentioned in the first edition of *Documents in Mycenaean Greek*[10] that some personnel in Mycenaean workshops (such as the bronzesmiths in the Pylos Jn series and the female textile workers on KN G 820), several flocks of sheep on the Knossos Dl tablets, and land on PY Eq 213 were picked out as being different by being recorded with the adjectival form of the word Potnia: *po-ti-ni-ja-we-jo* or "Potnian."[11] They translate this designation as "of or belonging to Potnia."[12] (Potnia itself can be translated literally as "Mistress," but it is generally thought to refer to one of the major goddesses (or to several individual female deities) of Mycenaean Greece.[13]) But besides a couple of suggestions made with reference to whichever particular series of tablets

---

[7] L. Bendall, "The Economics of Potnia in the Linear B Documents: Palatial Support for Mycenaean Religion," in *Potnia: Deities and Religion in the Aegean Bronze Age* (*Aegaeum* 22), R. Laffineur and R. Hägg, eds., Liège and Austin 2001, pp. 446-452.

[8] Bendall 2001, p. 449.

[9] S. Hiller, "Mykenische Heiligtümer: Das Zeugnis der Linear B-Texte," in *Sanctuaries and Cults in the Aegean Bronze Age*, R. Hägg and N. Marinatos, eds., Stockholm 1981, pp. 95-126; see p. 95. (My translation here and throughout.)

[10] M. Ventris and J. Chadwick, *Documents in Mycenaean Greek*, Cambridge University Press 1956; second edition, 1973, see p. 434; hereafter *Docs²*.

[11] For a discussion of the form of *po-ti-ni-ja-we-jo* see C.J. Ruijgh, "A propos de Myc. *po-ti-ni-ja-we-jo*," in *SMEA* 4 (*Incunabula Graeca* 23), Rome 1967, pp. 40-52.

[12] *Docs²*, p. 574. For instance, on p. 354 when discussing what it might mean when used within the Pylos Jn series to refer to a group of bronzesmiths, they suggested that it described "a class of persons specially subservient to Athena? or to the queen rather than the king?"

[13] For discussions of Potnia see J. Chadwick, "Potnia" *Minos* 5 (1957) 117-129. M. Gérard-Rousseau, *Les Mentions Religieuses dans les Tablettes Myceniennes*, Rome 1968, pp. 188-191. J.C. van Leuven, "Mycenaean Goddesses Called *Potnia*," *Kadmos* 18 (1979) 122-129. C. Boëlle, "*Po-ti-ni-ja* à Mycènes," *Minos* 27-28 (1992-1993) 283-301. And now see generally the *Aegaeum* volume dedicated to Potnia and associated religious topics: *Potnia: Deities and Religion in the Aegean Bronze Age* (*Aegaeum* 22), R. Laffineur and R. Hägg, eds., Liège and Austin 2001. I will briefly state here that I consider any reference to Potnia to indicate that we are dealing with the religious sphere. It has been suggested to me by Rehak (personal communication, December 1994) that in some cases the personage who was referred to on the tablets was actually the priestess of Potnia instead of the goddess herself. The term 'Potnia' then may have been used as a shorthand for 'the priestess of Potnia'. This makes sense particularly in cases where the action of a person rather than a deity would be expected.

they were discussing, Ventris and Chadwick left further speculation as to what the appearance of the epithet *po-ti-ni-ja-we-jo* might mean for our understanding of religion's role in Mycenaean economics for other scholars to consider.

Leonard Palmer, on the other hand, took a great interest in this topic and was keen to demonstrate the significant role that the religious sector played in the Mycenaean economy. Palmer showed that in many instances religion and industrial associations were found together on the same tablets, and instead of trying to discount one of those seemingly contradictory types of information in favor of the other, he tried to craft a picture of Mycenaean society that would account for the association of the two.[14] However, in the picture that he creates, the religious sector plays a more prominent part in both the economy and in Mycenaean society than the evidence of the tablets warrants.[15] Palmer's overall view is that the Mycenaean economy should be characterized as a "temple economy."[16] He says, "The picture which emerges is quite unlike that of Homer's Mycenae: it resembles rather the temple economy of oriental kingdoms with god-kings acting as stewards and vicars of the goddess."[17] In some instances Palmer promotes his view by elevating the religious sector's economic holdings to a level that cannot have been actually attained. For instance, he mentions in his summary of the Mycenaean economy that, "The CATTLE tablets likewise reveal the *wanax* along with the chief religious personages as owners of extensive herds scattered over the two provinces of the kingdom."[18] While it is true that the religious sector held flocks of sheep and one of pigs, the number of those flocks that are documented by the Linear B tablets (possibly 11) is very small compared to the numerous holdings of the palaces, and therefore certainly do not merit Palmer's implication that the two spheres were on the same level. Palmer goes on to say, "The BRONZE tablets show industrial establishments in full activity, the smiths being divided into *po-ti-ni-ja-we-jo* and secular..." Again, Palmer implies that the religious sector was on a level with the palace, but the tablets record that only 19 of nearly 300 bronzesmiths were designated as *po-ti-ni-ja-we-jo*. To provide a third example, when discussing the land held by religious personages Palmer says,

> The picture adumbrated in the above texts is quite unlike anything in the Hellas of post-Mycenaean times. It recalls rather the theocratic states like that of the temple of Olba, ... [where] the high priests and their colleagues continued to be lords and masters of all the inhabitants of the temple itself, the temple town, and the temple villages.[19]

As we will see in the chapter on land tenure, the number of religious personages who held land was quite significant, but there were large numbers of secular landholders as well, and more to the point, no real evidence that it was the sanctuary that owned any of the land.[20]

Palmer's exaggerated view of the religious sector's importance in the Mycenaean economy caused, somewhat understandably, a negative reaction to the entirety of his work on the religious sector. And, consequently, it also caused a reaction among Mycenologists against crediting the religious sector with any role in the Mycenaean economy. The evidence that sanctuaries and religious persons did participate in the economy was either downplayed or simply not addressed. Another factor at work here was the overall view of many scholars that the various palatial administrations were very much in control of all the economic activities that went on in their realms.

This view is seen, for example, in Hiller's seminal article on the Linear B evidence for Mycenaean sanctuaries.[21] Hiller's focus in this article was not the economic aspect of the sanctuaries; rather he was trying to answer questions such as, "What role did [the shrines] play in the political system? What was, in detail, their relation to the palace?"[22] But of course the issue of the religious sector's involvement in economic activities comes up in the course of his investigating the religious sector's social standing. For instance, when looking at the Theban Of series, in which deities and other personages associated with the religious sphere receive allocations of wool, he accepts the idea (first proposed by Chadwick[23]) that deities presided over *oikoi*, which he defines as industrial complexes that also had a sacred character.[24] Hiller also uses this concept to explain the economic activities of **ma-ri-ne-u* and *me-za-na* whom he accepts as deities, and many other instances where economic resources are associated with deities (such as the flocks of sheep and pigs found on PY Cc 665 that are associated with Potnia, the Potnian bronzesmiths of PY Jn 310.14 and Jn 431.16, the references to Potnia on PY An 1281 where she is allocated workers, and the flocks that are held by Potnia and Hermes in the Knossos D and Dl series).[25] The institution of the *oikos*, he says, "in a way seems to be a Mycenaean parallel to the oriental institution of the so-called 'temple economy'."[26] But he hastens to say that the *oikos* system makes up only a part of the Mycenaean

[14] See for example his interesting discussion on the connections between Pylian tablets An 1281, Fn 50, and Fn 187 in L.R. Palmer, *The Interpretation of Mycenaean Greek Texts*, Oxford University Press 1963, pp. 225-233.

[15] Palmer 1963, p. 95.

[16] Palmer 1963, pp. 95 and 220-221. Also see pp. 137, 230, 278, 280 and 482.

[17] Palmer 1963, p. 95.

[18] Palmer 1963, p. 95.

[19] Palmer 1963, pp. 220-221.

[20] I should add here that I do think the sanctuaries held their own land, but not the land recorded by the palace scribes, which was the evidence Palmer was using for his theories.

[21] Hiller 1981, pp. 95-126.

[22] Hiller 1981, p. 95.

[23] J. Chadwick, *The Thebes Tablets II, Minos Suppl.* 4, 1975; see p. 89.

[24] Hiller 1981, p. 103. The issues surrounding the Mycenaean *oikos* will be taken up in detail in Chapter 5.

[25] Hiller 1981, pp. 99-102, 110, and 114-115.

[26] Hiller 1981, p. 103.

economic organization, and that the production branch was under the control of the palatial administration.[27] Thus Hiller does not use the phrase "temple economy" in the same way that Palmer does. Hiller simply recognizes that sanctuaries were associated with economic resources, although he thought that they were ultimately under palatial control, whereas Palmer promoted the "temple economy" as one of the main economic forces in Mycenaean society.

In the end, when Hiller summarizes his thinking on the position the sanctuaries held in relation to the palace, he concludes that there were two types of sanctuaries, those that were administered by the palace and those that were independent of the palace.[28] He actually says, logically, although in contradiction to his initial statement on the topic, that the fact that the palace sent offerings to a sanctuary does not have to indicate *in every case* that the sanctuary was under the direction of the palace, although he does not say why he maintains that in some cases (in particular for *Pa-ki-ja-ne*) we should still take the palace's control for granted. And he makes it clear that he would include sanctuaries with *oikos* institutions in the category that was controlled by the palatial administration. He states,

> ...at least in the case of certain deities and their shrines – those in the scope of an oikos-institution, the shrine, together with the owner and the personnel of the oikos, was administered by the palace .... The cult personnel associated with these temple goods and their sanctuaries lay under the centralized control of the state (as is especially comprehensible for *pa-ki-ja-na*), and this accordingly also extends to ownership and economic output.[29]

Thus, Hiller recognizes that the members of the religious sector were involved in economic activities, but at the same time he feels it necessary to posit that they were controlled by the palace's economic system.

Chadwick, in his review of Mycenaean religious texts, also recognizes that industrial establishments "were sometimes under the control of a priesthood, or at least closely linked to the cult of a particular deity." But Chadwick comes to the conclusion that, "The concentration of records in palaces clearly demonstrates that the secular power was dominant over the religious."[30] It seems that Chadwick is making an implicit comparison with some Near Eastern societies where economic records are found in temples. He implies that since such records are not found in temples within the Mycenaean context then it is safe to say that the religious sector must not have been in control of their own economic resources. However, given the limited use of the Linear B texts,[31] I would think it is possible that the religious sector may have had their own resources but did not find it necessary to keep written records in the same way as the palaces did.

Killen, in his seminal article on Mycenaean economy and society, also recognizes that the industrial activities associated with the names of divinities are "most plausibly understood as references to workgroups and workshops 'owned' by these divinities."[32] But his understanding of their place in the Mycenaean economy is conditioned by his view of Mycenaean society as a whole and the position of the palace within it. Killen asserted (following Finley's conception of the character of the Mycenaean state[33]) that the best comparisons we have for Mycenaean society are to be found in the Near East.[34] Killen accepts that for the Mycenaean economy, as was thought to be the case at the time for the economies of the Near East, "the key role in the movement of goods and the employment of labour was played, not by a market or money, but by a central redistributive agent...," and in Mycenaean society, Killen saw that agent as the palace.[35] All other aspects of the economy were, therefore, thought to have been subordinated to the central agent, and no other economic force was considered to have had any power in relation to the palace.[36] Thus, even in cases where economically productive resources, such as tracts of land and sheep, were recorded against the names of private individuals (called "collectors"[37]), Killen pictured these assets as having been primarily owned and managed by the palace.[38] Furthermore, after noting that the palace was involved in "a wide variety of other activities, such as military and religious affairs" he states,

> Once we are faced with this evidence, it becomes in my view extremely difficult to avoid the conclusion that the role which the palaces played in the economy of Mycenaean estates

[27] Hiller 1981, p. 103. Hiller does not give a reason for this conclusion. He simply says that this "...does not need of course to be explained here in detail..."
[28] Hiller 1981, pp. 116-117.
[29] Hiller 1981, p. 116.
[30] Chadwick 1985, p. 200.

[31] K. Pluta,"Mycenaean Literate Administration," Talk presented at the 12th International Mycenological Colloquium held in Rome, Italy, 20-25 February 2006 discussed how overwhelmingly verbal the administration of economic matters must have been in Mycenaean society.
[32] J.T. Killen, "The Linear B Tablets and the Mycenaean Economy," in *Linear B: A 1984 Survey* (*BCILL* 26), A. Morpurgo Davies and Y. Duhoux, eds., Louvain-la-Neuve 1985, pp. 241-305; see p. 295.
[33] M.I. Finley, "The Mycenaean Tablets and Economic History," *Economic History Review* 10 (1957) 128-141. Finley of course was influenced by Polanyi and those scholars who adopted his substantivist view of ancient economies. See B. L. Sjöberg, *Asine and the Argolid in the Late Helladic III Period: A Socio-economic Study*, BAR International Series 2004, pp. 7-8 for a review of substantivist theories and their influence on the traditionally held view of Mycenaean economy and society. But also see P. deFidio, "Centralization and its Limits in the Mycenaean Palatial System, in *Economy and Politics in the Mycenaean Palace States*, S. Voutsaki and J. Killen, eds., Cambridge University Press 2001, pp. 15-24; p. 15, n. 3 for a reminder that while Polanyi "made a deep impression" on Finley, he nevertheless "distanc[ed] himself from all of Polanyi's formal conclusions."
[34] Killen 1985, p. 241.
[35] Killen 1985, pp. 241-242.
[36] Killen 1985, pp. 288 and 290-291.
[37] The status of the "collectors" within Mycenaean society will be discussed at length in Chapter 5.
[38] Killen 1985, pp. 245, 252.

> was not merely significant, but central and dominant.[39]

It is no surprise then that Killen sees the religious sector, like the rest of the constituents of Mycenaean society, as subject to the palace. He says that, "it would be dangerous to assume that there was a fundamental and clear-cut distinction in the Mycenaean economy between a 'religious' sector and the secular section represented by the palace."[40]

Aravantinos comes to similar conclusions in his analysis of the relationship between the Mycenaean sanctuaries and the secular power of the *wanax*. He takes the position that,

> ...the movement of goods and personnel in the texts from the "sacred" areas seems to indicate the central political power (palaces) as the only significant economic and administrative factor in the kingdom. During the Mycenaean period, economy, industry, trade and religion as well as other aspects of the economic, social and cultural life were most probably controlled and monitored by the palace.[41]

He concludes that the sanctuaries were dependent on the palace for their foodstuffs and raw materials,[42] and that religious authority had been incorporated into the palace's system of governance.[43] This way of thinking is found in many scholars' work. For instance, deFidio, even though she is at pains to point out that we do not really know the palace's "actual range of operation," nonetheless says, "[The palace] made offerings to the divinities as a form of ideological control, which was intended to foster social harmony and the consensus of its subjects."[44] Thus, as Sjöberg also shows in detail, the idea that the palaces were in control of all the economic transactions that took place within the Mycenaean economy was usually taken as a given in the majority of the work dealing with Late Helladic Mycenaean society.[45]

The conclusions these scholars came to are not entirely unreasonable considering the amount of evidence demonstrating the involvement of the palace in economic affairs. Also, most likely they are not incorrect in concluding that the palace was the most important single economic force in the realm. Recently, Voutsaki has argued, based on the distribution of prestige objects in mortuary and settlement contexts, that the elites of the palatial centers "exerted strict control over the production, circulation and consumption of prestige artifacts."[46] She contends that the Mycenaean elite did this as part of their strategy to create status and alliances through asymmetric gift exchange and conspicuous consumption. I find theories such as Voutsaki's concerning the elite's use of prestige goods to acquire and maintain control over their realms rather convincing.[47] However, I also think that there were elements of the economy that the palace did not have the wherewithal or perhaps even the desire to control, and I think the religious sector was one of those elements. Indeed, I think the relationship between the palatial elite and those who held upper positions in the sanctuaries must have been more complicated and varied (not all sanctuaries were as intimately involved with the palace at Pylos as *Pa-ki-ja-ne*) than the statements quoted above would allow for. And this is because I take the view, which I hope to show the value of in the course of this work, that the religious sphere did maintain control over their own resources, and therefore, that they constituted an economic force within their communities.

Several other Linear B scholars beside myself have also been reconsidering the position of the palace in the Mycenaean economy. The resulting general change in outlook has been underpinned (at least partially) by revisions to economic theory concerning the Near East and the ancient world in general.[48] Aubert, for instance, dismisses the idea that any ancient culture could have been so totalitarian as to have controlled every aspect of a society's economy:

> Thus, the organization of production, agricultural or not, depends at all times on the need and/or the willingness of 'entrepreneurs' to reach a level of productivity that would make their effort worthwhile: only an economic system like those established by some Communist regimes in the twentieth century would be able to subordinate economic rationalism to social priorities, an endeavour that

---

39 Killen 1985, p. 255.

40 Killen 1985, pp. 288-289.

41 V. Aravantinos, "Santuari e Palazzo: Appunti sui rapporti economico-amministrativi tra la sfera del culto e il potere politico in eta micenea," *Scienze dell'Antichita* 3-4 (1989-1990) 243-261; see pp. 260-261 (the quote is taken from the English summary; see pp. 259-260 for the same conclusions in Italian).

42 Aravantinos 1989-1990, p. 261.

43 V. Aravantinos, "Old and New Evidence for the Palatial Society of Mycenaean Thebes: An Outline," in *Politeia: Society and State in the Aegean Bronze Age* (*Aegaeum* 12), R. Laffineur and W.-D. Niemeier, eds., Liège and Austin 1995, pp. 613-622; see p. 618.

44 DeFidio 2001, pp. 17-18.

45 Sjöberg 2004, pp. 3-9.

46 S. Voutsaki, "Economic Control, Power and Prestige in the Mycenaean World: The Archaeological Evidence," in *Economy and Politics in the Mycenaean Palace States*, S. Voutsaki and J. Killen, eds., Cambridge University Press 2001, pp. 195-213.

47 And Killen's work on the An tablets supports her proposal by showing that the palatial elite recruited craftsmen from their home villages for service at Pylos (or some other central location) in order to produce their prestige goods ("Conscription and Corvée at Mycenaean Pylos," in *Fiscality in Mycenaean and Near Eastern Economies*, M. Perna, ed., Napoli 2006, pp. 73-87).

48 See in particular Chapter 1 in J.G. Manning and I. Morris, *The Ancient Economy: Evidence and Models*, Stanford University Press 2005 for full bibliography on the topic and for the most recent review of how ancient historians have handled economic issues. Also see M. Silver, *Economic Structures of Antiquity*, Greenwood Press 1995; *idem*, *Economic Structures of the Ancient Near East*, Croom Helm 1985. For a recent review of the varied natures of three different Near Eastern economies see N. Postgate, "System and Style in Three Near Eastern Bureaucracies," in *Economy and Politics in the Mycenaean Palace States*, S. Voutsaki and J. Killen, eds., Cambridge 2001, pp. 181-194.

> met limited success and saw the development of parallel economies (black market) ruled by profit.[49]

And Meijer (in his discussion concerning ancient Near Eastern economies) instead stresses the idea that palaces, as important as they may have been in economic matters, can be seen as "participants" in the economy rather than as the ultimate controllers that they have traditionally been seen as. He says that the "… general or "local" economy is an indispensable background for the elite economy, and therefore that "elite" economy cannot be separated from the "local" economy. They are both participants in the economy."[50] Warburton, who demonstrates that even in ancient Egypt (whose economic system is often cited as the best model case for a redistributionist economy) "there is no reason to believe that any form of 'redistribution' played a role in the system."[51] He therefore urges us to dispense with classifications of ancient economies as "redistributive" since it is clear that they were not primarily functioning in a way consistent with that label.

Such revisionist thinking on ancient economy has gone hand-in-hand with a movement among Mycenologists to read the Linear B tablets with a more open-minded outlook. One approach that has been particularly productive has been to look not only for the aspects of the economy that the palace recorded in detail, but also those areas which the palatial scribes did not record. The "gaps" found in the textual evidence, when paired with contemporaneous archaeological material, indicate that the palace was not producing certain goods within its own well-documented systems. In conjunction with this approach, scholars have also been able to recognize more clearly the bits of evidence found within the tablets that can be interpreted as glimmers of the extra-palatial economy interacting with the palatial one. The result of looking at the textual and archaeological evidence in this way has been to demonstrate that the palaces did not have such a controlling monopoly over all the industries and people surrounding their territories as was once thought to have been the case.

Halstead has been a major force in the reevaluation of the Mycenaean economy. In a series of articles he has shown that there were several types of resources that the palace must have obtained in some way, since they appear in the archaeological records of Bronze Age sites, but which, since they do not appear on the tablets, were most likely acquired through means other than one of the palace's closely managed systems (i.e., not through its taxation or *ta-ra-si-ja*[52] systems, or from workers who were wholly dependent on the palace).[53] Halstead points out, for instance, that certain foodstuffs like fruits, walnuts, chestnuts, millet, beans, lentils, vetch, and peas have been found at various sites (although not all of these are attested at every site), but that they are not mentioned on the tablets.[54] Halstead also points out that the importation of the raw materials used in the production of elite goods, such as ivory and blue-glass, is not mentioned in the tablets, although we do find ivory at palatial sites and blue-glass craftsmen in the tablets (*ku-wa-no-wo-ko-i* on e.g. MY Oi 701.7). To give a third example, Halstead has found that the palace's wool flocks must have been replenished from the non-palatial sector, while animals culled from the palatial flocks, which would have amounted to 10-12,000 sheep a year (a number that would have far exceeded the needs of the palace itself) were most likely given out to the non-palatial sector.[55] Halstead also, as others have done,[56] points out that there is some indication on the tablets that the palace actually "bought" certain items, such as the imported commodity alum (on PY An 35 and Un 443), with wool and other common commodities. He suggests that the rarity of such "purchase" records "should not be taken as an indication that such transactions were exceptional."[57] Taken together, Halstead thinks that these "unrecorded flows of commodities," may indicate that the palace engaged in "irregular, non-obligatory" and "opportunistic" transactions.[58] And he says that the fact that such transactions were possible, suggests that "a wide range of agricultural and craft production took place outside palatial control."[59] Hence he concludes,

> The palaces exercised only partial control over economic activity within their territories: the palaces directly controlled only a small fraction of the total labour force, palatial crop production was concentrated in the vicinity of major centres and sub-centres, and several commodities were only produced in the non-palatial sector.

[49] J.-J. Aubert, "The Fourth Factor: Managing non-agricultural production in the Roman world," in *Economies beyond Agriculture in the Classical World*, D. Mattingly and J. Salmon, eds., Routledge 2001, pp. 90-111; see p. 90.

[50] D. Meijer, "Polanyi, Markets and Ancient Mesopotamia and Syria," in *Fiscality in Mycenaean and Near Eastern Economies*, M. Perna, ed., Napoli 2006, pp. 123-131; see p. 126.

[51] D.A. Warburton, "The Egyptian Example and the Macroeconomic Implications," in *Fiscality in Mycenaean and Near Eastern Economies*, M. Perna, ed., Napoli 2006, pp. 255-266; see p. 262.

[52] In the *ta-ra-si-ja* system raw materials, such as wool or metal, were given out to workers who presumably were expected to return finished products to the palace.

[53] P. Halstead, "On Redistribution and the Origin of Minoan-Mycenaean Palatial Economies," in *Problems in Greek Prehistory*, E.B. French and K.A. Wardle, eds., Bristol Classical Press 1988, pp. 519-530; *idem*, "Agriculture in the Bronze Age Aegean: Towards a Model of Palatial Economy," in *Agriculture in Ancient Greece*, B. Wells, ed., Stockholm 1992, pp. 105-117; *idem*, "The Mycenaean Palatial Economy: Making the Most of the Gaps in the Evidence," *Proceedings of the Cambridge Philological Society* 38 (1992) 57-86; *idem*, "Towards a Model of Mycenaean Palatial Mobilization," in *Rethinking Mycenaean Palaces: New Interpretations of an Old Idea*, M.L. Galaty and W.A. Parkinson, eds., The Cotsen Institute of Archaeology at UCLA 1999, pp. 35-47.

[54] Halstead 1990, p. 107. Also see R. Palmer, "Perishable Goods in Mycenaean Texts," *Floreant Studia Mycenaea*, Acts of the 10th International Mycenological Colloquium held at the University of Salzburg, S. Deger-Jalkotzy, S. Hiller, and O. Panagl, eds., Wien 1999, pp. 463-485.

[55] See Halstead 1992, pp. 64-68 for an overview of all these examples.

[56] Killen 1985, p. 265. C.W. Shelmerdine, "Industrial Activity at Pylos," in *Tractata Mycenaea*, P. Ilievski and L. Crepajac, eds., Skopje 1987, pp. 333-342; see p. 337.

[57] Halstead 1992, p. 71.

[58] Halstead 1992, pp. 64 and 70.

[59] Halstead 1992, p. 64.

> Furthermore, exchange rather than redistribution seems to have been the basis on which many goods and services moved between the palatial and non-palatial sectors (and within the latter).[60]

Other scholars have also found that production activities must have been going on that were not necessarily controlled or even managed by the palatial administration. For instance, Galaty's analysis of the ceramic finds of the palace at Pylos has led him to conclude "with a high degree of probability" that "the Pylian LH IIIB ceramic industry was not centrally located and controlled."[61] This is because the palace's coarsewares in particular show significant variations in their chemical make-up, variations which can be traced to clays found in different regions of Messenia. Galaty found three main clay compositions: type 1a came from an area north of (but perhaps near to) the palace, while 1b was strongly associated with the southern area of Messenia, and 1c was classified as 'central' – also perhaps near to the palace.[62] Thus, "the bulk of utilitarian vessels were produced by at least three different craftsmen, workshops, or communities."[63] Galaty therefore proposes that the acquisition of such pots by the palace would have been "informal and irregular."[64] Whitelaw came to a similar conclusion after finding that different areas of the palace were stocked with distinct types of pottery.[65] Whitelaw argues that the different fabrics and intended uses of the palace's ceramic assemblages, coupled with the lack of Linear B documentation for the acquisition of pottery (which he says could indicate that records concerning the receipt of pottery were more ephemeral than those made up for goods that were under more centralized management), suggests that "the stocks of vessels were maintained independently" ... "and that the vessels entered the palace via different administrative routes."[66]

Galaty also found that the finewares, predominant among them of course being kylikes, were probably mass-produced and derived from "one large pottery workshop."[67] He points out that the acquisition of the kylikes was probably important to the elite of the palace, who most likely used them "in the political and religious context of animal sacrifice and feasting, which included the ritualized drinking of alcoholic beverages, most probably wine."[68] The ritual of feasting and drinking wine together at the palace probably served several important functions. Palaima has stressed that one of the prime functions was to spotlight the religious role of the *wanax*.[69] Another was to demonstrate to Mycenaean society at large the power held by the *wanax*, and a third was to reinforce the alliances the *wanax* had made with the regional officials who were invited to the feast.[70] The administration therefore would have wanted to ensure a regular supply of these kylikes, and in order to do that they would have focused their attention on one (or two) reliable workshops. Galaty also proposes that the single royal (*wa-na-ka-te-ro*) potter found on PY Eo 371.A (En 467.5) may represent the producer of the palace's finewares and that, since he also holds land, he was actually an independent entrepreneur rather than a servant who was dependent on the palace.[71] The honorary title of "royal" would then indicate his elevated status. Knappett basically agrees with this analysis and adds, "the 'royal' epithet was bestowed upon what was otherwise an independent producer, making pots for the wider populace within a market-like situation. In return for what may have resembled a form of 'royal seal of approval', a potter would have been expected to provide for palatial needs from time to time."[72]

Whitelaw's calculations concerning the palace's relative consumption of ceramics compared with that of the town of Pylos, and then also the entire region of Messenia underline the fact that potters would have only been required (or asked) to work for the palace from "time to time." He found that while the palace would have needed "perhaps 12,000 vessels a year," the community at Pylos would have used upwards of 75,000 vessels and the entire region could have required 612,500 to 1,225,000. To put

[60] Halstead 1992, pp. 72-73.

[61] M.L. Galaty, "Wealth Ceramics, Staple Ceramics: Pots and the Mycenaean Palaces," in *Rethinking Mycenaean Palaces: New Interpretations of an Old Idea*, M.L. Galaty and W.A. Parkinson, eds., The Cotsen Institute of Archaeology at UCLA 1999b, pp. 49-59; see p. 55; *idem*, *Nestor's Wine Cups*, British Archaeological Reports 1999a, p. 38.

[62] Galaty 1999a, pp. 69-70.

[63] Galaty 1999a, p. 69.

[64] Galaty 1999a, p. 75.

[65] T. Whitelaw, "Reading between the Tablets: Assessing Mycenaean Palatial Involvement in Ceramic Production and Consumption," in *Economy and Politics in the Mycenaean Palace States*, S. Voutsaki and J. Killen, eds., Cambridge 2001, pp. 50-79.

[66] Whitelaw 2001, p. 75. In contrast with Galaty, Whitelaw proposed that the pottery was acquired locally from one or two potters, but this proposal was made without the benefit of Galaty's information concerning the variety of fabrics found within the palace.

[67] Galaty 1999b, pp. 56-57.

[68] Galaty 1999a, p. 8. See J.C. Wright, "Empty Cups and Empty Jugs: The Social Role of Wine in Minoan and Mycenaean Societies," in *The Origins and Ancient History of Wine*, P.E. McGovern, S.J. Fleming and S.H. Katz, eds., Gordon and Breach Publishers1995a, pp. 287-309; p. 303 for his proposal that kylikes were specifically used for the consumption of wine at ceremonial banquets.

[69] T.G. Palaima, "The Nature of the Mycenaean *Wanax*: Non-Indo-European Origins and Priestly Functions," in *The Role of the Ruler in the Prehistoric Aegean* (*Aegaeum* 11), P. Rehak, ed., Liège and UT-PASP 1995b, pp. 119-139, pp. 130-131. Also see L.R. McCallum, *Decorative Program in the Mycenaean Palace of Pylos: The Megaron Frescoes*, Ph.D. Dissertation, University of Pennsylvania 1987.

[70] See J. Davis and J. Bennet, "Making Mycenaeans: Warfare, Territorial Expansion, and Representations of the Other in the Pylian Kingdom," in *Polemos: Warfare in the Aegean Bronze Age*, R. Laffineur, ed., Liège 1999, pp. 105-120 for a discussion of the fresco depicting a battle between Mycenaeans and barbarian warriors found in Hall 64 of the Palace of Nestor and its role in impressing the feasting guests who probably consisted of "the elite of the entire kingdom controlled by the Palace of Nestor in the 13th century B.C." (p. 111). Also see Wright 1995a for a discussion of the sociopolitical significance of the communal drinking and feasting ceremonies.

[71] Galaty 1999b, p. 57; *idem* 1999a, pp. 28, 77-78. Galaty also proposes (1999a, p. 78) that there could have been a "third-party agent [involved] in the distribution of Messenian finewares" who could have been a "professional merchant or cartel." Perhaps then the royal potter was this agent?

[72] C. Knappett, "Overseen or Overlooked? Ceramic Production in a Mycenaean Palatial System," in *Economy and Politics in the Mycenaean Palace States*, S. Voutsaki and J. Killen, eds., Cambridge 2001, pp. 80-95; see pp. 94-95.

that in more human terms, Whitelaw converted these numbers into the work hours necessary to produce the pots and found that the ceramic needs of the palace could have been fulfilled by only one or two full-time potters, while the kingdom as a whole would have needed 104 to 208 potters. These numbers show that, "the palace, while almost certainly the single most important consumer within the local region, was not necessarily determining or driving the demand for pottery production..." Rather, "in the context of the kingdom as a whole, the palace was, quantitatively, an insignificant player responsible for 1-2% of the ceramics consumed annually."[73] Galaty concludes that "in Late Helladic IIIB Pylos, the state center does not appear to have centralized and administered the production and redistribution of pots; rather ... patterns of ceramic distribution suggest localized exchanges of coarseware pottery, perhaps in the context of a system of reciprocal or market exchanges, and the professional merchandising of finewares."[74] Thus, Galaty's results concerning the provenance of the palace's pottery, coupled with Whitelaw's quantification of the palace's position in the region's ceramic industry, "appear to document the existence of an independent and parallel local economy that only superficially intersected with the palace economy."[75]

Parkinson presents similar conclusions concerning the relation of the obsidian blade industry to the palatial economy.[76] As a result of his analysis of the lithics data collected by the Pylos Regional Archaeological Project (PRAP) from the sites in Messenia that surround the palace at Pylos, Parkinson concludes that, "the production and distribution of obsidian blades in southwestern Messenia operated beyond the scope of the central authority."[77] His conclusion is based on the fact that although significant quantities of obsidian do appear at the palace, there is very little evidence at Pylos for the production of these blades. In fact, although 60-90% of the obsidian assemblages at the other Late Bronze Age sites in the area consisted of obsidian blades, the debitage that would have resulted from their production was found at only one site, called Romanou, which is located near the coast southwest of the Englianos ridge. Parkinson therefore thinks that it is most likely that the sites without debitage, including Pylos, were acquiring their blades from Romanou. Since the acquisition of the blades does not appear on the tablets, Parkinson concludes that, "it most likely operated independently of palatial control."[78]

Although these scholars are among the first to discuss the full implications of the fact that the palace did not have a monopoly on all economic activities, i.e., that there must have been a substantial extra-palatial economy, indications that this was the case have previously been recognized within the tablets by a few Mycenaean scholars. For instance, after noting that on KN Am 821 *e-qe-ta-e* are described as *e-ne-ka e-mi-to*, which could be taken to read "on account of */emmisthon/* or wage-earners," Shelmerdine proposed the possibility that "fully autonomous craftsmen, paid in some commodity or other, existed in Mycenaean Greece; these would appear in the tablets only when hired by the palace."[79] Laffineur has also proposed that workshops "were also active outside the palaces, in connection with the settlements."[80] The evidence he adduces for this proposal is found on PY Jn 829 and PY Jo 438, which record palatial collections of bronze and gold, respectively. He says that this type of collection "probably indicates that there was some circulation of metal in the periphery, and consequently some metallurgical activity, and that it escaped to a great extent the control of the palatial administration."[81] Killen himself has also recently recognized the likelihood that work went on in the Pylian realm that was not controlled by the palace. He says, "Whereas it is clear that the palace itself organised the production of high-quality, luxury manufactured goods, the evidence of [PY] Un 1322 suggests that it may have acquired goods of a simpler kind (like nets) from independent or semi-independent workers who were not located in palace-controlled workshops."[82]

H. Morris was actually among the first to analyze the Linear B texts for evidence concerning the extent and nature of the palatial economy. She demonstrated that the tablets at Pylos show very little evidence for the redistribution of goods to the society at large. When goods were given out by the palace, they almost always (70% of the instances) consisted of rations or raw materials that went to workers who were producing elite goods. Most of the remaining disbursement tablets recorded offerings to the religious sphere. She goes on to say that "This leaves only two tablets ([PY] Vn 20 and On 300) – about 0.1% of the total tablets – designating disbursements to major towns and not workshops or shrines."[83] Thus she demonstrated that the palace at Pylos was not involved in the business of redistribution for the benefit of the people of the region in which the

[73] Whitelaw 2001, pp. 64-67.

[74] Galaty 1999a, p. 9, p. 77. Also see pp. 24-25 for Galaty's discussion of markets in the Mycenaean period.

[75] Galaty 1999b, p. 59.

[76] W.A. Parkinson, "Chipping Away at a Mycenaean Economy: Obsidian Exchange, Linear B, and Palatial Control in Late Bronze Age Messenia," in *Rethinking Mycenaean Palaces: New Interpretations of an Old Idea*, M.L. Galaty and W.A. Parkinson, eds., The Cotsen Institute of Archaeology at UCLA 1999, pp. 73-85. Also see W.A. Parkinson, "Chipping Away at a Mycenaean Economy," *Bulletin of the Central States Anthropological Society* 32 (1997) 12-26.

[77] Parkinson 1999, p. 73.

[78] Parkinson 1999, p. 81. Parkinson also uses the fact that the obsidian blade industry was not centralized at the palace to support his argument, but since other industries that were palatially managed, such as the bronze-working and the textile industries, were actually conducted away from the palace, this argument is not a valid one.

[79] Shelmerdine 1987, p. 337.

[80] R. Laffineur, "Craftsmen and Craftsmanship in Mycenaean Greece: For a Multimedia Approach," in *Politeia, Society and State in the Aegean Bronze Age* (*Aegaeum* 12), R. Laffineur and W.-D. Niemeier, eds., Liège and Austin 1995, pp. 189-199; see p. 198.

[81] Laffineur 1995, p. 198.

[82] J.T. Killen, "Some Further Thoughts on 'Collectors'," in *Politeia: Society and State in the Aegean Bronze Age* (*Aegaeum* 12), R. Laffineur and W.-D. Niemeier, eds., Liège and Austin 1995, pp. 213-226; see p. 219.

[83] H. Morris, *An Economic Model of the Late Mycenaean Kingdom of Pylos*, Ph.D. Dissertation, University of Minnesota 1986, pp. 109-110.

palace was situated. Rather, the palace used its power to acquire the resources it needed to support its workers and to produce its prestige goods from local systems of production and exchange, which would have operated independent of the palatial economy. Parkinson suggests that these local production systems were in existence before the palace extended its influence over the region, and as the palace grew "it appears to have left these previously existing systems *in situ*...."[84] Since the palace must have turned to these local systems in order to fulfill many of its needs, the character of the palace's interactions with the community must have been much more complicated and varied than originally thought. At the same time it is also important to recognize that the local economic systems would have served the needs of, and must have existed primarily for, the people who lived outside of the palace and who did not participate directly in the palatial economic system.

With this more recent (and I think more likely) view of Mycenaean society and economy, it is fitting and logical to propose that the religious sector of Mycenaean Greece also had some economic independence from the palace. I think this is likely given the different types of economic activities that the sanctuaries and their personnel were involved in. I propose, therefore, that the religious sector, like the other non-palatial sectors of society, had its own systems of production. These systems would assuredly not have been on the same scale as those administered by the palace, but they would have served, at least, to fulfill the needs of the sanctuary and its associated personnel. I also think that the sanctuaries and their personnel participated in the local systems of exchange that operated around them, which means that they constituted independent economic forces within their communities. Economic influence coupled with religious authority could have been a powerful combination, and I will consider what that would mean for our view of Mycenaean society. I also think that the sanctuaries were active in their local economies before the palace's power became as far-reaching as it appears in the tablets. I have therefore proposed that "the palaces, as their administrative systems took shape and their economic interests expanded, had to deal with the already existing economic and social power wielded by the sanctuaries."[85] Shelmerdine has also proposed that the religious sector was a force that wielded power within Mycenaean society. She says, "The king, furthermore, seems to be just one of three sources of authority and administrative control in the Mycenaean state, along with the religious sphere and the *damos*."[86] As I will discuss in Chapter 4, I think the interaction between the palatial and the religious spheres over time may have resulted in a situation whereby each entity supported the other's claim to power – to their mutual benefit.

Thus our conception of the Mycenaean economy has been considerably altered in recent times. The palatial administration has gone from being conceived of as a centralized, almost totalitarian bureaucracy that collected and subsequently redistributed goods to the society at large, to one that is conceived of as predominantly interested in mobilizing resources almost solely for the purpose of producing its own elite goods. Alternative foci of economic power have been recognized, the *damos* and the religious sector. In this work I will thoroughly explore the clues to the latter's economic activities as they appear in the Linear B tablets and the archaeological record in order to better understand the economic role of the religious sector in Mycenaean society. In addition, I will bear in mind that economic power can bring social and political power. Indeed, they are very often intertwined. Therefore I will also examine, where possible, the indications that the religious sector wielded some influence within their communities and with respect to the palatial authority.

First, however, before delving into the archaeological and Linear B evidence concerning the economic activities of the religious sector, I will discuss exactly what I mean when I refer to a site as a workshop or a sanctuary, and the methods that I have used in identifying such places. Having clear definitions of each type of area will be important for evaluating the sites that I discuss throughout this work.

Then in Chapter 3 I will discuss the workshop-shrine connection as it is manifested in archaeological contexts outside of Mycenaean Greece. This discussion will provide us with some background and comparative material for our study of the relationship between religion and economic activities as it is found in the tablets. In Chapter 4 I will turn to one of the bodies of evidence that has proved most useful for this study: the Pylos land tenure tablets which deal with the landholdings of *Pa-ki-ja-ne*. Chapter 5 will focus on the religious sector's involvement in other economic activities, including

[84] Parkinson 1999, p. 83. Parkinson also suggests that by focusing on the elite, or "wealth-financed economy," but in neglecting to control the staple economy, upon which the palatial economy was dependent, the palace created a very unstable situation which could have contributed to the collapse of the entire palatial system (pp. 84-85). Also see T. D'Altroy and T.K. Earle, "Staple finance, wealth finance, and storage in the Inka ceramic political economy," *Current Anthropology* 26 (1985) 187-206.

[85] S. Lupack, "Palaces, Sanctuaries and Workshops: The Role of the Religious Sector in Mycenaean Economics," in *Rethinking Mycenaean Palaces: New Interpretations of an Old Idea*, M.L. Galaty and W.A. Parkinson, eds., The Cotsen Institute of Archaeology, UCLA 1999, pp. 25-34; see p. 34.

[86] C.W. Shelmerdine, "Administration in the Mycenaean Palaces: Where's the Chief?" in *Rethinking Mycenaean Palaces: New Interpretations of an Old Idea*, M.L. Galaty and W.A. Parkinson, eds., The Cotsen Institute of Archaeology at UCLA 1999, pp. 19-24; see p. 23. Shelmerdine mentions the *damos* because Killen had already proposed that the *damos* managed the cultivation of its own land, and therefore he posited the *damos* as an independent focus of power. Killen even argues against Halstead's assertion that the palace was in control of the grain production that went on near the palace. See J.T. Killen, "The Role of the State in Wheat and Olive Production in Mycenaean Crete," *Aevum* 72 (1998) 19-23; *idem*, "New Readings and Interpretations in the Pylos Tablets," in *Floreant Studia Mycenaea*, S. Deger-Jalkotzy, S. Hiller, O. Panagl, eds., Wien 1999, pp. 343-353; *idem* 1998, pp. 19-23. Halstead 1992, pp. 57-86; *idem*, "Plough and power: The economic and social significance of cultivation with the ox-drawn ard in the Mediterranean," *Bulletin on Sumerian Agriculture*, vol. 8, Cambridge 1995, pp. 11-22; see p. 18.

shepherding, textile production, bronze working, perfume production, and chariot and armor production. Finally, in Chapter 6 I will turn to the Mycenaean archaeological material that appears to support the evidence found in the tablets for the involvement of the religious sector in industrial production.

CHAPTER II

Discussion of Terminology

The Identification of a Workshop

In the course of this book I will present certain areas as representing ancient "workshops," "work areas," or storage areas for workshop materials. In some cases the industrial nature of the area is clear, but in other cases its nature may be debated, or perhaps should be. For this reason I would like to present at the start a set of basic criteria that I think can be helpful in making a decision concerning the nature of such an area, and the methodology that I prefer to use in applying those criteria.

In the past couple of decades, several scholars have attempted to arrive at a methodology by which industrial sites may be identified. Branigan was one of the first to try to sort out the different types of craftsmen (and by implication, the different types of workshops) that were in existence with specific reference to the Minoan world.[1] He takes as a basic premise that there were full-time resident craftsmen and part-time craftsmen.[2] The full-time craftsman, he says, can be found "permanently working in a single location and supporting himself entirely from the proceeds of his craft."[3] His work is in continuous demand and will show "a higher degree of standardization" than the part-time craftsman. In contrast, the part-time craftsman, "in addition to his agricultural labour, produces craft goods for the community ... requiring a low order of technology for which there is a lower demand."[4] Branigan also proposes that full-time craftsmen (and by implication, their permanent workshops) were to be found within the palaces, or were affiliated with the palatial administration, while part-time craftsmen operated outside the palaces' confines and purview.[5]

Clearly Branigan took a decent first stab at evaluating workshop types, but his view is fairly simplistic. While it may be true that many of the craft specialists within the palace were working full-time, it now seems that a much greater range of types of work was going on outside the palaces than Branigan at that point took (or could take?) into account. Also, Branigan's definitions of the different types of craftsmen are rather general, and do not help much in identifying the different types of area in which the work occurred. He distinguishes his part-time workshop from a full-time one by calling it a "work area" which can be identified by its "small isolated groups of tools without any trace of accompanying permanent workshops devoted to the craft."[6] However, he does not give any guidance as to how a permanent workshop should be identified, and the "small isolated groups of tools" that are supposed to identify part-time work areas may appear in the archaeological record because they were in storage or because they were simply lost or cast aside by their original owners. Hence his attempt at defining work areas does not provide any reliable criteria upon which we may judge whether an area was a workshop or not.

Tournavitou also attempts to classify different kinds of workshops. She suggests that we should distinguish between "permanent" and "domestic" workshops, instead of between "permanent" and "part-time" as Branigan had proposed.[7] Tournavitou defines the domestic workshops as "spaces within private domestic buildings, used as workplaces by the inhabitants of these buildings ... to fulfill household requirements." Another aspect of domestic workshops is that "the individuals working in this setting did not necessarily depend, at least wholly, on this one craft for their livelihood."[8] Tournavitou's definition of a permanent workshop is similar to Branigan's. She says that they "are spaces, not necessarily specifically designed for but certainly devoted to, all, or most of the year, workshop activities; spaces where a number of specialists are employed, i.e. individuals depending more or less completely on their craft for their livelihood."[9] Tournavitou does, however, recognize that permanent workshops can be of two kinds, either palatial or non-palatial.

This further delineation is certainly helpful, but classifying workshops as falling into two basic types, whether they be "permanent" and "part-time" or "permanent" and "domestic," only serves to obscure the reality that there are many types of workshops and many types of areas within which workshop activities took place. Attempts are being made, particularly within Roman archaeology, to look at the multiplicity of uses that a space might have had, and how that "spatial practice" was expressed in the artifacts.[10] For instance, in Berry's analysis of a Roman house in Pompeii (house I.8.14), she found the atrium, which was presumably used

[1] K. Branigan, "Craft Specialization in Minoan Crete," in *Minoan Society*, O. Krzyszkowska and L. Nixon, eds., Bristol Classical Press 1983, pp. 23-32.

[2] Branigan (p. 24) actually also mentions a third type, the itinerant craftsman. But archaeological evidence for this type is hard to identify and so will not be discussed here.

[3] Branigan 1983, pp. 24-25.

[4] Branigan 1983, pp. 24-25.

[5] Branigan 1983, pp. 28-29.

[6] Branigan 1983, p. 27.

[7] I. Tournavitou, "Towards and Identification of a Workshop Space," in *Problems in Greek Prehistory*, E.B. French and K.A. Wardle, eds., Bristol Classical Press 1988, pp. 447-467.

[8] Tournavitou 1988, p. 447.

[9] Tournavitou 1988, p. 447.

[10] R. Laurence, "Space and text," in *Domestic space in the Roman world: Pompeii and beyond*," R. Laurence and A. Wallace-Hadrill, eds., *Journal of Roman Archaeology*, Supplementary series no. 22, 1997, pp. 7-14.

at least part of the time as a meeting place for the *paterfamilias*, was also used for storage and workshop activities.[11] She proposes that "rooms in the Roman house were multi-functional and that activities were organised on a temporal rather than a spatial basis."[12] Thus, if we may assume that Bronze Age rooms were also multi-functional, it may be inappropriate to create a strict typology of room types and then expect the archaeological evidence to fit into it. As Whitelaw et al. have said, "The dichotomisation of specialisation as against household production over-simplifies a complex range of different production patterns and contexts."[13]

Nonetheless, the subject of what type of site may be called a workshop has continued to be a matter of contention. For instance, Schofield will only consider an area a workshop if it is "the centre of a single specialised craft..."; areas within domestic buildings that were used for one or several different types of industrial activities would be excluded by this definition.[14] Torrence objects to a stone-tool working area at Mallia being called a workshop even though "the types of waste by-products ... indicate that all stages of core preparation and blade production ... took place at this location."[15] Her reasoning is: "The quantities of material, however, do not confirm the presence of a workshop in the sense of a structure used frequently for the production of stone tools for consumers." Torrence therefore prefers the term "working area" or "activity area."

Evely, in his contribution to the topic, notes the "degree of contention" between scholars over what constitutes a workshop, and suggests that we should use a vaguer term: "Perhaps *work area* will do? It would mean nothing more than 'a place where some work activity occurred.'"[16] I am sympathetic with this point of view, and feel that more specific descriptive terms, such as permanent, domestic, craft, metallurgical, palatial, private, etc., could be attached to such a word when necessary. This is a nice solution, but, I have to admit, one which I find hard to enforce in my own work, partially because it seems to me (although I do not have as strong feelings on the topic as some) that some places *were* used as workshops and should therefore be recognized as such. I will therefore use the term "workshop" when it seems that we are dealing with a room, a group of rooms, or an entire building that was predominantly used for industrial activities, whether that be one or several, and "work area" when industrial activities are found in the midst of a building that is predominantly devoted to another function, such as religious activities.

While I may not have found Tournavitou's attempts to classify different types of workshops satisfying, she is however more helpful when discussing the means by which we may recognize and correctly identify a workshop or work area within an archaeological context.[17] Tournavitou starts from a very simple point, that our judgment of a site should be guided by the presence or absence of the artifacts that a particular craft or industry would require or produce.[18] She divides crafts into two groups, those that do not require built-in facilities (Group A) and those that do (Group B). Tournavitou then goes through a number of factors that one might look for in a workshop area and determines whether that factor can be used as a sound basis upon which we may judge the area to be a workshop. The different categories that she considers are: the architecture of an area, the pottery found within it, its permanent facilities, the tools found, the presence of worked material (this category includes raw material, half-worked material, waste material or mistakes, and finished objects), and an area's connection with the central administration. This leads to some rather obvious statements like, "Built-in facilities are only relevant in Group B workshops,"[19] i.e., in those types of workshops that would require built-in facilities. But the point that should be highlighted is that she finds the presence or absence of partly worked material, industrial waste, and pieces that show mistakes to be the most important factors in identifying a workshop space.[20] In other words, there must be material present that clearly demonstrates that work was actually going on in that particular place before one can safely call it a workshop. She also finds that tools are "very important for both craft groups, but ought to be corroborated by other evidence."[21] This is because tools found on their own may simply have been in storage, and cannot by themselves indicate a workshop space. Tournavitou builds a bit of flexibility into her system by saying that our judgment of an area cannot be simply based on the presence or absence of these things, but should take into account the possibility that such evidence might have been lost. For instance, the absence of tools or raw materials at a suspected workshop area may be due to looting, or simply to the inhabitants having carried such things away with them.[22] But for the most part, the most significant guideline that Tournavitou recommends is that waste material, raw material, and material showing mistakes in the manufacturing process

[11] J. Berry, "Household artefacts: towards a re-interpretation of Roman domestic space," in *Domestic space in the Roman world: Pompeii and beyond*," R. Laurence and A. Wallace-Hadrill, eds., *Journal of Roman Archaeology*, Supplementary series no. 22, 1997, pp. 183-195; see p. 193.

[12] Berry 1997, p. 194.

[13] T. Whitelaw, P.M. Day, E. Kiriatzi, V. Kilikoglou and D.E. Wilson, "Ceramic Traditions at EM IIB Myrtos, Fournou Korifi," in *TEXNH: Craftsmen, Craftswomen and Craftsmanship in the Aegean Bronze Age* (*Aegaeum* 16), Liège and Austin 1997, pp. 265-274; see p. 266.

[14] E. Schofield, "Evidence for Household Industries on Thera and Kea," in *Thera and the Aegean World* III, Vol. I: *Archaeology*, D.A. Hardy, ed., The Thera Foundation, London 1990, pp. 201-211; see p. 201.

[15] R. Torrence, *Production and Exchange of Stone Tools: Prehistoric Obsidian in the Aegean*, Cambridge University Press 1986, see pp. 150-152.

[16] D. Evely, "Minoan Craftsmen: Problems of Recognition and Definition," in *Problems in Greek Prehistory*, E.B. French and K.A. Wardle, eds., Bristol Classical Press 1988, pp. 397-415; see p. 399.

[17] Tournavitou 1988, *passim*.

[18] Tournavitou 1988, p. 448.

[19] Tournavitou 1988, p. 451.

[20] Tournavitou 1988, p. 459.

[21] Tournavitou 1988, p. 459.

[22] Tournavitou 1988, p. 452.

should be in evidence before we can confidently claim that an area was used as a workshop.

Evely also reviews the strengths and weaknesses of various criteria in identifying a workshop.[23] Like Tournavitou, he says that built-in or relatively immobile furniture, such as kilns, storage vessels and workbenches, can be good indicators that a place was a work area; but he warns that the latter two could not stand on their own as evidence for a workshop.[24] Evely is, however, a bit less confident than Tournavitou about using the presence of raw materials as the major criterion for judging whether an area was a workshop. Evely categorizes the materials that may be found in a work area as follows: (i) raw substances; (ii) objects in the course of manufacture, and debris resulting therefrom; and (iii) items from the tool-kit.[25] He concludes that the presence of raw material may indicate that a place was a workshop, but this criterion is not reliable on its own since it could also simply indicate "the proximity of a work area...."[26] As for unfinished objects and debris, Evely points out that craftsmen would from time to time clean up and dump their waste products some distance away from the work area, and that soils containing such debris could be moved away from their original context in the process of leveling floors or building walls. The redeposition of such material could "delude the archaeologist into believing himself to be in the presence of a work area." Like Tournavitou, Evely does not credit the presence of tools as a sure indicator either. The find of a single tool could represent one that had been lost or misplaced. Even what appears to be a tool-kit on its own can simply be in storage, although in this case work may have gone on near by. Evely stresses therefore that, "none of the above classes of objects (tools, debris, raw materials) can be relied upon of themselves to act as an infallible indicator." Rather, combinations of evidence are the thing to look for and his motto is "the more the better."[27]

The work of Tournavitou and Evely reflects the fact that in general scholars have been much more demanding of the evidence when evaluating workshop spaces. For instance, Schofield comments in the introduction to her discussion of industrial sites on Kea and Akrotiri that,

> ...a room is now accepted as a workshop if it contains waste material and rejects, together with examples of some of the following: raw material, unfinished objects, specialized equipment and perhaps a store of objects all of the same type representing finished products.[28]

This is perhaps a rather tall order. But the main policy for some, such as Krzyszkowska who works with ivory material, is that waste material, or debitage, must be present in order for a site to be accepted without question as a workshop.[29] A salient example of how this guideline has affected scholarship is found in the Cult Center of Mycenae. French originally published the material from area 36 of the Cult Center as representing a workshop.[30] However, in her forthcoming final publication on the service areas of the Cult Center, French will redefine area 36 as a storeroom – because no real debitage was found there.[31] This more exacting attitude is also apparent in Shelmerdine's reevaluation of both Spyropoulos' textile workshop at Thebes and the West House group of four buildings at Mycenae.[32] Shelmerdine concludes in both cases that they are more likely to have been used as storerooms or clearing houses than as workshops.

This stricter attitude has led to more precise assessments of the character of such sites, which can only produce a more informative picture of ancient society than what we were dealing with before. However, it seems to me that remaining flexible and keeping an open mind are also useful. As Tournavitou pointed out, it should be kept in mind that some types of evidence may be lacking because they were removed from the site by the inhabitants or the plunderers. Also, the hard and fast rule about debitage may not always be helpful. The absence of debitage in an archaeological assemblage may sometimes be the result of the excavation process, as French has agreed may have been the case for the Cult Center,[33] and as it certainly was the case at sites that were excavated for the most part in the early years of the twentieth century, such as Gournia and Palaikastro on Crete and Phylakopi on Melos.[34] Also, the requirement for the presence of debitage cannot apply to several types of industries that simply do not produce debitage in the way that stone or ivory working do. Textile manufacture comes immediately to mind. When looking for evidence for this industry we must rely on loomweights and/or spindle whorls.[35] Evidence for flour, wine and olive oil production may only amount to the equipment used to grind or press the grain and fruit, although in some cases we do have the remains of grapes or olive pits (and in one case even the flour[36]) to help us

[23] Evely 1988, pp. 401-410.
[24] Evely 1988, p. 402.
[25] Evely 1998, p. 407.
[26] Evely 1998, p. 408.
[27] Evely 1988, pp. 409-410.
[28] Schofield 1990, p. 201.

[29] O. Krzyszkowska in "Cult and Craft: Ivories from the Citadel House Area, Mycenae," in *TEXNH: Craftsmen, Craftswomen and Craftsmanship in the Aegean Bronze Age* (*Aegaeum* 16), Liège and Austin 1997, pp. 145-149; *idem*, "Aegean Ivory Carving: Towards an Evaluation of Late Bronze Age Workshop Material," in *Ivory in Greece and the Eastern Mediterranean from the Bronze Age to the Hellenistic Period*, British Museum Occasional Paper 85, J. L. Fitton, ed., British Museum 1992.
[30] French 1981, pp. 41-48.
[31] E. French, *Service Areas of the Cult Centre, Well Built Mycenae: The Helleno-British Excavations within the Citadel of Mycenae 1959-1969*, fascicule 13, Taylour, French and Wardle, series eds., Oxbow Books, forthcoming.
[32] See also Shelmerdine, "Workgroups and Record Keeping in the Mycenaean World," in *TEXNH: Craftsmen, Craftswomen, and Craftsmanship in the Aegean Bronze Age* (*Aegaeum* 16), R. Laffineur and P.P. Betancourt, eds., Liège and Austin 1997, pp. 387-396.
[33] French (personal communication, spring 1997).
[34] Schofield 1990, p. 202.
[35] B. Burke, "The Organization of Textile Production on Bronze Age Crete," in *TEXNH: Craftsmen, Craftswomen, and Craftsmanship in the Aegean Bronze Age* (*Aegaeum* 16), R. Laffineur and P.P. Betancourt, eds., Liège and Austin 1997, pp. 413-422; see pp. 414-415 for a discussion of loomweights, spindle whorls and the warp-weighted loom.
[36] S. Marinatos 1971, pp. 22 and 43. Also see plate 34a for a photo of the "flour."

in specifying which type of commodity was being produced. Shelmerdine identified the area where perfumed oil was most likely produced at Pylos (courts 42 and 47) by the equipment that was used in its manufacture and by the fact that the architectural setting would have been well suited for such an industry.[37] Thus, as Evely and Schofield note, the whole context of an area must be taken into account when deciding whether it may constitute a workshop or a work area, and the list of what one might expect to find "will depend entirely on the craft involved."[38]

With this philosophy in mind, I have decided that I will not specify a standard list of criteria which I would then apply to every area considered in this book in order to judge whether it is a workshop. Instead, I will evaluate each area individually, keeping, as Evely recommends, a "mental checklist,"[39] and decide on a case-by-case basis whether the material remains of a particular site constitute sufficient evidence upon which I may reasonably judge the function of an area to have been work-related.

This leads me to another point. In order to show a connection between industry and the religious sector, it will often be enough to show that work went on in the vicinity of the religious area in question. Thus, if the archaeological remains do not indicate that an area functioned as a workshop, but they do justify its being designated as a storeroom for a workshop, then in those cases, where other factors agree, I will consider a relationship between the religious area and industrial activities to have been established.

Sanctuary, Shrine, and Cult Building

There are two issues that must be addressed in this discussion. The first is how one should go about identifying an area or a building in an archaeological context as having had a sacred nature, and the second is defining the terms, such as "sanctuary" and "shrine," used to refer to those sacred places. The first issue pertains only to archaeological material, but the second is complicated by the fact that it pertains both to archaeological material and to the Linear B tablets. Thus, I will discuss the way in which the concepts are used in relation to each body of evidence.

The archaeological situation is perhaps the easier one to deal with since a typology can be derived from the material remains, whereas with the Linear B tablets we must try to understand what sorts of definitions were in the minds of the people who wrote the tablets, which is a difficult task. Thus I will begin with the archaeological material in the hopes that it will assist us in dealing with the Linear B evidence.

Nilsson was among the first to make an attempt at classifying Minoan and Mycenaean cult buildings. His general definition of a "temple" was "a separate building set apart to be the abode of the deity and to shelter its image and paraphernalia."[40] He was therefore able to claim, based on the evidence that was available to him at the time, that no temples existed in the Minoan civilization. He preferred instead to call the cult places of the Minoans (and of the Mycenaeans) "house sanctuaries." Taylour of course, once he had discovered the separate cult buildings of the Cult Center at Mycenae, was able show that the Mycenaeans did in fact have buildings of the type described by Nilsson, and decided to name one of his major cult buildings simply the "Temple."[41]

It was only later that scholars within the field tried to set up objective criteria which one could use in order to judge whether a site was actually religious or not. J.C. van Leuven, with much more material at his disposal than Nilsson had, actually attempted to create a typology of sanctuaries. But his sample included such a large number of possible cult buildings (over 100) from such a broad geographical area (Cyprus, Crete, and the mainland of Greece as far north as Macedonia) and chronological time periods (7000-1000 B.C.) that his conclusions had to be rather general.[42] Van Leuven's definition of a "sanctuary", however, stresses the idea that the presence of cult objects should generally be used as a basic criterion for identifying a sanctuary: "A sanctuary in the clearest sense must be a place of religious worship, and is normally identified by equipment suggesting a cultic purpose or ritual activity."[43] Rutkowski similarly stresses the importance of the objects that are found in a cult site over the type of building or area in which they are found. He says, "It is my contention that sacred objects and votive offerings are the only reliable indicators of Bronze Age cult places in Greece...."[44] This led him to eliminate "sacred crypts" from the types of areas usually considered religious, although he retained sites whose religious nature have since been questioned.[45]

---

[37] C.W. Shelmerdine, *The Perfume Industry of Mycenaean Pylos*, Paul Åströms Förlag: Göteborg 1985; see pp. 58-62.

[38] Evely 1988, pp. 409-410. Schofield 1990, p. 202.

[39] Evely 1988, p. 410. Mental checklists can be formed with the help of modern ethnographic parallels of work that is done in a manner presumed to be similar to the ancient techniques. Also, research into the topic of ancient technology is a great help in understanding what one is looking at (see in particular D. Evely, *Minoan Crafts: Tools and Techniques, An Introduction* (*SIMA* vol. XCII), Paul Astroms Forlag vol. 1: 1993 and vol. 2: 2000; and also K.D. White, *Greek and Roman Technology*, Thames and Hudson 1984 and H. Hodges, *Technology in the Ancient World*, Penguin Press 1970).

[40] M.P. Nilsson, *The Minoan-Mycenaean Religion and its Survival in Greek Religion*, Lund second edition, 1950 (first edition 1927), p. 77.

[41] W.D. Taylour, "New Light on Mycenaean Religion," *Antiquity* 44 (1970) 270-280; see p. 273.

[42] J.C. van Leuven, "Problems and Methods of Prehellenic Naology," in *Sanctuaries and Cults in the Aegean Bronze Age*, R. Hägg and N. Marinatos, eds., Stockholm 1981, pp. 11-26.

[43] van Leuven 1981, p. 11.

[44] B. Rutkowski, *Cult Places in the Aegean World*, Wroclaw 1972, p. 303.

[45] J. Wright actually refers to Rutkowski's criteria as "very loose" ("The Spatial Configuration of Belief: The Archaeology of Mycenaean Religion," in *Placing the Gods: Sanctuaries and Sacred Space in Ancient Greece*, S.E. Alcock and R. Osborne, eds., Oxford University Press 1994, pp. 37-78; see p. 37.

Fernandez objected to using the absence or presence of cult objects as the sole criterion for identifying cult places.[46] Instead she advocated an approach that takes into account several factors of the sites in question in addition to the presence of cult objects, such as orientation of the building, number of rooms, and the size of the rooms. The approach of taking several features of a site into account is certainly more appealing than the single criterion method, but the way in which she applies this theory relies on circular reasoning. In the end she uses cult buildings in order to establish the guidelines by which we may judge other cult buildings.[47]

Gesell makes a better case for judging a site on the basis of its entire context. She says, "The appearance of cult objects in situ in rooms architecturally suited for cult purposes identifies these rooms as sanctuaries or shrines. ... In order to establish a positive identification of the cult room, *distinctive architecture and cult objects both are necessary*."[48] Gesell leaves room for some flexibility though when she says, "If, however, a room in one building strongly parallels in location and architecture a sanctuary room in a second building but lacks the cult objects, it is still reasonable to conclude that it also is a cult room." In Mycenaean cult areas, the most common cult objects include terracotta figurines such as the Psi and Phi types, various other animal-shaped figurines (very often bulls and horses), and the larger and more elaborately decorated figures such as the Lady of Phylakopi.[49] Ritual vessels, in particular kylikes and rhyta (found in both conical and animal-shaped forms), but also bowls, cups, and stirrup jars, show that the pouring of libations played a large part in Mycenaean religion.[50] In some cases we find vessels whose bottoms have been deliberately broken and the necks of amphorae stuck in the ground, which must also have been used for libation rituals. Offerings of beads are sometimes found, as are sealstones, triton shells (which may have been used as trumpets), imported objects, and offering tables.

Knapp, taking a more theoretical viewpoint, points out the difficulties involved in defining a word like "sanctuary." He asks,

> ... what exactly constitutes a sanctuary? Its definition, like that of "sacred," "ritual," or even "religion," is somewhat arbitrary, and takes on subtle, subjective nuances depending on the theoretical stance of the interpreter, or on the particular disciplinary axe that one grinds.[51]

But Knapp does attempt to give some concrete elements that one can look for when attempting to identify a religious space:

> ...the following may be proposed as likely criteria for the identification of a "sanctuary": distinctive (e.g. monumental) architecture, units of construction (e.g. "cellas," "lustral basins"), or building material (e.g. ashlar masonry); "altars" or sacrificial blocks/tables; extensive remains of sacrificial victims; and precious or unique objects, distinguished by material, method of manufacture, or contextual associations (e.g. figurines, ceramic/stone vessels, bull's horns or "masks," and similar paraphernalia).[52]

The examples Knapp includes in his list of possible criteria fulfill his own prediction that such definitions will be shaped by the field within which one works.

Renfrew tried to create a less inherently biased set of criteria by delineating the basic features of cult practice that could be manifested physically in an archaeological site.[53] To do this Renfrew starts with the premise that in any religion there are belief systems to which people ascribe, and that, "Structure in the belief system should engender pattern in cult practice."[54] He goes on to say that such patterns are evidenced in sacred ritual or, in the "performance of expressive actions of worship," which produces "material correlates" of the religion.[55] Those material correlates are the artifactual remains that an archaeologist will be able to uncover at a future date. Those artifacts may consist of the objects offered to the deity, whether they be votive objects, sacrificed animals, or other food and drink offerings, pieces of cult equipment used in the rituals, one or several "attention-focusing devices," such as an altar, and some representation of the presence of the deity, such as a cult image, to which the offerings can be directed. Also, Renfrew points out that, due to the necessity of expressing the liminality of the religious area, the location used for the practice of rituals is very often distinguished as a special place, whether it be a natural setting like a cave, a grove, or a spring, or a special building or area within a building. The cult rooms may have special features such as platforms, basins, hearths,

[46] N. Fernandez, "Cult Places of the Bronze Age: The Identification Problem," in *Problems in Greek Prehistory*, E.B. French and K.A. Wardle, eds., Bristol Classical Press 1988, pp. 229-234.
[47] Fernandez 1988, p. 233.
[48] G. Gesell, *Town, Palace, and House Cult in Minoan Crete*, Paul Astroms Forlag, Goteborg 1985, p. 2.
[49] E. French makes the distinction between the figurines and the figures according to their relative sizes ("Mycenaean Figures and Figurines, Their Typology and Function," in *Sanctuaries and Cults in the Aegean Bronze Age*, R. Hägg and N. Marinatos, eds., Stockholm 1981, pp. 173-178).
[50] R. Hägg, "The Role of Libations in Mycenaean Ceremony and Cult," *in Celebrations of Death and Divinity in the Bronze Age Argolid*, R. Hägg and G.C. Nordquist, eds., Stockholm 1990, pp. 177-184.
[51] A.B. Knapp, *Copper Production and Divine Protection: Archaeology, Ideology and Social Complexity on Bronze Age Cyprus*, Göteborg 1986, see p. 45.
[52] Knapp 1986, pp. 45-46.
[53] C. Renfrew, *The Archaeology of Cult: The Sanctuary at Phylakopi*, British School at Athens Supplementary Volume No. 18, Thames and Hudson, 1985; see pp. 11-26. Also see his more recent presentation of these ideas in C. Renfrew, "The archaeology of religion," in *The Ancient Mind: Elements of Cognitive Archaeology*, C. Renfrew and E.B.W. Zubrow, eds., Cambridge University Press 1994, pp. 47-54; see 51-53.
[54] Renfrew 1985, p. 17.
[55] Renfrew 1985, p. 18.

or stones for sacrificial rites. Finally, Renfrew says that it is also likely that the symbols used to represent the important concepts of a religion will be repeated, and they will often appear in conjunction with other repeated symbols. This premise helps the archaeologist to identify symbols more readily when they occur on their own without their usual associated symbols.[56] After having listed these different types of material correlates that the archaeologist may hope to find, Renfrew emphasizes that "it is not, however, the presence or absence of specific diagnostic criteria of this kind which are significant, but rather the documentation of repeated actions of a symbolic nature which are directed, it may be inferred, towards non-terrestrial and therefore transcendent forces."[57]

Moore, in discussing his methodology for analyzing the Temple Complex of the Cult Center of Mycenae, has two points of criticism concerning Renfrew's work.[58] The first is that Renfrew starts "with a model which exists only in the mind of the investigator and may not be reflected in the thought of the subjects of study." Actually, this criticism is one that could be applied to any model theory, and is somewhat annulled by the fact that Renfrew was trying to find elements that would be common to all religious expression. Moore's second criticism perhaps carries more weight, and certainly more significance for the present study. Moore says that, "Renfrew's approach, may, in addition, serve to detract from the recognition of multiple functions in any given context."[59] The problem here is that by focusing so closely on the cult aspects of a site, and by being practically dependent on them to define the nature of a site, non-cult activity may get overlooked or even misinterpreted. This is in fact what I think happens when Renfrew attempts to explain the obsidian artifacts found in the sanctuary of Phylakopi. I will take up this point at greater length in Chapter 6, but let me say here that Renfrew attempts to find a religious explanation for the manufacture of obsidian blades within the shrine area, whereas I think a practical explanation for the blades' production would be more appropriate.

Despite these points, Moore says that "the approach to the identification of cult facilities suggested by Renfrew remains the most sound and sensible...",[60] and then he proceeds to evaluate the Temple Complex using Renfrew's guidelines. I will attempt to do the same in my work, looking primarily for repeated expressive action and some indication that a transcendent being is being worshipped. At the same time, I will also consider practical motivations for the presence of some items even though their contexts were religious.

To turn now to the issue of terminology, my specific definitions of "sanctuary" and "shrine" are derived from the sites that I discuss within this study. Phylakopi and Mycenae provide good examples of how I apply these two terms. Phylakopi has a definite religious area which comprises two separate cult buildings and a courtyard with a baetyl between them. This area I would term a sanctuary, while the separate buildings within it I call shrines. The shrines may themselves have had more than one room, as the West Shrine at Phylakopi did, or it may have had only one room, as the East Shrine did. Similarly at Mycenae, several individual cult buildings and courtyards are found within a fairly discrete area. I consider the whole area to constitute a sanctuary, while I designate the individual buildings as shrines. An individual cult installation, like a platform with religious objects found on or near it, can also be considered a shrine if it is without an associated building.

In Mycenaean contexts, the term "bench shrine" is often used to refer to a cult building that has a platform built along one or more of its walls that is used as an altar, while it is also used to refer to the altar itself. I will endeavor to use the term "bench shrine" only when I am referring to the platform type of altar so as to avoid any confusion. It is usually clear that the platforms were used as altars since offerings, cult objects, and terracotta figurines are very often found on or around them. Such altars are a very common feature of Mycenaean shrines, having been found at Mycenae, Tiryns, Berbati, Phylakopi, Methana, Kea and Asine, and can be interpreted as Renfrew's focusing-of-attention device.[61] Other fixed features found in shrines include hearths and altars that stood independent of the walls. Very often the altars are covered with white plaster, while the one that stood outside room 93 at Pylos and the one in the Room of the Painted Fresco in the Cult Center of Mycenae both bore painted decoration.

Whittaker in her study of Mycenaean sanctuaries prefers to use the term "cult building" (although she does use "sanctuary"), because it is the most "neutral" term. I also use this term because it is convenient. However, I do not think that the terms "sanctuary" and "shrine" are inappropriately applied to Mycenaean religious sites. On the other hand, I agree with Whittaker about the difficulties in using the word "temple" in Mycenaean contexts.[62] She points out that it "often carries connotations of major public monuments," and to my mind it conjures up an image of a Classical religious building. Hence I do not use the word "temple" except when referring to the building within the Cult Center at Mycenae that was originally so designated by Taylour.[63]

[56] Renfrew 1985, pp. 16-20. Renfrew goes on to give a more detailed list of items that one may look for when approaching a site on pp. 19-20. He presents a similar list in Renfrew 1994, pp. 51-52.

[57] Renfrew 1994, p. 52.

[58] A.D. Moore and †W.D. Taylour, *The Temple Complex, Well Built Mycenae: The Helleno-British Excavations within the Citadel of Mycenae 1959-1969,* fascicule 10, W.D. Taylour, E.B. French and K.A. Wardle, series eds., Oxbow Books 1999; see pp. 77-81.

[59] Moore and Taylor 1999, p. 77.

[60] Moore and Taylor 1999, p. 77.

[61] Renfrew 1985, p. 18.

[62] H. Whittaker, *Mycenaean Cult Buildings: A Study of their Architecture and Function in the Context of the Aegean and the Eastern Mediterranean,* The Norwegian Institute at Athens 1997; see p. 6.

[63] I also agree with G. Albers ("Rethinking Mycenaean Sanctuaries," in *Potnia: Deities and Religion in the Aegean Bronze Age* [*Aegaeum* 22],

The situation is a bit more complicated when we consider how the terms "sanctuary" and "shrine" should be used when referring to the religious places that are mentioned on the Linear B tablets. This is because it is not clear from the Mycenaean terminology what type of place was meant. It is possible that we have one or two words that the Mycenaeans themselves used to refer to sacred places. The first appears on PY Jn 829, where there is a reference to *ka-ko na-wi-jo*, which is most commonly read as "temple bronze,"[64] with the *na-wi-jo* representing *νάϝιον from ναός.[65] Thus a Mycenaean religious built structure could have been called a ναός. The Mycenaeans may also have used the word *i-je-ro*, or ἱερόν, to indicate a shrine as it appears on three tablets (KN Fp 363.2, Fh 5467.b and Fh 2013) where it could be interpreted as meaning "shrine." These tablets record offerings of oil that are being sent to different locations. On Fp 363.2 and Fh 2013 *i-je-ro* is found after the word designating the destination of the oil, and so could represent the word "shrine."[66] It is also possible that *i-je-ro* could be taken as an adjective, describing the oil as "sacred," rather than indicating an actual place of worship.[67] It is difficult to say for sure which of these two possibilities is correct.

Nonetheless, the fact that we have two possible words that the Mycenaeans could have used to designate their sacred places does not really help us in determining exactly what type of places they had in mind when they wrote these words. Were they what we would call sanctuaries, or were they simply shrines? PY Tn 316 helps a bit in this situation since its structure seems to indicate that separate shrines belonging to various deities existed within larger sanctuaries. This situation seems to parallel the arrangement of the religious sites of Phylakopi and Mycenae, which, as I mentioned, both had separate cult buildings within a larger sanctuary area. The first paragraph of Tn 316 demonstrates this:

Tn 316.1-5:
1. po-ro-wi-to-jo ,
2. i-je-to-qe , pa-ki-ja-si , do-ra-qe , pe-re , po-re-na-qe
3. pu-ro a-ke , po-ti-ni-ja AUR *215^{VAS}* 1 MUL 1
4. ma-na-sa , AUR *213^{VAS}* 1 MUL 1 po-si-da-e-ja AUR *213^{VAS}* 1 MUL 1
5. ti-ri-se-ro-e , AUR *216^{VAS}* 1 do-po-ta AUR *215^{VAS}* 1

In this paragraph we see that offerings of gold vessels (the *do-ra*) and women (referred to as the *po-re-na*) are being sent (or 'sanctified') to the sanctuary of *Pa-ki-ja-ne* (line 2). Potnia seems to have been the major deity of the sanctuary since she is listed first. But several other deities follow her on lines 4 and 5 (*ma-na-sa*, *po-si-da-e-ja*, *ti-ri-se-ro-e*, and *do-po-ta*) who also seem to be worshipped at *Pa-ki-ja-ne*. This implies that they too had shrines within the sacred precinct of *Pa-ki-ja-ne*. We can imagine that each one of these deities had, at least, their own bench shrine since, for instance, in both the West and the East Shrines at Phylakopi there was more than one altar, which could indicate that more than one deity was worshipped in each building. I may also mention that this type of arrangement has parallels in historical Greece. For example, the Athenian Acropolis also housed several deities, such as Poseidon, Hephaistos, Artemis, Zeus, and Kekrops, in addition to its major deity, Athena, and each one of these had his own shrine, or at least sacred area, within the sanctuary precinct. Thus, we can probably feel safe in saying that words such as *Pa-ki-ja-ne* or *po-si-da-i-jo* (*Posidaion*) represent actual sanctuaries. But, unfortunately, if a deity's name alone is used, we still cannot be sure if it was a sanctuary or a shrine.

Therefore, I have been guided both by the archaeological evidence and my own estimation of what each particular textual instance refers to in my choice of which word to use. In many instances I prefer to use the term "sanctuary," particularly in cases where there is any hint that there might have been more to a place than one cult building. In particular I feel that the use of the word "sanctuary" is justified if there are economic activities associated with the religious establishment. This is because economic activities, such as textile manufacturing, bronze working, and shepherding, imply the existence of buildings or installations in addition to the cult building, and a group of personnel who were needed to manage and conduct such activities. I do not, however, always mean to imply by the use of the word sanctuary that the sites were necessarily large or well-appointed complexes. Many of the places I will be discussing I imagine to have been quite modest. Nonetheless, the term sanctuary would be appropriate in any situation where the religious site in question most likely consisted of more than a single shrine.

R. Laffineur and R. Hägg, eds., Liège and Austin 2001, pp. 131-141; see pp. 139-140), who points out quite correctly that in actuality Mycenaean cult buildings can be called "temples" because they functioned as the dwelling or seat of the deity. She renders the issue of monumental architecture moot by showing that cult buildings in other disciplines are called temples even when they are not monumental because they served the "same essential purpose" as the larger cult buildings. The same reasoning could be applied to the Mycenaean situation. Nonetheless, I will restrict my use of the word "temple" because of the connotations it carries.

[64] The idea that *na-wi-jo* may derive from ναῦς, making this ship bronze, has been generally rejected. *Dic. Mic.* I, p. 466; S. Hiller, "*ka-ko na-wi-jo*, Notes on Interdependences of Temple and Bronze in the Aegean Bronze Age," in *Colloquium Mycenaeum*, E. Risch and H. Mühlestein, eds., Neuchâtel 1979, pp. 189-195; A. Leukart, "Autour de *ka-ko na-wi-jo*: quelques critères," also in *Colloquium Mycenaeum*, 1979, pp. 183-187. Both Hiller and Leukart discuss the possibility that in Linear B ναός may have retained an original meaning of "dwelling," but I think the fact that the religious officials called the *ka-ra-wi-po-ro* appear in the heading indicates that a religious building was meant. Also see Palmer 1963, pp. 283-284 and *Docs*[2], p. 513. Most recently M. Del Freo ("L'Expression *ka-ko na-wi-jo* de la Tablette Jn 829 de Pylos," in *Emporia: Aegeans in the Central and Eastern Mediterranean*, (*Aegaeum* 25), R. Laffineur and E. Greco, eds., Liège and UT Austin 2005, pp. 793-803) has argued that neither 'ship bronze' nor 'temple bronze' are satisfactory interpretations for *ka-ko na-wi-jo*, and proposes instead that Jn 829 should be interpreted as a record of bronze being called up for weapons that would be used on ships. If this is the correct interpretation, then obviously we would not be able to consider *na-wi-jo* as testifying to the word νάϝιον in Linear B.

[65] *Dic. Mic.* I, p. 466.

[66] *Dic. Mic.* I, pp. 275-276. Hiller 1981, pp. 96-97.

[67] *Dic. Mic.* I, pp. 275-276. *Docs*[2], p. 548.

With the words workshop, shrine, and sanctuary thus defined, and the methodology used to recognize these types of areas in the archaeological record thus laid out, I will now turn to an investigation of the archaeological sites outside of Mycenaean Greece that have been cited as demonstrating a connection between industry and religion.

CHAPTER III

The Workshop-Shrine Association in the Aegean Bronze Age

Archaeological Literature Review

When we look for evidence concerning the economic role of the religious sector in the archaeological record, particularly in a pre-literate society such as (the greater part of) the Bronze Age, we must necessarily look for situations where religious sites are found in close proximity to areas where industrial or workshop activities were conducted. Some sort of involvement of religious personnel in production work can reasonably be inferred from such close physical relationships.[1] In the Aegean Bronze Age, several sites have been noted as exhibiting a close connection between religious and workshop areas. In the Mycenaean world the sites that demonstrate such a connection are Pylos, Mycenae, Methana, Phylakopi, and Berbati. I will discuss these sites in Chapter 6 after I have reviewed the Linear B evidence for the involvement of the religious sector in economic activities. At this point I intend to discuss the Aegean Bronze Age religious sites that are associated with industrial activities that are outside the bounds of Late Bronze Age Mycenaean Greece either chronologically and/or geographically. In other words, I will be discussing many Minoan sites found on Crete and Thera, as well as those of Cyprus. I group the Cypriot sites with the Minoan because they do not, strictly speaking, belong with the Mycenaean ones in terms of culture, yet they are pertinent to our study both for the variety of religious-industrial associations they present and the scholarly discussion that has built up around them. Of course it would also be helpful if I were able to discuss pre-Mycenaean religious sites on the mainland of Greece, but unfortunately very few cult sites have been identified on the mainland that date to a time before the rise of the palaces in the Late Helladic period.[2] Wright in his review of Mycenaean sacred sites remarks that there is "virtually no evidence to go on for the Middle Bronze Age."[3] Hence it is to the Minoan and Cypriot sites that we must turn for relevant comparanda.

Indeed, a discussion of these sites on Crete, Thera, and Cyprus will serve several purposes. First, it will show that the phenomenon of sanctuaries being involved in economic activities was part of the larger Aegean cultural *koine* (although I do not mean to imply that the Mycenaean manifestation of this phenomenon was necessarily directly inherited from Crete or Cyprus, although some influence from Crete is possible). Second, since the associations between religion and industry manifested in the archaeological record were not always of the same nature, reviewing as many cases as possible will provide us with useful background material against which we may be better able to clarify our interpretation of the Mycenaean sites. And finally, there are several sites that scholars often refer to whenever they want to establish that there was a shrine-workshop connection in the Aegean Bronze Age, but the details of these sites and the validity of their being included in such an easy, standard list are not usually considered. I think it is necessary therefore to review the evidence of these sites to see whether any corrections to the list should be made.

At the conference that gave rise to the volume entitled *Sanctuaries and Cults in the Aegean Bronze Age*, the fact that religious areas are often found in close association with work areas was mentioned several times. It was brought up in the discussions following the papers given by Hiller (on Mycenaean sanctuaries[4]) and French (on the workshop areas in the Cult Center at Mycenae[5]), and Hägg and Marinatos paid special attention to this topic in their conference conclusions.[6] During those discussions the foundations for the "list" of sites that exhibit a relationship between religious and workshop activities were laid. The sites mentioned were: the Cult Center of Mycenae, Zakros, where "the shrine store filled with chalices and other valuable objects was right next to the craft workshop," the House of the Ladies on Thera, which was "next to what would appear to be a workshop, to judge from the unfinished marble jar found in it," and a room in the western part of the palace of Knossos where "fragments of gypsum stone vessels" had been found in the vicinity of the shrine area.[7] Hägg and Marinatos note that storage areas were also very often directly connected with shrine areas, as at Knossos, Phaistos, Mallia, Zakros, and many Minoan villas.[8] While this is a very interesting manifestation of the religious sector's involvement in economic activities, I will not be able to address this particular issue within the scope of this work.[9] More

[1] Whether that involvement entailed hands-on labor, managerial oversight of the production processes, or both must be determined, if possible, in each particular situation.

[2] See B. Rutkowski, *Cult Places of the Aegean*, Yale University Press 1986. H. Whittaker, *Mycenaean Cult Buildings: A Study of their Architecture and Function in the Context of the Aegean and the Eastern Mediterranean*, The Norwegian Institute at Athens 1997.

[3] J. Wright, "The Spatial Configuration of Belief: The Archaeology of Mycenaean Religion," in *Placing the Gods: Sanctuaries and Sacred Space in Ancient Greece*, S.E. Alcock and R. Osborne, eds., Oxford University Press 1994, pp. 37-78; see p. 38. The sanctuary of Ayia Irini on Keos, which dates to the MH and LH periods, has evidence that metal workers were worshipping within the shrine. I will discuss this site briefly in Chapter 6.

[4] Hiller 1981, pp. 95-126.

[5] E. French, "Cult Places at Mycenae," in *Sanctuaries and Cults in the Aegean Bronze Age*, R. Hägg and N. Marinatos, eds., Stockholm 1981, pp. 41-48.

[6] R. Hägg and N. Marinatos, "Conclusions and Prospects," in *Sanctuaries and Cults in the Aegean Bronze Age*, R. Hägg and N. Marinatos, eds., Stockholm 1981, pp. 213-217; p. 217.

[7] P. Warren, "Discussion" following Hiller's paper, p. 125.

[8] Hägg and N. Marinatos 1981, p. 217.

[9] See for an interesting discussion on the topic, E. Kyriakidis, "The Economics of Potnia: Storage in 'Temples' of Prehistoric Greece, in *Potnia: Deities and Religion in the Aegean Bronze Age* (*Aegaeum* 22), R. Laffineur and R. Hägg, eds., Liège and UT-PASP 2001, pp. 123-129.

pertinent to my work is that Hägg and Marinatos added the cave site of Arkalochori to the list of sites with a religious-industrial connection, "where the large amount of bronze (some of it not in the form of finished goods) suggested to the excavator, S. Marinatos, that the place was a sort of sacred smithy."[10] In discussing this phenomenon, French gave the opinion that the various workshops were organically connected with the sanctuaries,[11] and she said, "The shrines owned rich materials, which they gave out to be worked as in the Oriental system."[12] Hägg and Marinatos concluded, "The economy then, of both Minoan and Mycenaean societies, must have been stimulated by the production of the shrine workshops, and it may well be the case that these societies had sacred economies."[13]

Soon after the *Sanctuaries and Cults* conference, Tegyey examined the possibility that a "temple economy" existed at Pylos where the Northeast Building seems to have housed both a shrine and a workshop.[14] His work will be discussed in more detail in Chapters 5 and 6, but here it should be mentioned that Tegyey came to the conclusion, after analyzing both the archaeological and textual evidence found in the Northeast Building, that although "this modest shrine cannot be compared in influence to the wealthy temples of the Oriental societies" nonetheless, "the presence of a goddess ... in a shrine with priests and priestesses in her service, ... seem to point to an activity where the religious sphere could be a decisive element."[15] In making his case he mentions several of the sites mentioned above, and adds Myrtos, "where large buildings with specialized industries were attached to the shrine of the goddess," and Kition on Cyprus, "where a smithy was found in the immediate neighborhood of temples dating from the end of the Bronze Age."[16]

More recently Hägg has given us "a few glimpses of the relationship between religious cult and the production of goods."[17] His overview includes Arkalochori, Zakros, Mycenae, and the Cypriot sites of Kition, Enkomi and Athienou.[18] Hägg does not cover these sites in tremendous detail, but he does recognize (where others had not) that the different sites may have had different reasons for engaging in industrial work. The workshops at Zakros, for instance, seem to have produced goods that were to be used within a religious context, while "the metallurgical production associated with religion in Cyprus was of great economic importance and must be thought to have operated primarily to supply 'secular' needs."[19] Making such distinctions in purpose and scale are important for evaluating the role of a certain religious site within the overall economy of its community, and I will be paying attention to these types of distinctions in my analysis of the sites that follow.

Thus the archaeological evidence has indicated to several scholars that there was a connection between the religious sphere and the economy of Bronze Age society. The sites that have been mentioned, besides Pylos and Mycenae, are Arkalochori, Myrtos, Zakros, and Knossos on Crete, Akrotiri on Thera, and Kition, Enkomi, and Athienou on Cyprus. In the course of my research I have added three Cretan sites to this list, Mochlos, Pseira, and the Unexplored Mansion at Knossos, and one Cypriot, Myrtou Pigadhes. I will review the evidence for workshop-shrine connections in the Cretan and Theran sites first, and then I will discuss the situation on Cyprus separately.

Arkalochori

Arkalochori has probably been the most puzzling of the sites. The site called Arkalochori is a rock shelter about 30 m long and about 10 m wide that lies to the east of the central Cretan town of Arkalochori. Hazzidakis was the first to excavate there in 1912.[20] He undertook the project after hearing that the villagers were selling bronze artifacts they had found in the cave as scrap metal. He was told that approximately 20 kilograms of bronze had already been sold and melted down, and that the villagers had actually dynamited the cave in order to get more quickly to what they thought would be real treasure. Despite this treatment of the cave, Hazzidakis' excavation revealed many more bronze swords and double axes, and one small axe that was made of silver. Hazzidakis therefore interpreted the site as "a sacred cave."[21]

Hazzidakis left the site thinking of course that he had found all of its ancient material, but twenty-two years later, in 1934, Spyridon Marinatos was told that more material had been found there by children playing around the cave.[22] In the course of his investigation Marinatos discovered that Hazzidakis had thought he had hit rock bottom, so to speak, because the roof of the cave had collapsed in ancient times, thereby disguising the full extent of the cave.[23] Beyond the rock fall Marinatos found, in addition to the many artifacts that were

[10] Hägg and N. Marinatos 1981, p. 217.
[11] As I have mentioned in the section on identifying a workshop, French has changed her opinion on the site somewhat. That different opinion will be discussed at length in Chapter 5.
[12] French 1981, p. 48.
[13] Hägg and N. Marinatos 1981, p. 217.
[14] I. Tegyey, "The Northeast Workshop at Pylos," in *Pylos Comes Alive, Industry and Administration in a Mycenaean Palace*, C.W. Shelmerdine and T.G. Palaima, eds., New York 1984, pp. 65-79; see especially pp. 77-79.
[15] Tegyey 1984, p. 79.
[16] Tegyey 1984, p. 77.
[17] R. Hägg, "Sanctuaries and Workshops in the Bronze Age Aegean," in *Economics of Cult in the Ancient Greek World*, T. Linders and B. Alroth, eds., Uppsala 1992, pp. 29-32; see p. 32.
[18] Hägg (1992, p. 29) also includes workshops at Mallia because they have been proposed to have been producing cultic items. But since there was no shrine found in association with these workshops, I have not included Mallia in my study.
[19] Hägg 1992, p. 32.
[20] J. Hazzidakis, "An Early Minoan Sacred Cave at Arkalochori in Crete," *BSA* 19 (1912-1913) 35-47.
[21] Hazzidakis 1912-1913, pp. 35 and 46.
[22] S. Marinatos, "Zur Frage der Grotte von Arkalochori," *Kadmos* 1 (1962) 87-94; see p. 88; *idem*, *AA* 49 (1934) 251-254; see p. 252.
[23] Marinatos 1934, p. 253.

scattered all over the floor, two concentrations of finds, one in a corner and another in the center of the cave around what he (at that point) thought to be a small altar.[24]

The few sherds that were found show that the cave had been used in both the EM I-II and the MM III to LM I periods.[25] The bronze artifacts belong to the later period of use. Marinatos explained the different pottery dates by proposing that in the EM period the site had been used as a refuge, while it only became a sacred site in the MM III period.[26] The two excavations produced hundreds of votive bronze knives and double axes and many swords.[27] Many of the double axes were engraved with designs and one of them bore an inscription whose signs, as Marinatos said, look somewhat like a cross between the symbols on the Phaistos Disk and Minoan hieroglyphics.[28] The double axes range in size from only a few centimeters to those that were 0.65 and 0.70 m in breadth. Marinatos proposed that the larger double axes might have stood in wooden bases in a manner similar to those found at Knossos.[29] It is clear that most of the swords and blades were, like the double axes, made as votive offerings because they were too thin to be of any practical use. A few of the blades were thick enough to have been used, but these too, as Marinatos said, "never served in battle," because their bases were not made to attach to proper grips.[30] The swords were remarkable, though, in their exceptional length; most were more than 1 m long. In addition to the bronze artifacts Marinatos found 26 gold and 6 silver double axes as well as a piece of gold that he thought looked like a representation of a small ("sacred?") mountain.[31]

The interesting thing is that in addition to the votive objects, unworked bronze in bun ingots, sword blanks, and a bronze chisel were also found.[32] Marinatos originally thought that this unworked bronze had been brought to the site as offerings along with the other votive objects.[33] However, he later substantially revised his opinion of the cave's function, saying that he had been influenced by Nilsson's inclusion of the site in his list of cult sites[34] to see it as such, and to interpret the inner room as containing an altar.[35] However, by 1962 he decided that the cave was not a shrine at all, but must have been a metal-working shop. Marinatos says that two things speak against the cave as having been a sanctuary.[36] First, it lacks the abundant pottery and other finds that are very common in cave sanctuaries. Also, if it had been a religious site, the objects would have been distributed in such a way that the cave's sacred nature would have been indicated more clearly. He felt that this alternative explanation, that the site was a bronze-working shop, would better explain the bun ingots, sword blanks, and some of the swords, which he refers to as "half-finished."[37] He explains the presence of the votive objects by saying that they could have been made there (although he also implies that some of them could have been scrap metal). But despite his revised, more practical view of the site, Marinatos does not divorce the cave from the religious realm entirely. Rather, he proposes that the smithy was run by a rich priest guild that worshipped a deity who protected and fostered the art of metallurgy.[38] Evely says that this idea "may be feasible, but there is no evidence for a working area situated either in the environs of or within the cave itself."[39] Marinatos also recognizes that the cave itself could not have functioned as a workshop, but he believes that future excavation in the vicinity of the cave would confirm his proposition.

While it seems correct for Marinatos to reconsider his first theory, his second one has some problems as well. For instance, the presence of the double axe whose inscription demonstrates its great antiquity shows that at least some of the objects were treasured heirlooms. This seems to speak against the idea that the votives were being made there, or, for that matter, that they had been brought together as scrap to be melted down, at least by a priest guild. Also, the position of the cave on a rather inaccessible and steep hillside makes it and the surrounding area a very unlikely place for a bronze workshop. But the idea that Arkalochori was a cave sanctuary is not entirely satisfactory either. This has not, however, kept scholars from propagating the idea that Arkalochori was a sanctuary. Rutkowski for instance includes Arkalochori in his discussion of cave sanctuaries.[40] Tyree also included Arkalochori in her first survey of sacred caves (although she has since changed her mind),[41] and, as we have seen, it usually appears among the list of sites that are cited as exhibiting a connection between religion and industry.[42]

[24] Marinatos 1935, p. 250.

[25] Marinatos 1935, pp. 251 and 253. L. Tyree, *Cretan Sacred Caves: Archaeological Evidence*, Ph.D. Dissertation, University of Missouri 1974, see pp. 28-30 and 216.

[26] Marinatos 1935, p. 252.

[27] S. Marinatos *AA* 50 (1935) 248-256; see pp. 250-251.

[28] Marinatos 1935, p. 254.

[29] Marinatos 1935, p. 251.

[30] Marinatos 1935, p. 252.

[31] Marinatos 1935, p. 250.

[32] Marinatos 1935, p. 251.

[33] Marinatos 1934, p. 253.

[34] Nilsson, 1950; see pp. 60-61 and 459-460 where Nilsson discusses the possibility that it was to the Cave of Arkalochori that Zeus was brought to be hidden as an infant.

[35] Marinatos 1962, p. 89. Marinatos gives no real explanation as to what he originally thought constituted the altar or why he subsequently abandons it.

[36] Marinatos 1962, pp. 91-92.

[37] Marinatos 1962, pp. 91-92.

[38] Marinatos 1962, p. 92. Rutkowski proposes instead that it was a goddess of war that was worshipped at Arkalochori, "where long swords were offered up to the goddess in the hope that she would ensure long life to the weapons of the local population." (1986, pp. 65 and 227). Wherever these objects were originally offered, the two roles proposed for the deity who received them need not have been mutually exclusive.

[39] Evely 2000, p. 341.

[40] Rutkowski 1986, see pp. 64-68 and 227.

[41] Tyree 1974, pp. 28-30 and 216. Tyree has since changed her mind concerning Arkalochori and therefore in her forthcoming publication on sacred caves Tyree will not include Arkalochori (personal communication, October 2006).

[42] Hägg and Marinatos 1981 p. 217. Tegyey 1984, p. 77. M. Burdajewicz, *The Aegean Sea Peoples and Religious Architecture in the*

More recent work in the area, however, has taken a different approach. Tyree's current estimation of the site is that during the EM I-II period, it was most likely used as a burial place.[43] She comes to this conclusion partially because its pottery assemblage is similar to those found in other burial caves, and partially because Arkalochori's waterless crevice in the rock is not like the deep and usually rather moist caves with stalactites that were usually chosen to serve as sacred sites. Tyree also points out that Arkalochori should actually be classified as a rock shelter (because of its shallow depth), and that this is the type of place generally used as EM and MM burial sites. Thus Arkalochori could have served as a burial site during its earlier phase of use (EM I-II). As for the cave's use in its later period (MM III–LM I), Tyree does not think that it was considered sacred.[44] Rather, Tyree proposes that the metal objects found in the rock shelter simply constitute a hoard that was hidden in the cave. Rethemiotakis, who has been excavating the nearby Minoan palace Galatas, which happens to be in the vicinity of Arkalochori, has come to a similar conclusion.[45] The palace at Galatas was abandoned during the LM IA period, which seems strange when "contrasted to the historical background of the period which saw the peaking of the Minoan culture."[46] He attributes the decline and abandonment of the palace to local events that caused problems in the area, but which had no recognizable effects on the rest of the palaces of Crete. The treasure of the Arkalochori cave fits nicely into his picture of events. Rethemiotakis points out that many items that are commonly found at other cave sanctuaries, such as figurines, specialized vessels and large amounts of pottery, are missing from the Arkalochori cave. For this reason the cave itself should not be seen as a religious site, but rather simply as the place where the hoard was hidden away. But Rethemiotakis does think that the objects in the hoard did derive from "a sanctuary (or several), given that all the types (swords, daggers, double axes, ingots) have parallels in peak or hypaethral sanctuaries...."[47] The fact that the hoard was hidden in the cave indicates to Rethemiotakis that there was danger in the area, a danger which could have materialized at the palace, causing its abandonment.

The question then becomes, who left the hoard in the cave? Considering the overwhelming number of votive objects in the hoard, it certainly could have been religious personages attached to a certain sanctuary (or sanctuaries) who were trying to preserve their religious objects, and their wealth, for a better time. In this case, we can explain the bun ingots in one of two ways. Either they were also votive objects, offered by bronze workers seeking protection from the god(dess) for their industrial endeavors, or they were present because the priests themselves (somewhat as Marinatos had proposed) were smiths who ran a bronze-working shop at their sanctuary. A third possibility is that marauding bandits, who had plundered a sanctuary (or sanctuaries) and a smithy at around the same time, had hidden their collected treasure in the cave. Finally, a fourth possibility is that this was a smith's hoard and that the smith had acquired all the votive objects from sanctuaries that were, it would seem, very much in need of whatever the smith had to offer in exchange. Any one of these scenarios could account for the hoard of double axes and swords found in Arkalochori cave. Considering some of the evidence that I will discuss further on, the idea that priests were managing a smithy is not an unreasonable suggestion. Nonetheless, this proposal (like the others) is mere conjecture and therefore just as possible as the other possible explanations. This leaves us with no sure connection for the votive objects with an industrial workplace. Arkalochori, therefore, should not be cited as demonstrating a shrine-workshop connection.

Myrtos

Myrtos, however, provides us with a more certain example of the religious sphere's involvement in production. Myrtos is also the earliest of the sites that have been said to exhibit a shrine-workshop connection. The "large, single building complex"[48] of 93 rooms and areas situated on the hilltop of Fournou Koriphi belongs to the EM II period.[49] The majority of the remains, however, including those we will be discussing, derive specifically from the EM IIB period. In the southwest corner of the site a shrine and several other rooms that seem to have had a cultic nature were found. The western-most room of the complex, room 92, was designated as the shrine proper because a terracotta goddess figurine, clutching a jug to her side in the manner of the *kourophoros* figurines, was found next to a stone bench in the middle of the room.[50] Warren has proposed that, "one function of the goddess with her jug must have been the special protection of the water supply, something of crucial importance in the life of the settlement, since there were no wells on the hill and all water had to be carried up in jugs."[51] Room 91, which was just to the north of room 92, seems to have been the shrine's storeroom.[52] Its three surviving walls (those on the north, east and south) all had stone benches that must have served to support shelving for the 66 vessels that

Eastern Mediterranean at the Close of the Late Bronze Age (BAR International Series) 1990, see p. 64.

[43] L. Tyree, "Minoan Sacred Caves: The Natural and Political Landscape," in *Proceedings of the 9th International Congress of Cretan Studies, 1-7 October 2001*, pp. 329-342.

[44] L. Tyree, personal communication, October 2006.

[45] G. Rethemiotakis, "Τὸ νέο μινωικὸ ἀνάκτορο στὸν Γαλατὰ Πεδιάδας καὶ τὸ 'Ιερὸ Σπήλαιο' Ἀρκαλοχωρίου," in Κρήτες Θαλλασσοδρόμοι, Κύκλος Διαλεξέων, Ἰανουάριος - Ἀπρίλος 1996, A. Karetsou, ed., Herakleion, Crete 1999, pp. 91-111 (with an English summary). The new palace lies about 30 km southeast of Iraklion, close to the Medieval village of Galatas.

[46] Rethemiotakis 1999, p. 111.

[47] Rethemiotakis 1999, p. 111.

[48] P. Warren, *Myrtos: An Early Bronze Age Settlement in Crete*, Thames and Hudson 1972, see p. 260.

[49] Warren 1972, p. 269.

[50] Warren 1972, pp. 85-87.

[51] Warren 1972, p. 87.

[52] Warren 1872, pp. 84-85. Several tools, including a chisel, were also found in this room.

were found smashed on the floor. Only five of these vessels were large storage types, while nearly all the rest were fine wares. It seems likely that they could have been used in the religious rituals that were probably conducted in the area. Room 89, which adjoins the shrine room to the east, also seems to have had a cultic nature.[53] Against the east wall of this room was what Warren describes as "a tripartite structure consisting of two little, low benches or tables with a hearth between them."[54] Also, two shallow steps ran across the room from west to east at the northern and southern ends of the hearth. The steps would have obligated one to step down into the area directly in front of the hearth. The most remarkable find was uncovered on the southern step: the fragments of a human skull. The skull, which came from a young adult male, cannot have come from an unfortunate person who was unable to escape the final destruction of the site since no other bones were found in the room. It seems most likely that the skull was itself an object that played a role in the religion of the people who lived in the settlement. Warren says that "ancestor worship, or even human sacrifice cannot be ruled out."[55] In addition to this skull, a human figurine carved out of green steatite and several vases, including a pyxis and two piriform jars, were also found in room 89.

It seems that the religious personnel who were active in rooms 89 and 92 also engaged in some industrial activities, the most predominant of which was the production of wine. In room 90, which communicates directly with the shrine's storage area and, through that room, with the shrine itself, a stone bench was found against the north wall.[56] A large tub or lekane with a spout was found near to this bench and had most likely fallen from it. Warren says that the lekane probably had been positioned on the bench so that the spout would have projected over its edge. The liquid in the lekane could then pour out of the spout and into a jar that stood on the ground next to the bench.[57] A large deep bowl was found on a stone pot stand in the northwest corner, and inside this bowl were the remains of grapes, which most likely indicates that it was wine that was being produced in these vessels. The large quern, the pounder, and the perforated stone weight that were also found in room 90 would tend to support the idea that wine was made in this room. Thus it is likely that religious personnel were performing industrial work at Myrtos.

Concerning the purpose of the wine, Warren makes the reasonable suggestion that it was being made for offerings within the shrine. I have to wonder, though, if the wine was destined to be used not only within the shrine area, but if it was also used by the rest of the community. As Säflund pointed out, it is possible that room 80, which was the largest room of the settlement, and which was also in the southwestern area, may have been used in connection with the shrine for public ceremonial feasting and drinking rituals.[58] One of the few large pithoi in the room contained the remains of pressed grapes. This was the only other evidence on the site for the presence of wine, and it may have been the shrine's wine that was stored there. If this were the case, then the shrine was making an economic contribution to the community through its production of wine. And, perhaps, the goddess figurine found in room 92 had sacred wine in her jug, not water.

It should be mentioned that in Säflund's analysis of the site, she proposed that there was a much greater connection between the shrine and industrial production at Myrtos than Warren had envisaged. Instead of seeing Myrtos as a settlement with a shrine, Säflund saw a shrine with a settlement attached to it. She therefore thought that the influence of the goddess extended to all the industries of the site. It is true that within Myrtos there are several areas where specialized industries were conducted. These industries included pottery production (eight turntables were found in room 49), textile manufacturing and probably dyeing (evidence for warp-weighted looms was found in rooms 58 and 74), and a stone-working industry (two cores and chips and flakes were found throughout the site[59]).[60] Warren did see a relationship between the industries of the site and the goddess, but he saw her as a "household goddess" for whom the "protection and support of the household crafts and industries of the settlement must also have been her province."[61] In contrast, Säflund thinks that the goddess should be interpreted not as a "household goddess" but as "a patron goddess" who resides "in a sanctuary [that included] a specialized development."[62] Säflund sees the shrine as "an integral part of a substantial cult building, serving different ritual functions ..." and calls Myrtos a "sacred settlement."[63] Tegyey picks up on this line of argument and says of Myrtos that it had "large buildings with specialized industries ... attached to the shrine of the goddess."[64] If this were the case, then all of the industrial areas at Myrtos, even the ones that were not in particularly close physical proximity to the shrine, would be considered religious workshops. Of course it cannot be said with certainty which interpretation of the site is correct, but the evidence does not seem to support Säflund's idea that the entire settlement was a religious site. On the other hand, I would not call the deity of the shrine a "household goddess" since the term does not take into account the fact that her shrine probably served the entire settlement. Thus, while I think it is probable that she was considered the patron deity of the industries that were conducted within the settlement, it also seems

[53] Warren 1972, pp. 81-83.
[54] Warren 1972, p. 81.
[55] Warren 1972, p. 83.
[56] Warren 1972, p. 84.
[57] Warren 1972, p. 84.

[58] G. Säflund, "Cretan and Theran Questions," in *Sanctuaries and Cults in the Aegean Bronze Age*, R. Hägg and N. Marinatos, eds., Stockholm 1981, pp. 189-208; see p. 189.
[59] Warren 1972, pp. 263 and 326-327.
[60] See Warren's discussion of the industrial activities of Myrtos on pp. 255-265.
[61] Warren 1972, pp. 86-87.
[62] Säflund 1981, p. 189.
[63] Säflund 1981, pp. 189-190.
[64] Tegyey 1984, p. 77.

likely that the only industry that she and her personnel were directly involved in was the production of wine.

Pseira

On the island of Pseira, off the northeastern coast of Crete, a rather extensive community consisting of 60 buildings was built up over the course of the LM I period.[65] The largest of these buildings, the Plateia Building (or Building BS/BV) was located on the northern side of the town's plateia. The building's size, coupled with the range of activities that went on within it, have led the excavators to believe that this was the "residence of persons with elevated status in the LM IB community, and most probably the domicile of the 'rulers' on the island."[66] The area of the Plateia Building that holds the most interest for this study is the upper storey. Floyd found that several activities could be identified as having definitely gone on there, such as cooking and food preparation, weaving, the manufacture of stone vases, and cult activity.[67] Several other industrial activities, such as the manufacture of objects from quartz crystals and from shell, may also have occurred in the building.[68] The evidence for weaving consists of thirteen whole or fragmentary clay loomweights that fell together from the upper story into room BS 6, a room that was in the central part of the building.[69] Twenty-six more clay weights and two disks which might have been spindle whorls were found throughout the building, but the concentration of the thirteen seems to indicate that the main weaving locale may have been located above the area into which they fell. The location of the stone vase manufacturer's workshop was indicated by a cluster of pieces of ground stone hand tools, a chunk of emery, nineteen fragmentary or whole quartz crystals, pieces of unworked serpentine and one of obsidian with its cortex preserved, and unfinished stone vessels.[70] These objects all fell into room BS 14, which is in the center of the building. Floyd records that "numerous fragmentary and a few complete stone vessels" were found throughout the building, but it is again the cluster of the objects mentioned above which indicates where the stone vase manufacture most likely took place.

The evidence for cult activity came mainly from the floor above the western part of Wing BV, just to the west of the areas where the stone vase production and weaving were taking place. The evidence for the shrine consisted of fragments of a relief fresco,[71] a piece of a marble chalice, six rhyta, one cup rhyton, a horn from a bull rhyton, four "unusual footed vessels (possibly offering tables),"[72] a sherd from a fenestrated stand, and an almost complete triton shell.[73] It seems that access to the shrine could only have been gained by going through the area where the vases were being worked on. As Floyd says, "These three activities [weaving, stone vase manufacture, and cult activity], interestingly occurred in adjacent or contiguous areas on the upper story, i.e. they did not come from distinct, separate parts of the building. The persons involved in these various activities would have been in close proximity to each other and thus interaction seems likely."[74] It may have been that one of the responsibilities of the deity worshipped in that room was to watch over the manufacturing processes that went on so close to it.

This is not to say, however, that it was necessarily religious personnel who were employed in making the vases. The fact that the industrial areas and the shrine were so close to each other may be explained simply by the owners' desire to control access to these activities. Floyd mentions that "it is unlikely that each household produced its own stone vessels, and, indeed, few of the other buildings excavated or cleaned during the modern excavations produced evidence for stone vase manufacture…."[75] She also remarks that "Pseira is especially known for its abundant and beautiful LM I stone vases."[76] Thus, since the inhabitants of the Plateia House probably supplied these vases,[77] the stone vase workshop was probably a source of prestige and/or material wealth for its owners. They seem to have sought to protect this source of prestige by placing it within one of the most private areas of the building.[78] Floyd also says that the inhabitants of the building "...also played a significant role in the religious life of the community."[79] It seems possible then that they would have retained their positions as leaders at least partially through their possession of and ability to control access to the shrine.[80] Thus the same motivation could account for the fact that the shrine and the workshop were both located in the remotest parts of the building: the desire to control other peoples' access to them. This is the most logical conclusion if we take the Plateia Building, as the excavator does, as a residence.

[65] P.P. Betancourt and C. Davaras, "Excavations at Pseira, 1985 and 1986," *Hesperia* 57 (1988) 207-225; see p. 207.

[66] C.R. Floyd, *Pseira III: The Plateia Building*, University of Pennsylvania 1998, p. xiii.

[67] Floyd 1998, pp. 204-205. Also see C.R. Floyd, *The Plateia Building at Pseira: Evidence for Regional Style, Social Ranking, and the LM IB Domestic Economy*, Ph.D. Dissertation, University of Pennsylvania 1996, p. 361, which the author was kind enough to copy and mail to me herself.

[68] Floyd 1996, p. 361; *idem* 1998, p. 215.

[69] Floyd 1998, p. 206.

[70] Floyd 1998, p. 207.

[71] See Floyd 1998, pp. 167-169 for a discussion of the painted plaster.

[72] See Floyd 1998, pp. 186-188 for a discussion of the ritual vessels.

[73] Floyd 1998, p. 208.

[74] Floyd, personal communication, March 1997.

[75] Floyd 1998, p. 207.

[76] Floyd 1996, p. 363.

[77] Floyd 1998, p. 233.

[78] Floyd (1998, p. 207) remarks on how the workshop was not placed in an open space, but rather in one "where access could be easily controlled."

[79] Floyd 1998, p. 233.

[80] It should be noted that a more communal Shrine (Building AC, which is the source of the only relief fresco found on Pseira besides the one found in the shrine of the Plateia Building) has been identified within the settlement (Betancourt and Davaras 1988, pp. 215-218).

If, however, we saw the building primarily as a place where many industrial activities went on, that is, as a multi-purpose workshop, then the link between religion and industry could be drawn much more tightly. Floyd herself recognizes that some of the finds that came from the area, which she thinks might have been the sleeping/residential area of the house (the ground floor of the western BV Wing), "deviate from the profile established by Sandars for sleeping/guest/ceremonial areas."[81] Those finds are: "a large amount of small, badly worn pottery," twelve possible ground stone hand tools, two obsidian blades, a piece of a quartz crystal, and a clay weight.[82] Even the finds that Floyd records as being "personal possessions" fit easily into the industrial category: a stone seal and "a clay disk which could represent either a spindle whorl or a button."[83] The majority of the rest of the ground floor was used for storage.[84] Hence a case could be made for seeing this building as having a predominantly industrial nature. But still, the arguments for the Plateia Building being "the residence of persons of elevated rank on Pseira"[85] are strong. Floyd says,

> The Plateia Building has features that ally it both visually and conceptually (in terms of organization) to the Minoan palaces and differentiate it from other structures on the peninsula. Such architectural features of the Plateia Building include: the impressive Plateia facade wall, the irregular line of the Plateia facade, the large size of the structure, the relationship to the town square, the multiple benches, and the articulated entrance. ... Decorative features (such as the many floor pavings and the painted plaster, including fragments of a relief fresco) and portable luxury or ritual items (including rhyta, a marble chalice, triton shells, a sealstone, and imported pottery) serve to further underscore the importance and elevated status of the inhabitants of this building.[86]

Hence, it is probably safer not to deviate from the excavator's assessment of the building as a residence, and to conclude that the close proximity of the shrine and the principal areas of industrial activity may actually have been dictated by the needs of the owners of the building rather than by some close or special relationship between the craftsmen and those who conducted the religious rites.

Mochlos

On the mainland of northeastern Crete, opposite the island site of Mochlos, Soles has excavated the majority of two buildings (A and B) and parts of two more (C and D) in an area that he has identified as "an extensive Artisans' Quarter."[87] Both Buildings A and B contained industrial and religious artifacts. The main period of use for the industrial quarter is LM IB,[88] but it may have lasted into early LM II.[89] Room 4 of Building A, which was the largest (*ca.* 5.02 x 5.71 m) and most central room of the building, seems to have been the main workroom. The room had two stone platforms, one in the northwest corner and the other in the southeast corner, that were probably used as work surfaces, and a bench was located on the southern wall just to the west of the southeastern platform.[90] A stone bin, about 1.10 m deep, situated on the east wall was used for storage while a pit *ca.* 1 m in diameter near the southeastern bench was used for refuse. The finds show that various types of work went on in room 4,[91] including "stone vase making, bronze working and perhaps textile working."[92] But from the "numerous small pieces of bronze, which appear to be runoff or spillage from bronze casting,"[93] that were found in this room and several others of Building A, and the bronze foundry hoard that was found "against the southern wall of the destroyed northern room"[94] the main activity of Building A was metal working.[95] Room 1, which communicated directly with room 4, seems to have been a second intensively used work area.[96] It also had benches against its walls (one on the west and an L-shaped one on the south and east) and low flat stone stands were found in front of each bench which were probably used as work surfaces by those who sat on the benches.[97] Like room 4, room 1 was used for metal working as it contained a crucible fragment and three moulds, one of stone and two of clay. No hearths were found in these rooms though, which means that the actual melting and casting must have occurred outside the building. The most likely place for that was found on the northern side of the building, just outside of room 1, in an area that was most likely a porch or shed that was open to the sea.[98] Most of this area was lost to erosion, but two stone-lined pits were found against Building A's

[81] Floyd 1998, p. 217.
[82] Floyd 1998, pp. 78, 90-91, and 217.
[83] Floyd 1998, p. 217.
[84] Floyd 1998, pp. 212-214.
[85] Floyd 1998, p. 227.
[86] Floyd 1998, p. 233.

[87] J. Soles and C. Davaras, *Mochlos IA: Period III. Neopalatial Settlement on the Coast: The Artisans' Quarter and the Farmhouse at Chalimouri; The Sites*. Philadelphia 2003, p. 8; *idem*, "Excavations at Mochlos, 1990-1991," *Hesperia* 63 (1994) 391-436; see pp. 412-426; *idem*, "Excavations at Mochlos, 1992-1993," *Hesperia* 65 (1996) 175-230; see pp. 202-207. See also J. Soles, "A Community of Craft Specialists at Mochlos," in *TEXNH: Craftsmen, Craftswomen, and Craftsmanship in the Aegean Bronze Age* (*Aegaeum* 16), R. Laffineur and P.P. Betancourt, eds., Liège and PASP, University of Texas 1997, pp. 425-430.
[88] Soles and Davaras 2003, p. 10; *idem* 1994, p. 414.
[89] Soles and Davaras 2003, p. 10; *idem* 1996, p. 205. Radiocarbon results from the olive pits give the workshop area a 15th century date (Soles 1997, p. 426).
[90] The use of benches here does not indicate that the room was used for religious purposes because the finds associated with the benches were industrial in nature rather than cultic.
[91] Soles and Davaras 2003, p. 12.
[92] Soles and Davaras 2003, p. 13.
[93] Soles and Davaras 1994, p. 415.
[94] Soles and Davaras 2003, p. 94.
[95] Soles and Davaras 2003, p. 93.
[96] Soles and Davaras 2003, pp. 19-23.
[97] Soles and Davaras 2003, p. 19.
[98] Soles and Davaras 2003, pp. 19-20; *idem* 1997, p. 426.

northern wall, one of which contained two bronze bowls within which were casting debris and copper ingot fragments. Soles proposes that this deposit was "a small foundry hoard of used objects and new ingot pieces that was being stored to cast into new objects."[99] Soles also points out that this hoard, and the two others that were discovered in housed on the main settlement "demonstrate the importance of recycling in Minoan metallurgy."[100] Room 1 also seems to have been the main area for stone-vase manufacture in that it contained a drill guide and an amphibolite grinder and an amphibolite core, in addition to pieces of pumice and quartz crystal that could have been used as abrasives in the drilling process.[101]

Several other rooms in the building contained similar workshop remains, but one room, room 6, found to the east of room 4, was most likely a shrine. Unfortunately, much of this room could not be excavated since it lies under a modern building, but its special nature was indicated by the fact that it was the only room in the building whose walls and floor were covered with white plaster.[102] The finds were sparse but among them was a clay foot (which was found just underneath the foundation of the modern house) that measured only 0.114 m long and had an upturned toe. Soles says, "Because of its size and pointed, upturned toe, it should be identified as a votive foot, very similar to those from the shrine at Mallia."[103] Room 6 also contained a miniature jug "like those found in many peak sanctuaries and other shrines."[104] It seems possible then that this room was used for religious purposes, a possibility which is supported by the fact that Building B, which, like Building A, was used predominantly for industrial activities, also had a room that appears to have been a shrine.[105]

Building B seems to have functioned primarily as a pottery workshop.[106] Six potter's wheels, one with raw clay still attached to its surface (in room 8[107]), were found in the building, along with a pivot stone (in room 10), pits that "were probably being used as settling basins for the levigation of clay," a bronze cutting tool (possibly used as a spatula), and a variety of other tools that could have been used in the process of manufacturing pottery.[108] Several storage jars in the rooms could have held the potter's supplies of clay and temper, while stone pounders could have been used to crush the temper.[109] Nodules of red hematite, along with the larger stones upon which they were to be crushed (traces of red were found on these stones) were also found. The red of the hematite matched the color of the red paint found on pottery found in the building.[110] Finally, to complete the picture, two small updraft kilns were found outside the south wall of the building.[111]

In the midst of Building B, there appears to have been a room reserved for religious purposes: room 1.[112] Room 1's special nature was indicated by the fact that its entire floor was painted with white plaster. And by the objects that must have fallen from the low that bench ran *ca.* 1.65 m long on the east wall.[113] Among those finds were "two nearly identical clay stands with low flaring bowls on conical pedestals" and many other special dishes that were "designed to hold small offerings."[114] Also found was a hollow cylindrical tube that supported a small bowl that had been set into the tube at the top. Soles proposes that this object could be a prototype for the later "snake tube."[115] The assemblage in general resembles those from the contemporary shrines at Myrtos, Pyrgos, and Kommos.[116] The interesting thing about this shrine is that each of the crafts conducted within industrial quarter - metal working, pottery production and stone-vase production - are represented by votive objects: a miniature chisel that had no signs of wear, a miniature jug with a trefoil spout, and a piece of raw stone material.[117]

Soles proposes, considering the prominent place the work spaces occupied within the buildings and the more peripheral locations of the living/eating spaces, that the artisans who worked in these two buildings were full-time specialists whose markets were probably not confined to the immediate settlement in which they were located.[118] The buildings then were primarily industrial sites and not homes whose occupants happened to work on some craft activities. The religious rooms therefore must have been included in the building because they held some significance for the workers in relation to the industrial work that they were practicing there. Soles classifies them as "household shrines that played a supportive role in the artisan community."[119] It was probably hoped that the deity(ies) worshipped in the shrines would ensure the safety of the workers and a favorable outcome for their production processes. It is difficult to say however whether religious personnel were directly involved in the manufacturing processes. It is certainly possible, given the presence of the shrines, that religious personnel had a role in overseeing the production, and/or that they actually participated in the work, as a kind of monk-craftsmen. But it is also possible, and probably more likely that the shrines were used for worship by purely secular craftsmen who said

[99] Soles and Davaras 2003, p. 20; *idem* 1994, p. 416.
[100] Soles and Davaras 2003, p. 20.
[101] Soles and Davaras 2003, pp. 20, 93; *idem* 1994, p. 417.
[102] Soles and Davaras 2003, p. 33.
[103] Soles and Davaras 2003, p. 33; *idem* 1994, p. 419.
[104] Soles and Davaras, 2003, p. 33.
[105] Soles and Davaras 2003, p. 33; *idem* 1996, p. 204.
[106] Soles and Davaras 2003, p. 93; *idem* 1994, pp. 421-422; *idem* 1996, pp. 205-206.
[107] Soles and Davaras 2003, p. 49.
[108] Soles and Davaras 2003, pp. 53, 56, 94-95.
[109] Soles and Davaras 2003, p. 53; *idem* 1996, p. 205.
[110] Soles and Davaras 2003, p. 57; 1996, p. 206.
[111] Soles and Davaras 2003, pp. 81-86, 94-95; *idem* 1996, p. 206; *idem* 1997, p. 427.
[112] Soles and Davaras 2003, pp. 62-63.
[113] Soles and Davaras 2003, p. 62; *idem* 1994, p. 423.
[114] Soles and Davaras 2003, pp. 62-63; *idem* 1994, pp. 423-425.
[115] Soles and Davaras 2003, p. 63; *idem* 1994, p. 425.
[116] Soles and Davaras 2003, p. 63.
[117] Soles and Davaras 2003, p. 63.
[118] Soles and Davaras 2003, pp. 96-99; *idem* 1997, pp. 429-430.
[119] Soles and Davaras 2003, p. 99.

their prayers and made their offerings at the shrines' altars as part of rituals whose performance were important for their crafts. Perhaps they looked to a local priest to perform official rites for them. It is of course difficult to say what the exact role of religious personnel would have been in these particular shrines, but at least the evidence does show the importance of a religious presence for those who were involved in industrial work.

Thera

The site of Akrotiri on Thera is another one of the sites that was discussed at the Sanctuaries and Cults conference as having cult and craft in close association. The area that was referred to was the House of the Ladies, but subsequently other areas of Akrotiri have been cited as also having a combination of these two elements. First, however, I will consider the House of the Ladies, which is generally agreed to have housed a sanctuary because of the religious nature of the fresco in room 1.[120] Much of the extant fresco actually depicts a nature scene of large papyrus flowers, but fragments of three female forms were also found and pieced together.[121] The woman on the south wall appears to be processing towards the east, while one of the women on the north wall also faces east. This latter woman is bending over and offering a Minoan flounced skirt to the third female figure, which unfortunately is very poorly preserved, but may be a goddess or a priestess.[122] The fresco as a whole seems to depict a procession of women carrying gifts,[123] and/or a ceremonial robing scene.[124] Marinatos also found four clay chests or cists in the floor of the room that contained many ritual vessels, including painted ewers, one of which had a painting of polychrome swallows, a rhyton with tortoise-shell decoration, and many handleless bowls.[125] In contrast with S. Marinatos, Doumas thinks that these chests were actually part of the room below the shrine,[126] which would indicate that the sacred nature of the building extended to the story below. Room 2, which was immediately to the east of the room with the Ladies Fresco was filled with "a large number of cups and cooking vessels." Forsyth proposes that this room was used for celebratory feasts that were part of the ritual that took place in the shrine.[127] Room 7, just to the west of the shrine room, seems to have served as a storeroom for cult vessels.[128] No less than fourteen rhyta were found in room 7, along with a nippled ewer, several handleless bowls, and a "kymbe painted in a polychrome fashion and showing ibex-like animals grazing in a crocus field."[129]

It was in room 6, which was next to room 7, that "a half-finished vase of hard whitish stone was found."[130] This vase, which was 60 cm high and 40 cm wide at its upper end, was clearly not finished since it was rather thick and still bore tool marks. This stone vase has prompted some to call room 6 a "lapidary's workshop."[131] However, I find it difficult to think of room 6 as a full-scale workshop on the basis of this one vase. Warren proposes that "although workshop debris has not been reported, it must have been in the process of manufacture in this room or very near by."[132] It is unfortunate that Marinatos does not describe anything else that was found in room 6. He simply says, "Beam holes in the walls indicated the floor of the storey, but nothing of interest was found *in situ*.[133] I cannot help wondering if further indications of workshop activities may have been destroyed or obscured during the course of the excavation, which was very difficult at Thera, or in the destruction of the building. In any case, the evidence we do have only allows us to say that this one vase may have been worked on somewhere in the building, which does not constitute evidence that a full workshop operated there.[134] Thus any proposal that the personnel attached to the sanctuary were involved in the manufacture of stone vases is tentative at best.

It is possible, however, that cult and economic activities were associated in other shrines at Akrotiri. N. Marinatos actually describes seven instances in which shrines were associated with either storage, the preparation of food, or industry. Her criteria for identifying shrines are at times somewhat generous, and therefore I will only discuss those examples which have been more widely accepted as religious.[135] Also, because cooking and feasting can be considered part of ritual practice, I will not classify those activities as constituting economic activity. Finally, while I agree that the association of storage facilities with a shrine could represent the religious sector's involvement in economic activity, none of the rooms that N. Marinatos proposes as having had large storage areas

[120] S. Marinatos, *Excavations at Thera V (1971 Season)*, Athens 1972, pp. 11-16; *idem*, *Excavations at Thera VI (1972 Season)*, Athens 1974, pp. 8-11. Ch. Doumas, *Thera: Pompeii of the Ancient Aegean*, Thames and Hudson 1983, pp. 81-82. N. Marinatos, "Minoan Threskeiocracy on Thera," in *Minoan Thalassocracy: Myth and Reality*, R. Hägg and N. Marinatos, eds., Stockholm 1984, pp. 167-178; see pp. 171-172. P.Y. Forsyth, *Thera in the Bronze Age*, New York 1999, pp. 81-83. S.A. Immerwahr, *Aegean Painting in the Bronze Age*, Pennsylvania State University Press 1990; see pp. 54-59.

[121] S. Marinatos 1972, pp. 13-15.

[122] N. Marinatos 1984, p. 171. Doumas 1983, p. 82. Forsyth 1999, p. 82.

[123] N. Marinatos 1984, p. 171.

[124] Forsyth 1999, p. 82.

[125] Marinatos 1972, p. 13.

[126] Doumas 1983, p. 82.

[127] Forsyth 1999, p. 83.

[128] Marinatos 1974, pp. 10-11.

[129] Marinatos 1974, p. 10.

[130] Marinatos 1974, p. 9.

[131] N. Marinatos 1984, p. 172. Forsyth 1999, p. 83.

[132] P. Warren, "The Unfinished Red Marble Jar at Akrotiri, Thera," in *Thera and the Aegean World* I, C. Doumas and H.C. Puchelt, eds., London 1978, pp. 555-568; see p. 555. Note that after Marinatos' initial report the vessel was cleaned and the true color of the stone was revealed to be red, not white (Warren 1978, p. 556).

[133] Marinatos 1974, p. 9.

[134] Schofield 1990, p. 204.

[135] Nor do I agree with the conclusions that N. Marinatos' derives from these seven examples. She says (1984, p. 175), "We have seen that in Thera, just as in Crete, the shrines were intimately associated with the economy of the community and the production. The priests, who probably represented the nobility, were thus in charge of both the shrines and the economy..." Even if the priests were involved in some economic activities, I am not sure it is justified to go so far as to say that they were therefore in charge of the economy.

meet my criteria for actually being shrines. Thus of her seven, I would only propose two of them as valid examples of shrines that may have been involved in economic activities, and one of them is the House of the Ladies shrine, which I have already considered above.

The second is found in association with the Room of the Lilies (room D 2 in Complex Delta[136]), so named because of its fresco depicting the well-known lilies and the swallows that fly in and around them. Doumas (who is generally more critical in his assessment of religious spaces than some others[137]) is willing to call this building a sanctuary not only because of the numerous ritual vessels that were found within the Room of the Lilies, but also because of the "two plastered tripod 'offering tables' [one of which was painted with polychrome dolphins] and two rhytons in the form of a boar's head" that were found in the adjacent rooms to the east and north of the Room of the Lilies.[138] Also, Doumas was impressed by the fact that "the only well-preserved pair of 'horns of consecration'" at Akrotiri was found in front of the eastern facade of the house, just outside rooms 18 and 19.[139] A partial horns of consecration was also found to the south of the shrine in room D 11.[140] It is now thought that room 19 may have been the main entrance to this area, and it would have been through 19 that one would have come to the court in front of room 2, the Room of the Lilies. Room 18, with its mosaic floor, "being located directly in front of Room 2, may have served as an anteroom...."[141] Thus it seems that there was a group of religious rooms in this area for which the Room of the Lilies was the focus.

As for the economic activities that were associated with this sanctuary, S. Marinatos records that "a millstone and the relative installation" was found in what is now seen as the court in front of the Room of the Lilies.[142] This discovery indicates that the shrine's religious personnel were involved in producing flour. Immewahr, after noting that the cooking utensils and bronze sickle for cutting grain also found in the area may have been part of the cult equipment of the shrine, says, "If this were connected with the fertility of the land, a painting glorifying the rites of spring, with blooming lilies and courting swallows, would be entirely appropriate."[143] Immewahr, however, does not make note of the mill, and so does not consider the practical applications of the sickle. His point, though, may still be pertinent since the practical and the religious aspects of the mill may have been intertwined.

But for now let us consider the practical side of the mill. The fact that actual barley flour was found within the Room of the Lilies shows that the mill was definitely being used to provide for the needs of the shrine.[144] But it is interesting to consider whether the mill was also used to produce flour for other inhabitants of Akrotiri. Two other mill installations have been found in Akrotiri, so it cannot be argued that the villagers only used the one associated with the Room of the Lilies.[145] But it is possible, as we might imagine for the other mills, that the villagers of Akrotiri brought their grain to the mill, and that it was processed for them by the religious personnel of the shrine. It is conceivable that this might have been done for religious purposes, but even so, it would not be surprising if the shrine was able to derive some material gain from this activity.

Other finds could indicate that the shrine was also involved in the manufacture of textiles: in a compartment within the shrine a group of loomweights were found.[146] In general, a large number of loomweights were found at Akrotiri. Marinatos found 950, whereas, in contrast, only 185 were found at Ayia Irini on Kea in an area of similar size.[147] The other important thing about the Akrotiri loomweights is that they were found in concentrated groups in certain houses (e.g., more than 450 were found in the West House). Tzachili therefore concludes that weaving was a specialized craft within Akrotiri, and particularly at the West House, where the concentration of loomweights was the greatest.[148] She proposes that the people working there could have produced cloth for sails or for the elaborate garments seen on the frescoes. The deposit of loomweights in the Room of the Lilies is not as large as that in the West House,[149] and so the religious personnel associated with the shrine must not have produced cloth on the same scale as those who were working in the West House. But another clue may indicate that the shrine personnel were doing more than producing cloth for their own use. A large deposit of lead

[136] Forsyth (1997, p. 65) calls this building a complex because it "does not appear to be a single dwelling but rather an agglomeration of at least four architectural units...."

[137] For instance, Doumas (1983, p. 77) does not see a religious meaning in the frescoes of the West House while N. Marinatos does; see "The West House at Akrotiri as a Cult Center," *Ath. Mitt.* 98 (1983) 1-19.

[138] Doumas 1983, p. 54. Also see S. Marinatos, *Excavations at Thera IV (1970 Season)*, Athens 1971, pp. 21 and 26.

[139] Doumas 1983, p. 54. S. Marinatos 1974, p. 34; also see plate 83a. In his initial publication Marinatos says that the horn of consecration was found "before the crenellated facade of Xeste 1," but this name for the building was later dropped when it was found that these rooms were actually part of building Delta.

[140] S. Marinatos 1971, p. 27, plate 100b.

[141] Forsyth 1997, pp. 69 and 71.

[142] S. Marinatos 1971, p. 26. N. Marinatos (1984, p. 174) calls this the "anteroom" of the shrine.

[143] Immerwahr 1990, p. 47.

[144] S. Marinatos 1971, pp. 22 and 43. Also see plate 34a for a photo of the "flour."

[145] There was a mill house in sector alpha at the northern end of the site (Forsyth 1997, p. 85; S. Marinatos, *Excavations at Thera III [1969 Season]*, Athens 1970, pp. 13-15), and another was found within the Delta Complex (room D15) at the opposite end of the building from the shrine (S. Marinatos 1972, pp. 22-24).

[146] N. Marinatos 1984, p. 174. S. Marinatos 1974, p. 13. A room to the south of the shrine, D13, was also described as being "packed with loomweights" (S. Marinatos 1971, p. 27), but I would hesitate to associate D13 with the shrine because it is somewhat distant from the religious area and may very well be part of a separate household.

[147] I. Tzachili, "All Important yet Elusive: Looking for Evidence of Cloth-making at Akrotiri," in *Thera and the Aegean World* III, Vol. I: *Archaeology*, D.A. Hardy, ed., The Thera Foundation, London 1990, pp.380-389; see p. 381.

[148] Tzachili 1990, pp. 385-386.

[149] Unfortunately I have not been able to find an exact number for the shrine's loomweights, but it is likely that the deposit was not as great as that found in the West House or in room D13 because it is not discussed with them as having had one of the larger groupings.

weights was found in room D 8,[150] which can be associated with the shrine because of its own religious objects. Michailidou has found that at least some lead weights were found in every house at Akrotiri, which shows that the inhabitants used them on a regular basis and that it was not a central authority that did the weighing.[151] Also, the weights are associated in two cases with large groupings of loomweights, which indicates to Michailidou that the wool and cloth were being weighed for the purpose of exchange. Michailidou has difficulty explaining the concentration of lead weights in room D 8; she says that perhaps they were made there or that they were used to weigh something which left no evidence. But if we may associate the loomweights of the shrine with the lead weights of room D 8, then perhaps it was cloth that the shrine was weighing. Michailidou concludes, "So the presence of the lead weights is another useful indicator that specialized household industries were an essential part of the economic structure of the LC society at Akrotiri, along with the resulting exchanges (both internal and external)..."[152] The evidence suggests then that the shrine of the Delta complex also had its own specialized industries and that it too was part of the economic structure of Akrotiri's society.

It has also been pointed out to me by Maria Shaw that the main fresco of Xeste 3, whose religious significance is not debated,[153] may also have economic significance.[154] The fresco depicts young women out in the countryside collecting crocus flowers, whose stamens are the source of saffron. The baskets full of flowers are then being offered to a goddess who sits on a raised platform that is flanked by a griffin and a monkey.[155] Shaw suggests that the presentation of the saffron to the goddess symbolizes the fact that in the real world the saffron was given to her sanctuary. If this was the case, then it would be the personnel who were associated with the goddess's sanctuary who would have reaped the benefits of exchanging that saffron. N. Marinatos makes a similar suggestion, and supports it by pointing out that within the eastern part of the shrine room "there are two basins embedded in a structure adjacent to the wall and reminiscent of the N. mill installations."[156] She thinks it is possible that these were used in the extraction of saffron from the crocus flowers. Xeste 3 then, in its fresco and may represent another connection between cult and economic activities at Akrtotiri.

Zakros

The palatial site of Zakros, found on the eastern shore of Crete, was built towards the end of the MM III period and destroyed at the end of the LM II period.[157] Like other Minoan palaces, Zakros was arranged around a paved central court. The wing to the west of the court was occupied by the main shrine and its related cult rooms, while large storage rooms were located in the northwestern part.[158] The nature of the objects that fell into the rooms of the shrine complex from above indicates that the cultic area extended to the upper floor as well. Evidence for workshop activities, including stone vase manufacture and possibly metallurgy, were also found within the cult complex.[159]

The shrine complex on the ground floor contained rooms with many different functions, most of which were related to the performance of ritual. The religious nature of the rooms is emphasized by the tripartite entryway and the altar that stood in front of the central entrance. The southernmost door of the three opened into a large 10 x 12 m room that ran along the western side the central court. This room was furnished with pier and door partitions, a light well, frescos, and a floor paved in some mysterious substance. Hence Platon calls this the Hall of Ceremonies.[160] Amongst many other cultic items, two of the most important and well-known rhyta were found in this hall. The first is in the shape of a bull's head and the other bears the relief of the tripartite peak sanctuary with agrimi sitting on its roof. These vessels most likely fell from the floor above, thus indicating the religious nature of the area above the Hall. Directly to the south of this hall one could enter the Banquet Hall through a set of three doors. These rooms may have served as places for communal rituals and banqueting, which would actually have been important for both the religious and the state sectors of society.

After going through the center door of the entry hall one could either turn north towards the storage rooms or south to the religious complex. Platon remarks that the first two outer rooms of the religious complex (XI and XV) may have been used by "the priests, who controlled access to the shrine and managed its operations."[161] These rooms also seem to have been used for storage, as one had a niche and the other a cist built into their walls.

---

[150] Marinatos 1971, p. 38, plates 87b and 88. 102 weights were found at Akrotiri all together and 49 were found in Complex Delta, but the number found in room D 8 is not specified. Nonetheless, Michailidou considers this deposit as one of the most significant of the site (A. Michailidou, "The Lead Weights from Akrotiri: The Archaeological Record," in *Thera and the Aegean World* III, Vol. I: *Archaeology*, D.A. Hardy, ed., The Thera Foundation, London 1990, pp. 407-418; see pp. 408-409 and 417-418).

[151] Michailidou 1990, p. 418.

[152] Michailidou 1990, p. 418.

[153] S. Marinatos, *Excavations at Thera VII (1973 Season)*, Athens 1976, pp. 22-28 and 32-38. Doumas 1983, pp. 54 and 106. Immerwahr 1990, p. 59: "While the paintings of women from Knossos ... might suggest a secular society in which fashion dominated, it is clear from other paintings that this court dress was the costume in which the Minoan goddess was depicted (on the rare occasions in which she does appear) and that it was worn by her votaries, women and young girls, wherever Minoan culture and religion had spread. Nowhere does this close union between the goddess and her attendants come out better than in the beautiful paintings discovered in ... Xeste 3."

[154] M. Shaw, personal communication, summer 1998.

[155] Marinatos 1976, pp. 32-38.

[156] N. Marinatos 1984, p. 175.

[157] N. Platon, *Zakros: The Discovery of a Lost Palace of Ancient Crete*, Charles Scribner's Sons, New York 1971; see pp. 237-238 and 286.

[158] Platon 1971: for Platon's discussion of the Central Shrine and its associated rooms see pp. 115-173.

[159] Platon 1971, p. 121.

[160] Platon 1971, p. 155-160.

[161] Platon 1971, p. 115.

A room devoted to storage, which Platon calls the "Pantry of the Shrine" (room XIII) was to the east of these rooms. Carbonized remains of shelves were found along the walls of the room, along with many small clay vessels. The next room to the south was the Archives room of the palace (room XVI). Unfortunately, it seems that the roof must have collapsed and crushed most of the tablets that were stored in this room before the fire had hardened them: for the most part all that was left was shapeless masses of deep russet clay.[162] But thirteen tablets did survive, and Platon makes the conjecture that they recorded the business of the shrine.[163] The southernmost room of this area (room XXII) was called the Temple Repository.[164] In its mud-brick partitions were kept ritual vessels, a stone table for offerings and braziers for the burning of incense. This room communicated directly with the shrine itself to the northeast.

The main shrine room was actually located in the center of the shrine complex, with no windows to the outside.[165] Artificial light would therefore always have been necessary. No votive figurines were found within the shrine but a ledge was built into a niche in the south wall that may have been meant to hold a cult figure. A low bench with a mud-brick back support was found on the wall opposite the ledge. Pedestaled cups, one decorated with double axes, a dozen clay rhyta, and other ritual vessels were found around the bench and the east wall. The small size of the room and its location indicates that the shrine was meant only for a small number of worshippers and that access to it probably would have been restricted. Gesell says that "Since ... it was situated next to the Lustral Basin and the Archive Room in an area which must have been reserved for official state and cult functions, it surely was used as a sanctuary for the courtiers."[166]

The "Lustral Basin" (room XXIV) was located just to the east of the shrine and would have communicated easily with it through the shrine's northern door.[167] Room XXIV had steps leading down to a sunken chamber and a balustrade, all of which are characteristic of other rooms called lustral basins, but it is unlikely that the ritual performed in any of the lustral basins involved water.[168] N. Marinatos explains that Evans' original view of lustral basins as rooms that contained water is impractical because there are no drains in any of the lustral basins. The frescos and other objects generally found in these rooms do however point to cultic activity. N. Marinatos therefore calls such rooms "adyta" because they were constructed to facilitate the action of some ritual in a location that was set apart from the surrounding area.

South of this room and the shrine was a set of three rooms that seem to have been closely related to each other. The furthest east was the treasury of the shrine (room XXV). The finds from this room are quite remarkable. The stone vases particularly stand out. The three main types, rhyta, jugs, and chalices, show that the pouring of libations must have been a very important part of the cult's ritual. Of the many beautifully worked stone rhyta probably the most well known is the one carved out of rock crystal whose curved handle was made of crystal beads. An obsidian chalice, a faience vessel in the shape of a nautilus shell and two others in the shape of bull's heads, an ivory butterfly, a crown-shaped piece of bronze decorated with double axes, and two large bronze double axes decorated with engraved designs were also found in this room. All the objects had been stored in cists created by clay partitions that were built up against the walls of the room.

The room furthest to the south (room XXVII) was also a storeroom in that it contained 15 pithoi of various sizes that probably held olive oil. It is likely that this oil was used for offerings within the shrine, but the fact that there were 15 pithoi could indicate that more oil was stored here than was necessary for the shrine's cultic rites. If so, then the oil would represent part of the shrine's accumulated wealth, a part that could potentially be traded. I would suggest that this may be a case where large storage facilities could reasonably be said to indicate that the religious personnel who held them were involved in the economic interactions of their community.

In addition to this, between the treasury and the oil storeroom was a room that Platon calls a workshop.[169] The finds from this room consisted of piles of steatite fragments and cores of red marble or porphyry, which indicate that some of the stone vase manufacturing could have gone on in this room. Three tiers of stone slabs placed at the corner of the room may have served to support planks on which the craftsmen sat while doing their work. Many tools were also found along the room's walls. Evely, however, suggests that, since there was no worked debris found in the room, it could have functioned as a storeroom for the valued materials rather than the actual workshop.[170] In that case, the actual working of the materials would have gone on nearby, perhaps out in the Central Court where the light would have been better. Vessels made from the materials in this room could conveniently be stored in the treasury next door upon their completion, and were probably used in the rituals conducted in the Shrine complex. But as with the oil, it may also be possible that the shrine exchanged some of its stone vases with the elites of Zakros and the rest of Crete.

There is evidence that a mix of religious and craft activities were also taking place on the floor above the shrine complex. Religious vessels, including vessels with

[162] Platon 1971, pp. 151-152.
[163] Platon 1971, p. 159.
[164] Platon 1971, pp. 126-127.
[165] Platon 1971, pp. 124-126.
[166] Gesell 1985, p. 19.
[167] Platon 1971, pp. 127-132.
[168] N. Marinatos, *Minoan Religion: Ritual, Image, and Symbol*, University of South Carolina Press 1993; see pp. 77-87.
[169] Platon 1971, pp. 130-131.
[170] Evely 1988, pp. 402 and 407.

coiled figure-of-eight shaped handles and three plastered offering tables, fell from above into the rooms XI and XV. Further to the west the skull of a small child was found. Platon points out that it could not have been from a victim of the site's destruction since no other human remains have been found.[171] Therefore, the skull could very well have had some religious meaning. Between the vessels and the skull, in the western section of room XI, six bronze oxhide ingots (weighing 29-30 kilograms) and three large elephant tusks (the largest was 0.7 m) were found that had also fallen from the upper floor.[172] More workshop materials fell into the pantry (room XIII), including "several pieces of steatite, sheets of bronze, the handle of a gigantic cauldron, and a few bronze tools."[173] Several more bronze tools, including three saws (two for wood, one for stone), a kind of anvil, a curved hammer, some axes, chisels, small knives, drills and engraver's tools, as well as small white stone mortars, fell from above into the Lustral Basin (room XXIV) and the area near the Hall of Ceremonies.[174] A cultic amphora made of polychrome veined marble was also found shattered on the floor of the Lustral Basin. Platon thought that it could have been used in the purification rites of the Lustral Basin, but he also mentioned that it probably fell from above with more than 30 braziers and many vessels that he thought were for ceremonial use.[175] Thus in this area of the upper story too it seems that cult and industry were in close association with each other.

On the basis of the evidence related to industrial activities, Platon proposed that workshops for wood and stone workers as well as for stone vase manufacture and perhaps even metallurgy may all have been found on the upper floor.[176] Evely comments that it might be more appropriate to interpret these items (particularly the oxhide ingots) as having been in storage on the upper floor,[177] and he is almost certainly correct in this. Nonetheless, even if the ingots and the ivory were in storage, their close association with the religious areas seems to imply that the religious personnel had some interest, perhaps even a managing interest, in the costly raw materials and their use in industrial production.

This evidence seems to indicate that a substantial amount of craft and industrial work was going on in association with the Shrine complex. Much of the work was probably done with the intention of creating items destined to be used in the shrine itself, but it is possible that the religious personnel oversaw various industries (in particular metal working and stone vase manufacture) and accumulated large quantities of oil with the intention of trading some of the resulting goods. It is not clear, however, given that the religious area is situated within the palace, whether it was the religious personnel or the palatial administration that directed the trade and thereby gained the most from it. Clearly the reward would have been greater for the shrine if the religious authorities governed the trade of the items themselves, but even if it was the secular administration of the palace that handled the trade, the religious sphere probably would still have gained both materially and in prestige through having produced the items in the first place.

Knossos

At Knossos itself, there are two areas where cult and industrial activities may have been carried out in close association with each other. The first is a stone vase workshop that was recognized by Warren.[178] During his investigations into stone vase manufacture at Knossos, Warren noted that 73 "fragments of unfinished stone vases and waste pieces from the manufacture of stone vases"[179] had been found in cists 2 to 6 of West Magazine XII", which could be dated by the associated pottery to LM II-IIIA.[180] Evely, after re-examining the material, increased this number to 79 by including several pieces found in cist 1.[181] The fragments were predominantly of gypsum (although there were also a few pieces of limestone and one piece of marble[182]), and so Warren proposed that they had come from a workshop that specialized in small vases made out of gypsum.[183] He located that workshop in the floor above the Magazine in which the worked pieces were found, postulating that they had fallen from that room into the cists.[184] Evans had previously proposed that a sanctuary had been situated in this area of the upper floor based on the fresco fragments that were also found in the cists.[185] The fragments depicted "parts of architectural designs showing the facade of a Columnar Sanctuary..."[186] The fresco as it is reconstructed shows horns of consecration standing between sets of pillars and double axes that stick out of the upper parts of the pillars.[187] For this reason, Warren points out that this part of the first floor may have accommodated both religious and workshop activities.

There is, however, a problem with Warren's interpretation of the original location of the workshop. Both the gypsum and the fresco fragments were found in

[171] Platon 1971, p. 120.
[172] Platon 1971, pp. 116-117.
[173] Platon 1971, pp. 121-122.
[174] Platon 1971, p. 129.
[175] Platon 1971, p. 129.
[176] Platon 1971, pp. 121-122 and 129.
[177] Evely 2000, p. 341.

[178] P. Warren, "A Stone Vase-Maker's Workshop in the Palace at Knossos," *BSA* 62 (1967) 195-201. This and the other four stone vase workshops of Knossos are discussed in P. Warren, *Minoan Stone Vases*, Cambridge University Press 1969, pp. 157-158.
[179] Warren 1967, p. 195.
[180] Warren 1967, p. 198.
[181] D. Evely, "Some Manufacturing Processes in a Knossian Stone Vase Workshop," *BSA* (1980) 127-137; see p. 127.
[182] Evely 1980, p. 127.
[183] Warren 1967, p. 195. A. Evans (*The Palace of Minos*, vol. 1, London 1921, p. 443) had not published the gypsum pieces as a group or discussed the possibility that they might constitute evidence for a workshop. He mentions (p. 457) only that "many odd slips of gypsum slabs" had been found in "other Magazines" (meaning, not in the Eighth Magazine which he was at that point discussing), and that an inscribed piece of gypsum had come from the Thirteenth Magazine.
[184] Warren, p. 196
[185] Evans 1921, p. 445.
[186] Evans 1921, p. 443.
[187] Evans 1921, pp. 443-444.

the lower part of the cists, under second bottoms that were put in to make the cists shallower. This renovation of the cists must have occurred at a point before the final destruction of the Palace; the real destruction fill was found above the second bottoms, which effectively sealed the deposits below them.[188] One might ask then, how did stone fragments fall into the cists if the floor had not yet been destroyed? Hood proposed that the material was found in the upper, not the lower part of the cists, which would solve the problem by making the material part of the Palace's destruction debris.[189] Warren, however, dismisses this as unlikely "in view of the careful nature of the investigations here in 1904."[190] It may be pointed out that Evans does not say that the fresco fragments had fallen from above, but that they "had been evidently *derived from* upper chambers in this palace region" (my emphasis).[191] But Warren maintains that "the material did fall from an upper floor" and he says that "the fact that the material includes pieces of wall frescoes and the remains of a stone workshop would seem to support this."[192] Popham proposed to Warren what I think must be the most reasonable explanation which is that the stone fragments were actually part of a rubble fill that was brought in to support the second bottoms.[193] Evely supports Popham's theory and says that the material was most likely brought into the Magazine to fill in the cists from a "rubbish bin" outside the Palace.[194]

Evely also brings up the fact that "only one phase of manufacture (viz. that of the removal of the interior) is yet represented: exteriors, including handles and lugs are roughed out, but no waste chips from these shaping operations were preserved."[195] Hence it is unlikely that the stone pieces found in the cists represent the full assemblage of an active workshop, which we would expect if it had fallen from above. Thus it does seem most likely that the material did come from a trash heap of some kind, and the location of the workshop must remain a mystery.

Of course, whether the artifacts fell from the upper floor or not could be deemed immaterial to this study. The fact that the industrial and religious artifacts were found together in the same deposits could indicate that the two types of activities were going on in close proximity to each other wherever the finds came from. But, on the other hand, it is also possible that the trash heap contained things from widely separated areas. Thus it is impossible to number this particular example among those representing a workshop-shrine association.

[188] Warren 1967, pp. 196-198.
[189] Warren 1967, p. 197, n. 17.
[190] Warren 1967, p. 197, n.17.
[191] Evans 1921, p. 443.
[192] Warren 1967, p. 196, n. 5.
[193] Warren 1967, p. 196, n. 5.
[194] Evely 1980, p. 127, n. 4.
[195] Evely 1980, p. 127.

A more likely example at Knossos is provided by the Unexplored Mansion,[196] which was a large building (24.5 x 14.5 m) that was constructed in LM IA but only occupied in the LM II period.[197] It appears that the Unexplored Mansion, with its pillar hall and ashlar masonry, was constructed for a purpose other than the one it was actually used for.[198] It suffered a partial destruction by fire very soon after its construction, and subsequently the building was put to use for industrial purposes. Popham notes that the pillar hall "had never been paved with the customary stone flags ..." and "Indeed, its floor had not even been properly leveled."[199] Instead earthen floors were laid down and a large mud hearth, which the Catlings refer to as a "small furnace," was built in the main hall.[200] Considering the building's other finds, this hearth could very well have been used for the melting of scrap metal. A large number (256 from the LM II period) of bronze artifacts fell from the upper floor during the LM II destruction, which indicated that the main industrial occupation of the building had been the melting down of scrap pieces of metal for the production of new items. Every stage of the manufacturing process was represented among the artifacts, including pieces of scrap metal that had been broken up for easier melting, manufactured objects such as blanks that would have been forged into specific items, the waste droplets that spilled from crucibles, and pieces that had been broken off newly cast items after they had been removed from the mold.[201] Pieces of copper wire used to hold two-piece molds together, seventeen clay crucibles (ten of which were complete or nearly so), a bellows' nozzle, and other tools were also found. The concentration and the range of evidence led to the conclusion that, "The Mansion included, in one or more of its rooms, a bronzesmith's workshop."[202] In addition to the bronze working industry, the 150+ loomweights found in the southern part of the building indicate that textile production also went on in the building.[203] What seemed surprising to the excavator was that several ritual vases, including "a unique jug ... decorated with horns of consecration,[204] ... a rhyton,[205] several pyxides,[206] two unusual basket-shaped vessels,[207] and a large flat alabastron[208]" also fell with the bronzes from the upper

[196] M.R. Popham, "The Unexplored Mansion at Knossos: A Preliminary Report on the Excavations from 1967 to 1972: The Minoan Building and its Occupants," *AR* 19 (1973) 50-61; *idem*, *The Minoan Unexplored Mansion at Knossos*, *BSA* Supplement 17, Vols. I and II, Thames and Hudson 1984. H.W. Catling and E.A. Catling, "The Bronzes and Metalworking Equipment," in Popham 1984, pp. 203-222.
[197] Popham 1984, pp. 2 and 261.
[198] Popham 1984, pp. 2 and 261-262.
[199] Popham 1973, p. 52.
[200] Catling and Catling 1984, p. 206. Popham 1984, pp. 20-21; *idem* 1973, p. 61.
[201] Catling and Catling 1984, pp 203-221.
[202] Catling and Catling 1984, p. 207.
[203] D. Evely, "The Other Finds," in Popham 1984, p. 247.
[204] Popham 1984, p. 170, plate 60a.
[205] Popham 1984, p. 174, plate 65a.
[206] Popham 1984, pp. 172-173, plate 65b and c.
[207] Popham 1984, p. 174, plate 65d and e.
[208] Popham 1984, pp. 173-174, plate 66a and b.

floor.[209] The religious nature of this material was made clear by the fact that a figurine of a goddess wearing a painted flounced dress whose arms were stretched forward was also found in association with these items.[210] Thus it seems that there was a shrine on the upper floor alongside the industrial installation. Popham asks, "Were 'ploughshares' being converted into 'swords' under the protective care of the goddess of crafts?"[211]

This connection between industry and religion seems to have been carried forward in time within the building even after its main LM II destruction. The northern third of the building was not abandoned as the rest of the building was after the LM II destruction, but continued to be used for industrial activities until the final abandonment of the entire area in LM IIIB (1200 B.C.).[212] The deposits from this later period also produced a nearly complete askos of a horse carrying a jar,[213] a male figurine,[214] and a goddess with upraised arms[215] who seems to have replaced the original goddess figurine which had been lost at the end of LM II.[216]

It should be pointed out that this combination of industrial and religious finds caused some difficulty for Popham in interpreting the primary use of the Unexplored Mansion.[217] In a recent paper, Hitchcock made the point that neither body of evidence has to take precedence over the other. She says, "Rather than privilege one category of evidence over the other, I propose that both categories of evidence, ritual and industrial may be viewed as complementary...."[218] Of course I agree with this statement, and consequently see the Unexplored Mansion as providing another example of a connection between religion and industry. However, as with the shrines in the industrial buildings at Mochlos, it is difficult to say whether the religious personnel were involved in the industrial work, and if they were, it is impossible to discern the nature of their involvement (i.e., did they simply take a managerial role or were they also the craftsmen). The most we can definitely say is that the religious element was an important part of the production work that went on there, and that the religious personnel who conducted the rites associated with the shrine of the Unexplored Mansion probably acquired some benefit from that religious work, if not also from some participation in the building's industrial production.

Summary

The types of situations discussed above vary. I actually think three of the sites that are commonly cited as exhibiting a shrine-workshop connection do not provide clear evidence for that connection at all, and should not be referred to as providing proof of a shrine-workshop connection. Those sites are Arkalochori and the two postulated stone vase workshops in Akrotiri's House of the Ladies and Knossos's western wing. Another group of sites, among them Buildings A and B at Mochlos, the Unexplored Mansion at Knossos and possibly the Plateia Building at Pseira, provide us with fairly secure evidence for a connection between religion and industry. The connection for these sites, however, is manifested by the worship of a deity that was conducted within an industrial setting. These situations show that religion and industry were associated in that the deity was most likely expected to watch over and ensure the successful outcome of certain manufacturing processes, much as classical Athena or Hephaistos was expected to protect and foster their specific crafts and those who worked within them. But, while I think it is possible that religious personnel may have had an active role to play in the industries of these sites, and thereby in the economies of their communities, nonetheless, the evidence is not clear on this point and, therefore, the direct involvement of religious personnel in the oversight of the work should not be assumed.

The third group of sites, however, does provide such evidence. At Myrtos, the shrine was engaged in the production of wine, while in the Room of the Lilies shrine at Akrotiri we find clear evidence for the religious sector's use of a mill installation and for its involvement in the production and (possibly) the exchange of cloth. M. Shaw and N. Marinatos have also suggested that the sanctuary in Xeste 3 commanded control over the production of saffron at Akrotiri. Finally, at Zakros the religious sector stored costly raw materials, such as fine stone for vases, oxhide ingots and ivory, and was most likely also involved in the production of the items that were made from these goods. In all of these cases the goods that were produced by the sanctuary personnel were probably used in the sanctuaries themselves. But this does not overturn the proposition that the sanctuaries were involved in the economy of their societies. Engaging in any kind of industrial activity requires that the managers overseeing the work interact with other people in their communities on a very practical level. The shrines would have had to acquire the raw materials necessary to produce their goods, and possibly employ craftsmen to manufacture them (although the craftsmen could have been found among the religious personnel of the shrine). Furthermore, it is possible, and I think it is actually likely, that the shrines exchanged their finished goods for other items that the personnel of the shrines needed. The fact that they did participate in their

[209] Popham 1973, p. 58. Popham refers to the mix of religious and industrial materials as creating "A somewhat bizarre and unexpected picture." Also see Popham 1984, p. 21.
[210] Popham 1984, plate 191a. R.A. Higgins, "The Terracotta Figurines," in Popham 1984, p. 198.
[211] Popham 1973, p. 58.
[212] Popham 1984, pp. 263-264.
[213] Higgins 1984, p. 199, plate 192b.
[214] Higgins 1984, p. 198, plate 192a.
[215] Higgins 1984, p. 198, plate 191b.
[216] Popham 1984, pp. 8-12 and 263.
[217] Popham 1984, pp. 21 and 262.
[218] L.A. Hitchcock, "Cult, Context, and Copper: A Cypriot Perspective on the Unexplored Mansion at Knossos," in *Proceedings of the 9th International Congress of Cretan Studies, 1-7 October 2001*, In Press. Also see L.A. Hitchcock and D. Preziosi, "The Knossos Unexplored Mansion and the 'Villa-Annex Complex'," in *The Function of the "Minoan Villa,"* R. Hagg, ed., Stockholm 1997, pp. 51-62, where some of the same opinions are expressed although not in as developed a form.

community's systems of exchange, on however limited a basis, indicates that the religious personnel were less dependent on offerings from the rest of the society for their sustenance than one might otherwise assume.

It is this last type of connection between the religious sphere and economic activities that I will be exploring in Mycenaean society, the type in which sanctuaries and their religious personnel were active players in their economies. This is also the type of connection that is found on Cyprus and is demonstrated by the sites of Kition, Enkomi, Athienou, and Myrtou Pigadhes. It is to those sites that I now turn. This discussion will be informative both for its differences and its similarities to the Mycenaean situation.

The Involvement of the Religious Sphere in the Cypriot Copper Industry

Certainly on Cyprus there is an abundance of material that demonstrates a connection between copper production and religion. Several sites, both at major coastal centers and within rural areas, have shrines in close association with metallurgical installations. Also, the association between the two appears in the iconographical symbols used by the Cypriots. This material has given rise to two very different theories concerning the actual role that the religious sphere played in the copper production industry. The first type of interpretation, represented in particular by Catling, is that "the whole management of the copper industry in Cyprus may have been temple-based."[219] Knapp in contrast thinks that the Cypriot elites used religious iconography in order to legitimize and support their own control of the industry, and he pays very little attention to the question of how religious authorities might have fitted into the picture.[220] I would like to propose a compromise view that accepts Knapp's proposals concerning the elite's use of religious iconography to justify their control over copper production and trade, but one which would also acknowledge that the religious sector probably had some involvement in the management and material benefits of the industry. I will discuss both of these theories, as well as my own interpretation of the evidence, in more detail after I have presented the material that led to these different interpretations.

Archaeological and Iconographical Evidence

One of the major sites to demonstrate a close physical relationship between cult buildings and metallurgical workshops is Kition. The Late Bronze Age city of Kition, which for the most part still lies beneath modern Larnaca, was flourishing by the beginning of the 13th century B.C.[221] Due to its position on the eastern coast of Cyprus, its large size (at 70 hectares it was the largest settlement of its time), and the number of prestige goods found within its substantial city walls (average width, 2.4 m[222]), it has been classified as a primary coastal center.[223] Because of its position under Larnaca, only two areas of the ancient city have been fully excavated (although other sections have been investigated in the course of construction work), but we are fortunate in that Area II revealed a large temple and industrial complex. This complex stood at the northeast section of the city, just south of the city walls. The first temples (called temples 2 and 3) built in this area date to the beginning of the 13th century B.C. (the LC IIC period).[224] Karageorghis and Demas say that "a possible industrial quarter" also belongs to this period, but the evidence found on the floors was meager.[225] Copper slag was found in the fill used to level the ground for the next period, and so the excavators postulate that, "some metallurgical activity was undertaken in the vicinity of the temple precinct for floor IV."[226] Towards the end of the 13th century B.C., the site of Kition appears to have been abandoned. Karageorghis attributes the abandonment to the effects of a long drought that is thought by some to have affected much of the eastern Mediterranean at the time.[227] Nonetheless, the site was soon reoccupied, possibly by about 1200 B.C. A new city wall of Cyclopean masonry was constructed to replace the former mudbrick one, and in Area I a thick layer of soil (20-30 cm[228]) was laid over the buildings of the previous period. The new occupants also renovated the temple complex in Area II.

The major change that the new inhabitants made was to level Temple 3, cover over the gardens that were originally planted in that area, and build the much larger Temple 1 over both of these. Temple 1 measured 27.85 by 18.5 m, most of which was taken up by a large main hall whose roof was most likely supported by two rows of columns.[229] Three rooms whose "massive foundations must have supported an impressive superstructure"[230]

[219] H.W. Catling, "A Cypriot Bronze Statuette in the Bomford Collection," in *Alasia* I: *Mission Archéologique d'Alasia* 4, C.F.A. Schaeffer, ed., Paris 1971, pp. 15-32; see p. 30.

[220] Knapp, 1986; *idem*, "Ideology, archaeology and polity," *Man* 23 (1988) 133-163; *idem*, "Power and Ideology on Prehistoric Cyprus," in *Religion and Power in the Ancient Greek World: Proceedings of the Uppsala Symposium 1993* [*Boreas* 24], P. Hellström and B. Alroth, eds., Uppsala 1996, pp. 9-25.

[221] V. Karageorghis, "Kition: Mycenaean and Phoenician," *Proceedings of the British Academy* 59 (1973) 259-281; see p. 261.

[222] V. Karageorghis, *View from the Bronze Age: Mycenaean and Phoenician Discoveries at Kition*, E.P. Dutton Press 1976; see p. 60.

[223] A.B. Knapp, *The Archaeology of Late Bronze Age Cypriot Society: The Study of Settlement, Survey and Landscape*, University of Glasgow 1997; see pp. 53-57 for a discussion of primary coastal centers. See also P.S. Keswani, "Models of Local Exchange in Late Bronze Age Cyprus," *Bulletin of the American Schools of Oriental Research* 292 (1993) 73-83, who also discusses settlement hierarchy on Cyprus.

[224] Karageorghis 1973, p. 262.

[225] Karageorghis and Demas 1985, pp. 25 and 32-33.

[226] Karageorghis and Demas 1985, p. 37.

[227] Karageorghis 1973, p. 264.

[228] Karageorghis 1976, p. 58.

[229] V. Karageorghis and M. Demas, *Excavations at Kition V: The Pre-Phoenician Levels*, Nicosia 1985; see pp. 38 and 44. Karageorghis (1973, p. 267) says the dimensions of Temple 1 were 35 by 22 m. Reused column bases from the Late Bronze Age were found in the excavation of the 9th century Phoenician temple that stood on the same spot.

[230] Karageorghis and Demas 1985, p. 48. Karageorghis (1973, p. 267; 1976 p. 62) has interpreted the western walls to constitute a recess that

occupied the western end of the building. The rooms themselves may have served as storage space for cult paraphernalia. In building the 9th century temple of Astarte, which used the same foundations as the Bronze Age temple, the Phoenicians cleared the interior of the temple down to bedrock. Hence all Bronze Age floors and any evidence of the cult that was conducted there have been lost. Nonetheless, a sense of its monumental character can be gathered from the fact that all the interior walls and the exterior walls that would have been in sight of the public were built of ashlar masonry. This was a building style that was new to Kition[231] (although not to Cyprus[232]), and was meant to impress.

The plan of Temple 2[233] from the previous period was retained, but its walls were rebuilt with ashlar masonry blocks similar to those that were used for Temple 1. A hearth-altar used in the previous period was also retained, but a low table of offerings was added to the south, along with a bench-altar that was placed along the south wall.

Between the two temples was an open courtyard called Temenos B. The eastern wall of this courtyard, constructed of ashlar blocks, served as a monumental facade for the sacred complex, and its main entryway, the "propylaeum," was 4.25 m wide and 5.5 m in length.[234] Karageorghis and Demas say that Temenos B "may have served primarily as a monumental entrance hall and perhaps a processional route to Temple 1."[235] Two blocks in the southern portion of the Temenos may have supported the columns of a portico, which could have sheltered worshippers during ceremonies. Also found in Temenos B in the western end were two "heavy patches of burning and ash."[236] No bone was found amongst the ash so these areas could have been used for offerings that did not involve animal sacrifice. A limestone horns of consecration that had been broken in two can probably also be associated with this Temenos.[237]

A second enclosed courtyard called Temenos A could be entered through a door in the northern wall of Temenos B. The city wall created the northern boundary of Temenos A while its southern boundary was formed by the northern walls of Temple 1 and Temenos B. A small building (room 35) was constructed against the city wall in the northeast portion of the courtyard. Since it was clearly roofed it probably served as a storeroom.[238] In the northeast corner of Temenos A the excavators found a large oval area that was burnt and covered with ash. In the ash they found burnt stone chips and carbonized pieces of bone.[239] Another burnt area containing ash and pieces of carbonized matter was found over what had been the hearth-altar of Temple 3, the temple that had been removed for the new building project.[240] Two blocks of conglomerate lie to the south of this burnt area which may have been used as "tables of offerings or even slaughtering tables for sacrifices performed in Temenos A."[241] Another one or possibly two altars were found north of these features. The floor around one of these altars was heavily burned and carbonized animal bones and pottery were found on it.[242] The other altar, according to Karageorghis, was a stepped platform used to display the limestone horns of consecration (0.48 m in height and 0.43 m wide) that were found at its base.[243] Karageorghis notes that "the horns of consecration constitute, of course, a symbol of Aegean religion"[244] and infers from them that the people who rebuilt the temple complex at the end of the thirteenth century B.C. must have been Mycenaean. It may have been that Mycenaeans were involved in the reconstruction, but it should be noted that the temples do not seem terribly Mycenaean in nature, which Karageorghis himself points out: "It is doubtful, however, whether any Aegean elements may be found in the architectural plans of the two temples..."[245] Thus it seems likely that the Mycenaeans were not the only people involved in rebuilding the temple complex.[246] In any case, the religious nature of Temenos A is easily recognized and all the more interesting considering the industrial nature of the rooms that lie directly to the west of its altars.

The western end of Temenos A opens onto a series of workshops called rooms 12, 13, 14, 15, and 16. Copper slag, fragments of crucibles with copper still remaining within them, and fragments of bellows, in addition to thick layers of ash, were found on the floors of these workshops, indicating that they functioned as copper-working shops.[247] Area 16, which had two openings onto Temenos A, had several pits that were lined with hard whitish mud and were filled with either ash or dark soil. In the southwest corner of the room were found two small patches that were burned and covered with ash.[248] The exact purpose of the pits is hard to discern. Room 12, the westernmost of the group, provides the clearest evidence for metal working. In addition to a well and two benches, there was a pit whose sides were lined with baked clay on which "bits of a greenish substance (copper?) were found."[249] Two other pits in room 12 were partially filled

contained the image of the deity. He therefore called it a "holy of holies." Karageorghis and Demas (1985, pp. 249-250) discuss this proposition though and conclude that the rooms were more likely "sacred storerooms or treasuries."

231 Karageorghis and Demas 1985, p. 38.

232 Karageorghis and Demas 1985, pp. 92-93.

233 Karageorghis 1976, p. 67 gives the measurements as 14.5 x 9 m while Karageorghis and Demas (1985, p. 49) give 17.45 x 7.7 m.

234 Karageorghis and Demas 1985, p. 57.

235 Karageorghis and Demas 1985, p. 55.

236 Karageorghis and Demas 1985, p. 60.

237 Karageorghis 1973, p. 268; *idem* 1976, p. 71. Karageorghis and Demas 1985, p. 255.

238 Karageorghis and Demas 1985, p. 63.

239 Karageorghis and Demas 1985, p. 63.

240 Karageorghis and Demas 1985, p. 64.

241 Karageorghis and Demas 1985, p. 64.

242 Karageorghis and Demas 1985, p. 64. Karageorghis 1976, p. 70.

243 Karageorghis 1973, p. 268; *idem* 1976, pp. 69-70. Karageorghis and Demas 1985, pp. 107 and 128. The horns of consecration were actually found on Floor II (LC IIIB), but they were probably originally used on the earlier Floor III (LC IIIA).

244 Karageorghis 1976, p. 70.

245 Karageorghis 1973, p. 270.

246 Karageorghis and Demas 1985, pp. 261-262.

247 Karageorghis 1976, p. 72.

248 Karageorghis and Demas 1985, p. 65.

249 Karageorghis and Demas 1985, p. 82.

with "greenish coloured sand" mixed with "small pieces of copper slag," and their sides were lined with "hard-baked whitish mud."[250] A furnace was also found in room 12 whose interior was filled with ash and lumps of bone-ash. The same material was found in pits in a storeroom west of room 12. Karageorghis points out that bone ash was an important fluxing agent for the metallurgists of Cyprus. Because Cypriot ore is poor in silica, the bone ash allows them to extract more metal from the ore. Apparently they created this bone ash right on the spot for the metallurgical processing that was going on within these workshops.[251] Another nine pits were found in room 12, most of which were filled with black ashy soil while one contained greenish soil and pieces of copper slag.[252] It seems possible that room 12 also had a religious installation. A "huge stone anchor" was found lying against the western wall, and on top of and around this anchor were "three fragmentary skulls of horned animals and five horns."[253] Other bones were scattered on the floor near the anchor.

Rooms 13, 14 and 15 were situated between rooms 12 and 16. Unfortunately the floors of these rooms have been very disturbed by later digging in the area, but what does remain indicates that these rooms were also used for copper smelting. For instance, in room 13 there was a patch of burning and ash, and the center of room 14 was taken up by a large rectangular pit that was lined with clay and contained burnt soil and pieces of copper slag.[254] Approximately 45 pieces of copper slag were also found in room 14 along its northern wall. On the basis of this evidence Karageorghis and Demas conclude that, "The function of the workshops was surely not the production of bronze figurines for the needs of the temples but rather the actual refining of metallic copper."[255]

Another set of workshops, whose activities "may be indirectly related to the copper working of the Northern Workshops," were found to the west of Temple 1.[256] One could get from the Northern Workshops into the Western ones via a door in the western wall of room 12. Only one room produced finds that were occupation-specific: fifteen clay reels and six loomweights seem to indicate that weaving was one of the occupations pursued in this area.[257] This evidence brought Karageorghis and Demas to suggest that weaving could have been another "sacred industry related to the temples."[258]

The connection of the Northern and the Western workshops with the temples is made clear by their close association and the general ease of access between the two. The relationship with the copper-working shops in the northern section was especially close. In addition to the route that went from the Temple to Temenos A via Temenos B, a door in the western wall of Temple 1 led directly into the western area of the workshops, which means that the temple personnel would have had two access routes to the Northern workshops. Thus the temples and the workshops together formed an architectural unit.

A similar relationship between workshops and religious establishments was found at Enkomi, which, like Kition, was a primary coastal center. Two temples have been found at Enkomi, both of which can be dated to the LC III period (12th century[259]), and both are known by the bronze statues that were found in each of them. Thus the first of the two temples has been designated the "Sanctuary of the Ingot God,"[260] while the second is known as the "Sanctuary of the Horned God."[261]

The Sanctuary of the Ingot God was located on the east side of Enkomi's main north-south road, between the fourth and fifth streets that ran east-west. It consisted of a large 17.6 x 11.6 m^2[262] rectangular structure which was divided into a southern court and a northern hall by a 6 m long wall that ran east-west in the building's southern sector.[263] Access could be gained to the north hall on either side of the wall. Two large monolithic blocks with concave tops and ashes surrounding them were found about a meter apart to the west of, and practically in line with, this wall.[264] Courtois proposed that animal sacrifices were made on these altars.[265] A stone-lined hearth was found just to the south of the altars, and to their north was a massive stone block that was pierced with a large hole; the animals destined for sacrifice could have been tied to this block.[266] Scattered all over the floor of the sanctuary were the skulls of nearly a hundred bulls and deer, most with their horns still attached, along with the bones of sheep and goats.[267] Two double-headed centaur figurines found near the northern bench stand out among the numerous terracotta figurines.[268] In the northeastern corner of the building was a room that measured 2 x 1.9 m that Courtois called an adyton or cella.[269] A large bronze ox-horn, 13 cm long, was found just to the south of the threshold of the cella.[270] The Ingot

[250] Karageorghis and Demas 1985, p. 82.
[251] Karageorghis 1976, p. 73.
[252] Karageorghis and Demas 1985, pp. 82-83.
[253] Karageorghis and Demas 1985, p. 83. Room 15 also had four stone anchors while another one was found in room 14.
[254] Karageorghis and Demas 1985, pp. 83-84.
[255] Karageorghis and Demas 1985, p. 254.
[256] Karageorghis and Demas 1985, p. 77.
[257] Karageorghis and Demas 1985, p. 78.
[258] Karageorghis and Demas 1985, p. 254.

[259] J.-C. Courtois ("Le Sanctuaire du Dieu au Lingot d'Enkomi-Alasia," in *Alasia I: Mission Archéologique d'Alasia* 4, C.F.A. Schaeffer, ed., Paris 1971, pp. 151-362) calls this the Cypriot Iron I phase (p. 151).
[260] Courtois 1971, pp. 151-311.
[261] P. Dikaios, *Enkomi: Excavations 1948-1958*, Verlag Philip von Zabern 1969-1971, see pp. 191-220.
[262] Courtois 1971, p. 152.
[263] Courtois 1971, p. 159.
[264] Courtois 1971, pp. 159 and 178; *idem*, "Le sanctuaire du dieu au lingot d'Enkomi-Alasia (Chypre) et les lieux de culte contemporains en Méditerranée Orientale," *Académie des Inscriptions et Belles Lettres: Comptes Rendus des Séances*, Paris 1973, 223-246; see p. 235.
[265] Courtois 1971, pp. 178. Also see Karageorghis 1982, p 94.
[266] Courtois 1971, pp. 178-190 and 204.
[267] C.F.A. Schaeffer, "An Ingot God from Cyprus," *Antiquity* 39 (1965) 56-57. Courtois 1971, pp. 177-178 provides a partial list of the finds, but see figure 2 in Schaeffer 1971 for a visual impression of the spread of the animal skulls. Also see Courtois 1973, p. 227.
[268] Courtois 1971, pp. 280 and 326.
[269] Courtois 1971, p. 308.
[270] Courtois 1971, p. 310.

God himself, a 35-cm tall bronze statue, was found standing upright within a pit dug 80-110 cm deep into the floor of the cella.[271] The pottery found in association with the Ingot God had "affinities" with Mycenaean vessels of the LH IIIC period, and so the figure can be dated to the LC IIIA/B period (or one could argue, as Knapp does, that the figure had been manufactured and used in an earlier time period).[272] This figure was called the "Ingot God" because he stands upon what looks like a miniature oxhide ingot.[273] The Ingot God wears a horned helmet and greaves cover his legs. In his right hand he carries a small oval shield and in his left a raised spear. Speculation as to which god the figure represents has run the gamut from a Babylonian deity named Nergal to our familiar Hephaistos.[274] Knapp is probably correct though in saying that such attempts at a definite identification are futile.[275] The importance of the figurine is not in the name that he was worshipped under, but rather in that he represents a god who was probably the patron deity of those who worked in Cyprus's metal industry. A somewhat shorter female figurine (9.9 cm high), known as the Bomford Figurine after its original owner, also stands upon a base in the shape of an oxhide ingot.[276] Although the Bomford Figurine is without an archaeological provenience, Catling has compared her with other bronze figures on Cyprus and concluded that she too must have been manufactured in Cyprus.[277] He also thinks that she should be dated to the first half of the 12th century B.C., like the Ingot God.[278] Because of her similarity to the Ingot God, the Bomford Figurine is thought to represent his female counterpart who may have been expected to, as Catling puts it, "ensure the fruitfulness of the mines and even more of the smelting furnaces and the processes by which the raw copper is produced."[279] It is reasonable to propose that the two together may have been responsible for overseeing the continuing prosperity of the copper-producing industry. Karageorghis has even suggested that these two may have been the deities who were worshipped in the Temples 1 and 2 at Kition.[280]

[271] Schaeffer 1965, p. 56.
[272] Courtois 1971, pp. 151-152 (Cypriot Iron Age I); *idem* 1973, p. 233. Schaeffer (1965, p. 56) says, "...the earliest part of the Iron Age or Cypriot Iron Age I (Late Cypriot III), that is to say in the 12th century B.C." Knapp 1986, pp. 9 and 87.
[273] Schaeffer 1965, p. 56. E. Masson ("Le Dieu Guerrier d'Enkomi: Est-il Debout sur un Lingot? in *Studies in Honour of Vassos Karageorghis*, G.C. Ioannides, ed., Kypriakai Soudai, Leukosia 1992, pp. 155-156) disputes the idea that the object the deity is standing on is an ingot. She thinks instead that it might be the hide of an animal. While this is possible, Masson does not also consider the Bomford Goddess, the miniature ingots offered to the Horned God, nor the depiction of ingots in other media. Since she does not consider the entire context in which the Ingot God was found, I find her arguments unconvincing; it seems most likely that the shape beneath the feet of the deity is an ingot.
[274] A review of this material is provided by Knapp, 1986, pp. 9-11
[275] Knapp 1986, p. 11.
[276] Bomford purchased the figurine from Sotheby's in 1967, but the Ashmolean Museum acquired it from him "on extremely generous terms" in 1971 (Catling 1971, p. 32).
[277] Catling 1971, pp. 20-23.
[278] Catling 1971, p. 23. Knapp (1986, p. 87) has suggested that both of these figures could have been manufactured at an earlier date.
[279] Catling 1971, p. 30.
[280] Karageorghis 1973, p. 272.

The Sanctuary of the Horned God was actually found in a large 32.5 x 28.5 m building founded in the LC IIIA1 period (c. 1220/1210 B.C., Level IIIA) that its excavator, Dikaios, called the "Ashlar Building" because of its distinctive ashlar masonry.[281] The Ashlar Building was situated on the west side of Enkomi's main north-south street between the 4th and 3rd streets that ran east-west. Thus the two sanctuaries were located fairly close to each other with only about 50 m between them.[282] The Ashlar Building was constructed on top of the remains of a building called the "Fortress," which was used for "extensive copper work" (as were other areas in the immediate vicinity, which I will discuss below).[283] The Ashlar Building experienced three destructions, and the worship of the Horned God may only have been introduced after the first destruction which occurred in the middle of the LC IIIA period (Level IIIB, c. 1190 B.C.).[284] After the first destruction the building was substantially remodeled: the plan of the main hall or "megaron" was "obliterated," the main entrance at the northern end of the building, which had led to the megaron, was changed and a new one was built at the south side of the building which led into the substantial part of the building that was then given over to the cult of the Horned God.[285] The main room of the cult, room 45 (called the "west megaron"), was 8.75 x 6.75 m and had three pillars running down its longitudinal axis.[286] Near one of the room's hearths an ox skull was found lying face up, and two more fragmentary ox skulls were found near a second hearth in the northern part of the room. Another three skulls were found further to the north of the room with the bones of other animals. Near the doorway leading into room 9 (which led into room 10, the room in which the statue of the Horned God was found) Dikaios found miniature models of horns in gold leaf, fragments of gold leaf, an ivory lid and a miniature bronze spearhead. Room 9, at 2.45 x 1.55 m appears to have been a kind of ante-chamber for room 10.[287] It contained, among other things, a trough with a groove running to a hole at one end, gold pendants, and a miniature golden ox horn. Within room 10 (2.5 m^2), a similar trough was found along with 267 base-ring bowls and still articulated animal bones.

The Horned God himself, just like the Ingot God, was found standing upright in a pit dug into the floor.[288] The interesting thing is that the pit was dug through the second destruction layer (which initiated the IIIC Level at the end of the LC IIIA period, c. 1125/1100 B.C.) into the IIIB Level. Dikaios has reconstructed the following scenario: After the second destruction the inhabitants of the building came back to find the Horned God statue and

[281] Dikaios 1969-1971, p. 171. Knapp 1986, p. 21.
[282] Knapp 1986, p. 22.
[283] Dikaios 1969-1971, p. 18, see also pp. 21-24.
[284] Dikaios 1969-1971, p. 189.
[285] Dikaios 1969-1971, p. 210.
[286] Dikaios 1969-1971, p. 194.
[287] Dikaios 1969-1971, p. 197.
[288] Dikaios 1969-1971, pp. 197 and 295.

to re-establish his cult.[289] Disturbances in the destruction debris show that they rooted around until they found his statue (and probably also the more valuable of the cult items). But, instead of setting it up on the floor built on top of the destruction layer, the inhabitants dug a pit for the statue because, Dikaios reasons, they must have been afraid that another attack was imminent, and the pit seemed a safer hiding place for their deity.[290] The cult of the Horned God continued for a short period of time in room 13 (room 45 was beyond repair) where eight more oxen skulls were found.[291] Eventually the third and final destruction caused the final abandonment of both the building and the Horned God (c. 1075 B.C. in the LC IIIB period).[292]

At 55 cm the statue of the Horned God stands a good bit taller than the Ingot God and is actually modeled in a much more naturalistic way, but like the Ingot God he wears a horned helmet.[293] The Horned God's association with the copper-producing industry is implied by the fact that three miniature oxhide ingots, which are generally agreed to be votive objects, were found in the same area (Quartier 4W) as the sanctuary.[294] A miniature bronze sickle was found in the pit near the statue, which Dikaios classifies as a votive offering,[295] while in the fill a bronze pin and a bronze ribbon were found.[296] A cache of "miniature bronze weapons and tools which must have been offerings to the God" seems to have been gathered up after the second destruction and buried in the new wall of the room.[297] Courtois believes these were offered by a bronze workers' guild.[298] A female nude figurine made of bronze, which had faces on either side, was found in room 11 just to the east of room 10.[299] Several bronze objects, which were probably "remnants of offerings to the goddess," were also found in room 11.[300] The hair of this female figurine is arranged in tresses that fall on her chest in a way similar to the hair of the Bomford Goddess. It is possible then that both the Horned God and the Ingot God had female counterparts.[301]

Thus both sanctuaries at Enkomi seem to have housed cults whose deities may have had metallurgical production as their main concern. And, as at Kition, metallurgical workshops were found in close relation to the sanctuaries. One workshop was just 10 m to the northwest of the Sanctuary of the Ingot God, and a second was found in the block to the north of this sanctuary and just across the street from the Sanctuary of the Horned God (i.e., in Quartier 4E).[302] The remains of metal working in Quartier 5E actually date back to the late MC III/early LC I periods, but the most intense period of activity for both Quartiers 5E and 4E begins towards the end of the 13th century B.C. (Level IIIA) when the Ashlar Building was constructed.[303] It is at this time that the large industrial area at the northern end of the city (Quartier 1W) starts to shut down, which implies that the focus of the metal-working industry shifted to these central blocks.[304] Several hundred kilograms of slag, tuyeres, crucible fragments, stone molds, and areas that Courtois calls "cemented" (*bétonée*) were found in and around the workshop buildings of Quartiers 5E and 4E. In Quartier 4E a long piece of terracotta pipe was found *in situ* that ran from one of the cemented areas into a pit.[305] These workshops continued to be used through the 12th century B.C., and therefore their most intense levels of activity were contemporaneous with the Sanctuaries of the Ingot and Horned Gods. Courtois points out that the close physical relationship between the workshops and sanctuaries of Enkomi parallels the situation at Kition, and implies that the sanctuaries and the workshops were very closely tied.[306]

In addition to the bronze figures and the close proximity between religious and industrial areas that we have just discussed, other objects demonstrate that there was a relationship between religion and the copper-producing industry of Cyprus. For instance, I mentioned that three miniature oxhide ingots were found in association with the Horned God at Enkomi. These miniature ingots may have been fashioned as offerings for a deity who was thought to watch over the production of the full-sized ingots.[307] Other examples of these miniature ingots, of which Knapp lists fifteen, have been found at several different sites on Cyprus and at Thebes in Egypt, in Cilicia, on the Dalmatian coast and at Tell Beit Mirsim.[308]

---

[289] It seems that this must have been done very soon after the destruction since the animal bones, which were disturbed and mixed in with the destruction layer during the search, were still articulated when they were found. This means that the meat must have been still attached to the bones when the inhabitants were searching for the statue (Dikaios 1969-1971, p. 198).

[290] Dikaios 1969-1971, p. 219.

[291] Dikaios 1969-1971, pp. 201, 213 and 216.

[292] Dikaios 1969-1971, pp. 219-220.

[293] Dikaios 1969-1971, p. 295. Knapp 1986, p. 21.

[294] Dikaios 1969-1971, pp. 294 and 301. Knapp 1986, p. 28. For a discussion of the inscriptions found on the miniature ingots see O. Masson, "Deux petites lingots de cuivre inscrits d'Enkomi," in *Alasia I: Mission Archéologique d'Alasia* 4, C.F.A. Schaeffer, ed., Paris 1971, pp. 449-455.

[295] Dikaios 1969-1971, p. 301.

[296] Dikaios 1969-1971, p. 216. J.-C. Courtois, "L'activité métallurgique et les bronzes d'Enkomi au Bronze Récent (1650-1000 avant J.C.)," in *Early Metallurgy in Late Bronze Age Cyprus 4000-500 B.C.*, J.D. Muhly, R. Maddin and V. Karageorghis, eds., 1982, pp. 155-176; see p. 159. (The miniature spearhead is not mentioned by Dikaios.)

[297] Dikaios 1969-1971, p. 295. Dikaios proposes that these bronze tools and weapons were placed together as part of a foundation rite for the somewhat reconstructed room 10.

[298] Courtois 1982, p. 159.

[299] Dikaios 1969-1971, pp. 191, 200 and 295. Courtois 1982, p. 159.

[300] Dikaios 1969-1971, p. 200.

[301] Knapp 1986, p. 22. See also Dikaios 1969-1971, p. 191.

[302] Courtois 1982, pp. 161-163.

[303] Courtois 1982, pp. 160-161.

[304] Courtois 1982, pp. 157 and 160. Knapp (1986, p. 46) is misleading in that he says, "The main metallurgical production center at Enkomi lay near the north gate, in Quartier 1W", without mentioning that those workshops had "ceased their production" (Courtois 1982, p. 160) at the end of the 13th century. This leads the reader to think the workshops of Quartiers 5E and 4E were secondary to those at the north gate, which they were not.

[305] Courtois 1982, p. 161; see p. 162 for a figure showing the plans of the two workshops.

[306] Courtois 1982, p. 163.

[307] Catling 1971, p. 30. Knapp 1986, p. 25.

[308] Knapp (1986, pp. 26-27) lists the fifteen that he knew of at the time and their proveniences in a chart.

Despite their various findspots, Knapp is confident that most of them can "plausibly be traced to the island", i.e., Cyprus.[309] Several of them bear inscriptions in the Cypro-Minoan script, and it is possible therefore that they record the names of the deities to whom they were dedicated.[310]

Ingots have also been represented in other media. Two bronze four-sided offering stands, one from Kourion (now in the British Museum and therefore called the "London stand") and another probably made in Cyprus (the "Jerusalem stand"[311]), depict figures carrying full-size ingots in procession that they apparently intend to present as offerings.[312] On the London stand the ingot-bearer is bringing his offering to a divine tree. The intended recipient of the ingot on the Jerusalem stand is not extant but it seems possible that here too we would have seen a tree since Catling has proposed that the scenes on these stands drew upon a common model of much greater scale.[313] Catling also says that, "The ingot-bearer ... suggests that sometimes a full-size ingot was brought to the gods as a gift."[314] Knapp emphasizes the connection between religion and industry by saying, "Like the miniature ingots and bronze figurines, these bronze stands may somehow link the production of exotic goods, ritual and religious experience, and the sanctification of certain individuals or institutions in Cypriote society."[315]

Knapp goes on to argue that the common model may also have given rise to similar scenes found on pottery and seals. Knapp discusses three LH IIIA2 craters that depict figures that have been interpreted as ingot-bearers.[316] Two of these ingot-bearers are also found in front of trees.[317] Knapp uses these LH IIIA pots to demonstrate how early the sanctification of the copper industry must have begun. He says it must have been "in the 14th century, not the 12th."[318]

Knapp also discusses the ingots that appear on Cypriot seals, some of which can be dated to the 14th century B.C.[319] Knapp compiled a list of 33 seals that contained at least three of the following four iconographical elements: oxhide ingots, trees, anthropomorphic figures, and bucrania. The bucrania are significant when one recalls the large numbers of actual bucrania that were found in the sanctuaries of the Ingot and Horned Gods. Knapp proposes that these images may represent a narrative scene in which a "human figure bears a series of objects – including bucrania, a miniature and a full-sized ingot – to be placed before a tree..."[320] Knapp goes on to argue a native Cypriot inspiration for these seals and the imagery in general, contra Catling and others who proposed that the copper industry was spurred to its heights by the arrival of the Mycenaeans at the end of the 12th century B.C. He concludes his analysis of the seals by saying, "... it seems plausible to suggest that these seals connected symbolically the producers, overseers, or even the managerial elite of the Cypriote copper industry to some sort of political, religious, or economic authority."[321]

In addition to the sanctuaries of Kition and Enkomi, rural sanctuaries were also involved in the production of copper on Cyprus. Knapp mentions Alassa *Pano Mandilares*, an LC IIC–LC IIIA site, as a rural sanctuary that was associated with metal working activity.[322] The site actually had three cult areas and traces of metallurgical activity were found in four parts of the site.[323] One of these cult areas had among its finds "a bronze axe, slag pieces and natural copper alloys" which were found very near to "the best preserved bull figurine," a haematite cylinder seal, a bronze handle, and two more bull figurines which actually dated to an earlier phase.[324] Just north of this sanctuary "the finds indicate that some kind of metallurgical activity was taking place."[325] A second cult room, which contained five bull figurines and one of the miniature oxhide ingots, adjoined the room in which a bellows was found.[326] Thus here, as at Kition and Enkomi, religion and religious personnel could have been intimately connected to the copper-working industry of the site.

Two other frequently discussed rural sanctuary sites are Athienou *Bamboulari tis Koukounninas* and Myrtou *Pigadhes*. The shrine at Myrtou *Pigadhes*, a site in the northwest of Cyprus, was in use from the LH IIIB (late LC II) period to the very beginning of the LH IIIC (LC IIIA) period.[327] Its main feature was a large ashlar masonry altar situated in the shrine's courtyard that the excavator reconstructs as having been topped with horns of consecration.[328] A pile of antlers and rams' horns were found beside it and a small bronze bull figurine was

[309] Knapp 1986, p. 28.

[310] Catling 1971, p. 30. Masson 1971, p. 454.

[311] The exact provenience of the Jerusalem stand is not known, but Catling ("Workshop and heirloom: prehistoric bronze stands in the east Mediterranean," *RDAC* [1984] 69-91), pp. 83 and 90) argues that the iconography of this stand matches that of 31 (of the 60 extant) that were found on Cyprus and so should be included with them as a group.

[312] Catling 1971, p. 30, also see fig. 12 on p. 31; *idem*, 1984. Knapp 1986, p. 31.

[313] Catling 1984, p. 83.

[314] Catling 1971, p. 30.

[315] Knapp 1986, p. 34.

[316] They are the "Zeus crater" from Enkomi, Swedish Excavations Tomb 17, No. 1; another from Enkomi, Tomb 45, now British Museum C 341; and one from Pyla Verghi, Tomb 1, No. 37, now in the Cyprus Museum. See Knapp 1986, p. 35 for the references dealing with these pots.

[317] Knapp 1986, p. 35.

[318] Knapp 1986, p. 37.

[319] Knapp 1986, pp. 37-42.

[320] Knapp 1986, p. 41.

[321] Knapp 1986, p. 42.

[322] Knapp 1997, p. 35.

[323] S. Hadjisavvas, "A Late Cypriot community at Alassa," in *Early Society in Cyprus*, E.J. Peltenburg, ed., Edinburgh 1989, pp. 32-42; see pp. 35-39.

[324] Hadjisavvas 1989, pp. 37-38.

[325] Hadjisavvas 1989, p. 38.

[326] Hadjisavvas 1989, pp. 38-39.

[327] J. Du Plat Taylor, *Myrtou-Pighades: A Late Bronze Age Sanctuary in Cyprus*, Ashmolean Museum, Oxford 1957, pp. 22-23 and 114-115. The base of the altar was 2.5 m square and its height was at least 1.5 m, but probably was "actually considerably greater."

[328] Du Plat Taylor 1957, pp. 15-17.

found in the fill of the altar. Terracotta bull figurines and offering stands were also found.[329] Although the excavator did not discuss the possibility that workshop activities had gone on in the sanctuary, Knapp, after more recently analyzing the site, says that rooms 15, 16, and 17 within the sanctuary revealed "clear, albeit limited evidence for metallurgical activity."[330] Part of that evidence was a hoard of bronze tripods and rings stands that were "intertwined if they had been together in a bag,"[331] and which may therefore have been put aside as scrap metal for remelting. In room 16 a bronze shovel was found that contained traces of carbonized wood, and over the shovel were "two big lumps of fused copper and some slag."[332] Room 17 also revealed lumps of slag and a bronze knife. The metal working did not occur within these rooms since no hearth was found, and actually, no real hearth structure was found in the vicinity of these rooms (although Du Plat Taylor reports that the floor of the large room 12 was covered with a double layer of ash mixed with clay[333]). However, this may be due to the fact that many of the rooms in the area were not fully excavated or were left unexcavated. It does seem that this series of rooms was used for workshop activities since room 19 contained the base of a saddle quern and at least six upper quern stones and a thick patch of ash at the base of a bench.[334] The sanctuary then seems to have been involved in metal working as well as other types of industrial activities.

At Athienou *Bamboulari tis Koukounninas*, a large building complex was built in the 14th century B.C. (within the excavators' Stratum III), and continued to be used, with a few alterations, through the 12th century B.C.[335] The renovations occurred at the beginning of the 12th century (the initiation of Stratum II). The excavators found approximately 10,000 whole or fragmentary vessels, mainly within the courtyard of this building. Some of the vessels were normal-sized, but many were quite small, some no more than 1 cm high.[336] They have therefore been interpreted as votives.[337] The great majority of these were found in Stratum III, but some were also found in Stratum II.[338] Also found were an ivory conical rhyton decorated with stylized human heads, birds, fish, and gazelles, a tubular "snake house," a large limestone basin decorated with bull's head protomes, an Egyptian scarab, and a bronze ring inscribed with the hieroglyph group representing Ptah and the sign for 'Lord'.[339] Because of these finds the building has been interpreted as having been used for religious purposes.[340] Alongside these religious finds was an abundance of evidence for metallurgical production. About a half ton of copper ore and processed nodules or slag were found.[341] But no crucibles or tuyeres were found with them,[342] which led some people to speculate as to whether copper production had actually taken place there. Stech proposed that "the ore could have been roasted and smelted at the mines ... and the chunks brought to Athienou for processing and refining after the initial smelting."[343] Maddin, Muhly, and Stech Wheeler, however, subsequently explained the situation by saying that the nodules themselves could have been roasted in an oxidizing environment, and then after the sulfur had burned off, the ore would have been subjected to very high temperatures (at least 1100°C) within a reducing atmosphere.[344] The molten copper ore would form "prills" which could then be broken off manually after the ore had cooled. Their tests of slag found on the site showed that this process would have produced amounts of copper significant enough to make it worthwhile.[345] As to where this process took place, Stratum II produced several contiguous platforms, generally composed of a base layer of stones that were covered with 15 cm of lime plaster. It was clear that very intense fires had burned on the surfaces of these platforms (no trace of fire was found in the rest of the building), and the majority of the chunks of copper ore were found immediately to the east of them.[346] It seems most likely then that the platforms were used for the roasting and smelting of the ore.[347] Of course, the platforms were not associated with Stratum III, the level in which the majority of the votive vessels were found. This has led Muhly to debate whether we can associate the evidence for ore processing with the religious artifacts.[348] Dothan and Ben-Tor, however, point out that in the three trial sections that were cut through the northeast platforms chunks of copper ore were found in addition to the votive vessels.[349] Slag and ore was also found among the votive vessels in the courtyard, which suggests that the roasting and smelting took place nearby, perhaps even on installations that lie under the extant platforms. The excavators therefore concluded that the evidence indicates "that metal working at the site began as early as the 14th-13th centuries BCE

[329] Du Plat Taylor 1957, pp. 18-19.

[330] A.B. Knapp, "Ideational and Industrial Landscape on Prehistoric Cyprus," in *Archaeologies of Landscape: Contemporary Perspectives*, W. Ashmore and A. B. Knapp, eds., Blackwell Publishers 1999, pp. 229-25; see , p. 235.

[331] Du Plat Taylor 1957, p. 20.

[332] Du Plat Taylor 1957, pp. 20-21.

[333] Du Plat Taylor 1957, p. 20.

[334] Du Plat Taylor 1957, p. 21.

[335] T. Dothan and A. Ben-Tor, *Excavations at Athienou, Cyprus 1971-1972*, Jerusalem 1983.

[336] Dothan and Ben-Tor 1983, pp. 53 and 139.

[337] Dothan and Ben-Tor 1983, p. 25.

[338] Dothan and Ben-Tor 1983, p. 111.

[339] Dothan and Ben-Tor 1983, ivory rhyton: pp. 123-125; "snake house": p. 53; limestone basin: pp. 129-131 (this basin was found in Stratum I, but the excavator says it dates to the late 13th or beginning of the 12th century); scarab: p. 121; bronze ring: p. 121.

[340] Dothan and Ben-Tor 1983, p. 139.

[341] Dothan and Ben-Tor 1983, p. 140.

[342] Dothan and Ben-Tor 1983, p. 140. Also see R. Maddin, J.D. Muhly, and T. Stech Wheeler, "Metal Working," in *Excavations at Athienou, Cyprus 1971-1972*, T. Dothan and A. Ben-Tor, eds., Jerusalem 1983, pp. 136-138.

[343] T. Stech, "Urban Metallurgy in Late Bronze Age Cyprus," in *Early Metallurgy in Cyprus 4000-500 B.C.*, J. Muhly, R. Maddin and V. Karageorghis, eds., 1982, pp. 105-116; see p. 107.

[344] Maddin et al. 1983, pp. 132-134.

[345] Maddin et al. 1983, p. 137.

[346] Dothan and Ben-Tor 1983, p 12-14.

[347] Maddin et al. 1983, p. 137.

[348] J.D. Muhly ("The Late Bronze Age in Cyprus: A 25 year retrospect," in *Archaeology in Cyprus 1960-1985*, V. Karageorghis, ed., Leventis Foundation, Nicosia 1985, pp. 20-45; see p. 33, nn. 91-92).

[349] Dothan and Ben-Tor 1983, p. 20.

and was connected with a cult."[350] Also, the Stratum III platforms did have cultic associations in that two pits were found in the courtyard of the building that date to this period, one of which contained a "great number of bones ... including a pair of bull's horns" while the other had "mainly bones and ash."[351] These could have resulted from sacrificial rites, and the bull's horns recall the large numbers of such horns that were found in the temples of Kition and Enkomi.

In addition to its metallurgical activities, Athienou also seems to have been involved in the production and storage of olive oil. Keswani estimates Athienou's storage capacity to have been between 5,500 and 11,000 liters, which would have been "enough to support 180-365 adults for two years on a generous ration of 15 liters per year."[352] Keswani points out that the presence of such "supra-household" storage capabilities could have been "used to supply not only the officials and dependents of the sanctuary but also the full- or part-time miners who may have been drawn from the surrounding rural population."[353] Keswani proposes that the rural sanctuaries were actually involved in a variety of economic activities that linked them both to the mining sites and the primary coastal sites.

To summarize, the evidence for the involvement of the religious sphere in the metal-producing industry of Cyprus is great and varied. We find workshops in association with sanctuaries both in large primary coastal centers, such as Kition and Enkomi, and in rural or inland centers such as Alassa *Pano Mandilares*, Athienou *Bamboulari tis Koukounninas*, and Myrtou *Pigadhes*. These inland sanctuaries may also have been involved in storing and redistributing staple goods to those who were employed in the metal industry. Thus they were very much involved in the practicalities of the copper-producing industry. Iconographical evidence also links cult with the copper industry: bronze figurines, presumably of deities, were found within the sanctuaries that are associated with workshops, including two that stand upon miniature ingots, the miniature ingots themselves, some of which bear dedicatory inscriptions, and the ingot-bearers on pottery and bronze stands, which have been evaluated as "sanctuary furniture."[354] This evidence indicates that there was a major cult associated with copper production. It also seems that the religious sector took an active role in the production aspects of the industry. But the exact nature of that role has been debated.

[350] Dothan and Ben-Tor 1983, p. 140.
[351] Dothan and Ben-Tor 1983, p. 11.
[352] Keswani 1993, p. 78.
[353] Keswani 1993, p. 78.
[354] Catling 1984, p. 89.

"Ideology" and Religion in the Cypriot Bronze-working Industry

Catling saw the religious sector as playing a major role in the island's production of metal:

> I can believe that the whole management of the copper industry in Cyprus may have been temple-based, carried on in the name of the gods to whom the finished products were brought as their due, and on whose behalf the temple property was subsequently either issued to the city's bronzeworkers for the production of manufactured articles or disposed of by internal or foreign trade as surplus in exchange for other necessities.[355]

Thus Catling thought that not only was the industry protected by the gods, but that its management was in the hands of religious functionaries who were able to reap the benefits of the island's metal production through its manufacture and trade. Catling also suggested that "the religious centres may have acted as middlemen in [the island's] internal trade, and that commercial transactions may have been nominally on behalf of the gods."[356] Kassianidou, taking a diachronic view of the situation, proposed that originally (when copper alone, not bronze, was exported from the island) it was the rural sanctuaries and not the coastal centers that held the highest status on the island. This would make sense, she argues, because they controlled the production and distribution of both the food that was needed to sustain the system and the copper ore that was essential to the system.[357]

Keswani and Knapp both agree that the rural centers played a key role in the island's metal-producing industry. Keswani says, "the inland centers would have served not only as transshipment points for semiprocessed copper but also as the foci for the

[355] Catling 1971, p. 30.
[356] It is worth noting that the association between the religious sphere and the metal-working industry seems to have continued into the Archaic and Classical periods on Cyprus. For instance, at Tamassos slag, raw metal, and metal-working tools were found in close association with the temple of Aphrodite-Astarte (H.-G. Bucholz, "Der Beitrag der Ausgrabingen von Tamassos zur antiken Baugeschichte Zyperns," in *Archaeology in Cyprus,* V. Karageorghis, ed., Nicosia, Leventis Press 1985, pp. 238-255; see 241-243.) V. Kassianidou says, "The incorporation of copper workshops within temple complexes at the sanctuary of Aphrodite-Astarte and Cybele at Tamassos suggests that, just as in the Late Bronze Age, so too in the historical periods there was a connection between religion and copper production." ("Small-scale mining and smelting in ancient Cyprus," in *Social Approaches to an Industrial Past: The Archaeology and Anthropology of Mining*, A.B. Knapp, V. Pigott and E.W. Herbert, eds., Routledge Press 1998, pp. 226-241; see p. 236). Knapp 1999, p. 235.
[357] V. Kassianidou, "The Organisation of Copper Production in Late Bronze Age Cyprus: Thoughts from a Metallurgical Perspective," Paper Presented at the Seventeenth Annual Conference of the Theoretical Archaeology Group, University of Reading, 18-21 December 1995. She went on to say that the power of the coastal sites only increased when bronze became the favored export because at that time the coastal centers were able to take advantage of their ability to control the distribution of tin, which had to be imported to Cyprus.

collection of agricultural 'tribute'...."[358] Knapp voices a similar opinion:

> The chief role of secondary and tertiary centers was to control the production or distribution of copper and other traded items, and to provide storage facilities for staples and other localized goods.[359]

But Knapp differs from Catling in the amount of power that he would put into the hands of religious functionaries. Knapp[360] and Keswani[361] see the religious sphere as providing the ideological underpinnings of the system, but Knapp thinks the secular elites of Cyprus were the ones who managed the industry, and he gives no practical role whatsoever to the religious functionaries. Knapp stresses that the elites were using religious iconography to legitimize and support their controlling position, and that it was primarily ideological (i.e. not religious) in nature. It is worth quoting at length Knapp's own evaluation of his work because it seems that he has sometimes been misinterpreted as proposing something more akin to Catling's views.[362]

> In a short monograph entitled *Copper production and divine protection,* I questioned any sort of 'religious' domination over copper production on Bronze Age Cyprus. My intention was to demonstrate that several archaeological features of Late Bronze Age Cyprus previously regarded as religious in nature – figurines, representations of oxhide ingots, metallurgical workshops found in 'temples' – should in fact be regarded as ideological in nature. I argued that these material icons served the politico-economic ends of a newly-established, secular élite that sought to secure, legitimize and perpetuate their control over the Cypriot copper industry.[363]

Indeed in his original work, Knapp states that, "a single politico-economic institution, directly endowed with ritual sanctification to ensure that its dictates would be met, controlled both 'temple' and workshop."[364]

Knapp makes a reasonable case for the idea that the religious sector of Cypriot society was not in control of the entire metal-working industry of Cyprus, and I agree with him that ideology was probably used to legitimize and justify the control of certain elite groups. However, I take issue with the way that Knapp completely ignores the possibility that the religious sector might have played some role in the industry other than just providing for its ideological legitimization. For instance, in his eagerness to emphasize that the iconography was used to support the secular elites' claims to power (rather than that of any religious elite, whom he never mentions), Knapp seems to feel constrained from ever acknowledging that the iconography and the ideology it expressed was at base *religious* in nature. This is evident when he says,

> My intention was to demonstrate that several archaeological features of Late Bronze Age Cyprus *previously regarded as religious* in nature – figurines, representations of oxhide ingots, metallurgical workshops found in 'temples' – should in fact be regarded as *ideological* in nature."[365] (My emphasis.)

Note also how he applies quotation marks to the word 'temples', as if to imply that they were not actually temples at all. Concerning the close physical association between workshops and religious structures Knapp says very little, and when he does address the issue he uses vague and ambiguous terminology:

> But what of those public or ceremonial structures built in close proximity to areas of metalworking activity? ... General attitudes or *values*, as well as certain *institutions*, may also be sanctified and thus take on the nature of ultimate sacred propositions. The proximity to metalworking areas of the large-scale structures at Kition *Kathari* ("Temples" 1 and 2, and "Temenos" A), Enkomi *Ayios Iakovos* ("Ingot God sanctuary"), and Athienou *Bamboulari tis Koukounninas*, may signify such a sanctified value or institution. Like the ingot-bearer before a tree, this spatial situation may play on the familiarity of a well-entrenched, symbolic association between managers and producers, between the forces and the social relations of production.[366]

Knapp has to admit that the production of copper had become a sanctified institution, but again he uses alternate terms ("public or ceremonial structures" and "large-scale structures"), in order to describe buildings that are actually temples (note again how he puts quotes around the word when he has to use it). He also assumes that we will go along with him in seeing the managers of the metal industry as exclusively secular. As noted above, Knapp says that, "a single politico-economic institution, directly endowed with ritual sanctification to ensure that its dictates would be met, controlled both 'temple' and workshop."[367] But Knapp gives no real consideration to the role that religious personnel might have played in the metalworking industry, or the power that the religious sector could have wielded in the situation. Instead he credits the secular elite with all the power and control of not only the metal industry, but also of the religious hierarchy and the way in which its iconography was employed. Thereby, he neglects to address how the "single politico-economic institution" acquired its ritual

358 Keswani 1993, p. 79.
359 Knapp 1997, p. 67. Also see Knapp 1999, p. 247.
360 Knapp 1997, p. 67. Also see Knapp 1999, p. 247.
361 Keswani 1993, p. 79.
362 Knapp discusses this in 1996, p. 11.
363 Knapp 1996, p. 9.
364 Knapp 1986, p. 116
365 Knapp 1996, p. 9.
366 Knapp 1986, p. 81. He reiterates this thought on pp. 116-117.
367 Knapp 1986, p. 116.

sanctification in the first place, and how it maintained that crucial support through the years.

I think it is possible to admit the religious nature of the temples and the iconography, while also recognizing the function they had in supporting the secular elite's power. And I think it is possible to allow for the religious sector to have had some power of its own without implying that the secular elite had none. As Price says, "Religion just as much as politics is concerned with power."[368]

Therefore, I would advocate a theory concerning the management of the copper-producing industry of Cyprus that lies somewhere in between those proposed by Catling and Knapp. The secular elite may have held ultimate authority over the system as a whole, but it is difficult to deny that the evidence speaks for the active involvement of the religious sector in various points of the production system. Given the close proximity of the workshops at Enkomi and Kition to the temples, it is very probable that it was members of the religious personnel who were actually managing the production work at those sites. It seems most likely then, even if the secular elites were ultimately in control of the temple and workshop as Knapp asserts (although, in the end, there is no evidence that this was definitely the case either), that the religious personnel would have been able to reap the material benefits that resulted from that involvement. It should also be recalled that the inland rural sanctuaries were key players in the system, so much so that, as I mentioned, Kassianidou thinks that originally those were the sites that held the most power in the system. We might wonder then how great the control of the secular elites, who were based in the coastal sites, actually was over these inland sites. Did the secular elite really control them at all? Or was the relationship characterized more by cooperation and the recognition that each of the forces needed the other to make the business run smoothly and profitably? Indeed, the same questions could be applied to the workshop-temples in the coastal centers.

After all, the fact that the secular elite was successful in using the industry's religious associations in the consolidation of its power indicates that a basic concept of the sanctity of bronze working must have been an accepted feature of the Cypriot belief system prior to the elites' use of it. In other words, it was originally, and must have remained so to some extent, the religious hierarchy that held at least symbolic power over the metal industry. At some point the elites may have become powerful enough to override the religious hierarchy, but clearly the most convenient way to assert their power was to use the channels already established by the religious realm. The fact that they did not dispense with the religious connection seems to imply that they looked to the religious sphere to confirm their status. This may have been accomplished through a religious ceremony. And the fact that the Cypriot elite found this to be the most efficient way to continue to control the industry and the people who worked within it indicates that they must have continued to look to the religious hierarchy to confirm their status as controlling agents of the industry. Thus the ceremony would have been periodically re-enacted, which in effect would also have confirmed the power of the members of the religious hierarchy. In paying homage to the gods who were seen as the source of their power, the elites would in turn have conferred power upon the priests and priestesses who represented those gods. Hence the religious sphere would have gained in prestige from the situation.

The iconography that revolved around the copper industry demonstrates that the religious sector probably also benefited in a tangible way from their involvement in the copper industry. For instance, it is possible that the image of the ingot-bearer approaching a tree with his offering could symbolize actual offerings that were brought to the deities who were supposed to protect the copper industry. Such offerings would have functioned to bring the sanctuaries an income of their own. Also, the respect and reverence that was paid to the deities who were thought to care for the metal industry would probably have reflected upon the priests and priestesses who served those deities.

I have discussed the Cypriot material in such detail partially because it provides us with archaeological comparanda for the sites found on the mainland of Greece, and partially because the Cypriot sites have been discussed in previous literature in more detail than those found on the mainland. I think there are two important themes that we can take from the Cypriot material that are relevant to our study of the mainland situation. The first is that when workshops and religious structures are found together, it seems likely that the religious functionaries who managed the sanctuaries could have benefited materially from their involvement in the workshop's industrial activities. This basic premise has many implications for the status of the religious sector within Mycenaean society as well as for its relationship to the *wanax* and his administration. The second point to take from the Cypriot material is that religious iconography, and therefore also presumably religious belief and ritual, were used to secure and support the secular elite's claim to power over the society and its main means of production. Religious functionaries, as representatives of the deities, would have been the agents through which the elite's power would have been legitimized. I think a situation similar to this may have existed on the mainland of Greece, particularly at Pylos, where the religious sphere may have served to sanctify the *wanax*'s position as head of the realm and its most important industries. This second theme I will turn to in the next chapter as it lays the foundation for our consideration of the religious sector's role in Mycenaean society.

[368] S.R.F. Price, *Rituals and power: the Roman imperial cult in Asia Minor*, Cambridge University Press 1984, p. 247.

CHAPTER IV

Land Tenure at *Pa-ki-ja-ne*

In the previous chapter the involvement of the religious sector of several Aegean sites in economic (primarily industrial) activities was reviewed and evaluated. It was found that a few of them (Myrtos, Room of the Lilies shrine and the sanctuary in Xeste 3 at Akrotiri, and Zakros) provided evidence for sanctuaries that were actively involved in production work. The sites on Cyprus (Kition, Enkomi, Alassa *Pano Mandilares,* Athienou *Bamboulari tis Koukounninas* and Myrtou *Pigadhes* also seem to have been very much involved in the practicalities of the copper-producing industry. In interpreting the nature of the religious sector's role in the industry, Knapp proposed that the religious sector provided the ideological underpinnings for the Cypriot elite's controlling position at the head of that industry, but he downplayed the role of the sanctuaries in the actual management of the copper production. I propose that, as the religious sector must have been active in the Cypriot economy, it may also have acquired some social and political power of its own as a result of that involvement. Although there are major differences between the Cypriot and the Mycenaean situations - no major industry unites the purpose of the entire culture as the copper-producing industry seems to have done on Cyprus, and there is no religious iconography in the Mycenaean world related to craftsmanship or production - nonetheless I think the Linear B tablets and the archaeological evidence show that the religious sector did engage in economic activities within Mycenaean society, and it is possible that being engaged in such activities might have brought those at the top of the religious hierarchy some influence within their community, as I think it did for the Cypriot religious functionaries. Economic influence (especially when combined with religious power) may even have helped to give the religious sector a prestigious place in Mycenaean society.

Fortunately, for the Mycenaean period we have both textual and archaeological evidence, so here we are not limited to looking for sites where religious and industrial activities are found together. Rather, we can surmise from the Linear B tablets that the religious sector and the members of its religious hierarchy were involved in several different aspects of the economy. Therefore, rather than turning immediately to the archaeological evidence of the Late Bronze Age (which I address in chapter 6), I will start my investigation of the Mycenaean situation with the Linear B evidence. One of the most striking examples of the participation of religious personnel in the Mycenaean economy is found on the land tenure tablets from Pylos, where much of the land is held by people who were clearly associated with the religious realm, specifically in the area called *Pa-ki-ja-ne*. The bulk of this chapter will be taken up with an exploration into the details of these land tenure tablets.

But before I turn to these specific tablets, I will first discuss what we know about the sanctuary of *Pa-ki-ja-ne* itself and the area, also called *Pa-ki-ja-ne*, in which it was situated. The wide range of Linear B tablets that *Pa-ki-ja-ne* appears on certainly does seem to show that the sanctuary played an important role in the lives of the inhabitants of Pylos. We are also very fortunate in having a tablet, Un 2, which appears to demonstrate that a special relationship existed between the sanctuary of *Pa-ki-ja-ne* and the *wanax* of Pylos. Of course, information regarding such things as social standing and power relationships must be teased out of the Linear B records, given their laconic and predominantly economic nature. Nonetheless, the textual material does seem to provide us with information that seems to indicate that the Mycenaean *wanax* looked to the religious hierarchy for affirmation of his position as head of state. If the religious sphere was in the position of legitimizing the power of the *wanax*, no matter how symbolic that legitimization may have been, it most likely would have served to further enhance the prestige of those individuals who belonged to the religious community.

The rest of this chapter and those following will focus on the evidence for the religious sector's role in the Mycenaean economy, but I thought it would be useful to have an awareness of the elevated position a sanctuary could achieve in Mycenaean society as a foundation for both the main topic of this chapter, the role of the religious personnel of *Pa-ki-ja-ne* in land tenure, as well as for the role sanctuaries appear to have played in the various economic activities that I will discuss in chapters 5 and 6.

Pa-ki-ja-ne and its Relationship with the Inhabitants of Pylos and their Ruler, the *Wanax*

The place name *Pa-ki-ja-ne* is actually used to represent both a sanctuary site and one of the nine administrative districts of the Hither Province.[1] These nine administrative districts of the Hither Province are consistently listed in the same order on several tablets.[2]

[1] The area governed by the palace site of Pylos seems to have been divided into two geographical areas which the Pylians called "this side of Aigaleion" (*de-we-ro-a₃-ko-ra-i-ja*: Ng 319.1) and "beyond Aigaleion" (*pe-ra₃-ko-ra-i-ja*: Ng 332.1 and On 300.8). These are conventionally referred to as the Hither and Further Provinces. Within the Hither Province there seem to have been nine standard provinces, while in the Further there were seven (although this number and the place names are a bit more variable than those of the Hither Province).

[2] For a discussion of the tablets and their meaning for our understanding of Pylian political geography see J. Bennet, "Space through Time: Diachronic Perspectives on the Spatial Organization of the Pylian State," in *Politeia, Proceedings of the 5th International Conference held at the University of Heidelberg*, Vol. II (*Aegaeum* 12), R. Laffineur and W.-D. Niemeier, eds., Liège and PASP, University of Texas 1995, pp. 587-601. See also M. Lang, "Pylian Place Names," in *Texts, Tablets*

The district of *Pa-ki-ja-ne* is found, always fourth on the list, on the tablets Vn 20.6, Jn 829.7, and Cn 608.6.[3] The first of these tablets records wine that is being sent out to the districts, while Jn 829 records bronze that is being contributed by each of the districts to the palace for the manufacture of arrows and spears. Cn 608 records small numbers of pigs located at each district[4] that are to be "fattened" (*a-se-so-si*[5]), and which were most likely destined to be used in a communal feasting ceremony or religious celebration.[6] *Pa-ki-ja-ne* also appears within the taxation documents on Ma 221.1 and Na 561.1. Wyatt and Shelmerdine have shown that in the Ma taxation records the districts were arranged into fiscal groupings that each contributed their goods in fixed proportions of the total amount expected by the palace.[7] The goods on Vn 20 and Cn 608 also reflect these fixed proportions. Thus *Pa-ki-ja-ne* (the district) was part of the palatial economic system and its economic responsibilities vis-à-vis the palace were the same as those of the other districts.

The name of *Pa-ki-ja-ne*, however, may have arisen from a religious context. *Pa-ki-ja-ne* (found on Vn 19.4) would be transliterated as *Σφαγιᾶνες, a nominative plural form, while the alternate nominative form of *pa-ki-ja-na* (found on Na 561[8]) gives the singular feminine *Σφαγιᾶνα.[9] The root of *pa-ki-ja-ne* is most likely associated with the Greek root σφαγ-, which in historical Greek produces (among other related words) the verbs σφάζω and σφαγιάζομαι, which both mean "to slay a victim" or "to sacrifice," and the noun σφάγιον, which is the word for a "victim" or an "offering." A σφαγίς is "a sacrificial knife" while a σφαγεῖον is "a bowl for catching the blood of the victim." Lejeune mentions that the Greeks noted that their historical place name *Sphakteria* must be connected to the verb σφάζω.[10] There is no problem with seeing *pa-ki-ja-* as representing a word that starts with the consonant cluster /*sph*/ since usually, as in the case of *pe-mo* and *pe-ma* which represent σπέρμο/α, the initial "s" is dropped in the Mycenaean spelling of such words. A similar word, *sa-pa-ka-te-ri-ja*, which Killen thinks must also represent /*sphakteria*/,[11] is found, for example, on KN C 1561 and C(2) 941 in association with sheep and goats. In these instances Killen says that *sa-pa-ka-te-ri-ja* serves to describe the animals as "intended for slaughter or sacrifice."[12] Thus we may define *Pa-ki-ja-ne*, as Palaima has, as "the place of slaughter."[13]

Thus the name *Pa-ki-ja-ne* may indicate that religious sacrifices, or a festival during which such sacrifices were conducted, were associated with this place. Partially for this reason, I think that the place name *Pa-ki-ja-ne* was first applied to the sanctuary, and then the province around it also came to be known by the name of *Pa-ki-ja-ne*. Whether the district of *Pa-ki-ja-ne* was a religious institution akin to the Vatican City as Palaima has proposed,[14] or a secular one is a matter for debate, but I think the following discussion concerning the land tenure tablets will show that it is more likely that the district of *Pa-ki-ja-ne*, while it had grown up around the sanctuary and was heavily influenced by it, nevertheless was not a religious entity. It seems instead to be represented by the *damos*. Regardless of the secular base of power within

---

and Scribes: Studies in Mycenaean Epigraphy and Economy offered to E.L. Bennet, Jr., (*Minos* Suppl. 10), J.-P. Olivier and T.G. Palaima, eds., Salamanca 1988, pp. 185-212; and J.J. Carothers, *The Pylian Kingdom: A Case Study of an Early State*, Ph.D. dissertation, UCLA 1992. For the archaeological view on Pylos and its rise to power see J. Bennet and C.W. Shelmerdine, "Not the Palace of Nestor: The Development of the 'Lower Town' and Other Non-Palatial Settlements in LBA Messenia," in *Urbanism in the Bronze Age*, K. Branigan, ed., Sheffield Academic Press 2001, pp. 135-140.

[3] *Pa-ki-ja-ne* also appears on the more fragmentary lists found on Vn 19.4, On 300.3, and Jo 438.10, as well as on An 18.11, Vn 130.7, .9, Xa 113.1, and the land tenure tablets En 609.1, En 609.16/Eo 224.6, En 609.[18]/Eo 224.8, Eb 338.A, Eb 339.A, and Eb 1176.A. The religious tablets it appears on are Fr 1209.1, 1216.1, 1217.3, 1224, 1236, Fn 187.4, Tn 316.2 and Un 2.1. These will be discussed in more detail further on.

[4] Palaima notes that "certain place names on the tablet like *pa-ki-ja-si* are clearly in the locative...", hence we cannot speak of the animals as definitely being allocated to or requisitioned from the districts. "Perspectives on the Pylos Oxen Tablets: Textual (and Archaeological) Evidence for the Use and Management of Oxen in Late Bronze Age Messenia (and Crete)," in *Studia Mycenaea 1988, Ziva Antika Monographs* No. 7, T.G. Palaima, C.W. Shelmerdine, and P. Ilievski, eds., Skopje 1989, pp. 85-119; see p. 117-118.

[5] The majority of scholars take *jo-a-se-so-si* as consisting of ...ὡς + *ἀήσουσι, the latter being the 3rd person plural future indicative of ἀσέω (ἀσάω), meaning "thus they will fatten" (*Docs*[2], p. 534, also see *Dic. Mic.* I, p. 108). Risch proposed that instead *jo-a-se-so-si* could be broken down as οἵας ἥσουσι, using the future of ἵημι (*Etudes sur la grammaire et le vocabulaire du grec mycenien*, Amsterdam 1967, p. 168).

[6] Palaima 1989, pp. 117-118. On the idea that small numbers of livestock recorded in the Linear B texts were used in ceremonial banquets see Ch. Piteros, J.-P. Olivier, and J.L. Melena, "Les inscriptions en lineaire B des nodules de Thebes (1982): la fouille, les documents, les possibilites d'interpretation," *BCH* 114 (1990) 103-184; see pp. 171-184. J.T. Killen, "Observations on the Thebes Sealings," in *Mykenaïka* (*BCH* Suppl. 25), J.-P. Olivier, ed., Athens 1992, pp. 365-380; *idem*, "Thebes Sealings, Knossos Tablets and Mycenaean State Banquets," *BICS* 39 (1994) 67-84; see pp. 70-78; *idem*, "Thebes Sealings and Knossos Tablets," in *Atti e Memorie del Secondo Congresso Internazionale de Micenologia* (*Incunabula Graeca* 98), E. De Miro, L. Godart, and A. Sacconi, eds., Rome 1996, pp. 71-82.

[7] W.F. Wyatt, "The Ma Tablets from Pylos," *AJA* 66 (1962) 21-41. C.W. Shelmerdine, "Mycenaean Taxation," in *Studia Mycenaea 1988, Ziva Antika Monographs* 7, T.G. Palaima, C.W. Shelmerdine, and P. Ilievski, eds., Skopje 1989, pp. 125-148.

[8] It is possible that *pa-ki-ja-na* on Na 561 could be the locative (*Dic. Mic.* II, p. 68).

[9] *Dic. Mic.* II, pp. 68-69 discusses the alternation between the two. For a review of all the forms *pa-ki-ja-* appears in on the tablets see A.P. Sainer, "An Index of the Place Names at Pylos," *Studi Micenei ed Egeo-Anatolici* 17 (*Incunabula Graeca* 63), Rome 1976, pp. 17-63; see pp. 48-49.

[10] M. Lejeune, "Les Dérivés en –ter," in *Mémoires de Philologie Mycénienne*, Vol. II (*Incunabula Graeca* 42), Rome 1971c, pp. 199-224; see p. 203, n. 18 (first published in *Revue de Philologie* 34 (1960) 9-30).

[11] Killen 1996, p. 74. The idea was originally proposed by Lejeune 1971c, p. 203, n. 18.

[12] Killen 1996, p. 74. Killen (1996, pp. 79-81) also proposes that the adjunct *sa*, found in association with animals on KN C 394 and U 7063, may stand for *sa-pa-ka-te-ri-ja*, and serves to differentiate animals raised specifically for slaughter/sacrifice from those (designated as *pa* for *pa-ra-jo*, "old") that were being culled from breeding or wool-producing flocks because of their age.

[13] T.G. Palaima, "The Nature of the Mycenaean *Wanax*: Non-Indo-European Origins and Priestly Functions," in *The Role of the Ruler in the Prehistoric Aegean* (*Aegaeum* 11), P. Rehak, ed., Liège 1995, pp. 119-139; see p. 131.

[14] T.G. Palaima, personal communication, spring 2000.

the district, the sanctuary of *Pa-ki-ja-ne* also seems to have had an independent and somewhat special relationship with the palace.

This is not to say that *Pa-ki-ja-ne* was the only religious site that had close ties with the palace. Another sanctuary within the Hither Province district of *ro-u-so* also receives some attention from the palace.[15] Offerings of oil are sent to *ro-u-si-jo a-ko-ro*, which seems to have been the designation used to specify a sanctuary of *ro-u-so*, on Fr 1220.1 and Fr 1226.1. The tablet Un 47, which has as its heading: *ro-u-so* , *ro-u-si-jo* , *a-ko-ro*[, records foodstuffs, including grain, wine and sheep, that were probably destined to be consumed at a religious festival held at the sanctuary in *ro-u-so*. The worship of Poseidon (at one or more of his sanctuaries?) probably also played an important role in the religious life of the Pylians. The palace sends grain and figs to a sanctuary of Poseidon (*po-si-da-i-jo*, *Ποσιδάhιον) on Fn 187.2, and grain alone to a group that most likely represents his priests (*po-si-da-i-je-u-si*) on Fn 187.18.[16] Killen has recently proposed that the allocations on this tablet were probably for use in a religious festival.[17] A sanctuary of Poseidon is again recorded on Tn 316 *v*. 1, where gold vessels and human ministrants are sent to deities at Poseidon's sanctuary. Poseidon himself is not included among these deities, but the female version of Poseidon, *po-si-da-e-ja*, is listed in the first paragraph of Tn 316 with Potnia at *Pa-ki-ja-ne*. Poseidon is definitely not neglected as he receives offerings on Fr 343, Fr 1219.2, and Fr 1224, and the Un tablets 6, 718, and 853 seem to indicate that special festivals in his honor were of interest to the palace. Also, the Es series shows Poseidon as receiving special offerings or tribute(?) that was recorded by the palace.[18] Thus Poseidon, and presumably his sanctuary(ies?), held a prominent place in the religious life of Pylos.

The sanctuary of *Pa-ki-ja-ne*, though, is also very prominent, and as the textual evidence shows, it was perhaps the most important sanctuary in the religious life of the Pylians. To start with, *Pa-ki-ja-ne* is also sent an allocation of grain and figs on Fn 187.4, the tablet on which the *po-si-da-i-jo* and the *po-si-da-i-je-u-si* are recorded. In addition, the Fr series records *Pa-ki-ja-ne* six times: on Fr 1209.1, Fr 1216.1, Fr 1217.3, Fr 1224, Fr 1233.1, and Fr 1236.1.[19] Fr 1209 and Fr 1233 do not give us any information other than that the oil was going to *Pa-ki-ja-ne*, but the other Fr tablets do give us further information about the sanctuary and its significance in Pylian religion. For instance, Fr 1217 specifies that the oil was for use during the *re-ke-e-to-ro-e-ri-jo*, or the *Lekhestroterion*, which has been taken to represent a festival celebrating the "Spreading of the Couches." Two interpretations have been offered concerning the purpose of this festival: either the couches were being spread for a banquet of the gods,[20] or they were being prepared for a *hieros gamos* that was to take place between two deities.[21] In either case, *Pa-ki-ja-ne* may be said to have been the site of this important festival. On Fr 1224 *Pa-ki-ja-ne* is used as a month name: *pa-ki-ja-ni-jo-jo me-no*. Chadwick comments, "As in the classical world, it appears likely that month-names are sometimes derived from the festivals held in them."[22] Among the most recognizable months that are named after festivals in the Attic calendar are the Hekatombaion, Boedromion, Anthesterion, and Skirophorion.[23] Thus the use of *pa-ki-ja-* to create a month name underlines the importance of the place and its festival to the Pylians. Chadwick says, "thus the month called *pa-ki-ja-ni-jo* must be the time of the principal festival celebrated at that site...."[24] Another tablet, Fr 1216, records oil that was being sent to a group of people called the *pa-ki-ja-ni-jo-i*. This could have been a general term referring to those who were in the service of the deities worshipped at the sanctuary of *Pa-ki-ja-ne*. And finally, on Fr 1236, Potnia (specifically *u-po-jo po-ti-ni-ja*) is the deity designated to receive the tablet's offering of oil. This supports the idea that there was a link between *Pa-ki-ja-ne* and Potnia, as does Tn 316.3, where Potnia is listed first among the deities at that sanctuary.

Tn 316:

1. po-ro-wi-to-jo ,
2. -je-to-qe , pa-ki-ja-si , do-ra-qe , pe-re , po-re-na-qe
3. pu-ro a-ke , po-ti-ni-ja AUR **215*^{VAS} 1 MUL 1
4. ma-na-sa , AUR **213*^{VAS} 1 MUL 1 po-si-da-e-ja AUR **213*^{VAS} 1 MUL 1
5. ti-ri-se-ro-e , AUR **216*^{VAS} 1 do-po-ta AUR **215*^{VAS} 1
6. *angustum*
7. *vacat*
8. *vacat*
9. pu-ro *vacat*

[15] The district of *ro-u-so*, like *pa-ki-ja-ne*, appears on a variety of tablets, including Aa 717, Aa 798, Ab 383.B, Ab 1099, Cn 285.1, Cn 328.1, Jn 829.10, Jn 832.1, Jo 438.9, Ma 365.1, Mb 1398, Mn 456.7, Mn 1370.1, and Vn 130.12.

[16] The fact that two offerings are being sent to Poseidon on Fn 187 may indicate that two different sanctuaries were involved.

[17] J.T. Killen, "Religion at Pylos: The Evidence of the Fn Tablets," in *Potnia: Deities and Religion in the Aegean Bronze Age* (*Aegaeum* 22), R. Laffineur and R. Hägg, eds., Liège and PASP, University of Texas 2001, pp. 435-443.

[18] M. Lang, "Es Proportions," in *Mycenaean Studies: Proceedings of the 3rd International Colloquium for Mycenaean Studies*, E.L. Bennett, ed., University of Wisconsin Press 1964, pp. 37-55. Pia de Fidio, *I dosmoi pilii a Poseidon* (*Incunabula Graeca* 65), Rome 1977.

[19] If the first paragraph of Tn 316 may be taken to indicate that Potnia is the primary deity worshipped at *Pa-ki-ja-ne*, then the oil that was being sent to Potnia on the Fr tablets may also imply that the oil was being sent to the sanctuary of *Pa-ki-ja-ne*. Those tablets are Fr 1206, 1225, 1231, and 1235.

[20] *Docs*², p. 579.

[21] Bennett 1958, p. 31. The *Lekhestroterion* is also mentioned on Fr 343, one of the tablets that specifies Poseidon as the recipient. It has thus been proposed that the two deities who were to take part in the *hieros gamos* were Poseidon and Potnia.

[22] J. Chadwick, "What Do We Know about Mycenaean Religion?", *Linear B: A 1984 Survey* (*BCILL* 26), A. Moepurgo-Davies and Y. Duhoux, eds., Louvain-le-Neuve 1985, pp. 191-202; see p. 201. A similar type of thing seems to have occurred at Knossos where *di-wi-jo-jo me-no*, a month named after a deity, appears on KN Fp 5.1.

[23] W. Burkert, *Greek Religion*, trans. J. Raffan, Harvard University Press 1985, pp. 225-226.

[24] Chadwick 1985, p. 201.

10. *vacat*

v. 1: i-je-to-qe , po-si-da-i-jo , a-ke-qe , wa-tu
v. 2. do-ra-qe , pe-re , po-re-na-qe , a-ke
v3a. pu-ro -ja
v. 3. AUR *215^VAS 1 MUL 2 qo-wi-ja , ṇạ-[ ] , ko-ma-we-te-
v. 4. i-je-to-qe , pe-ṛẹ-*82-jo , i-pe-me-de-ja-qe di-u-ja-jo-qe
v. 5. do-ṛạ-qe , pe-re-po-re-na-qe , a , pe-re-*82 AUR *213^VAS 1 MUL 1
v. 6. pu-ro i-pe-me-ḍẹ-ja AUR *213^VAS 1 di-u-ja AUR *213^VAS 1 MUL 1
v. 7. e-ma-ạ2 , a-re-ja AUR *216^VAS 1 VIR 1
v. 8. i-je-to-qe , di-u-jo , do-ra-qe , pe-re , po-re-na-qe a-ḳẹ
v. 9. di-we AUR *213^VAS 1 VIR 1 e-ra AUR *213^VAS 1 MUL 1
v. 10. pu-ro di-ri-mi-jo⌞⌟di-wo, i-je-we , AUR *213^VAS 1 [ ] *vacat*
v. 11. *vacat*
v. 12. *angustum*
v. 13. *vacat*
v. 14. *vacat*
v. 15. pu-ro *vacat*
v. 16. *vacat*

The structure of Tn 316 highlights the importance of the sanctuary *Pa-ki-ja-ne*. While the sanctuary of Poseidon is recorded in the second paragraph on Tn 316 *v*. 1, the sanctuary at *Pa-ki-ja-ne* stands in the first.[25] Furthermore, it is possible, as Palaima seems to accept,[26] that all of the sanctuaries recorded on Tn 316 were located within *Pa-ki-ja-ne*.

Palaima also emphasizes the importance of *Pa-ki-ja-ne* for the town of Pylos and the *wanax*, whom Palaima believes played a large role in Pylian religion as the primary "intermediary between the human and divine spheres...."[27] As the representative of the community, "a chief function of the king or *wanax* was to preside over ritual sacrifices and feasts...."[28] One of those sacrifices may have been depicted on the wall of the Vestibule (Room 5) outside the Throne Room in the palace.[29] The fresco depicts a procession in which a bull is being brought as an offering to a shrine. Palaima interprets one figure, who is depicted on a larger scale than the others bringing offerings, as the *wanax*. Palaima also proposes that the open-air shrine depicted on the fresco may be identified as *Pa-ki-ja-ne*: "The tablet evidence might be taken to suggest that the destination would have been *pa-ki-ja-ne* with its many textually attested religious precincts (cf. Tn 316)."[30]

Thus the sanctuary at *Pa-ki-ja-ne* may be said to have held an important, perhaps even the preeminent, place in the religious life of the Pylians. It may also have played a key role in providing the means by which the *wanax* maintained his power. Palaima has said, "It is my own opinion that the powers and authority of the *wanax* are intimately connected with – and derived from – his religious associations."[31] Palaima based his opinion on an analysis of the Linear B tablets concerning the *wanax* and his activities. But it is not unusual for kings to base their claim to power at least partly on the role they played as representative of the people in the religious sphere, and the presumed connection they have with the divine. As we have seen, Knapp thinks the elite of the Cypriot Bronze Age depended upon religious ideology and iconography to support their controlling position of the copper-producing industry. Also, Earle points out that in many cultures it is typical for "chiefs and kings [to] maintain domination through perpetuating the belief that their superiority is part of the natural order, sanctioned by superhuman powers and authority."[32] Earle also says that ideological power is "characteristically backed by religious sanction." That is, religious sanction is often provided to the king through rituals or ceremonies that symbolically confer divine approval upon him. Galaty actually thinks that in the Mycenaean situation, the *wanax* chose to use religion and ritual to legitimate his increased political domination rather than doing so through increasing palatial control over the staple economy.[33] The *wanax* then may have needed the religious sector to sanction his religious role. The tablet PY Un 2 supports this theory and provides evidence that the religious personnel of *Pa-ki-ja-ne* may have had a role to play in legitimizing the position of the *wanax* in Pylian society.

Un 2:
1. pa-ki-ja-si , mu-jo-me-no , e-pi , wa-na-ka-te ,
2. a-pi-e-ke , o-pi-te-ke-e-u
3. HORD 16 T 4 CYP+*PA* T 1 V 3 *o* V 5
4. FAR 1 T 2 OLIV 3 T 2 **132* S 2 *ME* S 1
5. *NI* 1 BOS 1 OVIS^m 26 OVIS^f 6 CAP^m 2 CAP^f 2
6. SUS+*SI* 1̣ SUS^f 6 VIN 20 S 1 **146* 2

[25] See T.G. Palaima, "Kn02 – Tn 316," in *Floreant Studia Mycenaea*, Acts of the 10th International Mycenological Colloquium held at the University of Salzburg, S. Deger-Jalkotzy, S. Hiller, and O. Panagl, eds., Wien 1999, pp. 437-461; p. 452 on the hierarchical arrangement of Tn 316.

[26] Palaima never argues this explicitly, but it is implicit in statements such as "...Poseidon and the important Pylian deity *pe-re-*82* (Un 6), both of whom have sanctuaries in the district of *pa-ki-ja-ne* (cf. Tn 316)..." (1995, p. 131).

[27] Palaima 1995, p. 122.

[28] Palaima 1995, p. 132.

[29] See M. Lang, *The Palace of Nestor at Pylos in Western Messenia* II: *The Frescoes*, University of Princeton Press 1969, see pp. 38-40, 192-193, plate 119. L. McCallum, *Decorative Program in the Mycenaean Palace of Pylos: The Megaron Frescoes*, Ph.D. Dissertation, University of Pennsylvania 1987. Palaima 1995, pp. 132-133.

[30] Palaima 1995, p. 133.

[31] Palaima 1995, p. 129. K. Kilian also believed that the *wanax* derived much of his power from his position within the religious realm. See "The Emergence of Wanax Ideology in the Mycenaean Palaces," *Oxford Journal of Archaeology* 7 (1988) 291-302.

[32] T. Earle, "Political Domination and Social Evolution," in *Companion Encyclopedia of Anthropology: Humanity, Culture and Social Life*, T. Ingold, ed., Routledge 1994, pp. 911-931. (My thanks to J. Bennet for recomending this article to me.)

[33] M.L. Galaty, *Nestor's Wine Cups*, British Archaeological Reports 1999a, p. 79.

The body of the text of Un 2 records a list of foodstuffs similar to those found on other tablets (e.g., Un 718) that seem to have been destined to be consumed at a ceremonial or religious banquet. The first word of Un 2, *pa-ki-ja-si*, the locative form of *Pa-ki-ja-ne*, shows that the ceremony was to take place at *Pa-ki-ja-ne*. In the second line, *o-pi-te-ke-e-u* is thought to be an error for **o-pi-te-<u>-ke-e-u*, which Killen proposes may have been the title of an official "who is responsible for assembling or issuing the commodities" listed on the tablet.[34] The meaning of the verb *a-pi-e-ke* is undecided,[35] but may be related either to "ἵημι from the I-E root *isemi with the meaning 'to consecrate', or ἔχω, with the meaning 'to keep safely'...."[36] Thus the *o-pi-te-ke-e-u* is either consecrating or keeping the goods that are listed in the next four lines. The nature of the festival for which the goods were collected hinges on the phrase found in the first line, *mu-jo-me-no e-pi wa-na-ka-te*. The meaning of *mu-jo-me-no* has been debated,[37] but it is now generally accepted that *mu-jo-me-no* should be taken as a present middle/passive participle, *μυιόμενος, deriving from *μυίω with the meaning of μυέω, "to initiate."[38] The whole phrase, μυιομένῳ ἐπὶ ϝανάκτει could then be understood as denoting the time or occasion of the ceremony, and the *wanax* would either be seen as undergoing or presiding over an initiation.[39] The former interpretation has been deemed the most plausible, and thus the translation that Ventris and Chadwick gave is the one that is now generally cited: "on the occasion of the initiation of the king."[40] Un 2, therefore, is most likely a record of foodstuffs and sacrificial animals that were being gathered for a banquet that was meant to celebrate the initiation of the *wanax* at the sanctuary of *Pa-ki-ja-ne*.

If this interpretation of Un 2 is correct and the *wanax* was to be "initiated" at *Pa-ki-ja-ne*, we may wonder what the nature of this initiation was. Killen comments: "Though the initiation in question ... will be initiation into the mysteries, one wonders whether this did not take place as part of the installation of a new king."[41] It seems fitting that the *wanax* may have had to acquire his divine stamp of approval at the outset of his tenure as king, or perhaps this ceremony was done every year. In any case, it seems likely that the initiation provided the *wanax* with symbolic support from the religious sector, support that helped him to maintain, or could at least have enhanced, his position as head of state and as representative of his community in the religious realm. Un 2 shows that this religious sanction was bestowed upon the Pylian *wanax* specifically by the religious leaders at *Pa-ki-ja-ne*.

It would also seem reasonable to propose that the close relationship between the *wanax* and the religious sector seen on the Linear B tablets most likely developed before those tablets were written, perhaps even generations before. Palaima has proposed that the institution of the *wanax* was developed during "the period of the later Shaft Graves at Mycenae"[42] by a newly emerging class of persons who sought to impose their power over larger areas than had hitherto been dominated by a single paramount figure. Palaima says,

> There was a transition from a society with many locally based chieftains (each a *basileus*) to one in which single figures (each a *wanax*) held power over larger, separate territories and over local communities in which the *basilêes* continued to function. This transition would have entailed a process whereby the *wanax* could be singled out and placed at a level well above the *basilêes* and competing local aristocracy and the creation of an ideology that would justify and sustain this differentiation.[43]

He goes on to propose that the ideology used to set the *wanax* apart was derived from the Minoan culture (as may have been the word *wanax* itself, which is not Greek[44]), and that religion and religious iconography were very important elements in the establishment and perpetuation of this ideology. Divine sanctification of one's position as ruler would have been a very effective means of consolidating and legitimizing one's power, and

[34] The dative form of the word, *o-pi-te-u-ke-e-we*, occurs on Fn 41.14 and 50.8, and in the nominative plural on An 39.4, *o-pi-]te-u-ke-e-we*. The title has been interpreted as "the one in charge of the τεύχεα", which itself has been taken as "foodstuffs" such as the ones listed on Un 2 (POM, p. 179). Killen (1992, p. 376), however, points out that since τεῦχος in later Greek very often means "vessel" or "chest," it might be better to take the *o-pi-te-ke-e-u* as "a person who was in charge of the (palace?) cooking vessels or dining services (or, conceivably, of the chests in which stores of foodstuffs needed for the banquets, etc. were kept." Also see *Dic. Mic.* II, pp. 43-44 for previous proposals.

[35] Killen 1992, p. 376. Also see for somewhere in here on Un 2 and the other Un tablets: T.G. Palaima, "The Transactional Vocabulary of Mycenaean Sealings and the Mycenaean Adminiatrative Process," in *Administrative Documents in the Aegean and their Near Eastern Counterparts*, ed., M. Perna, Paravia Scriptorium 2000, pp. 261-276.]

[36] R. Palmer, *Wine in the Mycenaean Palace Economy* (*Aegaeum* 10), Liège and PASP, University of Texas 1994, pp. 105-106. *Dic. Mic.* I, pp. 80-81.

[37] Palmer (1963, pp. 258-259) for instance thought that *mu-jo-me-no e-pi wa-na-ka-te* could mean "making lament over the Wanax." See *Dic. Mic.* I, pp. 459-460 for a review of the proposed meanings. Also see for a more balanced appraisals M. Lindgren, "Two Linear B Problems Reconsidered from a Methodological Point of View," *Opuscula Atheniensia* 8 (1968) 71-76; see pp. 72-76; and P. Carlier, *La royauté en Grèce avant Alexandre*, Strasbourg 1984, pp. 91-94.

[38] *Docs*[2], pp. 221 and 440-441. *Dic. Mic.* I, pp. 459-460.

[39] Killen 1992, p. 376; *idem* 1994, p. 72. Palaima 1995, p. 131. C.W. Shelmerdine, "Administration in the Mycenaean Palaces: Where's the Chief?" in *Rethinking Mycenaean Palaces: New Interpretations of an Old Idea*, M.L. Galaty and W.A. Parkinson, eds., The Cotsen Institute of Archaeology at UCLA 1999, pp. 19-24; see p. 20. Also see Shelmerdine's discussion of Un 2 and the feasting tablets in "Review of Aegean Prehistory VI: The Palatial Bronze Age of the Southern and Central Greek Mainland," *AJA* 101 (1997) 537-585; see p. 579.

[40] *Docs*[2], pp. 221 and 440-441. Shelmerdine 1997, p. 579; *idem* 1999, p. 20. Killen 1992, p. 376; *idem* 1994, p. 72.

[41] Killen 1994, p. 72, n. 24.

[42] Palaima 1995, p. 130.

[43] Palaima 1995, p. 125.

[44] P. Rehak also mentions the foreign nature of the word *wanax* and proposes that the *wanax* as an institution did not come into being until LH IIA in "Enthroned Figures," in *The Role of the Ruler in the Prehistoric Aegean* (*Aegaeum* 11), P. Rehak, ed., Liège and PASP, University of Texas 1995, p. 116.

the *wanax* may have taken advantage of this in the early stages of the position's development. This implies that special religious personages, who would have been necessary associates in this process, may also have come into existence as the institution of the *wanax* was developing. In the case of Pylos, we can detect the existence of such a special religious community at *Pa-ki-ja-ne* in the textual evidence. Tentative archaeological evidence may support the proposition that they had already had a long history by the time those tablets were written.

Long ago Chadwick argued that the district (and the sanctuary) of *Pa-ki-ja-ne* was located close to Pylos. His reasons were twofold: first because the two are in close association on Tn 316, and second because (as we will discuss more fully further on) *Pa-ki-ja-ne* was designated as the place where "royal" craftsmen had their estates.[45] Chadwick therefore concluded that "we can place the fourth district as that close to, perhaps including, the palace...."[46] Bennet, however, has recently made a convincing argument that *pe-to-no*, the third of the nine districts, and not *Pa-ki-ja-ne*, was actually the district in which Pylos was located. This district would then encompass the area "to the north of the palace along the extensive coastal plain which runs essentially without interruption from south of Gargalianoi up to Filiatra."[47] However, Bennet agrees with Chadwick that the sanctuary of *Pa-ki-ja-ne* may have been located "at the village Hora, with its extensive chamber tomb cemetery at *Volimidia*."[48] Bennet explains:

I am inclined to follow this identification on locational grounds. It is attractive to see the palace site as lying at the intersection between two landscape units: the coastal area north of Navarino up to the Langouvardos and the uplands from Hora to Gargalianoi. We could argue that the palace dominates the lowland territory of *pe-to-no*, but also controls (and controlled from early on, since there is no tholos tomb at *Volimidia*?) the immediately adjacent upland territory of *pa-ki-ja-ne* with which it is directly linked by the Englianos ridge.[49]

Unfortunately, when Marinatos was excavating the chamber tombs at *Volimidia*, he found only scanty remains of actual habitation, but these did include LH I and LH III pottery.[50] McDonald and Hope Simpson remark that the "cemeteries surely presuppose an important habitation site in the vicinity, and this is all the more certain because of the magnificent springs at Kephalovrisi some 400 m N-E of the Volimidhia cemetery."[51] The remains of the habitation site may be under the modern city of Hora, or they may have been destroyed for the most part by the extensive cultivation that has taken place in the area. In either case, it is impossible at this point to identify *Volimidia* with *Pa-ki-ja-ne* for certain, but the cemetery, the presence of LH III pottery associated with walls, together with its close proximity to the palace, seem to make it a likely candidate.

Bennet also mentions that there was no tholos tomb found in the area of *Volimidia*. This may be significant given that tholos tombs have been interpreted as the "visible manifestations of the power of early Mycenaean elite families."[52] These tombs presumably indicate areas where powerful families or chiefs had established their centers.[53] Thus Bennet interprets the fact that the inhabitants of *Volimidia* never constructed a tholos tomb as "perhaps suggesting that [*Volimidia*] was already under the influence of the ruling elite at Ano Englianos" very early in its development, perhaps in the LH I period.[54] Thus, if the sanctuary of *Pa-ki-ja-ne* was located at *Volimidia*, it is possible that the relationship between the sanctuary and the palace may also date from this period. There would then have been a long period during which the two spheres, the palatial controlled by the *wanax*, and the religious directed by *Pa-ki-ja-ne*, co-existed and interacted.[55] I think it is possible that during that time the two may have bolstered each other's claims to power in order to further enhance their own.

If it is correct to see the religious sector as providing divine approval for the *wanax* and his right to rule, then it seems that the head priest or priestess of *Pa-ki-ja-ne* held some political power within Pylian society. Given that political and economic power are often intertwined, it seems appropriate that the religious personnel at *Pa-ki-ja-ne* also held a great deal of land within the district of *Pa-*

[45] J. Chadwick, *The Mycenaean World*, Cambridge University Press 1976; see pp. 41-46.
[46] Chadwick 1976, p. 43.
[47] J. Bennet, "The Mycenaean Conceptualization of Space, or Pylian Geography (...yet again!)," in *Floreant Studia Mycenaea*, Acts of the 10th International Mycenological Colloquium held at the University of Salzburg, S. Deger-Jalkotzy, S. Hiller, and O. Panagl, eds., Wien 1999, pp. 131-157; see p. 144.
[48] Bennet 1999, p. 147.
[49] Bennet 1999, p. 147. In a footnote to this statement (p. 147, n. 77) Bennet mentions that in the spoken version of this article that he delivered in Salzburg he had proposed that *Pa-ki-ja-ne* could be located at Myrsinohori *Routsi*. He has since that time reconsidered and decided that Myrsinohori was too far and too difficult to get to from the palace for it to have been *Pa-ki-ja-ne*.
[50] S. Marinatos, "Ἀνασκαφαὶ εν Πύλῳ," *Praktika* (1956) 238-250; see pp. 248-249. Approximately 100 m to the south of the chamber tombs Marinatos found traces of walls at the base of which he found a mass of LH III pottery. A test trench found LH I pottery, including Vapheio cups, about 1 m below the LH III material. Also see J.M. Cook, "Archaeology in Greece," *JHS* (1953) 118-119; J.M. Cook and J. Boardman, "Archaeology in Greece," *JHS* (1954) 155. For the chamber tombs see S. Marinatos, *Praktika* (1955) 473-496; (1956) 238-250; (1957) 299-316; (1966) 78-89 and 198-201; and (1967) 102-109.
[51] W.A. Mcdonald and R. Hope Simpson "Prehistoric Habitation in the Southwestern Peloponnese," *AJA* 65 (1961) 221-260; see p. 237.
[52] J. Davis "The Palace and its Dependencies," in *Sandy Pylos: An Archaeological History from Nestor to Navarino*, University of Texas Press 1998, pp. 53-68; see p. 60.
[53] C.B. Mee and W.G. Cavanagh, "Mycenaean Tombs as Evidence for Social and Political Organisation," *OJA* (1984) 45-64. J.C. Wright, "Death and Power at Mycenae: Changing Symbols in Mortuary Practice," *Thanatos: Les coutumes funeraires en Egee a l'age du bronze* (*Aegaeum* 1), Liège 1987, pp. 171-184.
[54] Bennet 1995, p. 597. Also see Davis 1998, p. 60.
[55] J. Wright discusses the idea that a cohesive Mycenaean religion was developing alongside the "formation and consolidation of Mycenaean political authority ("From Chief to King in Mycenaean Society," in *The Role of the Ruler in the Prehistoric Aegean* (*Aegaeum* 11), P. Rehak, ed., Liège and PASP, University of Texas 1995b, pp. 63-80; p. 72).

ki-ja-ne. But it is not enough to say simply that the religious functionaries held "a great deal of land." Rather, it is necessary to look in detail at the land tenure tablets that are concerned with *Pa-ki-ja-ne* in order to come to a more precise evaluation of the significance of the religious sector's presence in the region of *Pa-ki-ja-ne*, and, thereby, to better understand their position within the economic and political systems of Pylos.

The Land Tenure Series of *Pa-ki-ja-ne*: Who Owns the Land?

The land tenure series Ep/Eb and En/Eo,[56] which record landholdings within *Pa-ki-ja-ne*, further demonstrate both the interest of the Pylian administration in the district of *Pa-ki-ja-ne* and, as many of the landholders in these series are religious personages, the religious affiliations of many of its inhabitants. Whether the land recorded in the Ep/Eb and En/Eo series was actually religious land has been debated. The fact that the palatial scribes so carefully recorded the landholdings of this particular district demonstrates the interest of the palace in this land, and could indicate that it was under palatial control. Indeed Killen clearly states the two possible reasons for palatial interest in the land: 1. either all plots were owned by the palace and the tenants were supposed to render produce or services or both in exchange for the land, or 2. the plots were privately owned but the palace had the authority to collect taxes from the owners.[57] Killen clearly favored the former possibility. However, if we consider Killen's second possibility, there are a number of contenders for the position of primary landowner. For instance, the Ep series records land that is leased, for the most part, *pa-ro da-mo*, or from the *damos*. This would seem to suggest that perhaps the *damos* was actually the owner of this land. Also, in the En series leases are held from people called *te-re-ta*, which is a title of an official often thought to be in the service of the palace.[58] This could mean either that the *te-re-ta* themselves owned the land, or, if the connection with the palace is borne out, that the palace was in this case the actual owner, or at least the bestower, of the lands. And finally, a large number of the landholders on both sets are religious functionaries, which could, but does not necessarily indicate that these lands were somehow associated with the sanctuary of *Pa-ki-ja-ne*. Emmett Bennett in 1956 first discussed the preponderance of religious personnel found on these sets of tablets, and he proposed then that they probably recorded the landholdings of a large religious community.[59] Of course at this point there is no doubt that the sanctuary of *Pa-ki-ja-ne* did comprise a large religious community, but the question before us now is, exactly how did the sanctuary and the landholdings held by religious personnel fit into this rather complicated picture of land tenure at *Pa-ki-ja-ne*.

In order to answer this question, it is necessary to first review the land tenure series themselves to see what information they provide, and then to consider the most pertinent interpretations concerning Mycenaean society that these tablets have given rise to. Then, with this foundation having been established, i.e., with the view of Mycenaean society that I think is most likely having been sketched out, I will examine the landholdings of the religious personnel and their relationships to the other landholders of the series in order to determine the role the religious sector played as a landholder in the district of *Pa-ki-ja-ne*.

Review of the Ep/Eb and En/Eo Series

First I will review the basic characteristics of the two sets. Below are given examples of both an En and an Ep tablet. The patterns typical of each series are demonstrated by these tablets:

En 609:

1. pa-ki-ja-ni-ja , to-sa , da-ma-te , *DA* 40
2. to-so-de , te-re-ta , e-ne-e-si VIR 14
3. wa-na-ta-jo-jo , ko-to-na , ki-ti-me-na , to-so-de⌞ ⌟p̣ẹ-mo GRA 2 V 1
4. o-da-a_2 , o-na-te[-]ṛẹ , e-ko-si , ẉạ-na-ṭạ-jo-jo , ko-to-na ,

5a. GRA V 1

5. a-tu-ko , e-te-do-mo , wa-na-ka-te-ro , o-na-to , e-ke , de , pe-mo
6. i-ni-ja , te-o-jo , do-e-ra , o-na-ṭọ , e-ke , to-so-de , pe-mo GRA T 2 V 4
7. e-*65-to , te-o-jo , do-e-ro , o-na-to⌞ ⌟e-ke , to-so-de , pe-mo GRA T 2
8. si-ma , te-o-jo , do-e-ra , o-na-to , e-ke , to-so-de , pe-mo GRA T 1
9. *angustum*
10. a-ma-ru-ta-o , ko-to-na , ki-ti-me-na , ṭọ-so-de , pe-mo GRA 2 T 3
11. o-da-a_2 e-ko-si a-]ma-ru-ta-o , ko-to-na , o-na-te-re
12. so-u-ro te-o-jo do-]e-ro , o-na-to , e-ke , to-so-de , pe-mo GRA V 3
13. e-do-me-ne-u te-o-]jo , do-e-ro , o-na-to , e-ke , to-so-de , pe-mo G̣ṚẠ Ṭ 1̣
14. e-sa-ro te-o-jo do-]e-ro , ọ[-na-to]ẹ-ḳẹ⌞ ⌟ṭọ[-so-de]p̣ẹ-ṃọ GRA V 3
15. wa-na-ta-jo te-re-ta o-]ṇạ-ṭọ , e-ke , to-so-de pe-mo GRA T 1
16. e-ra-ta-ra i-je-re-ja do-e-ra]pa-ki-ja-na , o-na-to , e-ke , to-so-de , pe-mo GRA T 1

[56] The series designators Ep/Eb and En/Eo are written in this way to show that the Ep and En series were compiled from the preliminary documents of the Eb and Eo series, respectively. The two preliminary series were both written by Hand 41 and Hand 1 wrote both of the final series. E. Bennett gives an extremely detailed account of how the final Ep and En series were put together in "Pylian Landholding Jots and Tittles," in *Res Mycenaeae*, A. Heubeck and G. Neumann, eds., Gottingen 1983, pp. 41-54.

[57] J.T. Killen, "The Linear B Tablets and the Mycenaean Economy," *Linear B: A 1984 Survey*, *BCILL* 26, A. Morpurgo Davies and Y. Duhoux, eds., Louvain-la-Neuve 1985, pp. 241-305, see pp. 244-245.

[58] I will discuss the *te-re-ta* and their function in Pylian society further on in this chapter.

[59] E.L. Bennett, "The Landholders of Pylos," *AJA* 60 (1956b) 103-133; see especially pp. 129-133 for his discussion of the religious community of *Pa-ki-ja-ne*.

17. po-so-re-ja te-o-jo do-e-ra]o-na-to , e-ke , to-so-de , pe-mo GRA T 1 V 3
18. i-je-re-ja pa-ki-ja-na o-na-]to , e-ke , to-so-de , pe-mo GRA T 3

Ep 212:
1. re-ka , te-o-jo , do-e-ra , o-na-to , e-ke , ke-ke-me-na , ko-to-na , pa-ro , da-ṃọ , ṭọ-so pe-mo GRA T 6
2. e-ri-ko-wo , te-o-jo , do-e-ro , o-na-ṭọ , e-ke , ke-ke-me-na , ko-to-na , pa-ro , da-mo , to-so pe-mo GRA V 3
3. e-ko-to , te-o-jo , do-e-ro , o-na-to , e-ke , ke-ke-me-na, ko-to-na , ko-na , pa-ro , da-mo , to-so pe-mo GRA T 1 V 3
4. ko-ri-si-ja ⌊ ⌋te-o-jo , do-e-ra , o-na-to , e-ke , ke-ke-me-na , ko-to-na , pa-ro , da-mo , to-so pe-mo GRA 1
5. e-pa-sa-na-ti , te-o-jo , do-e-ra , o-na-to , e-ke , ke-ke-me-na , ko-to-na , pa-ro , da-mo to-so pe-mo GRA T 3
6. mu-ti-ri , te-o-jo , do-e-ra , o-na-to , e-ke , ke-ke-me-na, ko-to-na , pa-ro , da-mo to-so pe-mo GRA T 1
7. ka-wa-do-ro , te-o-jo , do-e-ro , o-na-to , e-ke , ke-ke-me-na , ko-to-na , pa-ro , da-mo , to-so , pe-mo GRA V 3
8. ḳọ-ṣạ-ma-to , te-o-jo , do-e-ro , o-na-to , e-ke , ke-ke-me-na , ko-to-na , pa-ro , da-mo , to pe-mo GRA T 1
9. i-do-me-ne-ja , te-o-jo , do-e-ra , o-na-to , e-ke , ke-ke-me-na , ko-to-na , pa-ro , da-mo to-so pe-mo GRA T 1 V 3
10. ra-su-ro , te-o-jo , do-e-ro , o-na-to ⌊ ⌋e-ḳẹ ⌊ ⌋ke-ke-me-na , ko-to-na[pa-ro] da-mo , to-so pe-mo GRA T 2

All of the records contain the ideogram GRA for *granum*, or wheat seed (**120*), which is often written out *pe-mo*, or σπέρμο,[60] within the text of the tablet.[61] Different quantities of GRA, which are thought to represent the sizes of the landholdings in terms of the surface area that would have been covered by that amount of grain,[62] are listed against various landholders who are recorded by name and, very often, title. The parcels of land can either be held outright, in which case they are called *ko-to-na* (as on En 609.3), or they are designated as being leased from another landholder's *ko-to-na*, in which case the land is called *o-na-to* (as on En 609.6 and all the records on Ep 212). *Ko-to-na* is interpreted as κτοίνα, a word which survived on Rhodes into the first millennium with the meaning of a "local division, like Attic δῆμος a township."[63] In the Mycenaean land tenure contexts *ko-to-na* simply meant a parcel of cultivable land.[64] It derives from the Indo-European root **ktei* meaning to "inhabit, settle, occupy." Several other Mycenaean words derive from the same root, including *ki-ti-me-na,* which is the type of land we see associated with the *te-re-ta* in the En series, as well as *a-ki-ti-to, ki-ti-ta*, and *me-ta-ki-ti-ta.* All of these words seem to relate to the settling or the cultivation of land and will be discussed in more detail further on. The leased *o-na-to* is generally taken as *ὀνατόν and is considered to be associated with the verbs *ὀνίναμι, *ὀνίναμαι, "to be profitable" or "to have or receive a benefit." Hence the *o-na-to* is considered to be a benefit, or to provide a profit for the people who lease the land, the *o-na-te-re.*[65]

We come across another landholding term in the heading of En 609. Line 1 records that there are forty *DA*, which can be identified as an abbreviation for the word *da-ma-te* in the same line. This term is only used to refer to the landholdings found within the En series. The most likely transliteration for *da-ma-te* is δάμαρτες, which Ventris and Chadwick translate as "family units" and "households," and they wonder if the term was originally used to refer to an amount of land that was "regarded as sufficient for one household, like the Old English 'hide'?"[66] The amounts of GRA that make up the *da-ma-te* on the tablets certainly varied within the En series, which shows that the term's meaning, if it had once meant "the land sufficient for one household," evolved into something a bit different. Bennett gives the effective meaning of *da-ma-te* as, "the total direct holding of the individual or of his household."[67] He comes to define *da-ma-te* in this way because there are forty names recorded as landholders in the En/Eo series (including both the *te-re-ta* and the *o-na-to* holders), but more than forty individual plots, so *da-ma-te* must refer to the total

[60] *Pe-mo* is the form found on the E tablets that we are dealing with, but it was also written *pe-ma*, for σπέρμα, on Pylian tablets Er 312.2 and Er 880.4, and on various Knossian tablets (*Dic. Mic.* II, p. 98).

[61] Ruth Palmer has concluded based on both archaeological and textual evidence that the ideogram **120*, which is traditionally read as GRA or wheat, should probably be taken as barley, and the ideogram **121*, which is traditionally read as FAR, should instead be read as wheat ("Wheat and Barley in Mycenaean Society," in *Mykenaïka, BCH Suppl.* 25, J.-P. Olivier, ed., 1992, pp. 475-497). I will however use the traditional readings within this paper, as Palmer herself recommends we do until we find more evidence to substantiate her theory (p. 491).

[62] Y. Duhoux ("Les mesures mycéniennes de surface," *Kadmos* 13 [1974] p. 27-38), concluded that of all the possibilities of what GRA could represent (1. the surface area, 2. a tax collected by the palace, 3. an allocation of grain given out by the palace, 4. the annual harvest of grain, 5. the value of the land or 6. the grain held in the palatial granaries for sowing the land), the most reasonable theory is that GRA represents the measure of the area in terms of seed required to sow the land.

[63] Liddell and Scott, *Greek-English Lexicon*," Oxford 1968. *Docs²*, p. 232. G. Dunkel, "Mycenaean *ke-ke-me-na, ki-ti-me-na*," *Minos* 17 (1981) 18-29; see p. 19.

[64] *Dic. Mic.* I, *s.v. ko-to-na.*

[65] M. Lejeune, "Sur le vocabulaire économique mycénien" in *Mycenaean Studies*, E. Bennett, ed., University of Wisconsin Press 1964, pp. 95-96. Duhoux sees the word *o-na-to* as representing the reciprocal nature of Mycenaean economics since he thinks the word indicates that the land was a benefit for both the person who grants the lease of the land and the one who receives it (*Aspects du vocabulaire économique mycénien*, Amsterdam 1976; see pp. 41-46).

[66] *Docs²*, pp. 242, 447, 538. Chadwick mentions that "the classical sense of δάμαρ'wife' [is] a specialisation of this (p. 447). See *Dic. Mic.* I, p. 151 for other possible interpretations of *da-ma-te.*

[67] Bennett 1956b, p. 118-121 for a full discussion of *da-ma-te*; see p. 121 for the quote. Duhoux (1974, pp. 36-37) reviews the literature on the subject of *da-ma-te* and also concludes that originally the word must have referred to the surface area necessary for the subsistence of one family, but that it evolved into a simple measure of surface area. This measure, he thinks, was being supplanted at Pylos by the land measure GRA. It does I think seem preferable to take it as a term used to refer to one individual's total lands, as Bennett proposes.

holdings of each of the persons recorded in the En series.[68]

In the En series all the *o-na-ta* are assumed to be leased from one of the *te-re-ta* who are first mentioned in line 2 of En 609. Each *te-re-ta* is given a separate paragraph, each of which lists first his landholding and then in succeeding lines the *o-na-ta* that are held from him. The standard formula for the introductory line of each paragraph is shown, for example, on En 609.3 where we see the *ko-to-na ki-ti-me-na* of *wa-na-ta-jo-jo*, and on En 609.10, which records the *ko-to-na ki-ti-me-na* of *a-ma-ru-ta-o*. The line that follows the introductory line introduces the landholders who are leasing land from that *te-re-ta*. An example of this formula can be seen on En 609.4, which reads, *o-da-a$_2$, o-na-te[-]re , e-ko-si , wa-na-to-jo-jo , ko-to-na*: and thus, the *o-na-to*-holders have [plots] of the *ko-to-na* of *wa-na-to-jo-jo*. Then the names of the *o-na-te-re* and the size of their plots in GRA follow in individual entries.

Whether the *ko-to-na* figure recorded for the *te-re-ta* included the parcels of land leased by the *o-na-te-re*, or if it represented the amount of land the *te-re-ta* had left after the *o-na-ta* were subtracted from some larger figure, is difficult to determine. Bennett has said, "For the principal subjects [i.e., the *te-re-ta*], the *da-ma-te* may be taken as the *ko-to-na* minus the *o-na-ta* within it."[69] This statement implies that the *ko-to-na* figure includes the *o-na-te-re*'s land. Chadwick, on the other hand, has gone about solving this problem with the help of a tablet that appears to record the total land of the *te-re-ta*, Ed 411.1.[70] The total land recorded for the *te-re-ta* on Ed 411 is GRA 44, while the total of the land held by the thirteen *te-re-ta* as *ko-to-na* on the En tablets is GRA 31 T 4 V 2.[71] This is a fairly large difference, but one that is lessened if we assume that the leases of *o-na-to* land are not included in the *ko-to-na* figures, but that they were included in the total on Ed 411. If we add the amount of land held by the *o-na-te-re*, which amounts to GRA 6 T 3 V 4, to the GRA 31 T 4 V 2 held by the *te-re-ta*, we get GRA 37 T 8. This figure at least brings us closer to the supposed total of GRA 44. Chadwick suggests that the missing GRA 6 T 2 would have been made up by what is often called the "missing fourteenth *te-re-ta*."

It is said that we are missing a *te-re-ta* because the second line of En 609 specifies that fourteen *te-re-ta* were supposed to be recorded in the En series, but only thirteen actually appear. There are several different ideas as to the identity of this *te-re-ta*. Bennett has proposed that the fourteenth *te-re-ta*, and the *o-na-to* that was held from his land, was recorded by mistake in the Ep series on Ep 613.11-12.[72] We know that this landholder, whose name was *pa-ra-ko*, was a *te-re-ta* because he is found twice on Eo 224 (lines 2 and 3), as the *te-re-ta* from whom two *o-na-to* holders were leasing their land. (The name *pa-ra-ko* was actually written in over the erased name *a-ma-ru-ta* on both lines 2 and 3, but in the final version of these lines, found on En 609.12 and 13, *a-ma-ru-ta* was retained as the *te-re-ta* and *pa-ra-ko* was left out.) Bennett suggests that *pa-ra-ko*'s *te-re-ta* landholding was misfiled with the Eb records, perhaps because it contained the word *ka-ma*, which is a particular type of landholding that does not appear at all in the En series but had a paragraph devoted to it in the Ep series.[73]

Carlier has proposed a different theory. He thinks that *su-ko* of Ep 613.4 may be the fourteenth *te-re-ta.*[74] The advantage to this theory is that *su-ko* is specifically recorded here as a *te-re-ta* who is obligated to *te-re-ja-e*, or to fulfill an obligation that is related to his position. Carlier also thought that the amount of GRA that *su-ko* holds (GRA 10[ ]) could make sense of the total amount of land that is recorded for the *te-re-ta* on Ed 411.1. As we saw, the total recorded on Ed 411 for the *te-re-ta* is GRA 44, while the total land recorded in the En series for the thirteen *te-re-ta* is GRA 31 T 4 V 2. *Su-ko*'s landholding of 10, or possibly more than 10 GRA, would bring the total closer to the 44 GRA recorded on Ed 411. It should be noted however that with this theory the *o-na-to* land that is leased from the *te-re-ta* could not have been included in the Ed 411 total; if it had been, the total would be significantly over 44 GRA (GRA 37 T 8 + GRA 10 = GRA 47 T 8). On the other hand, the total land held by Bennett's candidate for the fourteenth *te-re-ta, pa-ra-ko* (including his *o-na-to* holder's land), is only GRA 1 T 1 V 3. Adding his land to the total land of the En series (including both *ko-to-na* and *o-na-ta*), would only give us GRA 38 T 9 V 3, which does not get us to the 44 GRA. It would seem then that neither of these two theories works perfectly.

Lang, on the other hand, has proposed what is perhaps the most sensible solution.[75] The majority of her article actually concerns the Es series, which records the landholdings of thirteen men and their offerings to Poseidon (and three others). Lang showed that the magnitude of each person's offering was related to the size of that person's landholdings. More importantly for us, she also demonstrated that a fourteenth person had gone missing, and that his tax burden had been re-apportioned among the remaining thirteen men. After

[68] Bennett 1956b, p. 118. Bennett points out that in order for the names of the En series to add up to 40, we must ignore *ta-ta-ro* who appears on Eo 224.7 and does not reappear in the En series. He does however count *pa-ra-ko* of Ep 613.11 among the 40; see below on *pa-ra-ko*.

[69] Bennett 1956b, pp. 117-118.

[70] *Docs*[2], p. 453.

[71] The numbers given by Chadwick in *Docs*[2], p. 453 are slightly different from the ones given in this text since the numbers used here are taken from the most recent readings of the tablets given in *PoN IV*.

[72] Bennett 1956b, pp. 117. *Pa-ra-ko* also appears on Ep 301.12 holding a *ke-ke-me-na ko-to-na*. Bennett does not comment on this landholding, but perhaps he considered it to properly belong to the Ep series.

[73] Bennett 1956b, p. 117, see p. 122 for his suggestion concerning the *ka-ma* land. I will discuss *ka-ma* land more fully below.

[74] P. Carlier, "A propos des *te-re-ta*," in *Tractata Mycenaea, Proceedings of the Eighth International Colloquium on Mycenaean Studies*, P. Ilievski and L. Crepajac, eds., Skopje 1987, pp. 65-73; see p. 69.

[75] M. Lang, "Es Proportions," in *Mycenaean Studies: Proceedings of the 3rd International Colloquium for Mycenaean Studies*, E.L. Bennett, ed., University of Wisconsin Press 1964, pp. 37-55; see pp. 49-51.

dealing with the Es series, Lang turned her attention to the thirteen *te-re-ta* of the En series and concluded that in this series too a fourteenth member of the group had gone missing. She was even able to show the taxation groups that they fell into.[76] Therefore, according to Lang's scheme, there would be no need to look for a missing fourteenth *te-re-ta* in any of the land tenure records.

This conclusion puts us in a better position to answer Chadwick's question concerning the relationship of the *ko-to-na* to the *o-na-ta*.[77] Chadwick pointed out that if the missing *te-re-ta* was not recorded elsewhere within the series, then the totaling tablet Ed 411 must have been written before the final version of the En series had been compiled. As was mentioned above, the difference between the extant amount of land and the total on Ed 411, if the *o-na-ta* amounts are added to the *ko-to-na* total, is GRA 6 T 2; if the *o-na-ta* are not added, but assumed to already be counted in the *ko-to-na*, the difference is GRA 12 T 5 V 4. One of these two amounts presumably represents the missing *te-re-ta*'s landholding. The first is comfortably within the usual range of the *te-re-ta*s' landholdings, whereas the latter figure is significantly larger than the average size. Therefore it is more likely that the *o-na-ta* were not calculated in with the *te-re-ta*'s *ko-to-na*.

I would like to mention another bit of information that speaks for the *ko-to-na* figures not including the *o-na-te-re*'s land. There are a couple of cases where if we subtract the *o-na-ta* lands from the figure given for the *te-re-ta*'s *ko-to-na*, we end up with a very small figure. For instance *ru-*83-o* of En 74.1 would have T 6 V 5, and worse still, *a₃-ti-jo-qo* on En 74.11 would only be left with V 4, which, as we will see, is relatively a very small bit of land. Is it likely that a *te-re-ta* would have been left with such a small plot? Of course we cannot know for sure, but it would seem strange for one of the *te-re-ta* to have less land than most of those who were leasing the land.[78] For these reasons, in the calculations that follow in this chapter, I will not consider the land of the *o-na-te-re* to have been included in the figure given for the *te-re-tas*' *ko-to-na*.

In comparison with the En series, the primary landholder of the Ep series, the *damos*, does not ever appear as the subject of a landholding line in the way that the *te-re-ta* do. But it is clear that the *damos* was a primary landholder because so many *o-na-ta* are said to be held *pa-ro da-mo*. As we shall soon see, the Ep series is rather more complicated than the En series in the types of land that it records, but the most basic pattern is seen on Ep 212 above. The leaseholder is specified by his name and title and his *o-na-to* is specified as being held *pa-ro da-mo*, or from the *damos*. For example, on Ep 212.1 we read, *re-ka , te-o-jo , do-e-ra , o-na-to , e-ke , ke-ke-me-na , ko-to-na , pa-ro , da-mo , to-so pe-mo* GRA T 6, which translates as, *re-ka*, a servant of the deity, has a leasehold (*o-na-to*) of *ke-ke-me-na ko-to-na* from the *damos*; so much seed: GRA T 6.

Thus we can see that in both the En and Ep series, the most important information for the scribes to provide was 1. the identification of the holders of each parcel of land, and 2. the size of the landholding. The exact locations of the landholdings and the physical boundaries between them were not recorded. Uchitel points out that in most of the land cadastres put together by governmental officials (and his survey covers seventeen different lists that range from Uruk of the 4th millennium B.C. to a Theban Byzantine record) the detail that received the most attention was the exact location of every field.[79] The lack of such information led Bennett to propose that the most likely purpose of these documents would be "an assessment for the levying of taxes or of services"[80] and although there have been dissenters,[81] this has remained the generally accepted reason for their compilation.[82]

Another unifying feature of these series is that they both appear to have dealt with land in the same location, the district of *Pa-ki-ja-ne*. For the En/Eo series the connection with *Pa-ki-ja-ne* is made explicit on En 609, the tablet which, by virtue of its heading, is considered to be the first of the series. The heading reads as follows:

En 609.1-2:

1.	pa-ki-ja-ni-ja , to-sa , da-ma-te ,	*DA* 40
2.	to-so-de , te-re-ta , e-ne-e-si	VIR 14

The first word on line 1, *pa-ki-ja-ni-ja*, makes it clear that the land we are dealing with in the En series was located in the district of *Pa-ki-ja-ne*.
As for the Ep/Eb series, no heading like the one on En 609 has survived to tell us for sure where the landholdings of these tablets were located, but three factors support our associating them with *Pa-ki-ja-ne*. The first is that at least two of the landholders recorded in

[76] Lang 1964, p. 51.
[77] *Docs²*, p. 453.
[78] Shelmerdine has pointed out to me (personal communication, December 2001) that it may very well have been a desirable thing for the *te-re-ta* to lease out as much of their land as they could, that is if by doing so they escaped the responsibilities of managing the land themselves, but were still able to support themselves with the share of the goods that they would have received from the *o-na-te-re*. This is a very interesting idea, but I wonder if the *te-re-ta* might not have preferred to have a substantial amount of land under their own management in order to better ensure their income.

[79] A. Uchitel, *Near Eastern and Mycenaean Archives Compared*, Ph.D Dissertation, University College, London, p. 143.
[80] Bennett 1956b, p. 120.
[81] Most notably Deroy in "Quelques réflexions sur le cadastre mycénien de Pylos," *Minos* 24 (1989) 125-130. Deroy held the opinion that these texts were not primarily written to serve as the basis of a land tax but rather "for determining the classes of the inhabitants and fixing the divisions of the land so as to regulate the public life and to settle the eventual disagreements on clearly established bases." (p. 125).
[82] Killen 1985 (p. 244) for instance reasons that since "the land-holders of the Er tablets and on Es 650 were expected to make contributions, ... and that the amounts of those contributions were in some way related to the amounts in the GRA (WHEAT) entries that are shown at the ends of the records. ... it would seem a reasonable conclusion therefore that all these records were compiled for the same fiscal purposes as the Er, Es records: that in the case of each of the plots that is recorded a contribution ... was expected by the centre in respect of the holding, and that the size of this contribution was dependent on the size (or 'rateable value') of the plot, as indicated by the GRA entry."

the Ep/Eb series are specifically designated as being personnel associated with the sanctuary of *Pa-ki-ja-ne*: Eb 339.A records the landholding of the priestess of *Pa-ki-ja-ne* (*i-je-re-ja pa-ki-ja-na*), and Eb 1176.A lists a landholding held by a servant of the priestess of *Pa-ki-ja-ne* (*te-te-re-u i-je-re-ja pa-ki-ja-na do-e-ro*).[83] Secondly, several of the persons who hold land on the En series also hold land in the Ep series. For instance, six men designated as *te-re-ta* in the En/Eo series reappear on Ep 301.[84] Also, *pa-ra-ko* of Ep 301.12 appears on Eo 224.2 and 3, and *ta-ta-ro* of Ep 301.6 appears on Eo 224.7. Finally, *a-tu-ko* the royal armorer (*e-te-do-mo wa-na-ka-te-ro*) of En 609.5 holds land on Ep 301.5. This overlap of landholders, as we shall see, also occurs among the religious landholders. In contrast, the Ea series, which records landholdings in the same fashion as the Ep/Eb and En/Eo series, does not contain any of the landholders of those series. Bennett says that, "The Ea and En/Ep texts share only one name, probably no persons, and few of the qualifying words."[85] He therefore takes the Ea series to have been a land tenure record of a different location from the land recorded in the En and Ep series, which he considers to be *Pa-ki-ja-ne*.

The third indication that the land recorded in the Ep/Eb series was in the same area as that recorded in the En/Eo series has to do with the scribes who were responsible for writing these tablets. The preliminary series Eo and Eb were both written by the same scribe (Hand 41), while the final versions En and Ep, respectively, were also written by one scribe (Hand 1). Of course, as was natural for an upper-level scribe, Hand 1 also wrote other series (among them the Es and Eq series), and so cannot be said to have been looking after the land of *Pa-ki-ja-ne* exclusively. But Hand 41 had a much more limited scope. The two preliminary series Eo and Eb were his main body of work. In addition to these, Hand 41 wrote the first line of the totaling tablet Ed 411, which is also related to the land of *Pa-ki-ja-ne* in that it records the total land of all the *te-re-ta*. A sealing he wrote, Wa 784, reads]*o-na-te-re*[on line 1 and]*ko-to-na-o* on line 2, and may very well have labeled one of the baskets that held land tenure tablets.[86] Finally, Hand 41 wrote one tablet outside of the land tenure office, Fr 1207, which is part of the perfumed oil series. But he was clearly not usually involved writing the tablets for this industry which produced another 47 tablets.[87] Rather, Hand 41's main concern seems to have been the recording of land tenure records, and predominantly those of the Eo and Eb series. Given these three factors, the appearance of personnel designated as belonging to *Pa-ki-ja-ne* in the Ep series, the large cross-over of landholders between the two series, and the fact that it was the major concern of one scribe, it seems fairly certain that it was the land of *Pa-ki-ja-ne* that was being recorded in both the En/Eo and the Ep/Eb series.

One final indication that it was the land of *Pa-ki-ja-ne* that was being recorded in the Ep series as well as in the Eb series comes from the order in which the tablets were written. Hand 1, who compiled all the information from the preliminary sets, was fairly organized in putting the series together. The preliminary records of both the Eo and the Eb sets appear to have been sorted and put in a specific order before he began to write the series. We can determine this order by examining the shapes of the tablets, as well as the subjects they deal with. Thus the order of En 609, 74, 659, 467, Ep 301, 613, 705, 212, 539, and 704 has been accepted as the most likely arrangement of the tablets.[88] If we understand that Hand 1 compiled both sets together with this organization in mind, then we could take the heading of En 609, with its reference to *Pa-ki-ja-ne*, to stand for both the En series and the Ep series.

I will now review the reasoning behind this proposed order of the tablet, and in the process I will discuss the different types of landholdings in more detail.

En 609 with its heading is, of course, considered to be the first of the En series. En 74 is very similar to En 609 in that it details the land of three *te-re-ta*, each of whom have several *o-na-te-re*. It is therefore placed after En 609. The first paragraph of En 659 is similar to those on En 609 and En 74, but thereafter it records *te-re-ta* who have only one leaseholder associated with the land. Thus En 659 should be placed after En 74. En 467 records three *te-re-ta* who have no leaseholders at all, and is therefore placed last in the series. Thus the En series

[83] The corresponding Ep tablets (Ep 704.3 for the *i-je-re-ja* and Ep 539.8 for the *do-e-ro*) do not contain the reference to *Pa-ki-ja-ne*. It is possible that a third reference to *Pa-ki-ja-ne* was made in the Eb tablets: Eb 338.A has recently been restored by Melena (*PoN IV*) as *ka-pa-ti-ja, ka-ra-wi-po*[*-ro pa-*]*ki-ja-pi , e-ke-qe , to-so-de pe-mo*. Bennett in *PTT* (p. 105) notes that this restoration is "especially dubious," however, Melena seems to have greater faith in it.

[84] Those six are *a$_3$-ti-jo-qo* (Ep 301.2/En 74.11), *wa-na-ta-jo* (Ep 301.3/En 609.3), *a-da-ma-o* (Ep 301.4/En 659.8), *pi-ke-re-u* (Ep 301.8/En 74.20), *ra-ku-ro* (Ep 301.9/En 659.15), and *a-i-qe-u* (Ep 301.14/En 659.12).

[85] Bennett 1956b, p. 129.

[86] T.G. Palaima, *Scribes of Pylos* (*Incunabula Graeca* 87), Rome 1988, p. 102 says it is actually more likely due to its findspot that Wa 784 labelled a basket of Ea tablets.

[87] See C.W. Shelmerdine, *The Perfume Industry of Mycenaean Pylos*, *SIMA Pocketbook 34*, Åstroms, Göteborg 1985, for a detailed account of the Fr tablets.

[88] Bennett 1983, p. 41 says that "I shall call the tablets which record that [land tenure] document the Tertiary series, assuming that it was written, and was intended to be read, in the order: 609 74 659 467 301 613 705 212 539 704." Ventris and Chadwick (*Docs^2*, pp. 240-264) had sorted the Ep and En tablets into "sets" when they were first dealing with them. Their first set consisted of all the En tablets, and the Ep series was broken down into sets 2-4. The second set consisted solely of Ep 301, with its records of *ke-ke-me-na* plots that are mostly held by men familiar from the En series. The third set was also made up by one tablet, Ep 704, with its highly placed religious landholders and complicated land-holding formulae. Set four was made up of Ep 212, 539, 705 and 613, which took in all the rest of the landholders including the *te-o-jo do-e-ro/a* and the *ka-ma* holders. This grouping into sets seems simply to be an attempt on the authors' part to organize the tablets in some coherent way, but it was not an attempt to find the order in which the scribe organized and wrote them. Hence I have not made use of this system within this thesis.

starts out with the more complicated landholding situations and progresses to the simplest.

The Ep series is more complicated. The progression that is generally accepted is Ep 301, Ep 613, Ep 705, Ep 212, Ep 539, and finally Ep 704. It has been proposed that the organizing principle of the Ep series was to move from the secular landholders (Ep 301), to the secular and religious holders of *ka-ma* land (Ep 613), and then to the purely religious landholdings arranged in hierarchical order.[89] Bennett has confirmed this order through his extremely detailed examination of the physical characteristics of the tablets.[90] Ep 301 is considered to start off the series with its secular landholders, many of whom, as we have seen, are *ko-to-na*-holding *te-re-ta* or other leaseholders in the En series.

Ep 301:
1. ke-ke me-na , ko-to-na , a-no-no , to-so-de , pe-mo [GRA 1 T 1
2a. ko-to-no- -o-ko
2. a_3-ti-jo-qo , o-na-to , e-ke , pa-ro , da-mo , ke-ke-me-na , ko-to-na , to-so , [pe-mo] G̣ṚẠ 1 Ṭ 4 V 3
3. wa-na-ta-jo , o-na-to , e-ke , pa-ro , da-mo , ke-ke-me-na , ko-to-na , to-so-de ⌊⌋ pe-mo GRA T 5
4. a-da-ma-o , o-na-to , e-ke , pa-ro , da-mo , ke-ke-me-na, ko-to-na , to-so ⌊⌋ p̣ẹ-ṃọ GRA T 4
5. a-tu-ko , e-te-do-mo , o-na-to , e-ke , pa-ro , da-mo , ke-ke-me-na , ko[-to-na to-so pe-mo GRA *qs*
6. ta-ta-ro , o-na-to , e-ke , pa-ro , da-mo , ke-ke-me-na , ko-to-na , to-so pe-ṃọ[GRA V 3
7. *angustum*
8. p̣ị-ke-re-u , e-ke-qe , ke-ke-me-na , ko-to-na , ko-to-no-o-ko , to-so , pe-mo[GRA
9. ra-ku-ro , e-ke-qe , ke-ke-me-na , ko-to-na , ko-to-no-o-ko , to-so , pe-mo GRA[*qs*
10. ku-so , e-ke-qe , ke-ke-me-na , ko-to-na , ko-to-no-o-ko , to-so pe-mo GRA V [3
11. ke-ra-u-jo , e-ke-qe , ke-ke-me-na , ko-to-na , ko-to-no-o-ko , to-so pe-mo GRA T 4
12. pa-ra-ko , e-ke-qe , ke-ke-me-na , ko-to-na , ko-to-no-o-ko , to-so pe-mo GRA T 7
13. ko-tu[-ro_2] , e-ke-qe , ke-ke-me-na , ko-to-na , ko-to-no-o-ko , to-so , pe-mo GRA T 1
14. a-i-qe-u , e-ke-qe , ke-ke-me-na , ko-to-na , ko-to-no-o-ko , to-so , pe-mo GRA T 6

The first plot of land of Ep 301 is recorded as being *a-no-no*, *ἄνονος or *ἄνωνος.[91] The meaning of *a-no-no* must be contrasted to that of *o-na-to* in some way. Such land could have been without the same benefit that an *o-na-to* carried, perhaps, as Duhoux suggested, because it was not rented.[92] Ventris and Chadwick also took *a-no-no* to mean that it was not rented out, but to them this meant that "the holder does not have any *o-na-te-re*, but enjoys the full use of the land himself,"[93] which actually amounts to the exact opposite of what Duhoux proposed. It is difficult then to decide how exactly to define *a-no-no* land, but we can say that it probably was contrasted to the regular *o-na-to* holdings that follow, and was therefore placed first on the tablet. Lines 2-6 of Ep 301 are listed as having the more normal *o-na-to pa-ro da-mo*, but in lines 8-14 (line 7 is narrow and without an entry) *o-na-to pa-ro da-mo* is dropped and *ko-to-no-o-ko* is added. This could mean that those *ko-to-no-o-ko* held *ke-ke-me-na* land on their own, without having any relationship to the *damos*, which in turn could affect our definition of *ke-ke-me-na* land. I will take up this issue further on.

The next tablet in the series, Ep 613, like Ep 301, records the landholdings of several secular landholders, but it also records the land of many personnel who were associated with the religious sphere.

Ep 613:
1. ne-qe-wo e-da-e-wo ka-ma]o-pe-ro[du-]wo-u-pi , te-re-ja-e ,
2. e-me-de te-re-ja to-so-]de , [pe-mo] GRA 10 T 1
3.]*vestigia*[ke-ke-]me-na , ko-to-na , ka-ma-e-u , wo-ze-qe , to-so pe-mo [GRA] Ṭ 3̣
4. te-re-]ta , su-ko , po-ṛọ-du[-ma o-pe-ro-qe]du-wo-u-pi , te-re-ja-e ⌊⌋ o-u-qe , wo-ze[ ] *v*.
5. to-]ṣọ-de , p̣ẹ-mo GRA 10[ ] *vacat*
6. ạ$_3$-ḳẹ-re-u , ạ-si-to-po-qo , ka-ma , e-ke-qe , wo-ze-qe , to-so pe-mo GRA 1 T [2
7. a-•-ke-re-u , i-je-ro-wo-ko , ka-ma-e-u , o-na-to e-ke , wo-ze-qe to-so pe-mo GRA 1
8. sa-sa-]ẉọ , o-na-to , e-ke , ka-ma-e-u , e-pi-qe , to-me , te-ra-p̣ị[-ke]to-so , pe-mo GRA 1 T 5
9. e-u-]ru-wo-ta , te-o-jo , [do-e-]ro , e-ke-qe[ka-]ma , o-na-to , ẉọ-ze-qe ,ṭọ-ṣọ , pe[-mo] GRA 1 T 3
10. pe-]ṛẹ-qo-ta , pa-de-we-u[e-]ke-qe , ka-ma , o-na-to , si-ri-jo , ra-ke , to-so, pe-mo GRA 1
11. pa-]ṛạ-ko , e-ḳẹ-qe , ka-ma , ko-to-no-o-ko , e-o to-so , pe-mo GRA 1
12. po-]so-re[-ja te-]o-jo , do-e-ra , e-ke , o-na-to , pa-ro pa-ra-ko , to-so , pe-mo GRA T 1 V 3
13. ḳọ[-tu-ro_2 mi-]ka-ta , pa-de-we-u , ka-ma-e-u , e-ke-qe , wo-ze-qe , to-so , pe-mo GRA T 5
14. we-ra-jo[po-]ti-ni-ja-we-jo , o-na-to , e-ke , ke-ke-me-na , ko-to-na , to-so , pe-mo GRA T 2
15.a pe-mo
15. ko-pi-na , te-o-jo , do-e-ra , o-na-to , e-ke , ke-ke-me-na , ko-to-na , pa-ro da-mo to-so GRA T 2
16. mi-ra ⌊⌋ te-o-jo do-e-ra , o-na-to , e-ke , ke-ke-me-na , ko-to-na , pa-ro , da-mo , to-so pe-mo GRA T 1
17. qe-ri-ṭạ , te-o-jo , do-e-ra , o-na-to , e-ke , ke-ke-me-na , ko-to-na , pa-ro da-mo , pe-mo GRA T 2
18.]*vestigia*[te-o-]jo , do-e-ra , o-na-to , e-ke , ke-ke-me-na , ko-to-na , pa-ro, da-mo , to-so , pe-mo GRA V 3

[89] L.R. Palmer, *The Interpretation of Mycenaean Greek Texts*, Oxford University Press 1963, see p. 199.

[90] Bennett 1983, pp. 44-47. While Bennett says "...the order of these texts from the point of view of the characterization of the subjects and from the variation in formulae are fairly convincing" (p. 46) he also says, after detailing some possible alternative arrangements, like putting En 467 at the end of the two sets, or Ep 301 in the beginning, before even En 609(!), that he is "periodically skeptical" (p. 47) about the standard ordering of the tablets.

[91] *Dic. Mic.* I, pp. 68-69.

[92] Duhoux 1976, p. 45.

[93] *Docs*[2], p. 448.

19. te-o-jo], do-e-ṛọ , o[-]na-to , e-ke , ke-ke-me-na , ko-to-na , pa-ro, da-mo , to-so , pe-mo GRA V 4
20.]ra-so , te-o-jo , [do-e-ro o-]na-to , e-ke , ke-ke-me-na , ko-to-na , pa-ro da-mo , to-ṣọ[pe-mo GRA *qs*

For example on line 8 (Eb 842) we have a record of the landholding of *sa-sa-*]*wo*, who has no religious affiliation that we can detect, while line 7 records the land of a *i-je-ro-wo-ko*, or ἱερο-ϝοργός, which came into classical Greek as ἱερουγός, ἱεροεργός. This ἱερο-ϝοργός is interpreted as an officiating priest, perhaps in charge of sacrifices.[94] Thus the first paragraph of Ep 613, which runs from line 1 to 13, is made up of both religious and secular landholders. The unifying factor of this first paragraph is that it records land that is called *ka-ma*, which may be a special form of *ke-ke-me-na* land, but whose nature has been much debated. I will discuss this land type and how it should be defined further on.

The second paragraph of Ep 613 (lines 14-20) begins a long list of religious personnel that continues on the next several tablets. The first entry on line 14 records the landholding of *we-ra-jo* who is designated as [*po-*]*ti-ni-ja-we-jo*, or Potnian. Thus he is affiliated with the goddess Potnia and probably the sanctuary of *Pa-ki-ja-ne*. The rest of the paragraph provides us with the first of several lists of the *te-o-jo do-e-ro* and *do-e-ra* of the Ep series.[95] These records are very regular and for the most part follow the pattern shown on Ep 212 above. Ep 705 (which I will not reproduce here) follows Ep 613 with ten such records detailing the *o-na-ta* of the *te-o-jo do-e-ro/a*, and Ep 212 comes next with another ten. Ep 539 starts off with six more records of the *te-o-jo do-e-ro/a* and therefore should follow Ep 212.

Ep 539:
1. pi-ro-na , te-o-jo , do-e-ra , o-na-to , e-ke , ke[-ke-me-na ko-to-na
2. e-ri-qi-ja , te-o-jo , do-e-ra , o-na-to , e-ke , ke-ke-me[-na ko-to-na
3. i-na , te-o-jo , do-e-ro , o-na-to e-ke , ke-ke-me-na ko-to[-na pa-ro da-mo
4. po-so-re-ja te-o-jo , do-e-ra , o[-na-]to , e-ke , ke-ke[-me-na ko-to-na
5. po-so-re-ja , te[-o-jo]do-e-ra , o-na-to , e-ke , pa-ro[ ] , ka-ma-e-we , wo-ze-te , to-so , pe-mo[GRA *qs*
6. te-qa-ja , te-ọ-jo , ḍọ-e-ra , o-na-to , e-ke , ke-ke-me-na ko-to-na , p̣ạ-ṛọ⌞ ⌟da-mo to-so pe-mo GRA T 2
7. me-re-u , i-je-re-ja , do-e-ro , o-na-to , e-ke , pa-ro , [ ]re-ma-ta , ka-ma-e-ẉẹ⌞ ⌟o-u-qe , wo-ze , to-so pe-mo GRA[ ] V 2
8. te-te-re-u , i-je-re-ja , do-e-ro , o-ṇạ-to , e-ke , ke-ḳẹ[-]me-na , ko-to-na , pa-ro , da-mo , to-so⌞ ⌟pe-mo GRA V 3
9. pu-ṛụ-da-ka , ka-pa-ti-ja , do-e-ro , o-na-to , e-ke⌞ ⌟ḳẹ-ke-me-na , ko-to-na , pa-ro , da-mo , to-so pe-mo GRA T ̣3 V ̣3
10. e-ni-to-wo⌞ ⌟a-pi-me-de-o , do-e-ro , o-na-to , e-ke , ke-ke-me-na , ko-to-na , pa-ro , da-mo to-so pe-mo GRA T 1
11. to-wa-te[-u] a-pi-ṃẹ-ḍẹ-o⌞ ⌟do-e-ro , o-na-to , e-ke , ke-ke-me-na⌞ ⌟ko-to-na , pa-ro , da-mo to-so pe-mo GRA T 8
12. wi-dwo-i-jo , a-pi-me-de-o , do-ẹ[-ro] , o-na-to , e-ke , ke-ke-me-na , ko-to-na , pa-ṛọ⌞ ⌟da-mo , to-so pe-mo GRA T ̣2
13. we-te-re-u , i-je-re-u , o-na-to , e-ke , ke-ke-me-na , ko-to-na , pa-ro , da-mo[ ] *vacat*[ ]to-so , pe-mo GRA 2 T 3
14. a-pi[-me-]de , e-ke , e-to-ni-jo , ke-ke-me[-na-o ko-]to-na[-o] to-so , pe-mo GRA 4 T 6

On lines 7 and 8 of Ep 539 we move from the regular *te-o-jo do-e-ro/a* records to those of the servants of the priestess of *Pa-ki-ja-ne*. Line 9 records the *do-e-ro* of Karpathia, whom we know as the Keybearer of *Pa-ki-ja-na* from Ep 704.7/Eb 338A (Eb 338A : *ka-pa-ti-ja ka-ra-wi-po*[*-ro pa-*]*ki-ja-pi*). The next three records give the land of the *do-e-ro* of *a-pi-me-de-o*, whose own landholding is recorded on the last line of Ep 539. In between the *do-e-ro* and *a-pi-me-de*, we get the landholding of the priest *we-te-re-u*. Thus we seem to be going from the simple *te-o-jo do-e-ro/a,* to the *do-e-ro/a* who were attached to specific persons, and then to the persons themselves. These records reflect a kind of hierarchy which moves from the generic servants of the deity, to a higher class of servant who were associated with the more highly placed religious functionaries, to the functionaries themselves. This hierarchical arrangement continues on Ep 704 where we find two landholdings belonging to the priestess of *Pa-ki-ja-ne* (Ep 704.3 and 5-6) and Karpathia the Keybearer (Ep 704.7-8), both of whom had *do-e-ro/a* on Ep 539.

Ep 704:
1. o-pe-to-re-u , qe-ja-me-no , e-ke , ke-ke-me-na , ko-to-na , to-so , pe-mo[ ] G̣ṚẠ 2 T 5
2. u-wa-mi-ja , te-o-jo , do-e-ra , o-na-to , e-ke-qe , i-je-re-ja , ḳẹ-ra , to-so pe-mo GRA T 1 V 3
3. e-ri-ta , i-je-re-ja , o-na-to , e-ke , ke-ke-me-na , ko-to-na , pa-ro , da-mo , to-so , pe-mo GRA T 4
4. ki-ri-te-wi-ja , o-na-to , e-ko-si , ke-ke-me-na , ko-to-na⌞ ⌟pa-ro , da-mo , ṭọ-so , pe-mo GRA 1 T 9
5. e-ri-ta , i-je-re-ja , e-ke , e-u-ke-to-qe , e-to-ni-jo , e-ke-e , te-o , da-mo-de-mi , pa-si , ko-to-na-o ,
6. ke-ke-me-na-o , o-na-to , e-ke-e , to-so pe-mo GRA 3 T ̣9
7. ka-pa-ti-ja , ka-ra-wi-po-ro , e-ke , ke-ke-me-no , o-pe-ro-sa , du-wo-u-pi , wo-ze-e , o-u-wo-ze , [[ ]]
8. to-ṣọ[pe-mo GRA]4

Also on Ep 704 are: line 1: *o-pe-to-re-u qe-ja-me-no* (whose exact definition is uncertain and will be taken up later), line 2: *u-wa-mi-ja te-o-jo do-e-ra* (who may have been included here because she has a special kind of

[94] *s.v. Dic Mic.* I, p. 276.

[95] See M. Lejeune, "Textes mycéniens relatifs aux esclaves," in *Mémoires de Philologie Mycénienne* II (*Incunabula Graeca* 42), Rome 1971a, pp. 65-81, for a discussion of both the sacred and profane *do-e-ro/a* and a consideration of how the *te-o-jo do-e-ro/a* might compare to the rest.

landholding that seems to have been given to her by the priestess of *Pa-ki-ja-na* (*i-je-re-ja ke-ra*, ἱερείας γέρας[96]), and on line 4: a group called the *ki-ri-te-wi-ja* which seems to be best defined (albeit vaguely) as a group of women with cultic connections.[97]

Thus the Ep series does seem to move from secular landholders (Ep 301), through a mixture of secular and religious landholders grouped together because they hold a certain kind of land (the *ka-ma* on Ep 613.1-13), to a hierarchical organization of the religious landholders (Ep 705, 212, 539, and 704). This arrangement seems reasonable, but, there are a couple of landholders on Ep 539 and Ep 704, for instance *a-pi-me-de* of Ep 539.14 and *o-pe-to-re-u qe-ja-me-no* of Ep 704.1, whose religious associations are not readily apparent. I will classify such landholders, for now, as being of "uncertain" status. These landholders must be examined in more detail, but that task will be taken up in further on in the section on religious landholdings.

Despite the many similarities between the two sets, the differences are important and should be discussed. The Ep series records holdings of *ke-ke-me-na* land, while the En series records *ki-ti-me-na* land. As we have seen, the primary landholders, meaning those who do not lease the land but seem to hold it in their own right, are also different in each of the two sets. *Ke-ke-me-na* land is leased (usually) *pa-ro da-mo*, while the *ki-ti-me-na* land is leased from one of the *te-re-ta*. To put it another way, the En series never deals with *ke-ke-me-na* land or with the *damos*, while the Ep series never deals with *ki-ti-me-na* land. This dichotomy has given rise to various interpretations of these series, which in turn have given rise to different views of Pylian land tenure and the structure of Mycenaean society as a whole. Thus these tablets have become the subject of much debate. Now that we have reviewed the basic elements of the Ep and En series, we can turn to their interpretation.

The Societal Structure behind the Land Tenure Tablets

Ki-ti-me-na and Ke-ke-me-na

The dichotomy between the Ep/Eb, series with its *ke-ke-me-na* land being held *pa-ro da-mo*, and the En/Eo series with the *te-re-ta* as the main landholders of *ki-ti-me-na* land, is generally seen as the key to understanding these tablets. Although the interpretations of this dichotomy are varied, nonetheless, nearly every scholar who has dealt with this issue has subscribed to one of two basic approaches. The first approach assumes that the etymological meanings of the words *ki-ti-me-na* and *ke-ke-me-na* will give us the most reasonable indication as to the types of land that were signified by these words. Scholars who follow this approach generally find meanings for these words that have to do with their agricultural status or use. The dichotomy between the *damos* and the *te-re-ta* does not play a great role in these theories. In contrast, the second approach starts from the premise that the opposition between *ki-ti-me-na* land/*te-re-ta* and *ke-ke-me-na* land/*damos*, is of prime importance. Scholars who use this approach generally arrive at "juridical" meanings for the words *ki-ti-me-na* and *ke-ke-me-na*. In this review I will first evaluate the theories that look to the etymological meanings of the words *ki-ti-me-na* and *ke-ke-me-na*.

The basic etymologies of *ki-ti-me-na* and *ke-ke-me-na* will serve as the starting point for this discussion. *Ki-ti-me-na* is the present medio-passive participle of the verb *κτεῖμι, which is also found on the tablets in the third person plural, *ki-ti-je-si*, on Na 520.[98] The derivation of *ki-ti-me-na* land is fairly clear: as was mentioned when we were first discussing *ko-to-na*, it derives from the Indo-European root **ktei* meaning to "inhabit, settle, occupy." By the time of historical Greek, the root **ktei* was also used in words that had the meaning of "to cultivate," and it is often assumed that this meaning would already have been attached to the Mycenaean term,[99] but this may not have been the case.

The basic etymology of *ke-ke-me-na* is not as clear as that of *ki-ti-me-na*. It too is a participle (although a perfect medio-passive one instead of a present) but there are various roots from which *ke-ke-me-na* could have derived. Aura Jorro lists six possible derivations, but there are two main proposals that he considers to be morphologically the most likely.[100] The first is that it should be taken as *κ(h)εχεμένα from Indo-European **ghe*, which gives us the historical Greek χήρα, meaning "widow" and χῆτος, meaning "lack" or "want." Thus the *ke-ke-me-na* land could be thought of as "left as fallow land, not cultivated"[101] (which would better suit the situation of the land tenure records than taking it, as some scholars have, to mean "not inhabited, deserted, abandoned"[102]). The second main possibility is to interpret *ke-ke-me-na* as *κεκεσμένα from the root **kes*, which gives Classical Greek κεάζω, and would mean something like "divided" or "distributed" in the

[96] C. Ruijgh discusses this landholding in "*da-ma/du-ma* δάμαρ/δύμαρ et l'abbréviation *DA*, notamment en PY En 609.1," in *Tractata Mycenaea, Proceedings of the Eighth International Colloquium on Mycenaean Studies*, P. Ilievski and L. Crepajac, eds., Skopje 1987, pp. 299-322; p. 314, n. 67.

[97] *Dic. Mic.* I, p. 363. Also see M. Lindgren, *People of Pylos*, Uppsala 1973, pp. 81-82.

[98] *Dic. Mic.* I, pp. 366-367.

[99] Dunkel (1981, p. 19), for instance, bases his definition of *ki-ti-me-na* on this assumption. A related word found in Homeric contexts is ἐυκτίμενος and is seen in *Il.* 21.77. Carpenter ("*Ki-ti-me-na* and *ke-ke-me-na* at Pylos," *Minos* 18 [1983] 81-88; see p. 85), however, objects that even where ἐυκτίμενος is applied to gardens, it is more likely to mean "'well planted' (i.e. 'established')."

[100] *Dic. Mic.* I, pp. 338-339.

[101] C.J. Ruijgh, *Études sur la grammaire et le vocabulaire du grec mycénien*, Amsterdam 1967, p. 365. Duhoux 1976, p. 23-24 supports this interpretation but also gives us the problems with such a theory, as we will see below.

[102] L. Deroy and M. Gérard, *Le cadastre mycénien de Pylos* (*Incunabula Graeca* 10), Rome 1965, pp. 19-20. Deroy and Gérard actually proposed that the land was abandoned and deserted during a first stage that occurred before the land tenure records were written, but that in a second stage, which is reflected in the tablets, the *damos* took over the *ke-ke-me-na* land so that it became "public or communal land."

Mycenaean context. Lejeune, using this etymology, saw the lands of the *damos* as having been subject to a very varied distribution and therefore defined the *ke-ke-me-na* land as "terres de morcellement," or "lands of distribution."[103] (Lejeune also proposes that the *damos* had other tracts of land that was not subject to being parceled out, but that we are ignorant of the name of that type of land and its importance because it never shows up in the palatial records.[104]) Aura Jorro prefers this to κεκειμένα from **kei* meaning to "cut" or "divide,"[105] but Carpenter points out that "*-s-* is not usually ignored before *-m-* (cf. *do-so-mo*, etc.), and we should expect *ke-ke-se-me-na*."[106]

Duhoux has been one of the main advocates of the position that *ki-ti-me-na* and *ke-ke-me-na* should not be interpreted as juridical terms but rather as agricultural terms.[107] In order to show that we should not base our definitions of *ki-ti-me-na* and *ke-ke-me-na* on their relationships with the *te-re-ta* and the *damos*, Duhoux points out that not all the *ke-ke-me-na* land is associated specifically with the *damos*. In fact, seven of the Ea tablets record officials as the holders of *ke-ke-me-na* land and on three others it is held by individuals.[108] Duhoux also thinks that it is unlikely that the basic meaning of *ki-ti-me-na* of "settled" or "inhabited" should have evolved into "private." He proposes instead (as Carratelli originally did[109]) that we take *ki-ti-me-na* land as being "cultivated" and *ke-ke-me-na* as its opposite in agricultural terms: "left fallow."[110] Dunkel, through a similar line of reasoning, proposes the same meanings for *ki-ti-me-na* and *ke-ke-me-na*: "cultivated" vs. "fallow."[111]

Dunkel however goes into more detail than Duhoux in his consideration of the problem cases in the Ep series. By "problem cases" we mean those in which *ke-ke-me-na* land occurs without the words *pa-ro da-mo*, or those in which land of the Ep series was leased by an individual. These cases, by breaking the tie between *ke-ke-me-na* land and the *damos*, undermine the dichotomy between the *damos* and the *te-re-ta*. If that dichotomy can be discredited, then there would seem to be more support for those who try to define *ki-ti-me-na* and *ke-ke-me-na* according to their etymological meanings. In fact, there are several such problem cases, and it is worth going through each of them individually in order to see how well founded Dunkel's claims concerning their significance are.

First Dunkel considers the cases where the land is specified as *ke-ke-me-na ko-to-na*, but where there is no mention of the owner, and therefore stands a chance at not being owned by the *damos*. First he concedes that *pa-ro da-mo* could be supplied for Ep 539.3 and 704.5-6 since in the first case the parallel tablet supplies it, and in the second because it is clear that the *damos* has claimed to be the primary holder of the land.[112] It is good that Dunkel mentions these two examples, but one thing that he does not fully acknowledge is that the example of Ep 539.3 demonstrates that the scribe does not always necessarily include the words *pa-ro da-mo* when they are surely meant to be understood. There are two other examples of this, on Eb 1187 and 477, where *pa-ro da-mo* is left out, but we can be sure that it was meant to be understood because the final versions of the entries, Ep 539.10 and 13, do contain *pa-ro da-mo*.[113] Thus, it cannot be argued that simply because *pa-ro da-mo* is missing, the land was not associated with the *damos*.

Nevertheless, Dunkel says the situation is unclear for Ep 539.1, 2 and 4, where no owner is named. The space which could have held the owner's name is damaged, and because lines 5 and 7 of Ep 539 concern land held from individuals (which we will turn to in a moment), Dunkel says that the possibility exists that lines 1, 2, and 4 could also record land that was held *pa-ro* a personal name. I think this is unlikely. The corresponding tablet for line 2, Eb 1440, which is a complete record, does not include *pa-ro da-mo*, but neither does it record a personal name from whom the land was leased. It seems unlikely that if the land was leased from a personal name that the scribe would forget to note that down, since such information would be specific to this case. It would seem more likely that if the scribe were to omit an owner it would be one that could be assumed by the reader, such as the more common *damos*. For lines 1 and 4 we have no similar recourse since the parallel Eb tablets are lost, but I think

[103] M. Lejeune, "Le *damos* dans la société mycénienne," *in Mémoires de Philologie Mycénienne III* (*Incunabula Graeca* 43), Rome 1972, pp. 137-154; see pp. 142-145.

[104] Lejeune 1972, p. 145. Carlier (1987, pp. 65-73) suggests something very similar.

[105] Aura Jorro (*Dic. Mic.* I, *s.v. ke-ke-me-na*) gives Adrados, "Mas sobre el Culto Real en Pilos y la Distribucion de la Tierra en Epoca Micenica," *Emerita* 29 (1961) 53-116, p. 99 credit for this suggestion. Another suggestion that Aura Jorro does not favor is to relate *ke-ke-me-na* to κοινός (also through the root **kei*) to give a meaning of "public", "communal" as Palmer 1963, p. 187 does (on p. 426 Palmer defines *ke-ke-me-na* as "share-land").

[106] Carpenter 1983, p. 83.

[107] Duhoux 1976, pp. 9-65.

[108] Those tablets on which land is held by officials are: Ea 809, *ra-wa-ke-si-jo-jo a-mo-te-wo*; Ea 801, *ku-ru-no-jo me-ri-te-wo*; Ea 305, 757, 802, *qo-qo-ta-o*; Ea 59.3, 480: a *su-qo-ta-o*. The three that list an individual are: Ea 59.2, *ke-re-u*; 806, *ke-re-te-u*; and 922, *a-pi-a₂-ro*. Duhoux also brings up a few other tablets where *ke-ke-me-na* or a related word appears without *pa-ro da-mo*: An 830.6, Na 395. *lat. sup.*, and KN Uf 835 and 983.

[109] G. Pugliese Carratelli, "La decifrazione dei testi micenei," *Parola del Passato* 35 (1954) 81-117; see p. 102.

[110] For Duhoux's discussion of *ki-ti-me-na* see Duhoux 1976, pp. 12-22, and for *ke-ke-me-na* see pp. 22-27.

[111] Dunkel 1981, p. 18-29. I should also point out that Carpenter 1983, pp. 81-88, also proposed that these words should be defined according to their root meanings rather than as juridical terms. His proposal though, that *ki-ti-me-na* land, defined as "settled" or "inhabited," should be taken to indicate land that was immediately surrounding the settlement, and that *ke-ke-me-na* land, derived from *κίχημι, "to find, happen upon," should be taken as land that was farther away and probably of poorer quality, does not seem to have had great influence in the literature on the topic and so I will not discuss it in detail here.

[112] This entry concerns a dispute over the status of a plot of land between the *damos* and the priestess of *Pa-ki-ja-ne*. It will receive more detailed attention further on.

[113] This was pointed out by D. M. Jones, "Land Tenure at Pakijane: Some Doubts and Questions," in *Proceedings of the Cambridge Colloquium on Mycenaean Studies*, L. Palmer and J. Chadwick, eds., Cambridge 1966, pp. 245-249; p. 246.

it is more likely, given the majority of cases on the tablet, that these too would have been held *pa-ro da-mo*.

Dunkel also brings up Ep 613.14 as a record that does not specify an owner. Line 14 of Ep 613 though signals a break with the previous 13 lines of the text, which dealt with *ka-ma* land, by starting off a new paragraph (that runs to line 20) of entries that are exclusively concerned with religious holders of *ke-ke-me-na* land (not *ka-ma*). Bennett discusses the fact that the tablet shape of Ep 613 was too narrow for the long string of characters that needed to be fit onto each one of these lines, and mentions that on lines 15-20, where *pa-ro da-mo* was included, there was "regular crowding."[114] The crowding was such that "After this tablet, a different format is adopted and retained, i.e. the writing along the longer axis of the tablet, the better to fit in longer texts, beginning with 705 and 212...."[115] Thus it seems possible that on line 14 the scribe left out the *pa-ro da-mo* in order to avoid crowding the text, even though afterwards he felt it had to be included. Indeed, Bennett, after including line 14 with those that come after it as a group,[116] comments that "*pa-ro da-mo* seems to be implied in some texts which do not have it...", and then he mentions 613.14 as one of those texts.[117] Thus here too it would not be unreasonable to suppose that *pa-ro da-mo* was actually an assumed part of the record.

The same could be said for Ep 704.1 and 7, which Dunkel also brings up as records that lack the words *pa-ro da-mo*. Lack of space could particularly have been an issue for line 7 where even *ko-to-na* was left out. Bennett mentions that the omission of *ko-to-na* "might have made it seem possible to put the whole copied text on the single line."[118] Such a goal could have motivated the scribe to leave out *pa-ro da-mo* as well. Ep 704.1 may also lack these words for the same reason. The scribe knew such an omission would not cause any confusion since *pa-ro da-mo* would be readily understood from the context.

Dunkel finds additional challenges to the connection between *o-na-to ke-ke-me-na ko-to-na* and the *damos* on Ep 539.5 and 7 and Ep 613.12, where the land is stated as being *pa-ro* a personal name.[119] The word *ke-ke-me-na* is not actually included in these records either. However, Dunkel states that the entries on Ep 539.5 and 7, at least, should be considered to be *ke-ke-me-na* land since the rest of the tablet deals with *ke-ke-me-na* land.[120] Here Dunkel uses an argument that he eschews when considering the reasons for the absence of *pa-ro da-mo*. The interesting thing though about these cases is that they all appear to have been associated with *ka-ma* land. In Ep 539.5 and 7 the individual who owns the land is called a *ka-ma-e-u*, and the *pa-ra-ko* who is leasing out the land to *po-*]*so-re*[*-ja* on Ep 613.12, is recorded on Ep 613.11 as holding a *ka-ma*. Dunkel also considers many of the other records dealing with *ka-ma* land on Ep 613 (lines 1-2, 6, 11, and 13) as constituting problem cases since they too lack *pa-ro da-mo*. But Dunkel had not, it seems, fully investigated the meaning of *ka-ma* and its relationship to the *damos*. He does not really discuss *ka-ma* land *per se*, and he assumes that it is a type of land separate from *ke-ke-me-na* land.[121] It is worth looking more carefully at *ka-ma* land in order to see if this assumption is correct.

Ka-ma landholdings do seem to be different from most of the rest of the *ke-ke-me-na* lands. First, they are generally larger than most regular *o-na-ta*, which are usually in the range of T 1-3. In contrast, of the nine entries for *ka-ma* land on Ep 613 whose amounts we can be fairly sure of, eight are GRA 1 or more.[122] This has led some scholars to think that the *ka-ma* holders, or *ka-ma-e-we*, were privileged in some way. Another distinguishing factor of *ka-ma* land though is that it seems to carry with it special obligations which may relate to the working of the land. The *ka-ma-e-we* are said to have to *wo-ze* ("work" from the root **werg-*) or *te-re-ja-e* ("to fulfill or accomplish a purpose," from τέλος), and the scribes note when this obligation is not fulfilled.[123] Ep 613.4 provides us with an example of this: the *te-re-*]*ta su-ko* is said to be obligated (*o-pe-ro-qe*) to *te-re-ja-e*, but he does not: *o-u-qe wo-ze*.[124] The derivation of the word *ka-ma* is appropriate for land that had to be worked: the word *ka-ma* seems to be related to the verb κάμνω meaning to "labor" or "toil."[125] *Ka-ma* seems to have been carried into historical times on Crete as καμάν, which Hesychius glosses as the Cretan word for ἀγρόν. The Linear B derivative *ka-ma-e-u* (instead of **ka-me-u*) shows, however, that the Linear B *ka-ma* would have been neuter: *κάμας.[126]

Foster mentions that it was not only *ka-ma* holders who had the obligations attached to their lands spelled out: one holder of *ke-ke-me-na* land, *ka-pa-ti-ja ka-ra-wi-po-ro* on Ep 704.7-8, is also seen to carry such specified obligations.[127] But this is the only example of someone

[114] Bennett 1983, p. 46.
[115] Bennett 1983, p. 46.
[116] Bennett 1983, p. 49.
[117] Bennett 1983, p. 50.
[118] Bennett 1983, p. 50.
[119] Ep 539.5 actually has no name preserved, while on Ep 539.7 we have]*re-ma-ta*, and the land on Ep 613.12 is held *pa-ro pa-ra-ko*.
[120] Dunkel 1981, p. 23, n. 20.

[121] Dunkel 1981, p. 23, n. 23.
[122] The nine are on Ep 613 lines 1-2, 4-5, 6, 7, 8, 9, 10, 11, and 13. The record on lines 4-5 is not stated to be *ka-ma* land but it does have the same type of obligations associated with the landholding and is found in a paragraph that is otherwise devoted to records of *ka-ma* land. Only *ko-tu-ro*$_2$ the *mi-ka-ta* has less than GRA 1 with T 5.
[123] The *ka-ma* land on Ep 539.5 and 7 also carries the obligations of *wo-ze*.
[124] This line also shows that the meaning of the two words *wo-ze* and *te-ra-ja-e* must be similar since they can be used side-by-side in the same context.
[125] Duhoux 1976, p. 29-30. Also see *Dic. Mic.* I, pp. 309-311 for more bibliography on *ka-ma*.
[126] J. Chadwick, "The Muster of the Pylian Fleet," in *Tractata Mycenaea, Proceedings of the Eighth International Colloquium on Mycenaean Studies*, P. Ilievski and L. Crepajac, eds., Skopje 1987, pp. 75-84; see p. 81.
[127] E. Foster, "The Flax Impost at Pylos and Mycenaean Landholding," *Minos* 17 (1981) 67-121; see p. 80. Ep 704.7-8 reads: *ka-pa-ti-ja , ka-ra-wi-po-ro , eke , ke-ke-me-no , o-pe-ro-sa du-wo-pi , wo-ze-e , o-u-wo-ze*.

who was not a *ka-ma* holder having such requirements.[128] Thus, the correspondence between *ka-ma* holders and these specially delineated obligations is strong and has invited many attempts at explanation.

Lejeune thought that the obligation was to develop the land.[129] Duhoux, on the other hand, thought that it was not clear exactly what the obligations were, but that they probably had something to do with increasing the yield of the soil.[130] In his view, the plots of land were larger not because they were some kind of privilege, but rather because they were not of as good a quality as the regular *ko-to-na*. Bennett, in line with his thinking that the land tenure documents were made up as the basis for a tax assessment, thought that the obligation had to do with the amount of tax a *ka-ma* holder was expected to pay.[131]

Chadwick proposed that the obligation to *wo-ze* refers to the landholders' obligation to serve in the military during wartime and to provide other services in times of peace.[132] More importantly for our investigation, Chadwick also points out that on Ed 236 *ka-ma-e-we* is used as a general term for holders of *o-na-ta* of *ke-ke-me-na* land, and therefore suggests that, "*ka-ma* is the collective term for the land of which individual estates are described as *ke-ke-me-na ko-to-na*."[133]

Ed 236:
1. ka-ma-e-we , o-na-ta , e-ko-te , ke-ke-me-na-o , ko-to-na-o
2. wo-zo-te , to-so , pe-mo GRA 30 T 2 V 3

Deger-Jalkotzy notes this evidence (along with Eb 862.2 where *ka-ma-e-u* was written over an erased *pa-ro da-mo*) and says that this "may give cause to believe that *ka-ma* and *ke-ke-me-na ko-to-na* were the same."[134] But she also thinks that the different words must have been used to indicate some kind of differentiation between the two types of land and goes on to propose a logical solution to what *ka-ma* land must have been. She thinks that the obligation to *wo-ze* indicated that the *ka-ma* holder was obligated to do or contribute something that went beyond the normal obligations that were owed to the *damos* by all the regular *ke-ke-me-na* holders. Such obligations would only be applied to those whose plots of land were larger than what they needed for their normal obligations and their subsistence.[135] Thus, with the evidence of Ed 236 and Deger-Jalkotzy's understanding of the nature of *ka-ma* land, we can see that *ka-ma* land is actually a type of *ke-ke-me-na* land, and that it was part of the *damos* system. Therefore, the *ka-ma* records, such as those found on Ep 613 and on Ep 539.5 and 7, do not constitute sound evidence against the link between the *damos* and *ke-ke-me-na* land.

In support of his theory Dunkel also cites several cases where *ke-ke-me-na ko-to-na* occurs not only without *pa-ro da-mo*, but also without *o-na-to*. He considers such entries to be records of land owned by individuals just as the *te-re-ta* of the En series own their land. If this were true, then it would appear that *ke-ke-me-na* land could be held by someone other than the *damos*. Dunkel holds up Ep 301.8-14 as the best examples of private ownership, so I will take a close look at these records and the tablet on which they appear in order to determine whether his proposition is well founded. I will reproduce the tablet here again to make this discussion easier to follow.

Ep 301:
1. ke-ke-me-na , ko-to-na , a-no-no , to-so-de , pe-mo [GRA 1 T 1
2a. ko-to-no- -o-ko
2. a$_3$-ti-jo-qo , o-na-to , e-ke , pa-ro , da-mo , ke-ke-me-na , ko-to-na , to-so , [pe-mo] G̣ṚẠ 1 Ṭ 4 V 3
3. wa-na-ta-jo , o-na-to , e-ke , pa-ro , da-mo , ke-ke-me-na , ko-to-na , to-so-de ⌞ ⌟pe-mo GRA T 5
4. a-da-ma-o , o-na-to , e-ke , pa-ro , da-mo , ke-ke-me-na , ko-to-na , to-so⌞ ⌟pẹ-ṃọ GRA T 4
5. a-tu-ko , e-te-do-mo , o-na-to , e-ke , pa-ro , da-mo , ke-ke-me-na , ko[-to-na to-so pe-mo GRA *qs*
6. ta-ta-ro , o-na-to , e-ke , pa-ro , da-mo , ke-ke-me-na , ko-to-na , to-so pe- ṃọ[GRA V 3
7. *angustum*
8. p̣ị-ke-re-u , e-ke-qe , ke-ke-me-na , ko-to-na , ko-to-no-o-ko , to-so , pe-mo[GRA
9. ra-ku-ro , e-ke-qe , ke-ke-me-na , ko-to-na , ko-to-no-o-ko , to-so , pe-mo GRA[*qs*
10. ku-so , e-ke-qe , ke-ke-me-na , ko-to-na , ko-to-no-o-ko , to-so pe-mo GRA V [3
11. ke-ra-u-jo , e-ke-qe , ke-ke-me-na , ko-to-na , ko-to-no-o-ko , to-so pe-mo GRA T 4
12. pa-ra-ko , e-ke-qe , ke-ke-me-na , ko-to-na , ko-to-no-o-ko , to-so pe-mo GRA T 7
13. ko-tu[-ro$_2$] , e-ke-qe , ke-ke-me-na , ko-to-na , ko-to-no-o-ko , to-so , pe-mo GRA T 1
14. a-i-qe-u , e-ke-qe , ke-ke-me-na , ko-to-na , ko-to-no-o-ko , to-so , pe-mo GRA T 6

As was mentioned above, Ep 301 is separated into two paragraphs. The first is concerned (from line 2 to 6[136]) with *o-na-ta* of *ke-ke-me-na* land held *pa-ro da-mo*. The second paragraph (lines 8-14) deals with a list of

[128] The other two examples of landholders who are said to *wo-ze* who are not on Ep 613 are also associated with *ka-ma* holders: Ep 539.5 and 7.

[129] M. Lejeune, "Le Dossier *sa-ra-pe-da* du Scribe 24 de Pylos," *Minos* 14 (1975) 60-76; p. 65.

[130] Duhoux 1976, p. 40; see pp. 30-40 for his full discussion of *ka-ma*.

[131] Bennett 1956, p. 128.

[132] Chadwick 1987, pp. 75-84;

[133] Chadwick 1987, p. 82. Chadwick (p. 83) therefore explains the appearance of *ka-ma* on An 724.11 as indicating that "this land too [like all regular *o-na-to* holdings] was under obligation to provide fighting men in case of need."

[134] S. Deger-Jalkotzy, "Zum Charakter und zur Herausbildung der mykenischen Sozialstruktur," in *Res Mycenaeae*, A. Heubeck and G. Neumann, eds., Gottingen 1983, pp. 89-111; see pp. 97-98, see n. 50. This translation, and all others used herein of Deger-Jalkotzy's article are taken from Cynthia Shelmerdine's translation of the article which she has graciously given to me.

[135] Deger-Jalkotzy 1983, p. 100.

[136] Line 1 of Ep 301 is concerned with *a-no-no* land, which was discussed above as being somehow different from the rest of the *o-na-ta*.

landholders, described each time as *ko-to-no-o-ko*, who hold (*e-ke-qe*) *ke-ke-me-na ko-to-na*. In none of these records does *pa-ro da-mo* appear. Thus, at first glance, it appears that the two types of records are very distinct from each other. However, there are a couple of indications that this may not have been the case. First, the word *ko-to-no-o-ko* was actually written in above line 2, meaning that at least one of these *ko-to-no-o-ko* held his land *pa-ro da-mo*. Indeed Ventris and Chadwick believed that the *ko-to-no-o-ko* of line 2a "should be inserted at the end of each entry in the first section."[137] Also, on the Eb tablets that served as the basis for Ep 301.2-6, the formula included both *ko-to-no-o-ko* and *pa-ro da-mo*. Therefore, the two were not mutually exclusive. It seems the scribe left the word *ko-to-no-o-ko* out of lines 2-6 simply because of the difficulty he was having in fitting all his information onto these lines. Bennett comments, after discussing the problems the scribe was having with space, that *ko-to-no-o-ko* should probably be understood in the lines 3-6.[138] This leads one to wonder if we should likewise understand *o-na-to pa-ro da-mo* in the second paragraph where it is missing, but where *ko-to-no-o-ko* is kept in. The problem here is that *pa-ro da-mo* is also missing from the Eb tablets which were used in the compilation of Ep 301.8-14 even though on those tablets there probably would have been enough room to include it (see for example Eb 895, which corresponds to Ep 301.14). Nonetheless, I think it is possible that the scribe knew that *ke-ke-me-na ko-to-na* and/or *ko-to-no-o-ko* would imply *pa-ro da-mo* to anyone reading the tablet. The most compelling reason for thinking this is because on Eb 297, the word *ko-to-no-o-ko* appears in the place that the *damos* occupies on the final version that entry, Ep 704.5-6.[139]

Eb 297:
1. i-je-re-ja , e-ke-qe , e-u-ke-to-qe , e-to-ni-jo , e-ke-e , te-o
2. ko-to-no-o-ko-de , ko-to-na-o , ke-ke-me-na-o , o-na-ta , e-ke-e
3. GRA 3 T 9 V 3

Ep 704.5-6:
5. e-ri-ta , i-je-re-ja , e-ke , e-u-ke-to-qe , e-to-ni-jo , e-ke-e , te-o ? da-mo-de-mi , pa-si , ko-to-na-o ,
6. ke-ke-me-na-o , o-na-to , e-ke-e , to-so pe-mo GRA 3 T 9̣

This interchangeability of the two words indicates that the landholders designated as *ko-to-no-o-ko* are somehow a part of the *damos*. Perhaps they were its most prominent men, and therefore did hold *damos* land, but in a more privileged way. For example, they might have been able to retain a higher percentage of the produce than the rest of those who made up the *damos*. The fact that many of them are *te-re-ta*, as was shown above, would lead one to suppose that they did have an elevated status within the district of *Pa-ki-ja-ne*. Lejeune supposes that the *ko-to-no-o-ko* were listed at the beginning of the Ep series because of their importance within the *damos*, and that they could have constituted a sort of "conseil d'administration."[140] Deger-Jalkotzy proposes nearly the same thing, that they were "a group of /*damos*/ members ... which disposed of *ke-ke-me-na* estates."[141] The *ko-to-no-o-ko* then may have been the members of a kind of managerial board that directed the affairs of the *damos*. Perhaps this is what led to the confusion over whether *o-na-to pa-ro da-mo* should be included in the formula on Ep 301.8-14. Technically the land was *pa-ro da-mo* in that the collective body of the *damos* administered the land, but since the *ko-to-no-o-ko* were in charge of administering the *damos* land, and were therefore in a sense identified with it, it seemed strange or unnecessary to include the *pa-ro da-mo* in the description of their land. Thus, the *ko-to-no-o-ko* records of Ep 301, like the *ka-ma* records of Ep 613, cannot be disassociated from the *damos*.

It does seem then that the instances within the Ep series where a missing *pa-ro da-mo* can be assumed to indicate that the land was leased from some entity other than the *damos* are fewer than Dunkel has proposed. In several cases the *pa-ro da-mo* may have been left out due to lack of space on the entry's line, as on Ep 613.14 and Ep 704.1 and 7. In the case of the *ka-ma* and *ko-to-no-o-ko* land, it appears that these types of land were most likely associated with the *damos*, and therefore cannot be considered separate from it. Also, in the cases where the land is specifically said to be leased from an individual, as it is on Ep 539.5, 7 and Ep 613.12, it was shown that the *damos* is still likely to be associated with these landholdings since they are all *ka-ma* land, even though the authority of the *damos* may be more removed from the land's management than in most cases. As Lejeune and Foster point out, just because land is held by an individual does not necessarily mean that it has to be entirely disassociated from the *damos*.[142] Therefore, as is also noted by Lejeune and Foster, the relationship between the *damos* and *ke-ke-me-na* land is still a significant one, and that, along with the fact that the *damos* never holds *ki-ti-me-na* land, deserves serious consideration in our attempt to define *ke-ke-me-na* and *ki-ti-me-na* land.

In fact, there are actually several problems with seeing *ki-ti-me-na* and *ke-ke-me-na* as the agricultural terms "cultivated" and "fallow." Duhoux himself brings up one of them.[143] He finds it strange that so many people would only have the use of land that was left fallow, and says that it leads one to expect that each landowner should have one plot of each type of land. As we saw, there are several people who do own both types of land, but

[137] *Docs*², p. 250.
[138] Bennett 1983, p. 45.
[139] This was pointed out by Jones 1966, p. 246. Deger-Jalkotzy (1983) also points this out on pp. 90-91. The religious content of Ep 704 will be addressed further on.

[140] Lejeune 1972, p. 144.
[141] Deger-Jalkotzy 1983, pp. 90-91.
[142] Lejeune 1975, pp. 64-65. Foster 1981, p. 78, n. 42. This may also be true for the Ea tablets mentioned above on which *ke-ke-me-na* occurs without any mention of the *damos*.
[143] Duhoux 1976, p. 24.

certainly not all, and really not even close to the majority of landholders have a plot of each type. Dunkel also notes this problem and points out that the majority of the land surveyed was *ke-ke-me-na* land, which makes it even stranger that the *ke-ke-me-na* type of land should be the one to be left fallow. But Dunkel tries to answer this objection by pointing out that fallow land is actually quite useful as pasture land and he says that it might be of some significance that in the Ea series *ke-ke-me-na* land is often found to be held by oxherds and swineherds (*qo-qo-ta-o* and *su-qo-ta-o)* who would have been in a position to make the best use of the land.[144] Foster, however, states that if it makes sense that the *ke-ke-me-na* land on the Ea tablets was allocated to animal herders because it was useful to them as fallow land, then the distribution of *ke-ke-me-na* and *ki-ti-me-na* land in the Ea series is difficult to explain since *ki-ti-me-na* land is also held by oxherds (Ea 781) and two shepherds (Ea 71 and Ea 817).[145] It is true that this does not negate the fact that fallow land is useful, nonetheless, it does show that the fact that animal herders are associated with *ke-ke-me-na* land cannot be used as an argument that it was fallow.

Foster provides us with further reasons why we should reject the "cultivated" vs. "fallow" scenario. Her consideration of the word *ki-ti-me-na* takes into account the information of the Na flax documents. How she defines the words on those tablets that contain the root *kti-* sheds light on the way that we should define *ki-ti-me-na* in the En series. First she considers the word *a-ki-ti-to*, which appears on Na 406 and 926.[146] Since an alpha-privative appears before the root *kti-*, *a-ki-ti-to* would most likely have a meaning that is the opposite of *ki-ti-me-na.* Thus if *ki-ti-me-na* means "cultivated," then *a-ki-ti-to* would mean "uncultivated." However, this cannot have been the case since Na 406 and 926, like the other Na documents in the series, records a "forecast" of the amount of flax that was to be contributed to the central administration.[147] If a contribution of flax was expected of the land, then it could not have been "uncultivated."[148]

Second, Foster considers Na 520 which records *pu$_2$-te-re*, or planters, who are said to *ki-ti-je-si*, the third person plural present indicative derived from **ktei.*[149] The tablet reads as follows:

Na 520:
A. to-i̥-qe , e-re-u-te-ra
B.] pu$_2$-te-re , ki-ti-je-si *SA* 30

Foster (on the recommendation of Chadwick) reads the second line first, and translates: "The planters *ktiensi* and for them free of impost: *SA* 30."[150] She then says that, "*ktiensi* appears to refer to something the planters do, for which they are granted an exemption." She rejects the possibility that *ktiensi* means something along the lines of "are laying out the land," or "clearing, planting"[151] on the grounds that planters of trees and vines (as the *pu$_2$-te-re* are understood because of their relation to such in Classical Greek contexts and on Er 880)[152] would probably not, due to the specialized nature of their work, be involved in such activities. She rejects another proposed definition of "they settle, bring into cultivation"[153] since, as we have seen, *a-ki-ti-to* cannot mean the opposite of this, "unsettled" or "uncultivated." Instead of these meanings she proposes that we should actually take the root *kti-* with its meaning of "inhabited,"[154] and define *ktiensi* as "'they inhabit' in a specialized juridical sense of inhabiting on certain terms."[155] Foster proposes that the use of *ktiensi* on Na 520 may express "the close connection between the fact that the planters 'inhabit' on special terms, and the fact that they are given an exemption."[156] One might argue that *ki-ti-me-na* land was not always given an exemption since the En series was presumably drawn up as the basis from which taxes were to be determined. Therefore, the exemption given to those who *ki-ti-je-si* on Na 520 may have been particular to the contributions of flax. Within the En series the special terms under which the land was held may have been particular to the *te-re-ta*, whom Foster calls "individuals of local prominence at least," and whom she proposes may have been expected to render service in return for their land which they derived from the palace.[157] (This definition of the *te-re-ta* is akin to Palmer's original proposal that the *te-re-ta* were "Men of the burden (of service),"[158] which I will return to in a moment.)

We have at this point, I think, come to the point where we may agree that Ventris and Chadwick's first urge not to use etymological meanings to define *ki-ti-me-na* and *ke-ke-me-na* land was correct. As they said, "To make deductions about the precise conditions of Mycenaean land tenure from the apparent etymology of the terms used is of course rather precarious, in view of the historical adaptations which the system and its

[144] Dunkel 1981, p. 21; also see n. 12 where he credits Pugliese Carratelli (1954, p. 103) for first making this suggestion.

[145] Foster 1981, p. 78, n. 42.

[146] Foster 1981, p. 83-87.

[147] C.W. Shelmerdine, "Mycenaean Taxation," in *Studia Mycenaea 1988, Ziva Antika Monographs* 7, T.G. Palaima, C.W. Shelmerdine, and P. Ilievski, eds., Skopje 1989, pp. 125-148; see p. 139.

[148] Chadwick (*Docs*^{2}, p. 470) had actually already pointed this out.

[149] Foster 1981, p. 83.

[150] Foster 1981, p. 84.

[151] Palmer 1963, pp. 309 and 428.

[152] Foster 1981, p. 84.

[153] *Docs*^{2}, p. 554 gives this translation. Duhoux 1976, p. 18 applies the definition of "to cultivate" to the words with **ktei*.

[154] Foster 1981, pp. 82-83 points out that definitions related to "inhabited," such as "good to live in" would also fit many of the Homeric uses of ἐυκτίμενος and that that type of meaning is certainly preserved in words like περικτίμενος (*Il.* 17.220) which means "neighbors, those living around."

[155] Foster 1981, p. 85.

[156] Foster 1981, p. 86.

[157] Foster 1981, pp. 79-82, 91. Foster also discusses the fact that the *ki-ti-ta* and *me-ta-ki-ti-ta* of An 610 and An 724 probably should be defined as people who "inhabit (on specific terms, or, in return for service)" because they seem to be under obligation to row (An 724.3-4: ... *ki-ti-ta o-pe-ro-ta e-re-e...*) and because their obligation seems to be related to their land tenure status (the land tenure terms *ka-ma* and *e-to-ni-jo* also appear on An 724). Chadwick (1987) also proposes that the obligation to serve in the military was based on land tenure.

[158] Palmer 1963, pp. 190-196.

terminology may have undergone since the Greeks' original settlement of the country."[159] We may therefore now turn to an exploration of the possible juridical meanings of these terms.

Furumark, who wrote on the subject soon after the texts were first translated, did not search for etymological meanings for the terms *ki-ti-me-na* and *ke-ke-me-na*. Rather, he proposed that since the *ki-ti-me-na* land was always "owned" by the *te-re-ta*, the term *ko-to-na ki-ti-me-na* must indicate that the land was held by private individuals, and that *ko-to-na ke-ke-me-na*, which was in contrast (almost) always owned by the *damos*, was land held by the local government.[160] Ventris and Chadwick followed Furumark in privileging the dichotomy between the holders of the two types of land over their possible etymological meanings. They defined the two words simply as 'private' and 'communal', and called these their "effective rather than their etymological meanings."[161] Of course, this was only the beginning of the discussion concerning the juridical meanings since the definitions of both the *te-re-ta* and the *damos* have been much debated. How one interprets each of these terms will affect one's view of the lands that are associated with them.

The *Te-re-ta*

The root meaning of the word *te-re-ta* has suggested that the *te-re-ta* themselves did not actually hold the land in their own right, but that it had been bestowed upon them by some other power. It is generally accepted that the word *te-re-ta*, or τελεστάς, is related to the word τέλος, which would imply that the *te-re-ta* have some sort of purpose to fulfill or job to perform. The verb *te-re-ja* and its infinitive *te-re-ja-e* also appear in the Ep/Eb series, and may refer specifically to that purpose or job. It is possible though that it may have had a more general meaning since it is used in a parallel construction with *wo-ze* on Ep 613.4 (*su-ko* is obligated to *te-re-ja-e* but he does not *wo-ze*, or 'work').[162] Also, *te-re-ja* and *te-re-ja-e* appear on Ep 613.1-2 with *ne-qe-wo e-da-e-wo*, who is not designated as a *te-re-ta*. On the other hand, one has to wonder if the use of *te-re-ja* in itself indicated that the person was a *te-re-ta*. In either case, the fact that the *te-re-ta* bear this title has suggested to many that land of the En series was given to the *te-re-ta* in return for whatever service they were expected to perform. Palmer in particular took up this line of reasoning and proposed that the *te-re-ta* were actually associated with the palace, and that their land was granted to them by the *wanax* in return for their service to him. His interpretation rests not only on the derivation of the word *te-re-ta*, but also on a comparison with Hittite society. Palmer defines the *te-re-ta* as "Men of the τέλος" meaning that they carry a "burden of service."[163] Palmer saw this "burden of service" as being owed to the *wanax* because of a similarity between the *te-re-ta* and the Hittite LÚ *ILKI*, a term which is itself translated as "Man of the Service." It is clear from the Hittite texts that the LÚ *ILKI* received his land from the king. Palmer therefore thought that the Mycenaean "Man of the Service" should also receive his land from the king. The *te-re-ta* then, according to Palmer, was a sort of feudal baron who owed his service or support to the *wanax*, and who was supported in return by land grants. We can recognize those land grants in the *ki-ti-me-na* land. Thus, in Palmer's view, *ki-ti-me-na* land should not really be considered "private" in the sense that we understand the word, i.e., that individuals held it chiefly in their own right and for their own benefit. Rather, the land was held as a privilege from the palace, and the holders of such land were under obligation to provide some sort of service (such as military service) or contributions to the palace. This view has been supported by the fact that three craftsmen who are described as *wa-na-ka-te-ro*, and therefore seem to have been in the service of the *wanax*, also hold *ki-ti-me-na* land.[164] Thus it seemed plausible that *ki-ti-me-na* land was actually at the disposal of the *wanax* to bestow as he pleased. For this reason *ki-ti-me-na* land is very often seen as belonging to the palatial sphere.

Chadwick, on the other hand, proposed that the τελεστάς should be seen as a religious functionary since in historical Greek contexts "the terms τελεστής, τελετής or τελεστήρ are connected with mysteries and are either initiating priests or sometimes the initiated themselves."[165] If the *te-re-ta* are interpreted as priests on the Linear B tablets, they would hold their land in return for the religious duties they performed, the religious duties constituting the service they were expected to fulfill. Adrados also thought that the *te-re-ta* should be considered to have been religious functionaries.[166] He not only refers to the Classical religious associations for the τελεστάς, but he also brings up a reference made by Clement of Alexandria to a group of priests called the ἀνακτοτελέσται, who were involved in the mysteries of the Corybantes (probably at Thessalonika).[167] Adrados also brings in (as does Palmer) the fact that Pausanias (X.38.7) mentions that the

[159] *Docs*², p. 234.

[160] A. Furumark, "Ägäische Texte in griechischer Sprache," *Eranos* 52 (1954) 18-60, see p. 36. Furumark actually said that the *ke-ke-me-na* land could be owned by the state or the local government; it must not have been clear at that point whether the *damos* should be equated with the overall palatial government or with just the local government.

[161] *Docs*², p. 233.

[162] The full text of Ep 613.4 reads: *te-re-]ta , su-ko , po-ro-du-[ma o-pe-ro-qe]du-wo-pi , te-re-ja-e o-u-qe , wo-ze , to-so pe-mo* [GRA]T 3.

[163] Palmer 1963, pp. 190-196.

[164] Those three craftsmen are *a-tu-ko e-te-do-mo* (the armorer?) on En 609.5/ Eo 211.2, *pe-ki-ta ka-na-pe-u* (the fuller) on En74.3/Eo 276.2 and En 74.23/Eo 163.2, and *pi-ri-ta-wo ke-ra-me-u* (the potter) on En 467.5/Eo 371.

[165] J. Chadwick, "Potnia" *Minos* 5 (1957) 117-129 (see pp. 127-129 for his discussion of the *te-re-ta*).

[166] F. Adrados, "*Te-re-ta wa-na-ka-te-ro* y los ἀνακτοτελέσται," *Minos* 10 (1970) 138-150; see p. 138. Also see p. 148 where he does acknowledge that most of the *te-re-ta* were not associated with the *wanax*. Adrados also proposes that the *damos* gave the land to the priests in order to help the palace in supporting them.

[167] Clement of Alexandria, *Protr.* II.16. Clement of Alexandria is not clear on where these ἀνακτοτελέσται were located, but Adrados (1970, p. 143) follows Hemberg (*Die Kabiren*, Uppsala 1950, p. 253) in placing them at Thessalonika.

people of Amphissa celebrated a τελεστή, or a religious festival, for the two child kings (ἀνάκτων καλουμένων παίδων). And finally, Hesychius defines the ἀνακτοτελέσται as οἱ τὰς τελετὰς ἐπιτελοῦντες τῶν ἱερῶν, or those who organize the sacred ceremonies.[168] After citing all this Adrados proposes that the ἀνακτοτελέσται developed out of the Mycenaean *te-re-ta* who were designated as *wa-na-ka-te-ro*.[169] Those *te-re-ta* must have been, he believes, the priests in the service of the deity called *wanax*. But it should be mentioned that only one *te-re-ta* is actually described as *wa-na-ka-te-ro* in the Linear B corpus, *pi-ri-ta-wo* on Eo 371 (on En 467.5 the designation *wa-na-ka-te-ro* is dropped).

Eo 371:
A. ke-ra-me-wo , wa-na-ka-te-ro
B. pi-ṛị-ta-wo ? ko-to-na ⌊ ⌋ki-ti-me-na GRA [1 T 1

Also, as Carlier points out,[170] this association with the *wanax* is more likely due to the fact that this man was also a craftsman, specifically a potter (*ke-ra-me-wo*), since all the other persons described as *wa-na-ka-te-ro* in the En/Eo series are craftsmen.[171] Thus it does not seem likely that the ἀνακτοτελέσται of historical Greece developed directly from the *te-re-ta* of Mycenaean society. The religious connections for the τελέσται themselves seen in these examples are intriguing though, and Adrados adds several other citations to these that demonstrate the religious role of the τελεστήρ or τελεστής.[172]

Lejeune also saw the *te-re-ta* as possibly religious figures. He followed in the tradition of Furumark in that he considered *ki-ti-me-na* to be an abstract word concerning a landholding institution. He then proposed that this institution had to do with the distribution of lands among the members of the college of *te-re-ta*, and that the party which endowed the lands might have been a sanctuary.[173] Lejeune defined *ki-ti-me-na* land specifically as "terres de fondation," or "lands of the endowment."

Palmer, however (who actually has a reputation for seeing religion in many places where others would not), argues strenuously against the idea that the *te-re-ta* were religious in the Mycenaean period. He points out that despite the later religious associations for the word, nothing in the Linear B texts serves to associate the *te-re-ta* with the religious sector.[174] Palmer adds that in the earliest Classical use of the word, which was a sixth century B.C. inscription from Olympia, τελεστάς is put in opposition to the ϝέται:[175] αἴτε ϝέτας αἴτε τελεστά. This quote sets up a contrast between the τελεστάς, meaning some kind of official or magistrate, with ϝέτας, or private person, who held no such position. Thus he proposes that *te-re-ta* could have meant something like "magistrate" in its Linear B usage as well. Palmer also emphasizes that the majority of the citations that Chadwick and Adrados bring in to demonstrate the religious associations of the word come from later sources and should not be favored over the earlier citation.[176]

Chadwick and Palmer have also argued over what the tablet KN Am 826, which lists 45 *te-re-ta* alongside five carpenters (*te-ko-to-ne*), might indicate concerning the status of the *te-re-ta*. Chadwick argued that having 45 "barons" (as Palmer had originally defined the *te-re-ta*) at one place would be somewhat strange.[177] But Palmer countered by saying that having 45 "initiation priests" in one place would also be strange.[178] If, however, Palmer went on to argue, we consider the *te-re-ta* to be "Men of Service," then having so many of them at one place would be "less absurd than if we insert the modern word 'baron'."[179] Palmer goes on to point out that since the religious language is "a repository of archaisms" an ancient word can later be used in a religious context even though before it had not had such overtones. Such was the case for the development of the word *temenos*, which in Mycenaean Greek is used in secular contexts (to refer to the landholdings of the *wanax* and the *lawagetas* on Er 312), but which in Classical Greek is used for sacred precincts. The same kind of development could have occurred with τελεστάς. Palmer says that, "its original neutral significance "Man of the Service" could have passed to "Man of the Divine Service." Deger-Jalkotzy proposed something of a compromise between these two views. She thinks that the *te-re-ta* must have been in the service of the *wanax*, but that does not necessarily exclude the *te-re-ta* from having religious associations as well. In fact, there are two *te-re-ta* who do have religious associations (*qe/pe-re-qo-ta*[180] of En 659.1 and Ep 613.10 and *su-ko* of Ep 613.4). As she says, "in the Mycenaean period political and religious aspects certainly overlapped on all levels of public life, and like so many other functionaries the */telestai/* too could make religious contributions and fill religious offices."[181] Deger-Jalkotzy did not, however, consider the *te-re-ta* to be primarily religious. Rather she agrees with Palmer's comparison of the *te-re-ta* to the Hittite "Man of the Service," and brings in further examples from the Near East to bolster this case. For instance, in Ugarit there was a class of person called *bnsˇ mlk* or "people of the

[168] Hesychius, *s.v.* ἀνακτοτελέσται. Adrados 1970, p. 143.
[169] Adrados 1970, p. 138
[170] Carlier 1987, p. 66.
[171] On En 74.3/Eo 276.2 and En 74.23/Eo 160.3 we find *pe-ki-ta* the *ka-na-pe-u*, and on En 609.5/Eo 211.2 we have *a-tu-ko* the *e-te-do-mo* (who also has a landholding on Ep 301.5).
[172] Adrados 1970, p. 147. He also mentions the fact that the building in which the Eleusinian mysteries were held was called the Telesterion.
[173] Lejeune 1972, p. 148.
[174] Palmer does not consider being listed on the land tenure records of *Pa-ki-ja-ne* as a religious context.
[175] *SIG* 9 (W.D. Henberger, 3rd edition, Georg Olms Verlag 1982, pp. 8-9).
[176] Palmer 1963, p. 193.
[177] Chadwick 1957, p. 129.
[178] Palmer 1963, pp. 194-195.
[179] Palmer 1963, pp. 193-196.
[180] For the equation of *qe-re/pe-re* see *Dic. Mic.* II, *s.v. pe-re-qo-ta*. The two are used interchangeably on, for instance, En 659.
[181] Deger-Jalkotzy 1983, pp. 103-104.

king," who were obligated to provide their military and/or professional services in return for shares in the royal property sector.[182] The fact that the *te-re-ta* were also so obligated is shown by their being expected to *te-re-ja-e*, which Deger-Jalkotzy interprets as "to carry out that which belongs to the */telos/."

In the end, most scholars have decided that within the context of Mycenaean society as demonstrated by the Linear B tablets, the *te-re-ta* were not primarily associated with the religious realm.[183] This means of course that their *ki-ti-me-na* land cannot be considered to be religious either. We might then say that the *te-re-ta* did owe their service to the *wanax*. There is, though, a third possibility that has not yet been raised: that the *te-re-ta* actually owed their service to the *damos*. The *damos* is after all the third member, along with the palace and the religious sphere, of what seems to be the tripartite structure of power in Mycenaean society.[184] In order to understand how the *te-re-ta* may be related to the *damos*, we must first discuss the nature of the *damos* itself.

The *Damos*

After her detailed discussion of *ki-ti-me-na* land Foster does not actually go on to discuss in any great detail how we should understand *ke-ke-me-na* land. She follows Furumark though and says that *ke-ke-me-na* land should be "taken to mean approximately "communal'."[185] But there is still the question of how exactly the *damos* was related to its landholders, and what relationship it had with the palace. We have seen that the *damos* appears to have had a board of directors, so to speak, in the *ko-to-no-o-ko*, so it seems that the *damos* did manage the *ke-ke-me-na* land in a communal fashion. This type of land management system is also seen in several Near Eastern examples brought up by Deger-Jalkotzy in her treatment of the land tenure series.[186]

For instance, the Nuzi texts tell us that in the Hurrian state of Arrapha (15th-14th centuries B.C.), in addition to royal property there was also private real estate, and that the private real estate was owned by "extended family communes," not by private individuals.[187] Furthermore, the state expected certain obligations to be fulfilled with respect to these plots of land, but it did not deal with each individual owner in collecting these obligations, but rather with the extended family commune.[188] In the Middle Assyrian Empire, whether the villages owned their own land is debated. I.M. Diakonoff thinks that the village community was the proprietor of the land,[189] while J.N. Postgate believes that even private land was granted by the king to individual families.[190] P. Garelli endorses a kind of compromise view that both private and royal property existed, but the king could confiscate the village land for the use of his own family or his favored officials.[191] Despite this disagreement, Deger-Jalkotzy points out that the important factor for our purposes is that the villages of the Middle Assyrian Empire were the basic unit of the taxation system, and that the village elders were the ones to decide how much of the tax burden each member of the community should bear.[192] These decisions were based on the type and amount of land the members held. Thus the Middle Assyrian village communities acted as units in their dealings with the royal administration. The situation in Ugarit in the 14th and 13th centuries B.C. seems to be similar to that found in Arrapha. There the village communities were proprietors of their own non-royal estates and definitely had elements of self-government, such as village assemblies, councils of elders and various local officials.[193] The land though was not worked collectively, but was apportioned out to small individual families who then worked the land for themselves.

Deger-Jalkotzy takes the general pattern seen in these examples of the village community owning and administering land, and applies it to Mycenaean society. She proposes that the *damos* was collectively responsible for apportioning out the *ke-ke-me-na* parcels of land, and that they would have acted collectively in gathering together and handing over the agricultural produce that the palatial administration expected from the *damos* as tax. The theory that the *damos* itself acted as a corporate body in its dealings with the palatial administration, just as the Near Eastern village communities did, finds support within the Linear B tablets. One piece of evidence that the *damos* acts as a coherent legal entity appears on Ep 704.5-6. These lines hold important implications for our understanding of the *damos* as well as for our interpretation of the sanctuary's role in land tenure. I will therefore return to this tablet when I discuss the religious landholders. But for our current discussion concerning the *damos*, it is important to note that on this tablet the *damos* disputes the priestess *e-ri-ta*'s claim that her land should be classified as *e-to-ni-jo* land (meaning a privileged piece of land, presumably free of some

[182] Deger-Jalkotzy 1983, p. 104. M. Heltzer, "Royal Economy in Ancient Ugarit," in *State and Temple Economy in the Ancient Near East*, vol. II, E. Lipinski, ed., 1979, pp. 459-496.

[183] *s.v. te-re-ta* in *Dic. Mic.* II, pp. 334-335.

[184] Shelmerdine 1999, p. 23.

[185] Foster 1981, p. 77. On p. 80 she does discuss *ka-ma* land and the fact that its holders were under obligations to *wo-ze*, but she does not discuss what that would mean for the holders and their relationship to the *damos*, although there is an implication that they would owe their service to the palace (p. 81).

[186] Deger-Jalkotzy 1983, pp. 89-111; see pp. 103-104 for her support of Palmer on this point.

[187] Deger-Jalkotzy 1983, p. 92.

[188] Deger-Jalkotzy 1983, p. 92. N.B. Jankowska, "Extended Family Commune and Civil Self-Government in Arrapha in the 15th-14th Century B.C.," in *Ancient Mesopotamia: Socio-Economic History, A Collection of Studies by Soviet Scholars*, I.M. Diakonoff, ed., 1969, pp. 235-252; *idem*, "Communal Self-Government and the King of the State of Arrapha," *JESHO* 12 (1969) 233-282.

[189] Deger-Jalkotzy 1983, p. 93. I.M. Diakonoff, "Agrarian Conditions in Middle Assyria," in *Ancient Mesopotamia*, I.M. Diakonoff, ed., 1969, pp. 204-234.

[190] Deger-Jalkotzy 1983, p. 93. J.N. Postgate, "Land Tenure in the Middle Assyrian Period: A Reconstruction," *BSOAS* 34 (1971) 496-520.

[191] Deger-Jalkotzy 1983, pp. 93-94. P. Garelli, "Le problème de la 'féodalité' assyrienne," *Semitica* 17 (1967) 5-21.

[192] Deger-Jalkotzy 1983, p. 93.

[193] Deger-Jalkotzy 1983, p. 94. M. Heltzer, *The Rural Community in Ancient Ugarit*, 1976, see pp. 75 ff.

obligations[194]), rather than as an *o-na-to* (a regular leasehold that would have been subject to the usual taxes).

Ep 704.5-6: Eritha's Dispute
5. e-ri-ta , i-je-re-ja , e-ke , e-u-ke-to-qe , e-to-ni-jo , e-ke-e , te-o ? da-mo-de-mi , pa-si , ko-to-na-o ,
6. ke-ke-me-na-o , o-na-to , e-ke-e , to-so pe-mo GRA 3 T 9̣

Ἐρίθα ἱέρεια ἔχει εὔχετοικε *ἐτόνιον *ἔχehεν θεῷ δᾶμος δέ μιν *φασὶ *κτοινάων *κεκεμενάων *ὀνατὸν *ἔχehεν; τόσος *σπέρμο: GRA 3 T 9

Translation:
Eritha the priestess holds, and she claims that she holds for the deity, *e-to-ni-jo* land, but the *damos* says that she holds an *o-na-to* of *ke-ke-me-na* land; so much seed: GRA 3 T 9.

Deger-Jalkotzy interprets the fact that the *damos* disputes the priestess' claim as indicating two things. The first is that the *damos* (on Ep 704.5-6) and its board of *ko-to-no-o-ko* (on Eb 297) acted as its own governing body.[195] The second is that the obligation to pay a certain amount of taxes to the palace was shared communally by everyone in the *damos*. She deduces this by reasoning that if the obligations concerning tax due from the land were imposed on an individual basis by the palace, then it might be the palace who would object to *e-ri-ta*'s claim.[196] But since it is the *damos* that objects, then it must have been the *damos* that stood to lose in this situation. Certainly the *damos* would have lost whatever produce that could have been expected from the land if it had remained classified as a regular *o-na-to*, and if taxes were handled collectively, then the burden of the loss of *e-ri-ta*'s produce would have to be shared out among the rest of the members of the *damos* in order to come up to the amount expected by the palace.[197] As we have discussed, Lang has shown that such re-apportionings of tax burdens did occur in the tablets (in the Es series and perhaps also within the En series),[198] so it may have been the prospect of heavier burdens for each of its members that caused the *damos* to object. As Deger-Jalkotzy says, "It is no wonder that the /*damos*/ took no joy in the aspirations of *e-ri-ta* about her *e-to-ni-jo* land, *e-to-ni-jo* which meant freedom from burdens; her share in the collective obligations would then fall on the other members of the community!"[199] The fact that the *damos* did object to the reclassification of the land demonstrates, on this view, that the *damos* could act as a corporate body on behalf of its members in order to protect their collective interests in the land that it administered and, presumably, they all benefited from.

An alternative explanation for the text of Ep 704.5-6 could be that the *damos* was in charge of managing the land for the palace and that its objection was meant merely to alert the palace to the possible encroachment on its income. My feeling is, however, that Deger-Jalkotzy's evaluation of the situation is more likely because further evidence that the *damos* was a corporate body that acted as the representative of its community can be found within the tablets. For instance, Un 718.7 records that the *damos* provided an offering for Poseidon (on the occasion of what must have been a large religious festival) alongside other important individuals, such as *e-ke-ra$_2$-wo* (which may be the personal name of the *wanax*[200]) and the *lawagetas*. A similar situation is seen on Cn 608 where the *o-pi-da-mi-jo*, or, as Killen translates, "the people in the *damos*," of each of the nine districts of the Hither Province are to fatten (*a-se-so-si*[201]) the pigs that are recorded against their names.[202] Palaima has proposed that these pigs, since they are few in number, were probably meant for sacrificial purposes.[203] Thus, the *damos* could act on behalf of its constituents in providing religious offerings. In these cases the term *damos* or *o-pi-da-mi-jo* is used to refer to the collective group that constituted the community. Elsewhere, such as on Jn 829 and On 300, we see that the *damos* also had its own officials who seem to have been in charge of the collection of the taxes required by the palace. Jn 829 records a collection of bronze from the sixteen principal

---

[194] Deger-Jalkotzy 1983, p. 100. Ruijgh proposed that the etymological explanation for *e-to-ni-jo*, as ἐτώνιον, was that it was derived from a compound word *ἔτωνος, whose first element was ἐτός meaning "true" or "real," and whose second element was ὄνος, which we have already seen in *o-na-to* meaning "profit" or "benefit" (1967, pp. 109-110). Thus he translates *e-to-ni-jo* as a piece of land that was free of rent. Duhoux translates it as "that which is truly advantageous" (1976, p. 48).
[195] Deger-Jalkotzy 1983, pp. 90-91. Also see pp. 94-97.
[196] Deger-Jalkotzy 1983, p. 91; also see pp. 99-100.
[197] For a full account of the Mycenaean taxation system and the theory that the taxes were assessed in a "top-down" manner, see W.F. Wyatt, Jr., "The Ma Tablets from Pylos," *AJA* 66 (1962) 21-41; C.W. Shelmerdine, "The Pylos Ma Tablets Reconsidered," *AJA* (1973) 261-275; *idem*, 1989, pp. 125-148.
[198] Lang 1964.
[199] Deger-Jalkotzy 1983, p. 100. It should be pointed out that *e-to-ni-jo* land may not have been completely free of taxes since *a-pi-me-de*'s *e-to-ni-jo* was recorded by the palatial scribes in the Ep series. Since the tablets were compiled as a basis for a tax assessment, this would suggest that some tax would have been expected from his land. Perhaps *e-to-ni-jo* meant that the holder would pay a lower percentage of tax than those holding a regular *o-na-to*. On the other hand, it is possible that the scribes recorded *a-pi-me-de*'s *e-to-ni-jo* simply in the interest of keeping track of the landholdings, but they knew that the exemption would be applied.
[200] Palaima 1995, pp. 119-139.
[201] The majority of scholars take *jo-a-se-so-si* as consisting of ὡς + *ἀήσονσι, the latter being the 3rd person plural future indicative of *ἀσέω (ἀσάω), meaning "thus they will fatten" (*Docs*^{2}, p. 534, also see *Dic. Mic.* I, p. 108). Risch proposed that instead *jo-a-se-so-si* could be broken down as οἵας ἥσουσι, using the future of ἵημι (*Etudes sur la grammaire et le vocabulaire du grec mycenien*, Amsterdam 1967, p. 168).
[202] J.T. Killen, "The Role of the State in Wheat and Olive Production in Mycenaean Crete," *Aevum* 72 (1998) 19-23; see p. 20, n. 3. Killen mentions that Chadwick (in *The Mycenaean World*, Cambridge 1976, p. 76 ff.) had previously proposed that *o-pi-da-mi-jo* meant "those in charge of the *damos*." (Also see Chadwick 1979, p. 28.) Killen prefers "the people of the *damos*" because on PY An 830, "where it is used as a description of no fewer than sixty *qo-u-ko-ro*, oxherds," it would be difficult to see the word as applying to only those in charge of the *damos*.
[203] T.G. Palaima, "Perspectives on the Pylos Oxen Tablets: Textual (and Archaeological) Evidence for the Use and Management of Oxen in Late Bronze Age Messenia (and Crete)," in *Studia Mycenaea 1988, Ziva Antika Monographs* No. 7, T.G. Palaima, C.W. Shelmerdine, and P. Ilievski, eds., Skopje 1989, pp. 85-119; see pp. 117-118.

districts that made up the Hither and the Further districts of the Pylian realm, and it is the *ko-re-te* ('mayor') and the *po-ro-ko-re-te* ('vice-mayor') of each district who appear to be responsible for handing over the correct amount of bronze. Killen says that, "We can be reasonably confident that the districts in question are *damoi*, and that the *ko-re-te* and *po-ro-ko-re-te-re* are local *damos* officials..."[204] On 300 also records an official called the *da-mo-ko-ro*, whose first element shows that he was an official with some responsibility within the *damos*.

It seems then that the *damoi* were subordinate to the *wanax* of Pylos in that they were expected to pay taxes to the palace, but they also seem to have retained their own mechanisms for governing their people and managing their resources, which technically seem to have been owned by the community as a whole. I think this indicates that the *damoi* managed to remain somewhat independent of the palace. Lejeune, in his analysis of the *damos*, came to the conclusion that it was a fairly complex institution that would have been responsible not only for satisfying its financial obligations to the palace (which is the element that we see on the tablets), but also for ensuring the subsistence of its personnel, procuring (through barter) whatever was needed by the collective, and finally for providing and arranging the necessary offerings to the sanctuaries.[205] Deger-Jalkotzy also thinks that the *damos* had a greater presence in the Mycenaean economy than the evidence of the tablets indicates. She says, "... one suspects that the communities of the settlement called /*damos*/ in the individual districts were corporate bodies with a wider sphere of activity in property rights, and indeed also in economic activity, than the texts generally let us know..."[206] Killen also sees the *damos* as an entity that was separate from the palace.[207] In his consideration of how the palace went about acquiring all the grain that it needed for its general upkeep, Killen concludes that it must have been grown on *damos* land, and that the palace would sometimes loan out its own oxen in order "to assist with the cultivation of *damos* land (perhaps on the basis that the *damos* would contribute part of the harvest to the palace in return for its help)."[208] Such an exchange would not be necessary if the palace owned the land itself.

Thus, it seems most likely that *ke-ke-me-na* land was collectively owned and operated, and that it was the head men or village leaders of the *damos*, the *ko-to-no-o-ko*, who were responsible for apportioning out the plots of *ke-ke-me-na* land and the tax burdens that were attached to them. The palace had the power to tax the land, hence the detailed records concerning the potential production capacity of the plots, but I think the palace did not own the land outright.

[204] Killen 1998, p. 20.
[205] Lejeune 1972, p. 142.
[206] Deger-Jalkotzy 1983, p. 90.
[207] Killen 1998.
[208] Killen 1998, p. 23. I will come back to this theory in a moment.

As for the *ki-ti-me-na* land, Deger-Jalkotzy thought that this was land that the king had been able to commandeer for his own purposes from the communal property of the *damos*. He used the land predominantly for the support of the men who were in his service, i.e., the *te-re-ta*.[209] Deger-Jalkotzy also provides us with a diachronic view of how the snapshot image of Pylian society that we get from the Linear B tablets could have come into being. Originally, she says, there was the communally owned *damos* land (*ke-ke-me-na*), but as the *wanax* of Pylos grew in power he must have claimed part of that land for the "state property sector."[210] This land was then called *ki-ti-me-na*. The *wanax* was able to give out this land to the *te-re-ta* as he saw fit. At the time when the land tenure records were written, a substantial portion of communal *ke-ke-me-na* land remained, but it carried with it the obligation to provide support to the palace as needed, whether in the form of corvée labor or contributions of grain. Thus, according to Deger-Jalkotzy, the *ki-ti-me-na* land represents a state property sector belonging to the *wanax*, and the *ke-ke-me-na* land represents a private property sector belonging to the *damos*.[211]

The view that there was a substantial amount of land owned essentially by the palace that existed alongside landholdings that were owned by the *damos* is very attractive. In particular I accept Deger-Jalkotzy's understanding of *ke-ke-me-na* land and the *damos*. But it may be that the *ki-ti-me-na* land of the *te-re-ta* was not owned by the palace at all, but was also associated with the *damos*. This possibility is suggested by the tablets Un 718, Er 312 and Er 880, on which the *damos* and the *te-re-ta* appear to be equated with each other, and which therefore demand a separate discussion.

The Role of the *Te-re-ta* in the *Damos*: Un 718, Er 312 and Er 880

Un 718 records four payments or offerings (*do-so-mo*) to Poseidon that involve a place called *sa-ra-pe-da*.[212] Er 312 is a land tenure document that also has four entries. The two tablets appear to be linked to each other since three of the four entries on Un 718 can be readily equated with one on Er 312. Thus Er 312 is thought to have been an assessment document that was drawn up in order to determine how much each one of the individuals or groups on the tablet should give as their offering to Poseidon. Un 718 recorded those offerings once they were made.

[209] Deger-Jalkotzy 1983, p. 109.
[210] Deger-Jalkotzy 1983, p. 109.
[211] Deger-Jalkotzy 1983, p. 102.
[212] Even though Aura Jorro (*s.v. Dic. Mic.* II) prefers the theory that *sa-ra-pe-da* (*sa-ra-pe-do* on Er 880) was a type of landholding, Killen uses it as a place name (1998, p. 22), and Palaima has said that although it is difficult to say for sure which it is, he prefers to think of it as a place name (opinion given in a seminar, November 12, 1999). I prefer to follow Killen and Palaima.

Un 718:
1. sa-ra-pe-da , po-se-da-o-ni , do-so-mo
2. o-wi-de-ta-i , do-so-mo , to-so , e-ke-ra_2-wo
3. do-se , GRA 4 VIN 3 BOS^m 1
4. tu-ro_2 , $TURO_2$ 10 ko-wo , *153 1
5. me-ri-to , V 3
6. *vacat*
7. o-da-a_2 , da-mo , GRA 2 VIN 2
8. $OVIS^m$ 2 $TURO_2$ 5 a-re-ro , *AREPA* V 2 *153 1
9. to-so-de , ra-wa-ke-ta , do-se ,
10. $OVIS^m$ 2 me-re-u-ro , FAR T 6
11a. -ma
11. VIN S 2 o-da-a_2 , wo-ro-ki-jo-ne-jo , ka-
12. GRA T 6 VIN S 1 $TURO_2$ 5 me-ri[
13. *vacat* [me-]ri-to V 1

Er 312:
1. wa-na-ka-te-ro , te-me-no [
2. to-so-jo [[ ]] pe-ma GRA 30
3. ra-wa-ke-si-jo , te-me-no GRA 10
4. *vacat*
5. te-re-ta-o⌊ ⌋to-so pe-ma GRA 30
6. to-so-de , te-re-ta VIR 3
7. wo-ro-ki-jo-ne-jo , e-re-mo
8. to-so-jo , pe-ma GRA 7[
9. *vacat*

The conjectured correspondences between the two tablets are as follows: Er 312 starts off with the *temenos* of the *wanax*, which is 30 GRA. This entry is often seen as corresponding to the offering recorded on Un 718.2 that was given by the person named *e-ke-ra_2-wo*, which is thought by some to be the personal name of the *wanax*.[213] Next on Er 312 comes the *temenos* of the *ra-wa-ke-ta* (or *lawagetas*), who is ranked second with 10 GRA on line 3. This record corresponds to the offering of the *lawagetas,* which is listed third in the sequence on Un 718.9. In the final position on Er 312.7 comes the *wo-ro-ki-jo-ne-jo e-re-mo* which is recorded to have been at least 6 and perhaps 7 GRA. A *wo-ro-ki-jo-ne-jo ka-ma*, which seems to correspond to the *wo-ro-ki-jo-ne-jo e-re-mo*, is listed last on Un 718.11.[214] Since the three landholders of Er 312 seem to have a match on Un 718, the landholdings of the *te-re-ta* on Er 312.5 have been said to find their parallel in the offering of the *damos* on Un 718.7. If this correspondence is correct, the *damos* and the *te-re-ta* are not just linked with each other, but in some way equated with each other.

Lejeune though cast doubt on the correspondence between the *te-re-ta* and the *damos* when he proposed that Er 312 and Un 718 should not be considered alone, but rather in conjunction with Er 880. Er 880, like Er 312, records landholdings, but these landholdings are recorded with the term *sa-ra-pe-do*, the probable place name that is seen on Un 718.1 (as *sa-ra-pe-da*), but which is found on no other tablets.[215]

Er 880:
1.]ke-ra_2[ ]ti-me-no , e-ke
2. sa-ra-pe-do[ ]pu_2-te-me-no
3. to-so [ ] GRA 30[ ] *vacat*
4. to-so-de , [ ]to , pe-ma GRA 42[
5. to-sa , we-je[ ]1100[
6. to-sa-de , su-za[ ]1000[*vac.*
7. *vacat*
8. ku-su-to-ro-qa , to-so , pe-ma 94
9. *vacat*

Also, all three tablets are the work of one scribe, Hand 24, who did not write anything other than these three tablets and one label, Wa 731. This label was probably related in some way to the tablets since it repeats two of the key words found on Un 718: *do-so-mo* is found on line A of Wa 731 and line 1 of Un 718, while the second line of Wa 731 records *]o-wi-de-ta[*, which corresponds to the *o-wi-de-ta-i* seen on line 2 of Un 718.[216] Lejeune thought that this label could have served to mark the basket that held Un 718.[217]

With Er 880 in the picture, it is not so easy to maintain the previously outlined correspondences between Un 718 and Er 312. Palmer, who wanted to keep the dichotomy between *te-re-ta* and the *damos* intact for his explanation of the land tenure documents, was particularly against identifying the two on Un 718 and Er 312.[218] Lejeune also disputed the Un 718/Er 312 correspondences because he thought that *e-ke-ra_2-wo* could not have been the personal name of the *wanax*.[219] He pointed out that *e-ke-ra_2-wo* held two plots of land on Er 880, which meant that it was not necessary to consider that his offering of Un 718 was based on the *wa-na-ka-te-ro te-me-no* of Er 312. He reasoned instead that the offerings of Un 718 must be based on the landholdings of both Er 312 and Er 880. He set about proving this by calculating the percentages of the offerings that each person or group contributed, and then by trying to find matching percentages of the total land held by each person or group on Er 312 and Er 880. Lejeune actually did calculate the figures for situations where the *wanax* and *e-ke-ra_2-wo* were considered to be the same person, but his test cases did not work very well, so he thought that this approach was flawed. This allowed Lejeune to turn to a different approach. He saw that there are four offerings on Un 718, one each given by the *e-ke-ra_2-wo*, the *damos*, the

[213] Palaima 1995, pp. 119-139.
[214] The identification of these two seemingly different types of land is generally accepted (*s.v. wo-ro-ki-jo-ne-jo Dic. Mic.* II). Ventris and Chadwick (*Docs*[2] p. 261) originally proposed that *wo-ro-ki-jo-ne-jo* be associated with the Attic ὀργεῶνες, who were members of a sacred organization. Palmer objected to this due to the morphological difficulties of this interpretation. He did however consider this to be a description of 'cult land' (1963, p. 214). Killen has more recently proposed that instead of taking *wo-ro-ki-jo-ne-jo* as a religious group that it should be seen as a possessive adjective derived from a person's name *Wroikion* in "Mycenaean Possessive Adjectives in *–e-jo*," *TPhS* (1983) 66-99; see pp. 83-84.

[215] Lejeune 1975, pp. 60-76.
[216] The *o-wi-de-ta-i* seem to have been a group of people (dative plural), either priests or functionaries, who may have been responsible for overseeing the offerings. See *Dic. Mic.* II, p. 58 for this and various other interpretations.
[217] Lejeune 1975, p. 61.
[218] Palmer 1963, pp. 213-217.
[219] Lejeune 1975.

lawagetas and *wo-ro-ki-jo-ne-jo ka-ma*, but that the landholdings were six in number: on Er 312 we have a *temenos* of the *wanax*, another of the *lawagetas*, the land held by the three *te-re-ta*, and the *wo-ro-ki-jo-ne-jo e-re-mo*; and on Er 880, there are the two holdings that belong to *e-ke-ra$_2$-wo*. He reasoned therefore that two of these landholdings must be exempt from having to provide a *do-so-mo*. The situation that worked best with his calculations was for the landholdings of the *wanax* and the *te-re-ta* to be exempted. In this way the *wanax* was not equated with *e-ke-ra$_2$-wo*, and the *damos* was not equated with the *te-re-ta*, which would seem to work well, he said, considering the dichotomy of the Ep and En tablets. Instead he paired the *damos* with the landholding of Er 880.4, which could conceivably be detached from the land held by *e-ke-ra$_2$-wo*. The numbers he arrives at with this method are as follows: *E-ke-ra$_2$-wo* owns 45% of the land and he contributes 50% of the goods, while the *damos* owns 40% of the land and contributes 33% of the goods. The *ra-wa-ke-ta's* percentages are 10% of the land to 11% of the contribution, and those of the *wo-ro-ki-jo-ne-jo e-re-mo/ka-ma* are 5% land to 6% contribution. These figures may not seem entirely satisfactory, nonetheless, Lejeune accepted them as being "nettement plus satisfaisantes" than his previous attempts.[220] In this way he justifies rejecting the identifications of both the *wanax* with *e-ke-ra$_2$-wo* and the *te-re-ta* with the *damos*.

de Fidio, however, soon after Lejeune had published his work, did find a way to produce figures that were even closer than Lejeune's.[221] Like Lejeune, de Fidio also comes to the conclusion that exemptions must have been worked into the system, but she finds that the landholdings that should be considered exempt are those of the *wanax* on Er 312.1 and *e-ke-ra$_2$-wo*'s second landholding on Er 880.4. Within her system the *wanax* and *e-ke-ra$_2$-wo* are still not necessarily equated in that *e-ke-ra$_2$-wo*'s offering on Un 718 is not matched with the *wa-na-ka-te-ro te-me-no* on Er 312. But even though they may not be equated through their correspondence on Un 718 and Er 312, the possibility that they were the same person still exists. Palaima makes a strong case that *e-ke-ra$_2$-wo* was the personal name of the *wanax*, and his arguments remain strong without the direct equivalence of Un 718 and Er 312.[222] For instance, as he points out, it is *e-ke-ra$_2$-wo* alone who contributes a bull to this sacrificial feast.[223] This distinctive offering would seem to belong properly to the *wanax* himself. Also, if de Fidio is correct that one of *e-ke-ra$_2$-wo*'s landholdings is being exempted as well as the *temenos* of the *wanax*, we might conclude that it was among the privileges of the *wanax* to avoid certain tax requirements (it should be kept in mind though that *e-ke-ra$_2$-wo* does pay tax on his second piece of land on Er 880). Regardless of what we think of the identification of *e-ke-ra$_2$-wo* as the *wanax*, within de Fidio's system the entries concerning the *te-re-ta* and the *damos* are matched up with each other, and they must therefore be considered to be somehow equivalent.

Killen has recently picked up on de Fidio's work with these tablets and incorporated it into his own discussion on the management of agricultural resources at both Knossos and Pylos, which I have already mentioned above.[224] The following chart, adapted from the one provided by Killen,[225] shows how the equivalencies work:

Er 312 + 880	GRA	% of Taxed Land (of a total GRA 96)	% of *Dosmoi* (Un 718)
**wanax*	30	0	0
lawagetas	10	10.5	11
telestai (=*damos*)	30	31.5	33
Wroikion[226]	6[	6	6
e-ke-ra$_2$-wo (*pe-pu$_2$*)	50[	52	50
* *e-ke-ra$_2$-wo* (*a-ki*)	42[	0	0

.
* = Exempt from contributions.

A couple of notes are in order. Both Bennett in *PTT* and Melena in his most recent presentation of the tablets (*PoN IV*) felt that it was safer to print the first landholding of *e-ke-ra$_2$-wo* on Er 880.3 (listed as "*e-ke-ra$_2$-wo* (*pe-pu$_2$*)" in the chart above) as 30[GRA instead of the 50[that de Fidio and Killen used in their calculations. The assumption that the landholding of Er 880.3 would have amounted to 50 GRA is justified despite this reading of the tablet because the total on Er 880 is 94 GRA, so the two landholdings must add up to this amount. Lang says in her account of Er 880, "The two amounts are not completely preserved but the possibilities are virtually limited to 50 and 44 or 52 and 42."[227] Lang prefers the latter possibility for epigraphical reasons and because the numbers fit well into her scheme of taxation on the E tablets, but either would work for de Fidio's calculations. Also, Melena has restored a 7 on Er 312.8 where de Fidio and Killen used a 6. Using the 7 would not throw off the figures terribly much, but it should also be said that Melena's comment on this line is " 6[: probably complete, 5 units preserved, maximum 7." Hence a figure of 6 is not precluded either. In the end, it seems that de Fidio's system of correspondences between Un 718 and the two Er tablets should stand as the best

[220] Lejeune 1975, p. 69-70.
[221] Pia de Fidio, *I dosmoi pilii a Poseidon* (*Incunabula Graeca* 65), Rome 1977; pp. 114-118.
[222] Palaima 1995, pp. 132-135.
[223] Palaima 1995, p. 132.

[224] J.T. Killen, "New Readings and Interpretations in the Pylos Tablets," in *Floreant Studia Mycenaea*, S. Deger-Jalkotzy, S. Hiller, O. Panagl, eds., Wien 1999, pp. 343-353; *idem* 1998, pp. 19-23.
[225] Killen 1999, p. 352. Killen rightfully gives credit to Lejeune (1975, p. 67) for the "% of *Dosmoi*" column of the chart.
[226] As mentioned above, Killen (1983, pp. 83-84) thinks *wo-ro-ki-jo-ne-jo* is more likely to represent a possessive adjective derived from a man's name, and so uses that name in his chart.
[227] Lang 1964, p. 49. It should also be mentioned that Melena (*PoN IV*) now says in the notes to Er 880 that the 42 of line 4 might possibly be restored to 54, which would mean the number on line 3 would have to be 40. This would upset the scheme a bit more significantly, but since this is a restoration in which Melena did not have complete confidence, I think we may leave it aside for this discussion.

explanation of the numbers on these tablets. If this is accepted, then the *te-re-ta* may not be primarily associated with the *wanax*, but rather with the *damos*.

Killen has considered how this would affect our view of the manner in which the palace went about acquiring the great masses of wheat that it needed to support its personnel.[228] Halstead had proposed that the Knossos Ch series, which shows that the palace owned its own oxen and allocated them for use in agricultural work, indicated that the palace itself was growing the majority of the wheat it needed on palatial estates.[229] Killen wondered then how this was related to the stores of wheat seen on Knossos records such as F(2) 851 and 852.[230] Those records say that the *a-ma,* or 'harvest', was *e-pi-ke-re*, /*epi kherei*/ or, "in hand, in stock." On F(2) 845 the word *damos* also appears, and the question then becomes, as Killen puts it, "does the presence of the term here show that all crops on the *a-ma* records have a connexion with the *damos*, or only the crops on this record?"[231] In order to find an answer to this question Killen looks elsewhere within the tablets to see if the palace estates that Halstead proposed to have existed could be found. He determines that the lands attributed to the *wanax* himself are too small to have accommodated all the agricultural production that had to be taking place; and besides, those lands were probably for the personal use of the *wanax* and his family. Killen also notes that there are a couple of records (KN E 843 and 1035) which might record lands under the control of "collectors," but again, these are too few to constitute the lands we are looking for. Finally, Killen turns to the *ki-ti-me-na* lands of the En series. If the *te-re-ta* are associated with the palace, then these could be the palatial lands that Halstead thought existed. However, Killen says that "serious doubt" must be cast on the idea that the "*ki-ti-me-na* land constituted separate palace estates, distinct from the *damos*," because of the identification between the *damos* and the *te-re-ta* on Un 718 and Er 312. He continues to say that "this evidence makes it tempting to conclude that not only *ke-ke-me-na* but also *ki-ti-me-na* land was land held in or from the *damos*."[232] Killen therefore agrees with Halstead that the loaning of the palatial oxen indicates that the palace had a role in the agricultural process, but he thinks they were lent out, as was seen above, "to assist with the cultivation of *damos* land (perhaps on the basis that the *damos* would contribute part of the harvest to the palace in return for this help)."[233]

If it was the case that the *te-re-ta* and the *damos* were somehow identified with each other, the question that I cannot help considering is, what role did the *te-re-ta* play in Mycenaean society if they did not owe their service to the *wanax*. What position within the *damos* would the *te-re-ta* have held, and why, if they were associated with the *damos*, was their land recorded separately?

Carlier has proposed a solution to these questions. Through an entirely independent line of thinking, Carlier also decided that the *te-re-ta* should be associated with the *damos*.[234] While he accepts the meaning of *te-re-ta* as "gens de charge," or "men of service," he disagrees that we should so easily accept that the service was owed to the *wanax*. As was mentioned earlier in this text, Carlier noticed that the *te-re-ta* are explicitly associated with the *wanax* in only one case: on En 467.5/Eo 371 the *te-re-ta* named *pi-ri-ta-wo* is described as *wa-na-ka-te-ro*. But, Carlier adds, this association with the *wanax* is more likely to be due to the fact that this man was also a craftsman, specifically a potter (*ke-ra-me-u*), since the word *wa-na-ka-te-ro* is in all other cases applied only to artisans.[235] Carlier also points out that the contexts in which we find the *te-re-ta* are predominantly concerned with land tenure. All nine of the *te-re-ta*'s appearances in Pylian texts are within the E series.[236] The Knossian mentions of *te-re-ta* are a little more diverse: *te-re-ta* appear three times on land tenure documents (Uf 839.a, Uf 970.a and Uf 990), four times in lists of persons (Am 826.1, B 7036, probably B 779.1 and V 159.1), and twice on fragments (X 1018 and X 7741.b).[237] Thus, Carlier reasons, the *te-re-ta's* main association is with land tenure, not with the *wanax*. It should be noted that Hooker promotes the same view. He says, "The *te-re-ta*, as presented in the tablets, have an intimate connexion with land and land-holding (and it may be that their title defines this connexion more precisely) but they are never brought into relationship with the *wa-na-ka*."[238] To whom then, does the *te-re-ta* owe his service?

Carlier answers this question in a very interesting way. He proposes that the *te-re-ta* actually represent an ancient landholding group, to whom the *damos* gave certain lands in exchange for their service (hence their being named "Men of Service"). The custom of the *te-re-ta* owing their service was of such antiquity though that the obligations had fallen by the wayside. This is Carlier's

[228] Killen 1998, 19-23.

[229] P. Halstead, "The Mycenaean palatial economy: Making the most of the gaps in the evidence," *Proceedings of the Cambridge Philological Society* 38 (1992) 57-86; *idem*, "Plough and power: The economic and social significance of cultivation with the ox-drawn ard in the Mediterranean," *Bulletin on Sumerian Agriculture*, vol. 8, Cambridge 1995, pp. 11-22; see p. 18.

[230] Killen 1998, p. 19.

[231] Killen 1998, p. 19.

[232] Killen 1998, p. 23.

[233] Killen 1998, p. 23. Halstead, in response to Killen's demonstration that the oxen were assigned to the *damos*, retracts his proposal that large-scale grain production was accomplished on palace estates. However, he does maintain his opinion that the palace had a strong influence over the production of grain and points out that, "Killen's reconstruction leaves open the possibility of sharecropping, with the palace providing plow oxen and the *damos* providing human labor." ("Towards a Model of Mycenaean Palatial Mobilization," in *Rethinking Mycenaean Palaces: New Interpretations of an Old Idea*, M. Galaty and W. Parkinson, eds., UCLA Press 1999, pp. 35-41, see p. 36).

[234] Carlier 1987, pp. 65-73.

[235] Carlier 1987, p. 66.

[236] *Te-re-ta* appears in the nominative singular on Ep 613.4/Eb 149.1, En 609.15/Eo 224.5, in the nominative plural on Ed 411.1, En 609.2, Eq 146, and Er 312.6, and in the genitive plural on Er 312.5 (*Dic. Mic.* II, *s.v. te-re-ta*).

[237] Carlier 1987, p. 65, n. 2. Aura Jorro does not include X 7741 on which the *te* is missing and the *-re* is uncertain: .b]*re-ta ri-no* [(*Dic. Mic.* II, *s.v. te-re-ta*).

[238] J.T. Hooker, "Titles and Functions in the Pylian State," in *Studies in Mycenaean and Classical Greek Presented to J. Chadwick* (*Minos* 20-22), J. Killen, J. Melena and J.-P. Olivier, eds., Universidad de Salamanca 1987, pp. 257-267; quote from p. 261.

explanation for the fact that the thirteen *te-re-ta* of the En series are not recorded as having to *te-re-ja-e*. He thinks that *su-ko* (of Ep 613.4) was apparently the only *te-re-ta* whose obligation to *te-re-ja-e* was still considered viable at the time the tablets were written.[239] Also, in Carlier's scheme the *ka-ma-e-we* are explained as being the more recent group to receive appropriations of land from the *damos*. Since their obligations were spelled out on the tablets, he considers them to have been much more current than those of the *te-re-ta*.

This scheme is very interesting, but there are a couple of assumptions in his argument that one could dispute. Perhaps most importantly, Carlier assumes that all of the *te-re-ta* on the En series were no longer obligated to render their services simply because the word specifying that obligation has been omitted. Indeed, one could argue that just being designated as a *te-re-ta* would have been enough to indicate that one was under an obligation, and that the one instance in which the obligation was made explicit may have represented the only time the scribe bothered to write it in. Or, Shelmerdine has proposed that it could be explained by a difference between the two series: perhaps the obligation was assumed in the En series while it had to be stated in the Ep series.[240] Hence I am not convinced that the *te-re-ta* necessarily represent an ancient disbursement of land. However, I do agree with the basic premises of Carlier's argument, that the *te-re-ta* should be linked with the *damos* because of the *te-re-ta*'s associations within the tablets, and that therefore the *te-re-ta* most likely owed their service to the *damos* instead of to the *wanax*. But I one may still wonder about the nature of that service.

Another curious thing that we know about the *te-re-ta* is that they were able to lease out their land, under their own jurisdiction, just as the *damos* did. This could constitute the special leasing arrangements under which the *ki-ti-me-na* land was "inhabited," which Foster proposed to have existed.[241] It is likely that the *te-re-ta* stood to gain from this arrangement, which gives us an indication that it was a privilege within the *damos* to be a *te-re-ta*. It is also pertinent that many of the *te-re-ta* were also *ko-to-no-o-ko*, whom we have proposed made up the managerial board of the *damos*. Thus some of the *te-re-ta* were also the headmen of the *damos*. But it seems that the two positions were not identical since *te-re-ta* is a distinct title, and the holding of *ki-ti-me-na* land was also a distinct privilege, so the service could not have been to manage the land. It is still possible that the *te-re-ta* had some sort of managerial responsibility concerning the *damos* that was separate from the duties performed by the *ko-to-no-o-ko*, but what I think is most likely is that their responsibilities were more military in nature: perhaps the *te-re-ta* were expected to direct the defense of the *damos* when necessary. This position and its obligation of military service could have been institutionalized before the *wanax* had gained his power over the region, at a time when each of the *damos* centers had to defend themselves from external enemies as well as potentially hostile neighboring forces. Even with the *wanax* organizing some sort of defense of the region, I think the need to defend one's own local territory may have still been pressing, and, therefore, the position of *te-re-ta* may not have become merely honorific. The fact that the *te-re-ta* and the *ko-to-no-o-ko* were overlapping but not identical groups may indicate that there were age or financial requirements one had to meet before you could become a member of the *ko-to-no-o-ko*, whereas the *te-re-ta* class may have included the younger men among the elite families who were fit for battle. Once you met such requirements however, it is clear that you could belong to both groups at the same time. It is also clear that such men who belonged both to the *te-re-ta* and the *ko-to-no-o-ko* would have held a great deal of power within their communities.

To summarize then, the attempts to define *ki-ti-me-na* and *ke-ke-me-na* land based on their etymological meanings have proven somewhat fruitless for our purposes, and instead it was the pursuit of juridical or effective meanings based on the *ki-ti-me-na* and *ke-ke-me-na*'s relationships with other words in the tablets (such as the *te-re-ta* and *damos*, respectively) that led to a clearer concept of how the terms functioned in Mycenaean society. Deger-Jalkotzy's ethnographic comparanda taken from Near Eastern societies, in combination with evidence found within the tablets, support the idea that the *damos* acted as a separate governmental body in its relations with the palatial administration. Thus the *ke-ke-me-na* land on the Ep/Eb series can be said to be administered and most likely owned by the *damos*, which is managed by its counsel or managerial board of *ko-to-no-o-ko*. The palace's interest in the land derives from its desire to accurately calculate and collect the amount of produce due to it as tax from the landholders. Also, the *ki-ti-me-na* land recorded on the En/Eo series, due to the correspondence between the *damos* and the *te-re-ta* found on Un 718 and Er 312 and the associations of the *te-re-ta* with land holdings in the tablets, may also be associated with the *damos* rather than with the *wanax* (or the religious sphere). *Ki-ti-me-na* land then was granted by the *damos* to a group of local, probably elite men called *te-re-ta* under special conditions that required them to perform some service, possibly entailing military duties, in exchange for being able to manage and lease out their own plots of land. Since the *te-re-ta* and their *ki-ti-me-na* landholdings were recorded by the palace, they must also have been expected to contribute their share of the taxes that were owed by the *damos* to the palace. This review has been particularly interesting for the light it shed on the inner workings of the *damos*, which appears to have had its own fairly intricate internal government that must have developed separate from the palatial administration, and which seems to have remained independent even at the height of the *wanax*'s power. Now, with this foundation concerning the social structure of the individual districts

[239] As we mentioned above, Carlier considers the *te-re-ta su-ko* to be the missing fourteenth *te-re-ta* that was not recorded in the En series.
[240] Shelmerdine, personal communication, October 2001.
[241] Foster 1981, p. 83.

or *damoi*, we may turn to an examination of the role of the religious sector and its relation to both the *damos* and the palace.

The Religious Landholdings of *Pa-ki-ja-ne*

Now, with this foundation concerning the social structure of the individual districts or *damoi*, and the knowledge that it was most likely the *damos* of *Pa-ki-ja-ne* that owned and administered the land found on the Ep/Eb and En/Eo land tenure documents, we can turn to an examination of the role of the religious sector in these series. Through this investigation we will also be able to gain an understanding of the religious sector's role in Mycenaean society. This investigation should also shed further light on the position that the sanctuary of *Pa-ki-ja-ne*, with which many of these religious personnel can be associated, held within Pylian society.

With the knowledge that the lands recorded in both of these series were not only under the managerial control of the *damos*, but that they were also owned by the *damos*, we can say that the religious personnel were therefore leasing their lands from the *damos*, and were expected to pay their share of taxes along with all the other lease holders. And yet, a glance at the tablets shows right away that a rather substantial number of the landholders were religiously affiliated, which could indicat e that the religious sector was itself a force to be reckoned with.

The sheer numbers of religious landholders are impressive. In the En series, 31 of the 35 *o-na-ta* are leased by religious personnel, and one of the *te-re-ta*, *qe/pe-re-qo-ta* of En 659.1, may be counted as a member of the religious hierarchy since he is recorded as *i-je-ro*[(which should probably be restored as *i-je-ro-wo-ko*) on Eb 159.A.[242] The *i-je-ro-wo-ko* (as was mentioned above) should be interpreted as ἱερο-ϝοργός, which was a type of officiating priest, perhaps in charge of sacrifices.[243] As we have seen, the types of leases are more varied in the Ep series, but again, religious personnel dominate with 45 certain (and 9 more possible) landholdings, as opposed to the 15 certainly held by secular people. This preponderance of religious personnel serves to demonstrate the large number of religious persons who were active at *Pa-ki-ja-ne*, all of whom had to be supported in some way. Among the male personnel who have religious titles are the *i-je-ro-wo-ko* named *a-•-ke-re-u* on Ep 613.7, *qe/pe-re-qo-ta pa-de-we-u* (Ep 613.10/Eb 159.A) who was probably also a *i-je-ro-wo-ko*, a priest (*i-je-re-u*) named *we-te-re-u* on Ep 539.13 (as well as on En 74.16 and En 659.4), and a man named *we-ra-jo* who is designated as *po-ti-ni-ja-we-jo* on Ep 613.14. Among the female religious personnel there is a group of women called the *ki-ri-te-wi-ja* on Ep 704.4 who may be defined as *κριθηϝια (from κριθή).[244] Bennett renders this as the "barleyers," but he adds that this is "less an occupation than a religious title" and suggests a comparison with the κριθολόγος of the Opuntians (Plu. 2.292c).[245] Adrados says they were evidently priestesses who performed a religious ceremony that concerned barley,[246] and R. Palmer has discussed the role of these women and barley in a religious context.[247] In addition to these women, on Ep 704.7 we find *ka-pa-ti-ja* the *ka-ra-wi-po-ro pa-ki-ja-na*, or Karpathia the Keybearer of *Pa-ki-ja-ne*. *Ka-ra-wi-po-ro* is agreed to be *κλαϝιφόρος which is analogous to the Doric κλαδοφόρος and the Attic κλειδοῦχος (which uses ἔχω instead of φορέω as the second element).[248] This official in historical times was a priestess who had "charge or custody of a place,"[249] presumably by virtue of her keeping the keys to the place. This *ka-ra-wi-po-ro* probably held the keys to the sanctuary of *Pa-ki-ja-ne*. Finally, we also have *e-ri-ta* (Eritha) the *i-je-re-ja* of *Pa-ki-ja-ne* whom we have already discussed above in the context of her dispute with the *damos* on Ep 704.5-6. She holds a second landholding on Ep 704.3, and it is actually the Eb tablet that corresponds to this line, Eb 339.A, that tells us that she is the priestess of *Pa-ki-ja-ne*.

Eb 339:

A. i-je-re-ja , pa-ki-ja-na , e-ke-q̣ẹ [o-na-to ke-ke-me-na] x̣

B. ko-to-na , pa-ro⌞ ⌟ḍạ-mo [to-so-de]pe-mo GRA T 4

There is also a *i-je-re-ja* who holds an *o-na-to* of *ki-ti-me-na* land on En 609.18/Eo 224.8, and there she is also designated as being the priestess of *Pa-ki-ja-ne*. Lejeune has proposed that she is the same person in each case because one of the totaling tablets, Ed 317.1, records collectively the holdings of simply the *i-je-re-ja*, as it also does for the *ka-ra-wi-po-ro* (*ka-pa-ti-ja*) and the *e-qe-ta* (*a-pi-me-de*?[250]).[251]

Ed 317:

1. ọ-ḍạ-a_2 , i-je-re-ja , ka-ra-wi-po-ro-qe , e-qe-ta-qe [[ ]]
2. we-te-re-u-qe , o-na-ta , to-so-de , pe-mo , GRA 21 T 6

Because of this identification of *e-ri-ta* with the priestess of *Pa-ki-ja-ne*, the *do-e-ra* and *do-e-ro* who are recorded as belonging to *i-je-re-ja pa-ki-ja-na* (En 609.16) or

[242] See the notes on Eb 159 in *PoN IV* and *Dic. Mic.* I, *s.v. i-je-ro*[.

[243] *Dic. Mic.* I, p. 276.

[244] *Dic. Mic.* I, p. 363 lists the other two possible translations of the *ki-ri-te-wi-ja* as *χριστηϝια meaning "anointed," or *κριτεια meaning "chosen."

[245] Bennett 1956b, p. 132.

[246] F.R. Adrados, "El Culto Real en Pilos y la Distribucion de la Tierra en Epoca Micenica," *Emerita* 24 (1956) 353-416; see p. 377.

[247] R. Palmer 1992, pp. 48-49.

[248] *Dic. Mic.* I, p. 324.

[249] Liddell and Scott, *s.v.* κλειδουχέω.

[250] The identification of *a-pi-me-de* as the *e-qe-ta* on Ed 317 will be discussed below.

[251] M. Lejeune, "Prêtres et prêtresses dans les documents mycéniens," in *Mémoires de Philologie Mycénienne* II (*Incunabula Graeca* 42), Rome 1971b, pp. 85-93; see p. 91.

simply the *i-je-re-ja* (Ep 539.7 and 8) would also be associated with this one priestess even though her name is not specified each time. If it is true that there is only one priestess of *Pa-ki-ja-ne*, might she then be classified as the "head" of the sanctuary? The fact that it is *e-ri-ta* who represents the sanctuary and its deity in the dispute with the *damos*, and not any of the other religious functionaries, may recommend this view. *Ka-pa-ti-ja* the *ka-wa-ri-po-ro*, who can also be designated simply by her title or her name, one implying the other, may have been, in a sense, second in charge considering *e-ri-ta*'s status as the head priestess.

In the Ep series 31 individuals called *te-o-jo do-e-ro/ra*, or servants of the deity, hold 33 *o-na-ta,* and in the En series 22 of these *te-o-jo do-e-ro/ra* hold 27 plots (several of the *te-o-jo do-e-ro/ra* hold multiple plots). Seven of the *te-o-jo do-e-ro/ra* hold both *ke-ke-me-na* and *ki-ti-me-na* land, so we actually have a total of 46 individual *te-o-jo do-e-ro/ra* from both series.[252] There are also two *do-e-ro* (Ep 539.7 and 8) and one *do-e-ra* (En 609.16) who are in the service of the *i-je-re-ja* of *Pa-ki-ja-ne*, and one *do-e-ro* in the service of *ka-pa-ti-ja* on Ep 539.9, who is here recorded without her title. Thus we can see that the religious sector at *Pa-ki-ja-ne* had a substantial number of personnel, all of whom were probably associated with the sanctuary of *Pa-ki-ja-ne*.

While these numbers are impressive, they would not actually signify much if the aggregate amount of land held by the religious personnel turned out to be rather small in comparison with that held by the secular landholders. Therefore, to more accurately determine the extent of the sanctuary's presence in the area of *Pa-ki-ja-ne*, we should also look at the relative amounts of land, expressed in units of GRA, that each category of landholder held. In the following chart I have sorted the landholders of the Ep and En series into three categories: "secular," "religious," and "uncertain." In the En series the secular category is fulfilled predominantly by the *te-re-ta*, but there are other secular persons within the En series that are not *te-re-ta*, whom I have separated out so that the *te-re-ta* may remain distinct. The landholders whom I have designated as "uncertain" are those whose religious status is not clear from their entry within the land tenure tablets, but whose other associations within the Linear B corpus imply that they could be taken as persons associated with the religious sphere. [Please note that V 6 = T 1 and T 10 = GRA 1.]

[252] I will discuss the multiple landholdings of the *te-o-jo do-e-ro/a* in more detail below.

Chart 4.1: Distribution of GRA in the En and Ep Series:

	Type of Landholder	
En Series:	*te-re-ta*:	GRA 29 T 1 V 2
	Secular:	GRA T 4 V 1
	Religious:	GRA 8 T 2 V 3
Ep Series:	Secular:	GRA 7 T 8 V 3
	Religious:	GRA 15 T 4 V 4
	Uncertain:*	GRA 29 T 8

*Counted among the "uncertain" landholders are:
Ep 539.10, 11, 12: Three *do-e-ro a-pi-me-de-o*, all with *o-na-ta* totaling: GRA 1 T 1.
Ep 539.14: *a-pi*[*-me-*]*de* himself with an *e-to-ni-jo*: GRA 4 T 6.
Ep 613.1: *ne-qe-e e-da-e-u* with a *ka-ma*: GRA 10 T 1.
Ep 613.4: *te-re-*]*ta su-ko po-ro-du-ma*, unspecified land type: GRA 10.
Ep 613.6: *a$_3$-ke-re-u a-si-to-po-qo* with a *ka-ma*: GRA 1.
Ep 613.13: *mi-*]*ka-ta pa-de-we-u*, a *ka-ma-e-u*: GRA T 5.
Ep 704.1: *o-pe-to-re-u qe-ja-me-no* with a *ke-ke-me-na ko-to-na*: GRA 2 T 5.

Chart 4.1 shows that the *te-re-ta* dominate as landholders in the En series with over 29 GRA.[253] After that the religious *o-na-ta* landholders in the En series have a little over 8 GRA while the secular *o-na-ta* landholders make a rather small showing with only T 4 V 1. Considering the fact that the *ki-ti-me-na* land was most likely given over to the *te-re-ta* for their benefit, it would make sense that no one else should rival their landholdings in this category. The more pertinent comparison in this land category would therefore be among the *o-na-ta* holders, and in that area the religious sector dominates.

In the Ep series the situation seen among the *o-na-ta* holders of the En series is repeated, but on a larger scale. Considering only those landholders who can definitely be identified as either religious or secular, the religious landholders actually seem to have about twice as much land as the secular ones. The *ko-to-no-o-ko* of Ep 301 combined with the other definitely secular landholders in the Ep series have GRA 7 T 8 V 3. In comparison, the landholders whom we can identify as being definitely religious have over 15 GRA, and, if we were to include the lands of those that I left as "uncertain," they would have over 45 GRA. This number actually exceeds the amount of land that the *te-re-ta* hold in the En series,

[253] As was decided at the beginning of this chapter, I will consider the amounts given for the *ko-to-na* holdings of the *te-re-ta* as not including the amounts given for the *o-na-ta* leased from the *te-re-ta*.
The figure of GRA 29 T 4 V 2 does not match the 31 GRA quoted at the beginning of this chapter as the total land held by the *te-re-ta*. This is because, as mentioned above, there is one *te-re-ta*, *qe-re-qo-ta/pe-re-qo-ta* of En 659.1, who is classified in the Ep/Eb series (Ep 613.10/Eb 159.A) as a *i-je-ro*[*-wo-ko*, and therefore was affiliated with the religious realm. I have decided therefore to count his *te-re-ta* landholding of GRA 2 T 3 among the religious landholdings even though it would probably be difficult to say whether he held that land mostly because of his secular or his religious role in the community. Most likely it was because of both.

which would make the religious sector the largest landholder in *Pa-ki-ja-ne*.[254] To understand if this high number is likely to be accurate, we should examine each of the landholders who appear on the "uncertain" list.

Ep 539.10, 11, 12: Three *do-e-ro a-pi-me-de-o*, all with *o-na-ta* totaling: GRA 1 T 1. Ep 539.14: *a-pi*[*-me-*]*de* himself with an *e-to-ni-jo*: GRA 4 T 6: The first thing that indicated that *a-pi-me-de* should be counted as a member of the religious hierarchy is his position on Ep 539. As was discussed above, the order of the Ep series was determined through an analysis of the progression of the types of landholders within the series.[255] To review, the first six lines on Ep 539 finishes out the run of *te-o-jo do-e-ro/a* that started on the bottom of Ep 613 and continued through Ep 705 and Ep 212. Then Ep 539 records the *do-e-ro* of the priestess, then the one belonging to *ka-pa-ti-ja ka-ra-wi-po-ro*, and then we see the three *do-e-ro* belonging to *a-pi-me-de*. Following immediately after this we see the *o-na-to* of the priest named *we-te-re-u*, and then in the final position we see the landholding of *a-pi-me-de* himself. The next tablet in the series, Ep 704, records the landholdings of several others who held elevated positions within the religious hierarchy. Thus, by his position on the tablets it seems that *a-pi-me-de* should be counted as a member of the religious hierarchy.

It is true that *a-pi-me-de* is never designated explicitly as a priest, but a case can be made that he was known as such by the scribe and so it was not necessary for the word *i-je-re-u* to be included in the text. *We-te-re-u*, for instance, who is designated as a priest on Ep 539.14, is not designated as such in his corresponding Eb texts (Eb 472 and 477).[256] *We-te-re-u* must have been recognizable as a priest by his name alone since Hand 1 knew well enough to include the title in his own rendition of the entry after having read the preliminary text written by Hand 41, where it was lacking. It is possible then that *a-pi-me-de* was also known well enough by name that his official position would have been recognized despite the fact that it was not written on this record.[257]

Another indication of *a-pi-me-de*'s religious status is that the type of land he holds is designated as *e-to-ni-jo*. As we saw above, this is the type of land that *e-ri-ta* claimed she was holding for the god on Ep 704.5-6. The fact that *e-ri-ta* claimed that the land was held for the deity makes it seem as if the special status of the land was due to the fact that it belonged to the religious realm. *E-to-ni-jo* land could then be interpreted as being inherently religious and always associated with a sanctuary, which would confirm *a-pi-me-de*'s religious status. This is the easy way out, so to speak, but there is evidence that *e-to-ni-jo* was not necessarily a religious piece of land. This is because the religious affiliation for the third person who holds *e-to-ni-jo* land is doubtful. This person, whose name is *e-nwa-ri-jo*, is found on An 724.12. Scholars were at first tempted to associate *e-nwa-ri-jo* with the deity *e-nu-wa-ri-jo* of KN V 52, which would keep the *e-to-ni-jo* land within the religious realm. However, this identification has for the most part been rejected since it seems best to take *e-nwa-ri-jo* of An 724 as a person rather than a deity.[258]

An 724:
1. ro-o-wa , e-re-ta , a-pe-o-te ,
2. me-nu-wa , a-pe-e-ke , a-re-sa-ni-e [[ ]]
3. o-pi-ke-ri-jo-de , ki-ti-ta , o-pe-ro-ta , [[ ]]
4. e-re-e VIR 1 VIR
5. e-ke-ra$_2$-wo-ne , a-pe-e-ke , a$_2$-ri-e , [[ ]]
6. o-pe-ro-te , e-re-e VIR 5
7. ra-wa-ke-ta , a-pe-e-ḳẹ[ ]ẹ VIR 1̣[
8. ta-ti-qo-we-u , o-[ ]-qe-[•]- jọ , VIR 1
9. a-ke-re-wa , ki-e-u , o-pe-[ ]ẹ , a-ri-ja-to VIR 1
10. ki-ti-ṭạ VIR 1 o-ro-ti-jo , di-qo , a-[ ] *vest.*
11. o-pe-ṛọ , [ ] , e-ko-si-qe , e-qe-ta , ka-ma[ ]*vest.*
12. e-to-ni-jo , e-nwa-ri-jo VIR 1 [ ]*v.*
13. wo-qe-we , ḍị-qo-te , ru-ki-ja , a-ko-wo ṾỊṚ [*qs*
14. ri-jo , o-no ? e-qo-te VIR 1̣0

Much of An 724 is difficult to interpret. Ventris and Chadwick mention that "Any attempt to construct a regular formula encounters difficulties, and the frequent corrections lead us to suspect that scribal errors are present."[259] But the heading at least makes the context clear. It reads: "at *ro-o-wa* (a coastal town) rowers who are absent."[260] (On line 9 we switch to the location *a-ke-re-wa.*) The rest of the tablet seems to provide explanations as to why the rowers were absent. A couple of entries record a person in the nominative, such as *me-nu-wa* in line 2 and the *ra-wa-ke-ta* of line 7[261] who seem to be the subject of *a-pe-e-ke*, which Chadwick takes as "either the aorist or perhaps perfect" of ἀφίημι, meaning "letting go" or "releasing." In the first entry it is spelled out that those being released, the *ki-ti-ta*, were under an obligation (*o-pe-ro-ta*) to row (*e-re-e*). Thus, according to Chadwick, the use of *a-pe-e-ke* demonstrates that these rowers are absent not because they are missing, but

[254] Even though I have decided to use the amounts of GRA that are extant on the tablets in order to remain fair to all categories of land, it should be pointed out that 45 GRA also exceeds the GRA 44 that is recorded for the *te-re-ta* on the totaling tablet Ed 411 (which was discussed earlier in relation to the issue of the missing fourteenth *te-re-ta*).

[255] Palmer 1963, pp. 198-199. Bennett 1956b, p. 128, 130-131.

[256] On his two preliminary tablets *we-te-re-u* is actually designated by his ethnic: *o-pi-ti-ni-ja-ta*.

[257] *Ka-pa-ti-ja* on (Ep 539.9 and Un 443.3) and perhaps *e-ke-ra$_2$-wo* (on, e.g., Un 718.2), if indeed he is the *wanax*, constitute two other examples where a person's name was enough to indicate his or her title.

[258] Ruijgh 1967, p. 112, says that it is possible that the two are the same, but that the context of An 724 would then be difficult to interpret. Chadwick denies that it could be the deity's name (1987, p. 81) and Aura Jorro says that his identity with the theonym *e-nu-wa-ri-jo* ought to be rejected (*Dic. Mic.* I, p. 221). Of course, if *e-nwa-ri-jo* coild be seen as a deity it would simplify the situation regarding *e-to-ni-jo* land and the religious nature of *a-pi-me-de*, but the *communis opinio* has decided against it.

[259] *Docs^2*, p. 431.

[260] Chadwick 1987, see pp. 79-83 for his discussion of An 724.

[261] Chadwick (1987, p. 80) also takes *e-ke-ra$_2$-wo-ne* as a constituting a nominative despite its dative form. He says, "either *e-ke-ra$_2$-wo-ne* is an error for *e-ke-ra$_2$-wo*, or, more likely, the final *-ne* is an attempt to indicate the final /*-n*/ of the nominative."

because they have been "excused attendance."[262] Killen describes An 724 as "a record of exemptions from service as rowers (*e-re-ta*) which have been granted to landholders..."[263]

The record containing *e-nwa-ri-jo* is difficult to fit into the basic formula, but it does seem that he was being exempted from service due to the *e-to-ni-jo* land.[264] It is a question though as to whether *e-nwa-ri-jo*'s line should be read with the one (or even the two) above it. It is possible that these lines should be read together since we are lacking a VIR ideogram at the end of lines 10 and 11 that would tell us for sure that the entry had ended. Therefore Chadwick takes lines 10-12 as constituting one entry. He says that the beginning of the entry is "obscure" but that *e-re-e* may stand in the lacuna on line 11, which, when combined with *o-pe-ro*, "at least suggests that the theme is still the non-fulfillment of obligations." Chadwick then restores *ka-ma* as a genitive ("*kama*[*hos*?") in order to make sense of *e-ko-si-qe e-qe-ta ka-ma e-to-ni-jo e-nwa-ri-jo.* He does not give an English translation, but his rendering into Greek would translate as, "and the *e-qe-ta* have an *e-to-ni-jo* of *ka-ma* land, Enwalios VIR 1," which would make *e-nwa-ri-jo* the one who was being exempted, presumably because of the special holding of the *e-qe-ta.*

I have problems with this interpretation, which I will bring up in a moment, but I think it is only fair to mention at this point that if these lines are taken together then there is a way to read them that would preserve the interpretation of *e-nwa-ri-jo* as a god. The case of *e-nwa-ri-jo* is ambiguous; it could also represent a dative. If we were to take it in that way, then we might translate "and the *e-qe-ta* have an *e-to-ni-jo* of *ka-ma* land [which they hold] for [or in the name of] Enwalios VIR 1." If this was considered the best rendering of these lines then *e-to-ni-jo* land should be considered to be religious in nature. But I would object to this interpretation on the grounds that it would leave the entry without a reference to the person who was being exempted, which is a fairly usual characteristic of the other entries on the tablet.

Thus I would prefer Chadwick's interpretation that *e-nwa-ri-jo* is the person being exempted from service, which would remove any religious implication for the *e-to-ni-jo* land on this tablet, and thereby also on Ep 539 and Ep 704. But in addition to this I would also like to mention a couple of reasons why it might be preferable to interpret the lines concerning the *e-qe-ta* as a separate entry from *e-nwa-ri-jo*'s. First, as I said above, no VIR is preserved on line 11, but there are traces of writing at the end of line 11, and that brings up the possibility that a VIR originally did appear at the end of line 11. Also, Chadwick's interpretation ignores the words *o-ro-ti-jo* and *di-qo* on line 10, which could be men's names. Perhaps they were the ones being exempted on account of the *e-qe-ta* having a piece of *ka-ma* land. Finally, I do not think that *e-to-ni-jo* land would have been considered a species of *ka-ma* land. *Ka-ma* land is already a special type of land, and it seems unlikely, from the way they are each used in separate contexts on the land tenure tablets, that the two would be equated. It would be simpler to take *ka-ma* as the accusative subject of *e-ko-si.* What do we do then with the two-word entry on line 12? I propose that the verb in this entry is to be understood from the previous one: "Enwalios [has] an *e-to-ni-jo* [and is therefore excused]. If this reading of the tablet is accepted, then it is unlikely that *e-nwa-ri-jo* could have been a deity, since he was the one who held the *e-to-ni-jo* land and was consequently exempted from service on that basis.[265]

Thus the interpretation of *e-to-ni-jo* as a landholding that conferred privileges upon its holder is supported. Its religious association, however, is not borne out by the fact that it was *e-nwa-ri-jo* who held it. Therefore, the *e-to-ni-jo* land of *e-ri-ta* and *a-pi-me-de*, which may very well have been awarded because of their status within the religious sector, cannot be judged to have been inherently religious itself. *E-to-ni-jo* land must then be seen as, as Chadwick puts it, "a preferential holding which extinguished the obligation normally associated with the land,"[266] but not as one that is naturally entitled to preferential treatment because it is itself religious land. This has interesting implications for *e-ri-ta* and her dispute with the *damos* over the *e-to-ni-jo* land. As Shelmerdine has pointed out,[267] assessments of land such as the one found on the Ep tablets most likely occurred once a year. This means that the land which *e-ri-ta* is claiming to be *e-to-ni-jo* must have changed its status sometime within the previous year (otherwise the dispute would probably already have been resolved), and it is most likely that before that time it had been classified as a regular *o-na-to.* This brings up the question of what caused the status of the land to change. It is possible that *e-ri-ta* simply decided that the land should be privileged (possibly due to some service that she and the sanctuary had performed for the *damos*), and that she is now asserting that claim, but this seems unlikely. It seems even more unlikely that the *damos* had changed the status since they are protesting that change. The most likely scenario therefore is that it was the palace that granted the special status. Perhaps the *wanax* stepped in and, despite the fact that the land actually belonged to the *damos*, unilaterally conferred the status of *e-to-ni-jo* on this particular piece of land with the intention of making an offering to the sanctuary. As I discussed above, Palaima has detailed the religious duties of the *wanax* and shown that he was "concerned primarily with the performance of rituals that assured the benevolence of the gods towards his community."[268] Palaima brings in as comparanda the strong role the Hittite king played in religious matters to demonstrate that "society as a whole would have viewed

[262] Chadwick 1987, p. 80.
[263] Killen 1985, p. 249.
[264] Chadwick 1987, p. 81.

[265] It is possible that it was a human representative of the deity Enwalios who was exempted, but this seems less likely.
[266] Chadwick 1987, p. 81.
[267] Shelmerdine, personal communication, August 2001.
[268] Palaima 1995, p. 130 for this quote.

the role of the *wanax* as intermediary with the divine sphere as of overwhelming importance for the well-being of the entire community."[269] A similar situation can be seen in ancient Mesopotamia. Postgate says that in Sumerian society the king was responsible for the "community's maintenance of the temples" and that "on his effective fulfillment of this role depends the community's favor with the gods, and hence its prosperity; failure in this aspect of his duties would account for hardship and distress."[270] Thus, he says, "...there was a moral obligation on them to sustain the temples by granting them contributions and securing them in perpetuity."[271] This role, having been established in early Sumerian times, continued to be important for the kings of Mesopotamia regardless of which cultural group was in ascendance. "To the end of the last Mesopotamian dynasty, in 539, the kings included their care for the temples among their principal titles, this remaining integral to their moral claim to the right to rule."[272] Hence, Robertson notes that "Over many centuries, great kings and local rulers courted divine favor through their largess to temples..."[273] and among their offerings were "tracts of land."[274] In light of this I wonder if the king of Pylos might not also have granted land to the sanctuaries. If this was the case, then it is possible that here the *wanax* took lands that originally belonged to the *damos* in order to create his offering. The *damos* felt compelled to protest this move because of the loss of income that the change in the land's status would entail. Clearly the case had not yet been resolved when the scribe was making up the land tenure records. We can imagine that the complaint had been submitted to the palatial authorities and the parties were still awaiting a decision.

If this scenario seems likely, it would also hold implications concerning the relationship between the *damos* and the palace. Perhaps, as Shelmerdine has suggested,[275] the *damos* leaders had been, in the days before the *wanax* of Pylos came to hold the supreme position in Messenia, the highest authority for each of the districts. As the power of the *wanax* grew, it began to overshadow that of the separate *damos* leaders, and in particular, due to their close proximity to the palace at Pylos, the *damos* leaders of *Pa-ki-ja-ne*. Thus, even though the land of *Pa-ki-ja-ne* was still managed by the *damos*, nonetheless the *wanax* at that point had the power to co-opt some of the land for his own purposes. This could explain how *e-ri-ta* received her *e-to-ni-jo* land. The question may also be raised as to whether *a-pi-me-de* and *e-nwa-ri-jo* had also received their *e-to-ni-jo* land from the palace. This of course is impossible to know for certain, but it is curious that there are only three examples of *e-to-ni-jo* land. If the word did refer specifically to land reclassified by the *wanax* as privileged, then perhaps the *wanax* did not often make gifts of this kind. The *damos*' protest may indicate why: stepping on the *damos*' collective toes would probably not have been without consequences, even though the *wanax* clearly had the power to make such a re-classification if he chose to.

To sum up, it has been shown that *e-to-ni-jo* land was a privileged landholding that was presumably free of (some?) obligation and/or taxes. It is possible that it could have been conferred by the *wanax* on those whom he wanted to honor in some way. Those honorees were not all definitely associated with the religious sector, and therefore *e-to-ni-jo* land itself should probably not be considered to be inherently religious land. Thus, the fact that *a-pi-me-de* has *e-to-ni-jo* land says nothing either way as to whether he was a member of the religious hierarchy or not.

Nonetheless, *a-pi-me-de*'s position on Ep 539 does indicate that he was prominent in the religious sphere, and Lejeune has suggested that we may identify *a-pi-me-de* with the *e-qe-ta* recorded in the totaling tablet Ed 317 on this basis.

Ed 317:
1. ọ-ḍạ-a$_2$, i-je-re-ja , ka-ra-wi-po-ro-qe , e-qe-ta-qe [[ ]]
2. we-te-re-u-qe , o-na-ta , to-so-de , pe-mo , GRA 21 T 6

On Ed 317 we see three of the most prominent religious functionaries of the Ep series, the *i-je-re-ja*, the *ka-ra-wi-po-ro*, and the priest *we-te-re-u*, listed along with an *e-qe-ta*. Lejeune thinks that *a-pi-me-de* should be identified as the *e-qe-ta* since there is no *e-qe-ta* listed as such in the Ep series and since *a-pi-me-de* is the person who is grouped with the three others of Ed 317 within the Ep series.[276] A further indication that this might be likely is found on Ed 847, which records the total landholdings of the *e-qe-si-jo do-e-ro*:

Ed 847:
1. o-da-a$_2$, e-qe-si-jo , do-e-ro , e-ko-si , o-na-ta
2. [[ ]] , to-so-de pe-mo GRA 1 T 3 V 4

Again, we have no *do-e-ro* in the Ep series who are said to be associated with an *e-qe-ta*, but *a-pi-me-de* does have three *do-e-ro* ascribed to him on Ep 539.10-12. We could therefore identify these *e-qe-si-jo do-e-ro* with the *do-e-ro* of *a-pi-me-de* if we accepted that *a-pi-me-de* was the *e-qe-ta* on Ed 317. The amount of land the three *do-e-ro a-pi-me-de-o* on Ep 539 amounts to GRA 1 T 1, which does not exactly match the GRA 1 T 3 V 4 of the *e-qe-si-jo do-e-ro*, but it is fairly close.

Lejeune also suggests that the reason *we-te-re-u* is designated on Ed 317 by his name, whereas the others are designated by their titles, is because there was more than

[269] Palaima 1995, p. 131.
[270] N. Postgate, "Royal Ideology and State Administration in Sumer and Akkad," in *Civilizations of the Near East, Vol. I*, J. M. Sasson, ed., Charles Scribner's Sons, New York 1995, pp. 395-411; see p. 397.
[271] Postgate 1995, pp. 397-398.
[272] Postgate 1995, p. 398. Also see p. 408 for a similar thought.
[273] Robertson 1995, p. 445.
[274] Robertson 1995, p. 445.
[275] Shelmerdine, personal communication, August 2001.
[276] Lejeune 1971b, pp. 91-92, n. 34.

one priest in *Pa-ki-ja-ne*, while there was only one *i-je-re-ja* and one *ka-ra-wi-po-ro*.[277] Actually, Lejeune proposes this because the name *sa-ke-re-u* is described as a priest (*i-je-re-wo*) on Ea 756 and he therefore thought that *sa-ke-re-u* should be taken as one of the priests of *Pa-ki-ja-ne*. But since *sa-ke-re-u* only appears in the Ea series,[278] which records land in an area different from *Pa-ki-ja-ne*, *sa-ke-re-u* is probably not a priest of *Pa-ki-ja-ne* but of some sanctuary found in the land recorded in the Ea tablets.[279] Nonetheless, the idea that *we-te-re-u* was designated by his name in Ed 317 because there was more than one priest in *Pa-ki-ja-ne* would still make sense if we conclude that *a-pi-me-de* was a priest. The title "priest" could not be used on the totaling tablet because it would not have been specific enough a designation given that there were at least two of them. Therefore, each of the priests was designated by some other distinguishing feature. In the case of *we-te-re-u* it was his name, and for *a-pi-me-de*, it was his title *e-qe-ta*.

If this identification of *a-pi-me-de* as an *e-qe-ta* is correct, as I think is likely, then *a-pi-me-de* was prominent not only in the religious sphere but also in the secular hierarchy of Pylos. The likelihood that *a-pi-me-de* was a very important man is supported by his appearance on other tablets. For instance, *a-pi-me-de* also appears on Cn 655.5 where he is the holder, or "collector," of a rather large flock of male sheep: his flock consists of 190 sheep while seventeen of the twenty flocks on Cn 655 number 100 or less. It is interesting that *a-pi-me-de* appears on Cn 655 alongside another prominent sheep holder, **we-da-ne-u* (Cn 655.6, 13-20), who may also be interpreted as having been connected with the religious sector because he receives offerings at Poseidon's side in the Es series.[280] Thus it seems that **we-da-ne-u*, just like *a-pi-me-de*, played a role in both the secular and religious realms. As we have seen, another such person who was active in both realms was *qe/pe-re-qo-ta*. He is recorded among the *te-re-ta* on En 659.1, and so was active in the secular realm, but he is also described as *i-je-ro[-wo-ko* on Eb 159.A.[281] Thus *qe/pe-re-qo-ta* too seems to have been a prominent person in the secular activities of the district of *Pa-ki-ja-ne*, while he also held a religious post. Another such person may be *ko-tu-ro*$_2$. He is listed as a *ko-to-no-o-ko* on Ep 301.13 and so was a member of the managerial board of the *damos*. But *ko-tu-ro*$_2$ also appears with a religious title (*mi-ka-ta*[282]) on Ep 613.13. Thus he too held posts in both the religious and secular realms. As Deger-Jalkotzy has said, "in the Mycenaean period political and religious aspects certainly overlapped on all levels of public life."[283] It seems possible, and indeed likely, that men who were prominent in the community could hold multiple positions that would involve them in both religious and secular affairs. *A-pi-me-de,* as an *e-qe-ta*, a "collector," and a religious official, was one of those who seems to have attained a prominent position in politics, economic affairs and in the religious hierarchy. This makes sense of course: his prominence in one area probably led to high status positions in other areas of society. The fact that he was highly placed within the secular community must have been to the benefit of the sanctuary when he acted as its representative. But given his secular ties, it could be questioned as to whether we should classify *a-pi-me-de*'slandholding as secular or religious. To me it seems justified to count his holding among the religious lands because of the way the scribe recorded him among the other religious landholders. The fact that *a-pi-me-de* was associated with the religious realm (we could even say, with the sanctuary at *Pa-ki-ja-ne*) must have been the most significant factor when it came to classifying and categorizing his land. Thus I, as did the scribe, will count his land among the religious land holdings. *A-pi-me-de*'s *do-e-ro* then should also be classified as religious, both because of their association with *a-pi-me-de* and because they too are recorded amongst the religious landholders on Ep 539.

Ep 613.1: *ne-qe-wo e-da-e-wo* with a *ka-ma*: GRA 10 T 1: The next person on the "uncertain" list is *ne-qe-wo e-da-e-wo*, one of the *ka-ma* holders. *Ne-qe-wo e-da-e-wo* is the genitive form of the name and title found on Qa 1298, *ne-qe-u e-da-e-u*. These two are generally agreed to be the same person.[284] The Qa series (which will be more fully discussed in Chapter 5) provides a pretty sure link for *ne-qe-u* with the religious sector because the entire series seems to have had a religious subject. The exact religious content though has only recently been illuminated by Melena. This is because the Qa series records the disbursement of a commodity represented by the ideogram **189*, which looks something like a piece of cloth or a hide, but the exact nature of this ideogram had remained something of a mystery. The religious nature of the series was indeed implied by the fact that several tablets within the series record personnel who are readily identified as religious: *i-je-re-u* appears on Qa 1290 and 1296, *i-je-re-ja* on Qa 1289, 1300, and probably on 1303 (*i[-je-re-ja*). One man named *ka-e-se-u* on Qa 1299 is called Potnian (*po-ti-ni-ja-wi-jo*), and Qa 1308 records

[277] Lejeune 1971b, pp. 91-92.

[278] In addition to Ea 756, *sa-ke-re-u* also appears on Ea 56, 304 and 776. The name also appears on Jn 431.17 where it is listed among the Potnian bronzesmiths. The fact that *sa-ke-re-u* appears in a religious context on both Ea 756 and Jn 431 encourages Nakassis (*The Individual and the Mycenaean State: Agency and Prosopography in the Linear B Texts from Pylos*, Ph.D. Dissertation, University of Texas at Austin 2006, pp. 200-201) to see them as the same person. Nonetheless, even if the two are the same person, the Potnian bronzesmith of Jn 431 is located at *a-pe-ke-e*, which means that he is not linked with *Pa-ki-ja-ne*.

[279] Perhaps he would belong to the ἔσχαρα of Dionysus that Melena has recently proposed as being located in the land recorded in the Ea tablets ("Mycenaean Religious Texts: The Significance of New Joins and Readings," Talk Presented at the University of Texas at Austin, October 1999).

[280] See Palaima 1989, pp. 104-108 and 114, for a discussion of *we-da-ne-u* and his religious and secular associations. In the next chapter I will discuss more fully the implications of these men's appearance on the Cn tablets and their status as "collectors."

[281] Again, see the notes on Eb 159 in *PoN IV* and *Dic. Mic.* I, *s.v. i-je-ro[*.

[282] The religious nature of this title will be discussed below.

[283] Deger-Jalkotzy 1983, p. 104.

[284] *Dic. Mic. s.v. ne-qe-u*. There are two other places where the name *ne-qe-u* appears. The one who appears on Aq 64.15 described with the patronymic *e-te-wo-ke-re-wi-jo*, is thought to be the same person as the one who appears on Ep 613 and Qa 1298. The second *ne-qe-u* appears on Jn 725.14 and he is thought to most likely be a different person.

]*pa-ke-u* for σφαγεύς, a slayer or sacrificer. But other persons mentioned on the tablets, such as *ne-qe-u e-da-e-u,* were not so clearly related to the religious sector. Melena though has proposed that the syllabogram within the ideogram **189* probably represents the syllable *ke*, which he interprets as the first initial of *geras* or γέρας, an honorary gift that was often given to priests and priestesses.[285] Because of the shape of **189*, he thinks these gifts were probably the hides of sacrificed animals. Thus, *ne-qe-u e-da-e-u* on Qa 1298 was receiving a *geras*, and can therefore be considered to have held a religious position.

Ep 613.4: *te-re-]ta su-ko po-ro-du[-ma*, unspecified land type, but probably *ka-ma*: GRA 10: The *po-ro-du[-ma* of Ep 613 is probably the same title as the *po-ro-du-ma-te* of Fn 50.7 (where he receives a ration of HORD) and the *po-ru-da-ma-te* of An 39 *v.* 1 (which records a group of four of these officials). The title itself seems to be composed of two elements. The second element must be *du-ma*, which most likely has a meaning of "supervisor."[286] The *du-ma-te* recorded on Jn 829.1 were placed between the *ko-re-te-re* and the *po-ro-ko-re-te-re*, so it is thought that the *du-ma-te* must have held a position within the districts that was on a par with the *ko-re-te*.[287] The first element, *po-ro-* has been thought to represent either πολλο- (as a variant of the *po-ru-*, πολυ-, which we see on An 39), which gives a meaning of an official who supervised many things, or προ-, as in *po-ro-ko-re-te-re*, which would make him a vice-superintendent. The third possibility is to take *po-ro* as σπόρο(ς), which would make the *po-ro-du-ma* a "supervisor of grain."[288] Lindgren favors the last of these choices because the tablets that *po-ro-du-ma-te* appears on, Fn 50 and An 39, also record an official called *me-ri-du-ma-te* (Fn 50.5 and An 39.2; *me-ri-da-ma-te* on An 39.8), which is most likely translated as a "supervisor of honey."[289]

The religious connection for *po-ro-du-ma-te* derives from a theory proposed by Olivier that several tablets (Fn 50 and An 39 among them) contained a list of religious functionaries that was repeated in part or in whole in nearly the same order on each tablet.[290] These two titles, *po-ro-du-ma-te* and *me-ri-du-ma-te*, are part of that list. Olivier's idea that there was a standard list of religious personnel that was repeated several times was first inspired by his tracing the tablet associations of one functionary, the *di-pte-ra-po-ro*, or *διφθεραφόρος, "skin-bearer," whom Olivier thought probably wore his skin as the insignia of his religious position.[291] Olivier classified the *di-pte-ra-po-ro* as religious based on his appearance on Un 219.6, a tablet which records several deities and religious personnel.[292] Then he noticed that the *di-pte-ra-po-ro* also appeared on Fn 50.6, which suggested to him that the rest of the functionaries on Fn 50 might also be religious. Tracking the appearances of the names of the functionaries on Fn 50 led Olivier to realize that several of them also appeared on An 39 and several other An tablets (An 207, 424, 427 and 594). A few of the titles on the list lend themselves to religious interpretations. For instance, *pu-ka-wo*, *πυρκάϝοι, "persons in charge of the fire" can be taken as "guardians of the sacred fire" and, as we will discuss in a moment, *mi-ka-ta* or "mixer" can be taken as "a mixer of religious offerings."[293] This contributed to Olivier's conclusion that all of the functionaries on the list were workers attached to a religious sanctuary. To return to *po-ro-du-ma*, Olivier happens to prefer the proposal that the *po-ro-du-ma* was a vice-*du-ma*, thinking that he could perhaps be an assistant supervisor of the sanctuary.[294]

If the religious connection for *su-ko* is accepted, since he is recorded as a *te-re-ta* on Ep 613.4, he may also be counted among the prominent men of *Pa-ki-ja-ne* who were involved in both the secular and the religious realms. Of course it is possible that the title *po-ro-du-ma* was used in both secular and religious contexts, and that this *po-ro-du-ma* could have been a secular official. It should be noted though that one more definitely, and possibly two more of the titles found within Olivier's list are found on the same tablet as *su-ko* among the *ka-ma* holders: the *a-si-to-po-qo* of Ep 613.6 and the *mi-ka-ta* of Ep 613.13 (both of whom I will discuss below), which might lend credence to the idea that *su-ko* was also affiliated with the religious sphere.

Ep 613.6: *a_3-ke-re-u a-si-to-po-qo* with a *ka-ma*: GRA 1: There are several *a-to-po-qo*, or bakers (*ἀρτοποκ^{w}ος > *ἀρτοκ^{w}οπος (with metathesis) > ἀρτοκόπος) who show up on Pylian tablets Fn 50.7, An 427.3 and An

[285] J. Melena, "Mycenaean Religious Texts: The Significance of New Joins and Readings," Talk presented at the University of Texas at Austin, October 1999.

[286] *Dic. Mic.* I, p. 195.

[287] Lindgren 1973, p. 41.

[288] *Dic. Mic.* II, p. 145-146.

[289] Lindgren 1973, p. 96. *Dic. Mic.* I, pp. 439-440. J.-P. Olivier, *A propos d'une "liste" de desservants de sanctuaire dans les documents en linéaire B de Pylos*, Brussels 1960, p. 139.

[290] Olivier 1960, *passim*. I was very pleased to find that recently Killen ("Conscription and Corvée at Mycenaean Pylos," in *Fiscality in Mycenaean and Near Eastern Economies*, M. Perna, ed., Napoli 2006, pp. 73-87; see p. 79) has written in support of Olivier's theory concerning a list of temple servants: "Many of the workers on these records have been identified by J.-P. Olivier as 'desservants des sanctuaire': persons with duties concerned with religious ceremonial. Though not all scholars have accepted his conclusions, which inevitably rely in part on purely 'etymological' interpretations of occupational terms, they are I believe likely to be correct, and are supported by evidence elsewhere in the archives, some of which only became available since Olivier wrote." Also see Killen 2001a.

[291] J.-P. Olivier, "Étude d'un nom de métier mycénien: *di-pte-ra-po-ro*," *Antiquité Classique* 28 (1959) 165-185. Olivier 1960, p. 123. Olivier cites the figures on the Haghia Triada sarcophagus who wear skins as one example of such religious dress. See *Dic. Mic.* I for various other interpretations of this word.

[292] It should be pointed out that Un 219 also has the *a-ke-ti-ri-ja-i* on line 4, the female workers in the textile industry, and secular officials such as the *ra-wa-ke-ta*. Hence it is not a given that everyone on Un 219 should be classified as religious, per se.

[293] Olivier 1960, see p. 34 for *pu-ka-wo* and 47-56 for *mi-ka-ta*. Another example of one of these religious officials found on Un 219 (line 5) is *da-ko-ro-i* (Un 219.5), in which we can readily see the Classical word ζακόρος, which originally meant "the one who sweeps the floor of the temple," but came to mean "a servant of the temple." Hence the Mycenaean *do-ko-ro-i* could also be considered to have been "temple servants" (Olivier 1960, pp. 100-105).

[294] Olivier 1960, p. 47.

39.11 and who are part of Olivier's list.[295] Olivier proposes that the *a-si-to-po-qo* found here on Ep 613.6 (Eb 177.1) may have been a mistake for *a-to-po-qo*. Perhaps, Olivier suggests, the scribe was thinking of *si-to*, which evokes the work of the baker, when he made this mistake. R. Palmer agrees with the equation of *a-si-to-po-qo* with *a-to-po-qo* saying that "the word cannot be interpreted in its present form" and that he "has the same status as the *a-to-po-qo*."[296] Lindgren has proposed that the *a-si-to-po-qo* of Ep 613 could be identified with the one on Fn 50, who may also have been associated with *Pa-ki-ja-ne*.[297] Thus the *a-si-to-po-qo* may also be counted as religiously affiliated.

Ep 613.13: *ko-tu-ro₂ mi-]ka-ta pa-de-we-u*, a *ka-ma-e-u*: GRA T 5 (also holds *ke-ke-me-na* land on Ep 301.13/Eb 499.A[298]): The title *mi-ka-ta*, as was mentioned above, is one of those included by Olivier in his list of religious functionaries.[299] *Mi-ka-ta* is actually one of only two (*me-ri-du-ma-te* is the other) of Olivier's eight titles that appear on all of his major lists: Fn 50.5, An 594.2, and An 39.3 and .10 (restored from *]ta*). This word is easily associated with the religious sphere since it etymologizes as *μίκτας and would have a meaning of "mixer" (from μίγνυμι). Lejeune has proposed that the title "mixer" could refer to "those who mix and prepare the offerings (wine, oil, honey, etc.)."[300]

This *mi-ka-ta ko-tu-ro₂*, like the *i-je-ro*[*-wo-ko/te-re-ta qe/pe-re-qo-ta* on Ep 613.10, is also designated as a *pa-de-we-u* on Ep 613.13. The scribe of the Eb tablets uses an alternate form of the word, *pa-da-je-u*, both on the preliminary record for *qe/pe-re-qo-ta* (Eb 159.A) and on the one he wrote for *mi-ka-ta ko-tu-ro₂* (Eb 839.A). This word is generally taken as a title, which possibly also had religious associations.[301] *Pa-de-we* appears on Un 219.2, .2 among various deities and officials who are all receiving disbursements of commodities that are most likely aromatic spices. *Pa-de-we* is thought by some to be the name of a deity: *Πανδϝει, or the title of a priest of that god: *Πάνδης.[302] The title *pa-de-we-u/pa-da-je-u* seems to have been derived from the deity's name and may indicate that he was somehow in the service of that deity.[303]

Ep 704.1: *o-pe-to-re-u qe-ja-me-no* with a *ke-ke-me-na ko-to-na*: GRA 2 T 5: *O-pe-to-re-u qe-ja-me-no* is rather difficult to interpret. Instead of *o-pe-to-re-u*, which we see on Ep 704.1, other scribes wrote the word as *o-pe-te-re-u* on Eb 294.1 and Ea 805, and the interpretations of the word are generally based on the *o-pe-te-re-u* form since the *o-pe-to-re-u* is considered to be either a variant or a misspelling of the word.[304] Thus one interpretation of the word is that it should be taken as ὀφελτρεύς from ὀφελτρεύω to sweep, which would mean that this person was a "sweeper" of some sort.[305] Olivier compares this "sweeper" with one that is found as a member of his list, *da-ko-ro*.[306] He sees in this *da-ko-ro* the ζάκορος of historical Greek, which was the title of a temple servant. Olivier says that little by little temple servants such as this one abandoned their original functions in the shrine (the *da-ko-ro*'s would have been sweeping, keeping the shrine clean) to become a sort of religious functionary, and that in Mycenaean times this development had already occurred.[307] Hence it is possible that the "sweeper" ὀφελτρεύς had undergone a development similar to that of *da-ko-ro*. Alternatively, *o-pe-te-re-u* could simply be taken as a person's name, Ὀπτηρεύς (or Ὀφελτρεύς) which might make sense since, as Duhoux points out, it is the first word of the record and usually the first word in the Ep/Eb series is the landholder's name.[308] The word *qe-ja-me-no* then might give us the key to the associations this person had, but the meaning of *qe-ja-me-no* is also debated. Duhoux proposes that it specifies the conditions under which the land is held *τειάμενος, from τίνω, to pay, so we get "s'étant fait payer" or, more exactly "s'étant fait donner une compensation."[309] In other words, *o-pe-te-re-u* would be holding the land as a compensation.[310] A religious sense has been proposed for the word by Ruijgh. He sees *qe-ja-me-no* as *κ^wεγάμενος whose root *κ^wεγα- corresponds to the zero grade *κ^wι- which survives in τίω, to esteem, honor.[311] *Qe-ja-me-no* could be taken in either an active sense meaning "celebrant" or a passive sense meaning of "reverend, honored."[312] If this is accepted then *o-pe-te-re-u* here may be a priest himself.[313] His position within the Ep series on Ep 704.1

[295] Olivier 1960, pp. 72-73.
[296] R. Palmer 1992, p. 487.
[297] Lindgren 1973, pp. 25-26.
[298] According to the latest tablet joins, Eb 499 is the tablet that corresponds to Ep 301.13. This replaced Eb 892 which was used in Aura Jorro (*s.v. ko-tu-ro₂, Dic. Mic.* I, p. 393).
[299] Olivier 1960, pp. 47-56.
[300] Lejeune, *Mem.* I, p. 194: "celui qui mélange et prépare les offrandes liquides (vin huile, miel, etc.).
[301] See *Dic. Mic.* II, *s.v. pa-da-je-u* and *pa-de-we-u*. The genitive form of the word (*pa-da-je-wo*) appears on Eo 444.1, and the dative (*pa-da-je-we*) appears on Eb 1347.1 (which involves a *do-e-ro* of *ko-tu-ro₂* but which has no extant corresponding tablet) and Eo 444.2, 3, 4, 5, which deals with the *te-re-ta qe/pe-re-qo-ta*.
[302] Ruijgh 1967, p. 88, n. 73.
[303] Ruijgh1967, pp. 230-231. Lindgren 1973, pp. 110-111, considers all the different possible interpretations of the word and concludes "It thus seems reasonable to suppose that *Pereqota* was somehow attached to a cult of this divinity at *Puro/Pakijana*..."

[304] *Docs²*, p. 422. M. Lejeune, "Sur les Signes Notant des Syllabes a Groupe Consonantique Initial," in *Mémoires de Philologie Mycénienne* I, CNRS 1958a, pp. 257-282; see p. 265, n. 44.
[305] *Docs²*, p. 253.
[306] Olivier 1960, p. 104, n. 2. See pp. 100-105 for his full discussion of *da-ko-ro*, which is found on An 207.8, An 427.1, An 424.3 and Un 219.5.
[307] Olivier 1960, pp. 102-103.
[308] Duhoux 1976, p. 60.
[309] Duhoux 1976, p. 60-61.
[310] Killen (1992, pp. 379-380) has proposed that this *o-pe-te/to-re-u* may be the same as that on Ea 805, where he holds his land *e-ne-ka a-no-qa-si-ja*, which Killen takes (following the suggestion of Mühlestein) as "because of manslaughter" or "by way of compensation for manslaughter." If these two are the same person, then it may be that *qe-ja-me-no* of Ep 704.1 should be translated as either "taking compensation" (with a middle force) or as "being compensated" (with a passive force), with the meaning that he held this plot of land as compensation for manslaughter as well.
[311] Please see Ruijgh 1967, p. 376 for his full grammatical explanation.
[312] Ruijgh 1967, p. 376.
[313] See *Dic. Mic.* II, p. 193 for other possible translations of *qe-ja-me-no*.

would also recommend his being affiliated with the religious sector.

After discussing each of these "uncertain" cases on an individual basis, it seems that the arguments for the religious status of many of these persons are fairly strong, although not always conclusive. I feel certain that *a-pi-me-de*, his three *do-e-ro* (GRA 5 T 7), and *ne-qe-u e-da-e-u* (GRA 10 T 1) should be counted among the religious landholders, and relatively sure that the rest of the members of the "uncertain" list (including *su-ko* the *te-re-ta/po-ro-du-ma* with GRA 10, the *a-si-to-po-qo* with GRA 1, the *mi-ka-ta* with T 5, and *o-pe-to/te-re-u qe-ja-me-no* with GRA 2 T 5) could be included. It is not my point here to demonstrate conclusively that all of these "uncertain" landholders are definitely associated with the religious sector, but rather to show the possibility that they were, and thereby to strengthen the point that the religious sector had a significant presence in the land tenure system of *Pa-ki-ja-ne*.[314] If we do include all these lands in the total of the religious landholdings the grand total for the Ep series of religiously affiliated land comes to GRA 45 T 2 V 4, which far exceeds the amount of land held by the *te-re-ta* that is extant on the En tablets of 29 GRA, and even comes in a bit above the amount recorded as their total on Ed 411. Finally, the total land held by religious landholders in both series is GRA 53 T 5 V 1, which again surpasses the total secular landholdings, which amount to GRA 46 T 4 V 2.

In this vein it is also interesting to note that several of the religious landholders are individually on a par with the *te-re-ta* in the size of their landholdings. For example, on Ep 539.13 the priest *we-te-re-u* has GRA 2 T 3, and the *e-to-ni-jo* land that *e-ri-ta* claims as belonging to the deity on Ep 704, is GRA 3 T 9. The following chart provides a list of religious landholders with GRA 1 or more (I have left those who were classified as "uncertain" in that category at the bottom of the list for ease of comparison with the previous chart).

Chart 4.2: Religious Landholders with GRA 1 or More:

Ep 539.13: *we-te-re-u i-je-re-u* with an *o-na-to*: GRA 2 T 3.
Ep 613.7: *i-je-ro-wo-ko*, a *ka-ma-e-u*: GRA 1.
Ep 613.9: *te-o-jo [do-e-]ro* with a *[ka-]ma*: GRA 1 T 3.
Ep 613.10: *pe-]/*qe*-re-qo-ta pa-de-we-u* [Eb 159: *i-je-ro*] with a *ka-ma*: GRA 1.
En 659.1: *pe/qe-re-qo-ta* with a *ko-to-na*: GRA 2 T 3 (same person as above).
Ep 704.4: *ki-ri-te-wi-ja* with an *o-na-to*: GRA 1 T 9.
Ep 704.5-6: *e-ri-ta i-je-re-ja* [Eb 339: *pa-ki-ja-na*] with *e-to-ni-jo*: GRA 3 T 9.

(Previously)"Uncertain" Landholders with GRA 1 or More:
Ep 539.14: *a-pi[-me-]de* with an *e-to-ni-jo*: GRA 4 T 6.
Ep 613.1: *ne-qe-e e-da-e-u* with a *ka-ma*: GRA 10 T 1.
Ep 613.4: *te-re-]ta su-ko po-ro-du-ma*, unspecified land type: GRA 10.
Ep 613.6: *a_3-ke-re-u a-si-to-po-qo* with a *ka-ma*: GRA 1.
Ep 704.1: *o-pe-to-re-u qe-ja-me-no* with a *ke-ke-me-na ko-to-na*: GRA 2 T 5.

The landholdings of the *te-re-ta* range for the most part between 1 and 3 GRA. Six *te-re-ta* have between 1 and 2 GRA, five have between 2 and 3 GRA, and one has GRA 3 T 2. There is one *te-re-ta* who far surpasses these with 8 GRA, but, if we include *ne-qe-u e-da-e-u* in the list of religious landholders, his holding of 10 GRA is comparible with the 8 GRA.

Another point of comparison between the religious landholders and the *te-re-ta* is the fact that several of the higher status religious landholders, like the *te-re-ta,* hold more than one plot of land. In three of these cases, the landholdings include both *ke-ke-me-na* and *ki-ti-me-na* land, as was noted to have been the case for the secular landholders.

The priestess of *Pa-ki-ja-ne* (*i-je-re-ja pa-ki-ja-na*) *e-ri-ta* holds three plots of land (one under dispute) on Ep 704.3, Ep 704.5-6, and En 609.18/Eo 224.8 (this last she leases from a *te-re-ta* named *a-ma-ru-ta*).[315] The total then of the *i-je-re-ja's* land is GRA 4 T 6, quite a large amount. The priest *we-te-re-u* holds a plot of *ke-ke-me-na* land on Ep 539.13 (which may itself have actually been made up of two distinct holdings since the Ep record appears to be a combination of two Eb tablets: Eb 472, GRA 1 T 3 and Eb 477, GRA 1, which gives the total of his holding on Ep 539: GRA 2 T 3), and two plots of *ki-ti-me-na* land: En 74.16/Eo 247.7 and En 659.4/Eo 444.3. The total of *we-te-re-u's* land is therefore GRA 2 T 9. *Qe/pe-re-qo-ta*, whom we have seen was designated as a *i-je-ro[-wo-ko* on Eb 159.A (the tablet that corresponds to Ep 613.10) holds not only his *ka-ma* of GRA 1,[316] but also in the En series was counted among the *te-re-ta* and so is seen to hold GRA 2 T 3 on En 659.1/Eo 441.1. This would bring his total to GRA 3 T 3 (and if we were to consider the

[314] I will not therefore go back and add in *ko-tu-ro$_2$'s ko-to-no-o-ko* holding on Ep 301.13 of T 1 (which was originally counted as secular land) into the total of religious land.

[315] See Lindgren pp. 37, 56, 72, 81; Adrados 1956, p. 365 and *idem* 1961, p. 56.

[316] Deger-Jalkotzy (1983, p. 98) proposed that *qe/pe-re-qo-ta* may have obtained this piece "by lot" since *ra-ke*, which could be λάχε from λαγχάνω was included in the formula.

Chart 4.3: Highly Placed Religious Personnel with More than One Landholding

Name	*ke-ke-me-na*	*ki-ti-me-na*	Total
e-ri-ta	Ep 704. 3, 5-6 (GRA 4 T 3)	En 609.18 (T 3)	GRA 4 T 6
we-te-re-u	Ep 539.13 (GRA 2 T 3)	En 74.16 and 659.4 (T 6)	GRA 2 T 9
qe/pe-re-qo-ta	Ep 613.10 (GRA 1)	En 659.1 (GRA 2 T 3)	GRA 3 T 3
ko-tu-ro2	Ep 613.13 (T 5) and Ep 301.13 (T 1)		T6

holdings of his *o-na-te-re* on En 659.3-6/Eo 444.2-6[317] as land that he benefited from, the total would be GRA 4 T 4 V 3). As noted above, *ko-tu-ro2 mi-ka-ta* also has two landholdings. In addition to his *ka-ma* land on Ep 613.13/Eb 839.A of T 5 he also holds *ke-ke-me-na* land as a *ko-to-no-o-ko* on Ep 301.13/Eb 499.A[318] of T 1, and therefore holds T 6 all together.

The holding of multiple plots also occurs among the servants of the deity. In fact, nine *te-o-jo do-e-ro* and *do-e-ra* have more than one landholding. These personnel are listed in Chart 4.4[319]

Chart 4.4: *Te-o-jo Do-e-ro/a* with More than One Landholding

Name	*ke-ke-me-na*	*ki-ti-me-na*	Total
e-ko-to	Ep 705.8 (T 2)	En 74.7 (V 3)	T 5
	Ep 212.3 (T 1 V 3)	En 74.17 (T 1)	
e-sa-ro	Ep 705.4 (V 2)	En 609.14 (V 3)	V 5
*e-*65-to*		En 74.9 (V 1)	T 2 V 1
		En 609.7 (T 2)	
ra-su-ro	Ep 212.10 (T 2)	En 659.3 (T 1)	T 3
ta-ra₂-to		En 74.15 (T 1)[320]	T 5 V 4
		En 659.6, 10, 13 (T 4 V 4)	
e-pa-sa-na-ti	Ep 212.5 (T 3)	En 74.13 (T 2)[321]	T 5
ko-ri-si-ja	Ep 212.4 (GRA 1)	En 74.18 (T 5)	GRA 2
		En 74.24 (T 5)	
mi-ra	Ep 613.16 (T 1)	En 74.4 (T 1)	T 2
po-so-re-ja	Ep 613.12 (T 1 V 3)[322]	En 609.17 (T 1 V 3)	T 3 +?[323]
	Ep 539.4 and .5 (not extant)		

[317] You may note that En 659 has four records of people who hold land from *qe/pe-re-qo-ta* while Eo 444 has five such records. This can be explained by a note in *PoN IV* under Eo 444.6 that *tu-ri-ja-ti* of Eo 444.4 (En 659.5) may also be restored on line 6, in which case the T 9 that *tu-ri-ja-ti* holds on En 659.5 may be made up of two records in the Eo series.

[318] According to the latest tablet joins in *PoN IV*, Eb 499 is the tablet that corresponds to Ep 301.13. This replaced Eb 892 which was listed in Aura Jorro (*Dic. Mic.* I, p. 393).

[319] This list was inspired by a list compiled by Lejeune (1971a, pp. 65-81). On pp. 73-74 Lejeune gives all the persons listed as a *do-e-ro* or *do-e-ra* and the tablets they appear on.

[320] Written *ta-ra-to* on Eo 247.6. A *ta-ra-to* also appears on An 192.10, but the *communis opinio* seems to be that it must be a different person from the *te-o-jo do-e-ro* (*Dic. Mic.* II, *s.v. ta-ra-to*).

[321] The form that we find on Eo 247.4 and Eb 1350A is *i-pa-sa-na-ti.*

[322] *Po-so-re-ja's* land is *pa-ro pa-ra-ko*, who holds a *ka-ma* on Ep 613.11, right above *po-so-re-ja*.

[323] Unfortunately no figures are preserved for *po-so-re-ja* on either of her entries on Ep 539. It would have been interesting to know what her holding on line 5 was since it seems to have involved *ka-ma* land (*po-so-re-ja , te[-o-jo]do-e-ra , o-na-to , e-ke , pa-ro[ ] , ka-ma-e-we , wo-ze-te , to-so , pe-mo*[]), which, as we have seen, can be relatively quite substantial. Of course, this does not necessarily mean that an *o-na-to* of such land, such as *po-so-re-ja* holds, would have also been larger than other *o-na-ta*, but it is worth considering.

Of course, most of these *te-o-jo do-e-ro/a* end up with an aggregate amount of land that is more than what is commonly held by other *te-o-jo do-e-ro/a* who have only one landholding. It is worth looking in detail at the *te-o-jo do-e-ro/a*'s landholdings. Of the 60 total plots of land held by *te-o-jo do-e-ro/a* (counting the multiple landholdings held by one *te-o-jo do-e-ro/a* individually), we have an extant amount of GRA for 55 of them. 47 of those 55, or 85%, are T 2 V 4 or less (2 are T 2 V 4, 12 are T 2, 22 are between T 1 and T 2, and 11 have less than T 1). Thus only eight of the single plots are more than T 2 V 4.

Chart 4.5: *Te-o-jo Do-e-ro/a* with Single Landholdings of T 3 or More:

Name	Tablets	Landholding
**e-pa-sa-na-ti*	Ep 212.5	T 3
te-se-u	En 74.5	T 4
**ko-ri-si-ja*	En 74.18	T 5
**ko-ri-si-ja*	En 74.24	T 5
re-ka	Ep 212.1	T 6
tu-ri-ja-ti	En 659.5	T 9
**ko-ri-si-ja*	Ep 212.4	GRA 1
e-u-]ru-wo-ta	Ep 613.9[324]	GRA 1 T 3

Of these eight, four (those marked with an *asterix*) are held by one of the *te-o-jo do-e-ro/a* that also has more than one landholding (and three of those are held by the same person, *ko-ri-si-ja*).[325] As we can see in Chart 4.4, six of the nine multiple holdings of the *te-o-jo do-e-ro/a* are more than T 3, and a couple are significantly more so. The landholdings of *ta-ra₂-to* for instance amount to T 6 V 4, and those of *ko-ri-si-ja* come to exactly GRA 2. This amount actually brings *ko-ri-si-ja* into the same range as the *te-re-ta* and the larger religious landholders. It seems possible that in these numbers we may read a hierarchy of the *te-o-jo do-e-ro* and *do-e-ra*. As Chadwick mentions, these *te-o-jo do-e-ro/a* are not simply "slaves, since they hold plots of land; they must rather be temple servants or ἱερόδουλοι, a relatively honorific position."[326] It seems possible that the more respected *te-o-jo do-e-ro/a* (or deserving in some way that is now lost to us) had the resources to acquire more significant landholdings from which they presumably acquired a greater benefit than their counterparts. As we

[324] A man named *e-u-ru-wo-ta* also appears on Jn 310.4, but it seems that the two are likely to be different people (*s.v. Dic. Mic.* I)

[325] It is possible that *tu-ri-ja-ti* should also be included in this group of those who hold multiple plots since, as explained above (n. 317), *tu-ri-ja-ti*'s holding of T 9 may be found on two separate lines of Eo 444 (lines 4 and 6). This possibility rests on a very tentative restoration though so I have not included her in Chart 4.4.

[326] *Docs*², p. 445.

can see in Charts 4.4 and 4.5, larger than normal aggregate landholdings could be acquired either through multiple landholdings or landholdings that were large in themselves, or both.

Thus we can see that in terms of the size of individual holdings and in terms of the total amount of land the religious sector held altogether, the religious personnel in *Pa-ki-ja-ne* had a significant interest in the area, one that was on a par with the *te-re-ta* and the rest of the secular landholders. But there is a significant difference between the land held by the *te-re-ta* and that held by the religious personnel, which is that the *te-re-ta* seem to have more control over their land in that they had the right to lease it out if they chose to, whereas all of the land held by the religious personnel (except for the *e-to-ni-jo* land) was leased from others. This brings up two different questions. The first is, didn't the sanctuary have land of its own that it could support its people with? And the second, which I will discuss first, is, who exactly did the leasing? In other words, did each of the religious functionaries lease the land for themselves on an individual basis, or did some agent lease the land and then bestow parcels of it on the individuals? Several possibilities present themselves. Adrados early on proposed that the parcels of land were given to the sanctuary by the *damos* as offerings.[327] This might seem attractive since we have concluded that the land was owned by the *damos*, but the dispute with *e-ri-ta* seems to argue against Adrados' idea, since it seems apparent that the *damos* was expecting a return from these leased lands. It seems unlikely therefore that the *damos* would have given over so much land free of charge, so to speak. It could also be proposed that the *wanax* had bestowed the land on the sanctuary, but if we are correct in our understanding that all the land on the Ep and probably also on the En series was owned by the *damos*, then it seems unlikely that the palace would have been able to interfere to such an extent in the *damos*' sphere as to confer the large amount of land that we see on the Ep and En series upon the religious sector. Besides, the manner in which the records were written seems to speak against the idea that they had been especially conferred by the palace. The *e-to-ni-jo* land might have been bestowed upon *e-ri-ta* (and *a-pi-me-de*) by the *wanax*, but none of the other lands seem to carry any indication that they were any different from the rest of the *o-na-ta* (and *ka-ma*) leased from the *damos* and the *te-re-ta*.

It seems most likely then that it was the religious sphere that acquired the land, but it is not clear exactly who did the acquiring. Did the sanctuary (meaning, the sanctuary's representatives) lease the *damos* land and then parcel it out to its dependents as it saw fit, or did the religious personnel act independently in acquiring the leases of land from the *damos* as individuals? It is certainly possible to imagine a scenario in which all the *te-o-jo do-e-ro*/*a* had been granted the land by the sanctuary for their support. Indeed, if the *damos* did collectively own the land, it might seem anachronistic to presume that individual owners could operate on this scale. If this were the case, then the affiliation with the sanctuary was taken for granted by the scribe. But it does seem that the *te-re-ta* were able to manage their own landholdings, which opens the door for others to act independently as well. And in contrast with the religious-collector tablets that we will examine in detail in the next chapter, individuals' names are associated with each landholding rather than the name of the deity they were affiliated with (although this may have been simply because it was the same deity in each case and could be assumed by the scribe). This difference speaks for the idea that it was the individuals who managed the leasing (and the proceeds) of the land. The only piece of land that we may safely say was held by the sanctuary is the *e-to-ni-jo* land that *e-ri-ta* claimed on behalf of the god. Since she specifies that she was holding it for the deity, we may presume that it was in the hands of the sanctuary that served that deity. But the other entries have no such indication that the sanctuary was involved in the management of the lands.

There is also some indication that the lower ranked personnel were in some way indebted to those above them for their land. For instance, one might wonder if it is a coincidence that *e-ra-ta-ra* the *i-je-re-ja do-e-ra pa-ki-ja-na* holds land from the same *te-re-ta* as the *i-je-re-ja* herself (En 609.16 and 18). Could it be that the priestess granted land under her control to her *do-e-ro* and *do-e-ra*? There is one fairly sure instance of this. On Ep 704.2 we see the *te-o-jo do-e-ra* called *u-wa-mi-ja* holding an *o-na-to* that is said to be a *i-je-re-ja ke-ra*, ἱερείας γέρας, or a gift of honor from the priestess. Lejeune says that without a doubt this land was taken from *e-ri-ta*'s land.[328] Ruijgh also wonders if this *ke-ra* was a "retrocession" from *e-ri-ta*'s *e-to-ni-jo*.[329] This formula is found only once, but it does indicate that the higher ranked religious functionaries did have some control, or at least could successfully influence the way in which the land was distributed, even if it was leased from the *damos*.

Thus perhaps there were a variety of agents here. The elite of the religious personnel seem to have been able to acquire leases of land on their own, and this may have been the case for some of the *te-o-jo do-e-ro*/*a* as well (although it cannot be excluded that the sanctuary was the agent in some cases). If it was the individual members of the religious hierarchy who acquired the land, independent of the sanctuary, what then, if anything, did the sanctuary itself stand to gain from such a situation? At the least, it must have been a benefit that its constituents were provided for and therefore not a burden

327 Adrados 1961, pp. 53-116. Also see Adrados 1956, pp. 353-416.

328 Lejeune 1971, p. 78

329 Ruijgh 1987, p. 314, n. 67.

Chart 4.6: *Ka-ma* Holders of Ep 613 and their Affiliations:

Line, Name and Title	Pylian Tablet Associations	Status
1. *ne-qe-wo e-da-e-wo*	Qa 1298, Aq 64.15[333]	Probably relig.
4. *te-re-]ta su-ko po-ro-du[-ma*	Fn 50.7, An 39 *v*. 1	Possibly relig.
6. *a_3-ke-re-u a-si-to-po-qo*	Fn 50.7, An 39.11, 427.3[334]	Possibly relig.
7. *a-•-ke-re-u i-je-ro-wo-ko*	None	Religious
8. *sa-sa-]wo*	None	Secular
9. *e-u-]ru-wo-ta te-o-jo do-e-ro*	None[335]	Religious
10. *qe/pe-]re-qo-ta pa-de-we-u*	Eb 159.A: *i-je-ro[-wo-ko*	Religious
11. *pa-]ra-ko*	Ep 301.12; Eo 224.2, 3	Secular
13. *ko-tu-ro_2 mi-]ka-ta*[336]	Fn 50.5, Fn 970.2 An 594.2; An 39.3,10; An 128.1,2[337]	Possibly relig.

(or as much of a burden as they otherwise would have been) on the sanctuary's resources. It is also possible that the religious personnel were expected to pay taxes not only to the palace but also to the sanctuary. In most cases the *te-o-jo do-e-ro/a* may have had only enough to sustain themselves (and their families?), but the priests and priestesses may have had a sufficient amount of surplus that the expectation that a percentage should be given to the sanctuary might not have been unreasonable. And lastly, we can say that the prestige and power that the land represents, even if it was held individually by the higher members of the religious personnel such as *a-pi-me-de*, *we-te-re-u*, *e-ri-ta* and *ka-pa-ti-ja*, would have reflected well upon the sanctuary and enhanced its prestige within the community as well.

Now, to return to the first question raised above, it is surprising that the sanctuary seems to have had no land recorded on the tablets that was primarily its own. Of course, some have proposed that the *e-to-ni-jo* land was primarily religious. Indeed, I do think the *e-to-ni-jo* land of *e-ri-ta* (and *a-pi-me-de*?) did belong to the sanctuary, but we concluded that it was not inherently religious land, but rather a special grant given to the sanctuary. And besides, even if we did consider the *e-to-ni-jo* land as inherently religious, the three plots that we see on the tablets do not make up a very substantial amount of land. Another candidate that has been suggested as constituting land belonging to the sanctuary is *ka-ma* land. Adrados, for instance, thought that *ka-ma* land was given as a form of recompense to officials of a private cult. He based this theory on the association found on Un 718.11-11a between *ka-ma* land and the *wo-ro-ki-jo-ne-jo,* who were, he thought (along with several others[330]), related to the Attic ὀργεῶνες, "members of a religious association."[331] However, as we have seen, Killen thinks *wo-ro-ki-jo-ne-jo* is more likely to represent a possessive adjective derived from a man's name, so this association is no longer on firm ground.[332] In addition, while we have seen that many of the *ka-ma* holders had connections to the religious sector, this is not the case for all of them.

Chart 4.6 details the affiliations of the *ka-ma-e-we*.

Of the nine *ka-ma* holders, three are definitely religious: the *i-je-ro-wo-ko* named *a-•-ke-re-u* of line 7, the *te-o-jo do-e-ro* of line 9, and *qe/pe-]re-qo-ta pa-de-we-u i-je-ro[-wo-ko* of line 10. Four more may be associated with the religious sector: *ne-qe-wo e-da-e-wo* of line 1, *te-re-]ta su-ko po-ro-du*[*-ma* of line 4, *a_3-ke-re-u a-si-to-po-qo* of line 6, and *ko*[*-tu-ro_2 mi-*]*ka-ta pa-de-we-u* of line 13. Thus the majority of *ka-ma* landholders could be said to be affiliated with the religious sector. Nonetheless, there are still two *ka-ma* holders who do not have any relationship with the religious realm that we can determine. Those are *sa-sa-*]*wo* and *pa-*]*ra-ko* of lines 8 and 11, respectively.[338] Of course we could say that, on analogy with the other religious *ka-ma-e-we* on the text, that these too were probably related to the religious sector. But if we recall from our discussion concerning the arrangement of the Ep series, the tablet that appears right before this one, Ep 301, dealt predominantly with secular landholders, and it is only in the second paragraph of this tablet, Ep 613.14-20, that the entries of the religious personnel appear to start in earnest. Thus, it seems that this paragraph containing the *ka-ma* holders, Ep 613.1-13, could be made up of a mix of secular and religious landholders. Therefore, I think the safer route is to take the absence of a religious connection for *sa-sa-*

[330] *Dic. Mic.* II, *s.v. wo-ro-ki-jo-ne-jo*, n. 6.

[331] F.R. Adrados, "Les Institutions Religieuses Myceniennes," in *Acta Mycenaea* (*Minos* 11), 1972, pp. 170-203; see p. 196.

[332] Killen 1983, p. 83-84.

[333] There is a bronzesmith of the same name on Jn 725.14, but it is uncertain whether the *ne-qe-u* described as *e-da-e-u* on Qa 1298 and Ep 613.1 and the one on Aq 64.15 described as *e-te-wo-ke-re-we-i-jo* can be considered the same person as the bronzesmith (*Dic. Mic.* I, p. 470). Nakassis (2006, p. 202) says the identification is "possible" but does not argue that it should be classified as "probable" or" certain."

[334] These tablets contain *a-to-po-qo*, not *a-si-to-po-qo*. The possibility that the scribe mistakenly put in the "*si*" has been discussed above.

[335] There is a bronzesmith of the same name on Jn 310.4, but it is uncertain whether this *te-o-jo do-e-ro* and the bronzesmith can be considered the same person (*Dic. Mic.* I, p. 265). Here again, Nakassis (2006, p. 202) considers the identification to be "possible."

[336] Under his personal name this *mi-ka-ta*, *ko-tu-ro_2*, holds a *ke-ke-me-na ko-to-na* on Ep 301.13/Eb 892.A, and a slave holds land from him on Eb 1347.1. The same name appears on Cn 436.6 and Jn 431.2, but it is doubtful whether they are all the same person (*Dic. Mic.* II, p. 393.)

[337] On Fn 970.2 *mi-ka-ta* is restored from]*mi-ka*[, from]*ka-ta* on An 128.1, 2 and from *[ta* on An 39.10.

[338] As was discussed above, *pa-ra-ko* on Ep 613.11 and the *o-na-to* held from *pa-ra-ko* on line 12 were thought by Bennett (1956b, p. 117) to have constituted the misplaced record of the fourteenth *te-re-ta* who was not included in the En series by mistake.

]*wo* and *pa-*]*ra-ko* at face value and leave them in the secular sphere. Thus *ka-ma* land probably should not be associated with the religious sphere either.

But as we have seen, the sanctuary of *Pa-ki-ja-ne* played quite an important role in the life of the Pylians. It was also proposed that the sanctuary of *Pa-ki-ja-ne* had been in existence for quite some time, and that it had seen its influence grow over the years in conjunction with the palace and the *wanax* at Pylos. If the sanctuary had been there for a century or more, one would think that it would have had the opportunity to claim the land surrounding the sanctuary for itself.

Certainly this is what seems to have happened in the Near East, and considering that we know so much more about the sanctuary's involvement in land tenure within these societies, it might be helpful to take a look at how the sanctuaries there regarded and handled their land. Mesopotamian sources suggest that the vast landholdings that the sanctuaries held in historical times were gathered very early on in their history, and in fact, in pre-literate times. Postgate explains, "The pictographic tablets from Warka, which are the earliest written archive known, came from a temple precinct, and although they cannot be read, they demonstrably deal with agricultural affairs, so that the most we can say is that temples presumably had considerable land-holdings as early as 3000 B.C."[339] It seems that even during periods of extremely centralized secular rule, such as under the rule of Hammurabi of Babylon in 1750 B.C., while the palaces controlled extensive tracts of land, "the temples, however, seem to have continued to own sizable acreages."[340] Thus Robertson, in discussing the economic organization of Mesopotamian temples, points out that "throughout the history of ancient Mesopotamia, the harvests reaped from [the temples'] vast estates sustained a number of critical enterprises, and in so doing supported the laborers who cultivated the estates; the artisans who fashioned cultic paraphernalia and kept the temple buildings in good repair; and the attendants of the gods, for whose benefit the entire system existed."[341] So the sanctuaries were an important economic entity in ancient Mesopotamia, and the lands were used to support its many personnel. Besides the economic reasons, it was also important for the temples to have land for symbolic reasons. As Postgate says, even the smallest of temples must have held land since "the ownership of land was a sign of dignity, and as such could hardly be denied to the god (and his priest)."[342] This last comment brings to mind *e-ri-ta*'s emphatic claim that she was holding the land for the god. Of course the sanctuaries of the Mycenaeans were not built on the same scale as those in the ancient Near East, but it is possible, as we have seen, that they (or particularly we should say, the one at *Pa-ki-ja-ne*) had a large influence on the communities within which they were situated. It seems likely therefore, in a land where wealth and influence were probably measured in land (as it still was in Classical Greek times), that the sanctuary at *Pa-ki-ja-ne* also had its own lands.

But it has to be said that there is no sure evidence for such land on the tablets. Nonetheless, perhaps in this case the archaeological evidence is more of a help to us. As I mentioned in the Introduction, Halstead compared the wide range of cereal and pulse crops that are found at palatial and nonpalatial Late Bronze Age sites with the records for grain on the Linear B texts, and he found that the Linear B records fail to mention many of the crops that are found in the archaeological record. He has therefore proposed that, "textually attested palatial farming represents only a part of overall regional farming..."[343] In other words, there must have been large tracts of land that were not recorded on the Linear B tablets. Thus, it is possible that the sanctuary at *Pa-ki-ja-ne* did own lands but that they were simply not recorded by the palace.

A possible reason for their not being recorded was suggested to me by Killen's analysis of the tablets Nn 831 and Na 1357.[344] Na 1357 records the exemptions granted to three persons and the god Hermes. All the mortals from Na 1357 reappear on Nn 831 along with other persons, but the god is left off. Killen proposes that the reason Hermes does not reappear on Nn 831 while his three companions do, is because the god was granted a complete exemption from the payment of tax whereas the others were only granted partial exemptions. Of course *e-ri-ta*'s claim concerning her privileged land also comes to mind once again. It is often said that the palatial scribes did not record anything that was not of direct economic interest to them, and therefore I think it is possible that the sanctuary could have owned lands but that they were never recorded because they had been granted full exemptions from taxes, or more likely, because they had never been taxed at all. Lejeune has proposed that something similar was going on with the *damos* land; he said that much of the *damos* land might not have ever been recorded by the palatial scribes, but only that which had been disbursed and was taxed by the *wanax*.[345] Carlier also proposed that much of the *damos* lands would never be found in the palatial documents. He proposed this because all the land recorded on the tablets is leased out, but he thought that there must have been a substantial amount of *damos* land that was reserved for the use and support of the members of the *damos* on a collective basis.[346] This might also have been the case for the sanctuary at *Pa-ki-ja-ne*. If the sanctuary

[339] N. Postgate, "The Role of the Temple in the Mesopotamian Secular Community," in *Man, Settlement and Urbanism*, P.J. Ucko, R. Tringham and D.W. Dimbleby, eds., Duckworth and Co., 1972, pp. 811-825; see p. 816.
[340] J.F. Robertson, "The Social and Economic Organization of Ancient Mesopotamian Temples," in *Civilizations of the Ancient Near East*, Vol. 1, J. Sasson, ed., Charles Scribner's Sons, New York 1995, pp. 443-454; see p. 451.
[341] Robertson 1995, p. 445.
[342] Postgate 1972, p. 816.

[343] Halstead 1999, p. 38. See also Halstead 1992, p. 64.
[344] J. Killen, "*Ke-u-po-da e-sa-re-u* and the Exemptions on the Pylos Na Tablets," *Minos* 27-28 (1992-1993) 109-123.
[345] Lejeune 1972, pp. 137-154.
[346] Carlier 1987, p. 72.

had been in existence for decades, and if it had been established at a time before the *wanax* at Pylos had become as powerful as he appears to be in the tablets, then it would seem likely that the sanctuary could have been the owner of its own land for a long time before the Linear B tablets were written. These lands would never have been taxed by the palace, and therefore would never have been mentioned in the palatial records.

In sum, I think it is likely that the sanctuary at *Pa-ki-ja-ne* did hold land of its own, but even without taking that for granted, the Ep/Eb and En/Eo land tenure tablets demonstrate that the religious personnel at *Pa-ki-ja-ne* were major landholders in their district. It is not always clear who the agent was who did the leasing, but the fact that the lands were owned primarily by the *damos* shows that it was not the palace that was supplying the land to the religious functionaries. This speaks for the idea that the religious sphere was independent from the palace in how it conducted its affairs and in its financial transactions.

The Ep/Eb and En/Eo tablets also demonstrate that there was a large number of religious personnel at *Pa-ki-ja-ne* who had to be supported in some way. Other sanctuaries in the Late Bronze Age may also have had similar populations, although perhaps the numbers of associated *te-o-jo do-e-ro* and *do-e-ra* may not have been as great as those found at *Pa-ki-ja-ne*. Nonetheless, the priests and priestesses of any sanctuary would have to be supported, and the land tenure series demonstrates that a religious functionary's support was most likely not supplied exclusively by the palace. In the next chapter we will explore other situations in which it is clearer that it was the sanctuaries acting as corporate bodies who engaged in various economic pursuits with the aim, we can imagine, of supporting themselves and their personnel.

CHAPTER V

The Linear B Evidence for the Economic Involvement of the Religious Sector in Mycenaean Society

Introduction

In the previous chapter we noted the large presence of the religious sector in land tenure within the district of *Pa-ki-ja-ne*. The fact that religious personnel held tracts of land from the *damos* implies that they were also involved in the cultivation of that land and that they derived some of their support from the land's produce. If this was the case, then the religious personnel may have been able to support themselves with income that was not provided to them by the palace, and therefore they could have enjoyed a certain amount of economic independence from the palace. Is it possible then that the independence of the religious personnel could indicate that the sanctuaries they were associated with had a certain amount of independence from the palace and its administration as well? In this chapter we will look into the involvement of the religious sector in economic endeavors besides agriculture, such as animal husbandry, textile manufacture and other industrial activities, in order to consider the possibility that the products of these activities were also used for the support of sanctuaries and their personnel. We will also see how in one case in particular the religious sector's economic pursuits were intertwined with those of the palace.

Deities as "Collectors"

On several sheep and textile tablets from Knossos and Pylos the names of deities appear in the same position, or administrative slot, that is usually held by the personal names of secular individuals. These individuals are traditionally called "collectors." It seems likely then that the deities (or actually the personnel who worked in their names) held a position in society that was similar to that held by those individual collectors.[1] But what role exactly did the collectors fulfill? That has been one of the most hotly debated subjects in Mycenology. Therefore, before discussing 'deities as collectors', it is necessary to first discuss the collectors themselves.

The Collectors' Relationship with the Palace and their Position within the Mycenaean Economy

The origin of the term "collector" is found in the sheep tablets from Pylos. The typical pattern of these tablets is represented here by Cn 655.[2] Generally they record the place at which the flock was located (here *ma-ro-pi*), then the name of the shepherd responsible for the flock in the nominative or the genitive (*qe-re-wa-o* on line 1), and sometimes an indication as to the type of sheep the flock consisted of, such as *pa-ra-jo* for "old" on lines 1, 2, 7-10). The number of sheep in the flock was then listed against the ideogram for male or female sheep.[3]

Cn 655:
1. ma-ro-pi , qe-re-wa-o pa-ra-jo OVIS^{m} 136
2. ma-ro-pi , to-ro-wi-ko , pa-ra-jo OVIS^{m} 133[
3. ma-ro-pi , ke-ro-wo-jo OVIS^{m} 85
4. ma-ro-pi⌊ ⌋ra-pa-sa-ko-jo OVIS^{m} 69
5. ma-ro-pi , pu-wi-no , a-pi-me-de-o , a-ko-ra OVIS^{m} 190
6. ma-ro-pi , i-wa-so , we-da-ne-wo , a-ko-ra OVIS^{m} 70
7. ma-ro-pi , ti-ṛẹ-wo , pa-ra-jo OVIS^{m} 70
8. ma-ro-pi , o-ka-ri-jo , pa-ra-jo OVIS^{m} 95
9. ma-ro-pi , e-ti-ra-wo , pa-ra-jo OVIS^{m} 70
10. ma-ro-pi , a-ta-ma-ne-u , pa-ra-jo OVIS^{m} 60
11. ma-ro-pi , qi-ri-ta-ko , a-ke-o-jo , a-ko-ra OVIS^{m} 90[
12. ma-ro-pi , a-ri-wo , a-ke-o-jo , a-ko-ra [ ]ị4
13. ma-ro-pi , ṛọ-ḳọ- jọ , we-ḍạ-ne-wo , a-ko-ra [ ]80
14. ma-ro-pi , o-pe-re-ṭạ , we-da-ne-wo OVIS^{f} 86
15. ma-ro-pi , po-ro-qa-ta-jo , we-da-ne-wo OVIS^{f} 63
16. ma-ro-pi , to-ru-ko-ro , we-da-ne-wo OVIS^{f} 88
17. ma-ro-pi , ma-ma-ro , we-da-ne-wo OVIS^{m} 90
18. ma-]ṛọ-pi , ma-du-ro⌊ ⌋we-da-ne-wo OVIS^{m} 100
19. ma-ro-]pi , se-no , we-da-ṇẹ-wo OVIS^{f} 40
20. ma-ro-]p̣ị , ta-ta-ke-u , [we-]ḍạ-ne-wo OVIS^{f} 30

As we can see in Cn 655, some entries, such as the one on line 5, contain a second personal name in the genitive, which is very often followed by the word *a-ko-ra*, or ἀγορά Killen associates this second genitive with the term *a-ko-ra*: "it seems a plausible supposition that this is the term on which the genitive in all such entries depends."[4] Thus we would have the *a-ko-ra* of, or belonging to, for instance, *a-pi-me-de* (whom we

[1] Nosch came to a similar conclusion in her analysis of the flocks associated with Potnia and Hermes ("Schafherden unter dem Namenspatronat von Potnia und Hermes in Knossos," in *Wiener Forschungen zur Archäologie*, J. Borchhardt and F. Krinzinger, eds., Vienna 2000, pp. 211-215.)

[2] The tablets that follow this pattern are listed by Bennet as Cn 40, 45, 254, 453, 599, 600, 643 and 719 (""Collectors" or "Owners"? An Examination of their Possible Functions within the Palatial Economy of LM III Crete," in *Mykenaïka* [*BCH* Suppl. 25], J.-P. Olivier, ed., Athens 1992, pp. 65-101; see p. 67). Bennet also notes that another type of Cn tablet lacks the names of collectors and is given a heading that consists of a toponym followed by the word *we-re-ke*. Men's names are recorded after the heading along with the types and numbers of their animals. Tablets in this group are Cn 131, 202, 328, and 441.

[3] It should be noted that many of the Pylian Cn tablets also record goats.

[4] J.T. Killen, "Linear B *a-ko-ra-ja/-jo*," in *Studies in Greek, Italic and Indo-European Linguistics Offered to L.R. Palmer*, A. Morpurgo Davies and W. Meid, eds., Innsbruck 1976, pp. 117-125; see p. 117.

discussed in the previous chapter). Four names are found associated with *a-ko-ra* on the Pylian tablets. Three of those, *a-pi-me-de-o*, *we-da-ne-wo*, and *a-ke-o-jo* are seen above on Cn 655, and the fourth, *a-ko-so-ta-o*, is found, for instance, on Cn 40.3. A slightly different pattern is found on Cc 660. Here, one of the men whose names were associated with *a-ko-ra* on Cn 655, *a-ke-o*, is found in the nominative followed by the verbal form of *a-ko-ra*: *a-ke-re*, or ἀγείρει.

Cc 660:
a. a-ke-o , a-ke-re
me-ta-pa , pa-ro ka-ra-su-no CAP^m 30

Since ἀγείρω means "to gather together" or "collect," Ventris and Chadwick proposed that the use of ἀγορά indicated that "the men so designated are in some way responsible for 'collecting' the cattle."[5] They saw the sheep tablets themselves as "a record of tribute imposed on his subjects by the overlord."[6] Hence we could take the noun *a-ko-ra* in the sense of a "collection" or a "flock." Ventris and Chadwick therefore dubbed the men who were thought to do the collecting, "collectors." This designation is still used by convention, and I will retain it for this discussion, even though Ventris and Chadwick's original theory concerning the function of these men has been superseded.[7]

Collectors are also thought to have existed at Knossos since, even though the Da-Dg sheep tablets of Knossos do not contain the words *a-ko-ra* or *a-ke-re*, many individuals on them can also be identified as holding a position similar to that held by the collectors of the Pylian tablets. What the Da-Dg tablets do show is an alternation like that found on Pylian tablets between flocks that are recorded with only a shepherd's name and others that were recorded with a shepherd's name plus an additional man's name, often in the genitive. Compare the following two tablets:

Dd 1171:
A. OVIS^m 20 OVIS^f 72
B. po-ro / pa-i-to *pa* OVIS^m 8

Dd 1157:
A. we-we-si-jo-jo OVIS^m 56 OVIS^f 42
B. a-wo-ti-jo / pa-i-to , *pa* OVIS^m 2

On Dd 1171 we have the shepherd's name written in majuscule (*po-ro*) and a toponym indicating the location of the flock (*pa-i-to*). The rest of the tablet is used to record the details of the flock itself. On Dd 1157 the name of a second individual, *we-we-si-jo-jo*, is written in the genitive on line A. This second individual is thought to correspond to the collectors on the Cn tablets both because his name is, like those on the Cn tablets, in the genitive case, and because his position on the tablet is so similar to that of the collectors on the Pylian tablets.

Further support for these men being equated in function with the collectors of the sheep tablets from Pylos is found in the Knossian Co tablets. The word *a-ko-ra-ja* appears on several tablets of this series: 903.1, 904.1, 906.1, 909.1 and 910.1, and we see a slight variant, *a-ko-ra-jo*, on Co 907.1.[8]

Co 904:
1. ku-do-ni-ja / a-ko-ra-ja OVIS^m 117 OVIS^f 100[
2. CAP^m 54 CAP^f 151 SUS^f 87 ḄỌṢ^m[

Co 907:
1. si-ra-ro / a-ko-ra-jo OVIS^m 202 OVIS^f 750
2. CAP^m 125 CAP^f 240 SUS^m 21 SUS^f 60 BOS^m 2 BOS^f 10

Killen takes *a-ko-ra-ja* and *a-ko-ra-jo* as adjectival descriptions of the animals on the tablet: he says, *a-ko-ra-ja* is most likely a "neuter plural (understanding 'creatures' *vel sim*)," and *a-ko-ra-jo* would be a "masculine plural used (like the male SHEEP ideogram) to designate both male and female animals."[9] As we can see, neither of these tablets supplies an individual's name that could be associated with the terms *a-ko-ra-ja/-jo* and which would therefore be understood as the collector. Nonetheless, because the words *a-ko-ra-ja* and *a-ko-ra-jo* are derivatives of the term *a-ko-ra*, Killen suggests that whatever the precise meaning of these words, "the implication of *a-ko-ra-ja/-jo* is 'belonging to 'collectors'."[10] Thus, from the Co tablets as well as from the position and case of the second personal name on the Da-Dg tablets, we can surmise that 'collectors' existed at Knossos as well as at Pylos.[11]

Gradually it was found that the collectors' names appeared on several different kinds of records. In addition to those that recorded flock strengths (Da-Dg,

[5] *Docs²*, p. 200.
[6] *Docs²*, p. 198.
[7] Chadwick himself retracted this theory in the second edition of *Docs²*, p. 434.

[8] The term *a-ko-ra-ja* also appears on F 157 *v.* 1, a record of several agricultural commodities, which may indicate that the collectors were also active in agricultural pursuits. Also, the term *a-ko-ra-jo* appears as a man's personal name on As 1516.8 (*Dic. Mic.* I, p. 47).
[9] Killen 1976, p. 122.
[10] Killen 1976, p. 123. In addition to these Co tablets, we also find either *a-ko-ra-ja/-jo* or *a-ko-ra* itself (depending on whether there was a further syllable after the break in the tablet) on Dk(1) 969. I will reserve discussion of this tablet for later due to its connection to Potnia and religiously associated flocks of sheep.
[11] It should be noted that Godart disagrees with the idea that the term *a-ko-ra* should be taken as being directly associated with the person in the genitive on the Cn tablets, and therefore he also thinks that *a-ko-ra-ja/-jo* cannot be taken to indicate that a collector was associated with the flocks. Instead, Godart proposes that *a-ko-ra* is used to indicate flocks that were being gathered from breeding centers and brought in to the palatial centers in order to restock the palatial flocks of wool-producing sheep (L. Godart, "Les tablettes de la série Co de Cnossos," in *Acta Mycenaea II* [*Minos* 12], M. S. Ruipérez, ed., Salamanca 1972, pp. 418-424). Later Godart proposed that the men recorded in the collector position were palace functionaries who managed the flocks for the palace; he calls them "administrateurs des biens palatiaux" ("Les collecteurs dans le monde égéen," in *Mykenaika* [*BCH* Suppl. 25], J.-P. Olivier, ed., Athens 1992, pp. 257-283; p. 275). Godart's theories have not, however, found wide acceptance among Linear B scholars and so they will not be pursued in the present work.

Dv), they also appeared on sheep totaling tablets (Dn), tablets that gave targets for wool and lamb production (Dk and Dl), and tablets that recorded targets and subsequent deliveries of the cloth that was manufactured using the sheep's wool (Lc, Le and Ld). Lists of textile workers (Ak) also bore their names. In all of these series, there is a very careful and consistent distinction made between collector and non-collector records. The question that Mycenologists have been trying to answer is, what role does this collector play? What is the nature of his association with the sheep and the textile workshops, and what is his relationship with the palace?

As mentioned above, Ventris and Chadwick originally thought that the most likely explanation of the Cn (and the KN Da-Dg) records was that they recorded flocks that were being delivered to the palace as tribute. Hence they rendered the word *a-ko-ra* as "collection." Ventris and Chadwick also noticed that at least two of the four men were of some importance in Pylian society. For instance, *we-da-ne-u* receives contributions in the Es series alongside (but at a much lower rate than) Poseidon, while *a-ko-so-ta* appears to be responsible for inspecting land on Eq 213.1 and for allocating aromatic substances to the unguent-boiler *tu-we-ta* on Un 267.1. We can add that, as we saw in the previous chapter, *a-pi-me-de* was also a prominent personage at Pylos in that he was a landholder of a large tract of land (GRA 4 T 6) which was marked out as privileged by being designated as *e-to-ni-jo* (Ep 539.14). Thus it seemed reasonable to Ventris and Chadwick to propose that these men were palace officials who were sent out to 'collect' the animals recorded against their names.[12] Ilievski came to the same conclusion after recognizing that the word ἀγείρω was used in Homer to indicate the collection of different taxes, and that in later Greek a term for tax-collector, ἀγέρτας, was formed from the same root as that found in *a-ko-ra* and *a-ke-re*.[13]

However, this theory was objected to on the grounds that it does not explain why collectors were associated with some flocks but not with all of them. If these men were palatial agents who were sent out to collect the animals as tribute for the palace, one would expect that such an agent would be required for all the flocks that were being collected. But many of the flocks do not have the name of a collector associated with them.

Palmer, in his review of the first edition of *Documents*, proposed instead that the collectors were the actual owners of the flocks listed against them. The 'zero' records, or those without the name of a collector, should then be assumed to belong to the *wanax*.[14] Palmer did not go any further, though, in trying to explain all the various series dealing with sheep and the closely related textile industry. This task was taken up by J.T. Killen.

In 1964 Killen proposed a fairly comprehensive explanation for the D series, one that seemed to make better sense of many of the tablets' details than the tax-collection theory proposed by Ventris and Chadwick. Rather than interpreting these tablets as records of sheep brought to the palace as tribute, Killen proposed that the Da-Dg tablets were actually census records of entire flocks, and that the census was drawn up to serve as the basis for calculating the amount of tax the palace would eventually take from the flocks.[15] Killen was then able to explain the Dk and Dl series as recording production targets (and deficits) for the flocks on the Da-Dg tablets.[16] (The Dl tablets record targets for wool production and lambs while the Dk series records only wool targets.) Killen proposed, therefore, that the collectors could more plausibly be seen as the owners of the flocks they were listed against, and that they were required to fulfill certain tax obligations *vis à vis* the palace.

In a series of articles, Killen and Olivier subsequently affirmed the basic dichotomy between collector and non-collector flocks of sheep, and they demonstrated that the palace made this distinction at every level of the administration of the flocks, their wool, and the cloth made from that wool. For instance, Olivier showed that in the Dn series, which he saw were the totaling tablets for the sheep found on the Da-Dg series, the totals of the collector flocks were tallied and recorded separately from the non-collector flocks.[17] The non-collector flocks were totaled according to their place names, whereas the collector flocks were totaled under the name of the collector, regardless of where they were located. Killen observed that the cloth in the Lc tablets was characterized as either collector or non-collector,[18] while Olivier proposed that this distinction was also made in the totaling records for the Lc(1) cloth target records.[19] Olivier noted that the totaling tablet L 536 + Lc 7383 came up short if it was to account for all the *pa-we-a* cloth of the Lc series, and proposed that this was because the collector's cloth was recorded separately. Killen was able to confirm this proposition by joining Lc(1) 7392

[12] *Docs*², p. 200.

[13] P.H. Ilievski, "A Re-examination of PY Cn Tablets," in *Atti e Memorie del 1° Congresso Internazionale de Micenologia*, Rome 1968, pp. 92-96; see p. 92.

[14] L.R. Palmer, "Review of *Documents in Mycenaean Greek* by Ventris and Chadwick," *Gnomon* 29 (1957) 561-581; see pp. 569-570. Mabel Lang also found problems with the idea that the collectors were tax collectors. Her alternate suggestion, that the collectors were the "officials who first introduced, sponsored or made popular other new breeds," has not however been picked up in the discussion concerning the role of the collectors ("Cn Flocks," in *Cambridge Colloquium on Mycenaean Studies*, L. Palmer and J. Chadwick, eds., Cambridge University Press 1966, 250-259; see p. 258).

[15] J.T. Killen, "The Wool Industry of Crete in the Late Bronze Age," *ABSA* 59 (1964) 1-15.

[16] It has since been recognized that the Dl series, which will be discussed further below, is not as closely tied to the Da-Dg series as the Dk series.

[17] J.-P. Olivier, "La série Dn de Cnossos," in *SMEA* 2 (*Incunabula Graeca* 18), Rome 1967, pp. 71-93; see pp. 75-81. Also see Olivier's update on the Dn series in "La série Dn de Cnossos reconsidérée," *Minos* 13 (1972) 22-28, where he shows that recent joins confirm his earlier proposals.

[18] Killen 1966, p. 105.

[19] Olivier 1967, p. 91.

with 7398.[20] The resulting tablet recorded the *pa-we-a* cloth of *we-we-si-jo*, an individual who is often found in the collector's position on the Da-Dg tablets. As Olivier predicted, his 230(+) units of cloth were not included in the total of L 536 + Lc 7383. Killen later demonstrated that the same distinction was made in the Ld(1) cloth delivery totaling records.[21] Finally, the Ak records, which record the workgroups responsible for the production of the cloth, were also separated into collector and non-collector records.[22]

Thus the collectors of Knossos were shown to play a role not only in the sheep industry, but also in the textile industry. Killen pointed out that this made it even more difficult to believe that the collectors were mentioned on the tablets because they were palatial agents responsible for collecting tribute.[23] However, several scholars, including Killen, thought that defining the collectors as straightforward "owners" of their flocks was too simple. Carlier, for instance, asked why the palatial scribes should record the collector flocks with the same amount of detail that they used for the palatial flocks if they were owned solely by the collectors.[24] This type of question invited scholars to try to refine our understanding of the nature of the relationship between the collectors and the palace.

Driessen, for instance, saw the collectors basically as palace officials.[25] His proposition concerning the collectors is based on his view of the likely development of Cretan society, which he derives from a comparison of the elites recorded on the LM II tablets found in the Room of the Chariot Tablets (hereafter, RCT) and those who appear on the chronologically later tablets preserved in the final destruction of Knossos. According to Driessen, the RCT Sc series, which records the allocation of horses, chariots and cuirasses to men's names, demonstrates that the elite of Knossos at that time was primarily concerned with military matters. Other tablets within the RCT show that these men were also involved in economic matters, but the way in which they were recorded does not indicate that they were part of a system like the one seen on the later tablets involving the collectors. Driessen concludes that the military elite of LM II was independent of the palace and that the system of collectors had not yet come into existence.[26] In contrast, by the time of the destruction of the palace, the elite of Knossos are no longer primarily found on tablets that deal with military matters, but instead another category of elites has appeared, which Driessen classifies as the elite "de nomenclature," or the "titled elite,"[27] many of whom, such as the *ko-re-te*, were locally based. Existing alongside the titled elite, but not overlapping with them, was an economic elite, which included the collectors. In order to explain this change, Driessen proposes that once Crete had been pacified, different systems and obligations were put in place: e.g., the obligation of personal military service had probably been replaced by contributions of raw materials and finished products.[28] Also, over the course of time, the palatial bureaucracy had become more centralized, and an economic elite was created to oversee its concerns.[29] The collectors therefore were not beneficiaries who were semi-independent from the palace, but rather palatial functionaries. Driessen also thinks that the tablets on which the collectors are found "demonstrate the direct engagement of the palatial administration."[30]

I would say that Driessen's thesis concerning the development of the military elite into a titled elite is compelling, but his opinion of the collectors as officials with direct ties to the palace is problematic. If the collectors are managing palatial business and not their own, then we would have to ask the same question posed above to Ventris and Chadwick's theory that the collectors were tax collectors. If the palace saw fit to assign a collector to some flocks, why did it not assign one to all of them?

F. Rougemont has recently put forward a theory that also sees the collectors as being primarily associated with the palace. She thinks that some collectors (namely, the ones attested with deficits representing more than 15% of the production of flock) were palatial inspectors who were sent out by the palace because the flocks and textile workshops were not being productive enough to meet the palatial targets.[31] Rougemont came to this conclusion after looking at the deficits in the sheep records and finding that the tablets with collectors accounted for

[20] J.T. Killen and J.-P. Olivier, "155 Raccords de fragments dans les tablettes de Cnossos," *BCH* 92 (1968) 115-141; see p. 137. Killen also discusses these totaling tablets in Killen, "A Problem in the Knossos Lc(1) (Cloth) Tablets," *Hermathena* 118 (1974) 82-90; see p. 85.

[21] J.T. Killen, "The Knossos Ld(1) Tablets," in *Colloquium Mycenaeum*, E. Risch and H. Mühlestein, eds., Université de Neuchâtel 1979, pp. 151-179; see p. 155. Also see Killen 1976, p. 119.

[22] This fact was alluded to in Killen 1966, p. 105, and discussed more fully in Killen, "Epigraphy and Interpretation in Knossos WOMAN and CLOTH Records," in *Texts, Tablets and Scribes: Studies in Mycenaean Epigraphy and Economy Offered to E. L. Bennett* (*Minos* Suppl. 10), J.-P. Olivier and T.G. Palaima, eds., Salamanca 1988, pp. 167-183. The clearest and most complete summary of the alternation between collector and non-collector texts can be found in Bennet 1992.

[23] Killen 1976, p. 119.

[24] Carlier reviews the problems with using either the term 'collector' or 'owner' in "Les collecteurs sont-ils des fermiers?" *Mykenaïka* (*BCH* Suppl. 25), J.-P. Olivier, ed., Athens 1992, pp. 159-166.

[25] J. Driessen, ""Collectors' Items". Observations sur l'Élite Mycénienne de Cnossos," in *Mykenaïka* (*BCH* Suppl. 25), J.-P. Olivier, ed., Athens 1992, pp. 197-214.

[26] Driessen 1992, p. 205.

[27] Driessen 1992, p. 206. Bennet uses the term "titled elite" in 1992, p. 95, n. 90.

[28] Driessen 1992, p. 213.

[29] Driessen 1992, p. 212.

[30] Driessen 1992, p. 210.

[31] F. Rougemont, "La hiérarchie des responsabilités dans les économies palatiales mycéniennes: l'exemple de la gestion des troupeaux d'ovins et de l'industrie textile," in *Responsabilité et antiquité,* Paris 2003, pp. 37-59. *Idem*, "Quelques remarques sur les entrées *o-pe-ro* et les "collecteurs" dans les enregistrements de moutons, de laine et de tissues à Cnossos," in *The Proceedings of the 11th International Mycenological Colloquium, Hesperia* supplement, in press. Rougemont has pointed out to me that our thinking on the collectors may benefit from our considering the possibility that they may not have all played one and the same role. (Hence her theory that some were auditors should not be automatically applied to all the collectors.) She may be correct in this, but herein I will persist in my attempt to find the solution that best fits the majority of cases.

nearly 50% of the documents that recorded a deficit, while only 30% of all the tablets in those series record a collector's name. She thinks that this differential is significant and one of the keys to our understanding of the role of the collector. It may be objected though that this theory has the same failing as the idea that the collectors were palatial tax collectors: why would the palace deem it necessary to assign such auditors to some of the flocks but not to all of them? Rougemont deals with this objection in a clever way. She suggests that the palatial administration only inspected 30% of its productive force each year.[32] But if you accept this explanation, other problems arise. If only 30% of the flocks could be inspected in a given year, one might expect that the palace would do this as efficiently as possible. But it is quite common for the same collector to be found in a wide number of locations, while at the same time several different collectors often appear at the same location.[33] Also, there are some collectors who are quite active, such as *u-ta-jo* who appears 49 times (at 16 different locations in the Da-Dg, Dv, Dn series) and *we-we-si-jo* who appears 33 times (at 9 different locations in the same series), while others appear only once or twice.[34] These patterns do not seem to reflect an organized effort on the part of a centralized administration to inspect its holdings. Also, from an administrative point of view, one would expect that in the totaling records all the flocks from a certain location would be recorded together, regardless of whether they were being inspected, since at that level the fact that the flock had been inspected would not have been of much consequence. But, as I mentioned, the distinction between collector and non-collector flocks is maintained in the totaling records. Rougemont herself mentions another problem, which is that high deficits do not exist within the Pylian records. Therefore the idea that the collectors were auditors would not serve to explain their presence in those documents.[35]

From my point of view, the fact that greater deficits can be attributed to the collector flocks than the non-collector, or palatial, flocks may demand an explanation,[36] but I am not convinced that the deficits *per se* constitute the necessary starting point in our search for an understanding of the collectors. Rather, it seems to me that the most important aspect of these tablets is the fact that the palatial administration consistently distinguishes the resources associated with the collectors from those without one. To my mind, the fact that the names of the collectors are recorded at every administrative level must mean that the collectors were far more intimately concerned with the sheep and the manufacture of cloth than their being inspectors would account for.

A different line of approach was taken by Olivier, Chadwick, and Killen. Olivier was actually the first to propose that the collectors might be, in some way, "*beneficiaires*" of the produce of the flocks.[37] Chadwick, thinking along similar lines, proposed that the collectors were beneficiaries of the palace in that they were given the flocks so that the sheep might provide their sustenance.[38] Killen fleshed out the concept by proposing that:

> the 'collectors' [were] members of the nobility, the royal family, or the like who were allocated part of the productive capacity of the kingdom for their own benefit (hence their appearance as 'owners' of flocks, weaving workgroups, etc.)....[39]

In this view, the collectors could be seen nominally as owners of the flocks, but ones who owed their position to the palace, and who therefore owed a substantial part of their produce to the palace as tribute. At a later date Killen added to this definition in a fairly significant way. He proposed that instead of the collectors being directly involved in the care of the sheep, "[the collectors'] share, however, [was] still being *managed* on their behalf by the central authorities."[40]

Killen's theory has the advantage of providing a plausible reason as to why not every flock had a collector - the palace had only allocated a portion of its resources to the elite - and it made sense of the scribes' need to distinguish the flocks associated with the collectors - presumably the palace would want to know how much of the flocks, wool, and textiles was going to be available for their use as opposed to how much was going to the collectors. In support of the collectors being members of the nobility, Killen points out that a few of the names of the Knossian collectors are found on tablets from other sites in contexts which might suggest that they were persons of elevated status. For example, adjectival descriptions of workers derived from the names of two D series collectors, *a-ka-i-jo* (De 1084.a and Dv 1085.a)[41] and *ko-ma-we*[-*ta* (e.g., Dv 5278.B), are found in the Theban Of series: *a-ka-i-je-ja* appears on Of 27.3 and .3

[32] Rougemont 2003, n. 29.
[33] See Bennet 1992, Tables 7-10.
[34] See Bennet 1992, Table 8.
[35] Rougemont, *Hesperia* suppl., in press. Rougemont would say here that the Pylian collectors were performing some other function besides auditing, but that they were acting on behalf of the palace in some capacity.
[36] I have also noticed this phenomenon in my work, but I approach the problem from a different perspective. As we shall see, the Potnian flocks have nearly 100% deficits, and I wonder whether this fact signals that the religiously affiliated flocks were in some way special. However, as we shall see, it turns out that such deficits are not uncommon; both collector and non-collector flocks had very high deficits. I therefore conclude that this must be the result of a system-wide problem: perhaps it had been a bad year, or a series of bad years, for everyone involved in sheep rearing. The higher deficits among the collectors could be explained by the idea that the collectors were in a better position than the shepherds to avoid or even to refuse the demands of the palace.

[37] Olivier 1967, p. 84.
[38] *Docs*², p. 434.
[39] Killen 1979, p. 177.
[40] Killen first expressed this view of the collectors' status in 1983 (p. 85). This quote, however, is from J.T. Killen, "Some Further Thoughts on 'Collectors'," in *Politeia: Society and State in the Aegean Bronze Age* (*Aegaeum* 12), R. Laffineur and W.-D. Niemeier, eds., Liège and PASP, University of Texas at Austin 1995, pp. 213-226; see p. 213.
[41] Killen 1979, p. 176. The name *a-ka-i-jo* also appears on several other tablets (F 153 *v.* 5, Vc 68, Vd 62), but it is unsure whether he is the same person as the collector of the D tablets (*Dic. Mic.* I, pp. 31-32).

and *ko-ma-we-te-ja* on Of 35.[42] Also, the *we-we-si-je-ja* workers of PY Aa 762 may in fact be derived from the name *we-we-si-jo*, one of the most prominent collectors at Knossos. After noting the repeated appearances of such names, Killen comments that, "perhaps as members of the same dynasty, they tended to be given names from a certain limited stock."[43]

Nonetheless, despite the advantages of this theory, I cannot help wondering about the practical aspects of such a system. Earmarking the production of particular flocks for certain individuals while maintaining control over the management of those sheep seems elaborate way to reward your elite. Add to this that we would have to assume, given that the textile workshops are also carefully recorded with the collectors' names, that produce from those workshops was also meant to be for the benefit of the collector. Again, it seems a very unwieldy way of rewarding your constituents. Why not simply allot a certain amount of say, wool or cloth, and avoid the burdensome connection with certain flocks and workshops? Also, within this scenario, whose purpose is to reward the collectors with material benefit, we would expect some indication that this reward was being paid out, but we do not have any records that would reflect that such payments were ever made.

Indeed, I think that I would be better persuaded by the beneficiary theory if we assumed that the collectors did manage the resources associated with them. But then we should ask how the details of such a beneficiary system would work. What happened when a beneficiary died? Were the sheep passed on to his children, or were they returned to the palace for reallotment? Indeed, what if the beneficiary fell out of favor with the *wanax*? Could the sheep change hands at the whim of the palace during the lifetime of the beneficiary? Allotting and re-allotting flocks would most likely create an unstable system in which disputes among beneficiaries could easily arise. It would almost certainly also lead to diminished productivity. (Given the ultimate collapse of the palatial system, maybe this *was* how the flocks were handled.) We could introduce stability into the system by assuming that once allocated, the flocks were kept within a family, and perhaps this is more along the lines of what Killen meant when he originally proposed the idea. But then wouldn't we be talking about something more akin to ownership than a real system of perks and rewards?

Carlier also had an interesting theory concerning the position of the collectors. He proposed that they could have been enterprising men who leased the rights to manage the palatial flocks.[44] This explanation, like Killen's, has the merit of accounting for the detail with which the palatial scribes recorded the flocks, since they were still the property of the palace, as well as the need to distinguish the flocks associated with the collectors from those that were not. However, while I do find this proposal attractive, I do see one problem with it. If we propose that the palace was recording the collector flocks with such care because they were leasing them out, would we be happy offering the same explanation as to why the palace recorded the details of the collectors' textile industry in comparable detail? We would have to propose that the palace was also leasing out the textile workshops. I suppose this could have been the case, but it seems unlikely to me. Would the palace really have found it to their advantage to build textile workshops in various locations on Crete just so that it could rent them out? Surely it would have been more efficient if such palatially owned workshops were close to the palace itself. All in all, I think there is a simpler explanation for the situation we see on the tablets, and this is the theory that was first proposed by Palmer and recently revived by Bennet (in particular for Knossos): that the collectors were actually the owners of the sheep and the workshops.[45]

After a very detailed analysis of the tablets relating to the collectors, that is, of both the sheep and the cloth tablets, Bennet came to the conclusion that the collectors, particularly those recorded on the Knossos tablets, should be viewed as the owners of the sheep and all the resources that they are associated with.[46] He comes to this conclusion partially because on the Knossos tablets the collectors are rarely found in contexts outside of the sheep and textile industries. Indeed, Bennet points out that "there are no unequivocal textual associations between "collectors" and the site of Knossos itself,"[47] such as one would expect if there were close ties between them and the palatial elite. "Rather," Bennet continues, "the opposite is true: most associations they have seem to be with regions at some distance from the palatial center."[48] Therefore, Bennet concludes that the Knossian collectors were probably not palatial officials or associated with the elite of the palace in any way. Bennet also infers from the carefully maintained distinction between collector and non-collector records at Knossos (which, as we have seen, was maintained at all levels of production, from the shearing of the sheep, through the allocation of wool to workgroups, to the finishing of the cloth) that the collectors were responsible for organizing the management of the flocks and the production of the cloth.[49] He says, "This pattern strongly suggests that these individuals enjoyed a substantial degree of

[42] An alternative theory concerning *ko-ma-we-te-ja* will be considered below in the section on the Theban Of tablets.

[43] Killen 1979, p. 177. See also Ilievski ("Observations on the Personal Names from the Knossos D Tablets," in *Mykenaïka*, *BCH* Suppl. 25, J.-P. Olivier, ed., 1992, pp. 321-349) who discusses the fact that the names of shepherds, who would presumably be lower on the social scale than the collectors, are also found in other contexts both on Knossian and Pylian tablets.

[44] Carlier 1992.

[45] Bennet 1992. Also see Bennet, "The Structure of the Linear B Administration at Knossos," *AJA* 89 (1985) 231-249; and *idem*, "Knossos in Context: Comparative Perspectives on the Linear B Administration of LM II-III Crete," *AJA* 94 (1990) 193-211.

[46] Bennet 1992.

[47] Bennet 1992, p. 95.

[48] Bennet 1992, p. 95.

[49] Bennet gives the details of the collector name/toponym dichotomy on pp. 70-83. He makes his analytical deductions concerning the significance of the distinction on p. 96.

responsibility, forming small economic units of their own, albeit within the overall economy based on the palace at Knossos." Bennet then follows this with, "Probably the most convincing explanation for this situation is that they owned the flocks (and probably the work groups) they were recorded against, as Palmer suggested in 1957."[50]

Bennet also explains the development of the collector-owners of Knossos.[51] He believes that they were actually members of locally based elite groups that headed up economically productive communities which were in existence before the palace at Knossos had become powerful enough to incorporate these areas into its own economic network. Even after they had been incorporated, these local elites maintained some independence from the palace and were able to retain control over their own enterprises. Hence they were fully "owners" even though their resources were being taxed by the palace.

I agree with Bennet on this point, and I would like to extend Bennet's conclusions concerning the Knossos collectors to those at Pylos. In contrast to the Knossian collectors, Bennet thinks that the four collectors at Pylos "seem to be palace officials, perhaps based at Pylos itself, entrusted with the management and/or the produce of about 40% of the region's flocks...."[52] Bennet says this because, as we have seen, at Pylos the collectors are sometimes found in contexts that deal with matters related to the palace, such as *a-ko-so-ta* the land inspector of Eq 213. Thus it would be more likely for the collectors of Pylos than for those of Knossos that they were palatial functionaries who had been given the sheep by the palace in recognition of their service. This scenario is certainly possible, but I wonder if we might not see the Pylian collectors as owners of their flocks as well. The fact that the Pylian collectors are closely tied to the palace cannot be denied. But perhaps the prominent role they played in palatial interests derived from their being influential nobles in the vicinity of Pylos whom the *wanax* sought to incorporate into his ranks for his own purposes. That is, instead of thinking that the privilege of holding the flocks was bestowed upon them as a reward for their service to the palace, one could say that they held their palatial positions because they were influential men, and part of what made them influential was their control over the means of production such as sheep and textile workshops, which the *wanax* had a need for. The early *wanax* would have done well strategically to try to win over the support of such men since their influence could have helped him to solidify and maintain his position as head of the community. He might have tried to bind the collectors to him by offering them prominent positions within the palatial hierarchy. The relationships formed in this way between the Pylian *wanax* and the elites would then have been maintained and strengthened over the years until the possession of economic resources and elite positions within the palatial hierarchy went hand-in-hand. It seems to me that this historical development could account for the situation we see in the tablets just as well as the idea that the collectors were Pylian officials given flocks for their use, and it would avoid the problems I raised above to the beneficiary theory. Thus, as in the Knossian situation, the palace at Pylos might have been tapping into already existing systems of production.[53] The difference then between the situations at Knossos and Pylos may have been that at Pylos those who owned the systems of production were incorporated into the palatial elite, whereas at Knossos they were not.

This is not to say that the owner theory is without its own problems. The largest objection to this view is that the targets set for collector flocks and cloth are the same as those set for the non-collector resources. This sticking point could lead one back to the idea that the flocks must all belong to the palace. It led me, however, to consider another issue concerning the collectors, one that is arguably just as important as whether the collectors were actually owners, beneficiaries, or leasers: the question is whether the collectors would have been able to make a living from their sheep. Killen has also considered this question and he maintains, despite the fact that he thinks the flocks were given to the collectors as something of an honor and in order to provide for their sustenance, that the return on the flocks may not have been great enough to make managing them very profitable.[54] And Killen has a point, because the fact is that whatever relationship the collector held the sheep under, he was still required to

[50] Bennet 1992, p. 96.

[51] Bennet 1992, pp. 96-97.

[52] Bennet 1992, p. 97.

[53] R. Palmer (1999, p. 468) has suggested that this would have been the way the palace would have gone about procuring many of the perishable items the palace used on a daily basis. She says that the palace would have "relied upon the patterns of agriculture already present in each area...."

[54] J.T. Killen, "Critique: A View from the Tablets," in *Rethinking Mycenaean Palaces*, M. Galaty and W. Parkinson, eds., UCLA Press 1999, pp. 87-90, see p. 90. Also see Killen, "Records of Sheep and Goats at Mycenaean Knossos and Pylos," in *Domestic Animals of Mesopotamia* [*Bulletin on Sumerian Agriculture*, vol. 7], J.N. Postgate and M.A. Powell, eds., Cambridge 1993, pp. 209-218). In this article Killen proposes that in fact we might be able to detect a rather high turnover of shepherds on the Pylian Cn texts, which he credits to the possibility that "the shepherds suffered rather than benefited from their responsibilities as herders through being required to make good from their own resources any losses from the palace's flocks" (p. 215). His reasoning for this is as follows: Cn 131 can be seen as a record of flocks that are being allocated to shepherds as replacements for the *pa-ra-jo* sheep found on Cn 655 + 719 + 643. These latter tablets then would constitute a set that was recorded some time before Cn 131. If indeed the flocks on Cn 131 are meant to replace those found on Cn 655 + 719 + 643, then one would expect the names of the shepherds to be for the most part the same. But actually only twelve of the twenty-five shepherds found on Cn 131 are found on Cn 655 + 719 + 643, and of the thirty-five shepherds named on Cn 655 + 719 + 643, twenty-three do not appear on Cn 131. Killen suggests that this discrepancy can best be explained by "a considerable annual turn-over in shepherds willing (or being required) to offer their services to the centre as shepherds of palace-owned flocks" (p. 215). I might point out though that Killen is discussing shepherds here, not collectors, and even though one may suppose that the adverse conditions that affected the shepherds would also affect the collectors, nonetheless, it may be that the collectors had, as Killen himself argues, a higher social standing than the shepherds, which could mean that the collectors had access to more resources than the shepherds and therefore were better able to withstand difficult circumstances. (See pp. 212-216, for Killen's full discussion of the relationship between Cn 131 and Cn 655 + 719 + 643.)

pay a substantial amount of tax in wool and lambs to the palace. For instance, the Dk series, which records the wool targets for the sheep of the Da-Dg series, shows that the palace expected 750 g of wool per sheep.[55] That amount was reduced somewhat, to 600 g, for the breeding ewes found on the Dl(1) tablets. The targets for lambs varied: in the Dl series the palace expected to receive one lamb from each ewe, while the lambing target for those in the Dl(1) series was only one lamb per two ewes. Also, the breeding sheep of the Do tablets seem to have "had a variable lambing target of 80%, 50%, or 40%."[56] These targets were definitely not inconsequential, and in support of his view Killen has said that the palatial expectation of one lamb per breeding ewe (as on the Dl tablets) or 0.8 lamb per ewe (as on the Do tablets) was probably the maximum production that could be hoped for.[57]

Also, there is no denying that the texts record substantial deficits in the number of lambs that were actually given over to the palace, which could imply that the collectors, and the shepherds, since the deficits occur on both collector and non-collector tablets, had difficulty in meeting their targets. But the extremely high number of deficit lambs speaks for something else going on other than just shepherds having trouble meeting targets. Using only those tablets on which we can read both the female flock strength[58] and the deficit in lambs, the total number of both secular collector and non-collector (palatial) female sheep is 1286, while the deficits in lambs amount to 962 animals.[59] That is, nearly 75% of the lambs expected by the palace had not been handed over at the time that these records were drawn up. A lambing rate of 25% seems a bit extreme and I think indicates that we are dealing with a situation that could not have been business as usual. In other words, the deficits cannot be explained by simply saying that the palace's expectations were too high. It's true that there is a differential between collector and non-collector flocks in that the collector flocks definitely handed over fewer animals:[60] For the non-collector flocks, only 54%[61] of the animals were missing, vs. 89.9%[62] missing for collector flocks. But it is still remarkable how high the deficits were in both categories. One possibility is that the records were written after a bad year, or a series of bad years. Morrison talks about this in relation to the Nuzi texts, which provide a lambing rate of 78%. The *muddu* texts that she was dealing with only record the deficits, and therefore "reflect the years in which the herdsmen could not meet their obligations to the livestock owners."[63] She points out that these records do not take into account the "years in which herdsmen did not have deficits."[64] In other words, the unproductive years are the only ones that come to our attention because surpluses were never recorded. Morrison goes on to say, "In good years, the herdsmen would be able to build flocks of their own or accumulate other resources with which they could support themselves and their families." Something similar could be said of the records we have for the flocks at Knossos. It is possible that we are getting a skewed picture by having only one year's, or rather less than one year's, records available.

There could also have been another reasons for the deficits, one that would make sense of the fact that the collectors did not give over as high a percentage of the owed sheep as the shepherds of the palatially owned sheep. Carlier proposed that there might have been some abuse of the system on the part of the collectors. Perhaps they did not always provide the palace with as much of the goods as they were expected to, not because they did not have the produce to make up the full target amount, but because they did not want to give up the larger part of their produce, and they found ways around doing so.[65] Carlier even says that this abuse of the system might have been transformed into habit.[66] Morrison has shown how shepherds recorded in the Nuzi documents might have been able to defraud the flocks' owners by not revealing to the owners the full number of lambs that had been born during the year.[67] The Mycenaean collectors may have purposefully conducted a similar kind of skimming of lambs that were supposed to be sent on to the palace. The shepherds may also have tried to defraud the palace,

[55] Killen first derives and discusses these targets in 1964, pp. 9-13. Halstead's discussion of the different series and their targets is well laid out and benefits from being more current ("Lost Sheep? On the Linear B Evidence for Breeding Flocks at Mycenaean Knossos and Pylos," *Minos* 25-26 [1990-1991] 343-365).

[56] Halstead 1990-1991, p. 348.

[57] Killen (1964, p. 12) quotes an anonymous author of a treatise from 1890 as saying "each cow ought to answer for a calf a-year, and each ewe one lamb a-year" (*Walter of Henley's Husbandry*). From this and other such sources Killen deduces that sheep only produce one lamb a year. In a later article ("The Linear B Tablets and the Mycenaean Economy," in *Linear B: A 1984 Survey* [*BCILL* 26], A. Morpurgo Davies and Y. Duhoux, eds., Louvain-la-Neuve 1985, pp. 241-305; see p. 288), Killen says that the targets "in the case of the sheep on the D tablets evidently represents the total production of the animals."

[58] For these figures I am using what is called the "notional" flock strengths, which means that even if some female sheep were recorded as missing from the flock I have included those missing animals in the total for the flock. I have done this because the number of lambs that were supposed to be handed over to the palace was based on this total or "notional" figure.

[59] I have also limited the tablets used here to those on which we can tell whether the flock belonged to a collector or to the palace.

[60] The tablets that I have included in the collector category are: Dl 47, 412, 794, 932, 935, 938, 940, 944, 947, 948, 949, 952, and 7132. Those that I have used for the non-collector flocks are: Dl 463, 916, 790, 791, 792, 934, 1060, 7086, and 9174. I should mention that for some of these tablets in the latter group it was more difficult to say for sure that it was a non-collector tablet because several of them are not terribly well preserved in the area where a collector's name would have appeared. Nonetheless, I have only included those which I feel reasonably sure of.

[61] For the non-collector flocks there are 547 total female sheep and 297 missing lambs.

[62] For the collector flocks there are 739 total female sheep and 665 missing lambs.

[63] Morrison 1981, p. 284.

[64] Morrison 1981, p. 283.

[65] Carlier 1992, p. 164.

[66] Carlier (1992, p. 164, n. 25) goes on to point out that most of the collector tablets register significant deficits, which he implies could be explained by this refusal to give over the whole of the expected amount. It should be noted though that deficits are also recorded for flocks that do not have collectors associated with them, which could imply that the shepherds were skimming as well. Carlier also proposes that the deficits might not be failures to pay but rather an account of what remains to be paid after a partial payment had been made during the course of the year.

[67] Morrison 1981, p. 279, n. 149.

but, perhaps because they were not as powerful as the collectors, they were somewhat less successful.

Given that the percentage of missing lambs is so high, it cannot act as a true indicator of the profitability of the flocks. The real question is whether the collectors could have made a living from the animals under normal circumstances. Carlier is the one who has argued most convincingly for the profitability of the sheep. Carlier was interested in finding the ways in which a collector could have made a profit because his theory to a certain degree depends on it: in order for leasing contracts to have been desirable, Carlier reasons, the collector must have anticipated acquiring a profit, or at least a reasonable livelihood, from the flocks. Therefore Carlier cites several ways in which the collectors, if they were vigilant, might have been able to realize that profit.[68] First Carlier points out that it is not uncommon for a ewe to give birth to two lambs, an event which is called twinning.[69] In my investigation into the topic, I found that under the right conditions modern ewes give birth to twins on a regular basis. In one manual from 1924 on the topic of animal husbandry, the subject of twinning is not explicitly discussed, but it contains a quaint black and white picture of sheep standing on a hillside with the caption: "A flock of 105 Suffolk breeding ewes with their 210 lambs."[70] More recent advice as to the best way in which to produce a high occurrence of twinning is as follows:

> The feeding and management of the ewe prior to and during the breeding season can have a marked influence on the number of lambs produced. Ewes in moderate to thin condition respond to an increased feed intake by producing a higher percentage of multiple births. This practice of feeding at higher levels immediately prior to and during the early part of the breeding season is spoken of as 'flushing.'[71]

Thus at least in today's world of animal husbandry twinning is not an unusual event. But there is also evidence that twinning was not unheard of in the ancient world. For instance, in the *Historia Animalium*, Aristotle says that, "The ewe normally produces two lambs, and sometimes three or four."[72] He goes on to discuss the reasons why a ewe may give birth to twins, presumably because his readers would want to guarantee or at least maximize the occurrence of twinning: "The production of twin lambs and goats may occur because of good pasturage or because the ram or he-goat, or the dam, is a twin producer." Varro also addressed this issue and recommended that rams that were going to be used for breeding purposes should be chosen as much as possible from mothers that had given birth to twins.[73] Both of these authors show a knowledge of the effects of selective breeding, which the Mycenaeans may also have had some knowledge of. In reference to sheep herding at Nuzi (whose records date to the middle of the second millennium B.C.), Morrison says that at least one of the texts (HSS 16 234) may point to special feeding of ewes so as to improve the young stock they would bear or were nursing.[74] This could indicate that they were trying to promote twinning. As for the Mycenaean texts, it is true that twinning is not mentioned, nonetheless, simply because we have no reference to the phenomenon does not mean that it did not occur. I think this leaves open the possibility that in good years the collector may have been able to retain some lambs for his own use.

Carlier also proposed that the normal target of a quarter unit of wool, or 750 g (=1.6 lb), per sheep would not have been an unreasonable target. In fact, he cites figures of wool production targets from the Near East that are somewhat higher than the 750 g expected by the Mycenaean palace officials. For example, texts from Larsa (of the first third of the second millennium B.C.) record amounts that varied between 0.96 and 1.15 kg.[75] Tablets from Ur III (2100 B.C.) set targets of 1.3 kg per sheep.[76] Killen cites an example from Alalakh of the fifteenth century B.C. in which "308 sheep are recorded as having produced an average of just over 1.6 lb of usable wool per head."[77] This figure fits Killen's estimated yield of 0.73 kg[78] of wool per Mycenaean sheep perfectly, but it seems that there was a range of possible yields, or perhaps a range of what was considered reasonable to collect. From these target figures it seems likely that sheep in the ancient world produced about a kilogram of wool per head.[79] If this was so, then the Mycenaean collectors would have been able to keep approximately 0.250 kg of wool per sheep, or 50 kg from a flock of 200, for themselves. This would certainly add up to amounts that would have been useful for industrial purposes and as we have mentioned, many collectors are seen to be active in the textile industry.

The collectors who did produce textiles with the wool they collected from the sheep they were managing would have been able to substantially increase their income through this second business. Killen in particular has discussed this aspect of the collectors. He says:

[68] Carlier 1992.
[69] Carlier 1992, p. 165.
[70] M.W. Harper, *Animal Husbandry for Schools*, Macmillan Co., New York 1924, p. 389.
[71] W.C. Weir, "Management of Sheep and Other Fiber-Producing Animals," in *Animal Agriculture: The Biology, Husbandry, and Use of Domestic Animals*, 2nd edition, H.H. Cole and W.N. Garrett, eds., W.H. Freeman and Co. 1980, pp. 586-598; see p. 592.
[72] Aristotle, *Historia Animalium*, 6.19, A.L. Peck, translator, Loeb Classical Library 1970.
[73] Varro, *Rerum Rusticarum*, 2.2.18: "Quos arietes summittere volunt, potissimum eligunt ex matribus quae geminos parere solent."
[74] M.A. Morrison, "Evidence for Herdsmen and Animal Husbandry in the Nuzi Documents," in *Studies on the Civilization and Culture of Nuzi and the Hurrians in Honor of E.R. Lacheman*, M.A. Morrison and D.I. Owen, eds., Eisenbraums 1981, pp. 257-296; p. 275, n. 129.
[75] Carlier 1992, p. 165. Carlier takes this information from F.R. Krauss, *Die staatliche Viehhaltung im altbabylonischen Larsa*, 1966, pp. 55-57.
[76] M.L. Ryder, *Sheep and Man*, Duckworth and Co. 1983, p. 96.
[77] Killen 1964, p. 9. Killen takes the Alalakh figures from D.J. Wiseman, *The Alalakh Tablets*, London 1952, pp. 16, 100 (100 shekels of wool per sheep, tablet 361).
[78] Killen uses this figure while Carlier uses the 750 g.
[79] This is also the opinion of Ryder (1983, p. 96) who has surveyed all the ancient target figures for wool.

> There is some evidence to suggest that wool produced by 'collector' flocks was woven into cloth in 'collector' workshops. This is certainly the conclusion suggested by the figures for 'collector' workgroups on the Lc(1) records. On Da-Dg tablets, collector animals appear to account for approximately 30% of all the sheep listed in the set; and while we lack complete figures for the 'collector' wool on the Lc(1) tablets, this again looks as if it could have accounted for c. 30% of the total.[80]

Killen goes on to discuss the Lc(2) cloth records, on which the "density of 'collector's' names" was high,[81] but for which we do not have such a clear corresponding set of sheep tablets as we do for the Lc(1) set. For these records, however, he shows that the sheep listed on the Co series must also have belonged to collectors, and that it is most likely their wool that was used in making the textiles of the Lc(2) series.[82] Bennet has also discussed in detail the involvement of the collectors in all the sets of tablets that pertain to the textile industry.[83] Bennet concurs with Killen that, as he puts it, "...approximately 30% of the productive capacity of the Knossian state was in the hands of the "collectors"."[84] Thus we can easily say with Carlier that, "it is even possible that certain collectors had concentrated in their hands the complete chain of production, from sheep to the woolen cloth."[85] Of course the scale of textile production was probably variable. Some collectors, in particular those who show up on the palatial tablets with textile workshops may have been manufacturing cloth that they meant to exchange in local networks. Others working on a smaller scale may have been using the wool they had in excess of the palatial targets to make clothing for themselves. In both situations, the collectors would have profited from the textiles that they produced.

The potential for profit would have been substantially increased if, as Carlier and Killen have separately proposed, the collectors held flocks that did not appear on the tablets.[86] Halstead came to a similar conclusion based on his analysis of the Knossos D tablets. Halstead found that the records of palatial breeding flocks do not record a number of animals that would have been sufficient for replenishing the palatial flocks.[87] Therefore, he thinks it necessary to assume that there were other flocks not counted on the palatial records from which the palace must have gathered sheep. He goes on to say, "It seems likely that the palace of Knossos raised only a fraction of its numerous wool sheep and that large numbers of wethers were acquired from outside the 'palatial sector' of the economy."[88] It seems entirely possible then that the source from which the palace derived these large numbers of wethers could have been, at least in part, the collectors who were already engaged in the business of raising breeding flocks. Clearly, if the collectors did hold such sheep, they would have constituted a great source of income. For one thing, the palace would have had to compensate the collectors in some way for these animals. And having such a stock would have increased the amount of wool, and therefore textiles, that the collectors would have been able to keep and produce. Also, since such collectors would already have had the land, the facilities, and the personnel necessary for the care of the sheep, whatever profit they did realize from the taxed flocks would have been made at little extra cost.

In addition to the sheep's wool and the potential for cloth manufacture, it should not be forgotten that the animals produced a variety of other goods which the palace seems to have had no interest in collecting (under this taxation system at least[89]). For instance, the milk of the sheep was probably used to make cheese and yogurt, while the animals themselves could have been eaten once they were culled from the flock. Also, the animals' skins, tendons, and horns would have been useful in the manufacture of all sorts of domestic and industrial products. Thus the collectors would have had a productive source of food in the dairy products and meat that the animals produced, while their physical remains would have been useful in

[80] Killen 1976, p. 121.

[81] Killen 1976, p. 120.

[82] Killen 1976, p. 125.

[83] Bennet 1992, p. 94. Bennet also summarizes this information in a helpful table.

[84] Bennet 1992, pp. 86-87.

[85] Carlier 1992, p. 163.

[86] Carlier 1992, p. 165. Killen 1993, pp. 211-212. See Killen 1993, p. 217, n. 19 concerning evidence "for the possibility that shepherds in the Near East used their own animals to make good losses in centrally owned flocks under their care." I have to say that this particular proposition is difficult to reconcile with the idea that the collectors owned the flocks. The problem is that if we agree that the flocks are owned, then the reason they appear in the palatial documents is because they are being taxed. If we want to then propose that there were sheep that did not show up on the tablets, then we would have to assume that those sheep were not subject to taxation by the palace. But a good reason as to why the palace would tax some flocks but not all of them is not easy to find, whereas it would be easy to imagine that collectors held flocks of their own in addition to those that they had received from the palace either as beneficiaries or as leasers. I can offer one possible explanation: Perhaps the palace only taxed a certain percentage of the total flocks held by collectors, just as any tax is only a percentage of a person's total holdings, and those are the flocks that appear on the tablets. It may have been more convenient for the palace to take their percentage of the collector's produce from whole flocks which together represented 30% of the total holdings of each collector, rather than taking 30% of each flock. This would have saved time and energy in the collection process. Alternatively, there may be a reason that we are just not privy to and never will be.

[87] Halstead 1990-1991, pp. 343-365.

[88] Halstead 1990-1991, p. 360.

[89] We know from tablets such as Un 718 that the people living at the palaces certainly did consume cheese. From this tablet, and others like it, it seems that the palatial administration could requisition the cheese for ceremonial banquets along with other foodstuffs and the animals that were to be sacrificed. Un 718, though, records the preparations for a special banquet that was to take place in a religious context, and therefore one has to wonder if the palace used other means to obtain fresh foods on a regular basis. R. Palmer addresses this question in "Perishable Goods in Mycenaean Texts," *Floreant Studia Mycenaea, Acts of the 10th International Mycenological Colloquium held at the University of Salzburg*, S. Deger-Jalkotzy, S. Hiller and O. Panagl, eds., Wien 1999, pp. 463-485. See p. 467, where she says that the palace must have used "a procurement system for cheese outside of the standard assessment-collection systems." Also, perishable items probably could not have been carried long distances, but would have been gathered from producers who were close to the palace, which many of the collectors were not.

the manufacture of all sorts of domestic and industrial products.[90]

And finally, it should be mentioned that while the collectors clearly had a very important financial relationship with the palace, there is no reason to suppose that they didn't engage in financial transactions with other members of their communities.[91] The fresh products that the collectors derived from the sheep, and the textiles that were made from their wool, would certainly have been used by the collectors and their families, but the collectors could also have traded them for whatever other goods that they needed or even desired. We can imagine that the collectors were active members of their communities, and used their resources to maximize both their comfort and their standing within those communities.

Thus, the collectors may have been able, through a variety of means, to have made the business of shepherding somewhat profitable, even if they were obligated to give up a substantial portion of their wool and lambs to the palace. They would have been able to use the products of the sheep that were not collected by the palace, as well as possible surpluses of the goods that were, and it is likely that the collectors kept flocks in addition to those that were taxed by the palace. The fact that the collectors were able to retain some wool of their own is supported by the fact that many of the collectors were engaged in manufacturing cloth. This would not have been possible if the palace took all the wool produced by the collectors' flocks. Also, it is possible that the collectors received some sort of remuneration for what they supplied to the palace in excess of the targets, and they certainly would have benefited from trading their goods within local exchange networks.[92]

With all these possibilities for generating income open to them, it would be surprising if the collectors did not take advantage of them to add to their personal wealth. In dealing with both the palace and their local community they would have also ended up enhancing their prestige within their communities. Indeed, it is likely that they held economically significant positions within Mycenaean society. Their resources, at Pylos at least, do not seem to have been limited to sheep and textiles. For instance, *a-pi-me-de*, who can be classified as a collector through his appearance on Cn 655.5, is also seen with *e-to-ni-jo* land on Ep 539.14. At Knossos too, one of the collectors, *e-me-si-jo*, appears to own "large amounts of land or wheat at various places" on E 843.[93] Thus we know that collectors could also be substantial land holders. *A-ko-so-ta*, in addition to his position as a land inspector on Eq 213, allocated aromatic spices for use in the manufacture of perfumed oil (Un 267). On the basis of this connection Killen proposes that *ku-pi-ri-jo*, who, like *a-ko-so-ta*, is found in a managerial position on tablets that deal with the perfume industry (KN Fh, Fp, Ga and Gg series), should also be classified as a collector.[94] Killen also proposes, as we will soon discuss, that several of the bronzesmiths on the Pylos Jn series appear to be collectors.[95] Thus it seems that these Pylian collectors were active in many facets of the Mycenaean economy. If this was the case, then some of the collectors may have been able to become quite prosperous. And, having acquired some affluence, they would also have attained, thereby, a certain degree of influence within their communities.

In sum, we have considered several possibilities for the role of the collector. They could be either palatial agents, "beneficiaries" as Killen proposed, "leasers" (*fermiers*) as Carlier proposed, or "owners" as Bennet (and before him, Palmer) has proposed. Given the state of the evidence and the fact that problems could be raised for each one of these interpretations, it is impossible to determine for sure which is the correct explanation of the collectors. Nonetheless, it seems to me that Bennet's analysis and conclusions concerning the collectors at Knossos are the most compelling, and I would apply his conclusions to the collectors at Pylos as well. Thus I consider the collectors on the Knossian tablets, and probably also those at Pylos, to be the owners of the flocks listed against them. We have also seen that regardless of which one of these interpretations is preferred, there existed opportunities for the collector to make his situation economically productive for himself. With this in mind, I will now return to the deities who appear on the Knossos sheep tablets in the position of the collector.

The Religious Collectors

As I pointed out at the beginning of this chapter, the names of deities, sanctuaries, and religious personnel appear on the sheep tablets in the same administrative slot, so to speak, as the collectors. In particular, the Knossian D, Dl, and Dp series demonstrate the involvement of the religious sector in the business of sheep herding. For instance on tablet D 411 the deity Hermes (*e-ma-a$_2$-o*) is recorded in the position of the 'collector.'

[90] The one thing to keep in mind is that the shepherds working for the collectors would have expected some share of the available goods as well, which would necessarily reduce the profit for the collectors. But, considering the elevated positions held by the collectors (particularly the Pylian ones), we might think that they were probably able to commandeer the majority of the profits for themselves.

[91] See on this topic see P. Halstead, "The Mycenaean Palatial Economy: Making the Most of the Gaps in the Evidence," *Proceedings of the Cambridge Philological Society* 38 (1992) 57-86; *idem*, "Towards a Model of Mycenaean Palatial Mobilization," in *Rethinking Mycenaean Palaces: New Interpretations of an Old Idea*, M.L. Galaty and W.A. Parkinson, eds., The Cotsen Institute of Archaeology at UCLA 1999, pp. 35-47.

[92] Of course the shepherds working for the collectors would have expected some share of the available goods as well, which would have necessarily reduced the profit for the collectors. But, considering the elevated positions held by the collectors (particularly the Pylian ones), it seems likely that they would have been able to commandeer the majority of the profits for themselves.

[93] J.T. Killen, "The Role of the State in Wheat and Olive Production in Mycenaean Crete," *Aevum* 72 (1998) 19-23; see p. 22.

[94] Killen 1995, pp. 215-217.

[95] Killen 1995, pp. 214-215.

D 411:
di-ko-to / e-ma-a_2-o OVIS^f 60 *WE* 30[[96]

On analogy with the other D tablets, we can understand that the shepherd is *di-ko-to*, while *e-ma-a_2-o*, or Hermes, is the collector. This seems to indicate that the god Hermes was considered, if we follow Bennet's conclusions, to be the owner of the sheep listed with him on this tablet. We can imagine then that the people who actually owned and benefited from the sheep would have been the religious personnel working in Hermes' name.

In addition to this D tablet, we find that the adjectival form of Potnia (*po-ti-ni-ja-we-jo*) appears (or can be safely restored[97]) in the position of the collector on a full nine of the Dl tablets.[98] Dl 946 is a good representative of these tablets.

Dl 946:
A. po-ti-ni-ja-we-jo OVIS^f 70 LANA 7
B. ke-u-sa / si-ja-du-we , *o ki* OVIS^m 70 *o* LANA 7

Potnia is also recorded as the collector associated with the *ne-wa po-ka*, or new fleeces, on two tablets in the Dp series, 997 and 7742.

Dp 997:
a.] po-ti-ni-ja-we-ja [
b.]to-sa , / ne-wa , po-ka OVIS^f[

Unfortunately we do not have any figures preserved on either Dp 997 or 7742. We can be fairly sure, however, as Melena points out, that Dp 997 probably would have given the total of the Potnian Dl(1) fleeces if the number had survived.[99]

It may at first seem strange to see the adjectival form of Potnia's name being used here, but Killen points out that it is not unusual at all. In fact the scribe of the series, Hand 118, wrote many of the other collectors' names in this way. For instance, *sa-qa-re-jo*, "a derivative of the owner's name **sa-qa-ra, *sa-qa-ro vel sim,*" is found on ten of the Dl tablets (e.g., Dl 794), and *e-se-re-e-jo*, which Killen proposes to have been derived from the name *e-se-re-a_2*, is found three times on the Dl tablets (e.g., Dl 947).[100] In fact, Killen mentions that "...it is a regular practice on the Ak/Lc(1) and D tablets to describe 'collector' workgroups and flocks in terms of an adjectival derivative of a 'collector's' name (as e.g. *pe-ri-qo-te-jo < pe-ri-qo-ta*)..."[101] Thus Potnia is here to be understood as the collector, or owner, of the flocks on these tablets.

Killen has noticed that a similar parallel between collector's flocks and those belonging to a divinity is demonstrated on the Thebes sealings. The words *a-ko-ra* (Wu 49.γ, Wu 50.γ, Wu 63.γ) and *a-ko-ra-jo* (Wu 52.β, Wu 68.β) are found several times on the Theban sealings, and since these words are associated with 'collectors' or 'owners,' Killen proposes that "the animals recorded on those sealings are flocks 'belonging to' secular 'owners'."[102] On several other sealings, we find the words *i-je-ro* (Wu 66.γ, Wu 86.β, Wu 87.β) and *i-je-ra* (Wu 44.β). These words seem to correspond in function to the *a-ko-ra* and *a-ko-ra-ja* descriptions of the animals, and therefore would similarly indicate the person or institution responsible for delivering the animals. This led Killen to ask rhetorically,

> "Is the contrast between flocks 'of' secular 'owners' and those 'of' a divinity in this [the Dl] series also found on the sealings, with *a-ko-ra-jo* indicating animals 'belonging to' secular 'owners' and *i-je-ro/i-je-ra* indicating animals 'belonging to' divine 'owners', like Potnia at Knossos?"[103]

I would answer a resounding "Yes!" to this question.

At Pylos too we have a tablet that records Potnia as a collector. On Cc 665 Potnia is recorded against a herd of 100 sheep along with 190 pigs.

Cc 665:
ne-wo-pe-o , po-ti-ni-ja OVIS^m 100 SUS 190

Thus, not only at Knossos, but also at Thebes and Pylos, religious personnel were in possession of livestock.

On analogy then with the Knossos D tablets, we can see that Hermes and Potnia were considered to be collectors. This seems to indicate that these deities were, if we follow Bennet's conclusions, the nominal owners of the sheep recorded with them on their tablets. Clearly though, it was not the gods themselves who did the work of managing the sheep, but rather religious personnel who were working in their names. Because it is the deity's name that is mentioned on the tablets, rather than an individual's name, as was the case for the secular collectors, it seems most likely that these personnel were probably associated with a sanctuary that was dedicated to the deity recorded as the owner. Ilievski's understanding of the situation was that when a scribe used the adjectival form of a deity's name, it was probably understood that it was the deity's sanctuary that had possession of whatever commodity (or person) that was being described in this way.[104] Thus it is most likely

[96] In *KT6* the following notes concerning this text are recorded: *-ma-* and perhaps *e-* over [[ ]]. Perhaps to be read as *e-ma-a_2 o* OVIS^f. Perhaps traces after 30[."

[97] Dl 950 and 7771 both record *po-ti-ni*[, and Dl 7905 has *]ja-we-jo*, which is enough to safely restore the word as *po-ti-ni-ja-we-jo*.

[98] Dl(1) 930.A, 933.A, 943.A, 946.A, [950.A], 7147.A, 7503.A, [7771.A], and [7905.A].

[99] J.L. Melena, *Studies on Some Mycenaean Inscriptions from Knossos Dealing with Textiles* (*Minos* Suppl. 5), Salamanca 1975, p. 29.

[100] J.T. Killen, "Thebes Sealings and Knossos Tablets," in *Atti e Memorie del Secondo Congresso Internazionale de Micenologia* (*Incunabula Graeca* 98), E. De Miro, L. Godart, and A. Sacconi, eds., Rome 1996, pp. 71-82; see p. 81.

[101] Killen 1976, p. 124.

[102] Killen 1996, p. 81.

[103] Killen 1996, p. 81.

[104] Ilievski 1992, pp. 321-349.

the sanctuary of Potnia that was the collector of the flocks of female sheep listed on these Dl tablets, and it was her religious functionaries who managed them and made use of the benefits they provided. Such sanctuaries may have constituted mini-economic centers, just as the collectors may have headed up their own economic units. And just as the secular collectors were able to make use of the meat, dairy products, and physical remains of the sheep, and probably also the wool and lambs that were in excess of the palatial targets, so the religious personnel must also have been able to.

Obviously I think that the flocks were to be used by the sanctuaries in the same way that the other collectors used them: for their personal maintenance and in the hopes of being able to derive a profit. Others though have proposed, simply because a divinity's name was associated with the flocks, that they were destined to be used for religious purposes. Halstead, for instance, brought up the possibility that that the Potnian lambs "might have been destined as offerings to that divinity."[105] But if this was their purpose, I think the religious records would have been set off from the others in some way. However, this was not the case. In administrative terms, the Potnian flocks were treated exactly the same as all the other flocks within the series and their tablets display the same information: their flock strengths were recorded along with the number of lambs and amounts of wool that they were supposed to provide to the palace. There is no indication that the lambs or the wool were being used for any distinctive purpose.

A few other objections can be made to the idea that the Potnian lambs were to be sacrificed in rituals dedicated to Potnia. First, one would have to wonder why we do not also encounter flocks whose lambs were being raised as sacrificial animals for any of the other deities that are prominent at Knossos (or at Pylos for that matter). We have flocks attributed to Hermes and to Potnia, but this would hardly constitute evidence for flocks in general being described by the deity's name for which they were destined to be sacrificed. Second, several tablets from Pylos (such as Un 2, Un 6, Un 138 and Un 718[106]) provide evidence for the procedure that was followed when it was necessary to gather together the animals and goods required for sacrificial banquets. These tablets show that when a festival was being arranged, prominent personages within the community (for instance, as we saw in the previous chapter, *e-ke-ra$_2$-wo* and the *ra-wa-ke-ta* on Un 718.2 and 9, respectively) and groups of people (such as the *damos* and those of the *wo-ro-ki-jo-ne-jo ka-ma* on Un 718.7 and 11, respectively) were called upon to supply both the animals and the foodstuffs that would be needed. Palaima has deduced that when animals were gathered for sacrificial banquets, they were usually requisitioned in small numbers, as for instance on Cn 3 where we see individual bulls being sent by groups of men with military affiliations, and on Cn 418 where we see one pair and one single bull that were described by their physical attributes (e.g., "white, dark on the underbelly").[107] It is true that bulls were much rarer in general in Bronze Age Greece than sheep, but Cn 418 and the Un tablets show that sheep, goats, and pigs were also requisitioned in small numbers. Also, Killen has shown, using the Wu sealings found at Thebes and the C(2) series from Knossos, that other palatial administrations used similar systems to collect the animals that were intended for slaughter or sacrifice for ceremonial banquets.[108] This does not necessarily preclude the possibility that sacred animals were raised for sacrifice *en masse*, but it does make it less likely. The size of the flocks attributed to Potnia would also seem to speak against their being used exclusively as flocks that were bred as sacrificial animals. The total number of Potnian female sheep on the five Dl(1) tablets whose flock numbers are extant (Dl 930, 933, 943, 946, and 950) is 300. On four of the Potnian tablets the number of ewes is illegible (Dl 7147, 7503, 7771, 7905), but if we were to suppose, based on the numbers of the extant flocks, that a flock of 50 animals was a reasonable estimate,[109] then we would be able to raise the number of female sheep belonging to Potnia to 500. This seems to be a large number of animals of one type that would have been destined for rituals dedicated to one deity, especially since we know of other ways in which the animals were procured.

Finally, there is one more characteristic of the religious tablets that would make it unlikely that these flocks were destined for use in religious rituals. As we have seen, many of the tablets record large deficits in the number of lambs given over to the palace. In fact, very often the numbers recorded for the flock strengths and the deficit number of lambs (*o ki* OVIS^m) are exactly equal. In other words, for the flocks on these tablets, the religious personnel were not handing over any of the lambs that were expected from them.[110] It seems unlikely that the palace would have left the procurement of sheep for sacrifice to so unreliable a source.

Therefore, we may assume that the reason for their being kept should correspond to that of the other collectors' sheep in the series. The specific purpose for the Dl series

[105] Halstead 1990-1991, see p. 348.

[106] See J.T. Killen "Observations on the Thebes Sealings," in *Mykenaïka* (*BCH* Suppl. 25), J.-P. Olivier, ed., Athens 1992, pp. 365-380; *idem*, "Thebes Sealings, Knossos Tablets and Mycenaean State Banquets," *BICS* 39 (1994) 67-84; *idem*, 1996, pp. 71-82.

[107] T.G. Palaima, "Perspectives on the Pylos Oxen Tablets: Textual (and Archaeological) Evidence for the Use and Management of Oxen in Late Bronze Age Messenia (and Crete)," in *Studia Mycenaea 1988, Ziva Antika Monographs* No. 7, T.G. Palaima, C.W. Shelmerdine, and P. Ilievski, eds., Skopje 1989, pp. 85-119; see pp. 104-110.

[108] Killen 1996, pp. 72-73. [Also see T.G. Palaima, "The Transactional Vocabulary of Mycenaean Sealings and the Mycenaean Adminiatrative Process," in *Administrative Documents in the Aegean and their Near Eastern Counterparts*, ed., M. Perna, Paravia Scriptorium 2000, pp. 261-276; pp. 266-269.]

[109] The extant numbers of animals in Potnian flocks are as follows: Dl 930: 50, Dl 933: 40, Dl 943: 90, Dl 946: 70, Dl 950: 50.

[110] At first glance we might think that this kind of deficit could indicate that the religious flocks were being treated specially by the palace (i.e., that perhaps they were getting some sort of special exemption due to their religious status). However, we have already noted that this kind of deficit was quite common throughout the Dl series.

has been discussed by both Killen and Halstead. The Potnian Dl records actually belong to a subset of the Dl series, the Dl(1) set, whose 53 tablets (of the 76 in the entire Dl series) were all written by Hand 118.[111] Killen originally recognized that the Dl flocks, with their targets set in both lambs and wool, were probably being kept primarily for breeding purposes.[112] The Da-Dg flocks, in contrast, were made up of both wethers and ewes and therefore were unable to replenish themselves. Killen therefore proposed at first that the Dl flocks might have been used to maintain the main wool flocks of the Da-Dg series.[113] Later he modified this somewhat to say that:

> The breeding flocks on the Dl, Do records (which are in fact not very numerous) may have had the role of supplying replacements, not in all cases of loss, but only in circumstances where, for one reason or another, a shepherd was unable to make good a shortfall even with the help of his own resources.[114]

The fact that production targets were recorded for the Dl flocks in wool as well as in lambs means that the capacity for wool-production of these sheep was not ignored even though they were primarily used as breeding flocks. But the average wool target for the Dl sheep was lower than that set for the main flocks of wool-producing sheep: 1 unit of wool for 5 breeding ewes as opposed to 1 unit for every 4 wool sheep (the targets for which are found in the Dk series). The lower yield reflects the physical stress that the ewes experienced in giving birth and supporting the young lambs.

Halstead had a slightly different idea as to what the purpose of the Dl(1) sheep might have been.[115] The main point of the article in which Halstead discusses the Dl(1) sheep is to better understand the mechanism by which the Da-Dg flocks were replenished. He argues, as Killen had already acknowledged, that it would be impossible to replenish the Da-Dg flocks with only the breeding flocks that were recorded by the palace.[116] But in contrast with Killen, Halstead goes on to dispute the idea that the Dl sheep were used at all to restock the wool flocks of the Da-Dg series. Indeed, Halstead contends that there are some indications that the Dl(1) series flocks might have been part of a different group from those that made up the main Da-Dg flocks. The reasons he gives for this are as follows: First, although eight of the fourteen toponyms of the Dl(1) series do recur in the Da-Dg series, six of them do not. This seems odd considering there are over 400 occurrences of different toponyms in the Da-Dg series.[117] Also, 60% of the Dl(1) sheep are recorded as belonging to one of four collectors (among them Potnia), none of whom recur among the 138 references to the 15 collectors found in the Da-Dg series. Finally, the Dl(1) series records the wool targets on the same tablets that record the flock numbers, whereas, in contrast, separate records were kept for the Da-Dg flocks. Therefore, Halstead says that the Dl(1) tablets record sheep that "seem administratively isolated from the main block of records detailing palatial wool production and textile manufacture."[118] He goes on to point out that if the Dl(1) flocks were used for replenishing the main flocks, they could only have provided 7-8% of the necessary lambs. Halstead therefore infers that "the three largest groups of known or possible breeding ewes [including the Dl(1) series] may all have been linked to minor wool flocks quite separate from the main central Cretan group of 60-65,000 wool sheep."[119] Hence the collectors of the Dl series, among them being the servants of Potnia, were engaged in the specialized business of raising breeding flocks.

Halstead also suggests that it was a deliberate palatial strategy at Knossos to leave the riskier and more labor-intensive task of breeding sheep to the non-palatial sector.[120] As was discussed above, the collectors may very well have had flocks of their own that were not subject to palatial taxation, and it may have been from these flocks that the palace derived the lambs it needed. As Halstead says, "the fact that the procurement of these wethers is not recorded in the archives suggests that they were acquired not by taxation (which tended to be regular and documented) but by exchange."[121] He goes on to say that this exchange "may have been part of a complex series of transactions in which grain, livestock, agricultural and craft labour, and finished craft goods flowed between the palace and the non-palatial sector...."[122] This exchange would have brought the collectors, including those in the service of Potnia, a wide variety of goods, some economic security, and perhaps even the possibility of acquiring some real wealth.

Of course there is no way to prove that the personnel working for Potnia had such flocks in addition to the ones recorded in the Dl series, but it is certainly possible.

[111] Halstead reviews this information in 1990-1991, pp. 346-348.
[112] Killen 1964.
[113] Killen 1964, p. 14.
[114] Killen 1993, p. 212.
[115] Halstead 1990-1991.
[116] It is interesting to note that in contrast with sheep tablets of Knossos, the Cn records of Pylos do record a sufficient number of ewes from which the palatial flocks could have been restocked (Halstead 1990-1991, pp. 356-359). Killen had already noted that in general Pylos' textile industry was more centralized than Knossos' in "The Textile Industries at Pylos and Knossos," in *Pylos Comes Alive*, C.W. Shelmerdine and T.G. Palaima, eds., New York 1984, pp. 49-63; see p. 55.
[117] It should be noted that Halstead (1990-1991, p. 347) does say, in a somewhat contradictory manner, that the fact that eight of the fourteen toponyms *are* found in the Da-Dg series "suggests a connection between the Dl(1) and the Da-Dg series".
[118] Halstead 1990-1991, p. 347.
[119] Halstead 1990-1991, p. 360.
[120] It is interesting to note that a similar strategy may have been in use at Pylos. The Cn records do not record breeding ewes as clearly as the Knossos sheep records, but the flocks held by collectors both in the Hither and Further Provinces have a higher percentage of ewes than non-collector flocks (ewes compose 25% of collector flocks in the Hither Province vs. 9% for non-collector flocks, and 57% of collector flocks in the Further Province vs. 31% of the non-collector flocks; see Halstead, p. 358). The collectors of Pylos, therefore, also seem to have borne the greater burden of providing lambs to replenish the wool flocks.
[121] Halstead 1990-1991, pp. 360-361.
[122] Halstead 1990-1991, p. 361.

Nonetheless, even without the benefit of such speculation we are able to say, based on the Dl and Dp series, that religious personnel kept flocks of sheep for breeding purposes and that the lambs from those ewes may have been the source of some material benefit for the religious personnel.[123] Furthermore, just as the secular collectors were able to make use of the milk and cheese that the flocks produced, and probably also the wool and skins that were in excess of the palatial targets, so the religious personnel must have been able to exploit these goods for their own purposes. Thus, I think it is reasonable to suppose that the religious personnel participated in the economy in the same way that secular collectors did. Many sanctuaries probably did not aspire to accomplish much more than providing for their basic needs, but some sanctuaries, like some of the secular collectors, may have been able to become quite prosperous, acquiring material resources in excess of what they needed for their daily sustenance. And I think it is possible that the tablets provide us with evidence for such a sanctuary at a place called *si-ja-du-we*.

Si-ja-du-we and the Potnian Flocks

It is of great interest that six of the Dl tablets that record Potnia as the collector (Dl 930, 933, 946, 950, 7503, and 7905) also record that the flocks were located at one place, that is, *si-ja-du-we*. The following chart lays out the information found on the Potnian Dl tablets.

As we can see, the shepherds in charge of the Potnian flocks are all different, but six of them were operating in or around *si-ja-du-we*. The *po-ti-ni-ja-we-jo* flocks are found with three other place names but only one flock is associated with each toponym: *qa-nwa-so* on Dl 943, *ka-ru-no* on Dl 7147, and *ra-ja* on Dl 7771. The toponym *qa-nwa-so* appears nowhere else in the tablets but it is at this place that we find the largest of the Potnian flocks (90 sheep). The other two toponyms, *ka-ru-no* and *ra-ja*, do appear elsewhere on the Dl tablets, *ka-ru-no* on Dl 412, and *ra-ja* on Dl 7138 and 9862. Dl 9862 is too fragmentary to be able to read any more than *ra-ja*, so we have no way of knowing to whom that flock belonged. Thus it is possible that there was another Potnian flock at that location although there is nothing really to support that proposition. The remarkable thing is the clustering of flocks at *si-ja-du-we*.

It seems that the sanctuary dedicated to Potnia at *si-ja-du-we*, for which the flocks were being kept, had invested more in shepherding than the other three represented on the tablets. This could be taken to imply that it was a more substantial sanctuary, with more people to support and more resources dedicated to that purpose. The total extant number of sheep held at *si-ja-du-we* is 210, and if we add two flocks of 50 (a common flock size) for the two tablets where figures are not extant, we have 310, not an inconsiderable number of animals. It is possible that with those resources the sanctuary at *si-ja-du-we* was able to grow and become one of the prosperous collector-

Chart 5.1: The *po-ti-ni-ja-we-jo* Flocks in the Dl Series

Tablet	Toponym	Shepherd	Number of OVIS^f	*o ki** OVIS^m
930	*si-ja-du-we*	]*ma-di-qo*	50	50
933	*si-ja-du-we*	]-**83-re-to*	40 (*o* 20)	60
943	*qa-nwa-so*	*a-ko-i-da*	90	90
946	*si-ja-du-we*	*ke-u-so*	70	70
950	*si-ja-du-*]*we*	] **18-jo*[	50	50
7147	*ka-ru-no*	----	---	---
7503	*si-ja-du-we*	*te-wa-jo*	---	---
7771	*ra-ja*	]*qo-ta*	---	---
7905	*si-ja-du-we*	]*ra-ri-jo*	---	---

**ki* = "young" or "newborn."

sanctuaries that I think existed in Mycenaean culture.

Hiller though saw *si-ja-du-we* as a place that had primarily an economic significance (he called it a *Wirtschaftsverband*),[124] and said that we may not be correct in looking for a shrine belonging to Potnia at *si-ja-du-we* because other flocks belonging to Potnia are found at places that occur in locations where we know that secular activities were taking place. He is referring to the two places names that had Potnian flocks, but which were also found on tablets that recorded secular flocks: *ra-ja* and *ka-ru-no*. While I would hesitate to locate large religious communities at these places, it does not seem impossible that religious activities could go on in the same place as secular ones. Certainly, as was

[123] In Killen's seminal 1964 article (pp. 6-7) on the D tablets he compares the Bronze Age system to that of medieval England and it is interesting to note that several of his examples are sheep-holding establishments that were associated with the religious realm. For instance, he says that the Bishop of Winchester in 1259 held about 29,000 sheep, while about 50 years later the Priory of St. Swithun's is recorded as holding 20,000. Also, in the same time period as the latter example, "the Abbots of Crowland had a central headquarters, from which sheep were dispatched to the various manors; at this headquarters a general account was kept and the wool was stored for sale."

[124] Hiller 1981, pp. 114-115.

discussed in Chapter 4, we know that both religious and secular activities were taking place at *Pa-ki-ja-ne*. Hence I would not exclude the possibility that the same might be true of many villages.

Other tablets support the conclusion that *si-ja-du-we* was a religious center that supported itself through shepherding. On line 2 of Am(2) 821 *si-ja-du-we* is recorded as the location of a man named *ta-ra*, who is described not only as a shepherd (*po-me*), but also a priest (*i-je*[*-re-*]*u*). This is very significant because it not only connects *si-ja-du-we* with shepherding, but it also provides further confirmation that the business of shepherding at *si-ja-du-we* was conducted by religious personnel.

Am(2) 821 + *frr*.:
1.]ra-jo , / e-qe-ta-e , e-ne-ka , ẹ-mi-to VIR 2 ki-ta-ne-to , / su-ri-mo, e-ne-ka , 'o-pa' VIR 1
2. si-ja-du-we , ṭạ-ṛạ , / i-je[-re-]u , po-me , e-ne-ka , 'o-pa' X VIR 1 ko-pe-re-u , / e-qe-ta , e-ki-'si-jo' VIR 1
3.] *vacat*

Am 821 is a difficult tablet to interpret. Even Killen has had trouble discerning the relationship between the men's names and the numbers of VIR recorded after them. He says, "It is not clear whether these VIR entries refer to the *e-qe-ta*, etc. themselves or to separate individuals that these important personages have been (or will be) responsible for supplying to the palace or have under their care.[125] Melena has said that it is a "personnel record, whose ultimate intention escapes us."[126] In their analyses of the tablet though, they have each said things that relate to our priest-shepherd *ta-ra*.

When discussing this tablet Melena had trouble with the idea that a shepherd could also fulfill the official position of a priest.[127] He starts by noting that *ki-ta-ne-to*, the personal name on Am 821.1, must have been a shepherd even though he is not specifically described here as a *po-me*, because he is seen again on Da 1108 as the shepherd of a flock of wool-producing sheep. The identity between the two *ki-ta-ne-to*'s is fairly certain since he is located at the place *su-ri-mo* on both tablets. Thus *ta-ra* should also be interpreted as a *po-me* who actually handled sheep rather than as a figurative shepherd (which Melena was also considering given the connection we have of priests being seen as shepherds of the people in their care). Because Melena thought so strongly that a shepherd could not also be a priest, he proposed that *i-je*[*-re-*]*u* was more likely to be the man's name than an occupational title. This forces him to interpret *ta-ra* as a minor place name recorded in addition to *si-ja-du-we*, rather than as the man's name. Now, however, since we have seen that religious personnel were involved in economic activities and understand that they can have dual roles in society, we can dispense with Melena's difficulties and accept the simpler interpretation of these lines: that *ta-ra* was both a priest and a shepherd.

Killen in his analysis of Am 821 is more interested in the fact that we have two shepherds whose function is somehow designated as *e-ne-ka o-pa*.[128] In 1992 he posed the question as to what this phrase might mean, but was unable to answer it entirely to his own satisfaction.[129] More recently though Killen has proposed that *o-pa* could indicate the process of "finishing" or, in this case, the fattening of sheep for slaughter or sacrifice. He therefore says that the two shepherds of Am 821 "might have had special responsibilities in connexion with the fattening of sheep for sacrifice *vel sim.*"[130] Killen then brings up the fact that *ta-ra* is both a priest and a shepherd in support of this proposal, implying that the priest was involved in the process because of his relation to the religious sphere. I would point out though that *ki-ta-ne-to,* the other shepherd who is recorded as *e-ne-ka o-pa* on the tablet, is not explicitly associated with the religious realm (as Killen himself admits[131]). Therefore it seems more likely that what we have here is a priest who happens to be recorded because of his business interests and who was being treated in the same way as the rest of the secular personages on the tablet. I think Killen is likely to be correct here that *e-ne-ka o-pa* indicates that the shepherds were being asked to contribute sheep that were being finished for sacrificial purposes, but it does not appear that it was necessary to have a priest employed in the process.

I should also mention that the location *si-ja-du-we* is also found on Dk 969 with the word *a-ko-ra*, which, as we saw above, most likely indicates that a collector was involved. It is possible that Potnia was the collector that the scribe had in mind when he wrote the tablet.

Dk 969:
A.] si-ja-du-we , [
B.]ki-to / a-ko-ra[

Po-ti-ni-ja-we-jo does not actually appear on this tablet, but Killen and Bennet have both used Dk 969 to support their associating the word *a-ko-ra* with collectors based on the fact that *si-ja-du-we* consistently appears in the Dl series with *po-ti-ni-ja-we-jo*, which they considered to hold the position of a collector.[132] In doing this they were

[125] Killen 1992, p. 378.
[126] J.L. Melena, "Further Thoughts on Mycenaean *o-pa*," in *Res Mycenaeae*, A. Heubeck and G. Neumann, eds., Gottingen 1983, pp. 258-286; see p. 259. Melena (1975) also attempts to determine the general location of *si-ja-du-we*. He points out that "it cannot be merely a coincidence that the two most frequent place names in the documents of scribe 118, *si-ja-du-we* and *e-ko-so* recur together in Am 821" (p. 28). He goes on to say that the relationship between the two places within the tablets "may support a location of *si-ja-du-we* near *e-ko-so*", which he has already placed north of the Amari valley, on the banks of the Mylos river. Thus he places *si-ja-du-we* on his map (p. 30) somewhat west of Knossos.
[127] Melena 1975, p. 30.
[128] Killen 1992, pp. 377-378; *idem*, "Mycenaean *o-pa*," in *Floreant Studia Mycenaea*, Acts of the 10th International Mycenological Colloquium held at the University of Salzburg, S. Deger-Jalkotzy, S. Hiller, and O. Panagl, eds., Wien 1999, pp. 325-341; see p. 333.
[129] Killen 1992, pp. 377-378.
[130] Killen 1999, pp. 332-333.
[131] Killen 1999, p. 333.
[132] Killen 1976, p. 123. Bennet 1992, pp. 76-77.

assuming a connection between *si-ja-du-we* and *po-ti-ni-ja-we-jo*. Thus it seems that this tablet too could be considered part of the *po-ti-ni-ja-we-jo/si-ja-du-we* records. Unfortunately though, it does not really provide us with any more information that is terribly useful.

Nonetheless, the several tablets dealing with Potnian flocks at this location, combined with the priest-shepherd of Am 821, leads me to conclude that those flocks were indeed associated with a sanctuary dedicated to Potnia, and that the flocks were maintained at least partially in the interests of supporting the activities of the sanctuary and the religious personnel who were employed there. Deger-Jalkotzy, in a discussion of Am 821, came to a similar conclusion. She said, "there was a shrine belonging to Potnia in *si-ja-du-we*, to which the flocks in question belonged" and that "the flocks probably provided the economic basis for the shrine, which the priest managed in the name of the deity."[133] She goes on to compare this situation with the one on Ep 704.5-6, where we saw the priestess *e-ri-ta* managing a landholding on behalf of the deity. And like *e-ri-ta*, it seems to me that the sanctuary at *si-ja-du-we* may have been able to benefit from their possession of economically productive resources. The religious personnel who managed the sheep at *si-ja-du-we* may have also been using their wool to produce textiles – another source of material benefit.

Possible Textile Workshops at *Si-ja-du-we* and *Ne-wo-pe-o*

As we saw above, Killen has shown that many of the collectors were probably not only herding sheep and collecting wool, but also using that wool in order to manufacture textiles of their own. Therefore, it is worth considering whether the possible sanctuary at *si-ja-du-we* might also have engaged in such activities. In fact, the tablet KN Ak 830 may give us evidence, as Melena says, "testifying to the existence of a textile centre in this village."[134]

Ak 830:
1.]du-wi-ja , po-ṣi[
2. ko-]wa / me-zo-e [
3. ko-]wo / me-zo-e 3[

The Ak tablets seem to record the "working strength" of the female workgroups who were employed in the Cretan textile industry.[135] These records most likely served as the basis upon which the production targets for each group would be calculated. They would also have assisted the palatial administrators in determining the magnitude of the rations that were to be allocated to the women and their children. Melena proposes that the *]du-wi-ja* could be restored as the ethnic adjective **si-ja-du-wi-ja*, from *si-ja-du-we*.[136] If indeed this restoration is correct, it would constitute evidence that a textile workshop was located in *si-ja-du-we*.

It would, however, still be up for debate as to whether the workshop was associated with the sanctuary dedicated to Potnia or not. In general, collector workgroups were indicated by the genitive or adjectival form of the collector's name, and non-collector workgroups were indicated by the toponyms at which they were located.[137] Since it is the adjectival form of the toponym *si-ja-du-we* that we are proposing should be restored on Ak 830, then, according to the pattern, Ak 830 would be thought to record a palatial workgroup. But there are exceptions to this rule.[138] Indeed, Dk 969, which we recently discussed as probably belonging to the Potnian group of tablets because it bore the place name *si-ja-du-we*, was considered (implicitly) by Killen and Bennet to be one of those exceptions. Therefore, Ak 830 could also reasonably constitute an exception to the rule. It would then follow that the collector being indicated by the place name was also the same as that on Dk 969, that is, Potnia.

There is, however, another complicating factor concerning this tablet that has to be taken into consideration: it is unclear what the incomplete *po-si[* on line 1 might refer to.[139] It could be the beginning of a man's name, in which case Ak 830 would be classified as a collector tablet, although, not one associated with Potnia. This seems unlikely though because there are no collector names, and indeed no names in the entire Linear B corpus, that start with *po-si*, which would make this a surprising hapax. On the other hand, *po-si* is found at the beginning of several words that are related to the deity Poseidon, such as the female goddess *po-si-da-e-ja* on Tn 316.4, the *po-si-da-i-je-u-si*, or priests of Poseidon, on Fn 187.18, and the sanctuary of Poseidon, the *po-si-da-i-jo* on Tn 316 *v*. 1. If *po-si[* is related to Poseidon in some way, then Ak 830 could actually record a textile manufacturing shop dedicated to the service of Poseidon, and the management of this textile workshop would remain within the religious realm, although, again, it would not be Potnia who was nominally in charge of it. Instead, we would have to imagine another sanctuary in *si-ja-du-we* that had mercantile interests, which of course would not be a concern to me. But, finally, it is also possible that *po-si[* did not indicate the workgroup's affiliation, but instead referred to some other distinguishing quality of the group.

[133] S. Deger-Jalkotzy, *E-qe-ta: Zur Rolle des Gefolgschaftswesens in der Sozialstruktur mykenischer Reiche*, Wien 1978, p. 89.
[134] Melena 1975, p. 28.
[135] Killen 1988, pp. 168-169.
[136] Melena 1975, p. 28. Killen on the other hand proposes **o-du-wi-ja*, from *o-du-we*, which appears as a toponym on the wool tablet Od 696.1 ("Two Notes on the Knossos Ak Tablets," in *Acta Mycenaea* II [*Minos* 12], M.S. Ruipérez, ed., Salamanca 1972, pp. 425-440; see p. 429, n. 4).
[137] Killen 1976, pp. 118-120; *idem*, 1988, p. 171. Bennet 1992, pp. 72-73.
[138] For instance, line 1 of Ak 627 reads: *da-*22-to* , / *a-no-zo-jo TA* 1 '*DA* 1' MUL[ ]9 *pe di* 2". *da-*22-to* is a fairly common place name on the Knossos tablets, and *a-no-zo-jo* could be the genitive of a man's name (Killen 1972, p. 426).
[139] Even the entry for *po-si[* in *Dic. Mic.* II (p. 151) does not give any possible definitions or references.

With all of these possibilities concerning the interpretation of *po-si*[, and the uncertainty of the restoration of]*du-wi-ja*, it is difficult to say with any certainty whether this workshop was associated with the religious or the secular realm. If we can place it in the religious realm, and assume that it was Potnia who presided over its associated sanctuary, then the sanctuary's personnel were capitalizing on its possession of sheep by producing textiles from their wool just as other collectors were doing. On the other hand, Ak 830 may not be an exception, in which case its *ko-wa* and *ko-wo* were involved in a palatial enterprise. Actually, it would be just as interesting to find that there was textile manufacture going on at *si-ja-du-we* under palatial auspices as under religious, since in the former situation the sanctuary could have been supplying the palatial workshop with wool, and it may have been able to make some further profit for itself through that exchange. The same type of situation would apply if it were Poseidon (or one of his related manifestations) who owned the workshop. In any of these scenarios – whether the textile workshop was managed by Potnia, Poseidon, or the palace – the sanctuary of Potnia and its personnel stood to gain from its possession of flocks of sheep.

The evidence for textile manufacture at *si-ja-du-we* is admittedly somewhat tentative, based as it is on one problematic tablet, and it is certainly not clear what role the religious sector would have had within it even if we do follow Melena's restoration of]*du-wi-ja* as **si-ja-du-wi-ja*. The Pylian tablets, on the other hand, give us more certain evidence that textile production was taking place at a location that also had Potnian flocks. Nonetheless, they also present us with a problem concerning which institution was managing the textile workshop. As was saw, PY Cc 665 ascribes a flock of 100 male sheep to Potnia, along with a herd of 190 pigs.

Cc 665:
ne-wo-pe-o , po-ti-ni-ja OVIS^{m} 100 SUS 190

I see these animals, like the ones on the Potnian tablets from Knossos, as providing the sustenance for the religious personnel who were managing them in the service of Potnia. The situation gets more interesting when we realize that the location at which these animals were kept, *ne-wo-pe-o*, is also recorded, on tablets Aa 786, Ab 554, and Ad 688, as the location of some female textile workers (and their children). These tablets, like the Ak series from Knossos, seem to have been census records of female workgroups whose occupations indicate that they were involved in textile manufacture. Thus there was almost certainly a textile workshop located at *ne-wo-pe-o*.

However, just as with Ak 830, it is not clear whether these textile workers were associated with the religious sector or with the secular. Perhaps we could infer from the combination of Cc 665 and its associated A tablets that religious personnel not only kept flocks at *ne-wo-pe-o*, but that they were also managing a textile workshop there. However, it is also possible that the workers were associated with the palace. Hence, we cannot say for sure which institution was managing the workers. But, as with the *si-ja-du-we* example, the sanctuary of Potnia and its personnel stood to gain from their possession of sheep in either scenario: even if the textile workshop was operated by the palace, the sanctuary could have supplied the nearby palatial workshop with wool, and most likely would have derived some benefit from this exchange.

While the nature of the evidence from Knossos and Pylos leads us to be unsure as to whether textile manufacture was conducted under religious auspices at these places, the evidence from Thebes Of series is far more clear, and it indicates that there were several religiously associated textile workshops in operation there.

The Theban Of Series

The Theban Of series consists of sixteen tablets that were grouped together because their texts all contain the ideogram LANA, which represents the wool that the palace was allocating to the various workshops found in this series.[140] These tablets were also found together as a group "near the E end of the excavation of the Archive Room,"[141] and they have since been assigned to the same scribal hand, 303.[142] The wool on these tablets was being allocated for industrial purposes, as is shown by the inclusion of occupational terms commonly seen on the Knossos and Pylos tablets dealing with cloth and cloth workgroups, such as *a-ra-ka-te-ja* (Of 34.2; and e.g., KN Lc 531.B, PY Aa 89), *te-pe-ja* (Of 35.1; and e.g. KN Le 641.4, PY Ad 921 in the genitive plural *te-pe-ja-o*), and *a-ke-ti-ra$_2$* (Of 36.1; also seen as *a-ke-ti-ri-ja* on PY Aa 815 and KN Ai 739.1 and *a-ze-ti-ri-ja* on KN Ln 1568 *lat. inf.*). The first was probably derived from ἠλακάτη or 'distaff', which gives us a definition for *a-ra-ka-te-ja* of 'spinning women' (or 'woman', depending on whether we take *a-ra-ka-te-ja* as a nominative plural or dative singular, an issue to which I will return in a moment). The second term, *te-pe-ja*, is an occupational description of female textile workers who seem to be named after the kind of cloth they produced, the TELA + *TE*, or *te-pa*, cloth.[143] Killen has proposed that the third term, *a-ke-ti-ra$_2$*, are /*asketryai*/ from ἀσκέω, with the meaning that they were 'decorators' or 'finishers' who used the wool on their tablets to decorate already manufactured pieces

[140] Th. Spyropoulos and J. Chadwick, *The Thebes Tablets II, Minos Suppl.* 4, 1975. Chadwick is the author of the commentary on the Of tablets and it is from his text that I derive much of the information that follows. When I am drawing from material in his commentary I will use "Chadwick 1975" as the footnote.

[141] Spyropoulos and Chadwick 1975, p. 22. C.W. Shelmerdine has since shown that this room was probably not an Archive, but rather a storeroom from which the wool was disbursed ("Workshops and Record Keeping in the Mycenaean World," in *TEXNH: Craftsmen, Craftswomen, and Craftsmanship in the Aegean Bronze Age*, R. Laffineur and P.P. Betancourt, eds., Liège and the University of Texas at Austin, PASP 1997, pp. 387-396; see pp. 387-389.

[142] J.L. Melena and J.-P. Olivier, *Tithemy: The Tablets and Nodules in Linear B from Tiryns, Thebes and Mycenae* (*Minos* Suppl. 12), Salamanca 1991; see pp. 35-37.

[143] Killen 1966, p. 109.

of cloth.[144] For all of these terms the case is ambiguous, they can either represent dative the singular or the nominative plural. Palaima has pointed out that since there are several other datives in the Of series, such as *ma-ri-ne-we-ja-i* (Of 25.1, 35.2) and *po-re-si* (Of 26.3) in the plural and *a-re-i-ze-we-i* (Of 37.1) and *qa-ra$_2$-te* (Of 38.1) in the singular, we should take these three ambiguous terms as datives as well.[145] Postulating datives in the context of this series would make sense since the wool was presumably being sent to these people. However, the scribe who wrote the Of series (Hand 303) was not adverse to using the nominative instead of the dative at times, and so we see *ko-pe-re-u* on Of 30.1 and *di-u-ja-wo* on Of 33.2. This leaves open the possibility that these three terms, *a-ra-ka-te-ja*, *te-pe-ja* and *a-ke-ti-ra$_2$*, are also in the nominative rather than the dative, and I think it is actually more likely that they are in the nominative.[146] The reason for this is that in every other instance in which we find these occupational terms, both at Pylos and at Knossos, their context shows that they are they are in the plural, which seems to indicate that the people who are employed in these occupations usually work in groups. It would be strange to send wool to one spinning woman or to one *te-pe-ja* cloth maker. Consequently it seems preferable to take them as plural nominatives.

The address to which the cloth was being disbursed is indicated in several different ways. In some cases the address was given as a toponym in the accusative followed by the allative suffix '*-de*', such as on Of 25.2 where we find *a-ma-ru-to-de* ("to Amarynthos"). In this case, as in others, the address is further clarified by including a man's name in the dative (*pa-pa-ra-ki*).[147] In several cases the address was indicated by a man's name followed by *do-de*, which can be translated as 'to the house of X,"[148] while for many entries a personal name in the dative or nominative was considered sufficient (e.g., Of 26.1: *pu$_2$-re-wa* and Of 28.1: *pi-ro-pe-se-wa*). In some cases we see an occupational term standing on its own (Of 34.2: *a-ra-ka-te-ja*), but in several others we see groups of workers or even a woman's name modified by the adjectival form of a man's name (e.g., Of 27.2: *a-ka-i-je-ja du-qo-te-ja*).

Killen has noted that the form of this latter type of 'address' – the adjectival form of a man's name – provides an interesting parallel with the way many of the collectors are indicated on the sheep tablets of Knossos. He therefore proposed that, on analogy with the Knossos tablets, we should also see the Theban names associated with the textile workshops as "collectors."[149] As I brought up within the context of Killen's beneficiary theory, the fact that some of the same names are found at different sites led Killen to suggest that certain names were retained and reused within prominent, perhaps royal, families.[150] While I do not know whether these people need be royal, it does make sense that they held the same status: i.e., they were both collectors.

The collectors who were in charge of the textile workshops in the Of series were apparently doing work for the palace under the *ta-ra-si-ja* system. The word *ta-ra-si-ja* is not found on the Of tablets, but it is found elsewhere on tablets that deal with wool and cloth (e.g., KN Lc 535.A, 536.A, Le 642.1, MY Oe 110.1), and, as we will see, it was also used to refer to allotments of bronze in the Pylian Jn series, as well as to work that was to be done on wheels (KN So 4442.b). The word is generally interpreted as representing *ταλα(ν)σία,[151] which in Classical Greek was used mostly in wool-working contexts. In Mycenaean contexts it seems to have retained its relation to τάλαντον, which refers to something weighed out, since *ta-ra-si-ja* appears to refer to the raw materials that were presumably weighed out and given to workers, such as the wool of the Of series. The word *ta-ra-si-ja* also seems to have taken on a more general meaning though within the tablets of "work assigned," and Mycenologists use it to refer to the palatial system of production under which raw materials were allocated to various workers who were then expected to return the finished products to the palace.[152] It is in this sense that we say the workshops of the Of series were working under the *ta-ra-si-ja* system since the palatial administration issued raw materials to them, the wool in this case, presumably with the expectation that the textiles produced with this wool would be sent back to the palace when they were completed.[153]

I do not think, though, as is often assumed, that the work these textile manufacturers did for the palace under the *ta-ra-si-ja* system constituted the total amount of the work that they did all year. Chadwick remarks on the fact that all the Of tablets "deal with wool in relatively small quantities."[154] The largest amount is 10 units, which equals 30 kg. This amount is only allocated twice, and each time to the same person (*qa-ra$_2$-te* on Of 37 and Of 38). After this the next largest amounts are 18, 15, 12, 11, and 10 kg, each given once. The allocation amounts that are most frequently given out are between 1 and 6 kg (1 and 3 kg are each allocated seven times, 2 kg is allocated twice and 6 kg allocated four times).[155] Of course, even these amounts of wool should not be considered trivial. Nosch has impressed upon me (in

[144] Killen 1979, pp. 165-168. Chadwick (1975, p. 90, n. 1) also uses this definition and notes his thanks to Killen for making him aware of his interpretation prior to publication.

[145] T.G. Palaima in "*Po-re-na*: A Mycenaean Reflex in Homer? An I-E Figure in Mycenaean?" *Minos* 31-32 (1996-1997 [1998]) 303-312; see p. 309.

[146] Hooker ("The Language of the Thebes Tablets," *Minos* 16 [1977] 174-178; p. 174) actually implies that interpreting them as plurals would be more appropriate.

[147] Chadwick 1975, p. 104; cf. *pa-pa-ra-ko*, a man's name on PY Jn 845.5.

[148] Chadwick 1975, pp. 88-89.

[149] Killen 1979, pp. 176-178.

[150] Killen 1979, p. 177.

[151] *Dic. Mic.* II, p. 313.

[152] *Dic. Mic.* II, p. 313.

[153] Killen 1999, p. 327.

[154] Chadwick 1975, p. 95.

[155] Without factoring the two allocations of 30 kg, the average allocation is 5.18 kg, and the mean is 3 kg.

person and in print[156]) that the production of cloth is far more time consuming than we might think. The process of spinning the wool into thread takes up the bulk of the time: 1 kg of wool, depending on the fineness of the thread, can take from 195 to 700 hours to spin. Assuming a workday of 10 hours, that would mean 20 to 70 days. The weaving, however, goes much faster: it takes an average of four days to weave a kilogram's worth of wool thread into cloth. Nonetheless, despite the time-consuming nature of this process, given that there would most likely have been a group of women working together in a workshop, it seems unlikely that the palatial *ta-ra-si-ja* work was the sole occupation of these workshops.[157] Rather, the collectors who ran these shops probably took on work from local clients in addition to what they were required to do for the palace. It was probably through the latter kind of work that the collectors would have stood to gain the most significant portion of their livelihood.

The Religious Textile Workshops

Religious figures, as on the sheep tablets, also appear among the holders of textile workshops at Thebes. Therefore, the religious collectors may again be said to hold an economic position that was parallel to that held by collectors. Among the religious holders of Theban textile workshops we see Hera (*e-ra*) on Of 28.2, Hermes (*e-ma-a₂*) on Of 31.3, and Potnia (*po-ti-ni-ja*) on Of 36.2. There are several other possible deities within the Of series, but for now these three can stand as representative of all of them.

Of 28:
1. pi-ṛọ-pe-se-wa , *ku* LANA 2
2. i-da-i-jo *ku* LANA *PA* 2 e-ra , ke-o-te-ja *ku* LANA 1
3. *vacat*

Of 31:
1. do-]de *ku* LANA *PA* [
2.]ḍọ-de *ku* LANA *P̣Ạ* [
3.] e-ma-a$_2$, re-[

Of 36:
1. no-ri-wo-ki-de *ku* LANA 1 a-ke-ti-ra$_2$, wa-na-ka[
2. po-ti-ni-ja , wo-ko-de , a-ke-ti-ra$_2$ *ku* LANA 1

As with the flocks of sheep, since the workers are associated with a deity's name, rather than with a personal name, we may imagine that they were working for a religious group dedicated to the service of that deity, and that this group was most likely associated with a sanctuary. Such workshops may even have been located within the precincts of the sanctuaries.[158] Because of this religious affiliation, Chadwick suggested that the wool that was given to the deities was probably used for "garlands of honour or by suppliants," and he quotes Classical sources as parallels for such a proposition.[159] However, given the nature of the tablets, it seems unlikely that the allocations of wool sent by the palace were ever used in this way. Of 36.2, for instance, specifies that the wool was being sent to decorators or finishers of cloth (*a-ke-ti-ra$_2$*), that is, specialized wool workers. Hence it is clear that this wool was to be used in a workshop, which precludes the possibility that the wool was used as offerings. Nor do I think that the textiles the religiously affiliated workshops produced for the palace would necessarily have been used for religious purposes. The *a-ke-ti-ra$_2$* associated with Potnia were working under the *ta-ra-si-ja* system just like the other secular workers within the series. They were not separated out from the others in any way, and in fact on Of 36 the Potnian *a-ke-ti-ra$_2$* are found on the same tablet with secular workers. Under this system the religious workers would have been expected to return finished products to the palace just like their secular counterparts. This means that from the point of view of the palace, this was a financial transaction, and the fact that some of the textile workshops that it required to manufacture cloth were under religious jurisdiction seems not to have mattered. What did matter for the palace was that it had its quotas of cloth fulfilled, and it must have utilized every available workshop in order to ensure that this was accomplished, regardless of the affiliation of the workshop. The fact that a particular workshop was associated with a deity need not encourage one to find some religious purpose behind the transaction recorded or the work being done. Rather, it seems reasonable to suppose, as I have been suggesting, that sanctuaries found ways to support themselves, such as by producing textiles, and that this is what we see reflected in the tablets.

And just as the secular managers probably worked for themselves in addition to the work they did for the palace, so too were the religious workshops most likely producing their own cloth in addition to that which they were required to produce for the palace. It is interesting to think about how the palace might have chosen certain workshops to be part of their *ta-ra-si-ja* system. In order for the palatial administration to have known about certain workshops, and in order for those workshops to have been considered able to handle the palatial demands, they must already have been manufacturing cloth for various purposes and clients. That is, their production must have been significant enough for the palace to

[156] E. Andersson and M.-L. Nosch, "With a Little Help from My Friends: Investigating Mycenaean Textiles with Help from Scandinavian Experimental Archaeology," in *Metron: Measuring the Aegean Bronze Age* (*Aegaeum* 24), K. Polinger and R. Laffineur, eds., Liège and Austin 2003, pp. 197-205

[157] See Killen, "Some Thoughts on *ta-ra-si-ja*," in *Economy and Politics in the Mycenaean Palace States*, S. Voutsaki and J.T. Killen, eds., Cambridge Philological Society, Supplementary volume no. 27, 2001, pp. 161-175, p. 172 for a similar conclusion concerning the work required at both Knossos and Pylos.

[158] See Chapter 6 where I discuss the archaeological evidence from the Late Helladic III period for workshops that are located in close proximity to their shrines.

[159] Chadwick 1975, p. 91.

havethought that it could successfully tap into it. Of course, the religiously affiliated workers probably also produced the textiles that were to be used in the sanctuary. After all, it would make sense to use your own production capacity to make the things you need so you do not have to acquire them in some other more costly way. But it seems likely that the religious workshops gained a substantial portion of their income from the cloth they made that could be traded. This income must have enabled them to support themselves and could have provided the opportunity to build some real wealth.

Now I will turn to the more controversial aspects of the Of series. There are several other words on the Of tablets that have been thought to represent religious groups of workers: the *ma-ri-ne-we-ja-i* on Of 25.1 and Of 35.2,the *ko-ma-we-te-ja* on Of 35.1, the *po-re-si* on Of 26.1, and the *a-pi-qo-ro* on Of 34.1. The first comes up in relation to another debated topic, the status of the *wo-ko*, and so I will treat that topic and the *ma-ri-ne-we-ja-i* first.

Was the *Wo-ko* a Religious Workshop?

It has been proposed that Of 36, the tablet with the Potnian *a-ke-ti-ra₂*, also provides evidence that the Mycenaeans distinguished religious workshops from palatial ones linguistically, i.e., that they actually had a word for religious workshops that was different from the word they used for secular workshops. This is seen in the opposition that seems to have been set up between the words *do* and *wo-ko*, which was first discussed by Chadwick.[160] Chadwick noticed that both *do*, or δῶ meaning "house," and *wo-ko*, or ϝοῖκος were used with the allative suffix *-de* to indicate addresses for the wool deliveries.[161] *Do-de* is seen in four places in the Of series (Of 26.2, 26.3, 31.2, 33.1), and it is likely, Chadwick says, that it should be restored on other tablets as well (e.g., Of 31.1 and Of 40.1).[162] We have a name associated with *do* on only three of those entries, but in all three the recipient is indicated by a man's personal name.[163]

Of 26.2: ... ḳọ-ḍẹ-wa-o , do-de *ku* LANA *PA* 1

Of 26.3: di-u-ja-wo ̦ do-de *ku* LANA *PA* 1 ...

Of 33.1: ... o-*34-ta-o ̦ do-de *ku* LANA *PA* 1

Two of these names are in the genitive (Of 26.2:]*-de-wa-o* and Of 33.1: *o-*34-ta-o*), which would give a translation of "to the house of x." The third name is in the nominative (Of 26.3: *di-u-ja-wo*), which Chadwick interprets as either a "scribal inconsequence or error."[164] In contrast with this, Of 36.2 reads *po-ti-ni-ja wo-ko-de*, which we can translate as "to the house (*woikos*) of Potnia." Thus the two forms of the word "house" seem to have been used in distinct contexts. *Do* seems to have been used in secular contexts while *woikos* in seen in a religious one. This parallel construction has prompted Chadwick to define *woikos* as "the house of a deity" or a "temple" and *do* as "the house of a human being."[165]

The word *wo-ko* is also seen on As 1519.11, where it is used to refer to the workshop of another possible divinity named **ma-ri-ne-u*.

If **ma-ri-ne-u* was a god, then the fact that he is seen on As 1519 in association with a *wo-ko* could be used to support the interpretation of the *wo-ko* as a religious workshop. And, if we consider **ma-ri-ne-u* to be a god, then we would have two additional religious workshops in the Of tablets since his female workers, the *ma-ri-ne-we-ja-i*, are found on both Of 25.1 and Of 35.2.

Of 25:
1. ma-ri-ne-we-ja-i , / a₃-ki-a₂-ri-ja LANA 4[ ]*vest*.[
2. a-ma-ru-to-de , / pa-pa-ra-ki LANA 6
3-5.] *vacant*

Of 35:
1. ko-ma-we-te-ja , te-pe-ja , *ku* LANA 1
2.]ma-ri-ne-we-ja-i , a-ki-a₂-ri-ja-de *ku* LANA 3

But whether or not **ma-ri-ne-u* should in fact be seen as a deity has also been debated.[166] The structure of As 1519 does seem to argue for his divinity since he is set off from the other actual men on the tablet.

As 1519:
0. *sup. mut.*
1.] VIR 1
2. i-we-ro VIR 1
3. ne-o-to VIR 1
4. qa-ti-ja VIR 1
5. o-pi-si-jo VIR 1
6. pa-ja-ro VIR 1
7. ki-ke-ro VIR 1
8. i-to VIR 1
9-10. *vacant*
11. ṃạ-ri-ne-wo , wo-i-ko-de
12. to-so VIR 10
13-14. *vacant*
15. *inf. mut.*

The first eight lines of As 1519 record a list of individual men's names (only those on lines 2-8 are preserved) followed by VIR 1. After line 8, lines 9 and 10 were intentionally left blank. Then on line 11 the *wo-i-ko* of

[160] Chadwick 1975, p. 89.
[161] Chadwick 1975, pp. 88-89.
[162] Chadwick 1975, p. 88.
[163] We see]*-de-wa-o* on Of 26.2, *di-u-ja-wo* on Of 26.3 and *o-*34-ta-o* on Of 33.1.
[164] Chadwick 1975, p. 88.
[165] Chadwick 1975, p. 89.
[166] L.R. Palmer was among the first advocates of **ma-ri-ne-u*'s divinity. See Palmer, "War and Society in a Mycenaean Kingdom," in *Armées et Fiscalité dans le Monde Antique*, No. 936, *Colloques Nationaux du C.N.R.S.*, H. van Effenterre and C. Mosse, eds., Paris 1977, pp. 35-64; see p. 56; *idem*, "Some New Functional Gods?" *Nestor* 6 (1979) 1338-1339.

ma-ri-ne-wo is listed. The total number of men being sent to him is given as VIR 10. Thus we might think that the scribe had two groupings in mind when he was writing the tablet: first he listed the secular men and then he recorded the religious workshop. But the situation is less straightforward when we look at **ma-ri-ne-u*'s appearance on other tablets.

The name **ma-ri-ne-u* is also found at Knossos on Ga 674.b and Gg 713 in the dative (*ma-ri-ne-we*).[167] **Ma-ri-ne-u*'s connections with cloth are also evident in MY X 508 where we find *ma-ri-ne*[preceded by *pu-ka-ta-re-i-ja*, which is a common kind of cloth.[168] Palmer, who believed that **ma-ri-ne-u* was a god, said that **ma-ri-ne-u*'s tablet associations indicate that he was "a deity closely associated with industrial activities."[169] Palmer interpreted the name **ma-ri-ne-u* as representing *Mallineus*, the "God of Woollens," formed from "(*ta*) *mallina*, the substantivized material adjective in *-ino-* from *mallos* 'fleece'."[170] One of the reasons that Palmer and others thought that **ma-ri-ne-u* might be a deity was because he is found on Gg 713 receiving an amphora of honey.

Gg 713:
ma-ri-ne-we , / do-e-ra *'ME+RI'* *$*209^{VAS}$* + *A* [[171]

Many tablets of the Gg series record offerings to various deities such as Potnia of the Labyrinth (*da-pu$_2$-ri-to-jo po-ti-ni-ja*, Gg 702), all the gods (*pa-si-te-o-i*, Gg 702, 705, 712), Eleuthia (*e-re-u-ti-ja*, Gg 705[172]; classical Eileithuia), and most likely also Poseidon (]*si-da-o-ne*, Gg 712.2). All of these deities receive the same offering that is given to **ma-ri-ne-u* – an amphora of honey. Also, a *do-e-ra* appears on Gg 713 with **ma-ri-ne-u*, which seems to indicate that the honey was accepted by the *do-e-ra* on behalf of **ma-ri-ne-u*. Hiller mentions that the word *do-e-ra* brings to mind the many *te-o-jo do-e-ra* and *do-e-ro* that appear on the land tenure tablets.[173] Of course *do-e-ro*/*a* are seen in secular contexts as well, such as in the Jn series, but it seems here as if the *do-e-ra* is acting as a representative of the deity, accepting his offering for him.

However, as Foster has detailed, the same department at Knossos that recorded the cult offerings of honey, and other goods such as coriander and cyperus, also recorded disbursements of these goods for use in the manufacture of perfumed oil.[174] For instance, *ku-pi-ri-jo*, whom we can identify, with Killen, as "a palace official responsible for administering [the perfumed oil] sector of the royal economy,"[175] receives an allocation of honey on Gg 995 (a tablet which was written by the same scribe, Hand 135, who wrote Gg 713). Killen has therefore objected to **ma-ri-ne-u*'s being identified as a deity on the basis of his appearance on Gg 713.[176] He does note the dichotomy between *do* and *wo-ko* and concedes that **ma-ri-ne-u* could be divine, nonetheless he says, "there is I believe no positive evidence to confirm this"[177] since Gg 713 may also be classified as an industrial tablet. If the amphora of honey on Gg 713 changes from an *offering* of honey for the deity **ma-ri-ne-u* to an *allocation* of honey that was to be used for industrial purposes, then the arguments for seeing **ma-ri-ne-u* as a god would be significantly diminished.

Complicating this issue is the fact that **ma-ri-ne-u* also receives ten units of coriander seed on Ga 674, a tablet which was written by the same scribe (Hand 135) as Gg 713. Ten units is a very large amount of coriander; it is as much as the *wanax* receives on Ga 675, and more than the disbursements of 5 or 6 units that *ku-pi-ri-jo* receives on Ga 677 and 676, respectively, and hence this allocation was most likely to be used for industrial purposes, specifically for use in the manufacture of perfumed oil.[178] Foster points out that we may also be able to restore *ma-ri-ne-we* on Fh 5970 and Ga 7594.[179] In that case, **ma-ri-ne-u* would also have received olive oil and cyperus (AROM+PYC). These goods, in combination with the coriander of Ga 674 and perhaps the honey he receives on Gg 713, are all ingredients that could have been disbursed for use in perfume manufacture.[180] Killen puts this all together and says,

> It cannot be argued in favour of *ma-ri-ne-u* being divine that he appears on Ga(1) 674 as the recipient of coriander and on Gg(2) 713 as receiving honey. The scribe of both these tablets is 135; and it may well be a common factor

[167] Melena (1974, p. 135) discusses the possibility that Ga 7594 may also record a distribution to **ma-ri-ne-u*, but all we have on that tablet is *ma-ri*[, so we cannot be sure that it is **ma-ri-ne-u*.

[168] We know that this particular batch of cloth was being shipped to Thebes since we find *te-qa-de* on the line above this description of the cloth. Palaima discusses the reasons why such a common type of cloth might be shipped from one city to another in "Maritime Matters in the Linear B Tablets," in *Thalassa: L'Egee Prehistorique et la Mer* (*Aegaeum 7*), R. Laffineur and L. Basch, eds., Liège and PASP, University of Texas 1991, pp. 273-309; see pp. 276-277.

[169] Palmer 1977, p. 56.

[170] Palmer 1979, pp. 1338-1339.

[171] *KT* VI states that the number following "'*ME+RI*' *$*209^{VAS}$* + *A*" could be '1'.

[172] It is interesting that *e-re-u-ti-ja* or Eleuthia (Eileithuia), is also found on Od 714.b, 715.a, and 716.a, all in relation to wool.

[173] S. Hiller, "Mykenische Heiligtumer: das Zeugnis der Linear B-Texte" in *Sanctuaries and Cults in the Aegean Bronze Age*, R. Hägg and N. Marinatos, eds., Stockholm 1981, pp. 95-125; see p. 101.

[174] E.D. Foster, "An Administrative Department at Knossos Concerned with Perfumery and Offerings," *Minos* 16 (1977) 19-51.

[175] Killen 1979, p. 178. Killen reiterates this identification of *ku-pi-ri-jo* in Killen 1995 and successfully defends it against the idea that *ku-pi-ri-jo* might have been the adjective "Cypriot."

[176] Killen 1979, pp. 177-178. Hooker (1977, p. 176) also wrote that "there is still no assurance that [**ma-ri-ne-u*] is a divine name."

[177] Killen 1979, p. 177. I might mention that Killen is now wavering as to whether **ma-ri-ne-u* should be considered a deity (personal communication to J. Gulizio, May 2000).

[178] J.L. Melena, "Coriander on the Knossos Tablets," *Minos* 15 (1974) 133-163; see p. 159-160. Melena mentions that a few tablets record coriander that was being sent to divinities, which seems to imply that coriander was used "as an addition to the diet of the servants of the cult or in offerings to the gods." However, the tablet Ga 674(1) (written by Hand 135), because of the large amount of coriander that it records, does not seem to register an offering, but rather an allocation that was to be used for industrial purposes.

[179] Foster 1977, p. 30.

[180] Foster 1977, see pp. 29-32 for her full discussion of **ma-ri-ne-u*.

> between all the tablets written by this scribe that they deal with raw materials used in the production of aromatic unguents.[181]

If Killen is correct, then **ma-ri-ne-u*'s divine status would hang solely on the fact that he appears on As 1519 with a *wo-ko*. However, I think it is possible to interpret Gg 713 as recording a religious offering rather than an industrial allocation. Within the Gg series there seems to be a difference between the tablets that record religious offerings and those that deal with allocations of honey for industrial purposes. The industrial tablets generally record allocations of several jars of honey, e.g., *ku-pi-ri-jo* on Gg 995 receives at least 6 jars (6[ ), and there are 20 jars owed (*o-pe-ro*) on both Gg 706 and Gg 708. In contrast, all the Gg tablets that clearly record religious offerings list only 1 jar of honey per divine recipient. The number of jars of honey being given to **ma-ri-ne-u* on Gg 713 is not perfectly clear, but *KT* VI states that the number following "'*ME+RI*' **209*^{VAS} + *A*" could be '1'. This would indicate that **ma-ri-ne-u* was receiving his honey as an offering, and that he was a divinity. Also, Killen is of course correct that Hand 135 wrote predominantly industrial tablets, but this does not mean that he was necessarily restricted to this sphere of activity. In fact, one tablet, Ga 1058, which has been tentatively attributed to Hand 135, records the disbursement of PYC on the occasion of a religious festival, the *te-o-po-ri-ja* (θεοφορία).[182] Thus it is not necessary to class Hand 135 as a scribe whose responsibilities only encompassed industrial allocations. Given these two considerations, it seems most likely that **ma-ri-ne-u* should retain his divine status.

The fact that **ma-ri-ne-u* is found on other tablets which are clearly of an industrial nature should not at this point pose any problem. Melena, who accepted the possibility that **ma-ri-ne-u* was a god, says of the situation, "An explanation of **ma-ri-ne-u* as a theonym does not dispose of the labour relationships of the tablets under consideration. We might suggest that a [perfume] workshop was located at the shrine of **Ma-ri-ne-u*."[183] Based on the raw materials that **ma-ri-ne-u* receives, Melena also says that "we might suggest a perfume workshop at the shrine of Knossos, and a textile one at that of Thebes."[184] Foster, in her analysis of the G series and the administrative department at Knossos that wrote them, accepts this proposition as well.[185]

In addition to this, it may be possible to restore a *wo-ko* on KN Gg 7792.a. It reads:
Gg 7792:
a.]-ko-ḍẹ
b.] '*ME+RI*' **209*^{VAS}]̣[

Gg 7792 does not preserve the name of the recipient, but since there is probably only one jar of honey being sent, then it is likely, according to what I presented above, that Gg 7792 records an offering for a deity. Therefore it is interesting that *KT* VI lists *wo*]*-ko-de* as one of the two possible restorations for the first line of the tablet.[186] If this restoration is correct, then it would seem that the offering was being sent to the *woikos* or divine house of some deity, and the religious nature of the word *woikos* would thereby gain support.[187]

One contradiction of this religious *wo-ko*, secular *do* dichotomy can potentially be seen in one of the records on Of 26. The problem is that the name *di-u-ja-wo* (which seems to be a variant of the name *di-wi-ja-wo* of TH Ug 11, KN Vc 293 and PY Na 406.B[188]) appears on Of 26.3 with *do-de*. We can see *di-u-ja-wo* as *Διϝyάϝων which was very likely based on the divinity's name *di-wi-ja*, the feminine form of *di-we* or Zeus.[189] It has been assumed that the name alone served to associate this person with the religious realm. Ruijgh designates the name as an anthroponym, but then he adds in a footnote that an interpretation of *Δίϝyαρϝος as the 'priest of Diwia' would also be conceivable.[190] Palaima has also seen *di-u-ja-wo* as belonging to the religious realm; in fact he implies that *di-u-ja-wo* was the name of a deity.[191] If this is the case, then we would have a situation in which *do* was used in a religious context, which would call into question the validity of the dichotomy between the two words *wo-ko* and *do*. It should be noted though that several other scholars have not taken *di-u-ja-wo* as a religious figure. For instance, Ventris and Chadwick do not even consider the possibility that the name was associated with the religious realm, while Mühlestein says it is probably a man's name that could be derived from the name of the goddess Diwia, but he says nothing about a religious affiliation.[192] In fact, it is not uncommon to see personal names that are derived from theonyms, as for example *di-wi-je-u* on the An coastguard records. Thus, it is actually just as likely, if not more so, that *di-u-ja-wo* was a man's name, which would mean that *do* was here being used in a secular context as usual.

---

[181] Killen 1979, p. 178.

[182] *Docs*², p. 585. *Dic. Mic.* II, p. 327: "θεhοφόρια (cf. θεοφόρος), 'religious procession in which an image of the deity is carried'." Palmer (1963, p. 457) proposes that it could be either the "name of a functionary or a festival."

[183] Melena 1974; for his discussion on **ma-ri-ne-u* see pp. 135-139; the quote is from p. 139. It should be mentioned that Melena also brings up the possibility that **ma-ri-ne-u* was the name of an office (p. 138) or occupational term (p. 139) in *–eus*.

[184] Melena 1974, p. 139.

[185] Foster 1977, p. 31: "J.L. Melena has argued convincingly that a workshop for perfume manufacture was located at a shrine of **ma-ri-ne-u* at Knossos."

[186] The second possibility is *to*]*-ko-de*.

[187] This possibility was kindly pointed out to me by C. Shelmerdine (personal communication, October 2001).

[188] *Dic. Mic.* I, pp. 179; 181-182.

[189] *Dic. Mic.* I, pp. 178-179; 181-182.

[190] Ruijgh, *Études*, p. 130, n. 155.

[191] T.G. Palaima, "The Last Days of the Pylos Polity" in *Politeia: Society and State in the Aegean Bronze Age* (*Aegaeum* 12), R. Laffineur and W.-D. Niemeier, eds., Liège and PASP, University of Texas at Austin 1995, pp. 623-634; see p. 628, n. 22.

[192] *Docs*², pp. 473 and 540. Mühlestein, "Panzeus in Pylos," *Minos* 4 (1956) 79-89; see p. 86.

A variant of the word *wo-ko*, *wo-ke*, is also found on two tablets: PY Sh 736 and KN L 698.3.

PY Sh 736:
1. to-ra-ke , a-me-ja-to , o-pa , me-za-na , wo-ke , ne-wo
   ZE 5

KN L 698:
1.]ne-we , pe-ko-to **164'*[
2.]i-jo-te , 'ku-su-a-ta-o' 11[
3.] jo-du-mi 'wo-ke' P 1[

Two interpretations have actually been proposed for *wo-ke*. The first takes it as a verbal form: "aor. pas. in -ην, of the theme *wrg-ê-: ϝόργεν, referring to the *to-ra-ke*, "...having been made, fabricated."[193] Duhoux translates Sh 736 as "cuirasses of the present year: the workshop of *ameja*, those manufactured at Messenia."[194] Killen also proposed that *wo-ke* be taken as a verb form in his discussion concerning the word *o-pa*.[195] The word *o-pa* on Sh 736, which Killen proposes has to do with the work of finishing a product, shows that these *to-ra-ke* 'cuirasses' have just been refurbished. The person responsible for this *o-pa* work would be the man in the genitive preceding *o-pa* – *a-me-ja-to*. What then to do with *me-za-na wo-ke*? In his article, Killen asks whether, if *me-za-na* is taken as the nominative of a personal name, and with *wo-ke*, taken as the aorist ϝόργε, this could be "a note – in parenthesis as it were – that M. was the original maker of the armour??"[196]

But more recently Killen has changed his mind on this point. He says, "But if this is the case, it is not easy to give *me-za-na* the same or a similar sense to *me-za-na* on Cn 3 [which records the sending of oxen for sacrifice], if the latter is *Metsana(i?)*."[197] Hence, he ends up agreeing with the idea first proposed by Palmer (and supported by Hiller) that *wo-ke* should be taken as the locative form of *wo-ko*,[198] and that *me-za-na* is most likely the name of a deity. Killen does not agree with Palmer's particular translation of *me-za-na* as the deity Μέλαινα,[199] but instead proposes that *me-za-na* could be taken "as */Metsana/ viz.* as the name of a goddess after whom Μεσσάνα (and the later Μεσσηνία) has been called, just as Athens (Ἀθῆναι) is named after Athene (Ἀθήνη)."[200] Killen therefore also agrees with Palmer that the phrase *me-za-na wo-ke* translates as "in the house of the goddess *me-za-na*" and that, as on Of 36, "the 'house' in question is an 'industrial' establishment."[201]

As for L 698, Hiller points out that it may be part of the same tablet as Od 696.[202] Killen also thinks this is likely given that the two tablets were written by the same scribe (Hand 103) and found in the same spot.[203] If this is the case, then a religious context for L 698 is implied by the mention of the religious festival *te-o-po-ri-ja* on Od 696.1.[204] Hiller also says that given the religious context, it would make sense to restore *ma-ri-]ne-we* on L 698 instead of the name that Killen favors, *e-ta-wo-]ne-we*.[205] Killen's case though for restoring *e-ta-wo-]ne-we* is a good one. In his study of the cloth tablets, Killen has found that *e-ta-wo-ne-u* appears (or may be safely restored) on several other L tablets (e.g., Ld(1) 584.2 and L 695.1a), and that he is very often associated with words that describe the decorative elements that were added to cloth. Killen has deduced from this that *e-ta-wo-ne-u* was probably in charge of a workshop that was responsible for finishing cloth for Knossos.[206] If the name is restored as *e-ta-wo-]ne-we* then *wo-ke* here on L 698 could not be considered as a religious workshop. But, I have to wonder if this tablet were put before Killen today, whether he would still support the restoration of *e-ta-wo-]ne-we* so strongly since he most recently has said, "there is now more evidence available ... to support the contention that woikos can be used on the tablets to refer to an 'industrial' establishment 'owned' by a goddess." Perhaps he would now favor the restoration of *ma-ri-]ne-we*.

On balance, I think the evidence weighs most heavily in support of the proposition that the *woikos* was a workshop affiliated with the religious sphere. Palmer concluded that the "*woikos* was not simply the 'house' or 'temple', but the industrial village or quarter on a temple estate."[207] Hiller, who was also convinced by the arguments for *woikos* being a religiously associated establishment, stressed that the *oikos* must be both cultic and industrial in nature.[208] He says,

> At the head of an oikos can stand its "nominal" (*ideeller*) owner, either a masculine or feminine deity. An oikos constitutes because of this – also – a sacred institution. 2. The concrete area of responsibility of an oikos and its business function lie however not primarily in the cultic, but in the economic sector. ... 5. In its combination of economic and sacral structures the institution of the oikos in a certain way

193 *Dic. Mic.* II, p. 437.
194 Y. Duhoux, *Aspects du vocabulaire économique mycénien*, Amsterdam 1976; see p. 125.
195 Killen 1999, pp. 329-330.
196 Killen 1999, p. 330. In n. 26 Killen also explains how seeing *me-za-na* as a personal name would work in Cn 3: "...it would not seem impossible that M. is the individual responsible for sending (if that is what *i-je-si* refers to) the oxen which are referred to in the text, even though these have been contributed by the groupings named in each of the individual entries on the record."
197 J.T. Killen, "The Language of Religious Texts: Some Fresh Thoughts on Old Problems," in *Proceedings of the 11th International Colloquium on Mycenaean Studies*, T.G. Palaima and C.W. Shelmerdine, eds., forthcoming.
198 Palmer 1963, pp. 53, 330, 464. Hiller 1981, pp. 101-102.
199 Palmer 1963, pp. 175, 330. Hiller 1981, p. 102.
200 Killen forthcoming.
201 Killen forthcoming.
202 Hiller 1981, p. 101.
203 Killen 1979, p. 161.
204 Hiller 1981, p. 101.
205 Hiller 1981, p. 101.
206 Killen 1979, pp. 159-162.
207 Palmer 1977, p. 57.
208 Hiller 1981, p. 103.

> seems to be a Mycenaean parallel to the oriental institution of the so-called "temple economy".[209]

I do not think the last assertion really fits the situation that we find in the Mycenaean world, but it certainly is interesting that the Mycenaeans saw such a fundamental difference between secular and religious workshops as to have different terms for them.

Hiller also brings up the fact that the definitions that appear in Homer for the words *do* and *oikos* do not correspond to those that seem to best suit them as they are found in the Linear B texts.[210] Chadwick had already addressed this issue by saying simply that "in other cases too Homer has blurred a Mycenaean distinction."[211] Hiller though goes a bit further in explaining the situation. He says that, "Homer evidently did not know the institution of temple economy, which in the Mycenaean texts implies the assignation of oikos to the sacred sphere; household economy is here left to the people..."[212] In other words, if the term *oikos*, as the Mycenaeans used it, did indeed refer to an area in which goods were produced, it is possible that this industrial and economic aspect of the word was retained in historical times while the religious association dropped away. This would be a logical development for a society that no longer manifested such a concrete relationship between industry and deities. Since cult personnel no longer managed industrial production, *woikos* became the simple term used to denote the practical workings and economics of a household that we see in Homer.

Thus it seems possible to conclude, after this lengthy but, I hope, useful discussion of *wo-ko* and **ma-ri-ne-u*, that the arguments for placing both of these words within the religious realm are stronger than those used to challenge their religious status. Therefore, the proposal that the Mycenaeans differentiated linguistically between religious and secular workshops may be upheld. Another result of this conclusionis that **ma-ri-ne-u* can be seen as a deity's name that was used at both Knossos and at Thebes, and, finally, **ma-ri-ne-u*'s female workers, the *ma-ri-ne-we-ja-i* found on Of 25.1 and Of 35.2, can be thought to represent another religious textile workshop.

The *Ko-ma-we-te-ja*, the *Po-re-si*, and the *A-pi-qo-ro*

As I mentioned, in addition to the *ma-ri-ne-we-ja-i*, the Of series provides us with several other tablets on which the recipients of wool may be associated with the religious realm. The candidates for such a classification are the *ko-ma-we-te-ja* on Of 35.1, the *po-re-si* on Of 26.1, and the *a-pi-qo-ro* on Of 34.1.

I will take the latter term, *a-pi-qo-ro*, first.

Of 34:

1. a-pi-qo-ro , ne-wa , ko-tu-ro$_2$, *DA* , LANA 3 [[*PA* 1]] [
2. a-ra-ka-te-ja , pa-ra-ja LANA 1 [

Following *a-pi-qo-ro* is the word *ne-wa*, which is probably being used to describe the wool as 'new' in contrast with the *pa-ra-ja* ('old') wool found in line 2. Next we see a man's name *ko-tu-ro$_2$*, which seems to be qualified with *DA*. The *DA* most likely indicates that *ko-tu-ro$_2$* is a 'supervisor.'[213] Chadwick took *a-pi-qo-ro* as a dative singular and proposed that the most likely translation of *a-pi-qo-ro* on this tablet would be 'priest', 'priestess' or 'attendant of the deity.'[214] He supports this religious association by citing the *a-pi-qo-ro-i* that are found on PY Fr 1205 receiving an allocation, or offering, of oil. Chadwick says, "the context of the Pylos Fr tablets clearly points to divine cult." Shelmerdine, however, points out that female palace workers are designated as *a-pi-qo-ro* on Aa 804 and Ad 690, and that this could indicate a secular context for the attendants of the Fr series as well.[215] The same reasoning could be applied to the *a-pi-qo-ro* on Of 34. Hooker makes another good point in support of seeing the *a-pi-qo-ro* of Of 34 as secular workers.[216] As we saw, Of 34.1 includes a reference to a man named *ko-tu-ro$_2$*. If we take the *DA* that modifies *ko-tu-ro$_2$* to indicate 'supervisor', which Killen had proposed and Chadwick accepted,[217] then *a-pi-qo-ro* would be, Hooker says, "far more likely to be in the nominative plural than in the nominative singular or dative singular, since it is hardly conceivable that one *DA* should be required to supervise one ἀμφίπολος."[218] Hooker also points out that the meaning of 'priest' for *a-pi-qo-ro* would be less likely than the more practical 'attendant' or 'servant.' Thus it seems that *a-pi-qo-ro* need not necessarily be associated with the religious realm in this context.

Next I will consider the women described as *ko-ma-we-te-ja* on Of 35.1, whom Chadwick also includes among the religiously associated persons of the Of tablets.

Of 35:
1. ko-ma-we-te-ja , te-pe-ja , *ku* LANA 1
2.]ma-ri-ne-we-ja-i , a-ki-a$_2$-ri-ja-de *ku* LANA 3

Chadwick's reason for considering the *ko-ma-we-te-ja* as religious in nature is because we see this very word, *ko-ma-we-te-ja*, on Tn 316 *v.* 3, whose context is, as Chadwick says, "agreed to be religious."[219] This is of course true, but still there has been some discussion

[209] Hiller 1981, p. 103.
[210] Hiller 1981, p. 105.
[211] Chadwick 1975, p. 89.
[212] Hiller 1981, p. 105.

[213] Chadwick 1975, p. 92.
[214] Chadwick 1975, p. 92. Chadwick later said that perhaps we should consider the *a-pi-qo-ro* divine since otherwise they "would then be an unsightly blot on a predominantly divine picture..." ("What Do We Know about Mycenaean Religion?," in *Linear B: A 1984 Survey* [*BCILL* 26], A. Morpurgo Davies and Y. Duhoux, eds., Louvaine-la-Neuve 1985, pp. 191-202; p. 197).
[215] C.W. Shelmerdine, *The Perfume Industry of Mycenaean Pylos, SIMA Pocketbook 34*, Åstroms, Göteborg 1985, p. 97.
[216] Hooker 1977, p. 174.
[217] Chadwick 1975, p. 92.
[218] Hooker 1977, p. 174.
[219] Chadwick 1975, p. 93.

concerning the exact role that the word *ko-ma-we-te-ja* play on Tn 316. Here is the relevant paragraph:

Tn 316 *v*.1-3:
v. 1. i-je-to-qe , po-si-da-i-jo , a-ke-qe , wa-tu
v. 2. do-ra-qe , pe-re , po-re-na-qe , a-ke
v3a. pu-ro -ja
v. 3. AUR *215^{VAS} 1 MUL 2 qo-wi-ja , ṇạ-[ ] , ko-ma-we-te-

On Tn 316 *ko-ma-we-te-ja* appears on line *v*. 3 as the third in a list of three names. These three names would presumably be the divinities who are to receive the specified offerings of one gold vase and two women. But there is a problem here. Only two women are recorded among the offerings, and it is usually the case on Tn 316 that every deity was to receive one man or one woman (depending on the gender of the deity). The question then becomes, which of the three names was supposed to receive the two women, and what was the status of any name(s) that we do not consider to be a deity.

Del Freo, who has discussed this problem in detail, makes the assumption that among those three names only one is a divinity and that the other two must be the names of the women being offered to the deity.[220] He believes that the first two names, *qo-wi-ja* and *na-*[ ], must represent the names of the two women who are being dedicated since they are the ones closest to the ideogram that would presumably refer to them, the MUL 2. The third name then, our *ko-ma-we-te-ja*, is the name of the goddess.

Del Freo also mentions that previous commentators of this text (e.g., Bennett) have proposed that *na-*[ ] could be restored as *na-ti-qe*, which would further serve to unite the first two names in the same category. To explain why two women would be dedicated to one goddess, which happens nowhere else on Tn 316, Del Freo appeals to an explanation put forward by Hiller.[221] Hiller noted that this paragraph contains another anomaly, namely that this is the only paragraph in which the subject *wa-tu* or ἄστυ appears. Hiller proposed that the *wa-tu* was specified here because it was offering one of the women while the palace of Pylos was offering the other.

Some have not found Hiller's explanation concerning the MUL 2 to be satisfactory since the *wa-tu* may very well refer to Pylos itself. Another major objection has been made to this interpretation: It also seems strange that the names of the two women being offered should be mentioned here while nowhere else on the tablet are the names of the people being offered specified. Therefore, it seems more likely that there were actually two goddesses on *v*. 3, and no named mortals. Palaima, who agrees with this line of thinking, identifies *qo-wi-ja* and *ko-ma-we-te-ja* as the two goddesses, and says that the sign group that appears between them is "very difficult to interpret."[222] He does offer a way of seeing the line:

> If the final or the erased word-unit ended in *-qe*, we should perhaps see here the listing of another minor "deity" linked with *qo-wi-ja* by the enclitic conjunction. The following *ko-ma-we-te-ja* might then be taken as the genitive of the more prominent deity (cf. TH Of 35.1) who is the "mother" or somehow "possessor" of these minor *hapax* deities.[223]

Thus the status of *ko-ma-we-te-ja* as a deity would be upheld by Palaima's interpretation of the tablet as well.

Killen, on the other hand, has proposed a different interpretation of the word *ko-ma-we-te-ja*, particularly in relation to its appearance on Of 35.1.[224] Killen includes *ko-ma-we-te-ja* among the adjectival forms derived from men's names that he thinks were used to describe collector workgroups (such as *a-ka-i-je-ja* from *a-ka-i-jo*). He interprets the name in this way because the man's name *ko-ma-we*(*-ta*)[225] appears on several tablets dealing with sheep and the textile industry in the position of the collector (e.g., KN Dv 5278.B: nom., *ko-ma-we*; Dk 920.a: in the genitive *ko-ma-we-to*; and Dk 1049.a: in the dative *ko-ma-we-te*).[226] With this in mind Killen suggests a way in which we could explain the *ko-ma-we-te-ja* of Tn 316 as indicating a mortal collector's name. Killen proposes, as Del Freo does, that the two feminine names that come before *ko-ma-we-te-ja* should be identified as the MUL 2 that are being offered. But Killen differs from Del Freo in that he proposes that *ko-ma-we-te-ja* could have been used to describe those two women as belonging to the collector *ko-ma-we*(*-ta*).[227]

The problem with Killen's interpretation, which takes all three names on Tn 316 *v*. 3 as belonging to mortals, is that it would leave us without any indication as to which deity was supposed to receive the offerings. Hence for Tn 316 at least, the interpretation of *ko-ma-we-te-ja* as an adjective derived from a man's name should probably be abandoned. Del Freo actually counter-proposes that we should see *ko-ma-we*(*-ta*) of the sheep tablets as a deity.[228] He says that the masculine form could be an "epiclesi di Poseidon" since the ceremony for *ko-ma-we-te-ja* is celebrated in the sanctuary of Poseidon (*po-si-da-i-jo*, Tn 316. *v*.1), and the feminine deity of the same name would be the "paredra o la figlia di Komawe." If this were the case, we would have another example of a

[220] M. Del Freo, "Osservazioni su Miceneo *ko-ma-we-te-ja*," *Minos* 31-32 (1996-1997 [1998]) 148-158.

[221] Del Freo 1996-1997, p. 154 refers to S. Hiller, "Zu PY Tn 316," in *Palaeograeca et mycenaea Antonino Bartonek quinque et sexagenario oblata*, Brno 1991, p. 84.

[222] T.G. Palaima, "Kn02 – Tn 316," in *Floreant Studia Mycenaea, Acts of the 10th International Mycenological Colloquium held at the University of Salzburg*, S. Deger-Jalkotzy, S. Hiller, and O. Panagl, eds., Wien 1999, pp. 437-461; see p. 452 and n. 46.

[223] Palaima 1999, p. 452, n. 46.

[224] Killen 1979, p. 176.

[225] Killen 1976, p. 124 proposes that the *ko-ma-we-ta* that we see on KN B 798.5 may be a variant spelling of the collector *ko-ma-we*(*-to*) that we see on the D records. For this reason, in Killen 1979, he uses '*ko-ma-we*(*-ta*)' to refer to this collector.

[226] In addition to Killen 1979, p. 176, also see *Dic. Mic.* I, p. 374.

[227] Killen 1979, p. 177.

[228] Del Freo 1996-1997, pp. 156-157.

deity involved in animal husbandry. This is however a very tentative proposal, and one which therefore should not be insisted on. It might be best to leave *ko-ma-we(-ta)* as a mortal collector's name.

But this makes it very difficult to decide whether we should consider the *ko-ma-we-te-ja te-pe-ja* as belonging to the religious realm or not. If it is accepted that the root of *ko-ma-we-te-ja* and *ko-ma-we(-ta)* gave rise in one case to a feminine deity's name (on Tn 316) and in another to a mortal's name (on the Knossian sheep tablets), then it is possible that *ko-ma-we-te-ja* on Of 35 could just as easily have been derived from the mortal man's name as from the deity's. In support of a religious affiliation one could bring in the fact that the other entry on Of 35 concerns the *ma-ri-ne-we-ja-i*, whom we have decided are religious. The scribe may have been grouping religious entries together. Of 36 though provides us with an example of a tablet that has both a religious entry (the one dealing with Potnia) and a secular one (Of 36.1: *a-ke-ti-ra$_2$ wa-na-ka*[]), so this argument is not very strong. Since this is the case, then the religious nature of the *te-pe-ja* workers of Of 35.1 cannot be definitely determined. For this reason I will leave the affiliation of their workshop as uncertain.

We may turn now to the *po-re-si* of Of 26.3, for whom a religious association does seem relatively certain.

Of 26:

1. pu$_2$-re-wa	*ku* LANA *PA* 1	ka-ka[ ] *ku* LANA *PA* 1
2. su-me-ra-we-jo̤ ,	*ku* LANA *PA* 1	ḳo-ḍẹ-wa-o , do-de *ku* LANA *PA* 1
3. di-u-ja-wo , do-de⌊ ⌋	*ku* LANA *PA* 1	po-re-si *ku* LANA 1

The word *po-re-si* is generally interpreted as the dative plural form of the word *φορήν.[229] *Φορήν is related to φέρω and φορέω can be understood to mean "something brought or offered." As Hooker says, "a form of φερ/φορ- was used [in Linear B] with the specialized meaning of 'that which is brought for a god', just as in later Greek the word φερνά means 'the god's portion (of the sacrifice)'."[230] The question that has concerned many scholars is how precisely should *φορήν be interpreted in the Mycenaean texts, considering the fact that on TH Of 26 and PY Tn 316 it is applied to human beings. This discussion has focused primarily on the accusative form of *φορήν, *po-re-na*, which is found several times on Tn 316 within its repeated formula. It will be enough to reproduce here the first paragraph of Tn 316 in order to remind us of the formula.

[229] *Dic. Mic.* II, p. 139. G. Nagy ("A Mycenaean Reflex in Homer: ΦΟΡΗΝΑΙ," *Minos* 29-30 [1994-1995] 171-175; p. 173, n. 10) proposed that *po-re-si* be taken as *phórensi*, the 3rd person plural of *phórêmi* meaning 'they carry.' Palaima (1996-1997, p. 309) pointed out that this cannot be the case since that would leave this entry without any recipient or address for the wool.

[230] Hooker 1977, p. 178.

Tn 316.1-5:

1. po-ro-wi-to-jo ,
2. i-je-to-qe , pa-ki-ja-si , do-ra-qe , pe-re , po-re-na-qe
3. pu-ro a-ke , po-ti-ni-ja AUR **215*^{VAS} 1 MUL 1
4. ma-na-sa , AUR **213*^{VAS} 1 MUL 1 po-si-da-e-ja AUR **213*^{VAS} 1 MUL 1
5. ti-ri-se-ro-e , AUR **216*^{VAS} 1 do-po-ta AUR **215*^{VAS} 1

To review briefly, here we see the offerings being made to various divinities (*po-ti-ni-ja, ma-na-sa, po-si-da-e-ja, ti-ri-se-ro-e*, and *do-po-ta*) at the sanctuary of *Pa-ki-ja-ne*. The offerings consist of golden vessels and women (men are offered to male deities in other paragraphs on the tablet). Since the vessels are inanimate objects they are thought to correspond to the *do-ra*, or the gifts, and they are considered to be the objects of the verb *pe-re*, or φέρει, since they would logically be carried to the sanctuaries. The men and women then correspond to the *po-re-na*, who are taken as the direct objects of the verb *a-ke*, or ἄγει, since they would be led.[231] It is generally agreed that the men and women were, like the golden vessels, being offered to the deities, but several opinions have been offered as to the form that offering was to take. One school of thought was that the men and women were actually victims about to be offered in a ritual that involved human sacrifice. This theory was linked with the idea that Tn 316, which is perhaps not the best specimen of scribal organization, was written in frightened haste because there was an invading force bearing down on Pylos. It was thought that a ritual involving human sacrifice was being performed because of the extreme circumstances the Pylians were facing.[232] Palaima though has reviewed the tablet in detail and found that while its style of writing may not be terribly elegant, it does get across the necessary information, and therefore it would have been considered a satisfactory piece of writing by the scribes.[233] Also, Palaima has shown that it is likely that the tablet was not among the very last to be written.[234] Thus Tn 316 should not be understood as reflecting a "state of emergency" at Pylos, which in turn means that there is no compelling argument for seeing the *po-re-na* as sacrificial victims.

[231] Palaima 1996-1997 [1998], p. 304.

[232] The proponents of the "state of emergency" theory are primarily John Chadwick (*Docs*^{2} pp. 284-289, 458-464; *idem*, *The Mycenaean World*, Cambridge 1976, pp. 89-96) and Lydia Baumbach ("An Examination of the Evidence for a State of Emergency at Pylos c. 1200 B.C.," *Res Mycenaeae*, A. Heubeck and G. Neumann eds., Gottingen 1983, p. 33). J.T. Hooker ("The End of Pylos and the Linear B Evidence," *SMEA* 23 [1982] 209-217) argues that the evidence usually adduced in support of the state of emergency, such as the scarcity of metals on the Jn tablets and the small sizes of the land holdings of the E series, could instead indicate that the destructions resulted from internal disturbances and the general weakness of the palace system on mainland Greece in the 13th century B.C.

[233] Palaima 1995, pp. 623-633. Also see Palaima 1999; pp. 437-461.

[234] Palaima 1995, p. 624, 628-632 and 1999, p. 439 points out that other texts, including Un 718, the Ta series and the Sh series were all brought to the Archives Complex and were awaiting processing after Tn 316 had already been received and stored away in its basket.

Another more reasonable theory is that the *po-re-na* were people who were being dedicated to their respective deities for service within their sanctuaries. Sacconi has proposed that they were actually priests and priestesses.[235] It could also have been that they were about to be initiated as *te-o-jo do-e-ra* and *do-e-ro*, or servants of the gods, like those found on the land tenure tablets. These servants of the gods could have been ceremonially dedicated to the deity they were to serve, and such a ceremony may be reflected here on Tn 316. Whether they were actually priests or *te-o-jo do-e-ro/a*, I would use the word 'dedicants' rather than 'victims' to define the *po-re-na* of Tn 316. Thus, the *po-re-si* of Of 26.3 could also have been people who had been dedicated to the service of a deity within a sanctuary, and the main occupation, or job, of these *po-re-si* was to work in their sanctuary's textile workshop.

It should also be mentioned that the word *φορήν is also found in two compound formations which further serve to establish the religious nature of the *po-re-na*. On PY Un 443 we find the term *po-re-no-zo-te-ri-ja*, while *po-re-no-tu-te*[*-ri-ja* appears on PY Ua 1413.

Un 443:
1. ku-pi-ri-jo , tu-ru-pte-ri-ja , o-no LANA 10 **146* 10
2. po-re-no-zo-te-ri-ja LANA 3
3.]ḍọ-ke , ka-pa-ti-ja , HORD 2 te-ri-ja GRA ̣1 LANA 5
4. [[ ]]

The first compound of *po-re-na*, *po-re-no-zo-te-ri-ja*, has been thought to represent *φορενο-ζωστήρια, the latter element being derived from ζωστήρ, which could have something to do with 'ceintures' or bindings(?).[236] Duhoux was among those who saw the *po-re-na* as 'victims', and since *po-re-no-zo-te-ri-ja* is here followed by an allocation of wool, he thought this might have something to do with the custom of putting ribbons of wool on the victims before they were sacrificed. Thus he proposed that these were "bandelettes pour les victimes."[237] Of course taking the *po-re-na* as dedicants instead of victims, we could say instead that the *po-re-no-zo-te-ri-ja* were a special type of clothing or accessory worn by the new initiates during the ceremony in which they were dedicated to their sanctuaries. Another possibility was proposed by Maurice who saw the *po-re-no-zo-te-ri-ja* as the word for the religious festival itself during which the **po-re-ne* took on their special clothing.[238]

The religious nature of Un 443 is further supported by the fact that *ka-pa-ti-ja*, the person who is designated by the religious title *ka-ra-wi-po-ro*, or Keybearer, on Ep 704, appears on line 3 of Un 443. It is also significant, as Palaima has pointed out, that Un 443 was written by the same scribe, Hand 6, who wrote Un 6 and Un 853. Both of these tablets "record contributions of mixed items including cloth, wool, oil, wine, and animals in quantities that suggest that they were to be used as sacrificial victims for ceremonial commensual banquets as attested clearly on such tablets as PY Un 2 and PY Un 718."[239] Thus it seems that Hand 6 was responsible for compiling information that had to do with religious festivals, and the *po-re-no-zo-te-ri-ja* seems to have been among them.

Ua 1413, upon which we find *po-re-no-tu-te*[*-ri-ja*, is a different type of document, but connections with the religious realm can also be discerned here.

Ua 1413:
.a **146* 7 **166+WE* 1 [
1. ro-u-si-jo a-ko-ro , po-re-no-tu-ṭẹ[

As was the case for *po-re-no-zo-te-ri-ja*, the first propositions for the definition of *po-re-no-tu-te*[*-ri-ja* had at their base the idea that the *po-re-na* were sacrificial victims. Ruijgh thus proposed that *po-re-no-tu-te*[*-ri-ja* or *φορενο-θυ(σ)τήρια, could be taken as "objects pertaining to victims,"[240] while Palmer says that Ua 1413 "records [the] offering of the sacrificial substances at *ro-u-si-jo a-ko-ro* on the occasion of the *po-re-no-tu-te*[*-ri-ja*, which may be a festival name."[241] Because this tablet records the cloth ideograms **146* and **166+WE*, Duhoux interprets this tablet as recording the clothing that was provided for the sacrifice.[242] As with *po-re-no-zo-te-ri-ja,* we may reinterpret these ideograms instead as representing the special clothing that was worn by the dedicants during their ceremonial induction into the religious community, and the word *po-re-no-tu-te*[*-ri-ja* may have referred specifically to that clothing or other objects used by the dedicants. Chadwick says that the -*tu-te*[*-ri-ja* "could easily be interpreted as θυ(σ)τήρια 'offerings.'"[243] Could then this word refer to the dedicants themselves? Palaima supports the idea that the **146* and **166+WE* were used in religious contexts by pointing out that both appear together on Un 6.6, which, as we just mentioned, records the commodities and sacrificial animals that were being gathered for a commensual ceremony.[244] Palaima goes on to propose that Ua 1413 may represent the kind of 'single entry' tablet that was used to compile the larger tablets like Un 2 and Un 718.[245]

---

[235] A. Sacconi, "La tavoletta di Pilo Tn 316: Una registrazione di caraterre eccezionale?" in *Studies in Mycenaean and Classical Greek Presented to John Chadwick* (*Minos* 20-22), J.T. Killen, J.L. Melena and J.-P. Olivier, eds., Salamanca 1987, pp. 551-555; see p. 554.

[236] Ruijgh, *Études*, p. 115. Palaima discusses this in 1996-1997, p. 306. Also see *Dic. Mic.* II, p. 140.

[237] Y. Duhoux, "Ideogrammes Textiles du Lineaire B: *146, *160, *165 et *166," *Minos* 15 (1976) 116-132; see pp. 127-128.

[238] N. Maurice, "Analogie et Flexion Nominale en Grec Mycénien: Le Datif-Locatif Pluriel des Thèmes en *-n-*," *Minos* 23 (1988) 117-146; see p. 131.

[239] Palaima 1996-1997, p. 306. Killen (1994, see pp. 71-78) also discusses the tablets and the fact that they may represent the makings of commensual banquets.

[240] Ruijgh 1967, p. 115, n. 79.

[241] Palmer 1963, p. 447.

[242] Duhoux 1976, pp. 127-128.

[243] J. Chadwick, "Pylos Tablet Un 1322," in *Mycenaean Studies*, E.L. Bennett, ed., University of Wisconsin Press 1964, pp. 19-26; see p. 23.

[244] Palaima 1996-1997, p. 307.

[245] Palaima 1996-1997, p. 307, n. 19.

It is also interesting that *ro-u-si-jo a-ko-ro* was the location specified on Ua 1413 since this was one of the places to which perfumed oil was sent as a religious offering in the Fr series. *Ro-u-si-jo a-ko-ro* appears twice in the Fr series: on Fr 1226, the oil is specified as being sent to the gods (*te-o-i*) at *ro-u-si-jo a-ko-ro*, and so we may presume it was being sent to a sanctuary there that was dedicated to all the gods. A recipient is not specified on the second Fr tablet (1220) that has *ro-u-si-jo a-ko-ro* as its address, but perhaps on analogy with Fr 1226 we may understand that it was again being sent to the *te-o-i*. In addition to these tablets, *ro-u-si-jo a-ko*-ro is also found on Un 47 as the site where another commensual banquet was to take place.[246] Un 47, like Un 6, records the foodstuffs that were being collected for such a banquet, including wine, grain, and male and female sheep. Considering all of these religious contexts in which *ro-u-si-jo a-ko-ro* appears, it seems likely that it was a place at which a religious sanctuary of some importance to the Pylians was located. It would make sense then that a festival involving new dedicants would occur at that place.

Thus the contexts in which we find *φορήν and its various formations all seem to testify to its religious nature. As dedicants (*po-re-na*) they are offered to divinities on Tn 316, and the word is used in compounds which refer either to a religious festival or the paraphernalia used in the rituals associated with such a festival.[247] The *po-re-si* recorded on Of 26 therefore must have been people who had been dedicated to the service of a deity within a sanctuary, and their responsibilities seem to have included working with wool and producing textiles in the workshop affiliated with the sanctuary to which they had dedicated their service. The question may be asked, to which deity were they dedicated? It must have been a well-known one for the scribe to leave the name out, which would lead me to speculate that it might have been Potnia herself. Perhaps since the allocation on Of 36 was meant specifically for the finishers, whose work was specialized, we might see here wool being allocated to the general staff of her workshop, who were responsible for producing the cloth itself.

Thus we have at least four or five textile workshops at Thebes that were affiliated with the religious sphere. Three of these belong to the deities Hera (Of 28.2), Hermes (Of 31.3), and Potnia (Of 36.2). A fourth seems to have belonged to the deity **ma-ri-ne-u*, and the entry in which the *po-re-si* appear may indicate a fifth workshop, or, what I think is also possible, another allocation to Potnia's workshop. It is also likely that the workshop of the *ko-ma-we-te-ja* women (Of 35) was religiously affiliated, but this case is not as certain as the others. These workshops must have been managed by religious personnel who were working in the name of their deity, and I think that these workshops would have been affiliated with their own sanctuaries. Just as I have proposed for the Potnian sheep on the Dl tablets, the fact that the owner is indicated by a deity's name (or a generic religious title such as *po-re-si*), rather than by a personal name, probably indicates that the official owner was that deity, but obviously it was the religious personnel managing the work who reaped the material benefits.

[246] Palaima 1996-1997, pp. 307-308.

[247] Palaima 1996-1997, p. 306. It seems likely that one of the words referred to the festival and the other referred to the special clothing or accessories worn during the rituals of that festival, but it is difficult to say which was which.

I will turn now to a consideration of the Pylos Jn series since a similar system may have been in operation within the bronze-working industry.

Potnian Workers in the Jn Bronze Series

There are twenty main Jn tablets,[248] eighteen of which record allocations of metal to bronzesmiths who were apparently working under the *ta-ra-si-ja* system, while the remaining two tablets record collections of bronze (Jn 829 and 881+896). We will be focusing on the eighteen tablets that recorded the allocations of bronze.

The allocation records are organized by toponym, and generally the smiths from a certain location are recorded together on one tablet.[249] Thus the bronzesmiths who were employed in this system were located at various towns that were scattered around the Pylian realm. The allocation tablets actually contained more information than their name implies. The first paragraph of these tablets is used to record the smiths who were to receive an allocation and therefore usually bears a heading similar to the one on Jn 310.1, which reads, *a-ke-re-wa ka-ke-we ta-ra-si-ja e-ko-te*, which translates as "at *a-ke-re-wa*, the bronzesmiths having an allocation."

Jn 310:
1.]a-ke-re-wa , ka-ke-we , ta-ra-si-ja , e-ko-te ,
2. ti-qa-jo AES M 1 N 2 qe-ta-wo AES M 1 N 2
3. a_3-so-ni-jo AES M 1 N 2 ta-mi-je-u AES M 1 N 2
4. e-u-ru-wo-ta AES M 1 N 2 e-u-do-no AES M 1 N 2
5. po-ro-u-te-u AES M 1 N 2 wi-du-wa-ko AES M 1 N 2
6. *vacat*
7. to-so-de , a-ta-ra-si-jo , ka-ke-we[ ] *vacat*
8. pa-qo-si-jo 1 ke-we-to 1 wa-[ ]re-u[1] *vacat*
9. pe-ta-ro 1
10. *vacat*
11. to-so-de , do-e-ro , ke-we-to-jo 1 i-wa-ka-o 1
12. pa-qo-si-jo-jo 1 po-ro-u-te-wo 1

[248] In J. Smith's analysis of the Jn series ("The Pylos Jn Series," *Minos* 27-28 [1992-1993] 167-259; p. 168) she says, "The Jn series consists of twenty main tablets and several fragments from page-shaped tablets."

[249] Two tablets that seem to have been working tablets record more than one location: Jn 725 is concerned with four localities (*e-ni-pa-te-we*,]-*nu-we-jo*, *a-ke-re-wa* and *na-i-se-wi-jo*), and Jn 693 is concerned with two (*a*[-*ke*-]*re-wa* and *a-pu*$_2$-*we*). The real exception to this principle of organization seems to have been the place *a-ke-re-wa* which is found on three tablets, Jn 310, 693 and 725. But the smiths on these three tablets belong to different groups, and maybe even to different workshops, so it is understandable that they were recorded separately.

13. [[ ]] *vacat*
14. po-ti-ni-ja-we-jo , ka-ke-we , ta-ra-si-ja , e-ko-te ,
15. i-ma-di-jo AES M 3 tu-ke-ne-u AES M 3
16.] AES M 3 i-wa-ka AES M 3
17. a-]ta-ra-si-jo , pu$_2$-ṣị-ja-ko 1

Then follows the names of the smiths and the amounts of their allocations. As we discussed in reference to the allocations of wool given to the textile workers in the Of series, workers who received raw materials from the palace and were expected to return the finished products are thought of as working under the *ta-ra-si-ja* system. Here on the Jn tablets we see that, unlike in the Of series, the allocation of raw material is specifically referred to as a *ta-ra-si-ja*.[250] On most tablets a second paragraph is created for smiths who were called *a-ta-ra-si-jo*, or smiths who were not going to receive an allotment, or an assignment of work, at that time. Thus on Jn 310.7 we see, *to-so-de a-ta-ra-si-jo ka-ke-we*, "so many bronzesmiths without an allocation." A third paragraph was set up on the tablets to record *do-e-ro* or slave(?)-assistants associated with the workshops. Their names were not given, but instead they were indicated by the numeral "1" following the genitive of one of the smiths' names that had already appeared on the same tablet (see Jn 310.11).

Since the *a-ta-ra-si-jo* smiths were recorded despite the fact that they were not receiving any bronze at the time that these records were drawn up, it appears that the palace kept a standard list of smiths who could be called upon when the need arose, but that not all of them were required to work for the palace at the same time. We can see how this system worked since we have both a preliminary and a final record concerning the smiths at a place called *na-i-se-wi-jo*. On Jn 725, which is the preliminary tablet, a whole paragraph concerning the smiths of *na-i-se-wi-jo* is legible even though it had been erased. In that paragraph eight smiths are recorded above the total amount of bronze that was to be distributed among them: AES M 12[251]. However, at this stage the bronze had not been allocated to any smith in particular. Apparently, it was still to be decided which of the eight smiths was to receive an allocation and a work assignment at that time. But on the final version of the record, which was drawn up on Jn 692, two of the smiths recorded on Jn 725 have been chosen to receive AES M 6 (Jn 692.2), while the other six smiths who appeared with them are recorded as *a-ta-ra-si-jo*.

The fact that not all the smiths received an allotment has been taken by some to indicate that there was a shortage of bronze at Pylos, which had been caused by a disruption of trade routes by the so-called "sea-raiders."[252] It may be true that unrest in the area affected the supply of bronze, but it has to be said that the amount of bronze being allocated on the Jn series is not insignificant. The total of the extant allocations is 645 kg,[253] and if Ja 749 is the totaling tablet for the Jn series, then the entire total would have been 1,046 kg.[254] These numbers seem to indicate that the palace was not facing a major shortage of bronze. Ventris and Chadwick have estimated that "The smaller of the two most common allotments at Pylos (that of 1.5 kg) would be sufficient for making 1000 arrow-heads, the larger (5 kg) enough for at least fourteen swords or spears."[255] Thus, at least 131 swords could have been produced with the extant figure of 645 kg or, if we use the figure on Ja 749 of 1,046 kg, as many as 209. Also, there is nothing that speaks against the *a-ta-ra-si-jo* smiths being called upon at some future date. Therefore, the fact that many of the smiths were not given an allocation should more likely be explained by the idea that the palace shared out the work that they needed done among a large group of smiths, rather than that the palace was facing a shortage of bronze. This, along with the fact that the individual allotments given over to each of the smiths were in themselves generally not large (3-4 kg is the norm[256]) implies that the palace was probably not the only customer that these bronzesmiths worked for. Rather, as I proposed for the textile workshop collectors, the bronzesmiths probably also served the needs of others who lived in the vicinity of their bronze-working shops.[257] Repair work and recasting of scrap metal could have been among their more common tasks. And indeed, the fact that the smiths very often they had *do-e-ro* associated with them indicates that they were establishments that were set up to handle more work than what we see being ordered by the palace. Indeed, Nakassis has proposed that some of the bronzesmiths actually attained quite a high status in Mycenaean society due to their management of smithing workshops and their involvement in other economic and political activities. He says, "The Linear B evidence at Pylos indicates that individuals who engage in smithing are involved in a wide variety of activities designed to enhance their

[250] As we saw above, the word *ta-ra-si-ja* was also used in wool-working contexts within the Linear B tablets, e.g., KN Lc 535.A, 536.A, Le 642.1, MY Oe 110.1, but it is also used in reference to wheels on KN So 4442.b.

[251] The weight measurements are: L = 30 kg, M is equal to 1 kg and N, which we will see in a moment, is equal to 0.25 kg.

[252] *Docs*^{2}, pp. 509-510, see also p. 513. See n. 227 above for references concerning the "state of emergency."

[253] I am basing this figure on the following numbers: Jn 310: 24 kg; Jn 320: 56 kg; Jn 389: 28 kg; Jn 410: 30 kg; Jn 415: 34 kg; Jn 431: 81 kg; Jn 478: 26 kg; Jn 601: 108 kg; Jn 605: 9 kg; Jn 658: 80 kg; Jn 692: 12 kg; Jn 693: 42 kg; Jn 706: 30 kg; Jn 725: 28 kg; Jn 750: 24 kg; Jn 832: 3 kg; Jn 845: 12 kg; Jn 927: 18 kg. I have only included extant tablet totals and restorations that one can be very confident of. Therefore, the totals for some of these tablets probably would have been higher. Also, I included the amounts recorded as *e-pi-da-to*, or "distributed" (*Docs*^{2}, p. 544; *Dic. Mic.* I, *s.v. e-pi-da-to*) found on Jn 389.7 and Jn 601.7.

[254] M. Lejeune, "Les forgerons de Pylos," in *Mémoires de Philologie Mycénienne* II (*Incunabula Graeca* 42), Rome 1971, pp. 169-195; see p. 194. Also see *Docs*^{2}, pp. 356, 508. Smith (1992-1993, p. 171, n. 4) disagrees that Ja 749 is the totaling tablet for the Jn series since she thinks that the majority of the series has been preserved. She points out that this tablet does not have the ideogram for bronze nor the word *ka-ko* on it, but only the signs for weight that can be used for metals (among other things).

[255] *Docs*^{2}, p. 356.

[256] *Docs*^{2}, p. 509.

[257] Smith 1992-1993, p. 180 also discusses this possibility.

material standing and social status in the community."[258] In his work Nakassis details the variety of other administrative and economic fields that the smiths were involved in, and comes to the conclusion that, "some bronzesmiths appear to be involved in "collector"-like behavior" with some of them "among the 'entrepreneurial elite' of the Pylian state."[259] Thus, the traditional characterization of the bronzesmiths as low status workers who were dependent on the palace for their sustenance is unlikely to be true.

As in the Of series, the Jn tablets also record allocations that were assigned to workers who were affiliated with the religious sphere. These religious collectors, designated as *po-ti-ni-ja-we-jo*, or Potnian, are found on two tablets, Jn 310 and Jn 431. Jn 310 is the tablet that I used above to show the general pattern of the Jn tablets, and Jn 431 is shown below.

Jn 431:
1. a-pe-ke-i-jo , ka-ke-we , ta-ra-si[-ja e-ko-te
2. wi-ja-ni-jo AES M 5 ka-ra-*82[ ] AES M 5[ ] ko-tu-ro$_2$ AES M 5
3. ma-na-si-we-ko AES M 5 da-ṃạ-so AES M 5 qe-ta-ko AES M 4
4. a-ko-to-wo AES M 7 ụ[ ]ị-jo AES M 6 [[ ]]
5. ma-wa-si-jo AES M 5 qe-ṭọ-ro-no AES M 7
6. qa-si-re-u , a-pi-qo-ta 1 [ ]i-*65-qe 1
7. to-so-de , ka-ko , AES [L 1] M 24
8. *vacat* [ ] *vacat*
9. to-so-de , a-ta-ra-si-jo , ka-ke[-we] *vacat*
10. a-ta-tu-ro 1 i-ta-ra-jo 1 sa[1] *vacat*
11. wi-ja-te-wo 1 no-e-u 1 tu-ri-ja- jọ 1 qe-ṭạ-ḳọ-jo , do-e-ro 1
12. a-ka-ma-wo 1 e-pe-ke-u 1 *82-de 1 pu-te-u 1
13. ko-ne-wa-ta 1 qe-to-ro-no 1 mo-re-u 1 a-e-ri-qo 1
14. *vacat*
15. *vacat*
16. a-pe-ke-e , ka-ke-we , po-ti-ni-ja-we-jo , ta-ra-si-ja , e-ko-te
17. ko-za-ro AES M 6 a-ke-wa-ta AES M 3 sa-ke-re-u AES M 6
18. we-we-si-jo AES M 3 ko-ta-wo AES M 3 da-u-ta-ro AES M 6
19. *vacat*
20. to-so-de , ka-ko AES M 27 [
21. *vacat* [ ]
22. to[-so-de]a[-ta-]ra-si-jo , ka-ke-we , ka-ri-se-u 1 du-ko-so[1
23. ko[ ]ḷ e-u-wa-ko-ro 1 ke-we-no 1 a-ta-o 1 [
24.]wa-ti-ro 1 me-ri-wa-[•] 1 [
25.] i- jẹ-re[-wo]V̩ỊṚ 10 to-sa-no-jo VIR 5
26. VIR] 1 a-mu-ta-wo-no VIR 31

The Potnian bronzesmiths are marked out as distinct in some way from the other secular smiths by being set off in their own paragraphs (Jn 310.14 and Jn 431.16). Indeed, it looks as if the scribe of Jn 431 had considered making the Potnian record a separate tablet entirely. In the middle of line 15 there is a deep scoring which evidently was made in order to separate the two parts, although in the end the scribe retained the two parts as one tablet.[260] It seems, however, that the scoring must have weakened the tablet, causing it to break in the destruction of the palace, because it was indeed found as two separate tablets, and two separate numbers were assigned to them, 431 and 433. It seems that originally the fact that the break was not made by the scribe was overlooked since Chadwick says that the tablet had been "cut apart after writing."[261] If the tablet had been broken, the Potnian group of bronzesmiths would have stood on its own within the file, separate from the secular smiths. However, both Smith and Melena noticed that after the tablet had been scored, an attempt was made to repair it either with the scribe's thumbnail or some other type of "eraser."[262] Perhaps the scribe reconsidered how the file should be organized and decided that all the bronzesmiths from *a-pe-ke-e* should stand together regardless of their different classifications. Nonetheless, the fact that he did use separate paragraphs for the Potnian smiths on both Jn 310 and 431, and the fact that his initial impulse with Jn 431 was to physically separate the two records, indicate that the Potnian smiths were considered to be distinct from the others in some way. I think this was probably not just because the smiths had different affiliations, but because they were located at different workshops. Both the secular and the religious smiths of each tablet were in the same villages: the smiths of Jn 310 were located at *a-ke-re-wa* and those of Jn 431 were all at *a-pe-ke-e*, but they had to be separated out in order to indicate the different places to which the bronze was being sent. Since, as I proposed for the sheep and the textile workshops, the deity's name is used to describe the workers, I think that they were working for a shop that was organized and managed by religious personnel who were dedicated to a sanctuary. It is possible that the religious workshops may have been located within or near to the confines of sanctuaries dedicated to Potnia.[263]

There is one detail that can be interpreted as arguing against the idea that the religious workshops were separate from the secular ones. On Jn 310.11, one *do-e-ro* (*i-wa-ka-o* 1), who appears to belong to one of the Potnian smiths (*i-wa-ka* of line 16), is recorded in the same paragraph as the *do-e-ro* belonging to the secular

[258] D. Nakassis, *The Individual and the Mycenaean State: Agency and Prosopography in the Linear B Texts from Pylos*, Ph.D. Dissertation, University of Texas at Austin, p. 294.

[259] Nakassis 2006, p. 296.

[260] Smith 1992-1993, p. 228. Melena *PoN* IV, Jn 431.

[261] *Docs*^{2}, p. 354.

[262] Smith 1992-1993, p. 228; Melena *PoN* IV, mentions the "eraser" in his comments to Jn 431. A fragment from the right end of the tablet covering lines 14-17 has been found that retains the original connection, which assures the break between the lines was not made by the scribe who wrote the tablet.

[263] As was discussed in Chapter 2, on Cyprus, where the religious sector clearly took an active role in the production aspects of the copper industry, several Late Bronze Age sites, such as Kition (Karageorghis and Demas 1985), Enkomi (Dikaios 1969-1971), Athienou (Dothan and Ben-Tor 1983) and Myrtou Pigadhes (Du Plat Taylor 1957 and Knapp 1999, p. 235) had metal-working facilities in close association with a sanctuary site. Keswani (1993) and Knapp (1986, 1997, 1999) in particular have discussed this phenomenon.

smiths. In this one instance the sharp distinction between the two groups breaks down. The fact that this *do-e-ro* of the smiths was recorded with the secular *do-e-ro* could be taken to indicate that they were indeed one group, and that all the smiths, Potnian and secular, were working side-by-side in the same workshop. On the other hand, this conflation of the *do-e-ro* could just as easily have been motivated by the scribe's concern for a neat and compact presentation of the information, and so may not indicate anything in particular about the organization of the bronzesmiths' workshops. The scribe did, after all, have only that one *do-e-ro* belonging to the Potnian smiths to record, and he may not have thought it worthwhile to separate him out in his own paragraph. In contrast, the separation of the Potnian and secular smiths into separate paragraphs seems to have been the more important organizational distinction that the scribe wanted to make. It seems more likely, therefore, that the religious and secular smiths were actually working in separate workshops.

There is an interesting addendum to Jn 431 that supports the idea that the Potnian workshop at *a-pe-ke-e* was actually being run by religious personnel.

Jn 431:
25.] i- je̩-re[ ]V̩I̩R̩ 10 to-sa-no-jo VIR 5
26. VIR] 1 a-mu-ta-wo-no VIR 31

On the last two lines of Jn 431, 25-26, right beneath the record of the Potnian smiths who were *a-ta-ra-si-jo*, we see a group of 10 men, the first in a list of four such groups, listed against *i-je-re*[, which can be restored as either *i-je-re*[*-ja* or *i-je-re*[*-wo*, the genitive forms of 'priestess' and 'priest'.[264] This makes sense because the other two records that are fully extant have the groups of men recorded against names that are also in the genitive (*to-sa-no-jo, a-mu-ta-wo-no*). These groups then were most likely under the management of the person whose name or title is given in the genitive. Presumably this *i-je-re*[was the priestess or priest of Potnia at *a-pe-ke-e*. This group of ten men then is certainly associated with the religious realm. Actually, some have considered all of the groups to have had religious affiliations simply because of the fact that they were positioned right underneath the Potnian bronzesmiths. Smith in fact says "it is clear that the men listed at the bottom of Jn 431+433 have a connection with the smiths of the goddess Potnia, as a larger labor force or something analogous...."[265] The fact that the scribe who wrote Jn 431 did think about separating the bottom half of the tablet from the upper could be seen to support the idea that all the workers in this last paragraph were religious.[266] However, it is also possible that the reason he did not separate the two is because he realized that he would have to add this group of men at the end, and since they were associated with both the secular and the religious shops, he had to keep the two records together. It is true that the workgroups were appended to the bottom of the tablet without regard for which shops they were affiliated with, but this could have been because the names of the men they were allotted to would have served as identification enough. It may be safer therefore to consider only the group of ten men recorded with *i-je-re*[*-ja/wo* as definitely associated with the religious realm.[267]

In any case, the fact that we have a *i-je-re-ja* or a *i-je-ro* in a managerial position with whom workers were affiliated seems to imply that there was a separate religious workshop in *a-pe-ke-e*, which, since the bronzesmiths are designated as *po-ti-ni-ja-we-jo*, was considered to belong to Potnia.

Despite the distinction made because of the smiths' religious affiliation and location, the palatial administration seems to have treated the Potnian smiths in the same way as the other bronzesmiths. We can immediately dismiss the idea that the allotments of bronze were actually given as offerings since the Potnian smiths are clearly shown to be working under the *ta-ra-si-ja* system, which indicates that the metal was to be worked and returned to the palace once it had been turned into finished products. Also, the amounts of bronze allotted to the Potnian smiths is similar to those given to secular smiths. On Jn 310 the four Potnian smiths are all listed as receiving AES M 3, while three of the six Potnian smiths on Jn 431 also receive AES M 3 and the last three receive AES M 6. These numbers are well within the normal range of allocations given to secular smiths. Ventris and Chadwick record that 123 of 144, or 85% of the smiths whose allotments are extant receive between AES M 1 N 2 and AES M 5.[268] A smaller number of smiths receive between AES M 6 and 8, and the largest amount found on the Jn tablets is AES M 12, but this amount is only allocated once (Jn 601.6). Thus, the seven Potnian allotments of M 3 are well within the normal range of allocations given to secular smiths, while

[264] Smith discusses this emendation on p. 184, n. 50.

[265] Smith 1992-1993, p. 184.

[266] If all 47 men were associated with the religious realm it might seem a bit excessive to have 47 laborers at one bronze workshop. In that case, we might wonder if the common factor between the Potnian smiths and these workers was that they were associated with the sanctuary dedicated to Potnia.

[267] There has also been some debate concerning the status of these men. Lejeune (1971, p. 183, n. 60) proposed that "*do-e-ro*" should be restored at the beginning of line 25 as a kind of heading for the rest of the two lines. (1992-1993, p. 184) Smith does not agree with this, saying that, "In writing tablets of the Jn series Hand 2 was careful to note whether a man was or was not a *do-e-ro*.... Therefore we would expect him to have used the word *do-e-ro* to describe the men on Jn 431+433 if they had been classified as *do-e-ro*." Whether or not these men were actually *do-e-ro*, their appearance on the Jn tablets without any specification as to their function would seem to suggest that they were unskilled labor forces. We may presume that they were working for the bronze-working shops, even though *to-sa-no* and *a-mu-ta-wo* are not found elsewhere on the Jn tablets (*to-sa-no* does appear on Fn 79.4 and *a-mu-ta-wo* is found on Nn 831.7), since the *i-je-re*[is presumably affiliated with the Potnian shop and because it would seem strange if they were just appended to the tablet without any indication of what they were to do unless we were to assume it was to take part in the bronze work. If they were working with the bronzesmiths, the shops themselves must have been pretty sizable operations.

[268] *Docs*², p. 356. Smith 1992-1993, p. 179.

the allotments of M 6 are a bit on the high end, but still not abnormal.

It should also be noted that the Potnian smiths were just as likely to have been left without an allotment of bronze as the secular ones. On Jn 310.17 there is one Potnian smith described as *a-ta-ra-si-jo*, and on Jn 431.22-24 there are at least eight Potnian smiths in this category. Finally, both secular and religious smiths had *do-e-ro*, which implies that both types of workshops were run internally in a similar fashion as well. Thus it seems the Potnian workshops on Jn 310.14 and Jn 431.16 were active, functioning production facilities that were working under the *ta-ra-si-ja* system, producing goods for the palace when required just as the secular shops did. The religious smiths, like the secular, probably did work for local customers in addition to the *ta-ra-si-ja* work they did for the palace. It was probably through that work that the religious personnel would have been able to acquire the goods that the sanctuary needed. Thus, it seems likely that the Potnian bronzesmiths, like their secular counterparts, were engaged in the production and repair of items made from bronze and that the goods they received in exchange for their work most likely provided for, at least, the general maintenance of the sanctuary and its personnel.

General Summary

From the Linear B evidence it seems that the Mycenaean religious sector was not only involved in animal husbandry, but also textile manufacture and metal working, and it seems that the religiously affiliated collectors interacted with the palace in the same way that the secular collectors did. In the case of the sheep tablets, the religious personnel in the service of Potnia were expected to fulfill their targets of lambs. In the Theban textile workshops and the Pylian bronze workshops allocations of raw materials were given to the religious workers under the *ta-ra-si-ja* system in the same way that they were given to secular ones, and presumably finished goods were expected to be returned to the palace once those raw materials had been worked on. The religious collectors therefore held a position in the Mycenaean economy that was commensurate with that held by the individual collectors, the secular entrepreneurs of Mycenaean society. This means that the religious personnel were, like the secular collectors, most likely engaged in procuring their own livelihoods, and that they probably traded their goods and services within local exchange networks, as well as with the palace. It is from these local transactions that both types of collector most likely gained the more substantial portion of their income.

If indeed, as I believe was the case, the religious collectors were working for sanctuaries dedicated to their deities, then the proceeds from their work was probably used by the sanctuary to finance its own operations and to support its personnel. Therefore, it seems possible that sanctuary sites, such as the one we have posited to exist at *si-ja-du-we*, with it several hundred sheep, and the one we can be more certain of at *Pa-ki-ja-ne*, could have acted as economic centers just as the palaces did. In the same vein, the fourteen Potnian smiths on Jn 431 (both *ta-ra-si-jo* and *a-ta-ra-si-jo*), along with the ten men who were recorded with the *i-je-re*[in the appended paragraph would have constituted quite a workforce. I do not mean to overestimate the role of the religious sector in the Mycenaean economy. I would agree with Killen when he says that, "it is difficult to believe that the so-called 'owners' or 'collectors' [among whom we can now number religious personnel] can have formed a genuinely independent sector of the economy...."[269] Hiller has a similar opinion. In discussing the workshops of the religious personnel he says, "the sacrally organized *oikos*-system makes up only a part of the Mycenaean economic order."[270] This is of course true. We can see, for instance, within the bronze-working industry that the religious workshops were clearly not a large part of the economic sector; only 19 of the 286 extant bronzesmiths[271] are described as Potnian, and only two towns (that we know of) seem to have had religiously affiliated bronze workshops. Also, the religious collectors were well integrated into the organizational systems the palace used to procure the goods it needed. They had to comply with the palace's demands for wool, lambs, and manufactured goods just as the secular collectors did. The sanctuaries were therefore subordinate to the economic power of the palace and any talk of a "temple economy" is inappropriate for the Mycenaean situation.[272] But neither do I think that the religious hierarchy relied on the support of the palace for its sustenance, nor do I think that their economic activities were controlled by the palatial administration.

Of course, many of the sanctuaries must have been fairly modest in size, and the proceeds from their economic endeavors may have been intended simply to provide for the maintenance of the inhabitants of the sanctuary. In this category I would put the religious collectors associated with the single flocks of Potnian sheep on KN Dl 943, 7147 and 7771. But in some cases, the religious collectors could have created surpluses, which would have given the religious personnel more opportunity to barter and exchange their goods. They would also have been able to take on additional roles within the community, such as landlord, employer, and loan provider. It is possible then, as seems to have been the case for several of the collectors, that the sanctuaries and their personnel may have been able to acquire some real material wealth. This wealth would have served to

[269] Killen 1984, p. 288.
[270] Hiller 1981, p. 103.
[271] My count of 286 smiths includes the *a-ta-ra-si-jo* smiths, but not the *do-e-ro* associated with them. For the following, the number of smiths is given after the tablet number: Jn 310: 17; Jn 320: 17; Jn 389: 16; Jn 410: 4; Jn 415: 12; Jn 431: 39; Jn 478: 8; Jn 601: 19; Jn 605: 9; Jn 658: 16; Jn 692: 8; Jn 693: 12; Jn 706: 14; Jn 725: 21; Jn 750: 19; Jn 832: 22; Jn 845: 15; Jn 927: 18. For Jn 693 and 725, which are working tablets, I included only those smiths who were not recorded on other tablets.
[272] As discussed in Chapter 1, Palmer (1963, *passim*) is the biggest proponent of a "temple economy" having existed in Mycenaean Greece. I. Tegyey considers the question in "The Northeast Workshop at Pylos," in *Pylos Comes Alive*, C.W. Shelmerdine and T.G. Palaima, eds., New York 1984, pp. 65-79; see especially pp. 77-79.

enhance the prestige that was already attached to the religious personnel because of their cultic knowledge, and would have provided them with a more concrete base for their influence within society. Thus, although the religious sector may not have rivaled the political authority and economic force wielded by the palaces, nonetheless prosperous sanctuaries and their personnel may have held an elevated standing within their communities.

Other Religious Workers Associated with the Palaces

The tablets provide several other examples of workers who were affiliated with the religious sphere, but the relationship of those individuals with the palace is markedly different from those I have just considered in the sheep, textile, and bronze-working industries. In these next instances the religious workers are much more closely tied with the palace than the people I call the religious collectors.

***Pi-ra-jo* the Potnian Unguent Boiler**

For instance, *pi-ra-jo* of Un 249 is described as an unguent boiler (*a-re-pa-zo-*[*o*]), but he is also designated as *po-ti-ni-ja-we-jo*.

Un 249:
.a po-ti-ṇị-ja-we-jo
1. pi-ra-jo , a-re-pa-zo[-o] ku-pa-ro$_2$ AROM 2 T 5
2. wi-ri-za LANA 2 [ ] **157* 10
3. *vacat* [ ] *KAPO* T 6
4. *vacat*

There are three other unguent boilers recorded at Pylos (on Un 267, Ea 812, and Fg 374, connected by name and context to Gn 1184), but only one of them is listed against aromatics in the same way as Potnian *pi-ra-jo* is. This secular unguent boiler is named *tu-we-ta*, or Thyestes, and he is recorded as receiving aromatics and wool from *a-ko-so-ta* on Un 267.

Un 267:
1. o-do-ke , a-ko-so-ta
2. tu-we-ta , a-re-pa-zo-o
3. tu-we-a , a-re-pa-te [[ ]]
4. ze-so-me-no [[ ]]
5. ko-ri-a$_2$-da-na AROM 6
6. ku-pa-ro$_2$ AROM 6 **1̣5̣7̣* 1̣6
7. *KAPO* 2 T 5 VIN^a 20 *ME* 2
8. LANA 2 VIN^b 2
9-11. *vacant*

Thus we do not actually have much material with which to compare the relative positions of Potnian and secular unguent boilers. However, what we do have indicates that they were fairly similar. Both *pi-ra-jo* and *tu-we-ta* receive 6 kg of wool. *Tu-we-ta* receives more cyperus seed than *pi-ra-jo* (720 l vs. 300 l) and more of **157*, although this difference is not quite as striking as that in the case of the cyperus seed (16 units vs. 10). Nonetheless, the differences in the quantities do not indicate that *pi-ra-jo* had a different function from *tu-we-ta* since they are fairly large in both cases and can be understood to have been allocated for industrial purposes. Also, since Un 249 has no indication of place on it, we may consider that *pi-ra-jo* was working at the palace center itself. Shelmerdine concurs with this. At first she considers the possibility that *pi-ra-jo* might actually be located at a shrine dedicated to Potnia, but she comes to the conclusion that it would be more likely for him to be working at the palace.[273] This means that, in contrast to what seemed most likely for the religious collectors associated with sheep, textiles and the bronze workshops, *pi-ra-jo* was not (or probably not) employed in a workshop that was associated with a religious sanctuary. Rather, *pi-ra-jo* seems to have been working within the palace-run perfumed oil industry. The question then is what did his being designated as Potnian signify? The easy solution is to propose tha *pi-ra-jo* managed the production of the oils that were to be sent to Potnia as offerings. But this seems unlikely: why would only one deity be specified in this way when oil was sent to many deities? It seems more likely that he was simply a priest dedicated to Potnia, who happened to be working in the palace. As we saw in the previous chapter, there were several people at Pylos who held religious positions who were also active within the secular sphere. *Pi-ra-jo* seems to have been among those persons. And perhaps he was able to (or was required/expected to) pass on some of the benefits that he accrued through working in the palatial workshop to the sanctuary to which he belonged, but there is no evidence for that one way or the other.

The Potnian Women of KN G 820

A group of women on the Knossos tablet G 820 should also be discussed here since they are described as Potnian (*po-ti-ni-ja-we-ja*).

G 820:
1.] ̦ [ ]-ṇạ , e-ko-si , a-pi , ku-do-ni-ja / pa-sa 'ki-ri-ta' LUNA 1
2. ja-]pu$_2$-wi-ja-qe , *56-ko-we-i-ja-qe LUNA 4
3. da-]*22-ti-ja , ku-ta-ti-ja-qe , po-ti-ni-ja-we-ja , a-pu , ke-u-po-de-ja
4.] LUNA 4

The Potnian women of G 820 appear amongst several other groups of women, most of whom are designated by ethnic adjectives derived from toponyms (such as the *da-*]**22-ti-ja*, who were presumably from or working at *da-*22-to*, a common place name in the Knossian texts). The women are receiving rations of *ki-ri-ta*, or barley, and therefore were probably doing some work for the palace, most likely in the textile industry.[274] The Potnian women, therefore, were most likely also doing work for the palace like the other groups of women. So again we

[273] Shelmerdine 1985, pp. 44-45.

[274] J.T. Killen, "Mycenaean Possessive Adjectives in *-e-jo*," *TPhS* (1983) 66-99; see p. 71.

have a case of dual affiliation: the fact that this group of women was designated as Potnian could indicate that they were primarily affiliated with a sanctuary of Potnia. But they were working for the palace. Several scenarios could be imagined. One is that they usually worked in a religious textile workshop, but the palace had requisitioned their labor from the sanctuary, as a kind of corvee labor. Another possibility is that the sanctuary did not need their labor at the moment and so hired them out to the palatial workshop. A third possibility is that the women were not usually employed in a sanctuary's workshop at all and were working for the palace independent of their religious affiliation. There is however an indication that the religious affiliation of the women was significant in this context.

The barley is said to be given to the Potnian women *a-pu ke-u-po-de-ja*, which could mean, "from the χευσπόνδεια," or female libation pourer.[275] Perhaps this was an important religious official within the palace, so well known that her name did not need to be specified, who dealt with the religious workers. The masculine form of this title, *ke-u-po-da*, is attested on several tablets, both at Pylos and Knossos (e.g., PY Na 395.B, KN C 1044.b and Dq 442). Killen points out that on the Knossos tablets *ke-u-po-da* is found in the collector position,[276] which could indicate that this was another example of a religious official who was also active in the secular realm. Killen however does not mention any sort of religious affiliation for *ke-u-po-da*, but he does take *ke-u-po-de-ja* of G 820 as the adjectival form of this man's name (or title). This would give us the "Potnian women of *ke-u-po-da*." If we retain the interpretation of *ke-u-po-da* as a religious title meaning 'libation pourer', then perhaps we could say that these women were being managed by *ke-u-po-da*, and that they were all working in the name of Potnia.

Aura Jorro puts forward an interesting suggestion of his own concerning this word *ke-u-po-de-ja*.[277] For the word itself he proposes **xeu-spondeia* or **geus-spondeia*, meaning "ceremony of the libations," and he asks, "could *ke-u-po-de-ja* be interpreted as the name of a religious ceremony of initiation, of the sort that, once accomplished, the women would acquire the rank of *po-ti-ni-ja-we-ja*?" If this is the case, then maybe these women were given their allocation of barley upon the occasion of this initiation ceremony.
In either case, it does seem as if the religious affiliation of the women is important here even though they were doing something that was a service to the palace.

R. Palmer compares G 820 with KN E 777, which also records rations, this time in GRA, that were being given both to groups of women designated by their toponymic adjectives and to a group of female religious personnel.[278]

[275] Palmer 1963, p. 307.
[276] Killen 1979, p. 176.
[277] *Dic. Mic.* I, p. 356.
[278] R. Palmer, "Wheat and Barley in Mycenaean Society," in *Mykenaïka* (*BCH Suppl.* 25) J.-P. Olivier, ed., Salamanca 1992, pp. 475-497; see pp. 48-49.

The religious women found on E 777.1 are the *ki-ri-te-wi-ja-i*, which Bennett renders as the 'barleyers,' but he adds that this is "less an occupation than a religious title."[279] We have also seen these *ki-ri-te-wi-ja-i* in the land tenure series of *Pa-ki-ja-ne*, where they were recorded among other religious personnel on Ep 704.4.[280] R. Palmer therefore seeks to elevate the ration to a kind of offering and says of the *ki-ri-te-wi-ja-i*, "Their status and privileges show that even if they do prepare barley in some way, this would not be considered a menial occupation but rather an honor."[281] While this may be true, I wonder if perhaps we should also interpret E 777, like G 820, as recording a ration or payment of sorts, given to workers who happen to be associated with the religious realm. This would not necessarily detract from the status of the *ki-ri-te-wi-ja-i* since it is possible that they were not the ones actually doing the work; rather they could have had craftswomen working in their name.

An 1281 and the Northeast Building/Workshop of Pylos

Further evidence for the involvement of the religious sector in industrial activities, and in those that were very important to the elite of the palace, is found in a tablet that was discovered in the Northeast Building of Pylos, An 1281. Before turning to a consideration of An 1281 though, I will discuss the nature of the Northeast Building, since the tablet's archaeological context is important to its interpretation.

The Industrial and Administrative Aspects of the Northeast Building

The Northeast Building is a rectangular structure of c. 32.6 m long by 16 m wide that consisted of six rooms of various sizes (numbered 93, 96-100 on the plan). The Northeast Building stood separate, but not far from, from the Main Building.[282] Rooms 93, 99, and 100 looked out onto a porticoed courtyard within which was situated a frescoed block of poros that Blegen and Rawson identified as an altar.[283] Despite the presence of this altar, Blegen and Rawson interpreted the Northeast Building as the "Workshop belonging to the palace."[284] They came

[279] E.L. Bennett ("The Landholders of Pylos," *AJA* 60 (1956b) 103-133, see p. 132) suggests a comparison with the κριθολόγος of the Opuntians (Plu. 2.292c).
[280] The *ki-ri-te-wi-ja-i* also appear on KN Fp 363.2 receiving an offering of oil on the same line as a *i-je-ro*, on PY Un 1426.6 (*ki-ri-te-wi-ja-pi*) receiving an allocation of figs, and on An 607.1 in the heading of a tablet that seems to record the parentage of several persons.
[281] R. Palmer 1992, p. 486.
[282] C.W. Blegen and M. Rawson, *The Palace of Nestor at Pylos in Western Messenia,* Vol. I: *The Buildings and their Contents*, Princeton University Press 1966, pp. 299-325.
[283] Blegen and Rawson 1966, pp. 301-302.
[284] Blegen and Rawson 1966, p. 299. This identification has also been made by subsequent scholars. For instance, T.G. Palaima ("The Transactional Vocabulary of Mycenaean Sealings and the Mycenaean Administrative Process," in *Administrative Documents in the Aegean and their Near Eastern Counterparts*, M. Perna (ed.), Paravia Scriptorium 2000, p. 261-276; p. 270) says that the wheel assembly workshop (or chariot workshop) mentioned on Vn 10.2 (*a-mo-te-jo-na-de*) "seems indeed archaeologically to be the Northeast Workshop, judging from the references to *a-ko-so-ne* found on tablets therein."

to this conclusion because the building itself was constructed in a more utilitarian manner than the Main Building had been, with clay floors, wide doorways, and shelving in Room 99, all of which indicated that it was well suited for workshop activities. They also based their conclusion on the Linear B tablets found within the building, many of which deal with industrial work. In this section I will focus on the tablets and the evidence they provide concerning the use of the Northeast Building and the role of the religious sector within it. In the next chapter I will take up the issue of the altar and whether we are justified in seeing room 93 as a shrine.

Blegen and Rawson's interpretation of the Northeast Building as a workshop stood for several decades. But recently both Hofstra[285] and Bendall[286] have argued that we should abandon the traditional way of referring to and thinking about the building (as Northeast Workshop of Pylos) and use instead the more generic term, "Northeast Building." This is because Hofstra's and Bendall's independent analyses of the structure and its contents have shown that the Northeast Building was not used *solely* as a workshop dedicated to specific types of production. Hofstra has stressed that large-scale manufacturing processes requiring facilities for tanning hides or kilns for bronze working could not have been conducted on this site.[287] Her analysis of the small finds from the Northeast Building revealed that it "preserves only a relatively small number of lithics, no bone tools, and only (according to Rawson's field notes) six or eight ground stone tools."[288] These are enough, however, for Hofstra to think that some workshop activities were conducted within the building.[289] For instance she says that, "there is evidence for lithics production, leather working, wood-working, [and] possibly chariot repair" but that this "repair and 'production' work of different sorts" was not the primary focus of the building's occupants.[290] Rather, Hofstra and Bendall agree that the building must have served predominantly as a storage facility and administrative clearinghouse that managed the collection and subsequent disbursal of livestock, various goods, raw materials, and groups of workers. Shon too had concluded that,

> Although, due to space requirements, the Northeast Building may not have been the actual location of all the production needed by the chariot industry, it was certainly the location where this industry was administered and where raw materials for it were collected and stored.[291]

The bulk of the tablets that deal with industrial matters are concerned with weapons, chariots and items that would have been made for the chariots, like reins and halters. Because of the tablets' connections with military items, Bendall actually finds more value in Blegen's original interpretation of the Northeast Building as an armory of sorts.[292] Shon, in his analysis of the Northeast Building has said, "of the items for which there is evidence of manufacture in the Northeast Building, chariots are the most proliferate."[293] The tablet An 1282 actually lists men in groups of 18 (one group seems to have been split into 13 and 5 and two groups seem to have been combined to make 36), who are being put to work on manufacturing chariots and their constituent parts.

An 1282:

1. a-qi-ja-i	VIR 18	a-mo-si	VIR 18
2. ki-u-ro-i	VIR 13	po-qe-wi-ja-i	VIR 5
3. do-ka-ma-i	VIR 36		
4.	*vacat*		

A-qi-ja-i as the first entry are the chariots[294], while *a-mo-si* gives us 'wheels', *ki-u-ro-i*, 'baskets'(?), *po-qe-wi-ja-i*, 'halters' or 'bridles' and *do-ka-ma-i*, 'handles or shafts'. Hofstra comments that it is unlikely that these men were producing the items listed "since there is little regard for precisely adapting the number of men to the type of labor involved in manufacturing, and one would expect specialists such as the sewers, leatherworkers and woodworkers known from other Pylos documents to be involved in the manufacture of chariots and harnesses."[295] Perhaps, she goes on to say, "they are movers or porters." I would suggest that, on the other hand, they probably were involved in the production work since much of it could be done by people who had a basic knowledge of what had to be done, especially if they had an overseer, which is likely.

The tablets of the Ub series continue the chariot workshop theme of An 1282. Ub 1318 for instance records the allocation of of hides to various craftsmen, the number of hides being disbursed to each of them, and the items they were supposed to make out of those hides.

Ub 1318:

1. au-ke-i-ja-te-we , ka-tu-re-ẉị-ja-i di-pte-ra 4 [•-•-•-•]ḍị-pte-ra 2 au-ke-i-ja-te-we , o-ka , di-pte-ṛạ[
2. au-ke-i-ja-te-we o-pi-de-so-mo ⌊ ⌋ka-tu-ro$_2$, di-pte-ra 4 ka-ne-ja ⌊ ⌋wo-ro-ma-ta 4
3. me-ti-ja-no , to-pa , ru-de-a$_2$, ḍị-pte-ra 1 a-re-se-si , e-ru-ta-ra , di-pte-ṛạ 3 wo-di-je-ja , pe-di-ra 2
4. we-e-wi-ja , di-pte-ra , 10 wi-ri-no , we-ru-ma-ta , ti-ri-ṣị , ze-u-ke-si 1
5. wi-ri-no , pe-di-ro , e-ma-ta 4 e-ra-pe-ja , e-pi-u-ru-te-we , *E* 2

[285] S. Hofstra, *Small Things Considered: The Finds from LH IIIB Pylos in Context*, Ph.D. Dissertation, University of Texas at Austin 2000.

[286] L. Bendall, "A Reconsideration of the Northeastern Building at Pylos: Evidence for a Mycenaean Redistributive Center," *AJA* 107 (2003) pp. 181-231.

[287] Hofstra 2000.

[288] Hofstra 2000, p. 273.

[289] Hofstra 2000, p. 273; personal communication, August 2006.

[290] Hofstra, personal communication, August 2006.

[291] Schon 1994, p. 50.

[292] Bendall 2003, p. 184.

[293] Schon 1994, p. 43.

[294] *A-qi-ja-i* being a mistake for *i-qi-ja-i* (J.T. Killen, "New Readings and Interpretations in the Pylos Tablets," in *Floreant Studia Mycenaea*, S. Deger-Jalkotzy, S. Hiller and O. Panagl, ed., Vienna 1999, pp. 343-353; see p. 349. Also see *Dic. Mic.* I, *s.v. a-qi-ja-i*, p. 92.

[295] Hofstra 2000, p. 288.

6. a-pe-i-ja , u-po , ka-ro , we-[ ]-ja 1 u-po , we-e-wi-ja , e-ra-pe-ja *E* 1
7. mu-te-we , we-re-ne-ja , ku[ ]pe-re 1 mu-te-we , di-pte-ra , a_3-za , pe-di-ro-i 1
8. *vacat*
9. *vacat*

Thus, in the first line we have four hides (*di-pte-ra*) that were to be made into saddlebags (*ka-tu-re-wi-ja-i*) being given to *au-ke-i-ja-te-we*. Other items being manufactured are straps (*o-ka*), bindings of pack saddles[296] (*o-pi-de-so-mo ka-to-ro$_2$*), and sandals (*pe-di-ra/ro-i*), which could have been made to be worn by those driving the chariots. Ub 1315 seems to be an inventory of similar items such as reins (*a-ni-ja*), 16 red hides (*di-pte-ra e-ru-ta-ra*), and 11 pairs of new halters (*ne-wa po-qe-wi-ja ZE*).

Ub 1315:
1.]-wo-ja a-ni-ja , te-u-ke-pi , 5 di-pte-ra$_3$ e-ru-ta-ra 16[
2. ro-u-si-je-wi-ja 6 ra-pte-ri-ja a-ni-ja 3

a.

3. ne-wa , a-ni-ja , a-na-pu-ke , 5 dwo 2 a-pu-ke 9 a-ni-ja-e-e-ro-pa-ja-qe-ṛọ-ṣạ

a. 1

4. a-pe-ne-wo 4 a-pu-ke , a-pe-ne-wo ne-wa po-qe-wi-ja *ZE* 11

Ub 1316 and 1317 also record hides, but do not specify what the hides were to be made into. We can, however, speculate that they were to be used in the manufacture of items similar to those on Ub 1316 and 1318.

Va 1323, Va 1324 and Vn 1339 contribute to the image of the Northeast Building as a center associated with chariots and military equipment in that they record axles (*a-ko-so-ne*, 1323, 1324 and 1339), spears (*e-ke-i-ja*, 1324, 1339), and infantry spears (*pe-di-je-wi-ja*, 1324), while Vn 1341 records 200 darts or javelins (*pa-ta-jo*). Killen proposes that words such as *e-ke-ja* (Vn 1339) and *a-ko-so-ne* (Va 1324) may refer to wood for making spears and axles rather than the finished products.[297] Sealings found in the Northeast Building demonstrate that some of these materials were delivered to and perhaps also stored in the Northeast Building. Wr 1328, for instance, records a delivery of infantry spears[298] and Wr 1480 records a delivery of darts or javelins (*pa-ta-jo*) and handles or shafts (*do-ka-ma*). Ja 1288, which most likely records an allocation of bronze to a man named *ka-ra-wi-so*,[299] shows that the bronze used in the construction of the chariots, wheels, and weapons was also a concern of the Northeast Building. In addition to the tablet evidence, over 600 arrowheads were actually found in the Northeast Building.

The Northeast Building managers also monitored the finished weapons and their condition. The Sa series, which was found in the Archives Complex, but which was probably written in the Northeast Building, inventoried and assessed the quality of 85 pairs of chariot wheels. Sa 682, for example, records wheels that were "unfit for service" (*no-pe-re-a$_2$*), while Sa 287 describes its wheels as "bound with silver" (*a-ku-ro de-de-me-no*).[300] The one tablet of this series, Sa 1313, that was found in the Northeast Building, was identified as belonging to the Sa series because it was written by the same hand as the rest of the series (Hand 26) and because the one full word found on Sa 1313, *we-je-ke-e*, which most likely means "serviceable,"[301] is also found on many other tablets within the Sa series.[302] This makes it likely that the Sa tablets were all written within the Northeast Building and subsequently transferred to the Archives Complex.[303] The same might be conjectured for another set of tablets found in the Archives Complex, the Sh series, which records another item of military equipment: corselets.[304] We can conclude therefore that the Northeast Building was the site of an inventory of chariot wheels,[305] and most likely of corselets as well. Hence the administrators of the Northeast Building were responsible not only for the production of chariots and weaponry but also for their maintenance and repair.[306] Clearly this was a prime concern of those working in the Northeast Building. But, as Hofstra points out, the facilities necessary for doing the heavy work are not present in the Northeast Building, and therefore cannot have served as the workshop where the metal working and leather tanning was done. Rather, the managers of the Northeast Building were overseeing the practical steps necessary for the palace's military preparedness.

Another group of tablets, the Ac series, indicates that the Northeast Building was used as an assembly point for large groups of workmen. From the six extant place names on the Ac tablets,[307] it is clear that the men were called up from the main districts of the Hither Province and at least one of the districts of the Further Province (*ti-mi-to-a-ke-e*). Tegyey had extrapolated, based on the

[296] See Tegyey 1984, p. 74.

[297] Killen 1999, p. 348.

[298] *Pe-di-e-wi* appears on the sealing but it is probably an error for *pe-di-je-wi-ja*, which is found on Vn 1338.

[299] The case of *ka-ra-wi-so* is ambiguous but C.W. Shelmerdine ("Industrial Activity at Pylos," in *Tractata Mycenaea*, P. Ilievski and L. Crepajac , eds., Skopje 1987, pp. 333-342; p. 334, n. 8) points out that it is more likely that *ka-ra-wi-so* is in the dative "since the amount [of bronze, which is AES M 4 N 1 P 6] is the most common allotment size for individuals on the Jn tablets."

[300] M. Ventris and J. Chadwick, *Documents in Mycenaean Greek*, Cambridge University Press, 2nd edition 1973, pp. 373-375.

[301] Shelmerdine 1987, p. 335.

[302] To be precise, the dual form *we-je-ke-e* appears most often in this series (a total of eighteen times) but three Sa tablets actually have the regular plural *we-je-ke-a$_2$*: Sa 787.A, 791, and 843.

[303] T.G. Palaima, *The Scribes of Pylos* (*Incunabula Graeca* 87), Rome 1988, p. 156. Shelmerdine 1987, pp. 333, 335.

[304] Shelmerdine 1987, p. 335. Killen 1999, pp. 345-347.

[305] It is also pertinent that the word *wo-ka*, which can be translated as 'chariot' (*ϝοχά) appears on many of the Sa tablets (see *Dic. Mic.* II, p. 437).

[306] See Palaima 1988, pp. 269-271) for a discussion on how these sealings and tablets reflect Pylian administrative methods of monitoring deliveries and production work.

[307] The place names are *me-ta-pa*, *a-ke-re-wa*, *pi-*82*, *ka-ra-do-ro*, and two, *pe-ti-ni-jo* and *te-mi-ti-jo* seem to be the adjectival forms of *pe-to-no* and *ti-mi-to-a-ke-e*.

original readings of the extant number of men (which he calculated as 178), that there would have been more than 500 men if all the tablets had been preserved.[308] Even though the latest readings of the Ac tablets give us a lower number than Tegyey had counted (102 men present and 36 missing[309]), we can still say that there would have been at least a couple hundred men congregating at the Northeast Building. As for the purpose for which the men were requisitioned, we can be fairly sure that they were workmen being assembled for some corvée labor since, as Lang said, "the anonymous and summary form of the record on these tablets ... makes it more likely that these groups of men presented and owed to the palace are slaves or workmen for some activity of which Room 87 [now 99] was the headquarters than that they were fighting men being mobilized."[310] Lang uses the word "headquarters" advisedly since the size of the Northeast Building, as Bendall works out in detail,[311] was not large enough to accommodate such a large number of workmen. Thus it is likely that these workers were being assembled in the area of the Northeast Building and that they would have been sent elsewhere for specific assignments.

There are also a couple of tablets that seem to record rations for workforces associated with the Northeast Building. Un 1322, which was found in the Northeast Building, records either rations, or what could actually be payments (*o-no*), in wheat and figs that were given to workers such as a net-maker and a weaver.[312] Also, on Fn 50, which can be associated with the Northeast Building even though it was actually found in the Archives Complex, rations are given to the *do-e-ro* of three workshop managers who are recorded on a tablet that was found in the Northeast Building, An 1281. Thus the managers of the Northeast Building oversaw various types of work, or, they were involved in various aspects of personnel management.[313] It seems then that the majority of the work implied by the tablets found in the Northeast Building must have been conducted elsewhere, although some of the raw materials required for the work were stored there and the work was administered by managers who were located there.

Other tablets indicate that the Northeast Building was also used as a "general receiving depot for the Main Building...."[314] For instance Cc 1283-1285 and Cn 1286-1287 record deliveries of small numbers of sheep and goats from various individuals. Several sealings (e.g., Wr 1325, 1331 and 1334) also demonstrate that small livestock were being delivered to the Northeast Building. How these animals were to be used has been a topic of debate. Tegyey thought that they were to supply the workshop with the leather needed for the bridles and straps found on other tablets.[315] Hofstra disagrees with this view since no tanning facilities were found near the Building. Instead she thinks it is more likely that they were to be slaughtered for food, or, given the fact that many of the animals were female (those on Cn 1287), that they could have been used for their milk or in religious ceremonies.[316] The idea that the animals were used in religious contexts has been proposed by both Aravantinos[317] and, more recently, Killen.[318] Killen though does not see the sacrificial and industrial uses of the animals to be contradictory since once an animal had been sacrificed its hide and other useful parts could be used for industrial activities. He points out that "in the Classical period the skins of animals consumed at sacrificial banquets were often sold to tanners by the organisers of the festivities."[319] It also seems possible that the hides of the animals, once sacrificed, could have been tanned elsewhere and returned to the workshop for use in the chariot industry. The fact that the animals were delivered to the Northeast Building may indicate that this is where they were ultimately supposed to be used.

The contexts of Un 1321, which deals with wine and grain, and Un 1319, which deals with grain and other foodstuffs, are unclear. It can be said though that these tablets show that the administrators of the Northeast Building were involved in handling goods that were not connected with industrial activities, thereby contributing to the definition of the Northeast Building as a clearinghouse. The Qa series, which most likely records disbursements of a type of cloth (**189*), also contributes to this view. I will return to the religious associations of these tablets and their significance further on.

Thus, it appears that the administrators working in the Northeast Building were involved in a variety of activities. They handled the receipt and subsequent

[308] Tegyey 1984, p. 69. It was originally proposed by Lang (1958, p. 190), and supported by Shelmerdine (1987, p. 339), that the men were requisitioned in numbers that were proportional to the tax assessments on the Ma tablets, Cn 608, and Vn 20. Shelmerdine, however, has since pointed out that because subsequent readings of the tablets have produced different numbers for the men, the proposed correspondences with the Ma tablets are no longer valid ("Mycenaean Taxation," in *Studia Mycenaea 1988, Ziva Antika Monographs* 7, T.G. Palaima, C.W. Shelmerdine, and P. Ilievski, eds., Skopje 1989, pp. 125-148; see p. 147, n. 49).

[309] The tablets and their figures are 1272: VIR 2, *o* 8; 1274: VIR 6, *o* 13; 1275: VIR 25, *o* 1; 1276: VIR 20; 1277: VIR 10, *o* 6; 1278: VIR 17, *o* ?; 1279: VIR ?, *o* 1; 1280: VIR 22, *o* 7.

[310] Lang 1958, p. 190.

[311] Bendall 2003, pp. 203-206.

[312] Chadwick 1964, pp. 19-26. The first three lines of Un 1322 seem to represent a regular ration except for the inclusion of the word *o-no*, which may indicate that these workers were actually being paid for their work rather than simply receiving rations. Lines 4 and 5 of Un 1322 are slightly different in that they seem to represent an actual exchange of goods: payments in wheat were being given in exchange for the type of cloth represented by the ideogram **146* (p. 25). Also see Killen's discussion of this tablet in Killen 1995.

[313] Bendall 2003, pp. 209-211.

[314] Hofstra 2000, p. 60.

[315] Tegyey 1984, p. 71.

[316] Hofstra 2000, pp. 274 and 290-291.

[317] V.L. Aravantinos, "Santuario e Palazzo: Appunti sui rapporti economico-amministrativi tra la sfera del culto e il potere politico in età micenea," in *Scienze dell'Antichità* 3-4 (1989-1990) pp. 243-261; see p. 257. *Idem*, "The Mycenaean Inscribed Sealings from Thebes: Problems of Content and Function," in *Aegean Seals, Sealings and Administration* (*Aegaeum* 5), T.G. Palaima, ed., Liège and PASP, University of Texas 1990; see p. 162.

[318] Killen 1999, p. 334.

[319] Killen 1999, p. 334.

disbursal of various goods,[320] many of which were raw materials that were being allocated to workers for specific tasks, they managed large groups of personnel who were being assembled at the Northeast Building, and they oversaw the production and upkeep of chariots and other items of military equipment. It is this latter area of responsibility that seems to have been prime among the concerns of the Northeast Building's administrators. Clearly the Northeast Building acted as an administrative center for an industry that was of great importance to the elite of the palace. With this context in mind, I propose to look at the religious associations of the Northeast Building. Among its nearly 60 Linear B tablets there is one in particular, An 1281, that merits our attention because of the link it provides between the religious sector and the industrial activities administered in the Northeast Building.

An 1281 and the "Seat of Potnia"

An 1281 is, like the majority of tablets found in the Northeast Building, an industrial tablet, but it has very significant religious associations as well. The goddess Potnia appears twice on An 1281, and in each instance the scribe makes it clear that he is referring to a different manifestation of this goddess.

An 1281:
1. po-]ti-ni-ja , i-qe-ja
2.]-mo , o-pi-e-de-i
3. a-ka , re-u-si-wo-qe VIR 2
4. au-ke-i-ja-te-we [[ ]]
5. o-na-se-u , ta-ni-ko-qe VIR 2
6. me-ta-ka-wa , po-so-ro VIR 1
7. mi-jo-qa[ ]e-we-za-no VIR 1
8. a-pị-e-ra ⌞ ⌟to-ze-u VIR 1
9.]-a-ke-ṣị , po-ti-ni-ja , re-si-wo VIR 1
10. au-ke-i- ja̧-ṭẹ-ẉẹ[ ]ro VIR 1
11. mi-jo-qa , ma-ra-si-jo [ ] VIR 1
12. me-ta-ka-wa , ti-ta-ra-[ ] VIR 1
13. a-pi-e-ra , ṛụ-ḳọ-ro VIR 1
14. *vacat*
15. *vacat*

On line 1 she is Potnia *i-qe-ja*, which can be read as ἱππεία or Hippeia.[321] On line 9 she is the Potnia of *]a-ke-si*, which is generally restored as the locative of *po-ti-ja-ke-e*, or *Potijakee*, a toponym which appears on two other tablets: An 610.11 as a site for which there are recorded six *e-re-ta* or 'rowers', and on An 298.2 in association with *ra-pte-re* or 'tailors'.[322] The two references to Potnia, and the fact that each one is given a location while the rest of the people on the tablet were not, sets up a two-paragraph structure for An 1281 with Potnia at the head of each one. We may therefore infer that the records following heading were meant to be associated with the first.

What follows each heading are records of men's names in the nominative who are being allocated to men and women in the dative. For example we have *o-na-se-u* and *ta-ni-ko* of line 5 being allocated to *au-ke-i-ja-te-we* on line 4. The names of the people in the dative in the first paragraph are repeated in the second paragraph: *au-ke-i-ja-te-we* is seen on lines 4 and 10, *me-ta-ka-wa* is on lines 6 and 12, *mi-jo-qa* on lines 7 and 11, and *a-pi-e-ra* on lines 8 and 13. We can infer that these were managers or, as Shelmerdine calls them, "craftsmen in charge of workshop operations,"[323] since they are supervising men here on An 1281. Three of these managers appear again on other tablets in positions of authority. For instance, *au-ke-i-ja-te-we* appears three times on Ub 1318 (twice on line 1, and once again on line 2), a tablet which was mentioned above as recording allocations of hides to various people who must have been responsible for seeing that they were made into the leather goods specified on the tablet. This would indicate that *au-ke-i-ja-te-we* was to oversee the production of these items, which puts *au-ke-i-ja-te-we* again in the position of a manager of workshop activities. Also, as was pointed out above, on Fn 50.11-13 we find grain rations being allocated to the *do-e-ro* of three of the four managers found on An 1281 (*au-ke-i-ja-te-we*, *mi-jo-qa* and *a-pi-e-ra*).

Fn 50:
1. a-ki-to-jo , qa-si-re-wi-ja HORD [*qs*
2. ke-ko-jo , qa-si-re-wi-ja HORD [*qs*
3. a-ta-no-ro , qa-si-re-wi-ja HORD T[*qs*
4. me-za-ne HORD V 2 a_3-ki-a_2-ri-jo V 2[
5. me-ri-du-te HORD V 3 mi-ka-ta HORD V 3
6. di-pte-ra-po-ro HORD V 2 e-to-wo-ko V 2
7. a-to-po-qo HORD V 2 po-ro-du-ma-te HORD V 2
8. o-pi-te-u-ke-e-we HORD V 2 i-za-a-to-mo-i HORD V 3
9. ze-u-ke-u-si HORD V 4
10. *v.* [ ] *vacat*
11. au[-ke-i-]ja-te-wo , do-e-ro-i HORD T 1
12. mi-jo[-qa] do-e-ro-i HORD V 3
13. a-pi-ẹ-ṛạ⌞ ⌟do-e-ro-i HORD V 3
14.]-ẉọ[ ]ṇẹ[do-e-ro-]i HORD T 3
15.-18. *vacant*

It must be no coincidence that these names were grouped together on Fn 50 just as they were on An 1281. They were probably well known to the scribes as the managers

[320] See Shelmerdine (1987) for a detailed discussion of the mechanisms by which the Northeast Building acquired its goods.

[321] L.R. Palmer ("Some Points for Discussion," in *Proceedings of the Cambridge Colloquium on Mycenaean Studies*, Palmer and Chadwick, eds., Cambridge 1966, pp. 275-284; see p. 277) discusses the possibility that Potnia Hippeia is a theriomorphic deity: "I too find it difficult to dissociate the Potnia Hippeia of our text from one of the female figures in this complex of theriomorphic divinities. It is tempting to equate her with the Despoina fathered by Poseidon Hippios."

[322] Ruijgh 1967, p. 265, n. 150, sees the name as consisting of two parts: Ποτὶ ἀγκέει, 'close to the valley', but he also says that *po-ti* could be a doublet for *po-si*. Pugliese Carratelli ("Aspetti e Problemi della Monarchia Micenea," *La Parola de Passato* 14 [1959] 401-431; see p. 417) thinks that the word is a compound of Πότις (= Poseidon) and ἄγος meaning 'a sacred place,' which would give us the "sanctuary of Poseidon." See *Dic Mic* II, p. 155 for a summary of the interpretations of *po-ti-ja-ke-e*.

[323] Shelmerdine 1987, p. 340.

of operations in the Northeast Building, and therefore their *do-e-ro* were known by their affiliation with these managers rather than by their own names.[324] It should also be mentioned that three of the managers of An 1281 appear to be women (*me-ta-ka-wa*, *a-pi-e-ra* and *mi-jo-qa*). As we saw in the land tenure tablets, it seems that a position within the religious realm afforded women the ability to act in the world in contexts that might not otherwise have been open to them.

It is interesting that other religiously associated workers, besides the An 1281 managers, appear on Fn 50. The first paragraph of Fn 50 records secular workers: three groups described as belonging to *qa-si-re-wi-ja* appear on lines 1-3, and since *qa-si-re-u* appears with secular bronzesmiths in the Jn series (as on Jn 431.6), it is likely that the groups on Fn 50.1-3 are also secular.[325] It is in the second paragraph that we begin to see workers who could be religiously affiliated. For instance, as we saw in the previous chapter, religious interpretations have been proposed for the two titles recorded on line 5: the *mi-ka-ta* (*μίκτας, from μίγνυμι) may be a "mixers of libations"[326] and the *me-ri-du*[*-ma-*]*te* (*me-r*i interpreted as μέλι, or honey, and *du-ma* taken as "superintendents" or "overseers" on analogy with the *du-ma* found in official contexts on Jn 829.1) could be seen as the "superintendent of the (sacred) honey."[327] We may also recall that Olivier thinks that these occupational terms are part of a master list of religious personnel that appears on several tablets including Fn 50, An 39, An 424, An 427, and An 594.[328] In addition to the *mi-ka-ta* and the *me-ri-du*[*-ma-*]*te*, the four titles recorded on Fn 50.6-7 (*di-pte-ra-po-ro*, *e-to-wo-ko*, *a-to-po-qo* and *po-ro-du-ma-te*) and the *o-pi-te-u-ke-e-we* of line 8 are all included on Olivier's master list, while he considers *i-za-a-to-mo-i* and *ze-u-ke-u-si* (on Fn 50.9) to be part of a daughter-list.[329] One might wonder whether these religious personnel were also associated with the Northeast Building. They may have been, but since they are separated off in a different paragraph, it seems equally likely that they were not. Nonetheless, it is interesting to see the large number of religious personnel who were recorded on Fn 50.

To return to An 1281, we have established that the four people named in the dative are managers of workshop activity that was administered (and probably at least partially conducted) within the Northeast Building. The question then is: how does Potnia fit into this scenario? In thinking about this question I think it is significant that the second line of An 1281 reads *o-pi-e-de-i*, or *ὀπὶ *hεδε(h)ι, the latter from ἕδος, or seat.[330] Killen defines the *o-pi* element as meaning "chez," or, in industrial contexts, "at the workshop of."[331] He uses the latter translation for tablets such as KN Ln 1568, *lat. inf.*, where we find groups of workers who are said to be *o-pi* a personal name in the dative.

Ln 1568, *lat. inf.*
a. a-ze-ti-ṛị-ja ne-ki-ri-de [
b. o-pi , ma-tu-ẉẹ o-nu-ke LANA 1 o-pi , po-ni-ke-ja [

Killen translates this as, "At the workshop of *ma-tu* one unit of *o-nu-ke*. At the workshop of *po-ni-ke-ja*...."[332] Therefore it seems reasonable to translate *o-pi-e-de-i* as "at the seat of Potnia," meaning most likely "at the shrine of Potnia."[333] Ventris and Chadwick saw Potnia Hippeia as receiving the workers who are recorded on line 3. They translate, "For the Mistress of the Horses, [contribution] *at the shrine*: A. and R.: 2 men."[334] The fact that Potnia Hippeia and the Potnia of line 9 were receiving workers could indicate that there was a religious functionary in charge of each workshop who worked specifically in the name of his or her particular Potnia. It could have been this religious functionary who was receiving the workers and directing the affairs of the workshop. The managers listed below each Potnia were identified by Ventris and Chadwick as "priests or religious functionaries of some sort."[335] Lang also seems to take all the managers as religiously associated; she says, "the tablet lists men (nominative) serving Potnia Hippeia (genitive or dative) for various persons (dative)."[336] Olivier brings up the fact that three of the managers of An 1281 are women in support of taking them as priests and priestesses of Potnia. He points out (as I mentioned above) that nowhere else on the tablets do we see women in charge of men unless they held titles within the religious hierarchy (such as *e-ri-ta* the *i-je-re-*

[324] A *do-e-ro* of *mi-jo-qa* is also seen on line 12 of Fn 837 + 867 receiving grain (Before these two tablets were joined, this *do-e-ro* was on Fn 867.4). Another link between Fn 867 and An 1281 is that on line 9 of Fn 837 + 867 we find *i-qe*[, which may be compared with *po-ti-ni-ja i-qe-ja* of An 1281.1. See J.T. Killen, "Thoughts on the functions of the new Thebes tablets," in *Die Neuen Linear B-Texte aus Theben: ihr Aufschlusswert für die Mykenische Sprache und Kultur*, S. Deger-Jalkotzy and O. Panagl, eds., Wien 2006, pp. 79-110; pp. 94-95 for a discussion of these tablets and their relation to each other.

[325] L.R. Palmer ("Review of Olivier's *Liste*," *Gnomon* 34 [1962] 707-711; see p. 708) points out that there is no *qa-si-re-u* associated with the Potnian smiths on Jn 431 (or 310), even though one does appear on Jn 431.6 with the secular smiths.

[326] M. Lejeune "Mycénien *da-ma/du-ma* 'Intendant'," in *Mémoires de Philologie Mycénienne* I, CNRS 1958, pp. 187-201; see p. 194) has proposed that the title "mixer" could refer to "those who mix and prepare the offerings (wine, oil, honey, etc.)."

[327] J.-P. Olivier, *A propos d'un 'liste' de desservants de sanctuaire dans les documents en linéaire B de Pylos*, Brussels, Presses Universitaires 1960, p. 42.

[328] Olivier 1960, *passim*.

[329] Olivier 1960, p. 31.

[330] *Docs*^{2}, pp. 483-484. *Dic Mic.* II, *s.v. o-pi-e-de-i*.

[331] J.T. Killen, "The Knossos *o-pi* Tablets," in *Atti e Memorie del 1º Congresso Internazionale de Micenologia*, vol. II, Rome 1968, pp. 636-643.

[332] Killen 1968, p. 641.

[333] A. Morpurgo Davies, who reviewed all the contexts of *o-pi* and *e-pi* in an attempt to understand the relationship between the two and their precise Mycenaean definitions, agrees with this interpretation and said, "the interpretation *opi hedei* "at her shrine" is possible and would suit the context we have" ("Mycenaean and Greek Prepositions: *o-pi*, *e-pi*, etc.," in *Res Mycenaeae*, A. Heubeck and G. Neumann eds., Gottingen 1983, pp. 287-310; see p. 292).

[334] Ventris and Chadwick (*Docs*^{2}, p. 483), on analogy with the Es tablets, restored the]*-mo* of line 2 as *do-so*]*-mo*, meaning "contribution," or more properly "imposition" according to Shelmerdine 1987, p. 337. Shelmerdine (p. 341) also proposed that the]*-mo* could be restored as *a-to*]*-mo*, */arthmos/*, which enables her to translate An 1281.1-2 as "guild at the shrine of Potnia Hippeia."

[335] *Docs*^{2}, p. 483.

[336] Lang 1958, p. 190.

ja pa-ki-ja-na and *ka-pa-ti-ja* the *ka-ra-wi-po-ro* who have *do-e-ro* on Ep 539.7-9), and since *mi-jo-qa*, *a-pi-e-ra* and *me-ta-ka-wa* are women who were in charge of men, then they could very well be priestesses as well.[337] Killen has added to their religious associations by showing that the disbursements of grain on Fn 50, the tablet that lists three of An 1281's managers, were being allocated in connection with a religious festival.[338] Thus, the workers of An 1281 were being sent to two workshops that were being managed by personnel who were working in the name of Potnia, and who could have been members of the religious hierarchy themselves.

The identity of the first workshop/shrine, the seat of Hippeia Potnia, is most likely the Northeast Building itself, the building in which the tablet An 1281 was found. It is possible to make this assertion because the Northeast Building has within it a room that was identified as a shrine by its excavator Carl Blegen, partially because of the altar that stands in the courtyard directly in front of the shrine door. We will discuss the archaeological circumstances of the Northeast Building in more detail in the next chapter, but we can say here that a religious presence at the Northeast Building seems to be supported by the remains at the site. Also, it is notable that on line 1 of An 1281 Potnia Hippeia is not given a specific place name (as she is on line 9), which would therefore imply that her seat was located at the palace site itself.[339] Finally, the industrial activities that were conducted at the Northeast Building seem particularly well suited to the deity mentioned on An 1281.1, whose epithet "Hippeia" connects her to horses and chariots. Indeed, Shelmerdine has pointed out that it may have been the epithet Hippeia itself which served to indicate the specific place at which the shrine of this particular manifestation of Potnia was located.[340] As Blegen first pointed out, Potnia Hippeia, or "Mistress of the Horses," "would certainly not be out of place in an armory where appurtenances of horse-drawn chariots were kept."[341] It seems, therefore, that this workshop in the Northeast Building, which was producing objects and equipment of great importance to the palatial elite, was presided over by the goddess Potnia Hippeia and managed by the religious personnel working in her name.

Now we should address the fact that there is a second Potnia. The word appearing with the Potnia of line 9,]-*a-ke-si* (or *Potijakee*) has no such fortuitous connections to the workings of the Northeast Building like the epithet Hippeia. Rather, as I have mentioned, it is thought to be a place name. This indicates that there was probably a second workshop located at a place separate from the palace over which Potnia was considered to preside.[342] If this was the case, the fact that the managers listed after each Potnia are the same four people could argue for a certain closeness of purpose between the two workshops. As we have seen, the majority of the work recorded on the tablets found within the Northeast Building could not have taken place there. Perhaps then the second workshop was the site used more predominantly for manufacturing purposes. Positing this second workshop helps us to better understand why the Northeast Building was the center of administrative activities for the chariot industry even though it did not have the room that would have been necessary for the actual manufacture and storage of the chariots: the processes that required more space were probably done at the *Potijakee* site. Having a second workshop would also make better sense of the large numbers of men listed on An 1282 and the Ac tablets (1272-1280). Of course it is possible that these workers were being assembled in the area of the Northeast Building so that they could be sent out from there for specific assignments around the palace. But perhaps some of these workers were actually being assembled for the workshop at *Potijakee*. The 90 workers on An 1282 were certainly being allocated for work that was in line with the interests of the Northeast Building, so we can at least consider these workers to have worked at the shop at *Potijakee*. The men of the Ac series may also have been destined to work there.

It is significant in this context that Cooper has confirmed that the Northeast Building complex was the last building project that the Pylians accomplished before the palace was destroyed.[343] Shelmerdine has proposed that it was deemed necessary, at a time when there was unrest in the area, to bring the production of special goods, such as perfumed oil and bronze weaponry, close into the palace.[344] This idea is consistent with the theory put forth by Wright to explain the modifications made in the palace towards the end of its existence.[345] The changes made to the palace, such as the addition of courts 42 and 47 for the sake of industrial purposes, to what was originally a rather impressive facade, make it clear that the Pylians modified the palace so that it would be a more

[337] Olivier 1960, p. 135-136. Olivier actually sees the men on An 1281 as *do-e-ro*, and makes his assertion on the basis that nowhere else do we see women who have *do-e-ro* except in religious contexts (as on Ae 303, Ae 110, En 609.16/Eo 224.6, Ep 539.7, Ep 539.8/Eb1176.1, and Ep 539.9). I am personally not sure we can assume that the men being allocated on An 1281 are *do-e-ro*, but the point can be made more broadly that women are not found to be in charge of other people in secular contexts.

[338] J.T. Killen, "Religion at Pylos: The Evidence of the Fn Tablets," in *Potnia: Deities and Religion in the Aegean Bronze Age* (*Aegaeum* 22), R. Laffineur and R. Hägg (ed.), Liège - Austin 2001, pp. 435-443.

[339] E.L. Bennett, "Correspondances entre les textes des tablettes pyliennes des séries Aa, Ab et Ad," in *Études Mycéniennes*, M. Lejeune, ed., Paris 1956a, pp. 121-136.

[340] Shelmerdine, personal communication, October 2001.

[341] C. Blegen, "The Palace of Nestor Excavations of 1957: Part I," *AJA* 62 (1958) p. 177.

[342] Lang 1958, p. 190 was the first to propose that there were two workshops represented on An 1281.

[343] F.A. Cooper, "Minnesota Archaeological Researches at Pylos, 1991-1993 Seasons" at http://clvl.cla.umn.edu/marwp/pylos.html.

[344] C.W. Shelmerdine, "Architectural Change and Economic Decline at Pylos" in *Studies in Mycenaean and Classical Greek Presented to John Chadwick* (*Minos* 20-22), J.T. Killen, J.L. Melena and J.-P. Olivier, eds., Salamanca 1987, pp. 557-568. Shelmerdine reiterates this view in "Workshops and Record Keeping in the Mycenaean World," in *Mykenaïka* (*BCH* Suppl. 25), J.-P. Olivier, ed., 1992, pp. 387-396; see p. 394.

[345] J. Wright, "Changes in Form and Function of the Palace at Pylos," in *Pylos Comes Alive: Industry and Administration in a Mycenaean Palace*, T.G. Palaima and C.W. Shelmerdine, eds., Fordham University Press 1984, pp. 19-29.

utilitarian complex.[346] Morris has also considered the character of the changes that were made to the palace after its initial construction. She calculates that 59% of the later additions to the main building consisted of workshop space, while 29% were for storage space.[347] Thus nearly 90% of the alterations were made for the purpose of giving the elite Pylians within the palatial complex readier access to, and control over, the prestige items that were important to their way of life. Such alterations to the original building at Pylos are paralleled at Mycenae, where workshops and storerooms were built within the areas encompassed by the newly extended Cyclopean masonry walls. The changes at both sites could imply that the Pylians and Mycenaeans were aware that their strategic positions were not as secure as they had been when the palaces were first built. Hence their desire to have the industries that were vital to them, or at least the administration of those industries, close by, despite the fact that these changes detracted from the impressive nature of the building's original architecture.[348]

Given that the Northeast Building was added onto the palace late in its history, we can imagine that before the Northeast Building was constructed, the workshop at *Potijakee* had housed the same industries as the workshop in the Northeast Building, but that it had been located further away from the palace. Thus the second workshop listed on An 1281 at *Potijakee* could actually have been that original workshop. If so, then it is clear that the original workshop had not ceased to function when the Northeast Building was constructed, but rather the two workshops were operating in conjunction with each other. We may presume then that the Northeast Building was built to bring the administration of the important industries, and perhaps some of the more costly materials involved in those industries, close to the palace.

If the operations of the two workshops were closely intertwined (as the fact that the same managers governed the activities of both shops would suggest) then we may have to reconsider the identity of An 1281's *]ja-ke-e*. Palmer places the *po-ti-ja-ke-e* of An 610 and An 298 within the Further Province because it appears on An 610 after *ri-jo*, the last Hither Province town on Jn 829.12 and Vn 20.11.[349] Sainer says that it has "associations in the south HP, possibly on the east of the central range of hills...."[350] This makes one wonder, could the managers at both workshops have been the same if they were so far apart? I think the fact that they show up on the same tablet in this way might indicate that the two places were rather closer to each other than would be the case if one were at Pylos and the other were in the Further Province. This could mean that the *]ja-ke-e* of our tablet may not actually have been the same place as the *po-ti-ja-ke-e* of An 610 and An 298, but a place closer to Pylos that happened to have the same name.[351]

Through this discussion we can see that the workshop activities of the Northeast Building were very much connected to the main administration of the palace. As we saw, records such as the Sa tablets were made up in the Northeast Building, but were then transferred to the Archives Complex to be filed and stored for future reference. Also, on Vn 10, which was found in the Archives Complex, we see saplings and axles being sent to the 'chariot workshop'.[352] It seems likely that the workshop referred to on this tablet was one of the two on An 1281, which would mean that the palace collected and kept track of materials that were going to be used in the workshops. Despite this Tegyey considered the Northeast Building to have been a separate entity from the palace. In support of his view he cited the fact that the Northeast Building "was a separate unit (like the Southwestern unit and the Wine Magazine) where the conditions for a separate and independent activity were present."[353] While it is true that the Northeast Building stood separate from the palace's Main Building, the two were actually very close to each other. Communication between the two buildings would have been quite easy. And besides, a bit of physical distance does not necessarily imply an administrative division. Tegyey also appeals to the tablet evidence saying that within the Northeast Building "we can establish the consecutive steps of the administrative process, from the stage of procuring raw materials to the exchange of finished goods."[354] While this is true, and could on its own indicate that the Northeast Building was somewhat independent in its operations, nonetheless, it must be remembered who was keeping the records in the first place. It was not the religious personnel but rather the palatial administration that was keeping track of the goods that were going in and out of the Northeast Building. Also, the fact is that the more important records of costly materials were stored in the Archives Complex. This indicates that, as Shelmerdine says,

> ...work in the Northeast Building, though physically set off from the palace proper, is probably subject to the same organization and

[346] For a specific discussion concerning the use of these courts in the production of perfumed oil see Shelmerdine 1985, pp. 59-62.

[347] H.J. Morris, *An Economic Model of the Late Mycenaean Kingdom of Pylos*, Ph.D. Dissertation, University of Minnesota 1986, p. 144.

[348] Galaty has also discussed how "Industries appear to have been pulled into the palace's workshopping system when the item produced was of prestige or ritual value and/or used in great amounts and regularly by central elites." And he implies that this was done simply because it was to the elite's advantage. (*Nestor's Wine Cups*, British Archaeological Reports 1999a, p. 75; also see p. 28). Surely this was the most basic reason for the physical shift of the workshops.

[349] Palmer 1963, p. 69.

[350] A.P. Sainer, "An Index of Place Names at Pylos," in *SMEA* 17 (*Incunabula Graeca* 63), Rome 1976, pp. 17-63; see p. 53.

[351] Of course it is also possible that the *]ja-ke-e* of An 1281 should be restored differently.

[352] See *Docs*^{2}, pp. 350, 371: *a-mo-te-jo-na-de*, *ἁρμοτεγωνα-δε: "allative in *–de* of a workshop noun in -εών (cf. Hom. χαλκεών 'smithy') formed from the word *a-mo-ta* seen on the WHEEL tablets." Also see Palmer 1963, p. 406; Shelmerdine 1987, p. 335; and *Dic. Mic.* I, pp. 59-60 for discussions of *a-mo-te-jo-na-de*.

[353] Tegyey 1984, p. 75. Tegyey reiterates this proposition in "Scribes and Archives at Knossos and Pylos: A Comparison," in *Tractata Mycenaea*, P. Ilievski and L. Crepajac, eds., Skopje 1987, pp. 357-366; see p. 362.

[354] Tegyey 1984, p. 75.

> administration as other palace industrial activities; this is not likely to be an independent or unusually organized place.[355]

Given that this must be true, how then do we understand the references on An 1281 to Potnia? It does seem that we can build a case from An 1281 for religious personnel managing workers within the Northeast Building under the auspices of Potnia, as well as at another religious workshop somewhat removed from the palace. Also, the fact that three of the managers of An 1281 are found again on Fn 50, this time with their *do-e-ro*, and that *au-ke-i-ja-te-we* is found three times on Ub 1318 with hides, indicates that the extent of their managerial control went beyond the workers named on An 1281. It is an open question though as to how far the managerial control of the religious personnel extended within the workshops. It is certainly possible that these religious managers were operating alongside secular managers. However, the fact that An 1281 speaks of the "seat of Potnia," compels me to propose an alternative scenario. If the "seat of Potnia" can be equated with the Northeast Building, which includes both the shrine and the workshop, then I think it is likely that both of the workshops listed on An 1281 were considered to be functioning under the auspices of Potnia, and that a large part of those two workshops' operations (although not necessarily all) were managed by the religious personnel working in Potnia's service.

And yet, the palace clearly held the position of upper management, so to speak, in that it arranged for raw materials to be brought in, allocated workers to the necessary tasks, issued rations to some of those workers (the *do-e-ro* of Fn 50), and probably controlled the types and quantities of goods that were to be produced. Of course the palace also had the power to dispose of the finished goods as it saw fit, and, as Hofstra points out, most of the goods produced in the Northeast Building were predominantly for the use of the elite who lived in the palace site and its immediate surroundings.[356] It seems to me then that religious and secular authority were very much intertwined in the Northeast Building at Pylos. But how did this come about?

I think it would be helpful here to look at the situation diachronically. If, as I have proposed, there was an original workshop that had been in operation for quite some time before the Northeast Building was constructed, then it is possible that religious personnel had also been involved in managing the workshop for quite some time. Perhaps originally it was the religious personnel who had sole control over that workshop, as we have proposed was the case for the religious textile workshops at Thebes and the Potnian bronze-working shops of the Jn series. If this was the case, then this original workshop at]-*a-ke-si* could have been quite independent of the palatial administration when it was first founded, and the personnel may instead have been associated with a shrine or sanctuary that was dedicated to Potnia.

It may be significant then that the Qa series was also found within the Northeast Building. As was discussed in the previous chapter, Melena has recently proposed that the Qa series records honorary gifts, or γέρα, that were to be given to titled members of the religious hierarchy.[357] To review, the common factor in all the Qa tablets is the presence of a commodity represented by the ideogram **189*, which looks a bit like a piece of cloth or a hide, but whose exact nature had previously remained something of a mystery. Melena's solution is that the syllabogram written within the ideogram represents the syllable *ke*, which he interprets as the first initial of *ke-ra* or *geras* (γέρας),[358] an honorary gift that was often given to religious personnel. Because the ideogram **189* looks like a hide, Melena surmised that the *geras* probably consisted of the hide of an animal that had been sacrificed. These *gera* then were being given out to the religious personnel on the tablets, among whom are two priests (*i-je-re-u*: Qa 1290 and 1296), two priestesses (*i-je-re-ja*: Qa 1289 and 1300), and probably another priest or priestess on Qa 1303 (*i*[*-je-re-ja*/*-u*). There is also a man named *ka-e-se-u* who bears the title "Potnian" (*po-ti-ni-ja-wi-jo*) on Qa 1299, and Qa 1308 records a]*pa-ke-u*, which can be taken as σφαγεύς, a slayer or sacrificer.[359]

It is of course possible that these *gera* were being given to a group of religious personnel who were not associated with the Northeast Building, but it would be interesting to consider the possibility that they were actually meant for the religious staff of the shrine or sanctuary attached to the original workshop at]-*a-ke-si*. One might even wonder if the *gera* were being given to the religious functionaries by the palace in recognition of, or in exchange for, their efforts in the workshop. Since it was indeed the elite of the palace who benefited from the products that were manufactured in the workshop, it may have been in the palace's best interests to pay their respects to the religious personnel who were nominally in

[355] Shelmerdine 1987, p. 336.

[356] Hofstra 2000, p. 293: "...there is little evidence to show that the activities of the Northeastern Building were directed beyond the interest of the palace itself. The chariots and associated equipment mentioned in the documents and perhaps represented by some of the finds were likely to have been the province of the elite who formed the dominant users of the palace. The small amounts of leather recorded in the Ub series are also unlikely to have been for anything beyond local consumption."

[357] J. Melena, "Mycenaean Religious Texts: The Significance of New Joins and Readings," Talk presented at the University of Texas at Austin, October 1999.

[358] This was actually one of the suggestions for the ideogram that Lang made in 1958, p. 191. Her other suggestions were that the *KE* could represent *ke-se-nu-wi-ja* or *ke-ra-a*, the horns from the animals brought to the Northeast Building or for one of the products made there.

[359] It should also be mentioned that the scribe who wrote the majority of the Qa series, Hand 15 (his tablets are Qa 1259, 1290-1299, 1301-1304, 1306, 1308-1312; another four Qa tablets, 1289, 1300, 1305, and 1307, were written by Hand 33), also wrote Un 219, a tablet which records the allocation of a variety of goods to several divine recipients, such as Artemis, Hermes, Potnia, *pa-de-we*, and perhaps Hera (*e*-[ ], line 8). As we have seen in the previous chapter, Olivier thought that other personages on Un 219 could be interpreted as religious personnel, such as the *di-pte-ra-po-ro* of Un 219.6 (Olivier 1960, pp. 122-125), and the *da-ko-ro-i*, literally "sweepers," found on line 5 (1960, p. 101). With the evidence of Un 219 we could say that Hand 15 was concerned with allocations to the religious sphere.

charge of the production of these goods. One more thing could be added here. Above I mentioned the possibility that the Cc 1283-1285 and Cn 1286-1287 tablets recorded animals that were brought into the Northeast Building to be used in sacrificial ceremonies, and it was also suggested that their hides could have been used to make some of the items produced in that building. But one might wonder if perhaps the hides from animals such as these were given over to the religious personnel as *gera*. Again, this would not preclude the possibility that they were ultimately used for industrial purposes, which would further benefit the religious personnel.

How then did the workshop and its religious personnel become so much governed by the palatial administration? It is possible that something similar happened with the workshop as I have proposed for the sanctuary at *Pa-ki-ja-ne*. As the influence of the *wanax* of Pylos and his administrators grew, perhaps they saw the original workshop as a perfect spot to manufacture the goods that were of great importance to the palatial elite, and to the defense of their city. The original workshop could have been brought, maybe gradually, maybe all at once, into the palatial system. Eventually, as we have seen, at a time when the first workshop may have seemed vulnerable because of its distance from the palace, the palace must have decided to move the headquarters of the operation closer to the palace site, for which purpose they constructed the Northeast Building. Whether the workshops had always produced goods such as chariots for the palatial elite, or if it was put in the position of doing so by the palace is impossible to say. But it does seem that despite the very active role the palace took in the industrial production of the Northeast Building, some managerial responsibility within the workshops was at least partly retained by Potnia's religious personnel. The relationship between the secular administration and the religious personnel can only be guessed at. Perhaps the take-over of the workshop had been a somewhat hostile one. The presence then of the religious managers might indicate that it would have been impolitic for the palace to entirely eliminate the religious element. On the other hand, perhaps the palace was glad to keep the religious association with Potnia through her managers, thinking that Potnia's presence carried with it a beneficence that would positively affect the workings of the shop. In either case, the fact that religious personnel were acting as managers implies that they had attained some status within both the economic and religious realms of their society.

Thus one of the more significant manifestations of the religious sector's involvement in economic activities may be found in the Northeast Building. The religious personnel seem to have had some managerial control within an industry that must have had great importance for the Pylian elite – the manufacture and repair of the chariots they used in hunting and warfare. The fact that these workshops produced such items must have given the religious personnel working within them some prestige within the community and perhaps even some influence with the palace.

Conclusions

The Linear B evidence gives us a variety of ways in which religiously affiliated persons acted within the economy of Late Bronze Age Mycenaean society. Many deities are seen in the position of the collector, especially in the fields of animal husbandry, textile manufacture, and bronze working. I think that in these cases the fact that a deity's name is used as the collector implies that it was the sanctuary dedicated to that deity who was in possession of the resources recorded on those tablets. In practical terms then, it would be the personnel of the sanctuary who managed those resources. Those sanctuaries then acted as mini economic centers, albeit on a smaller scale than the palaces themselves. The interest of the religious collectors in owning sheep, producing cloth and working bronze must have been the same on a certain level as the that of the other collectors: to provide themselves and their dependents with a reasonable livelihood through the use of their resources and productive capabilities. This would involve interacting with others in the economic community in order to acquire the goods that they did not produce on their own. It also entailed, apparently, being subject to the requirements of the palaces. This requirement to fulfill certain quotas for the palace does not however mean that the sanctuaries were subject to the palace or that they looked to the palace for support. On the contrary, it highlights the active and prominent role that these sanctuaries must have played in the economic life of their communities since their workshops must have been significant enough for the palaces to see them as worth tapping into.

In addition to these religious collectors, the tablets also show us religious personages who seem to have been more closely associated with the palace than the religious collectors. *Pi-ra-jo* the unguent boiler, for instance, seems to have been working for the palatial perfumed oil industry, irrespective of his religious affiliation. He may be compared with some of the religious personages who held land in the Ep and En series. I proposed that it may not have been the sanctuary at *Pa-ki-ja-ne* that gave them their land, but rather that they were able to acquire the land on their own. Thus they may have been acting in their own interests, i.e., without the benefit of a sanctuary in mind. The Potnian women and the barleyers may also have been working for the palace irrespective of their religious affiliation, but it is also possible, given the fact that they are not named and it is their association with the religious sphere that is their most salient feature, that they were associated with a sanctuary that expected some return from their labor, even though it was conducted under palatial auspices.

The managers of An 1281 employed in the name of Hippeia Potnia, and the Potnia of]*-a-ke-si*, seem to have been working under yet another set of conditions. I have proposed that they, or those at the top of the larger religious hierarchy they belonged to, were originally in charge of their own workshop, perhaps in a situation similar to that of a collector sanctuary, but that at some point the palace saw fit to, and had the power to, appropriate the top managerial position in order, presumably, to be better able to direct the workshop's production. In this situation though, managerial control was not entirely in the hands of the palace, and the religious affiliation of the workshop had not been dispensed with. Whether this was due to the power of the priests and priestesses who were in charge of this particular sanctuary and its workshop, or because the palatial inhabitants believed they were better off retaining the religious association, cannot be decided. But the fact that the religious personnel were in positions of authority within the "seat of Potnia" (which I think should be equated with the Northeast Building), a shrine-sanctuary that was overseeing industries and interactions that were of great importance to the elite of the palace, shows that the religious hierarchy of these sanctuaries were indeed not only active within the palatial economy, but also held positions of some importance within it.

It seems then that persons affiliated with the religious sector various types of resources, and various ways in which they could act within the Mycenaean economy. They were involved, to varying degrees, depending on their circumstances, in both the palatial and non-palatial sectors of society. They would have been able to barter and exchange goods within their communities as well as deal with the palace when the opportunity presented itself, or when put in the position of having to. This involvement would at least have brought them, perhaps as individuals, and probably also in most situations the sanctuaries they were affiliated with, the goods and services they needed. In some cases they may also have been able to acquire some real wealth. We may consider then how this affected their status within Mycenaean society. The priests and priestesses would already have held prestigious positions within their communities due to the fact that they were the people's representatives to the gods. If some of these religious officials were also relatively wealthy, then they would have had access to another source of influence within the community, one which would have been founded on a more concrete base than the first. Prosperous sanctuaries and their personnel, therefore, may have had a certain amount of *auctoritas* with which they would have been able to command the respect of the secular sphere. This *auctoritas* may not have rivaled the actual authority of the palace, but it may have guaranteed that the palace itself could not escape showing the proper respect for it.

In the next chapter I will consider the archaeological evidence for the involvement of the religious sector in economic activities. This will mostly consist of sanctuaries or shrines that were active in industrial production of some kind. As we will see, the archaeological evidence seems to confirm the proposition made here, based on the textual evidence, that religious personnel were involved in industrial production.

CHAPTER VI

Archaeological Evidence for the Involvement of the Religious Sector in Industrial Activities in Late Bronze Age Mycenaean Greece

Introduction

In Chapter 3 the involvement of the religious sector of several Aegean sites in economic (industrial) activities was reviewed and evaluated. It was found that a few of the sites (Myrtos, Room of the Lilies shrine, and the sanctuary in Xeste 3 at Akrotiri, and Zakros) provided evidence for sanctuaries that were actively involved in production work. The sites on Cyprus (Kition, Enkomi, Alassa *Pano Mandilares,* Athienou *Bamboulari tis Koukounninas*, and Myrtou *Pigadhes*) in particular also seem to have been very much involved in the practical aspects of the copper-producing industry. In the previous two chapters I have reviewed the Linear B evidence for the Mycenaean religious sector's involvement in various economic activities, some of which would not have been known if we only had archaeological evidence to consider. At this point though it is important to turn to a consideration of the archaeological evidence for the Mycenaean world so as to demonstrate how the material evidence complements the textual, thereby reinforcing the view that the religious sector actively participated in the economy of the Mycenaean world. The sites of the Late Bronze Age at which I think a connection between religious and industrial activities can be established are Pylos, Mycenae, Phylakopi, Ayios Konstantinos at Methana, and Berbati.

Pylos and the Northeast Building

As I have previously discussed,[1] and as I review in chapter 5 of this work, I think the textual evidence from Pylos indicates that religious personnel were involved in managing the various economic activities that were administered within the "seat of Potnia" mentioned on An 1281, and I think that "seat of Potnia" can be identified with the Northeast Building. The archaeological evidence from the site can also be seen to support the proposition that religious personnel were working in the Northeast Building, particularly if we credit Blegen's identification of room 93 as a shrine. This view has been challenged by Bendall,[2] and if indeed the Northeast Building was to lose its shrine, then the identification between the "seat of Potnia" and the Northeast Building would be on shakier ground. It would not, however, undermine the textual evidence that members of the religious sector were in charge of workshop activities at Pylos. Rather, it would remove an important example of the complementary, physical manifestation of a relationship between the religious sphere and industrial production. Nonetheless, I do think that a strong case can be made for room 93 having been a shrine, and therefore also for an active religious presence in the economic activities that went on in the Northeast Building. Since I have presented this case elsewhere,[3] here I will review the most important points in order to show clearly why I credit this identification. I will also review some of the more basic archaeological attributes of the Northeast Building so as to demonstrate its predominantly utilitarian nature.

The Northeast Building (Figure 1) is a rectangular structure approximately 32.6 m long and 16 m wide that consisted of six rooms of various sizes (numbered 93 and 96-100 on the plan), with a corridor (95) running between 93, 96 and 97 on the southwest and 98, 99, and 100 on the northeast, and a courtyard (92), which was bordered by a roofed colonnade (94) on its northeast side.[4] Carl Blegen and Marion Rawson noted that the building had been constructed relatively simply, without stucco floors or stone thresholds, which they thought suited its use as a workshop.[5] Such construction is also appropriate for the more recent interpretation of the building as an administrative center that was also used for storage and small-scale, possibly *ad hoc* workshop activities. The wide corridor that ran down the center of the building and the entryways into most of the rooms would also have facilitated the activities of a storehouse and small scale workshop, allowing the transportation of bulky raw materials, finished items that were packed-up and ready for shipping out, and perhaps even chariots, through its passageways.[6] Many of the items found within the rooms also helped the excavators to come to the conclusion that this building had been used as a workshop.[7] For instance, among the pots found in room 98, there were two large jars (one still standing upright) that were filled with colored earth and shiny granular matter that looked to

[1] S. Lupack, "The Northeast Building of Pylos and An 1281," in *The Proceedings of the 12th International Mycenological Colloquium*, A. Sacconi, L. Godart and M. Del Freo, eds., Biblioteca di Pasiphae series, Rome 2008, pp. 467-484.

[2] L. Bendall, "A Reconsideration of the Northeastern Building at Pylos: Evidence for a Mycenaean Redistributive Center," *AJA* 107 (2003) 181-231.

[3] Lupack 2008.

[4] C.W. Blegen and M. Rawson, *The Palace of Nestor at Pylos in Western Messenia,* Vol. I: *The Buildings and their Contents*, Princeton University Press 1966, pp. 299-325.

[5] Blegen and Rawson 1966, p. 299.

[6] The width of the corridor was 2.8 m wide while the widths of the doors were: room 97: 2.75 m, room 98: 2.98 m, room 99: 2.95 m.

[7] Actually, Blegen in his very first summary of the site said that, "it is tempting to recognize in the building the quarters of the palace guard or garrison, and perhaps the armory." ("The Palace of Nestor Excavations of 1957: Part I," *AJA* 62 [1958] 175-181; see p. 177). But by the next year Blegen was calling it "the Palace Workshop" (C. Blegen, "The Palace of Nestor Excavations of 1958: Part I," *AJA* 63 [1959] 121-127; see p. 121).

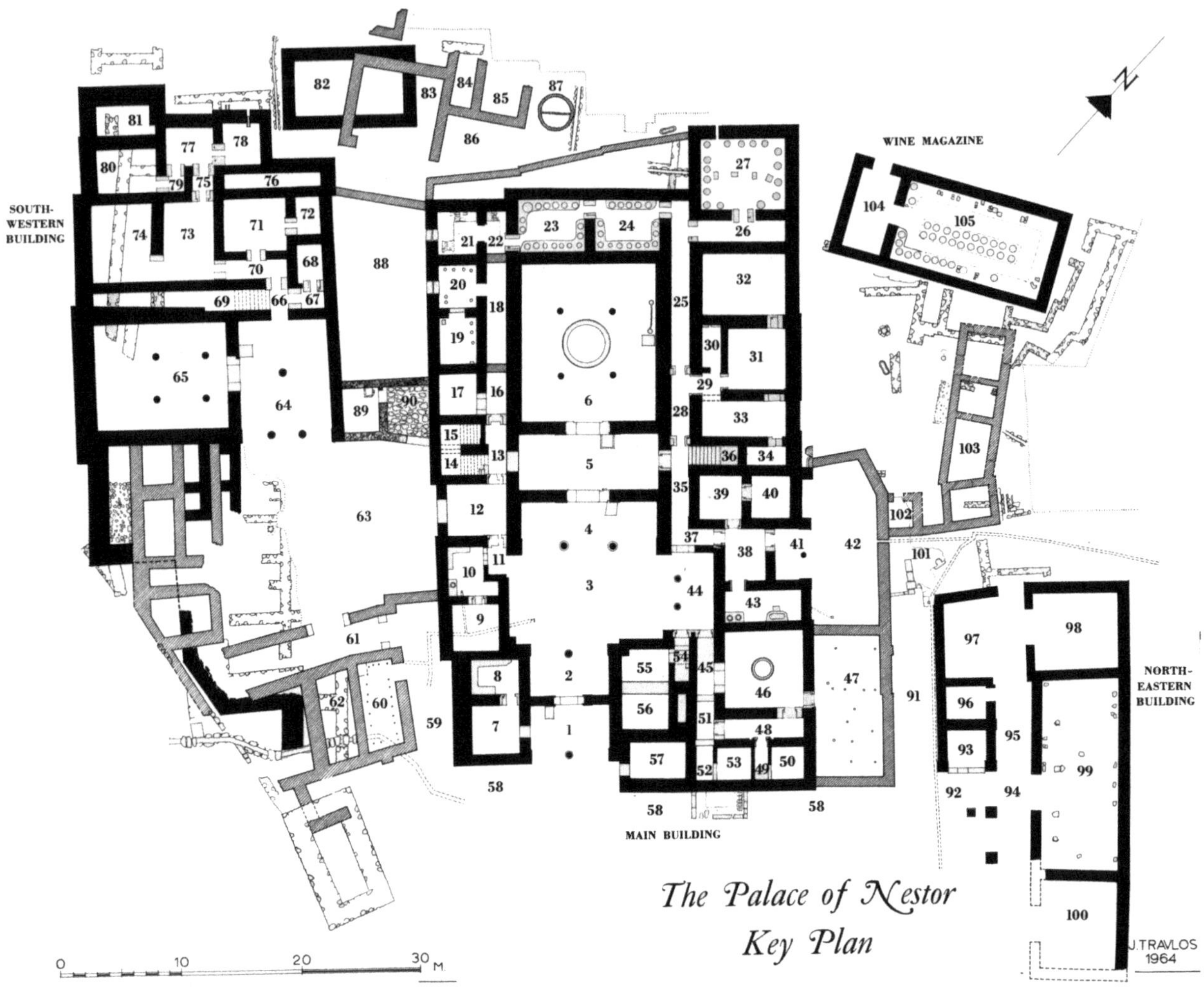

Figure 1. Plan of the Palace of Nestor at Pylos with the Northeast Building.

Blegen like ground-up stone.[8] These materials could have been used to make faience or glass. Hofstra points out that the material was probably not worked in the Northeast Building since no large heating installations were found.[9] Perhaps instead the materials were stored here and allocated when necessary to the glass workers. There were also bright yellow and red patches of color on the ground in the western corner of the room, which may be the remnants of minerals or dyes used as coloring agents.[10] Also in room 98 was a mass of bronze nearly a kilogram in weight, which appeared to have been poured out onto the ground forming a metallic puddle. Hofstra points out that "sustained temperatures over 1000° C would have been required to melt a bronze vessel into such a puddle, yet the pottery standing only two or three meters away was not vitrified, which should also have occurred near 1000-1100° C."[11] Thus we are left to wonder whether the bronze had been poured out before the destruction, and if so, why. A considerable quantity of bronze was also found in this room in the form of sheeting, strips, wire, pins, and shapeless chunks that had been melted by the intense fire. Blegen and Rawson suggested that this room functioned in part as a storeroom, while actual work was carried out in room 97.[12] This is because room 97 was quite large, but did not contain the abundance of material and storage facilities that were found in rooms 98 and 99. Schon, too, comments that room 97 may have been large enough to accommodate different types of work, including chariot assembly.[13] Nonetheless, signs of such work were not actually found within the room so it cannot be confirmed that workshop activities were performed here. Room 97 did however have bright yellow and red patches under its burnt destruction layer, like those found in room 98, so it may have acted as a supplementary storage room.

Room 99, the largest of the six rooms at 15.9 m long on its northeastern side and 6.5 m wide on the northwestern side, seems to have been one of the main storage areas of

[8] Blegen and Rawson 1966, p. 315.

[9] S. Hofstra, *Small Things Considered: The Finds from LH IIIB Pylos in Context*, Ph.D. Dissertation, University of Texas at Austin 2000, p. 68.

[10] Blegen and Rawson 1966, p. 316.

[11] Hofstra 2000, p. 70.

[12] Blegen and Rawson 1966, p. 316.

[13] R. Schon, *Pu-ro a-mo-te-jo-na-de: The Northeast Building at the Palace of Nestor*, M.A. Thesis, Bryn Mawr College 1994, p. 43. See Chapter 4, n. 305 of this thesis for a fuller discussion of room 97.

the building. A dozen flat stones, spaced at intervals along the northeastern wall, must have served as supports for posts that "held up wooden shelving along this whole side of the room."[14] Three or four more of these flat stones were found along the southwestern wall, which means that much of the room was taken up with shelving upon which raw materials, tools, and items that were in the process of being manufactured or repaired could have been stored. Many pieces of bronze, including some curved strips (0.06-0.08 m) furnished with rivet holes (and in some cases extant rivets) and decorated with incised spirals were also found.[15] These strips and much of the rest of the bronze that was found may have been used in the construction and repair of chariots, although the bronze could have been put to many other uses as well. Several twisted pieces of lead (possibly from clamps), 45 nearly complete arrowheads (and fragments of many more), and two tools made of bronze, a blade and a chisel, were also among the items found in room 99.[16] Finally, an obsidian blade was found in room 99. This blade, along with the six others found in the Northeast Building, do not actually constitute a high rate of blades on a per meter basis when compared with the rest of the palace.[17] But the interesting thing is that not only did the Northeast Building contain these finished blades, but it also had many chips and flakes, in addition to chunks and flakes with cortex on them. Cortex is the outer surface of naturally occurring obsidian, which shows that raw obsidian had been brought to and worked on at the site. This suggests that one of the jobs of the Northeast Building was to manufacture the obsidian tools needed by the rest of the palace. Room 99 may also have acted as something of an office for the Northeast Building since the majority of the tablets found in the building (50 of 59[18]) were discovered in this room.

Unfortunately, the southern part of room 100 has been lost due to the erosion of the slope upon which the Northeast Building sits. But its northern section produced *ca.* 300 fragments of ivory, some of which were decorated with spirals and connected concentric circles.[19] Hofstra has suggested that these thin strips were used to decorate a piece of furniture or even a piece of military equipment such as a chariot.[20] Hofstra also points out that it is unlikely that such a costly item would have been kept and used within such a utilitarian building, and that therefore the item was probably "in storage, or in the process of being repaired."[21] It also seems possible that the piece, or, for that matter, the several pieces that were all being made with the same design, were in the process of being assembled in room 100. Also found in room 100 were more than 501 tiny bronze arrowheads that had been stored together in a box. A flint blade with "one edge straight and coarsely serrated; the other curved" was another interesting item found in room 100.[22] Blegen postulates that this room was "devoted to the making of delicate objects in bronze and ivory."[23] Again though, no signs of actual bronze working were found in the Northeast Building, and the items that bore the ivory might have been awaiting repair. So we might rather say, with more caution, that room 100 was devoted to the storage of such items. Nonetheless, the fact that this room and rooms 97, 98, and 99 held tools, raw materials, and storage space for an abundance of materials now lost to us, does indicate that work may have been conducted in the vicinity of the Northeast Building if not also at times (as was the case for the obsidian blades) within its confines.

Room 96 is smaller than the rooms just discussed (2.68 by 3.38 m) and it is also different from them in its relative lack of industrial materials. It did however have a couple of interesting features. Two irregular niches seem to have been carved into the northwest and southwest walls. The one in the northwest wall was 1.03 m long and extended down to about floor level. The one in the southwest wall was semicircular, 0.43 m wide, and had stepped sides so that the depth of the niche was 0.4 m at the bottom (at floor level) and 0.2 m at the top, which was 0.6 m above the floor level.[24] A group of sherds were found in front of the northwestern niche. It seems likely then that these niches were created to hold "shelving, wooden bins, or a countertop" as Hofstra has suggested.[25] But one can wonder about the nature of the objects that were placed on that shelving. Blegen and Rawson speculated that room 96 "might have been an adjunct to the neighboring shrine on the southeast, or it could have been the office of the management of the Workshop." As was discussed in Chapter 5, I think the management of the Northeast Building consisted of religious personnel working in the service of Potnia. Therefore it is tempting to propose that room 96 served both of the purposes that Blegen and Rawson suggested. However, since there were no Linear B tablets and only one sealing found in room 96, it seems unlikely that it could have served as the office of the Building. Even if this room was used to store documents that had been transferred onto more perishable material, one would still

[14] Blegen and Rawson 1966, p. 319.
[15] Blegen and Rawson 1966, pp. 319 and 321.
[16] Blegen and Rawson 1966, p. 322.
[17] Hofstra 2000, pp. 264-265.
[18] Taking into account the most recent joins and reclassifications as reflected in *PoN* IV, the 49 tablets found in room 99 are: Ac 1272, 1274-1280, An 1281, 1282, Cc 1284, Cn 1286, 1287, Ja 1288, Qa 1289-1306, 1308-1312, Ub 1315-1318, Un 1319-1321, Va 1323, 1324, Vn 1314, 1339, 1341, Xa 1342. The other nine found in the area are: court 92: Cc 1285, Un 1322, Xa 1337, colonnade 94: Cc 1283, room 97: Mb 1336, Xa 1343, room 98: Sa 1313. Cc 1258 and Qa 1259 were actually found in court 47, but, as Shelmerdine says, "are to be associated with their workshop sets" (C.W. Shelmerdine, "Industrial Activity at Pylos," in *Tractata Mycenaea*, P. Ilievski and L. Crepajac, eds., Skopje 1987, pp. 333-342; see p. 333, n. 4).
[19] Blegen and Rawson 1966, pp. 324-325. See Hofstra's discussion of this group of ivories on pp. 155-158.
[20] Hofstra 2000, p. 158.
[21] Hofstra 2000, p. 158.
[22] Blegen and Rawson 1966, p. 325.
[23] Blegen and Rawson 1966, p. 325.
[24] Blegen and Rawson 1966, p. 309; also see n. 10. Hofstra 2000, p. 66 supplies the height of the wall.
[25] Hofstra 2000, p. 67. Hofstra also points out that "the stratigraphic notes do not mention disturbed fill" (p. 67), which could indicate that even though the excavators were unsure if the niches existed when the building was in use or if they were created later by casual digging, it seems most likely that they were made to be used with the building.

expect to find tablets since information would have had to have been taken from them to make up the documents written on 'paper.' On the other hand, the fact that room 96 is so lacking in material remains makes it similar, as we shall see, to room 93, the postulated shrine. I will return to this issue once I have discussed room 93.

Thus, the archaeological evidence (in conjunction with the textual) found in rooms 97-100 demonstrates that the Northeast Building was used for storage, record keeping, and the organization of various activities. It may also have served as the base for smaller workshop functions since the materials stored in the Northeast Building could have been worked on in an open area near to the Building, and then returned when the work (or the workday) was finished. The major work may have occurred at the second workshop that I think is referred to on An 1281.9 at *]a-ke-si*, or *Potijakee*).[26] The relative scarcity of tools and finished objects may be due to their having been removed by the owners when the site was abandoned. Scavenging may also have been a factor, as may be the fact that many of the items that would have been stored in the Northeast Building, such as the leather mentioned on the tablets, would not have been preserved. Nonetheless, the tools and materials that are extant show that some workshop activities could have taken place near to the Northeast Building, and that the organization of other activities was among its main concerns.

The archaeological evidence that there was a religious presence in the Northeast Building comes from room 93 and the altar in the courtyard that room 93 looks out upon. The only area at Pylos (other than possibly the megaron[27]) that is considered to have had a religious function is room 93, which was dubbed "the Shrine" by Blegen.[28] Room 93 was, in fact, an integral part of the Northeast Building,[29] the site in which An 1281, with its references to two different manifestations of Potnia, was found. It has to be said though that not much of a clearly cultic nature was found within the shrine; there were no cult figures found in the room, nor was there any sign of a bench upon which cult figures might have been placed. As I have discussed elsewhere,[30] it would be easy to appeal to Blegen's statement that the floor of the shrine must have "vanished altogether" in order to explain the lack of a bench and other cultic finds. However, many of the other facts of the site indicate that Blegen could have been mistaken when he proposed that the floor of room 93 had vanished. First of all, one of the room's walls was preserved to a height of 0.78 m, and the other two, while somewhat less well preserved, nonetheless were found with two courses intact. It seems unlikely that the floor had been lost while the walls were left standing. The fourth side consisted of the doorway of the room that looked out onto the courtyard. This door was framed by poros blocks which were neatly dressed and meant to be seen; in other words, they were not undressed foundation blocks which would only be expected at a basement level. Furthermore, the threshold blocks are extant and seem to be at the same level as the floor that they give entrance to. But Blegen proposed that two or three more steps should be reconstructed on top of these threshold blocks. However, following the suggestion of Joseph Shaw,[31] I have proposed that room 93 is too small to have accommodated these two or three extra steps, and that Blegen, with Classical models in mind, may have been misled by his own conception of what a shrine should look like when he reconstructed the shrine's entrance in this way.[32] In fact, in Blegen's account of the room, the two issues are immediately juxtaposed:

> Between the two anta bases ... is a row of four flat poros blocks which *evidently* formed the bottom step of two or three that rose to the level of the floor inside the shrine. The upper steps and the floor itself have vanished altogether since they *must have* reached a level higher than that of the modern ground. (My emphasis.)[33]

If we remove the postulated steps, then the floor level does not have to be, and in fact should not be, higher than the threshold blocks. Blegen's description of the floor of room 93, "Only the clayey broken-up stereo that supported them was left,"[34] might have presented problems to this proposal, but only if the rest of the rooms in the Northeast Building had possessed nice clear floors. In fact, the floors were evidently somewhat

[26] Please see chapter 5 for a detailed discussion of An 1281 and *]a-ke-si*, or *Potijakee*.

[27] Miniature votive cups and a table of offerings were found in the megaron at Pylos to the right of the area where the throne would have stood. A channel is cut into the floor to the right of the throne which could have been used in conjunction with the miniature cups for the pouring of libations (W.D. Taylour, *The Mycenaeans*, Thames and Hudson 1983, p. 47). For a discussion of the religious meaning of the hearth see for example, J. Wright, "The Spatial Configuration of Belief: The Archaeology of Mycenaean Religion," in *Placing the Gods: Sanctuaries and Sacred Space in Ancient Greece*, S.E. Alcock and R. Osborne, eds., Oxford University Press 1994, pp. 37-78; see pp. 56-60. P. Rehak suggests that the person who took the throne in the megaron was a woman, and that her role was to lead the toasting for important drinking ceremonies, which may very well have had a religious nature ("Enthroned Figures and the Function of the Mycenaean Megaron," in *The Role of the Ruler in the Prehistoric Aegean* [*Aegaeum* 11], P. Rehak, ed., Liège 1995, pp. 95-118). For a discussion concerning religion in Cretan throne rooms see W.-D. Niemeier, "On the Function of the 'Throne Room' in the Palace at Knossos," in *The Function of Minoan Palaces*, R. Hägg and N. Marinatos, eds., Stockholm 1987, pp. 163-168.

[28] Blegen and Rawson 1966, pp. 303-305.

[29] It has been suggested that the shrine was built first as an independent structure, and that the rest of the Northeast Building was added on afterwards, at which point the shrine went out of service (Bendall 2003, p. 186, n. 31; and implied in C.W. Shelmerdine, "The World According to Perimos: A Mycenaean Bureaucrat Talks Back," in *Autochthon*, A. Dakouri-Hild and S. Sherratt eds., BAR 2005, pp. 200-206; see p. 202). I have spoken to Cooper on this point, who, as director of MARWP, led the re-excavation of the palace at Pylos, and he has confirmed that the entire building was constructed simultaneously. Hence room 93 must be construed with the rest of the Northeast Building.

[30] S. Lupack, "Palaces, Sanctuaries and Workshops: The Role of the Religious Sector in Mycenaean Economics," in *Rethinking Mycenaean Palaces: New Interpretations of an Old Idea*, M.L. Galaty and W.A. Parkinson, eds., The Cotsen Institute of Archaeology, UCLA 1999, pp. 25-34.

[31] Joseph Shaw, personal communication, 1997.

[32] Lupack 1999, p. 28.

[33] Blegen and Rawson 1966, p. 304

[34] Blegen and Rawson, 1966; p. 304.

difficult to distinguish and are variously described as, "The floor [in corridor 95] was made of a clayey earth and could hardly be recognized..." and "the clay floor [of room 96], which rested on a fill of greenish stereo-like earth..." and "the floor [of room 97] itself was of earth," and, finally, of room 99 he said, "The best indication of [the floor level] seemed to be a stratigraphic change from the fallen reddish disintegrated crude brick to the greenish-white stratum resembling stereo." It could very well have been that what Blegen accepted as floor levels in other rooms did not impress him as constituting a floor in room 93 because he had already decided that the floor must have vanished.

If indeed what we have is the actual floor level, then we must attempt to explain the lack of finds in light of that fact. Actually, the room was not devoid of finds, and what we do have is at least consistent with the interpretation that it was used as a shrine. Fragments of 32 normal-sized kylikes were found, as well as one miniature votive kylix. In addition there was a fine ware dipper and other vessels used for the pouring and storage of liquids. Very often items of this type are found within religious contexts and are thought to be used in ritual drinking and the pouring of libations.[35] I would like to suggest that this was their function within room 93.[36]

Also, it may be significant that three terracotta figurines were found in other parts of the building. A female figurine with a bird-like head was found in room 97,[37] while the head of a female figurine, also with a bird-like face, was found in room 99.[38] An animal figurine, most likely a horse, was found in the corridor (95).[39] The date of this figurine has been questioned,[40] but if upon further examination its Mycenaean provenience were to be confirmed, it would provide an interesting link to Potnia Hippeia of An 1281. It is possible that these figurines could be the remnants of a more substantial assemblage of religious items that were originally used within the building, but which were left behind when the occupants were gathering up the things they wanted to save from the other rooms.

Another interesting point concerning the nature of the finds in room 93 is that there was a distinct lack of any kind of industrial materials. A few stone chips and flakes were found within room 93, but these possibly stray pieces are insignificant when compared with the abundance of material that was found in the other rooms of the complex (except room 96). No pots that would indicate that the room was used for storage were found either, nor were any of the building's tablets or sealings found in room 93, so it could not have served as an office either. Because such materials were so plentiful in the other rooms of the building, it is unlikely that their absence in room 93 could be explained simply by proposing that they had been thoroughly cleaned out or scavenged. Instead, I think that the room served some purpose different from that of the other rooms.

The special nature of room 93 is further indicated by its architectural details. As I mentioned, two large poros blocks framed the room's wide door, and in the upper surfaces of these blocks were dowel holes into which further blocks or wooden beams may have been fitted. Here I think Blegen was correct when he called the poros blocks "decorative antae."[41] In addition, the room's threshold was marked by four stone slabs, a feature that was not found anywhere else in this otherwise utilitarian building. Hofstra has noted that the façade of room 93 "resembled the architectural façades depicted in fresco at Pylos, surmounted by lions and sphinxes."[42] Although there is no evidence that such animal figures were once sitting atop the façade of room 93, it is interesting that the frescoed façades that Hofstra refers to, 1 A 2 and 2 A 2, are interpreted as representing shrines.[43] Also, it seems that room 93 and the colonnade that bordered the open court were meant to form a cohesive visual unit. The stuccoed floor of the colonnade was raised 0.47 m above the floor of the courtyard and its roofed area was 3.76 m deep.[44] The foundations of two columns survive, but a third one most likely originally stood at the southeastern end of the building so that the colonnade would have extended all along the front of rooms 99 and 100. Two nearly complete blocks of poros and several pieces of other blocks were found in the courtyard which Blegen and Rawson think most likely fell from the entablature of the colonnade. They say though that the blocks could have come from the façade of the Shrine.[45] It seems possible that these blocks could have come from either structure, and if similar blocks were used for the shrine and the colonnade the area would have had a unified and somewhat monumental aspect. Blegen and Rawson also mention that "The columns and the woodwork as well as the whole façade of the shrine were almost surely decorated in bright colors as intimated by the frescoes on the altar..."[46] Bendall has suggested that the effort the Pylians put into dressing up the façade of the Northeast

[35] For example see A.D. Moore and †W.D. Taylour, *The Temple Complex, Well Built Mycenae: The Helleno-British Excavations within the Citadel of Mycenae 1959-1969,* fascicule 10, W.D. Taylour, E.B. French and K.A. Wardle, series eds., Oxbow Books 1999; see pp. 79-80. Also see R. Hägg, "The Role of Libations in Mycenaean Ceremony and Cult," in *Celebrations of Death and Divinity in the Bronze Age Argolid*, R. Hägg and G.C. Nordquist, eds., Stockholm 1990, pp. 177-184.

[36] Votive kylikes were also found in rooms 96, 98, and 99 of the Northeast Building, as well as in room 7 of the Archives Complex, where they were found with burnt ox bones. Perhaps they were used in these rooms too for some libation ritual connected with the rooms' industrial activities.

[37] Blegen and Rawson 1966, pp. 311-312.

[38] Blegen and Rawson 1966, p. 322.

[39] Blegen and Rawson, 1966; pp. 307-308.

[40] M. Popham says that this figurine may be dated to the Geometric period ("Pylos: Reflections on the Date of its Destruction and on its Iron Age Reoccupation," *OJA* 10 [1991] 315-324; see p. 324).

[41] Blegen and Rawson 1966, p. 304.

[42] Hofstra 2000, p. 65.

[43] M.L. Lang, *The Palace of Nestor at Pylos in Western Messenia, Vol. II: The Frescoes*, Princeton University Press 1969. See pp. 131-140 for a discussion of the façades and plates 75, 76, 136, and I and R for photos and reconstructions.

[44] Blegen and Rawson 1966, p. 305.

[45] Blegen and Rawson 1966, p. 302.

[46] Blegen and Rawson 1966, p. 306.

Building was made in order to "maintain architectural coherence for the palace's frontal aspect,"[47] and I agree that this may have been part of the Pylians' motivation. However, I also think that at this late stage of the palace's life, after the industrial courts 42 and 47 had already obscured the monumental nature of the palace's northeastern entrance, the Pylians would not have made such efforts unless the nature of the building itself merited them. Thus I think that while the portico was certainly used at times to shade those who worked in the Northeast Building, it probably also provided shade for those who gathered to watch the enactment of cultic rites that were performed in the courtyard.

That religious rituals were performed in the courtyard is indicated by another rather distinguishing element associated with room 93. Within the court is situated a squared, painted poros block, measuring 0.64 x 0.60 m, that stands about 3 m southeast of the shrine, very nearly, but not quite, on its longitudinal axis.[48] Blegen and Rawson identified the block as an altar (Figure 2).[49] This identification has, however, been challenged. Cooper argued (to me in person) that since there were no signs of burning on the top of the block it could not have been used for offerings.[50] Bendall also finds it significant that the Pylos altar shows no signs of burning, but she limits her comparison to the freestanding features found at Mycenae.[51] Restricting one's comparanda in this way cannot be justified; the comparison should more logically be made between all Mycenaean features that were used for religious offerings. If we look at the numerous Mycenaean altars we find that it is fairly common for them to show no signs of burning. For instance, in the Cult Center at Mycenae the Temple had three features that must have been used for offerings that were not burnt: in the main room of the Temple (room 18) neither the central dais (which Taylour says may have been used for libations[52]) nor its bench shrines were burnt,[53] and in the anteroom of the Temple (room XI) the rectangular feature made of white clay was also free of burning.[54] The platform in room 32 of the Room of the Fresco Complex was also used for offerings that were not subject to being burnt.[55] Furthermore, one of the altars that Bendall lists as having been used for burnt offerings, the Round Altar,[56] may not have been used for such. It is understandable that she listed it in this way because Taylour says that there was "a quantity of ashes around it."[57] However, Mylonas, who wrote in more detail about the area (and was its excavator), says that the altar was covered by a thick coat of plaster and "does not exhibit signs of fire or burning." He goes on to say that, "at a distance of 1.2 m west of the altar a pit was found, filled with ashes, bones of small animals and sherds.[58] There was also a pit containing burnt material in corridor 35 that was later covered over when room xxiv was built onto room xxviii in the middle of the LH IIIB period.[59] A new basin was built in room xxiv that seems to have been made to replace the earlier pit in that it too contained burnt material; bones were definitely found in this second feature.[60] French and Taylour associate these features with the Round Altar in that they imply the date of the Altar likely corresponds to that of the first ash pit, but they do not assume that any material was burnt on the altar itself. Rather they say, "...the ash pit below xxiv indicates burnt residues, presumably offerings, somewhere in the area."[61] The offerings could have been burnt on a large brazier.

The rectangular altar that stood outside of Tsountas' House Shrine (now officially referred to Shrine Gamma), or the "edicule" as it is sometimes called, is similar to the Round Altar in that the main part of the altar was coated with fine plaster and did not exhibit any burning; but it had a round hole near to it that contained ash and fragments of burnt bones.[62] In both of these cases burnt offerings were connected with the cults associated with the altars, but the actual burning must have taken place somewhere else, possibly on portable braziers. The published reports concerning the horseshoe-shaped altar within Tsountas' House Shrine can also be confusing because Mylonas says that its plaster bore "slight traces of smoke."[63] But Mylonas goes on to emphasize the libation aspects of the altar,[64] as does Taylour, who does not mention any smoke.[65] Shelton, who will soon be publishing a full account of Tsountas' House Shrine, was able to clear up this confusion. She says that "The very slight burning on the surface was from the burned destruction of the shrine itself," and that the altar was

[47] Bendall 2003, p. 186.

[48] Blegen and Rawson 1966, p. 302: The block is actually 0.25 m to the northeast of the longitudinal axis.

[49] Blegen and Rawson 1966, p. 302.

[50] F. Cooper, personal communication, 1996. Cooper offered the alternative explanation that it could have served as a column base. I, however, think this could not have been the case since there are two extant column bases nearby of an entirely different construction.

[51] Bendall 2003, p. 186; and even with this limited sample, only three of her five examples, two of which were built as hearths, display signs of burning.

[52] W.D. Taylour, *The Mycenaeans*, Thames and Hudson 1983, p. 50. Also see Moore and Taylour 1999, p. 82.

[53] W.D. Taylour, "New Light on Mycenaean Religion," *Antiquity* 44 (1970) pp. 270-280; see p. 273-274.

[54] Moore and Taylour 1999, p. 12. Moore proposes that this feature may have been used as a basin.

[55] Taylour 1970, p. 275.

[56] Bendall 2003, p. 186, n. 27.

[57] Taylour 1983, p. 61.

[58] G. Mylonas, *Mycenae Rich in Gold*, Athens 1983, pp. 141-142.

[59] Please note that contrary to what Taylour originally said, no reference to animal bones can be found in the excavation notes (E.B. French and †W.D. Taylour, *The Service Areas of the Cult Centre, Well Built Mycenae: The Helleno-British Excavations within the Citadel of Mycenae 1959-1969*, fascicule 13, Oxbow Books 2007; see pp. 10 and 43, n. 6).

[60] French and Taylour 2007, p. 15.

[61] French and Taylour 2007, p. 10

[62] Mylonas 1983, p.137.

[63] Mylonas 1983, p. 135.

[64] On the western side of the altar there are two projections; one is circular and had a hole in the center, which was coated with lime and seems designed as a receptacle for libations. The other projection created a groove between it and the circular projection, which was also plastered. The neck of an amphora was set in the floor at the end of the groove (Mylonas 1983, p. 135).

[65] Taylour 1983, p. 49. In an earlier publication Mylonas himself (*The Cult Center of Mycenae*, Athens 1972, p. 38) does not mention any smoke.

used "probably for libations exclusively."[66] Just to the north of the horseshoe-shaped altar there was another feature: a large boulder (1.15 x 0.70) wedged into the ground, with the plaster of the floor overlapping its base. Its exact use is unclear but Mylonas suggests that it was "a 'slaughtering stone' on which sacrificial animals were laid to be killed and their blood collected, to be used for libations" presumably on the horseshoe-shaped altar nearby.

In addition to the features from Mycenae's Cult Center, there was also a low rounded altar found in the porch of Mycenae's great megaron that was associated with an alabaster slab that Hägg thinks must have been used for libations.[67] We can add to this that none of the four altars in the two shrine buildings at Phylakopi show any sign of burning.[68] Nor does the altar inside room 117 (and its subsequent manifestation, room 110) in the Lower Town at Tiryns,[69] nor do the three cult features found at Berbati.[70] The bench altars of Methana and Asine were also free of any sign of burning.[71] More significant than these perhaps is the LH IIIB round altar (max. diam. 1.21 m, ht. 0.35 m) that stood in the courtyard in front of the main Megaron of Tiryns.[72] In LH IIIC the Megaron was rebuilt on a smaller scale (Building T),[73] and the round altar was renewed in that it was encased in a larger rectangular altar (3.25 x 2.68 m). In addition to the fact that no burning was found in association with this altar, it also parallels the one at Pylos in its being placed opposite the room it was associated with, and in its being set in the open air. Unfortunately we do not know what the exterior of the Tiryns altar looked like since only the stones were preserved, but Dörpfeld thought that it must at least have been covered in plaster.[74]

To be sure, there are religious features in the Mycenaean world that do exhibit signs of being used for burnt offerings. For instance, the main room of the Room of the Fresco Complex (room 31) did contain a hearth that appears to have been built specifically for cult purposes.[75] The Citadel House Megaron and the anteroom of the Temple also had hearths,[76] the first one of which Bendall includes in her list of altars with burning.[77] Also at Methana and Asine,[78] hearths were found within the cult rooms, but they were separate from the bench altars that had not been used for burnt offerings. As for actual altars that do show signs of burning, the altar on the eastern wall of the room 31 of The Room of the Fresco Complex had three disc-shaped features along its western edge that had some ash on them.[79] Moore calls these "miniature hearths and suggests that there was a "second use of fire within the room."[80] There was also an oval altar to the north of the cult room 117 in the Lower Town of Tiryns whose associated layers preserved slight traces of ash.[81]

From this survey it seems that Mycenaean altars did not always, or even usually, show signs of burning, and if the cult practices of a certain shrine did involve burnt offerings, a separate hearth or a brazier was usually provided to accommodate them. Thus it seems that the evidence would not support the assertion that the painted block at Pylos could not be an altar simply because it did not exhibit signs of burnt offerings.

Also, while it is true, as Bendall asserts,[82] that the most common type of Mycenaean altar is the bench shrine set against a wall, there are at least four freestanding altars within the Cult Center at Mycenae: the dais in the Temple, the horseshoe-shaped altar inside Tsountas' House Shrine, the edicule outside Tsountas' House Shrine, and the Round Altar outside of the Temple. A fifth may be added if you consider the hearth in the Room of the Fresco Complex to be equivalent to an altar,[83] and even a sixth if you include the "slaughtering stone" in Tsountas' House Shrine. The rounded altar in the porch of Mycenae's great megaron is also a freestanding structure. Furthermore, the edicule and the Round Altar, like the one at Pylos, stand outside of their shrines. They are not, it is true, centered in front of their entries, but they are clearly associated with them. Taylour says of the Round Altar that "it fronts on to the southwest entrance of the Temple"[84] and the edicule is placed very

---

[66] K. Shelton, personal communication, September 2006.

[67] Hägg 1990, p. 180.

[68] For a discussion of these altars and their assemblages see C. Renfrew, "The Sanctuary at Phylakopi," in *Sanctuaries and Cults in the Aegean Bronze Age*, R. Hägg and N. Marinatos, eds., Stockholm 1981, pp. 67-80.

[69] K. Kilian, "Zeugnisse Mykenisher Kultausubung in Tiryns," in *Sanctuaries and Cults in the Aegean Bronze Age*, R. Hägg and N. Marinatos, eds., Stockholm 1981, pp. 49-58; see pp. 53-54. Also see K. Kilian, "Ausgrabungen in Tiryns 1977," *AA* (1979) 379-411; see p. 389 and *ibid*, "Ausgrabungen in Tiryns 1976," *AA* (1978) 449-470; see p. 460. These two altars are actually of IIIC date, but I think they may be included in this survey (particularly the earlier one) since they and their finds demonstrated clear continuity from the IIIB period.

[70] A. Akerström, "A Mycenaean Potter's Factory at Berbati near Mycenae," in *Atti e Memorie del I Congresso Internazionale di Micenologia, Roma 1967* (*Incunabula Graeca* 25), Rome 1968, p. 4.

[71] E. Konsolaki, "The Mycenaean Sanctuary on Methana," *BICS* 40 (1995) 242. R. Hägg, "The House Sanctuary at Asine Revisited," in *Sanctuaries and Cults in the Aegean Bronze Age*, R. Hägg and N. Marinatos, eds., Stockholm 1981, pp. 91-94; see p. 93.

[72] H. Schliemann (with contributions by Dörpfeld), *Tiryns*, London 1886, pp. 206-208, 337-340. K. Müller, *Tiryns III: Die Architektur der Burg und des Palastes*, Augsburg 1930, p. 137. Also see R. Hägg 1990, p. 181, n. 36 and K. Kilian, p. 184 in the same volume.

[73] C. Blegen, "The So-Called Temple of Hera at Tiryns," *Korakou*, Boston 1921, see pp. 130-134. J. Maran, "Das Megaron im Megaron," *AA* (2000) 1-16; *idem*, "Political and Religious Aspects of Architectural Change on the Upper Citadel of Tiryns. The Case of Building T," in *Potnia: Deities and Religion in the Aegean Bronze Age* (*Aegaeum* 22), R. Laffineur and R. Hägg, eds., Liège and UT-PASP 2001, pp. 113-122.

[74] Schliemann (Dörpfeld) 1886, p. 206.

[75] W.D. Taylour, *Well Built Mycenae: The Helleno-British Excavations within the Citadel of Mycenae 1959-1969*, fascicule 1, Aris and Phillips 1981, p. 17.

[76] Taylour 1983, p. 59 and Moore and Taylour 1999, p. 11, respectively.

[77] Bendall 2003, p. 186, n. 27.

[78] Konsolaki 1995, p. 242. Hägg 1981, p. 93.

[79] W.D. Taylour, "Mycenae, 1968," *Antiquity* 43 (1969) 91-97, see pp. 94-95. Taylour also says that it wasn't clear whether the ash came from the original use of the rings or from the destruction layer, and doesn't mention them again in subsequent publications.

[80] Moore and Taylour, *Fresco Complex*, forthcoming.

[81] Kilian 1979, p. 390.

[82] Bendall 2003, p. 186.

[83] As Bendall does (2003, p. 186, n. 27).

[84] W.D. Taylour 1983, p. 61.

near to the entrance to Tsountas' House Shrine. It should be recalled that during the first phase of Tsountas' House Shrine its front entryway was entirely open to the court in front of it, which meant that the edicule was even more a part of the shrine than it would seem if there had been walls and a door.[85] Again, Tiryns should not be overlooked since two of its altars are freestanding, and are situated in the open air: the one in the Lower Town that stands outside room 117, and the round altar in front of the Megaron. The latter of these two is, as I mentioned above, most like the altar at Pylos in that it is centered in front of the entryway to the room it served.

All in all, it seems that one of the most notable characteristics of Mycenaean altars and cultic features is their diversity of form. Bendall advises caution in our interpretation of the frescoed block at Pylos, and she is correct in doing so, but to object to its being an altar on the grounds that it "has no certain parallel"[86] is not well-founded. It is true that none of the altars provide an exact parallel for the Pylos altar, but they are all fairly idiosyncratic, with none of them providing a good parallel for any of the others.

Furthermore, positive arguments can be made for the block having been used as an altar. While it is common for altars in Mycenaean shrines to be coated with white plaster, only one, the altar inside the Room of the Fresco (room 31), was as elaborately painted as the one at Pylos. As it was found, the northwestern and northeastern sides of the block had less of their faces left above ground due to the rising slope of the floor of the courtyard, which must have been re-finished several times in order to facilitate the movement of goods in and out of the Northeast Building. However, the altar had not been neglected: the fresco that covered its sides as well as its top surface had been repeatedly renewed, and the same design was applied each time, which speaks of a long-standing tradition that one would expect in a religious setting. It is true though that the design of the fresco on the Pylian altar is not as clearly religious as the one at Mycenae: it consists of a repeated pattern of three parallel dark wavy lines that run nearly vertically at intervals up the altar. Within the intervals are cream and red-colored bands. Lang says that this type of design is "a stylized imitation of *ca.* 0.60 m. plaques of cut stone which are imagined to be various in color and marked with darker veins" and actually, this motif is not uncommon in secular areas of the palace where it is often used in dadoes.[87] But the design was not confined to secular sites. For instance it is also seen on the Hagia Triada Sarcophagus on the base of the double axe. Blegen proposed that the Pylian altar could be considered analogous to the tables of offering that are "familiar at Pylos and at other Mycenaean sites ... since they too bear painted decoration, not only around the rim, but across the top."[88] On the other hand, we may compare the Pylian altar with the many freestanding, externally placed altars that are pictured on sealings and seal rings found in Mycenaean contexts. These images may have been created at an earlier date than the Pylos altar,[89] nonetheless, I think it is not too far-fetched to suppose that such altars were not unknown in Late Mycenaean times, and that the altar at Pylos was among those in use.

All in all, the arguments for this frescoed block having been used as an altar are fairly strong, and therefore support the interpretation that room 93 was a shrine. The architectural details of room 93 and the colonnade also suggest that the people who built this area were trying to set it off from the more utilitarian parts of the building. Thus the archaeological evidence, combined with the many tablets that were found in the Northeast Building, which demonstrated a religious connection for workshop personnel, lead me to conclude that room 93 was a shrine whose personnel were directly involved in the industrial activities that were performed in the workshop.

The Cult Center of Mycenae

At Mycenae, too, there is evidence for a connection between the religious sector and industrial production. In 1959 William Taylour undertook the excavation of an area of Mycenae that up until that point had been left untouched. By 1969, after a series of tense seasons, each of which were supposed to be his last on the site, Taylour had revealed a series of new cult buildings that have added immeasurably to our knowledge of Mycenaean religion.[90] This area, which Alan Wace had originally called the "Citadel House" when its religious nature was still unknown,[91] is now appropriately known as the Cult Center of Mycenae (Figure 3).[92] The Cult Center comprises the Megaron, the Temple, the Room with the Fresco Complex, and, to their south, two buildings that are named after their initial excavator, Tsountas, who dug there in 1886: Tsountas' House Shrine (or now, Shrine Gamma) and Tsountas' House.[93] The Cult Center is situated to the south of Grave Circle A, the South House and its Annex, but the orientation of the cult buildings and the fact that some of them are at a significantly lower

[85] Mylonas 1972, p. 38; *idem* 1983, p. 135.
[86] Bendall 2003, p. 186.
[87] Lang 1969, pp. 164-165.
[88] Blegen and Rawson 1966, p. 302.

[89] J. Younger, "Aegean Seals of the Late Bronze Age: Stylistic Groups, VI. 14th Century Mainland and Later 14th-Century Cretan Workshops," *Kadmos* 26 (1987) 44-73.
[90] Preliminary results of Lord William Taylour's excavations of the Cult Center are found in Taylour 1969, pp. 91-97, and *idem* 1970, pp. 270-280. His full publication of the excavation is presented in *Well Built Mycenae: The Helleno-British Excavations within the Citadel of Mycenae 1959-1969*, fascicule 1, W.D. Taylour, E.B. French and K.A. Wardle, series eds., Aris and Phillips 1981.
[91] Wace actually started to excavate the site in 1954 but was prevented from working any further there because of the Anglo-Cypriot crisis of 1956 and 1957, and then in the autumn of 1957 Professor Wace died. The results of his one season are published in *ABSA* 50 (1955) 177-179.
[92] Taylour discusses changing the name for the area to more accurately reflect its character in "A Note on the Recent Excavations at Mycenae, and the Scheme Proposed for their Publication," *ABSA* 64 (1969) 259-260. The terms "Citadel House" or "Wace's House" or even "Wace's Citadel House" were used to refer to this area before "Cult Center" was settled upon.
[93] C. Tsountas, "Ἀνασκαφαὶ Μυκηνῶν τοῦ 1886," *Praktika* (1888) 59-79.

Figure 2. The Altar in the courtyard of the Northeast Building.

level shows that they should be seen as forming a discrete area in themselves. Wace[94] and then Mylonas[95] also worked in this area, and based on their combined efforts French has determined that Tsountas' House and its Shrine may date to the late LH IIIA2 period (late 14th century B.C.) while the rest of the buildings were constructed by the middle of the 13th century B.C., or in the IIIB1 period.[96] It was originally thought that the later cult buildings were constructed soon after the LH IIIB western extension of the citadel's cyclopean walls,[97] but now French believes that the western citadel wall was built after the Cult Center was completed, which means that as it was first laid out and used, the Cult Center would have been open and easily accessible through its lower courtyard (now Court 35).[98] French has proposed that even after the western extension of the citadel wall was built, there may have been a gate into the citadel at the point where the Hellenistic tower still stands.[99] She says that "this hypothesis would help to explain the fine stairway ... at the southern end of Tsountas' House."[100] If the gate was (is) there, then the Cult Center would still have been accessible from the west, i.e., from the lower town of Mycenae, although that access would have been more controlled. If there was no gate at that point, then the cult buildings could only have been approached from the northern Processional Way leading down from the palace and via passages along the interior of the citadel wall. In either case, access to the Cult Center must have been made more limited after the citadel wall was built.

During the LH IIIB 2 period, after the citadel wall was completed, a disaster of some kind (most likely an earthquake as French proposes) caused the Mycenaeans to radically alter many of the Cult Center's shrines.[101] The fresco in the Room of the Fresco was covered up, the alcove and room 19 of the Temple were walled up, along with rooms xxv and xxviii, and the Room of the Fresco Complex and the passageway between the Temple and the Fresco Complex were filled with earth. In the terms used by the scholars who are working with the Mycenaean material, this disaster brought Phase VII to a close. The rest of the Cult Center remained in use in a limited way until a second, more significant disaster at the end of the 13th century B.C. destroyed the area so completely that reoccupation only occurred at a higher level. This latter part of the Cult Center's history is called Phase VIII.

Mylonas revealed that the long Processional Way led from the palace at the summit of the acropolis to the Cult Center's buildings on the lower terraces of the site.[102] The highest portion of the Processional Way that has been excavated is a passage that runs at an incline from north to south. Then comes a 1.7 m wide stairway whose steps (8 are extant; Mylonas projects that there were 14 in all[103]) are 0.36 m deep and had a rise of 0.10 m. Mylonas points out that such dimensions would have given the

[94] A.J.B. Wace, "Mycenae 1950," *JHS* 71 (1951) 254-257.
[95] G. Mylonas, Τὸ Θρησκευτικὸν Κέντρον τῶν Μυκηνῶν, or *The Cult Center of Mycenae*, Athens 1972 (with English summary on pp. 36-40).
[96] E. French, *Mycenae: Agamemnon's Capital: The Site and its Setting*, Tempus Publishing Ltd. 2002, p. 85. Also see C.W. Shelmerdine, "Review of Aegean Prehistory VI: The Palatial Bronze Age of the Southern and Central Greek Mainland," *AJA* 101 (1997) 537-585; p. 571, n. 214 for the acknowledgement of French's personal communication of this information.
[97] Taylour 1981, pp. 8-9. E. French, "Cult Places at Mycenae," in *Sanctuaries and Cults in the Aegean Bronze Age*, R. Hägg and N. Marinatos, eds., Stockholm 1981, pp. 41-48; see p. 43.
[98] French 2002, p. 85.
[99] French 2002, p. 92; *idem*, 2007, p. 43, n. 5.
[100] French 2007, p. 43, n. 5.
[101] French 2002, p. 85. Also see the chronological chart on p. 10.
[102] Mylonas 1972, pp. 36-37; *idem* 1983, pp. 127-133.
[103] Mylonas 1983, p. 130.

stairway a monumental aspect.[104] At the bottom of this stairway was a 1.9 m wide path that ran north for 9 m until it arrived at a large wooden doorway whose threshold was marked by a conglomerate block measuring 2.5 by 0.9 m. This portion of the corridor was roofed and painted with a fresco that was found *in situ*. Along with a marbling motif was the remains of a chariot procession that faced north, towards the Cult Center.[105] From the doorway an interior corridor with plastered floors continued northward and gradually downward for 28 m, at which point the corridor comes out onto a broad platform. At the northern end of this platform there was a doorway into Room 4, through which one could have gained access to the main path leading to the Lion Gate. The corridor itself makes a sharp turn at the platform and continues southward to the Cult Center. Near the turn a bench 2.3 m long and 0.45 m wide was found. Six meters further on there was a stairway that led westward, down into the Cult Center. If one followed the corridor instead of going down the stairway it led to the courtyard of Tsountas' House Shrine (which is designated on the figure by its new name 'Shrine Gamma'), which, along with Tsountas' House on the levels below it, constitutes the southern boundary of the Cult Center.

Tsountas' House Shrine had two phases of use. During the first phase (now dated to LH IIIA2[106]), the low (0.2 m above the ground) horseshoe-shaped altar (measuring 1.29 by 1.33 m), which was mentioned previously, was used in the front room of the shrine. Two projections came off the west side of the altar. The southernmost was circular and had a hole in it that could have been used for libations, while the northern one stuck straight out from its side and had a curved upper surface (it is often described as "bolster-like.")[107] Mylonas reported that "a mass of clay had been attached to the side of the altar, leaving a groove of 0.8 m in width between it and the circular projection."[108] The groove came to an end at a two-handled jar that had been set into the floor.[109] This installation was probably also used for libations. As mentioned above, less than a meter to the north of the altar a large boulder (1.15 x 0.7 x 0.65 m) was also set into the floor. It is clear that the boulder is contemporaneous with the altar and that it was not part of any later building project because the plaster that was used to coat the floor of the shrine is found on the sides of the boulder.[110] It has been proposed that the boulder was a "slaughtering stone" upon which animals would have been sacrificed.[111] At some point the area was filled in and a new floor, probably dating to LH IIIB, was constructed 0.37 m above the original floor. The top of a piece of bedrock that had been projecting into the room was leveled at that point. (Tsountas in his excavation of the area had stopped at the leveled bedrock thinking he had reached the only floor of the building. Wace was the one to go further and expose the horseshoe-shaped altar.[112]) The Processional Way also seems to have been re-paved and its second floor is on the same level as this leveled piece of bedrock. In the northeastern corner of the shrine an almost elliptical clay ring with a diameter of 0.75 m formed a hearth that was found to contain ash and burnt remains. This structure may have replaced the horseshoe-shaped altar of the earlier phase. It was in the smaller room to the south of this one that Tsountas had found the plaque that bore the painting of a female divinity covered by a figure-of-eight shield with two women on either side of her in worshipping poses.[113] A rectangular altar (1.15 by 1.55 m), sometimes referred to as the "edicule," was positioned within the courtyard of the shrine, immediately to the left of its entrance.[114] French says that "This is the spot to which the 'Processional Way' led from higher on the slope."[115] Its sides and surface were also covered in fine plaster, and at its southwest corner a hole of 0.24 m was found to contain ash and fragments of burnt bones. Tsountas' House, down the slope from Tsountas' Shrine, has been interpreted as a priest's house since "it is so closely connected with the shrine and seems to have no exit except through it"[116] and because, as French points out, it was more likely to have been used for domestic purposes.[117]

It was the area to the north of Tsountas' Shrine that Taylour set out to excavate in 1959. As very often seems to happen in archaeological undertakings, it was not until the end of his tenure there, in 1968 and 1969 when his team was removing the "Great Baulk" which ran through the site, that the most spectacular finds were revealed. At that time he found two more buildings that were clearly used for cult activities, which are now called the House of the Idols, or the Temple, and the Room of the Fresco Complex.[118]

The Temple is made up of four rooms: the vestibule (room XI), the main room (room 18; also referred to as the Temple), the room 18 Alcove, which is to the northwest of the main room, and room 19, which is up a flight of stairs from room 18.[119] Room 19 was dubbed the Room of the Idols because within this 2 by 2 m room

[104] Mylonas 1983, p. 130.
[105] French 2002, p. 85.
[106] Shelmerdine 1997, p. 571, n. 214.
[107] Wace 1951, p. 254. See *Archaeological Reports* (1972-1973) p. 13 for a good picture of this feature.
[108] Mylonas 1983, p. 135.
[109] Wace 1954, p. 254.
[110] Mylonas 1983, p. 136.
[111] Mylonas 1972, p. 38; *idem* 1983, p. 136.
[112] Wace 1951, p. 254.
[113] Wace 1951, p. 254.
[114] French 2002, p. 87.
[115] French 2002, p. 97.
[116] Wace 1951, p. 255. Also see French 2002, p.87, who seems to agree that the house may have been used for this purpose.
[117] French 2002, p. 87.
[118] Moore and Taylour 1999. A.D. Moore and Taylour, *Room with the Fresco Complex, Well Built Mycenae: The Helleno-British Excavations within the Citadel of Mycenae 1959-1969,* fascicule 11, W.D. Taylour, E.B. French and K.A. Wardle, series eds., Oxbow Books, forthcoming. The text of Moore and Taylour's *Room with the Fresco Complex* that I used in preparing this manuscript is an edited version of Moore's doctoral thesis, which was kindly provided to me by E.B. French. I warmly thank both French and Moore for the use of this work. See also French 2002 and 2007.
[119] The most recent and complete account of this building is found in Moore and Taylour 1999.

a great many idols were found scattered over the ground, some of which were of a type that had never before been seen in the Mycenaean world.[120] Similar items were actually also found in the room 18 Alcove. The figures are fairly large, ranging from 0.35 to 0.69 m, and are characteristically painted in a dark color all over the body and face except for some reserved areas around the eyes and mouth. This kind of decoration gives the figures a rather forbidding appearance. Twenty-seven of these "Type B" anthropomorphic figures (of which seventeen are complete or nearly so) were found along with fifteen examples of another type of figure, the coiled clay snake figures, which were also painted a dark monochrome color. There were also three pieces of Type A anthropomorphic figures (two of which are substantially complete), which are similar in appearance to figures that had already been found at Phylakopi and Tiryns.[121] The Type A figures are smaller (0.22 to 0.29 m), and are more finely made and decorated than the Type B ones. Moore considers these to have been actual representations of deities while he thinks the Type B figures, because of their larger numbers and the way they hold their hands in offering positions, were probably cult celebrants or officiants.[122] Many beads of amber, rock crystal, lapis lazuli, carnelian and glass paste were also found. These beads are thought to have played a part in the adornment of the idols.

It appears that the first LH IIIB disaster, the one that ends Phase VII, caused the Mycenaeans to take many of their cult items and store them away in this fashion. They must already have been broken when they were stored away since in several instances fragments of the same figures were found separately in the two rooms, but whether they were broken as a result of an earthquake or if they were broken on purpose is impossible to say. In any case, the figures were clearly being decommissioned, although not discarded. Room 19 was literally walled up and sealed, so the figures put in there were never to be used again. It is interesting though that the Alcove of room 18, unlike room 19, "does not appear to have been permanently sealed during Phase VIII, and it is therefore possible that the objects deposited in the Alcove continued to be used in Phase VIII."[123] Moore proposes that some of the pottery and the less fragmentary figures could have continued in use, although of course it is impossible to be sure of this.

It is, however, certain that the main room of the Temple continued to be used until the entire palace was destroyed at the end of the LH IIIB period. In the center of the main room of the Temple was found a slightly concave rectangular dais that was coated with plaster. Because there was no sign of burning on the dais, Taylour thinks that it must have been used to receive libations.[124] At the far end of the room, along its northern wall, there were a series of platforms, all of varying heights and sizes. These too were covered with plaster. Incredibly, a large monochrome Type B figure was found *in situ* on the easternmost platform, unharmed by the destruction of the site. In front of this idol was a clay offering table. Both of these were set into the plaster that covered the platforms and so were definitely in use after the disaster,[125] which shows that the Temple continued to be used for religious devotions despite the decommissioning of so many figures.[126] The figure on the platform actually would not have been visible from the door of the room since one of the three columns that lined the east side of the room would have blocked it from sight. This is a further reason why Moore has proposed that this and the other Type B figures found in the room 18 Alcove and room 19 were not representations of deities. He reasons that the important thing about this figure was the action it was performing, that of offering something to the deity, "permanently making the gift," rather than that she be seen by the human celebrants of the cult.[127] In addition to the main room of the Temple, the vestibule itself may also have been used for religious rites since there was a hearth in the eastern part of the room, a bench along the wall to the northeast of the hearth, and a basin made of white clay mixed with earth on the northwestern wall right next to the entrance to the main room.[128]

To the west of the Temple was the Room with the Fresco Complex, so called because of the fresco found on the southeast wall of its main shrine room. The entrance to the first room of the building, a kind of vestibule (38), was marked, like the Processional Way, by a large (1.7 m) conglomerate block. After moving through the vestibule one entered the main room, which measured c. 5.3 by 4.0 m. Two rooms came off of room 31, room 33 to the west and room 32 to the east. Not much was found in room 33, but Mylonas reported that he found a jug set in the floor, which could have been used for libations.[129] Moore mentions this jug and says, "It is not clear from his account at which level this jug lay but it may well have been the Phase VII floor [i.e., before the minor disaster]."[130] Room 32 was actually added onto the building at some point after the building was first constructed (but before the end of Phase VII). Thus, the door in the east wall of room 31 originally led onto the corridor (34) that ran between the Temple and the Room with the Fresco Complex. Room 32 has been dubbed "the Shrine" because of the Type A female figurine with upraised arms (often called the "Lozenge Lady" because of her distinct decoration) that was found on a platform covered with clay in the southwestern corner of the room. A group of forty-four glass beads was found at the foot of

[120] Taylour 1969, p. 91.
[121] Moore and Taylour 1999, p. 90.
[122] Moore and Taylour 1999, pp. 93-101.
[123] Moore and Taylour 1999, p. 31.
[124] Taylour 1983, p. 50.
[125] Moore and Taylour 1999, p. 30.
[126] It is likely that other cult figures were being used during Phase VIII, but that these figures were taken by the priests and priestesses of the cult as they fled the site before the final destruction. This scenario would be similar to what I think happened at the shrine in the Northeast Building of Pylos.
[127] Moore and Taylour 1999, p. 98.
[128] Moore and Taylour 1999, pp. 11-12.
[129] G. Mylonas, "ΑΝΑΣΚΑΦΗ ΜΥΚΗΝΩΝ," *PAE* (1973) 101.
[130] Moore and Taylour, *Room with the Fresco Complex*, forthcoming.

this platform,[131] and may have been meant as an offering to the cult figure.[132] In his first publication of the room Taylour said that room 32 "appears to have been an ivory workshop" because several partly worked pieces of ivory were found in its northern section.[133] But when the remainder of the Main Baulk was removed from the southern half of the room in the next season, the discovery of the cult figure indicated that the room had been used for religious purposes as well.[134] I will return to this combination of cult and industrial materials in a moment.

Within the main room itself an undecorated but complete clay larnax was found along the northern wall of the room, and an elliptical hearth occupied the center of the room. Plesia (or thick clay) -covered features built higher than the hearth were found on either end of it. The one on the west was circular, while on the east two rectangular blocks were placed so that they were "not quite parallel but converging on one another towards the E like the arms of a horse-shoe."[135] Three post-holes were worked into these features. Moore suggests that the wooden columns would have been protected from the fire by coatings of plesia.[136] Two platforms that would have been visible from the doorway that led into room 32, the first rather low (0.10+ m high; Moore calls it a "step or plinth"[137]), and the next quite a bit higher at c. 0.65 m. The western edge of the main platform was raised 0.10 m above the rest of the surface, and a series of three clay discs, or "small hearths," [138] that were full of ash were found on this ledge. Both of the platforms were plastered and a fresco was painted onto the plaster of the north face of the main altar: a series of three horns of consecration set atop circles representing the beam ends of a building. This decoration appears to have been part of the whole scheme of the fresco for which this room is famous. The fresco actually consists of two paintings that were found *in situ* in two panels, one above the main altar and the other in the space above the lower platform.

The upper register of the fresco depicts two women facing each other and two small male figures who float in the air between them.[139] The woman on the left wears a fringed robe and holds the hilt of a downward-pointing sword while the one on the right, dressed in a Minoan-style flounced skirt, holds a staff that has been interpreted as either a spear or a scepter. On the lower register to the left of these figures is another woman who holds a sheaf of wheat in each of her upraised hands. The identities of these figures have been much debated, but it is generally agreed that the one in the upper register on the left, being the largest, is most likely the main deity of the shrine. The female figure facing her is also accepted by Moore as a deity, although a lesser one, perhaps the larger one's daughter.[140] The identity of the wheat-holding woman on the lower register is thought to be either a minor goddess who holds the attribute that identifies her, or a highly ranked priestess who is presenting the wheat to the goddesses above to the right.[141] The fact that she is accompanied by an animal that could be either a lion or a griffin[142] accentuates the religious aspect of the fresco, but does not serve to identify the figure necessarily as a deity, since griffins and lions appear with both divine and mortal figures.[143] Marinatos favors the interpretation that this female figure is a priestess because she is facing, and so much smaller than, the larger female figures. She also suggests that the fresco may mirror a ritual that was actually enacted within the shrine.[144] Rehak, on the other hand, believes that the figure should be considered a divinity since the fresco is also positioned above a platform (although it is quite low), and because the way in which she holds the wheat "seems to be more hieratic than a pose of attention or respect directed toward the higher bench or even the figures in the upper register."[145] In contrast, Moore's opinion of the figure's pose is that it is similar to the way several of the Type B figures from the Temple held their arms, and he points out that these have been interpreted as "offerants." Moore therefore identifies her as a priestess.[146] So it seems that the iconography is open to debate and I do not intend to try to solve the question of these figures' identities here. Nonetheless, the fact that one of these figures holds sheaves of wheat in her hands is important because a goddess called *si-to-po-ti-ni-ja*, either "Lady Sito" or the "Mistress of the Grains,"[147] appears on MY Oi 701.3, a tablet which was found within the Cult Center.[148] Rehak identified the figure holding the wheat as this goddess. The identity of the main goddess he left open, although in a previous article he had supported the view that she was a War Goddess.[149] On the other hand, Moore credits N. Marinatos with suggesting that

[131] Taylour 1970, p. 277.
[132] Moore and Taylour, *Room with the Fresco Complex*, forthcoming.
[133] Taylour 1969, p. 94.
[134] Taylour 1970, p. 277.
[135] Moore and Taylour, *Room with the Fresco Complex*, forthcoming. A good picture of this hearth can be seen on p. 54 of Taylour 1983.
[136] Moore and Taylour, *Room with the Fresco Complex*, forthcoming.
[137] Moore and Taylour, *Room with the Fresco Complex*, forthcoming.
[138] French 2002, p. 91.
[139] Rehak (1992, p. 49) proposes that these floating men are votaries, while Marinatos thinks they are spirits ("The Fresco from Room 31 at Mycenae: Problems of Method and Interpretation," in *Problems in Greek Prehistory*, E.B. French and K.A. Wardle, eds., Bristol Classical Press 1988, pp. 245-251; see p. 248).

[140] Moore and Taylour, *Room with the Fresco Complex*, forthcoming.
[141] See Rehak 1992, p. 50, n. 118 for a summary of which theory the different scholars have favored on this question.
[142] Marinatos (1988, p. 246) says that the animal is a flying griffin while Rehak (1992, p. 55) argues that it must be a lion because it is painted yellow while griffins are usually white.
[143] Marinatos 1988, p. 247.
[144] Marinatos 1988, p. 247.
[145] Rehak 1992, pp. 50 and 57.
[146] Moore and Taylour, *Room with the Fresco Complex*, forthcoming.
[147] *Docs*^{2}, p. 507. *Dic. Mic.* II, p. 295. The word *si-to-po-ti-ni-ja* can be interpreted in three ways. First it could simply be a compound of *si-to* and *po-ti-ni-ja*, or, if we were to admit a division between the two parts, then *si-to* could either represent the dative of Σιτῷ (as a divine epithet) or the genitive plural σίτων (hence, "Mistress of the Grains"). Chadwick points out that in Sicily Σιτώ was used as an epithet for Demeter.
[148] This tablet and the Oi series will be discussed further in a moment.
[149] P. Rehak, "New Observations on the Mycenaean 'War Goddess'," *AA* (1984) 535-545; see p. 540 where Rehak says that this figure in the fresco must be the "same divine being" as the "warrior goddess" seen on the plaque discovered in Tsountas' House that is covered by a figure-of-eight shield and holds a spear or sword.

> "... an underworld or chthonic deity and her daughter are depicted who are linked with vegetation by virtue of the cereal offerings being made to their altar. The sword [of the main figure], it is suggested, may not be a specifically martial aspect, but may symbolise power, for example over life and death."[150]

Thus it is possible that the main deity represented in the fresco could have been *si-to-po-ti-ni-ja*. In either case we would have a case for identifying one of the female figures of the fresco as *si-to-po-ti-ni-ja*. The Oi series and its *si-to-po-ti-ni-ja* have further significance for this study since these tablets have primarily industrial associations, which I will consider in a moment.

In contrast with the Temple, the Room with the Fresco Complex may not have been used at all in Phase VIII. It seems that rooms 31 and 32, the main cult rooms of the building, were purposefully filled in with earth after the minor disaster. Also, large stone slabs were laid along the south side of the main room about 1 m above the floor, effectively sealing the backfill and the religious objects beneath it. The stone slabs, however, did not run across the entire surface of the backfill, and so when room 31 was initially excavated Taylour was under the impression that the stone slabs indicated that a bench had been constructed in that spot.[151] Moore, however, says that the slabs were used to mark the filling-in of the shrine in some way, and that all the earth in the room, including that beneath the slabs, was part of the backfill. In other words, according to Moore's latest study of the material, there never was a bench on the southern wall of room 31.[152] Moore also proposes that the filling in of the Room of the Fresco probably occurred at the same time that the figures were sealed up in the Temple, and that both events were in response to the same catastrophe.[153] Thus this building, as well as the Alcove and room 19 of the Temple, were probably in full use as cult sites for a fairly short period of time, perhaps no more than a few decades.

Nonetheless, during Phase VII many artifacts of an industrial nature were also deposited within its confines. It was noticed early on in the course of Taylour's excavation that different types of workshop materials were appearing in several areas of what was still at that time called the Citadel House.[154] In 1962 Taylour found "not only masses of pottery but valuable objects such as boars' tusks, ivory strips and inlays, in abundance"[155] in the Basement II room of the building on the terrace above the Temple called the Megaron. Room 2, the large upper floor of the building, did not produce many finds, but the hearth in the center of the room combined with the fact that a stairway off the Processional Way led to this building caused Taylour to consider that "it undoubtedly was yet another cult room."[156] Its close relation to Tsountas' House Shrine may also be taken as support for its being used by the religious personnel who were operating in the area, although whether they used it specifically for the performance of religious rituals is uncertain.

After these discoveries, in 1965 Taylour found in area 36 "complete and many shattered vases, bronze implements, numerous tiny disc beads, steatite 'spindle whorls', little strips of ivory, horn implements, and the impression in the soil of a basket."[157] In addition to these items, a "brick-shaped block of steatite, deeply carved on all four principal faces with characteristic Mycenaean motifs"[158] was also found in area 36. This mold still had some glass attached to its surface, indicating that it had been used for the manufacture of glass beads.[159] Taylour concluded that area 36 was "used as a workshop for the production of objects of high quality not very different from those found in the basement of the Megaron (II)."[160] Finally, it was in 1968 that he revealed "several pieces of partly worked ivory" and a "cube of the raw material" that was clearly "a core from which layers or segments of ivory have been cut" in the northern half of room 32 of the Room with the Fresco Complex. At the time he called this room an "ivory workshop,"[161] but changed the designation to the "Shrine" once he unearthed the cult figure that was situated in the southern half of the room.[162]

French picked up the task of interpreting and organizing the publication of the finds from the Cult Center. In her initial publication of the site she pointed out that the lighting in both the basement room II of the Megaron and in the Shrine (room 32) would have been inadequate for actual work to have gone on in them and that instead we should interpret these areas as storerooms.[163] She also proposed that the materials would have been given out from these rooms to be worked in open areas on the site and then, when the object had been finished, it, along

[150] Moore and Taylour, *Room with the Fresco Complex*, forthcoming. Moore is quoting work that Marinatos has done for her forthcoming volume in the *Well Built Mycenae* series, *The Painting from the 'Room with the Fresco*,' fascicule 29.

[151] Taylour 1970, p. 275; *idem* 1983, p. 55.

[152] Moore and Taylour, *Room with the Fresco Complex*, forthcoming. Taylour actually says in his publication of the site (1981, p. 52) that "It was thought at first that these slabs were supported by a mud-brick or pisé wall but tests showed that this was not so and that in fact they were laid on earth. Slabs and earth were therefore removed." But it seems that he may still have been in doubt as to whether the slabs represented a bench or not since two years later (1983, p. 55) he published that there was a bench on the south side of the room.

[153] Moore and Taylour, *Room with the Fresco Complex*, forthcoming.

[154] Taylour 1981, pp. 17-19, 33, 40.

[155] Taylour 1981, p. 40.

[156] Taylour 1983, p. 61.

[157] Taylour 1981, p. 40.

[158] *Archaeological Reports* for 1966-1967, p. 9.

[159] D. Evely, *Ground Stone, Well Built Mycenae: The Helleno-British Excavations within the Citadel of Mycenae 1959-1969,* fascicule 27, Taylour, French and Wardle, series eds., Oxbow Books 1992; see pp. 22, 29-31. Evely mentions that the mold could also have been used for creating ornaments out of gold foil. Photos of all six sides of the stone can be found in this publication on p. 30, but a more easily accessible photo can be found in O. Dickinson, *The Aegean Bronze Age*, Cambridge University Press 1994, p. 187.

[160] Taylour 1981, p. 40.

[161] Taylour 1969, p. 94.

[162] Taylour 1981, p. 52.

[163] French 1981, p. 45.

with any scrap material, would have been returned to the storeroom. Initially French considered area 36 to be the main candidate for the actual workspace and consequently it was labeled "Workshop" on the general plan of the Cult Center found in her first publication that dealt with the site.[164] Several factors recommended that area 36 be classified as a workshop. For instance, it was "basically an open area,"[165] and so there would have been plenty of light to work by. Shade was provided for as well; two postholes indicate that the western section of 36 may have been covered by reed/brush roofing.[166] Also, the finds of the two proposed storerooms (room II of the Megaron and room 32 of the Room of the Fresco Complex) were very similar in nature to those found in area 36, which indicated that there probably had been a connection between the three areas. Among the items found in French's more detailed list of the items found on Floor 2 of area 36, the floor that belonged to Phase VII, or early to mid LH IIIB,[167] are three bronze tools (a serrated sickle, a blade, an awl mounted on a bone handle), bone tools, five tools made of antler, two three-legged mortars, a pestle, a pounder, lead sheeting and rivets, glass beads, a glass lily ornament, and several pieces of ivory. Among the ivories were two pieces of worked ivory, three inlay strips, and one ivory attachment.[168] The finding of fragments of gold and the steatite mold contributed to the picture that the manufacture of luxury items was one of the main focuses of the presumed workshop. During the discussion that followed her original presentation of this material, French expressed the opinion that "The shrines owned rich materials, which they gave out to be worked as in the Oriental system."[169]

However, French and other scholars working on the material have since raised a problem with the above interpretation of the evidence, particularly in relation to the idea that there was an ivory workshop in area 36. The difficulty is that no debitage was found in the area.[170] In other words, no flakes or tiny chips of ivory that would serve to positively indicate that the ivory had been carved there have been preserved. Krzyszkowska in particular is very cautious in her interpretation of the ivory material found in the Cult Center, and reasonably so given the nature of the material. It is worthwhile at this point to provide a detailed list of the ivory pieces found in room II of the Megaron and in room 32 so that it is clear what kind of material we are talking about. Krzyszkowska records that room II "contained numerous inlays" (she lists 12) including strips, some of which "certainly seem to require additional work, e.g., trimming and polishing" and rosettes and lilies that "could be construed as left-overs from larger job-lots."[171] There were also some unfinished pieces that were "perhaps abandoned during the course of manufacture" and "several blanks," and she mentions that another piece "may have been intended as a knife handle [although] perhaps it was damaged and retained as salvage."[172] In addition to the ivory there was also a "large unworked segment of hippopotamus lower canine and a quantity of unworked boar's tusk."[173] Several more pieces, including "a few inlay fragments, a waste segment, a bone pin and a marble pommel," were found in a disturbed area over room II. Krzyszkowska recommends that these should be associated with ivories found in room II.[174] Among the pieces found in the Shrine, room 32, was "a sizeable cube of ivory, which might yield several blanks for combs, plaques or inlays."[175] "Also found were two inlay strips, one perhaps unfinished, and a damaged spoon."[176] Krzyszkowska goes on to say, "Remarkable is the quantity of partly worked ivory, including unfinished items, a blank, and irregular off-cuts" (which are the "remains from secondary sectioning of tusks"[177]). In addition to these items there were two Naue II hilt-plates and a knob that should be considered as salvage. Finally, a worked horn

[164] French 1981, p. 42.

[165] E. French, *Service Areas of the Cult Centre, Well Built Mycenae: The Helleno-British Excavations within the Citadel of Mycenae 1959-1969,* fascicule 13, Taylour, French and Wardle, series eds., Oxbow Books 2007, p. 18. (Please note that through the kind generosity of E. French I was working with the proofs of this fascicule (for which I am very grateful), and therefore it is possible that the page numbers may change in the final published version.)

[166] French 2007, p. 18.

[167] It is important to note that originally two floors of area 36, Floor 1 and Floor 2, were thought to belong to nearly the same time period, and their finds were considered together. After a full study of the stratification of the area French has determined that Floor 1 belongs to the post-destruction phase (i.e., LH IIIC) and that Floor 2 is the one that belongs to the LH IIIB occupation and use of the site. The artifacts discussed here are exclusively from Floor 2, following French 2007. See pp. *iv* and 1 of French 2007 for a discussion of the reevaluation of the floors of area 36.

[168] French 2007, p. 19. Krzyszkowska's (2007, p. 9) account differs a bit. She says, "The ivories found include two fragmentary inlay strips, not necessarily finished and in use; two unfinished items [on p. 40 described as: "a small plaque" and "a curious object shaped rather like a mushroom"], perhaps damaged during manufacture; and a waste segment. ... A small T-shaped inlay and a small piece of scrap come from phase IX levels but should probably be seen as strays from LH IIIB. It is most likely that the stray pieces mentioned above were stored in Area 36 at the time of the catastrophe, as the infill from here was clearly moved in Phase IX."

[169] French 1981, p. 48.

[170] French, personal communication, 1997; *idem*, 2007, p. *iv*. O. Krzyszkowska, "Cult and Craft: Ivories from the Citadel House Area, Mycenae," in *TEXNH*: Craftsmen, Craftswomen and Craftsmanship in the Aegean Bronze Age (*Aegaeum* 16), Liège and PASP, University of Texas 1997, pp. 145-149; *idem*, "Aegean Ivory Carving: Towards an Evaluation of Late Bronze Age Workshop Material," in *Ivory in Greece and the Eastern Mediterranean from the Bronze Age to the Hellenistic Period*, British Museum Occasional Paper 85, J. L. Fitton, ed., British Museum 1992. And now see O. Krzyszkowska, *The Ivories, Well Built Mycenae: The Helleno-British Excavations within the Citadel of Mycenae 1959-1969,* fascicule 24, W.D. Taylour, E.B. French and K.A. Wardle, series eds., Oxbow Books 2007; see p. 9. It might also be mentioned that French (2007, p. 1) has pointed out that "In considering all the materials from 36 it must be noted that almost no sieving was carried out and that other methods of fine retrieval had not yet been developed." Therefore, the smaller pieces that would have constituted debitage could very well have been lost. But French (2007, p. *iv*) also states that this area "was excavated with great skill and attention" and so we must take the material as we have it and build our theories from there.

[171] Krzyszkowska 2007, p. 6.

[172] Krzyszkowska 2007, p. 6.

[173] Krzyszkowska 2007, p. 6.

[174] Krzyszkowska 2007, p. 6.

[175] Krzyszkowska 1997, p. 147.

[176] Krzyszkowska 2007, p. 9.

[177] Krzyszkowska 1997, p. 147.

core and two antler tools were also found in room 32.[178] Overlying room 31 and in the early LH IIIC strata of rooms 33, 38, xxiv and xxviii there were a few more stray pieces that Krzyszkowska considers to have belonged to the main group sealed in room 32.[179]

Krzyszkowska says of this collection of pieces that they "smack of that bottom drawer where we stow things that 'might come in handy' – but never do."[180] She also emphasizes that not only was there no debitage found in the Cult Center, but also "very few blanks, i.e., work in progress" and she says that "primary materials are all but lacking."[181] More recently she has said, "In short, it is virtually impossible to interpret our material as ivory stored *for use* in a workshop."[182] This has caused her to doubt whether the material that was found was even in storage.[183] Krzyszkowska nevertheless goes on to say, "This is not to deny that the material had originated in a workshop – its very nature makes that clear."[184] And therefore she suggests that the ivory pieces were all dedicated as offerings by a workshop or by individual craftsmen.[185] This explanation may have been suitable for the material found in room 32, and perhaps possible for the ivory found in room II (but whether this room was used for the performance of religious ritual is very unclear since we do not know exactly what the building was used for), but I think it is not appropriate at all for the material found in area 36. Hence an explanation for the presence of the ivory and bone pieces in all these areas is still needed.

I would like to put forth my own very tentative suggestion even though I am sure that it is not without its own problems. I can not help wondering if perhaps the items that were of real value, the more useful raw materials and any high quality (nearly) finished items that are missing from these assemblages, were cleared out of the rooms before they were filled in or abandoned. This would have been possible for room 32 and area 36 since they were both filled with earth after the destruction.[186] This means that there would have been time for the people who used the area to remove the most valuable items before the earth was brought in. With room II of the Megaron, and actually with the other two areas as well, we would have to presume there was some sifting through the debris to find the best pieces. Moore has proposed that something similar occurred in the Temple. He says, "material from the Temple may have been deliberately removed in antiquity, especially objects of intrinsic value."[187] It seems possible that the same may be true for other areas of the Cult Center. If this scenario is deemed plausible, then the assemblages that we have are merely poor reflections of all that was once stored in these rooms. French herself does not doubt that there was an ivory workshop "somewhere at hand"[188] although she adds, "The actual location of the ivory workshop remains a major puzzle."[189]

A puzzle it certainly is. But further clues to the nature of the Cult Center's possible involvement in industrial activities can be obtained by considering the rest of the material that was found in association with the ivory. French still feels that many of the objects found within the area indicate that several different types of manufacturing processes could have been conducted in the vicinity of area 36 and the shrines. For instance, French refers to Mossman's suggestion that the lead sheeting found in area 36 could have been "used in the manufacture of gold jewellery for beating out the gold foil without marking it."[190] Also, the five antler tools found on the LH IIIB floor (Floor 2), which could not have been used for cloth or leather working because their points were not sharp enough for piercing and because their wear patterns do not suggest scraping, could instead have been used for rubbing or polishing. French suggests that they may also have been used in gold working, perhaps for opening out gold leaf.[191] These tools, along with the two fragments of gold, provide evidence that gold jewelry or ornaments could have been manufactured in the area. Also, there is evidence that glass beads were made nearby. The fact that glass was found on the steatite mold found in area 36, even though it was not in its original context, shows that it was indeed used for the production of glass items.[192] Also, a quadruple ivy glass plaque was found in area 36 that was most likely made from the same mold (although not the one we have preserved) as two other pieces that were found in rooms II and 2 of the Megaron. Significantly, the latter of these two pieces was warped while being made, as were several other glass pieces found in room 11. The warped pieces actually do constitute debitage, and therefore contribute to the idea that there was a glass-working shop in the vicinity.[193] Furthermore, Evely suggests that two small mortars and the pestle that were found in area 36 could have been used to grind up glass or faience ingredients.[194] Evely cautions that we should be wary in our evaluation of this evidence since no debris or tools were found in the area, but he does say, "It is very tempting, taking into account the two stone mortars also found in Area 36 and the Oi series of Linear B tablets ... dealing with the *ku-*

[178] Krzyszkowska 2007, p. 9.
[179] Krzyszkowska 1997, pp. 147- 148. *Idem* 2007, p. 9
[180] Krzyszkowska 1997, p. 148.
[181] Krzyszkowska 1997, p. 148.
[182] Krzyszkowska 2007, p. 51.
[183] Krzyszkowska 1997, p. 148. Although in her 2007 fascicule (pp. 9, 31 and 51) she does say that room 32 was "evidently a storeroom-cum-shrine" and that (p. 51) "Room II was apparently a storeroom."
[184] Krzyszkowska 2007, p. 51.
[185] Krzyszkowska 2007, p. 51.
[186] No backfill layer was actually found in area 36, but since corridor 34 certainly was backfilled, and the IIIC floor in area 36 lies almost directly over the IIIB floor without much indication even of the destruction layer that lies so deeply over the rest of the Cult Center, it seems likely that the early IIIC builders cleared the area of both the backfill and the destruction layer when preparing it for re-use (French, personal communication 1997; *idem* 2007, p. 12.)
[187] Moore and Taylour 1999, p. 83.
[188] French 2007, p. 30.
[189] French 2007, p. 30.
[190] French 2007, p. 26. Mossman's full analysis of the lead material will be published as *WBM* 23.
[191] French 2007, p. 30.
[192] Evely 1992, p. 31. French 2007, p. 25
[193] French 2007, p. 30.
[194] Evely 1992, p. 22.

wa-no-wo-ko-i (held by Chadwick to be specialist craftsmen working in blue-glass paste), to postulate that some jeweller could have been working here."[195]

Area 36 also contained 55 steatite conuli, 20% of which were unused or unfinished. The Room with the Fresco Complex also had a large number of conuli: 27 were found in room 31 and another 55 in room 32. French most recently says that "No comprehensive explanation of the function/s of conuli exists but what is clear is that with 145 examples (27 from room 31, 55 from room 32, 55 from area 36, and 8 from between floors 2-5 of area 36) out of a total of 383 for the whole Citadel House Area ... one, at least, of their functions must be relevant to this area."[196] Originally French suggested (and Moore follows this suggestion) that they could have been used as part of "a tally system used to keep record of disbursements of raw materials to craftsmen."[197] A small number of worked steatite nodules were also found in room 32. Evely suggests that their wear patterns indicate that they were either used to rub other objects, perhaps in order to polish them, or they were themselves rubbed. He says, "With a substance as soft as steatite (1-1+ on the Mohs' scale), abrasion would produce large quantities of powder – talc powder in effect."[198] This powder could then have been used in various manufacturing processes, particularly in stone working.[199] It could also have been used to line the inside of molds so that whatever material was poured or pressed in would come out of the mold easily after it had set.

Finally, objects similar to the ones discussed above were found in the earth that was used to fill in rooms 31 and 32 of the Room of the Fresco Complex and corridor 34. It is impossible to know the exact source of the soil, but it would make sense that it was taken from an area relatively nearby the rooms that it was used to fill. If this is so, then those objects would provide further evidence for industrial activity in the area. Evely discusses this issue and says, "If [the soils] were taken from a tidying up of the locality, then potentially they provide evidence for some artisan activity or storage in the region; but if carried in from elsewhere, then the focus of labour must remain unknown – though the assumption of craft practice may stand."[200]

Linear B evidence can also be adduced in support of the religious sector having been involved in workshop activities. As I mentioned above, several tablets, Oi 701-706, which had both industrial and religious associations, were found in the eastern section (predominantly in room 4) of the Cult Center.[201] The tablets from this series must have fallen from the terrace above room 4 to their findspots during the LH IIIB destruction.[202] Taylour characterized the layer in which they were found as "calcined stone and rubble, which had been fused by the heat of the great conflagration to the consistency of concrete."[203] This calcined stone and rubble represents the remains of a stone building within which the tablets must have been stored. Taylour calls this building a "record office,"[204] but since the tablets that were found there belong exclusively to one series, the Oi series, it seems that the building's functions must not have been limited to record keeping. Rather, the building must have been used for other activities, activities which may very well be implied by the tablets found within it. Since the Oi series records the allocation of a certain as yet unidentified commodity (**190*) to several different types of workers, I think it is possible that the building was used, among other things, as a clearinghouse for the commodity **190*.

Oi 701 is the most complete tablet of the set:

Oi 701:
sup. mut.
1. *vestigia*[
2. *vacat* [
3. si-to-po-ti-ni-ja **190* [
4. po-ro-po-i **190* 10
5. ka-na-pe-u-si **190* 6
6. [• •]-ta do-ke-ko-o-ke-ne **190* 5
7. [ku-wa-]no-wo-ko-i **190* 2
8. *inf. mut.*

The ideogram **190* is now considered to be the same as **134*, which was at first kept separate because of slight epigraphical differences.[205] But the two are now considered to represent the same item, and we can therefore use all of its appearances in trying to deduce what it was. Many attempts have been made at identifying this commodity.[206] But the fact that on some tablets the commodity was counted (as on KN U 7063 and here in the Oi series) while on MY Go 610 it is

[195] Evely 1992, p. 22.

[196] French 2007, p. 25.

[197] French 1981, p. 45. Quote from Moore and Taylour, *Room with the Fresco Complex*, forthcoming.

[198] Evely 1992, p. 34.

[199] Moore and Taylour, *Room with the Fresco Complex*, forthcoming.

[200] Evely 1992, pp. 22-23.

[201] One tablet, Oi 701, was actually found in Room 1, but the rest of the series was found in the northwest section of corridor 4. Oi 708 is included in this series because it was found with the others, but since no writing was preserved on it I have not included it in this discussion. Another tablet, X 707 was found in the southwestern part of room 4, but does not seem to be part of the Oi series. (W. Taylour, "The Citadel House" in *The Mycenae Tablets III, Transactions of the American Philosophical Society*, Vol. 52, Part 7, Philadelphia 1963, pp. 35-46; see pp. 37-41; and J. Chadwick, "Texts and Commentary," pp. 54-67 of the same volume, 1963, see p. 57.)

[202] Taylour 1963, *passim*. Chadwick 1963, pp. 48-50.

[203] Taylour 1963, p. 37.

[204] Taylour 1963, p. 45.

[205] Killen 1992, p. 366. P. Ilievski, "Some Observations on Mycenaean Epigraphy," *Klio* 50 (1968) 39-52; see p. 49. C. Piteros, J.-P. Olivier, and J.L. Melena, "Les inscriptions en linéaire B des nodules de Thèbes (1982): la fouille, les documents, les possibilités d'interprétation," *BCH* 114 (1990) pp. 103-184; see p. 163. The reason the two ideograms had been separated was because on the tablets from Mycenae the ideogram's horizontal lines did not cross the vertical ones while on the Knossos tablets they did. Piteros, Olivier and Melena (1990, pp. 163-166) found that on the Theban nodules both types were exhibited, thus making the distinction unnecessary.

[206] See C. Boëlle, "*Po-ti-ni-ja* à Mycènes," *Minos* 27-28 (1992-1993) 283-301, see pp. 296-297 for a summary of the different propositions. Also see Piteros, Olivier and Melena 1990, pp. 163-166 for another helpful summary.

measured in the units used for liquids, adds to the confusion. Nonetheless, given the fact that liquid measurements are used for *190, it does seem most likely that it was a liquid substance.[207] Killen deduces from its contexts that it is most likely some kind of foodstuff.[208] It is listed on KN U 7063.2 after sheep and before wine, and on MY Ue 661 on the same line with an allocation of figs. The first word of Ue 661 is *jo-po-ro-te-ke*, which can be interpreted as "*ho protheke*, 'thus he set out'" from the verb προτίθημι, which "is the technical term for serving food."[209] Killen compares this tablet with others that seem to record lists of food items that were "being supplied to the palace for a ceremonial banquet *vel sim.*" *190 appears in a similar context on the Theban Wu sealings which Killen thinks must record the delivery of food items to the palace. Thus, although its exact identity is still unknown, *190 can be understood as a food item. Such a commodity might have been given by the palatial administration to the recipients on the Oi tablets in exchange for (or, as payment for) services they had already rendered, or were supposed to accomplish in the future. It is also possible that the palace was allocating the commodity for use in some industrial process, although, if this were the case, we would have to find a substance that would suit the work of all the professionals who appear on the series, and so seems much less likely.

Those industrial workers listed on the Oi tablets are the *ka-na-pe-u-si*, or fullers, who appear twice in the series (Oi 701.5 and 704.2), and *ku-wa-no-wo-ko-i*, the cyanus, or blue-glass workers, who appear (or can be restored) four times (Oi 701.7, 702.4, 703.2, and 704.4).[210] *Ko-o-ke-ne* of 701.6 is generally agreed to be a man's name. This name is recorded three times in the Oi series, on Oi 701.6, 703.3, and 704.3. In two of these instances, Oi 701.6 and 703.3, *ko-o-ke-ne* appears with the verbal form *do-ke*, which is the 3rd person singular aorist form of δίδωμι, meaning "he gave" or "contributed." Even though the nominative is used in one of these instances (Oi 701.6) and the dative in the other (703.3) it seems more likely that the nominative is a mistake or a nominative of the rubric because on Oi 701.6 a word precedes *do-ke* which very well may be the subject of the verb.[211] Also, on Oi 704.3 the dative form can be reasonably restored even though no verb stands with the name. This means that *ko-o-ke-ne* is receiving an allocation along with the others recorded on the Oi series.[212] Perhaps he was an individual craftsman or a foreman in charge of others. A religious professional occupation may also be recorded in the Oi series. The word *po-ro-po-i* (Oi 701.4, *po-po-i* on 702.3) has been interpreted as the dative plural of the noun *πρόπος or augur (cf. θεοπρόπος).[213] These augurs may have been religious officials who worked within or for the Cult Center.

The religious nature of the Oi series is also signaled by the fact that Potnia is found among the professionals on three of the Oi tablets: *si-to-po-ti-ni-ja* appears on Oi 701.3, and may perhaps be restored from]*po-ti*-[on Oi 702.2 since there is room on the tablet for at least two signs before the]*po-ti*-[.[214]

Oi 702:
0. *sup. mut.*
1.] *vacat*
2.]p̣ọ-ti-[ ]**190* 3
3.]ne-ja , po-po-i **190* 5
4. ku-wa-]ṇọ-wo-ko-i **190* 2
5.] **190* 2
6.]*vest.*[
inf. mut.

The third appearance of Potnia is found on Oi 704.1, where *po-ti-ni-ja* appears without further qualification.

Oi 704:
1. po-ti-ni-ja **190* 15
2. ka-na-pe-u-si **190* 6
3. ko-o-ke-ne-ị **1̣9̣0̣*[
4. ku-wa-ṇọ[-wo-ko-i
5.]*vest.[*
inf. mut.

Because these Potnias are found listed alongside professional titles it seems likely that they were, like the others, receiving their allocations of *190 in return for work that was being done for the palace. That work then would have been conducted in a workshop over which Potnia or Sito Potnia was considered to preside. Each of these deities, or rather the priests or priestesses who worked in their names, may have had separate managerial duties or spheres of influence within the sanctuary's industrial endeavors.[215]

It is of course possible to interpret the allocations of *190 to *po-ti-ni-ja* and *si-to-po-ti-ni-ja* on the Oi tablets as religious offerings. But I think this is unlikely first because the Potnias are listed along with professional

---

[207] It should be noted though that on KN U 7063, however, *190 is counted.
[208] Killen 1992, p. 376.
[209] Killen 1992, p. 376. Chadwick 1963, p. 62.
[210] For a discussion of the exact identity of *ku-wa-no* see R. Halleux, "Lapis-lazuli, azurite, ou pâte de verre? A propos de kuwano et kuwanowoko dans les tablettes mycéniennes," in *Studi Micenei ed Egeo-Anatolici* No. 9 (*Incunabula Graeca* 39), Rome 1969, pp. 47-66.
[211] I thank C.W. Shelmerdine for pointing this out to me.
[212] J.-P. Olivier, "En marge d'une nouvelle édition des tablettes de Mycènes," *Kadmos* 8 (1969) 46-53; see p. 53. Also see *Dic. Mic.* I, p. 379.
[213] *Docs*², p. 507. *Dic. Mic.* II, p. 144.
[214] J. van Leuven, "Mycenaean Goddesses Called *Potnia*," *Kadmos* 18 (1979) 112-129; see p. 117. This proposition has been generally accepted.
[215] It is debatable whether *si-to-po-ti-ni-ja* and *po-ti-ni-ja* of Oi 704.1 should be taken as referring to the same goddess. Chadwick (1963, p. 59) thinks that they should be seen as one, and while this is certainly possible, Boëlle (1992-1993, pp. 298 and 300) has made a good case for the idea that they were different goddesses. She points out that the same scribe (Hand 64) wrote both Oi 701, which records *si-to-po-ti-ni-ja*, and Oi 704, which has *po-ti-ni-ja*. She reasons that the scribe would have used the same form of the goddess's name on both tablets if he meant the same deity. On the other hand, it could also be argued that he was using *po-ti-ni-ja* as a shorthand version of *si-to-po-ti-ni-ja*. I think it is a tricky question.

workers, and second because of the quantities of **190* that are being allocated. The amounts of **190* listed on the Oi series are rather large, larger than what would be expected if these were simply offerings. If the numbers on the Oi series do indicate liquid measures, an allocation of one whole unit would equal 28.8 liters. Thus, on Oi 702.2 *si-to-]po-ti[-ni-ja* receives 3 units, or 86.4 liters and on Oi 704.1 *po-ti-ni-ja* receives 15 units, or 432 liters.[216] Even though the commodity being recorded is different, it is worth noting that the quantities of the Oi series are much larger than those that are recorded as offerings in the Pylos Fr series. In the Fr series average offerings are significantly less than one unit, and range between a quarter of a liter to 9.6 liters. Thus the allocations on the Oi series were more likely intended for industrial purposes or as payments for work than as offerings.[217]

Killen points out that **190* "seems always to occur ... in religious, or at least arguably religious, contexts."[218] And he includes in that category "KN U 7063.2.3, where the single animals recorded in the same registers suggest a sacrificial context, the Thebes sealings Wu 48, Wu 80+ (contributions to the 'menu' of a state-sponsored banquet) and the new Thebes tablet Uo 121, all the rest of whose contents again suggests that it is a list of offerings."[219] He therefore syas, "There seems little question, incidentally, that Oi 704, and the other thablets in the same 'set', are wholly religious texts, rather than part religious and part secular (something which it would be difficult to parallel elsewhere in the records.)"[220]

Given this evaluation, we may wonder about the exact nature of the relationship between those professional workers and the Potnias. Should the fullers and blue-glass workers be seen as working for the sanctuary? Boëlle assumes that the professionals all belonged to the religious sector and makes the suggestion that since the same type of worker reappears on different tablets of the Oi series, these groups could have been employed in different shrines belonging to the different goddesses.[221] But this seems unlikely for a couple of reasons. First, if the tablets did record different sets of fullers and blue-glass workers, one would expect the scribe to have made it clear which set of workers was meant in each case, i.e., to which shrine the workers belonged. Since this is not made clear, it would seem that the same groups were meant each time they were recorded. Also, it would seem strange to have a set of fullers and a set of blue-glass workers attached to different shrines, especially if those shrines can be identified (as I think they can) with the fairly modest ones in the Cult Center. The fact that the occupational designations on the tablets recur could instead be taken to indicate that allocations were given to the same groups of people but at different times. The question remains though as to whether we should consider these groups of workers as having been associated with the sanctuary on a permanent basis. A case may be made, through the steatite mold and glass wasters that were found in the Cult Center, that the blue-glass workers were associated with the sanctuary. The augurs too could be said to have been working within the Cult Center. PY An 1281 constitutes a comparable example of a tablet on which groups of workers were recorded in a list on the same tablet as the Potnias with whom they were working. But it has to be said that in the case of An 1281 the hierarchical manner in which the tablet was written made the association of the workers with the Potnias much more clear. In the end, it is very difficult to say for sure whether the workers were associated with the sanctuary on a full-time basis, but I tend to think that at least the blue-glass workers were.

In sum then, the archaeological and the textual evidence tend to indicate that the religious officials of the Cult Center were engaged in industrial activities. Indeed, because of this evidence, French has not changed her interpretation of the areas of the Cult Center that she originally saw as storerooms. Nonetheless, the lack of debitage has caused French to conclude that area 36 was not a workshop, but rather more like an "*apotheke* of sorts"[222] or, more recently, "a repository or distribution point."[223] This leaves us still wondering about the mystery of the missing workshop.

In a previous publication I proposed that the area between the Room of the Fresco Complex and Tsountas' House (sometimes designated as court 35) may have served as at least one of the workshop areas for the site.[224] Mylonas, who excavated the area in 1973, did not publish a detailed account of this area, but he does give an overview of its main features, while French gives her own description and interpretation of the area in her most recent publication.[225] As I mentioned above, Mylonas found a circular altar (0.68 m high and 1.4 m across) within the courtyard[226] close to the entryway of room xxiv. Three deposits of burnt matter can be associated with this altar. (I say "associated with" because there was no sign of burning on the altar itself.) The first was a deposit found by Mylonas: "at a distance of 1.2 m west of

[216] Unfortunately the amount that *si-to-po-ti-ni-ja* receives on Oi 701.3 has not been preserved.

[217] If payment for work seems the most likely alternative, then one more possibility must be mentioned, and that is that the Potnias were receiving the allocations as payment for services rendered in the religious realm rather than the industrial. This would be different from offerings *per se*, in that a financial agreement would have been entered into, and the transaction would have been recognized by both parties as an outright exchange. If this was the reason for the large allocations of **190*, then the religious sector could be seen in this way to have engaged in economic activities of a different sort than industrial.

[218] J.T. Killen, "Thoughts on the functions of the new Thebes tablets," in *Die Neuen Linear B-Texte aus Theben: ihr Aufschlusswert für die Mykenische Sprache und Kultur*, S. Deger-Jalkotzy and O. Panagl, eds., Wien 2006, pp. 79-110; see p. 89.

[219] Killen 2006, pp. 89-90.

[220] Killen 2006, p. 89.

[221] Boëlle 1992-1993, p. 298.

[222] French, personal communication, 1997.

[223] French 2007, p. 41.

[224] Lupack 1999, pp. 30-31.

[225] Mylonas 1983, pp. 141-142. (Also see Mylonas 1972, p. 38 where he mentions the altar.) French 2007.

[226] Mylonas said that the altar was covered with thick clay, but French (2007, p. 12) suggests that the clay layer was the result of "the wash down of mudbrick debris" and that it was not applied on purpose to the altar.

the altar a pit was found, filled with ashes, bones of small animals and sherds.[227] The second was a pit that was found below the floor of room xxiv, in what was originally part of the passage.[228] This indicates that the altar itself most likely also belongs to an earlier period than room xxiv;[229] it would be reasonable to assign it to the same building period as the Temple and the Room of the Fresco Complex (early in LH IIIB1[230]). The third was found as part of room xxiv and consisted of a basin that was lined with two layers of plesia. This basin definitely had burnt bones in its black soil.[231] Thus the religious nature of the area is assured. The area was also decorated in a special manner. The courtyard "itself was floored with coloured slabs"[232] and Mylonas mentions that "the southwest side of the court of the altar was lined by a shallow stoa.[233] French also tells us that the entryway into room xxiv "was emphasized by a shallow porch with wooden columns."[234] This arrangement calls to mind the stoa that lined the court of the Northeast Building at Pylos and the entrance to its shrine, room 93.

French provides further details in her description of rooms xxv and court 35 which indicate that the personnel of the Cult Center were engaged in industrial activities. Although French says that court 35 did not yield finds that seemed to derive from primary contexts, nonetheless she states that "a remarkable quantity of small pieces of lead" were found "on the floor levels covered with the destruction debris."[235] This takes on further significance when we consider the fact that a lead 'bun ingot' and two more pieces of lead were found in room xxv. Also found in room xxv was a tripod mortar and some organic coloring matter. Of this assemblage French says, "Though restricted in quantity the material *in situ* on the floor of xxv is of very considerable interest for its range."[236] Certainly these materials indicate that the area was being used as for industrial activities. French goes on to say, "The presence of the lead 'ingot' would seem to preclude purely domestic usage and some kind of manufacturing purpose seems likely."[237] The location of court 35 would also recommend its being interpreted as a workshop area since it is convenient to all three areas that had workshop materials and for the most part it was open to the sky, which would allow for light to work by and the ventilation of any smoke. Also, the stoa would have provided shade for the craftspeople working there.

A second possible location where industrial activities may have been conducted, which I have also previously proposed, is in or around the stone building within which the Oi series was found.[238] The tablets may have been written in that building because it was used to store the commodity that they recorded, but it is also possible that the workers listed on them worked nearby, as was the case for some of the workers listed on the tablets from the Northeast Building at Pylos and probably also for those listed in the ration tablets of the Ivory Houses of Mycenae.[239] Since the area from which the Oi tablets fell has not been excavated, this hypothesis cannot be confirmed. There are, however, other clues in the archaeological evidence that support this theory. At least one major piece of evidence for industrial activity occurring in the area, the elaborately worked steatite mold, which was found on Floor 2 of area 36 and so belongs to Phase VII, is thought to have been brought to area 36 from the place in which it was originally used.[240] French has agreed that it could have originally been used in the building on the terrace above room 4.[241] In this the tablets and the archaeological evidence seem to support one another since, as we saw, blue-glass workers (*ku-wa-no-wo-ko-i*), who would have used such a mold, are frequently mentioned in the Oi series which definitely came from this area.

In addition to these two possible (and not necessarily mutually exclusive) workshop sites, Moore has proposed that the abundance of vessels found in room 31, the Room of the Fresco itself, along with the hearth in the center of the room, may indicate that the shrine personnel were involved in the production of perfumed oils and unguents.[242] He says, "When the evidence of the contents of the rooms is also taken into account we have at the least a strong suggestion that the cult of the Room with the Fresco Complex not only used perfumed oil but may have had a hand in its production."
In this context we may remember that at Pylos *pi-ra-jo* the unguent boiler was one of the workers designated as Potnian.

Thus, even though we do not have unequivocal evidence for an actual workshop in close proximity to the shrine complexes, nonetheless, there are enough indications that one, or more than one for that matter, did exist for us to work with the assumption that the religious personnel of the Cult Center were involved in industrial activities. The goods produced by the workshop seem to have consisted largely of prestige items: beads and decorative pieces, ivory inlays for furniture and decorative boxes, and personal objects like combs, and probably items made of gold. These goods may have been made for export, or for use by the elite of the palace and those favored by the elite. Conceivably, the objects could have

[227] G. Mylonas, *Mycenae Rich in Gold*, Athens 1983, pp. 141-142.
[228] French 2007, pp. 10 and 15.
[229] French 2007, p. 15.
[230] French 2007, p. 4.
[231] French 2007, p. 15.
[232] French 2007, p. 15
[233] Mylonas 1983, p. 141. In Mylonas 1972, p. 38 the facts he gives about the stoa are different, but I have followed the later version assuming that it was written after the area had been more carefully studied.
[234] French 2007, p. 15.
[235] French 2007, p. 36.
[236] French 2007, p. 36.
[237] French 2007, p. 36.
[238] Lupack 1999, pp. 30-31.
[239] I. Tournavitou (*The 'Ivory Houses' at Mycenae*, British School at Athens 1995, pp. 257-269) discusses the tablets found within the West House, the House of the Oil Merchant, the House of the Sphinxes, and the House of the Shields at Mycenae and their possible relation to the types of work that went on in those buildings.
[240] Evely 1992, pp. 22, 31.
[241] French, personal communication, 1997.
[242] Moore and Taylour, *Room with the Fresco Complex*, forthcoming.

been made for both foreign and domestic use. Whether the palatial administration had any control over the work that the religious sector engaged in, and if it did have some, to what extent that control went, is of course difficult to say. One could propose that the palace must have organized the acquisition of the raw materials and dictated to the sanctuary's personnel the type of objects that they were to be made into. Alternatively, it is possible that the religious hierarchy was more independent in their actions. I do not think that the physical proximity of the Cult Center to the palace necessarily indicates that the palatial administration managed the details of the industrial production that went on in the area. And since it is not made clear in the tablets which sphere (or spheres) of society was (were) able to acquire imported items such as the blue glass needed by the *ku-wa-no-wo-ko-i*, there is no reason why religious personages could not have been active in such acquisitions. The Oi series could have helped in sorting out the issue of the exact nature of the palace's involvement in the industrial production that went on in the Cult Center, if it were clear what **190* was being used for. If **190* was a raw material, then the palace was involved in production, and the situation would parallel that of the Northeast Building at Pylos where the religious and palatial authorities seemed to have been working together. If, on the other hand, **190* was a foodstuff that was meant to be consumed (as is thought to be more likely), then the palace was merely paying for work and one could argue that the personnel in the Cult Center were more independent. In either case, it can be positively said that the religious personnel who were involved in the production work most likely gained materially from their efforts.

The Sanctuary of Ayios Konstantinos at Methana

The first non-palatial site that I will consider is the recently excavated LH IIIA-B site of Ayios Konstantinos, Methana which is situated in the northeastern area of the Peloponnese called Troizen.[243] Ayios Konstantinos has produced a very interesting shrine complex that appears to have been built within a Mycenaean settlement. Its finds date to the LH IIIA-B period, although the majority came from the LH IIIB period. The presence of carinated kylikes (FS 267) and a deep bowl of Group B (FS 284) demonstrate that this room was in use up until the end of the LH IIIB2 period.[244]

The religious complex consists of five rooms arranged around a courtyard. The main shrine room, room A, was of a good size, 4.35 x 2.65 m, and its main axis ran east-west. It contained a stepped bench shrine in the northwest corner, directly opposite the entrance in the northeast corner. The shrine was remarkable for its extremely large number of terracotta figurines: approximately 150 were found on and around the platform. The large number of figurines led the excavator to propose that there had been a shelf above the platform, which would have served to hold many of the figurines. This assemblage of figurines is also distinguished by the types it exhibits, some of which are fairly rare. Most of the figurines are individual bovids, but many are composite constructions of animals with riders. Konsolaki records that there were 10 chariot groups, 5 horses with helmeted riders, 3 oxen with riders, and 17 driven oxen depicted with reins.[245] The rider on one of the three ridden oxen is actually attached to the top of the bull's head clasping its horns. Konsolaki proposes that this may be an image of a divinity.[246] Remarkable also was the fact that there was only one female figurine: a hollow Psi type. This too could reflect something about the type of worship that was conducted in the shrine.[247]

Several other features in the room are worthy of comment. A deposit in the southwest corner included an animal-head rhyton, a plain two-handled cup, a dipper, and a fragmentary jar neck. The combination of these items could indicate that a libation ceremony, possibly one that involved blood, was part of the rites that were conducted in this shrine.[248] This sanctuary has also yielded secure evidence of burnt animal sacrifice, as the hearth in the southeast corner of room A contained a large number of burnt animal bones, mostly from juvenile pigs, that were very different from the bones found in other areas of the site that resulted from sacrificial meals.[249] A big conch shell, which could have provided some sort of music, was also found with these items.

Just south of this main shrine was a room (called *delta*) that did not contain any finds of a religious character. Instead, its contents indicated that it was used for industrial purposes. In addition to some stone tools, the excavators found bits of corroded metal, a few lead blobs, and a crucible. Also, there was a whitish substance which has not yet been analyzed, but which could indicate, especially when considered in conjunction with

[243] E. Konsolaki-Yannopoulou, "Mycenaean Religious Architecture: The Archaeological Evidence from Ayios Konstantinos, Methana," in *Celebrations: Selected papers and discussions from the tenth anniversary symposium of the Norwegian Institute at Athens, 12-16 May 1999*, M. Wedde, ed., Paul Astroms Forlag 2004. E. Konsolaki, "A Mycenaean Sanctuary on Methana," in *Peloponnesian Sanctuaries and Cults*, R. Hägg, ed., Stockholm 2002, pp. 25-36; *idem*, "Methana, Agios Konstantinos," *B' Ephoreia Proistorikon kai Klassikon Archaioteton, Archaiologikon Deltion* 46 (1991) [1996], 71-74; *idem* 1995, p. 242. Much of the information presented here, especially that concerned with the industrial remains, has been generously supplied by the excavator herself, Eleni Konsolaki, through personal communication, 1997. Also see Shelmerdine 1997, pp. 574-575.

[244] Konsolaki 1995, p. 242.

[245] Konsolaki 1991, p. 72. Konsolaki discusses the horses with helmeted riders in detail in "A Group of New Mycenaean Horseman from Methana," in *Meletemata: Studies in Aegean archaeology presented to Malcolm H. Weiner as he enters his 65th year*, vol. II (*Aegaeum* 20), P. Betancourt, V. Karageorghis, R. Laffineur and Niemeier, eds., Liège and PASP, University of Texas 1999, pp. 427-433.

[246] Konsolaki 1995, p. 242.

[247] As we will see below, a separation of figurines by gender also existed at Phylakopi.

[248] E. Konsolaki-Yannopoulou, "New Evidence for the Practice of Libations in the Aegean Bronze Age," in *Potnia: Deities and Religion in the Aegean Bronze Age*, *Aegaeum* 22, R. Laffineur and R. Hagg, eds., Liège and UT-PASP 2001, pp. 213-220.

[249] Konsolaki-Yannopoulou 2001, p. 215.

the lead blobs and crucible, that the extraction of silver from lead, or cupellation, was performed on the site.[250] The courtyard around which the building was situated could have provided a good work area. If this very tentative hypothesis turns out to be correct, then Ayios Konstantinos, Methana constitutes a non-palatial example of a shrine engaged in the manufacture of a precious commodity.

Phylakopi and the Production of Obsidian Blades

Phylakopi on Melos provides us with another example of a sanctuary that appears to have been involved in production work (Figure 4). Even though Phylakopi is located in the Cyclades, its inclusion here among the Mycenaean sites is justified because it had a definite Mycenaean character during its later phases: Late Helladic IIIA-C. As Barber has discussed, in its earlier phases, Phylakopi's main affiliations appear to have been more Minoan.[251] This connection with Crete seems to have peaked in the earliest stage of Phylakopi's Third City, which is equivalent in date to the late LM IA-B periods. During this period a building called the "Mansion" was constructed, which may have served as the administrative center for the site. In the vicinity of the Mansion fragments of a Linear A tablet were found. These fragments "could be a relic of the administrative system in use – whether operated by Minoans, or simply on Minoan lines."[252] Minoan-inspired religious objects also date from this time, such as a "tripod table" or "tripod hearth" in the LM IA style and a mold for a double axe.[253]

The Minoan influence on the site came to an end during the LM IB period at which time Phylakopi underwent a major burning destruction.[254] Barber conjectures that the destruction of the site "may well be connected with the arrival of the Mycenaeans."[255] Renfrew says simply, "We know little of the events which led to the remodeling of the Mansion..."[256] But it is clear that after this destruction the Minoan cultural influence was replaced with Mycenaean. This is seen most clearly in the replacement of the Mansion with a much more Mycenaean megaron-centered palatial structure, the construction of which can be dated to the early stages of the Late Helladic III A1 period. It is during the same period that the West Shrine of Phylakopi was built. Renfrew, discussing the differences between Minoan and Mycenaean religion, points out the very Mycenaean character of the Shrine. For instance, the animal figures and figurines and group figures can be set firmly within the Mycenaean tradition, as can be the Psi figurines,[257] which were locally made.[258] Also, the way the sanctuary was laid out, with low benches that functioned as altars, is typical of Mycenaean shrines. Renfrew's conclusion was this: "...I am inclined to see in the West Shrine at Phylakopi the adoption of mainland cult practices, which were conducted in a building having possible mainland predecessors."[259] It is justified then to include the evidence from Phylakopi in this study.

The history of the Shrine complex, or sanctuary, of Phylakopi is long, and it is worth briefly reviewing its major phases, the events that differentiate them, and the significant artifacts that appear in each phase. The Shrine was in use from the LH IIIA period until the mid LH IIIC period. In terms of absolute chronology, Renfrew dates the construction of the Shrine to *ca.* 1360 B.C., and its abandonment to the end of the 11th century B.C., a span of approximately 260 years.[260] During this long time period a couple of major events affecting the Shrine can be used to distinguish three main phases of use, which Renfrew outlines as follows:[261] The first phase is initiated with the construction of the West Shrine (LH IIIA), which seems to have been built soon after the Megaron. The West Shrine (see Figure 4) consisted of a main room, axially arranged with platforms, or altars, in the northwest and southwest corners. On and around these altars were found several human figures and interestingly, they seem to have been separated by gender: only female figures were found on the southwest altar while only male figures (during phases 1 and 2) were found on the northwest altar.[262] At the western end of the main room, between the two altars, there was a doorway that led into two smaller rooms, A and B. These rooms seem to have been used for storage, but there are indications that they also served as special cult rooms. Particularly this might have been true of their use in phase 1, since beads were

[250] Konsolaki, personal communication, 1997. A similar "whitish substance, much like pumice, but heavier" was found in a "cooking pot" and a bowl in a basement room of the West House at Akrotiri. Marinatos took this as evidence that cupellation of silver from lead minerals was taking place there (S. Marinatos, *Excavations at Thera VI (1972 Season)*, Athens 1974, pp. 29-30, plates 63b and 64).

[251] R.L.N. Barber, "The Status of Phylakopi in Creto-Cycladic Relations," in *Minoan Thalassocracy: Myth and Reality*, Hägg and Marinatos, eds., Stockholm 1984, pp. 179-182.

[252] Barber 1984, p. 181.

[253] C. Renfrew, "Questions of Minoan and Mycenaean Cult," in *Sanctuaries and Cults in the Aegean Bronze Age*, R. Hägg and N. Marinatos, eds., Stockholm 1981, pp. 27-31; see p. 28. (Hereafter "Renfrew 1981b.")

[254] For a full discussion of the Mycenaean influence on the Cyclades see R.L.N. Barber, *The Cyclades in the Bronze Age*, University of Iowa Press 1987, pp. 224-246.

[255] Barber 1984, p. 180.

[256] Renfrew 1981b, p. 28.

[257] C. Renfrew, *The Archaeology of Cult: The Sanctuary at Phylakopi*, British School at Athens Supplementary Volume No. 18, Thames and Hudson, 1985; see p. 428.

[258] French 1985, *passim*. Renfrew 1985, p. 415.

[259] Renfrew 1985, p. 436. Whittaker in her study of Mycenaean cult buildings agrees that the shrines at Phylakopi should be regarded as in the Mycenaean tradition (*Mycenaean Cult Buildings: A Study of their Architecture and Function in the Context of the Aegean and the Eastern Mediterranean*, The Norwegian Institute at Athens 1997; see pp. 28-31.)

[260] See the chronological chart in Renfrew 1985, p. 86.

[261] Renfrew 1985, pp. 71-87; see especially the chart on p. 86. Also see Renfrew 1981a.

[262] This gender separation recalls that on Tn 316 where female *po-re-na* were only offered to female deities and male *po-re-na* were only offered to male deities. One might wonder if this was a common aspect of Mycenaean religious practice.

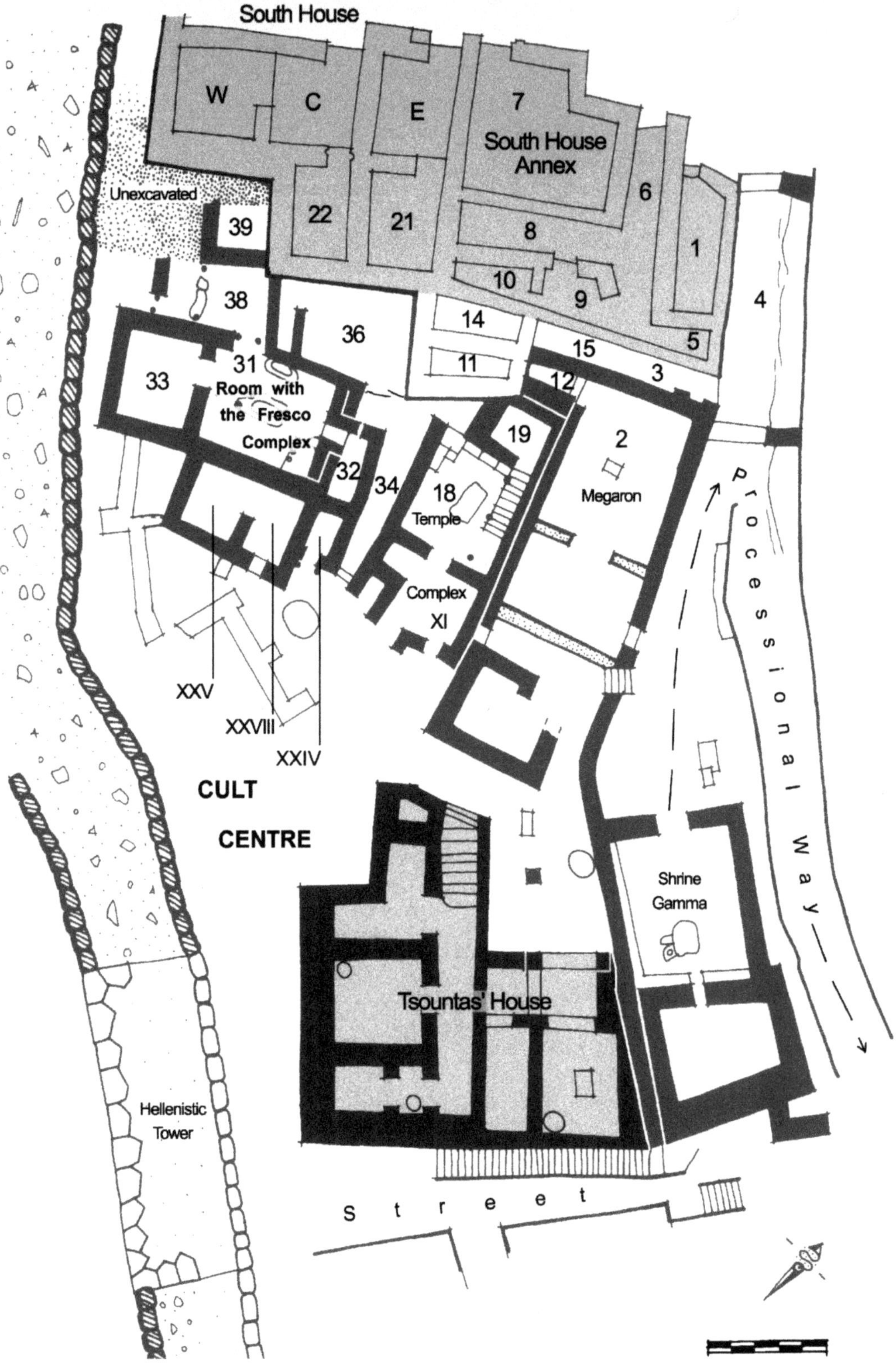

Figure 3. Plan of the Cult Center at Mycenae.

found in phase 1 levels that could have been offerings.[263] Room A, the room that held, in addition to other figures and figurines, the Lady of Phylakopi, the most elaborate and well-made figure of the Shrine's entire assemblage, could be considered as Renfrew suggests, "an *adyton*, a 'Holy of Holies', a place apart, where the most important cult image could be venerated away from the eyes of the general congregation. The Lady of Phylakopi was judged by French to have been a Mycenaean import, probably brought in from the Argive area.[264] French dated this

[263] Renfrew 1985, p. 378.

[264] E. French, "Chapter VI: The Figures and Figurines," in C. Renfrew, *The Archaeology of Cult: The Sanctuary at Phylakopi*, British School at

figure by stylistic analysis to the early LH IIIA period, which probably means that it was brought into the Shrine at or near the date of its construction. The Lady of Phylakopi continued to be used in the Shrine until the end of the site's second period, up until *ca.* 1120 B.C. If we can estimate the date of the construction of the Shrine as occurring a couple of decades after the Megaron was built in 1360 B.C.,[265] and if indeed the Lady of Phylakopi's acquisition by the Shrine was contemporaneous with the building of the Shrine (or nearly so),[266] then the Lady was in use in the Shrine for approximately 220 years.[267] Renfrew says that she was "used singly as the principal cult figure."[268] Renfrew goes on to say though that no beads were found in Room A with the Lady of Phylakopi, which could be taken to indicate that she was indeed simply in storage and not in an adyton.[269]

The construction of the East Shrine marks the beginning of the second phase of the Shrine complex. Renfrew dates the construction of the East Shrine to the IIIB 1 period (*ca.* 1270 B.C.), and believes that it was built soon after the Mycenaean fortification wall was put up. With the construction of the East Shrine a small courtyard was created between the two shrines which also seems to have been used for religious purposes. A purposely (but roughly) rounded stone, or baetyl, was placed "at the intersection of the entrance axes of both shrines."[270] The assemblage of this courtyard contained twenty or so pots, a significant number of which would have been involved in the handling of liquids. Renfrew suggests that they were probably used for the pouring of libations, and points out that since pots were rarely found in the rest of the Shrine complex their existence and use in the courtyard makes it an important focus of the cult area.[271] In the East Shrine one low platform was used and upon it was found, among other things, wheel-made bovid figures and a cache of ten sealstones (one other was found in the West Shrine) which Younger proposes were deposited here as votive offerings.[272] No human figures or figurines were found here at all in this time period.[273] A male gold facemask was found in the latest level of the East Shrine, and it is possible that this mask and the figure upon which it originally was fitted could have been reused from earlier periods, as we know other figures in the shrine had been. So it may have been the case that this platform did have a male figure, although we have no way of positively establishing this. Phase 2, which lasted for a century and a half, was the most prosperous years of the Shrine's existence.

In the mid LH IIIC period (*ca.* 1120 B.C.) Phylakopi suffered major damage, whether from an earthquake or a purposeful destruction is uncertain, although Renfrew favors the idea that the "collapse" was caused by "enemy action, to be interpreted as the consequence of unrest in the Cyclades at that time."[274] The shrine continued to be used after this destruction but in a more limited way. It is at this time that the Blocking Wall was built, which closed off the southern half the West Shrine. The Blocking Wall also shut off access to Rooms A and B, effectively sealing in the now broken Lady of Phylakopi (her head had come off) and the other figures that accompanied her. The sealing off of the Lady of Phylakopi and the other figurines may have seemed appropriate as her main altar at the southwest of the West Shrine was also put out of use.[275] A new altar was set up in the northeastern area of the West Shrine, which may have been meant to take the place of the now inaccessible southwestern one.[276] It should be mentioned that in the phase 3 deposits of the northwestern altar, which previously had only male figures associated with it, a female Psi figurine was found along with the male figures. This means that at this time the male/female dichotomy that had been adhered to in phases 1 and 2 of the Shrine was now dispensed with. Among the finds of the East Shrine were several animal figurines as before, but now for the first time the animal figurines were accompanied by two female figurines. Thus at the very end of the Shrine's history there may have been a blurring of the "distinctions in function which were seen in phase 2b."[277] Also it seems that at this time the baetyl in the courtyard had been buried by the accumulating floor levels. This "shabby and impoverished"[278] state may have only lasted a couple of decades before the Shrine was abandoned altogether in the later part of the mid LH IIIC period, at *ca.* 1100 B.C.

It is interesting that, as at Mycenae, several objects were found within the sanctuary area that in other contexts might have been interpreted as indicating a domestic setting.[279] For instance there were querns, mortars, rubbers, and ceramic vessels that could have been used in the preparation of food. Some of this food, as Renfrew points out, "could have been used in the celebration of the cult."[280] These more practical objects were not, however, found with the cult assemblages on the platforms, but rather, mainly in the street and courtyard area. As Renfrew says, "The East and West Shrines, it has been argued, were constructed and used for cult

Athens Supplementary Volume No. 18, Thames and Hudson, 1985; see pp. 215-216.

[265] Renfrew 1985, p. 436.

[266] French 1985, pp. 215-216.

[267] Please see Renfrew 1985, p. 86 for a chart that gives the dates for the relevant events.

[268] Renfrew 1985, p. 415. It is at this point that he brings up the similarities between the Lady of Phylakopi and the female figure found in the Shrine at Mycenae in room 32 of the Room with the Fresco Complex.

[269] Renfrew 1985, p. 373.

[270] Renfrew 1981a, pp. 73 and 79.

[271] Renfrew 1985, p. 374.

[272] J. Younger, "Chapter VII: The Sealstones," in Renfrew 1985, pp. 281-297.

[273] Renfrew 1985, p. 370.

[274] Renfrew 1985, p. 379.

[275] French (in Renfrew 1985, p. 279) discusses the question of whether the Lady's head had been broken in Room A or if it had been broken elsewhere and both pieces were removed to Room A for the purpose of sealing them in there. She also mentions the parallel situation in the Cult Center at Mycenae.

[276] Renfrew 1985, p. 380.

[277] Renfrew 1985, p. 381.

[278] Renfrew 1985, p. 391.

[279] Renfrew 1985, p. 387-388.

[280] Renfrew 1985, p. 387.

purposes. This does not, however, of necessity imply that other more mundane, and obviously functional activities were not carried out within them."[281]

What then do we make of the fact that several practical-looking metal objects were found within the shrines? This set of finds included twelve pieces that were considerably corroded and unrecognizable, seven pieces of slag, and several lumps of bronze, one of which looks like a puddle ingot. A terracotta mold was also found that was probably used in the manufacture of metal axes or chisels.[282] These pieces could represent the raw materials and by-products of a metal working industry that was being managed by the personnel of the sanctuary, but since there was no indication of a furnace or industrial-sized fires in the area, and since no crucibles were found with the metal objects, this is probably not the best explanation for this set of finds. Rather, it has been proposed that these metal objects were brought to the shrine as votives.[283] A similar situation is seen on Kea at the site of Ayia Irini. Within the Temple of this site a crucible and a tuyère were found in a Middle Bronze Age context and portions of larger crucibles and tuyères were found in Late Bronze Age levels.[284] Evidence for metal working dating to the LH II period was however found nearby in House A.[285] This suggests that bronze workers worshipped at the shrine and must have propitiated the deity in the hopes that (s)he would favor their work by offering items that related to the practice of their industry. Renfrew says that offerings of this type "do perhaps suggest some connection between some of the smiths of Phylakopi and the sanctuary."[286] Schallin, on the other hand, who has reviewed all the evidence for metal working in the Cyclades, does not propose that the bronze workers had some special relationship with the shrine, but rather that smiths brought these objects to the deity because they had significant symbolic value. She says, "To the metal worker the metallurgical objects may have represented a skill inspired by the gods," and that they may have offered such objects "in gratitude for the ability to perform their craft."[287] Caskey says, "...for throughout the history of religion it is common enough to dedicate objects connected with what you do or with what you hope to accomplish..."[288]

Thus, the metal objects found within the sanctuary at Phylakopi do not provide evidence that the personnel in the sanctuary were engaged in metal-working processes. Nonetheless, there is evidence that the religious personnel were involved in a different manufacturing activity: the production of obsidian blades.

A significantly large number of obsidian artifacts were found within the shrine: 2,724 to be exact.[289] Among these artifacts were finished blades, cores, and the chips and flakes produced during the manufacture of blades, leaving no doubt that a blade-manufacturing industry was conducted within the confines of the sanctuary. Also, the types of artifacts being produced by the sanctuary's flake industry were "broadly similar in character to debitage from other areas at Phylakopi and found at other Aegean bronze age sites (personal observations at Agia Irini, Lerna, and Knossos)...."[290] Thus they were not necessarily special in any way despite their religious context. This would seem to speak against the obsidian artifacts being classified simply as votive offerings,[291] as was concluded for the metallurgical material. Instead it seems that the religious personnel of the Phylakopi sanctuary were actively engaged in a form of industrial production. But to what end? Were the obsidian tools being produced solely for use within the shrine? Torrence proposes that the obsidian might have played a role in ritual activities, and well they might have given the special nature of obsidian and its singular relationship to the Melians.[292] But I think it is worth considering that there may have been a more practical reason for the obsidian production.

Two facts set the Shrine's obsidian apart from other obsidian deposits found at Phylakopi. The first is that the quantity of obsidian found within the sanctuary's precinct increased over time, and the second is that the increase took place at a time when the obsidian found in domestic areas of Phylakopi where blade manufacture also occurred went down. It appears that between Phases 1 and 2 of the sanctuary's use "the relative quantity of obsidian in the sanctuary increases by a factor of 2.5..."[293] Torrence compares this figure with data that was collected from a trench that was excavated immediately to the east of the sanctuary area. This trench, *Pla*, provided a perfect comparison for the sanctuary since its deposits were considered to come from a domestic context and because the chronological sequences could be matched up. It seems that while the amount of obsidian found in the sanctuary during Phase 1 was less than half that of the obsidian deposited in *Pla* during the same time, in phase 2, the situation reversed itself. Torrence measured the relative abundance of obsidian in the sanctuary area and in area Pla by dividing the total number of obsidian pieces by the number of *zembils* of

[281] Renfrew 1985, p. 387.
[282] Renfrew 1985, p. 388; see also Chapter VIII.
[283] Renfrew 1985, p. 388.
[284] M.E. Caskey, "Ayia Irini, Kea: The Terracotta Statues and the Cult in the Temple," in *Sanctuaries and Cults in the Aegean Bronze Age*, R. Hägg and N. Marinatos, eds., Stockholm 1981, pp. 127-135; see p. 132.
[285] W.W. Cummer and E. Schofield, *Keos, vol. III: Ayia Irini: House A*, Mainz 1984, p. 38: Crucibles, an ingot, copper slag, and litharge fell from above into rooms 19, 20, 21 and 25-27. Offerings from the bronze workers, including a crucible and an ingot, were also found in the shrine of House A in room 7 (p. 39) during the same time period.
[286] Renfrew 1985, p. 388.
[287] A.-L. Schallin, "Metallurgy, a Divine Affair?" in *Trade and Production in Premonetary Greece: Production and the Craftsman, Proceedings of the 4th and 5th International Workshops, Athens 1994 and 1995*, C. Gillis, C. Risberg and B. Sjöberg, eds., Paul Aströms Forlag 1997, pp. 139-172; see pp. 160-161.
[288] Caskey 1981, p. 133.

[289] R. Torrence, "Appendix C: The Chipped Stone," in Renfrew 1985, pp. 469-478.
[290] Torrence 1985, p. 470.
[291] Renfrew tentatively suggests this as a possible explanation for the worked stone (1985, p. 386).
[292] Torrence 1985, p. 474.
[293] Torrence 1985, p. 472.

earth excavated from the deposits. In this way she found that in all deposits of Phase 2 in the sanctuary the number of artifacts could be expressed as 3.6, while during the same time period the number of artifacts from all deposits of trench *Pla* could be expressed as 1.8. If we look at the numbers for the floors of those periods the numbers are slightly less striking, although still significant: 3.86:2.81.[294] Torrence concludes that, "From these data one can surmise that as the frequency of obsidian discard (and, by implication, its use) declined in the domestic contexts at Phylakopi, relatively more obsidian was being brought into the sanctuary area."[295]

Torrence seems to imply that this was because the religious use of the obsidian tools became more important than the domestic uses. But Kardulias and Runnels say that

> Lithics continued to be used for important tools in the Bronze Age, even though implements made of other materials increased in quantity (pottery) or appeared for the first time (e.g. metals). The introduction of metallurgy did not displace flintknapping as the key process for the production of many tools because bronze remained a relatively expensive commodity throughout the Bronze Age. Sickle elements, projectile points, knives, and other tools for everyday use continued to be made of stone to the end of the Mycenaean period.[296]

Kardulias and Runnels also point out that within their sample of the Southern Argolid at least, there was a greater number of Bronze Age types of stone tools than in the previous periods, which they say "suggests Helladic peoples engaged in a wider range of tool-using behavior than did their predecessors."[297] It seems more likely then that the tools produced in the sanctuary were meant to be used for practical purposes rather than for some unknown religious purpose. Where then were the tools destined to be used? Some of them could have been used in domestic contexts within the site of Phylakopi, but the tools made in trench *Pla*, and elsewhere in Phylakopi, make this unlikely since it seems that a sufficient number of stone tools were made at these sites for immediate household use. It seems unlikely that the sanctuary's blades were meant to be used within the shrine since its scale of production certainly surpassed the immediate needs of the shrine and its personnel. It seems possible then that the shrine's obsidian tools were destined for external trade.

It is also interesting that from Phase 1 to Phase 2 of the sanctuary there is a rise in the proportion of blades in comparison to flake cores, which Torrence says could indicate a greater emphasis on blades than on "expedient flake tools."[298] It should be noted that Torrence also says this trend could be due to the fact that "the majority of Phase 1 deposits corresponds to the building of the West Shrine rather than to the use of its floors. In other words, it might be expected that construction fills would contain a higher proportion of large cortical waste by-products in relation to tools than would the material discarded on floors."[299] Nonetheless, if what we are seeing is a rise in the production of finely manufactured blades, then it might seem that the personnel of the shrine were consciously specializing in the production of these blades. Thus it is interesting that Kardulias and Runnels also mention that the production of blades in particular was an important part of the Bronze Age lithic industry, and that the techniques for producing them had been refined in the Bronze Age.[300] Torrence has argued that the obsidian on Melos was readily available to those who came to the island in search of it.[301] Whether this was actually true has been disputed,[302] but the evidence shows that even if the obsidian itself was easily obtainable, the availability of the blades that were subsequently produced from the raw material was often controlled. For instance, in Messenia, Parkinson has found that the production of obsidian blades seemed to have been localized at one site in the area, a site called Romanou.[303] No other site in Messenia, including the palace at Pylos itself, had extensive evidence for blades being manufactured on-site. This would mean that all the other sites in the area were probably getting their obsidian blades in their finished form from Romanou. Kardulias and Runnels also found that in the southern Argolid the obsidian cores were concentrated in one area (at Fournoi) although the blades were found fairly regularly throughout the area.[304] They go on to suggest that in the Argolid, blades were produced "for export to other settlements in the region" and that "it was, perhaps, as an exchange commodity that obsidian acquired its greatest economic significance."[305] Runnels had earlier observed that there was a concentration of cores at Lerna in the northern Argolid, and that blades struck from those cores were being traded as far north as the furthest areas of northern Greece.[306] Thus the skill and knowledge involved in producing the blades was not as commonly available as the obsidian itself may have been. Perhaps this was also the case on Melos itself. It seems possible that the sanctuary's personnel were engaged in the

[294] Torrence 1985, p. 478, Chart C.7.
[295] Torrence 1985, p. 473.
[296] N. Kardulias and C. Runnels, "The lithic artifacts: Flaked stone and other nonflaked lithics," in *Artifact and assemblage: The finds from a regional survey of the southern Argolid, Greece*, C. Runnels, D. Pullen and S. Langdon, eds., Stanford University Press 1995, pp. 74-139; for a discussion of the Bronze Age material see pp. 93-97; for the quote see p. 93.
[297] Kardulias and Runnels 1995, p. 96.

[298] Torrence 1985, p. 471.
[299] Torrence 1985, p. 471.
[300] Kardulias and Runnels 1995, p. 96.
[301] R. Torrence, "The obsidian quarries and their use," in *An island polity: The archaeology of exploitation in Melos*, C. Renfrew and M. Wagstaff, eds., Cambridge University Press 1982, pp. 193-221.
[302] Barber 1984, p. 181, n. 26. Also see the *Discussion* section of Barber's paper on p. 182.
[303] W.A. Parkinson, "Chipping Away at a Mycenaean Economy: Obsidian Exchange, Linear B, and Palatial Control in Late Bronze Age Messenia," in *Rethinking Mycenaean Palaces: New Interpretations of an Old Idea*, M.L. Galaty and W.A. Parkinson, eds., UCLA Press 1999, pp. 73-85; see p. 77.
[304] Kardulias and Runnels 1995, p. 94.
[305] Kardulias and Runnels 1995, p. 96.
[306] Kardulias and Runnels 1995, p. 94.

production of obsidian blades for the purpose of trading them to areas where the blades were not commonly made.

In light of Renfrew's estimation of the sanctuary's place in Phylakopi's society, the sanctuary may have been in need of such an income. Renfrew does believe that the sanctuary may have been supported to some extent by the ruling authority,[307] but he also brings up the fact that the offerings found in the Shrine were "individually attractive but certainly not princely,"[308] and that they were therefore probably offered by individuals in their own right. In other words, Renfrew sees no "representative communal offerings made by the ruler on behalf of the community."[309] In fact, Renfrew considers the Shrine at Phylakopi to have been rather modest. It is true that its construction was superior to any other building's in the settlement except for the palace itself, nonetheless, Renfrew points out that the Shrine was of a relatively small size and that it was positioned on the edge of the community. Hence, even if the ruling authority did support the sanctuary in some way, that support must not have been very lavish. The shrine's distance from the palace and its lack of obvious palatial support may seem to argue that the sanctuary was left somewhat on its own in terms of supporting itself. I think, therefore, that the religious personnel used the blade-manufacturing industry to provide for its daily maintenance. Even if the palace taxed the sanctuary's production in some way (and we have no way of knowing whether it did or not), it is likely that the shrine would still have commanded some payment or privilege because of its handling of the manufacturing process. Indeed, the value of the blades may have been enhanced by the fact that they were manufactured by priests (and priestesses?) because of their connection to the divine world, which would thereby enable the religious personnel to increase the price that they asked for their handiwork.

Renfrew actually remarks upon the similarity between the situations at Mycenae and Phylakopi. At Phylakopi, the obsidian was concentrated in Rooms A and B (during Phase 2). As mentioned above, these rooms probably functioned basically as storage rooms for the shrine, but, in the case of Room A in particular, where the Lady of Phylakopi was found, they might also have been considered to be special inner rooms sacred to the goddess who resided therein. This situation is very similar to that found at the Shrine of Mycenae (room 32), where much of the ivory in the Cult Center was stored, and where, as I mentioned, a goddess figure was found *in situ* on her platform.[310] Perhaps it was thought at Phylakopi, as was suggested for Mycenae, that the goddess would keep watch over the costly materials whose successful manufacture was her responsibility.

Whether or not the obsidian blades did have an enhanced worth because of the circumstances of their manufacture, I think it is possible to say that the obsidian industry was very important to the sanctuary in a practical way. I think this is shown most clearly by the fact that in Phase 3, after the Blocking Wall had been put in place, the manufacture of obsidian blades fell off only slightly from the previous period's rates. This means that the religious personnel of the sanctuary continued to invest their time and energy in the production of blades despite the relatively poor quality of the shrines and the artifacts that at that point were surrounding them. Since the production work continued practically unabated, perhaps the religious personnel saw their work, and what they could acquire through trading the blades, as a way for them to improve their situation. Sadly, as we know, that upturn in their fortunes never came about.

The Potter's Workshop at Berbati

With the material from Methana and Phylakopi we have established that non-palatial sanctuaries engaged in economic, specifically industrial activities. This indicates, as I have already proposed based on the textual evidence, that the phenomenon of sanctuaries supporting themselves was an established part of Mycenaean society. At this point I know of no other Mycenaean sanctuaries that were clearly producing products in quantities large enough to be used as a means of support for that sanctuary's personnel. However, at the site of Berbati we find a pottery workshop that had three religious installations within its confines. I include Berbati not to imply that it was necessarily a monk's workshop (which is not entirely impossible, but certainly not provable), but rather to show that a relationship between the religious and industrial spheres existed prior to the time when the Mycenaean palaces' elaborate economic system was beginning to take on the form that we see reflected in the tablets.

We can tell from the wasters that range in style from Grey Minyan and Matt Painted wares to late pictorial kraters that a pottery workshop was in operation at Berbati from the late Middle Helladic period until the end of the Late Helladic IIIB period (Figure 5).[311] As Akerström points out, "the conditions for the ceramic industry were ideal here."[312] There is a stream about 100 yards below the factory that could have provided the water necessary for processing the clay, and the opposite bank of this stream has beds of clay that may have been used in the Bronze Age workshop. Fuel for firing the pottery could have been collected on the slopes of the hills surrounding the site. It must have been this ideal combination of resources that enticed the original potters

[307] Renfrew 1985, p. 391.
[308] Renfrew 1985, p. 390.
[309] Renfrew 1985, p. 391.
[310] Renfrew 1985, p. 408.

[311] Akerström 1968, pp. 3-6; *idem*, *Berbati Volume II: The Pictorial Pottery*, Stockholm, Svenska Institut i Athen; Göteborg, Paul Aströms Förlag 1987. A.-L. Schallin, "The Late Bronze Age Potter's Workshop at Mastos in the Berbati Valley," in *Trade and Production in Premonetary Greece: Production and the Craftsman, Proceedings of the 4th and 5th International Workshops, Athens 1994 and 1995*, C. Gillis, C. Risberg and B. Sjöberg, eds., Paul Aströms Förlag 1997, pp. 73-88.
[312] Akerström 1968, p. 5.

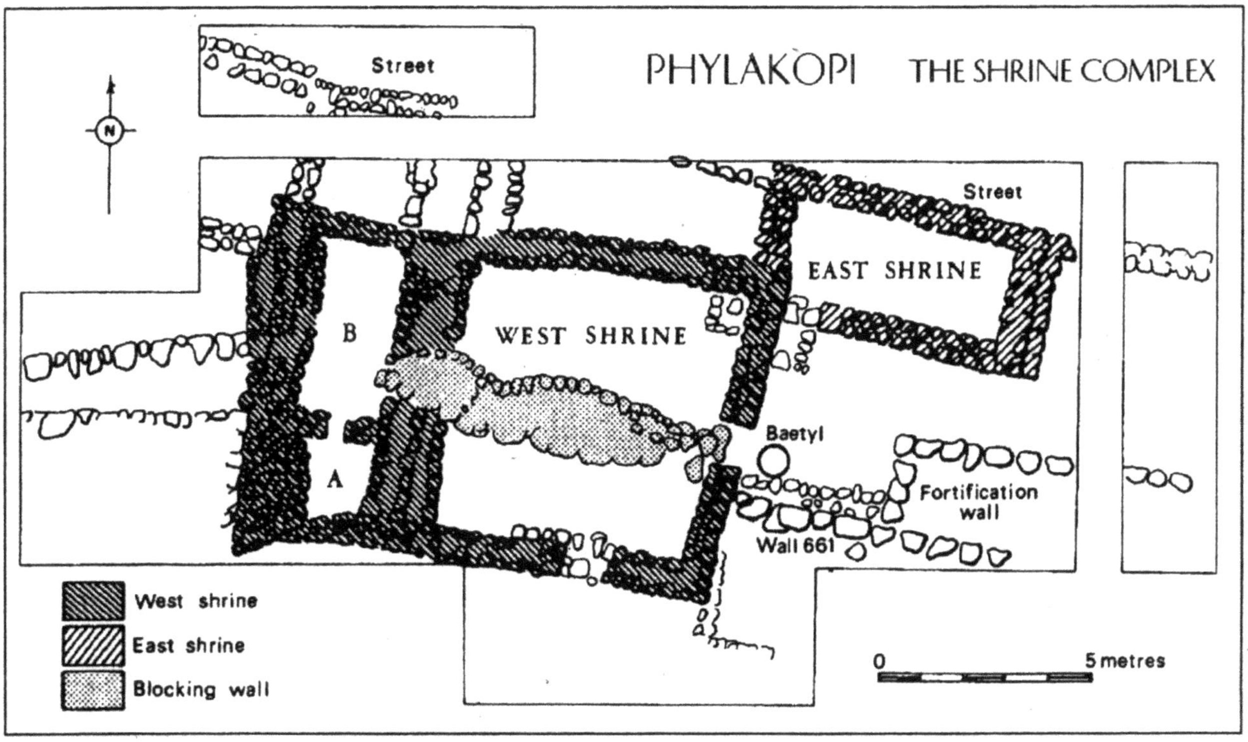

Figure 4. Plan of the Shrine Complex at Phylakopi, post IIIB destruction phase.

to set up their workshop in this location since there seems to have been no other settlements in the area in the MH period. In fact, the Berbati-Limnes Archaeological Survey found that there was no other habitation in the area during the late MH[313] or the LH I periods.[314] It was only in LH II that people started to settle in the area, and it was not until the LH III period that there was extensive use of the area. This settlement pattern seems to be linked to the gradual growth of nearby Mycenae. As Mycenae grew, and as its need for agricultural produce grew, the areas around the citadel were more intensively exploited. In the same way, after the destruction of Mycenae, the area was significantly depopulated; only a few sherds from the LH IIIC period were found.[315] The workshop at Berbati was abandoned, peacefully it seems, around the time of Mycenae's final destruction.

Even though the end of Berbati's life must have been linked to the destruction of the citadel of Mycenae, the workshop itself may have been independent of Mycenae for most of the time it was in operation, at least from the beginning of its use in the MH period until the LH IIIA period. We actually have no evidence for the site's relationship with Mycenae in its earlier periods, but in the LH IIIA1 period a tholos tomb was built and used for a single burial near the site.[316] Bennet has proposed that we may use such tholos tombs to "posit the existence of power centers – chiefdoms, perhaps – ...centered on locations where tholos tombs existed."[317] Thus it seems likely that one of the chiefs of Berbati was interred in that tomb, and perhaps up until that point Berbati had not been ruled by Mycenae. The tomb, however, went out of use in the LH IIIA1 period, which suggests that soon after it was built the chiefs of Berbati had become subject to those of Mycenae.[318] This seems to coincide with the pattern of pottery production at Berbati. During the LH IIIA period the workshop began producing pictorial amphoroid and open kraters decorated with chariot scenes and bulls shown fighting or running. These pots are found in abundance on Cyprus,[319] but the ones that have been found elsewhere on mainland Greece are thought to have been locally made.[320] Also, Akerström points out that "there are, with two exceptions, no amphoroid kraters in the hundreds of Mycenaean tombs of the Argolid."[321] Thus it seems likely that from the later LH IIIA1 period on, Berbati had become a factory that produced specialty pots particularly for export, and it is thought that those pots were being produced at the behest of the palatial agents at Mycenae who then handled the actual trade of the pots.[322] Akerström says, "these vases ... were meant for overseas customers,

[313] J. Forsén, "The Early Helladic Period," in *The Berbati-Limnes Archaeological Survey 1988-1990*, B. Wells, ed., Paul Åströms Förlag, Stockholm 1996, pp. 75-120; see p. 75.
[314] A.-L. Schallin, "The Late Helladic Period," in Wells 1996, pp. 123-175; see p. 124.
[315] Schallin 1996, p. 170.
[316] Schallin 1996, p. 123. B. Santillo Frizell, "The Tholos Tomb at Berbati," *Op. Ath.* 15 (1984) 25-44; see p. 32.

[317] J. Bennet, "Space through Time: Diachronic Perspectives on the Spatial Organization of the Pylian State," in *Politeia*, Proceedings of the 5th International Conference held at the University of Heidelberg, Archäologisches Institut, 10-13 April 1994, Vol. II (*Aegaeum* 12), R. Laffineur and W.-D. Niemeier, eds., Liège and PASP, University of Texas 1995, pp. 587-601.
[318] Schallin 1996, pp. 170-171.
[319] Akerström 1987, p. 110.
[320] Schallin 1997, pp. 80-81.
[321] Akerström 1987, p. 119.
[322] Schallin 1996, p. 170-172; *idem* 1997, pp. 81-83.

evidently for Cyprus, the main recipient, and the Near East."[323] Whether it was specifically palatial agents or not who handled the trade, it does seem that the existence of the palace promoted a smoothly operating economy that was key to facilitating such international exchange. During the LH III period the factory must have become fairly dependent on the orders from abroad considering its inability to persevere once the infrastructure that supported foreign trade was disrupted.

As for the material evidence of the workshop itself, we have no architectural remains from the MH or LH I periods; the misfired pieces and broken pots with attached lumps of unfired clay or patches of glaze stand as our evidence that workshop activities were indeed going on at the site.[324] We do, however, have a building whose first use seems to date to the LH II period, which was contemporaneous with the only actual kiln that is extant at the site.[325] Judging from the misfired sherds found near the kiln it was in use at least until the LH IIIA period, but possibly it was still being used in the LH IIIB period.[326] The kiln and its associated building were then covered over and a larger building was constructed in its place. Even though another kiln has not been found in the area, nonetheless the large numbers of pottery sherds and misfired pieces ensure that the next phase of the building was also used for the production of pottery.

It is within the initial LH II-IIIA building that we find the first indications of cult activity on the site. Room A in Figure 5 indicates the location of a bench made of unworked stone. Pieces of two female Psi figurines were found in association with this bench, indicating its religious nature.[327] A spoon was also found *in situ* on this bench shrine whose special nature was indicated by the fact that its interior was also decorated, thus precluding that it was used for everyday purposes.[328] An amphora was also found on the bench along with a clay plaque.[329] The bottom of the amphora was missing.[330] This spoon and the amphora, along with other vessels that were found around the bench, indicate that some sort of libation ritual was conducted in this area.

Two other cultic installations were found in the larger building that covered over the kiln and the first structure. The first of the later (LH III) cultic installations may have been built specifically to replace the original one since it was constructed quite close to the location of the original one. The new installation (Figure 5, B) consisted of a channel of stones that terminated on the left in the earth. On the right the channel was blocked off by more stones, and in these stones was fixed the base of a "huge stemmed bowl or cup."[331] Akerström also mentions that one of the stones of the channel was much larger than the others and could have served as a table for cultic paraphernalia.[332] It looks as if this installation, like the bench shrine that preceded it, was used for some libation ritual. This theme is continued in the third installation (Figure 5, C), which was constructed after the channel with the kylix, although the two seem to have been used contemporaneously. It consisted of a large krater that was "sunk to half of its height into the earth." The bottom of this krater had been deliberately pierced, which means that liquids poured into the krater would have seeped away into the ground. Such deliberately broken vessels are seen elsewhere in Mycenaean religious contexts. I have already mentioned the amphora neck that was set in the floor in room 33 of the Room of the Fresco Complex.[333] Another such amphora was discovered by Mylonas below the floor level of room 32, next to the possible door pivot. Moore conjectures that this may indicate that before room 32 was built onto room 31, libations were poured upon entering room 31.[334] Also at Mycenae, within Tsountas' House Shrine, was a groove that ended at the neck of an amphora that had been set into the floor.[335] Deliberately broken drinking vessels were also found at other sites, such as Asine where a deliberately broken jug was fixed upside down in the bench that was associated with the head of the "Lord of Asine" (now thought to be not a "Lord" at all, but a "Lady").[336] Another has recently been found at Ayios Konstantinos, Methana where the upper part of a large coarse ware jar with its neck facing down was found in the southwest corner of room A.[337] Finally, Kilian reports a similar vessel at the open-air site located near a chapel of Agia Triada near Klenies, where 123 Phi figurines made in LH IIIB style were also found.[338] All of these vessels were probably used in libation rituals. The deliberately broken amphora that was used at Berbati was decorated with fighting bulls,[339] a design that was one of the specialties of this workshop. The potters at

[323] Akerström 1987, p. 120.
[324] Akerström 1987, p. 70.
[325] Akerström 1968, p. 4. Schallin 1997, p. 77.
[326] There seems to be some disagreement or confusion over the date at which the kiln and its associated structure went out of use. Akerström 1968, p. 4 says LH IIIA, but then in a subsequent publication he dates its last use to LH IIIB based on the amphora found in association with the bench ("Cultic Installations in Mycenaean Rooms and Tombs," in *Problems in Greek Prehistory*, E.B. French and K.A. Wardle, eds., Bristol Classical Press 1988, pp. 201-209; see p. 201.) Schallin, however, in a later publication (1997, p. 77-78) says, "In LH IIIA the kiln and the associated building were abandoned and subsequently overbuilt (perhaps not until LH IIIB).... The larger [new] building belongs to LH IIIB (and perhaps to LH IIIA)."
[327] A.W. Persson and A. Akerström, "Zwei mykenische Hausaltäre in Berbati," *Arsberättelse* (1937-1938) 59-64; see p. 61. Akerström 1988, p. 201.
[328] Persson and Akerström 1937-1938, p. 61.
[329] Akerström 1988, p. 201. It is the amphora that Akerström dates (in this publication) to LH IIIB.
[330] Akerström 1968, p. 4.

[331] Akerström 1968, p. 4.
[332] Akerström 1988, p. 201. Photos of this installation and other items found with the cultic installations can be seen in Plates 8 and 9 of Akerström 1988.
[333] Moore and Taylour, *Room with the Fresco Complex*, forthcoming.
[334] Moore and Taylour, *Room with the Fresco Complex*, forthcoming.
[335] Mylonas 1983, p. 135.
[336] Hägg 1981, p. 93.
[337] Konsolaki-Yannopoulou 2001, p. 215.
[338] K. Kilian, "Patterns in the Cult Activity in the Mycenaean Argolid: Haghia Triada (Klenies), the Profitias Elias Cave (Haghios Hadrianos and the Citadel of Tiryns," in *Celebrations of Death and Divinity in the Bronze Age Argolid*, R. Hagg and Nordquist, eds., Stockholm 1990, pp. 193-196.
[339] Akerström 1967, p. 4.

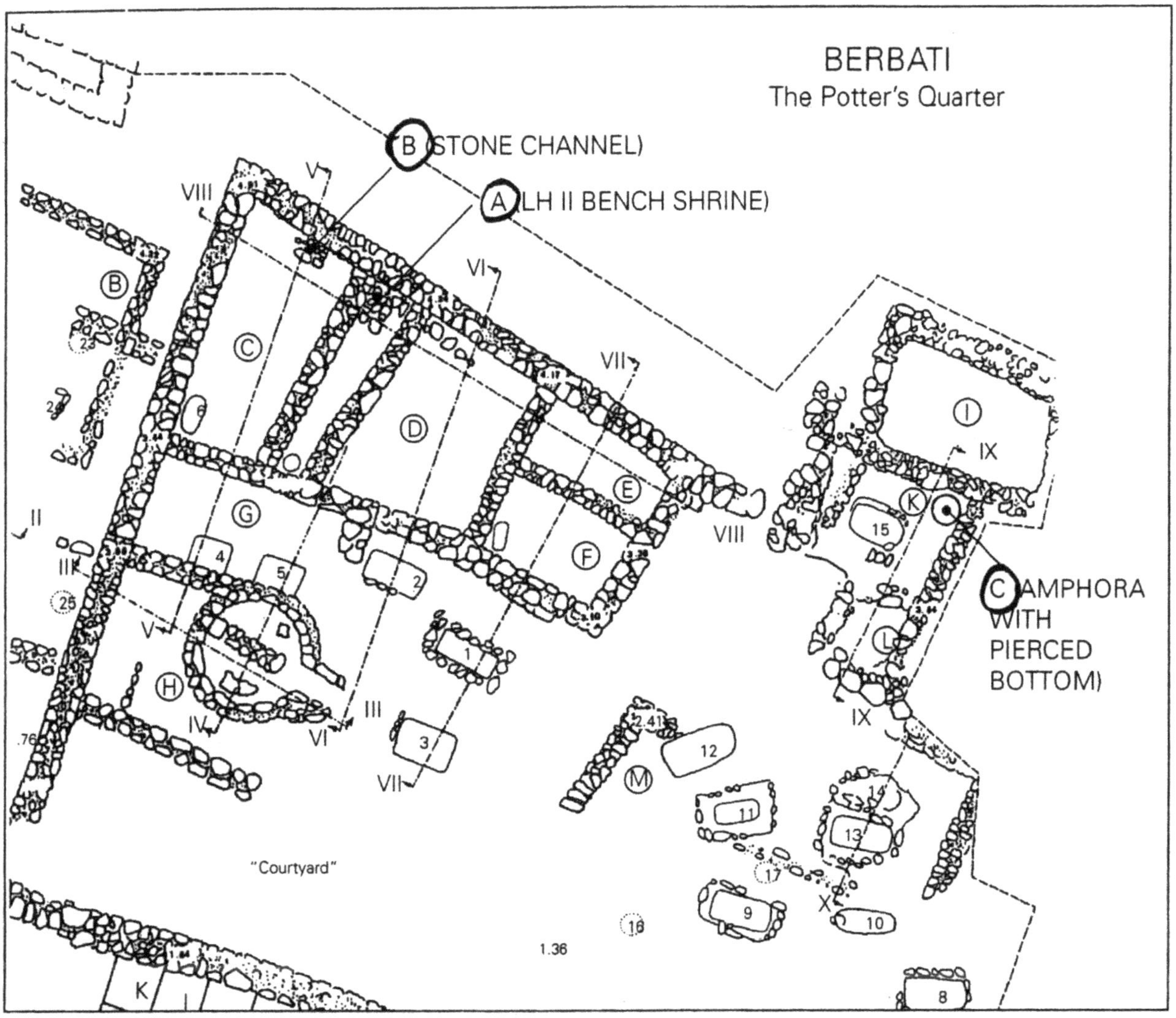

Figure 5. Plan of Berbati, The Potter's Quarter.
A: LH II bench shrine; B: stone channel; C: amphora with pierced bottom.

Berbati must have been intent on asking the gods for a favorable outcome for their endeavors and clearly it was through the pouring of libations that their particular god was supposed to be petitioned.[340]

One thing that remains to be discussed is the nature of the buildings in which the altars were found. When these installations were first published by Persson and Akerström they were called "house altars," which indicates that they thought the religion practiced at Berbati was of a domestic sort.[341] This designation was continued by Akerström in his next publication of the site in 1968,[342] even though he calls the complex a "factory."[343] It seems that the excavators may have used the term "house altar" because they had in their minds the examples of religious installations that were found prior to their own discovery that were located in Minoan houses. That is, they used the Minoan examples as parallels for their finds in Berbati. Actually, the shrine at Asine had also been classified as a house sanctuary based on the same idea,[344] and in their first publication on Berbati, Persson and Akerström say that, "we may now place the two [house altars] from Berbati next to the one at Asine."[345] It now seems though that neither of these two shrines should retain the classification of "house altar." Hägg in his reevaluation of the shrine at Asine, said in conclusion that "It is still an open question, whether this is a private house with a small domestic altar

[340] The only person to debate the religious nature of these cultic installations has been Schallin 1997, p. 79 where she says, "According to Akerström, the various stages of the workshop were equipped with cultic installations in the corner rooms, such as benches, vessels with perforated bases, a water channel, a spoon and some figurines. However, these religious features may as easily be seen as signs of the profane occupation of pottery making." I am happy to say that at a conference where I gave a talk on the topic Schallin approached me afterwards and said that she was convinced by my evaluation of the site that these installations were made for religious use.

[341] Persson and Akerström 1937-1938.

[342] Akerström 1968, p. 5.

[343] Akerström 1968, p. 4.

[344] Hägg (1981, p. 91) says, "[The shrine at Asine] was characterized by Nilsson as the first example on the Mainland of a cult room for domestic cult comparable to the Minoan cult rooms in houses."

[345] Persson and Akerström 1937-1938, p. 63.

or a complex of primarily religious function."[346] Certainly the plan of the house and the room in which the bench shrine was found, with its two columns down the center, does not look like a domestic shrine.[347] As for the buildings at Berbati, both the LH II one and the one from the later periods were probably used primarily as workshop space. From analogies taken from early modern Greece we know that a pottery workshop had to have a significant amount of space for all the processes that went on there.[348] For instance, you had to have a place for the wheel, or wheels, on which the vessels were to be made, as well as "a stamping floor, an extensive drying area for the vessels, a place for the glazing of those pots which required it,"[349] and, in the case of Berbati you would certainly have needed a place for the painters of the pots to do their work. In addition you would need room to store the water jars, the wet clay, the temper that would be mixed with the clay, and the kiln implements used to load and stack the pots. The outdoor space of the workshop would have contained baskets of clay, an area for beating the clay, and troughs for mixing the clay and to use as settling basins. Finally you would need space to store the pots that were ready for market. A potter's workshop then has to be fairly sizable in order to accommodate all of these stages in the production of the pots. Akerström says of the LH II remains that they had found "the circular foundation of a potter's kiln and part of a house, possibly the potter's abode."[350] But it seems more likely that a structure situated so close to the kiln should be classified as the workshop that produced the pots for the kiln. And as for the larger establishment built in the LH IIIA period, considering the extensive manufacture of the pictorial vases (and other pots) that went on there, it seems likely that this too was mainly a workshop, and in this case, I think we may say along with Akerström, a proper "factory." It should not be surprising if some domestic-looking elements are found within these buildings since the workmen presumably ate and maybe even slept nearby. Blitzer mentions that some workshops also had a hearth and other items that were used by the potters during meals and rest periods.[351] But that does not eclipse the fact that these buildings were most likely used predominantly as workshops and that the cult installations within them were probably built there because of the industrial work that was going on. In other words, I do not think these are domestic altars, but ones whose worship was associated with the craft of pottery production.

Conclusions

Berbati is different from the other sites discussed thus far in that it does not consist of a shrine with an industrial component. Rather, it is a workshop with a religious aspect. Therefore, it cannot be said to constitute an example of religious personnel managing the production of an important commodity. Nonetheless, Berbati does demonstrate that a link between the two realms of religion and industry existed on the Mainland of Greece just as we saw, in Chapter 2, that it had on Crete. It is possible that the potters at Berbati were worshipping a deity whose responsibility it was to oversee and ensure the positive outcome of what was a tricky manufacturing process, as I have suggested the goddesses at Mycenae and Phylakopi were expected to do. This patronage of a certain deity could have translated into prestige and influence for the religious personnel who performed the rites and rituals for that deity.

I also think that it is likely that shrines and sanctuaries were managing their own workshops (as well as tending their own sheep) prior to the palatial period. Creating and maintaining financial independence and stability would have been important for sanctuaries because it would have enabled them to support their personnel and the operations of the sanctuary. If the sanctuary was successful in its endeavors it could have taken on additional roles within the community, such as landlord, potential employer, and loan provider, which would have given the sanctuary added prestige and influence. These two factors may both have been at work at Phylakopi, where the religious personnel were engaged in making a product out of a material that was probably rather special to the Melians and which required a great deal of skill to produce. Also at Methana the religious personnel may have been engaged in producing costly prestige items. The religious workshops at Pylos and Mycenae also seem to have produced items that were important to the elite of the palaces near which they were located. At Pylos the Potnian workshop probably produced chariots and other goods for the palatial elite, and at Mycenae it seems that the workshop manufactured decorative items of blue glass, ivory and gold, also items designed for the elite. In these two cases I think it is possible that the sanctuaries were involved in economic activities before the palaces had gained the extensive power that is reflected in the tablets. The palaces then, as their administrative systems took shape and their economic interests expanded, may have had to deal with the already existing economic power wielded by the religious sector (just as the palaces probably had to work with other pre-existing elements of the culture from which they emerged, such as the *damos*[352]). As I have discussed, it is difficult to say

[346] Hägg 1981, p. 94.
[347] Hägg 1981, p.92.
[348] H. Blitzer, "KORONEIKA Storage-jar Production and Trade in the Traditional Aegean," *Hesperia* 59 (1990) 675-711; see pp. 683-684 for a discussion of the pottery workshop.
[349] Blitzer 1990, p. 683.
[350] Akerström 1968, p. 4.
[351] Blitzer 1990, p. 684.

[352] J.T. Killen, "The Role of the State in Wheat and Olive Production in Mycenaean Crete," *Aevum* 72 (1998) 19-23. Also see, for his side of the debate, P. Halstead, "The Mycenaean palatial economy: Making the most of the gaps in the evidence," *Proceedings of the Cambridge Philological Society* 38 (1992) 57-86; *idem*, "Towards a Model of Mycenaean Palatial Mobilization," in *Rethinking Mycenaean Palaces: New Interpretations of an Old Idea*, M. Galaty and W. Parkinson, eds., UCLA Press 1999, pp. 35-41; see p. 36.

exactly how much control the palatial administrations had over the economic activities of the Northeast Building and the Cult Center. It may have been that the sanctuaries and their industries were simply incorporated into the palaces' developing economic system because the palace saw the advantages of doing this and the power to accomplish it. Or the sanctuaries may have moved closer to the palaces in an attempt to avoid the unrest in their areas. Either way, the result was that the palaces must have benefited from the situation considering the types of goods that were made in the religious(/palatial) workshops. Nonetheless, maintaining a good relationship with the sanctuaries, as was discussed in Chapter 4, was probably also of importance to the *wanax*. His position as head of the community most likely had to be sanctioned by the deities, and this could only occur through rituals conducted by the religious sphere.[353] The religious(/palatial) sanctuaries, in their turn, probably also benefited both materially and in more intangible ways from the situation. Their prestige and influence within their society must have increased because of the patronage they received from the ruler of their community, and since that patronage was probably also manifested in material terms, the wealth of the sanctuary would also have increased. In turn, this further increase in wealth would also have increased the power of the religious leaders. It may have been, then, that the two realms operated in a system of economic cooperation that was presumably to their mutual benefit, in both economic and more intangible terms.

[353] T. Palaima, "The Nature of the Mycenaean *Wanax*: Non-Indo-European Origins and Priestly Functions," in *The Role of the Ruler in the Prehistoric Aegean, Aegaeum 11*, Paul Rehak, ed., Liège, 1995, pp. 119-139. See also Shelmerdine, "Administration in the Mycenaean Palaces: Where's the Chief?" in *Rethinking Mycenaean Palaces: New Interpretations of an Old Idea*, M. Galaty and W. Parkinson, eds., UCLA Press 1999, pp. 19-24.

CHAPTER VII

Conclusions

At the beginning of this work I proposed to investigate the role of the religious sector in the economy of Late Bronze Age Mycenaean Greece. I was trying to understand how religious institutions, the sanctuaries, and the personnel that made up the communities of those sanctuaries, interacted with the palatial administration on a practical level, specifically on an economic level. I also wanted to consider the relative amounts of power, both economic and political, that each sector might have wielded in respect to the other, and the positions the sanctuaries might have held within their communities. Up to now, the prevailing opinion has been that the religious sector was subordinate to the palace, and it was thought that the sanctuaries were controlled by the palatial administration.[1] It was recognized that the sanctuaries found on the tablets, and at archaeological sites, may have had some involvement in economic activities, but that involvement was downplayed and considered to be merely a part of the palatial economic system, and a small part at that. In this work I propose, and try to demonstrate, that the sanctuaries most likely managed their own economic resources and therefore were able to provide for their own livelihoods. If this was the case, then the sanctuaries maintained some economic independence from the palace, which I think means that they were not administered or controlled by the palace. Economic independence also has implications for the position of the sanctuaries in their own communities. As I discussed in the Introduction to this work, in recent years, several scholars have been contributing to a new, more balanced concept of the Mycenaean economy, one that allows for systems of exchange that were not dominated by the palace. It now seems that a wide range of economic activities were being pursued outside of the palatial system.[2] I think that the sanctuaries and their personnel also participated in those local systems of exchange, and indeed, that they were integral parts of those systems. The religious personnel must have had, therefore, some economic power that enhanced the power they already possessed because of their relationship with divine forces. This means that the members of the religious hierarchy were probably seen as fairly influential personages within their communities. Furthermore, if the religious sector was the agent responsible for legitimizing and supporting the power of the *wanax* (as may have been the case at Pylos), then the religious sector may have held a substantial amount of prestige and power within the palatial centers. Such prestige may be reflected, for instance, in the large amount of land held by religious personages in the land tenure documents of the Ep/Eb and En/Eo series.

In investigating the land tenure documents of *Pa-ki-ja-ne* in Chapter 4, it was found that the most likely owners of both the *ke-ke-me-na* land of the Ep/Eb series and *ki-ti-me-na* land of the En/Eo series was the *damos*. This was judged to be the case for the Ep/Eb series because the *o-na-ta* leases are consistently designated as *pa-ro da-mo*, and because the *damos* appears to act as an independent body in several instances, such as on Ep 704.5-6, Un 718, and Cn 608. The land of the En/Eo series, which is leased from *te-re-ta*, was also deemed to have belonged to the *damos* because of the correspondence on Un 718, Er 312, and Er 880 between the *te-re-ta* and the *damos*. The *te-re-ta* may have held their privileged positions as landholders who were able to lease out their land because they were among the head men of the *damos* and because they were expected to render some service to the *damos* in return for the land rights. The *damos*, managed by village leaders on the board of *ko-to-no-o-ko*, seems to have retained its own mechanisms for governing its people and managing its resources. I think this indicates that the *damos*, although it was required to pay tax to the palace, nonetheless managed to remain somewhat independent of the palace financially and in their systems of self-governance. The interest of the palace in the land derives from its desire to accurately calculate and collect the amount of produce due to it as tax from the landholders.

This of course means that the religious personnel were leasing their land from the *damos*, and did not own it outright themselves. Nonetheless, the fact that the religious landholders did lease land (and were expected to pay their share of taxes along with all the other leaseholders) indicates that they were active players in the area's economy, and the amount of land they leased shows that they held a significant portion of the land of *Pa-ki-ja-ne*.

Both in terms of the number of landholdings, and in the total amount of land held, the religious landholders of *Pa-ki-ja-ne* are superior to the secular landholders. In the En series, 31 of the 35 *o-na-ta* holders and one of the *te-re-ta* are religious personnel. In the Ep series religious personnel have 45 certain (and 9 more possible) landholdings, as opposed to the 15 certainly held by

[1] S. Hiller, "Mykenische Heiligtümer: Das Zeugnis der Linear B-Texte," in *Sanctuaries and Cults in the Aegean Bronze Age*, R. Hägg and N. Marinatos, eds., Stockholm 1981, pp. 95-126. J.T. Killen, "The Linear B Tablets and the Mycenaean Economy," in *Linear B: A 1984 Survey, BCILL* 26, A. Morpurgo Davies and Y. Duhoux, eds., Louvain-la-Neuve 1985, pp. 241-305; see pp. 241-242, 295.

[2] P. Halstead, "On Redistribution and the Origin of Minoan-Mycenaean Palatial Economies," in *Problems in Greek Prehistory*, E.B. French and K.A. Wardle, eds., Bristol Classical Press 1988, pp. 519-530; *idem*, "Agriculture in the Bronze Age Aegean: Towards a Model of Palatial Economy," in *Agriculture in Ancient Greece*, B. Wells, ed., Stockholm 1992, pp. 105-117; *idem*, "The Mycenaean Palatial Economy: Making the Most of the Gaps in the Evidence," *Proceedings of the Cambridge Philological Society* 38 (1992) 57-86; *idem*, "Towards a Model of Mycenaean Palatial Mobilization," in *Rethinking Mycenaean Palaces: New Interpretations of an Old Idea*, M.L. Galaty and W.A. Parkinson, eds., The Cotsen Institute of Archaeology at UCLA 1999, pp. 35-47.

secular people. It is true that in the En series the *te-re-ta* hold the majority of land with over 29 GRA, as opposed to the religious *o-na-ta* landholders' 8+ GRA. In comparison though, the other (secular) *o-na-ta* holders of the En series make a rather small showing with only T 4 V 1. In the Ep series, however, the religious landholders clearly hold the majority of land leased from the *damos*. The landholders who can definitely be identified as secular in the Ep series have GRA 7 T 8 V 3, while the landholders whom we can identify as being definitely religious have over 15 GRA. If we were to include the lands of those that I originally identified as "uncertain," most of which probably belong to the religious sector, the amount held by religious landholders would amount to over 45 GRA. This number actually exceeds the amount of land the *te-re-ta* hold in the En series, which makes the religious sector the largest landholder in *Pa-ki-ja-ne*. The total land held by religious landholders in both series is GRA 53 T 5 V 1, which again surpasses the total secular landholdings of GRA 46 T 4 V 2. Finally, it was also found that several of the religious landholders are on a par with the *te-re-ta* in the magnitude of their individual landholdings.

Thus the evidence of the land tenure tablets allows us to surmise that many of the religious personnel, since they were leasing these plots from the *damos*, must have had their own means of support and would not have been beholden to the palace for their entire maintenance. In fact, many of the plots held by religious landholders were as large as those held by the *te-re-ta* (who were officials with elevated positions within the community). It also seems to have been the case that some men who were highly placed in the religious hierarchy were also highly placed in the secular hierarchy. This could indicate that some positions within the religious realm were acquired because of the status that one held in the secular realm, or *vice versa*. I tend to think that the two may not have been easily separated out, and that it would have been natural for an upper-class Pylian to hold a religious position, perhaps on a hereditary basis.

Where though does this leave the sanctuary of *Pa-ki-ja-ne*? There is no evidence to suggest that the land held by the religious personnel had been given to them by the sanctuary. Nonetheless, the fact that religious personnel held so much land in *Pa-ki-ja-ne* must have positively affected the sanctuary in several ways. First, if the personnel associated with the sanctuary were able to support themselves, and were therefore independent of the palace, then the likelihood that the sanctuary was also financially independent increases. With land comes produce, and with produce comes the ability to participate in the local economic systems of exchange (after taxes are paid of course). Thus, the religious personnel may have been active players within the area's economy, which would have increased the influence of the institution they were associated with, their sanctuary. Also, the religious personnel may have been expected to donate a portion of their produce to the support of the sanctuary, which would have increased the sanctuary's resources and its own ability to act independently within the exchange systems of the community. Finally, the prestige of those who were highly placed within the religious (and secular) hierarchies, such as *a-pi-me-de*, *we-te-re-u*, *e-ri-ta*, and *ka-pa-ti-ja*, and the fact that they were able to amass large landholdings, must have reflected well on the sanctuary.

It is also possible that the sanctuary at *Pa-ki-ja-ne* (and probably also at other locations), held its own land apart from the leases that we see on the land tenure tablets. We have an indication that this was the case in the dispute on Ep 704.5-6 between the *damos* and *e-ri-ta*, the priestess of *Pa-ki-ja-ne*, who claims that she holds the land for the god. The dispute may have arisen because land held on behalf of a deity may not have been taxed like the other types of land owned by the *damos*. Thus the *damos* may have been protesting *e-ri-ta*'s claim that the land belonged to the god because if that claim was allowed to stand, then the *damos* would have lost the revenue it would otherwise have received from the land. Thus, I think it is possible that the sanctuary held its own land, but that those plots were never recorded because they had been granted full exemptions from taxes, or more likely, because they had never been taxed at all. If the sanctuary of *Pa-ki-ja-ne* had been established as early as LH I or II, the sanctuary could have acquired its land before the *wanax* had fully developed his power. The lands of the sanctuary would have served to support, at least partially, the activities and personnel of the sanctuary, and later, in the LH period when the palaces had established themselves, they would have helped the sanctuary to retain its economic independence from the palace.

In Chapter 5 it was found that the religious sector was involved in other economic endeavors besides agriculture, such as animal husbandry, textile manufacture, bronze working, perfumed oil production, and the manufacture of prestige items such as chariots. In some of these industries it seems that the religious sanctuaries are positioned on the tablets and treated by the palace in the same manner as were the individuals designated as "collectors." Therefore, I propose that the sanctuaries were acting in the Mycenaean economy in the same fashion as the collectors.

These collectors were originally identified on the sheep tablets of Pylos and Knossos. On many Knossos sheep tablets only a shepherd's name is found, but on some a second individual's name is added. This person is traditionally called the "collector." The relationship of the collector with the palace has been debated. One theory, espoused particularly by Killen,[3] sees them as beneficiaries of the palace, nobles who were given their flocks by the palace. Killen also assumes that the palace managed the flocks for the collectors. However, I think this proposal is unlikely because of the difficulties in

[3] J.T. Killen, "The Knossos Ld(1) Tablets," in *Colloquium Mycenaeum*, E. Risch and H. Mühlestein, eds., Université de Neuchâtel 1979, pp. 151-179; see p. 177; *idem*, "Some Further Thoughts on 'Collectors'," in *Politeia: Society and State in the Aegean Bronze Age* (*Aegaeum* 12), R. Laffineur and W.-D. Niemeier, eds., Liège and PASP, University of Texas at Austin 1995, pp. 213-226

parceling out wool and textiles to certain collectors from the certain flocks with which they are associated. I think there must have been a much closer relationship between the collectors and the flocks, i.e., that the collectors were actively involved in the management of the sheep. Killen's theory also assumes that all the flocks on Crete were at some point taken over from the previous owners and subsequently parceled out to the palace's favorites. Bennet however has demonstrated that the collectors recorded on the Knossos tablets were not involved in palatial affairs, and are unlikely therefore to have been palatial nobles. Bennet therefore proposed an alternate theory,[4] which takes into account the probable development of Knossos' authority in Cretan society. Bennet sees the collectors as members of locally based elite groups that headed up economically productive communities that were in existence before the palace at Knossos had incorporated these areas into its own economic network. Bennet also proposed that after the local elites had been incorporated, they maintained some independence from the palace and were able to retain control over their own enterprises. Hence Bennet sees the collectors of Knossos as the actual owners of the resources recorded against them on the tablets, even though these resources were being taxed by the palace. I propose that the same type of development could apply to society on the mainland of Greece, but that the Pylian collectors were given positions in the palatial administration because the *wanax* thought they were worth courting for their access to substantial economic resources. Because the collectors were active in several other industries, such as textile manufacture and bronze working, I see them as the entrepreneurs of Mycenaean society.

Sanctuaries and their religious personnel are often seen to be engaged in economic activities in ways that are similar to the collectors. For instance, on D 411 the deity Hermes (*e-ma-a$_2$-o*) is recorded in the position of the collector, and the adjectival form of Potnia (*po-ti-ni-ja-we-jo*) appears (or can be safely restored) in the position of the collector on a full nine of the Dl tablets. Also, Potnia is recorded as the collector associated with the *ne-wa po-ka*, or new fleeces on Dp 997 and 7742. A similar parallel between collector's flocks and those belonging to a divinity is demonstrated on the Thebes sealings, where we find the words *i-je-ro* (Wu 66.g, Wu 86.b, Wu 87.b) and *i-je-re-ja* (Wu 44.b) in parallel with *a-ko-ra* (Wu 49.g, Wu 50.g, Wu 63.g) and *a-ko-ra-jo* (Wu 52.b, Wu 68.b), the terms thought to indicate animals that belong to collectors. Thus the sanctuaries most likely operated within Mycenaean society as the collectors did.

Six of the Potnian Dl tablets (Dl 930, 933, 946, 950, 7503, and 7905) locate the flocks at the same place name: *si-ja-du*-we. Another instance of *si-ja-du-we* is found on Dk 969 with the word *a-ko-ra*, and on Am(2) 821.2 a man who is recorded as being both a shepherd (*po-me*), and a priest (*i-je*[*-re-*]*u*) is located at *si-ja-du-we*. Thus it seems that the Dl flocks were associated with a sanctuary dedicated to Potnia, and that the flocks may have been maintained in the interests of supporting the activities of the sanctuary and the religious personnel who were employed there.

Also, in the Theban Of series we see textile workshops that are held by deities or religious groups alongside those that were held by secular collectors. Among the religious holders of Theban textile workshops were Hera (*e-ra*) on Of 28.2, Hermes (*e-ma-a$_2$*) on Of 31.3, and Potnia (*po-ti-ni-ja*) on Of 36.2. A fourth seems to have belonged to the deity **ma-ri-ne-u* (indicated by the word for his female workers, the *ma-ri-ne-we-ja-i*, on Of 25.1 and Of 35.2). The *po-re-si* on Of 26.3 may indicate a fifth workshop, or, possibly, if the *po-re-si* were in the service of Potnia, the tablet may actually refer to Potnia's workshop. It is also likely that the workshop of the *ko-ma-we-te-ja* women (Of 35.1) was religiously affiliated. It was also concluded that the word *wo-ko*, seen in association with Potnia on Of 36 and **ma-ri-ne-u* on KN As 1519.11, most likely referred to a religious workshop, while *do*, seen on Of 26.2, 26.3, 31.2, and 33.1, was used to refer to secular workshops, most likely belonging to collectors.

There is also evidence for religious textile workshops in the Knossos and Pylos texts. A flock of 100 male sheep is ascribed to Potnia at *ne-wo-pe-o* on PY Cc 665, along with a herd of 190 pigs. Female textile workers (and their children) are also found at *ne-wo-pe-o* on tablets Aa 786, Ab 554, and Ad 688. These tablets seem to have been census records of female workgroups whose occupations indicate that they were involved in textile manufacture. Cc 665 and its associated A tablets may therefore indicate that religious personnel not only kept flocks at *ne-wo-pe-o*, but that they were also managing a textile workshop there. At Knossos Ak 830 records a female group described as]*du-wi-ja*, which could be restored as the ethnic adjective **si-ja-du-wi-ja*. If so, then there may have been a textile workshop in *si-ja-du-we*, in addition to Potnia's flocks of sheep. However, it is possible that the workers recorded on PY Aa 786, Ab 554, Ad 688, and KN Ak 830 were associated with the palaces of Pylos and Knossos, respectively, instead of with the religious sector. If so, then the religious personnel at *ne-wo-pe-o* and *si-ja-du-we*, while they may not have been engaged in textile manufacture, may nonetheless have been able to exchange the wool of their flocks with the palatially owned workshops.

In the Pylos Jn series, which records allocations of bronze to different sets of bronze workers at various locations, bronzesmiths described as Potnian are set off in their own paragraphs on Jn 310.14 and Jn 431.16. I think that this distinction was made because they were located at workshops separate from their secular counterparts. On the bottom of Jn 431.25, a group of 10 VIR described as *i-je-re*[(which could be restored either as *i-je-re*[*-ja* or *i-je-re*[*-wo*, the genitive forms of 'priestess' and 'priest'),

[4] J. Bennet, "'Collectors' or 'Owners'? An Examination of their Possible Functions within the Palatial Economy of LM III Crete," in *Mykenaïka* (*BCH* Suppl. 25), J.-P. Olivier, ed., Athens 1992, pp. 65-101.

is found beside two other groups of VIR that are ascribed to men whose names are in the genitive. If the 10 VIR were overseen by a priest it would make sense that he was associated with a religious workshop, while the other groups were associated with secular workshops overseen by collectors.

Thus, religious personnel were engaged in animal husbandry, textile manufacture, and the bronze-working industry. We can assume that these enterprises were meant to provide at least for the daily maintenance of the religious personnel engaged in these economic endeavors. Also, the fact that the position of the collector is filled by a deity's name (or a generic religious title such as *po-re-si*), rather than by a personal name, probably indicates that the official owner of the workshop was that deity. But of course, the religious workshops must have been managed by religious personnel who were working in the name of their deity, and who were probably associated with the sanctuary dedicated to that deity. The proceeds from their work could have been taken in by the sanctuary and used to support its personnel as was deemed necessary. It seems possible then that sanctuary sites, such as the one we have posited to exist at *si-ja-du-we* and the one we can be more certain of at *Pa-ki-ja-ne*, could have acted as economic centers just as the palace sites did, albeit on a much reduced scale.

The religiously affiliated workshops interacted with the palatial administration in the same way that the secular collectors did. The palace set the same targets for the sheep and wool of the religious collectors just as it did for the secular ones, and in the religious textile workshops and the Potnian bronze workshops goods were expected to be manufactured under the *ta-ra-si-ja* system just as they were in the secular ones. Thus the religious workshops were well integrated into the economic systems the palace used to procure the goods it needed; this shows that they were subordinate to the palace in that they had to comply with its demands for wool, lambs, and manufactured goods. Therefore, to refer to the economic activities of the religious sector as constituting a "temple economy" along the lines of those seen in the Near East would be inaccurate.[5] The magnitude of the religious economy in relation to the secular, from what we can see in the tablets, seems rather small. For instance, within the bronze-working industry only 19 of the 286 extant bronzesmiths are described as Potnian, and only two towns (that we know of) seem to have had religiously affiliated bronze workshops. Therefore, it is clear that the economic interests of the religious personnel did not rival those of the palace, but rather, I think the individual sanctuaries filled a role that was commensurate with that held by the individual collectors. This means that the religious personnel were, like the secular collectors, most likely engaged in procuring their own livelihoods, and that they probably traded their goods and services within local exchange networks, as well as with the palace. It is from these local transactions that the religious workshops, like the secular collectors, most likely gained the more substantial portion of their income. It is also possible, as seems to have been the case for several of the collectors, that the possession of such resources gave the religious personnel, and their sanctuaries, the possibility of acquiring some real wealth, which could have translated into power and influence within their societies.

In addition to these independent religious workshops, there also seems to have been religiously affiliated workers who were more closely associated with the palace than those that I have just considered in the sheep, textile, and bronze-working industries. For instance, *pi-ra-jo* the unguent boiler (*a-re-pa-zo-*[*o*]) on Un 249 is described as *po-ti-ni-ja-we-jo*, but works within the palace's perfumed oil industry. Also, KN G 820 records an allocation of grain for women who are described as Potnian and who are affiliated with a *ke-u-po-da*, which has been interpreted as a religious title meaning 'libation pourer'.

Another such situation is presented by the Northeast Building at Pylos, which acted as an administrative center for industries that were of great importance to the elite of the palace: the manufacture of chariots, weapons, and other leather goods. Within the Northeast Building, craftsmen and managers appear to be associated with the religious sector through PY An 1281, even though they were working within a palatial workshop. Other tablets found within the Northeast Building, such as Ub 1318 and the Qa series, also demonstrate a connection with the religious sector. An 1281 can be broken down into two paragraphs, each of which is headed by a different manifestation of Potnia, Potnia *i-qe-ja* (Hippeia) and Potnia of]*a-ke-si*, which was a place name. Within the paragraphs workers are being sent to a list of four managers that was the same in each of the paragraphs. The heading of An 1281 records that the workers were "at the seat or shrine of Potnia." Thus, the workers of An 1281 were being sent to two workshops that were being managed by personnel who were working in the name of Potnia, and who were therefore members of the religious hierarchy themselves. The seat of Potnia Hippeia was most likely the Northeast Building itself, which actually has a shrine room and a frescoed altar in its courtyard, while the second workshop may have been located at]*a-ke-si*, apart from the palace.

It seems possible, since the Northeast Building was only built very late in the history of the palace, that the second workshop on An 1281 was operating prior to the one in the Northeast Building. This earlier workshop at]*a-ke-si* may have been managed (at least when it was first founded) solely by religious personnel who were associated with a sanctuary dedicated to Potnia. Towards the end of its existence, the palatial administration brought industries, such as the perfumed oil industry, within the immediate environs of the palace, and it may also have wanted to bring the chariot-making industry closer. Hence they built the Northeast Building to house

[5] L.R. Palmer characterized the Mycenaean economy in this way in *The Interpretation of Mycenaean Greek Texts*, Oxford University Press 1963.

the administrative center and possibly also some of the workshop activities of the industry. The Linear B tablets show that by the time they were written the palace definitely held the position of upper management. But the religious component had by no means been totally eclipsed, and in fact the religious personnel seem to have retained some managerial control of the workshop. Thus the two different authorities seem to have worked side-by-side in the Northeast Building, and it seems likely that the religious managers benefited from working within an establishment that was of such great importance to the palace.

The evidence of the Linear B tablets for religious personnel supporting themselves through various economic activities is supported by archaeological evidence found both in Mycenaean Greece and in other geographical areas and time periods of the Bronze Age. In Chapter 3, I reviewed several sites on Crete, Thera, and Cyprus that demonstrated a connection between the practice of cult and industrial activities. It was found that the connection was manifested in two different ways. First, there were workshops or work areas that also had a room or an area dedicated to worship within them. Such sites were found at Buildings A and B at Mochlos, the Unexplored Mansion at Knossos, and perhaps the Plateia Building on Pseira. Second, there were sanctuary sites within which evidence for industrial activities was found. The sites that fit into this category are Myrtos *Fournou Koriphi*, and the shrine area in the western wing of the palace at Zakros on Crete, the Room of the Lilies shrine at Akrotiri on Thera, and Enkomi, Kition, Athienou, and Myrtou *Pigadhes* on Cyprus. It seems likely that in the sanctuaries where industrial activities were going on, it was the religious personnel who were engaged in them. The sanctuaries and their religious personnel were therefore involved in the economy of their societies.

On Cyprus this was true on a large scale as the religious sector was involved in various stages of the island's copper-producing industry. The religious sector also provided the ideological underpinnings that supported and justified the mobilization of labor and resources that was necessary to keep the system running. Knapp, in reaction to Catling's view that the religious sector controlled the copper-producing industry, downplayed the role of the religious sector in the practicalities of the industry.[6] But I think the evidence indicates that, even though the secular elites probably were the directors of the entire system, the religious personnel of the sanctuaries of Enkomi, Kition, Athienou, Myrtou *Pigadhes*, and Alassa *Pano Mandilares* were very active in managing the workshops and in acquiring, storing, and distributing the foodstuffs needed to support them. They would therefore have been able to reap the material benefits of their direct involvement with the workshops. Also, the religious sphere would have gained in prestige from its position as the ideological force behind the industry. Furthermore, the secular elite may have had to look to the religious sector to actively confirm their status as controlling agents of the industry, which would have further enhanced the prestige and power of those at the top of the religious hierarchy of Cyprus.

In Chapter 6 I discussed several sites of Mycenaean Greece that also demonstrated a connection between cult and industry. At four of these sites, the Northeast Building at Pylos, the Cult Center of Mycenae, *Ayios Konstantinos* at Methana, and in the East and West sanctuaries of Phylakopi, the connection consisted of a sanctuary that was engaged in industrial activities, while a fifth site, Berbati, consisted of a production site that had places of worship within it. At Pylos, room 93 of the Northeast Building, with its frescoed altar standing in its courtyard, can be categorized as a shrine. This is most likely the "seat" of Potnia that is referred to on An 1281.2. The rest of the Northeast Building functioned as an administrative center and clearinghouse for several industries including the production of chariots, arrows, and other prestige goods. The Cult Center at Mycenae, with its Room of the Fresco Complex, Temple with the Idols and Tsountas' House Shrine (or Shrine Gamma), also contained a variety of workshop materials including a variety of tools, ivory pieces, gold foil, warped pieces of glass, and a steatite mold that had glass clinging to one of its surfaces. The actual workshop of the site has not been identified, but I propose that the workshop(s) may have been located either (or both) in the area between the Room of the Fresco Complex and the lower level of the Tsountas' House Shrine, or on the terrace above the Cult Center. The Oi series, which records Potnia in association with other craftsmen, fell from the upper terrace into the Cult Center, and may therefore support the location of a religious workshop in that area. Unfortunately, since neither of these areas has been thoroughly excavated, these proposals cannot be confirmed. Nonetheless, the workshop materials found within the Cult Center make it likely that one or several work areas were probably located in or near the Cult Center. The secular administration of Mycenae may very well have been involved in the acquisition and manufacture of the goods produced in the Cult Center's workshop, as was the case at the Northeast Building's seat of Potnia, but the fact that the workshop materials were found within the Cult Center indicates that the religious personnel also had a substantial role to play in the production activities that went on there and most likely benefited materially from their involvement.

At Methana, *Ayios Konstantinos*, evidence for silver cupellation was found in the room next to the main shrine room, and at Phylakopi 2,724 obsidian artifacts were found within the shrine. There is no doubt that a blade-manufacturing industry was conducted within the confines of the sanctuary since every stage of manufacture was found among the obsidian artifacts, including blades, cores, and the chips and flakes produced during the manufacture of blades. At Berbati,

[6] H.W. Catling, "A Cypriot Bronze Statuette in the Bomford Collection," in *Alasia* I: *Mission Archéologique d'Alasia* 4, C.F.A. Schaeffer, ed., Paris 1971, pp. 15-32. A.B. Knapp, *Copper Production and Divine Protection: Archaeology, Ideology and Social Complexity on Bronze Age Cyprus*, Göteborg 1986.

where the pottery wasters indicate that the site had been used for ceramic production from the late Middle Helladic period until the end of the Late Helladic IIIB period, three cultic installations were found. The first, which was built in the LH II-IIIA period, was replaced in nearly the same spot when a LH III building covered it over. A third, also belonging to the LH III period, was found in another building on the site. Hence the worship of some deity who was probably expected to watch over the production process was an important part of the industry for the craftsmen who worked at Berbati.

Thus the archaeological evidence of Mycenaean Greece supports the idea that the religious sector was actively involved in economic activities. Indeed, the evidence from these sites shows that the sanctuaries were engaged in producing goods, such as the chariots of the Northeast Building at Pylos and objects made of blue glass, gold, and ivory at Mycenae, that would have been valuable to the elite of Mycenaean society. Through the exchange of these items the religious personnel would have, at the most basic level, been able to support themselves, which would have provided them with financial independence. But they may also have been able to acquire some real material wealth from their endeavors. If so, such sanctuaries may have been able to take on additional roles within the community, such as landlord, employer, and loan provider, which would have given the sanctuary added prestige and influence. The prestige derived from economic influence would have enhanced that which the religious sector already derived from its role as intermediary between the divine and mortal realms. For the sanctuaries that were particularly successful, the combination of economic and religious power may have given their priests and priestesses influence within the social and political spheres of Mycenaean society.

Such influence may be reflected in the tablets concerning *Pa-ki-ja-ne*. The economic capabilities of the religious personnel associated with the sanctuary are seen in the large plots of land that those at the top of the religious hierarchy held in *Pa-ki-ja-ne*, while the political influence may be demonstrated by Un 2, where we see the *wanax* being initiated at *Pa-ki-ja-ne*. As I have proposed, the sanctuary of *Pa-ki-ja-ne* may have been in existence for several generations, and it may have grown in power alongside, and in conjunction with the *wanax* of Pylos. It is possible that the sanctuary of *Pa-ki-ja-ne* was responsible for bestowing the approval of the divine realm upon the *wanax*, thereby legitimizing his right to rule. The *wanax* in turn provided the sanctuaries with offerings and goods for large religious festivals, which symbolized his acceptance of their religious power. Thus the two spheres, the religious and the secular, may have had a relationship that was to their mutual benefit.

Of course, not every sanctuary held a position like that of *Pa-ki-ja-ne*. But I think those at the top of the religious hierarchy at Mycenae may also have enjoyed an elevated status, both within the community and in relation to their *wanax*. It may have been because of their importance to the *wanax* that the shrines of the Cult Center were built within the newly extended LH IIIB city walls. Other smaller sanctuaries, such as the one I have postulated as being located at *si-ja-du-we*, would have had a much more limited sphere of influence, but still, they too must have benefited in both material and less tangible ways from their economic activities. Thus, although the religious sector may not have rivaled the political authority and economic force wielded by the palaces, nonetheless prosperous sanctuaries and their personnel may have had a certain amount of *auctoritas* within their communities that was made more effectual because it was based not only on religious authority, but also on economic power.

Bibliography

F.R. Adrados, "El Culto Real en Pilos y la Distribucion de la Tierra en Epoca Micenica," *Emerita* 24 (1956) 353-416.

F.R. Adrados, "Mas sobre el Culto Real en Pilos y la Distribucion de la Tierra en Epoca Micenica," *Emerita* 29 (1961) 53-116.

F.R. Adrados, "*Te-re-ta wa-na-ka-te-ro* y los ἀνακτοτελέσται," *Minos* 10 (1970) 138-150.

F.R. Adrados, "Les Institutions Religieuses Myceniennes," in *Acta Mycenaea* (*Minos* 11), 1972, pp. 170-203.

A. Akerström, "A Mycenaean Potter's Factory at Berbati near Mycenae," in *Atti e Memorie del I Congresso Internazionale di Micenologia, Roma 1967,* vol. I (*Incunabula Graeca* 25), Rome 1968, pp. 3-6.

A. Akerström, *Berbati Volume II: The Pictorial Pottery*, Stockholm, Svenska Institut i Athen; Göteborg, Paul Aströms Förlag 1987.

A. Akerström, "Cultic Installations in Mycenaean Rooms and Tombs," in *Problems in Greek Prehistory*, E.B. French and K.A. Wardle, eds., Bristol Classical Press 1988, pp. 201-209.

G. Albers, "Rethinking Mycenaean Sanctuaries," in *Potnia: Deities and Religion in the Aegean Bronze Age* (*Aegaeum* 22), R. Laffineur and R. Hägg, eds., Liège and UT-PASP 2001, pp. 131-141.

E. Andersson and M.-L. Nosch, "With a Little Help from My Friends: Investigating Mycenaean Textiles with Help from Scandinavian Experimental Archaeology," in *Metron: Measuring the Aegean Bronze Age* (*Aegaeum* 24), K. Polinger and R. Laffineur, eds., Liège and UT-PASP 2003, pp. 197-205.

V. Aravantinos, "Santuario e Palazzo: Appunti sui rapporti economico-amministrativi tra la sfera del culto e il potere politico in età micenea," *Scienze dell'Antichità* 3-4 (1989-1990) pp. 243-261.

V. Aravantinos, "The Mycenaean Inscribed Sealings from Thebes: Problems of Content and Function," in *Aegean Seals, Sealings and Administration* (*Aegaeum* 5), T.G. Palaima, ed., Liège and UT-PASP 1990, pp. 149-167.

V. Aravantinos, "Old and New Evidence for the Palatial Society of Mycenaean Thebes: An Outline," in *Politeia*: *Society and State in the Aegean Bronze Age* (*Aegaeum* 12), R. Laffineur and W.-D. Niemeier, eds., Liège and UT-PASP 1995, pp. 613-622.

J.-J. Aubert, "The Fourth Factor: Managing non-agricultural production in the Roman world," in *Economies beyond Agriculture in the Classical World*, D. Mattingly and J. Salmon, eds., Routledge 2001, pp. 90-111.

R.L.N. Barber, "The Status of Phylakopi in Creto-Cycladic Relations," in *Minoan Thalassocracy: Myth and Reality*, Hägg and Marinatos, eds., Stockholm 1984, pp. 179-182.

R.L.N. Barber, *The Cyclades in the Bronze Age*, University of Iowa Press 1987, pp. 224-246.

L. Baumbach, "An Examination of the Evidence for a State of Emergency at Pylos c. 1200 B.C.," in *Res Mycenaeae*, A. Heubeck and G. Neumann, eds., Gottingen 1983, p. 33.

L. Bendall, "The Economics of Potnia in the Linear B Documents: Palatial Support for Mycenaean Religion," in *Potnia: Deities and Religion in the Aegean Bronze Age* (*Aegaeum* 22), R. Laffineur and R. Hägg, eds., Liège and UT-PASP 2001, pp. 446-452.

L. Bendall, "A Reconsideration of the Northeastern Building at Pylos: Evidence for a Mycenaean Redistributive Center," *AJA* 107 (2003) 181-231.

J. Bennet, "The Structure of the Linear B Administration at Knossos," *AJA* 89 (1985) 231-249.

J. Bennet, "Knossos in Context: Comparative Perspectives on the Linear B Administration of LM II-III Crete," *AJA* 94 (1990) 193-211.

J. Bennet, ""Collectors" or "Owners"? An Examination of their Possible Functions within the Palatial Economy of LM III Crete," in *Mykenaïka* (*BCH* Suppl. 25), J.-P. Olivier, ed., Athens 1992, pp. 65-101.

J. Bennet, "Space through Time: Diachronic Perspectives on the Spatial Organization of the Pylian State," in *Politeia,* Proceedings of the 5th International Conference held at the University of Heidelberg, Archäologisches Institut, 10-13 April 1994, Vol. II (*Aegaeum* 12), R. Laffineur and W.-D. Niemeier, eds., Liège and UT-PASP 1995, pp. 587-601.

J. Bennet and C.W. Shelmerdine, "Not the Palace of Nestor: The Development of the 'Lower Town' and Other Non-Palatial Settlements in LBA Messenia," in *Urbanism in the Bronze Age*, K. Branigan, ed., Sheffield Academic Press 2001, pp. 135-140.

E.L. Bennett, "Correspondances entre les textes des tablettes pyliennes des séries Aa, Ab et Ad," in *Études Mycéniennes*, M. Lejeune, ed., Paris 1956a, pp. 121-136.

E.L. Bennett, "The Landholders of Pylos," *AJA* 60 (1956b) 103-133.

E.L. Bennett "Pylian Landholding Jots and Tittles," in *Res Mycenaeae*, A. Heubeck and G. Neumann, eds., Gottingen 1983, pp. 41-54.

E.L. Bennett, L.L. Melena, J.-P. Olivier, T.G. Palaima, and R. Palmer, eds., *The Palace of Nestor at Pylos in Western Messenia, Volume IV: The Inscribed Documents*, UT Press, forthcoming.

J. Berry, "Household artefacts: towards a re-interpretation of Roman domestic space," in *Domestic space in the Roman world: Pompeii and beyond*," R. Laurence and A. Wallace-Hadrill, eds., *Journal of Roman Archaeology*, Supplementary series no. 22, 1997, pp. 183-195.

P.P. Betancourt and C. Davaras, "Excavations at Pseira, 1985 and 1986," *Hesperia* 57 (1988) 207-225.

S. Blakely Westover, "Smelting and Sacrifice: Comparative Analysis of Greek and Near Eastern Cult Sites from the Late Bronze through the Classical Periods," in *Metals in Antiquity* (BAR International Series 792), S. Young, ed., Oxford University Press 1999, pp. 86-90.

C.W. Blegen, "The So-Called Temple of Hera at Tiryns," *Korakou*, Boston 1921.

C.W. Blegen, "The Palace of Nestor Excavations of 1957: Part I," *AJA* 62 (1958) 175-181.

C.W. Blegen, "The Palace of Nestor Excavations of 1958: Part I," *AJA* 63 (1959) 121-127.

C.W. Blegen and M. Rawson, *The Palace of Nestor at Pylos in Western Messenia,* Vol. I: *The Buildings and their Contents*, Princeton University Press 1966.

H. Blitzer, "KORONEIKA Storage-jar Production and Trade in the Traditional Aegean," *Hesperia* 59 (1990) 675-711.

C. Boëlle, "*Po-ti-ni-ja* à Mycènes," *Minos* 27-28 (1992-1993) 283-301.

C. Boëlle, "*Po-ti-ni-ja*: Unité ou Pluralité?" in *Potnia: Deities and Religion in the Aegean Bronze Age* (*Aegaeum* 22), R. Laffineur and R. Hägg, eds., Liège and UT-PASP 2001, pp. 403-409.

K. Branigan, "Craft Specialization in Minoan Crete," in *Minoan Society*, O. Krzyszkowska and L. Nixon, eds., Bristol Classical Press 1983, pp. 23-32.

H.-G. Bucholz, "Der Beitrag der Ausgrabingen von Tamassos zur antiken Baugeschichte Zyperns," in *Archaeology in Cyprus, V.* Karageorghis, ed., Nicosia, Leventis Press 1985, pp. 238-255.

M. Burdajewicz, *The Aegean Sea Peoples and Religious Architecture in the Eastern Mediterranean at the Close of the Late Bronze Age*, BAR International Series 1990.

B. Burke, "The Organization of Textile Production on Bronze Age Crete," in *TEXNH: Craftsmen, Craftswomen, and Craftsmanship in the Aegean Bronze Age* (*Aegaeum* 16), R. Laffineur and P.P. Betancourt, eds., Liège and UT-PASP 1997, pp. 413-422.

P. Carlier, *Le royaute en Grece avant Alexandre*, Strasbourg 1984.

P. Carlier, "A propos des *te-re-ta*," in *Tractata Mycenaea, Proceedings of the Eighth International Colloquium on Mycenaean Studies*, P. Ilievski and L. Crepajac, eds., Skopje 1987, pp. 65-73.

P. Carlier, "Les collecteurs sont-ils des fermiers?" *Mykenaïka* (*BCH* Suppl. 25), J.-P. Olivier, ed., Athens 1992, pp. 159-166.

M. Carpenter, "*Ki-ti-me-na* and *ke-ke-me-na* at Pylos," *Minos* 18 (1983) 81-88.

M.E. Caskey, "Ayia Irini, Kea: The Terracotta Statues and the Cult in the Temple," in *Sanctuaries and Cults in the Aegean Bronze Age*, R. Hägg and N. Marinatos, eds., Stockholm 1981, pp. 127-135.

H.W. Catling, "A Cypriot Bronze Statuette in the Bomford Collection," in *Alasia* I: *Mission Archéologique d'Alasia* 4, C.F.A. Schaeffer, ed., Paris 1971, pp. 15-32.

H.W. Catling, "Workshop and heirloom: prehistoric bronze stands in the east Mediterranean," *RDAC* (1984) 69-91.

H.W. Catling and E.A. Catling, "The Bronzes and Metalworking Equipment," in *The Minoan Unexplored Mansion at Knossos, BSA* Supplement 17, Vols. I and II, Thames and Hudson 1984, pp. 203-222.

J. Chadwick, "Potnia," *Minos* 5 (1957) 117-129.

J. Chadwick, "Texts and Commentary," in *The Mycenae Tablets III, Transactions of the American Philosophical Society*, Vol. 52, Part 7, Philadelphia 1963, pp. 54-67.

J. Chadwick, "Pylos Tablet Un 1322," in *Mycenaean Studies*, E.L. Bennett, ed., University of Wisconsin Press 1964, pp. 19-26.

J. Chadwick, *The Thebes Tablets II, Minos Suppl.* 4, Salamanca 1975.

J. Chadwick, *The Mycenaean World*, Cambridge University Press 1976.

J. Chadwick, "The Use of Mycenaean Documents as Historical Evidence," in *Colloquium Mycenaeum*, E.

Risch and H. Mühlestein, eds., Neuchâtel 1979, pp. 21-33.

J. Chadwick, "What Do We Know about Mycenaean Religion?" *Linear B: A 1984 Survey* (*BCILL* 26), A. Morpurgo Davies and Y. Duhoux, eds., Louvain-la-Neuve 1985, pp. 191-202.

J. Chadwick, "The Muster of the Pylian Fleet," in *Tractata Mycenaea, Proceedings of the Eighth International Colloquium on Mycenaean Studies*, P. Ilievski and L. Crepajac, eds., Skopje 1987, pp. 75-84.

J.F. Cherry and J.L. Davis, "Under the Sceptre of Agamemnon': The View from the Hinterlands of Mycenae," in K. Branigan, ed., *Urbanism in the Bronze Age*, Sheffield Academic Press 2001, pp. 141-159.

Clement of Alexandria, *Protr.* II.16.

F.A. Cooper, "Minnesota Archaeological Researches at Pylos, 1991-1993 Seasons" at http://clvl.cla.umn.edu/marwp/pylos.html.

J.-C. Courtois, "Le Sanctuaire du Dieu au Lingot d'Enkomi-Alasia," in *Alasia I: Mission Archéologique d'Alasia* 4, C.F.A. Schaeffer, ed., Paris 1971, pp. 151-362.

J.-C. Courtois, "Le sanctuaire du dieu au lingot d'Enkomi-Alasia (Chypre) et les lieux de culte contemporains en Méditerranée Orientale," *Académie des Inscriptions et Belles Lettres: Comptes Rendus des Séances*, Paris 1973, 223-246.

J.-C. Courtois, "L'activité métallurgique et les bronzes d'Enkomi au Bronze Récent (1650-1000 avant J.C.)," in *Early Metallurgy in Late Bronze Age Cyprus 4000-500 B.C.*, J.D. Muhly, R. Maddin and V. Karageorghis, eds., 1982, pp. 155-176.

J.H. Crouwel, *Chariots and Other Means of Land Transport in Bronze Age Greece*, Amsterdam 1981.

W.W. Cummer and E. Schofield, *Keos, vol. III: Ayia Irini: House A*, Mainz 1984.

T. D'Altroy and T.K. Earle, "Staple finance, wealth finance, and storage in the Inka ceramic political economy," *Current Anthropology* 26 (1985) 187-206.

J. Davis and J. Bennet, "Making Mycenaeans: Warfare, Territorial Expansion, and Representations of the Other in the Pylian Kingdom," in *Polemos: Warfare in the Aegean Bronze Age,* R. Laffineur, ed., Liège 1999, pp. 105-120.

P. de Fidio, *I dosmoi pilii a Poseidon* (*Incunabula Graeca* 65), Rome 1977.

P. de Fidio, "Centralization and its Limits in the Mycenaean Palatial System, in *Economy and Politics in the Mycenaean Palace States*, S. Voutsaki and J. Killen, eds., Cambridge University Press 2001, pp. 15-24.

S. Deger-Jalkotzy, *E-qe-ta: Zur Rolle des Gesellschaftswesens in der Sozialstruktur mykenischer Reiche*, Wien 1978.

S. Deger-Jalkotzy, "Zum Charakter und zur Herausbildung der mykenischen Sozialstruktur," in *Res Mycenaeae,* A. Heubeck and G. Neumann, eds., Gottingen 1983, pp. 89-111.

M. Del Freo, "Osservazioni su Miceneo *ko-ma-we-te-ja*," *Minos* 31-32 (1996-1997 [1998]) 148-158.

M. Del Freo, "L'Expression *ka-ko na-wi-jo* de la Tablette Jn 829 de Pylos," in *Emporia: Aegeans in the Central and Eastern Mediterranean*, (*Aegaeum* 25), R. Laffineur and E. Greco, eds., Liège and UT Austin 2005, pp. 793-803.

L. Deroy, "Quelques réflexions sur le cadastre mycénien de Pylos," *Minos* 24 (1989) 125-130.

L. Deroy and M. Gérard, *Le cadastre mycénien de Pylos* (*Incunabula Graeca* 10), Rome 1965.

I.M. Diakonoff, "Agrarian Conditions in Middle Assyria," in *Ancient Mesopotamia*, I.M. Diakonoff, ed., Moscow 1969, pp. 204-234.

O.T.P.K. Dickinson, *The Aegean Bronze Age*, Cambridge University Press 1994.

P. Dikaios, *Enkomi: Excavations 1948-1958*, Verlag Philip von Zabern 1969-1971.

T. Dothan and A. Ben-Tor, *Excavations at Athienou, Cyprus 1971-1972*, Jerusalem 1983.

Ch. Doumas, *Thera: Pompeii of the Ancient Aegean*, Thames and Hudson 1983.

J. Driessen, ""Collectors' Items" Observations sur l'Élite Mycénienne de Cnossos," in *Mykenaïka* (*BCH* Suppl. 25), J.-P. Olivier, ed., Athens 1992, pp. 197-214.

Y. Duhoux, "Les mesures mycéniennes de surface," *Kadmos* 13 (1974) pp. 27-38.

Y. Duhoux, *Aspects du vocabulaire économique mycénien*, Amsterdam 1976.

Y. Duhoux, "Ideogrammes Textiles du Lineaire B: *146, *160, *165 et *166," *Minos* 15 (1976) 116-132.

G. Dunkel, "Mycenaean *ke-ke-me-na, ki-ti-me-na*," *Minos* 17 (1981) 18-29.

J. Du Plat Taylor, *Myrtou-Pighades: A Late Bronze Age Sanctuary in Cyprus*, Ashmolean Museum, Oxford 1957.

A. Evans, *The Palace of Minos*, vol. 1, London 1921.

D. Evely, "Some Manufacturing Processes in a Knossian Stone Vase Workshop," *BSA* (1980) 127-137.

D. Evely, "The Other Finds," in *The Minoan Unexplored Mansion at Knossos, BSA* Supplement 17, Vols. I and II, Thames and Hudson 1984.

D. Evely, "Minoan Craftsmen: Problems of Recognition and Definition," in *Problems in Greek Prehistory*, E.B. French and K.A. Wardle, eds., Bristol Classical Press 1988, pp. 397-415.

D. Evely, *Ground Stone, Well Built Mycenae: The Helleno-British Excavations within the Citadel of Mycenae 1959-1969,* fascicule 27, Taylour, French and Wardle, series eds., Oxbow Books 1992.

D. Evely, *Minoan Crafts: Tools and Techniques, An Introduction* (*SIMA* vol. XCII), Paul Aströms Förlag vol. 1: 1993; vol. 2: 2000.

M.I. Finley, "The Mycenaean tablets and economic history," *Economic History Review* 10 (1957) 128-141.

N. Fernandez, "Cult Places of the Bronze Age: The Identification Problem," in *Problems in Greek Prehistory*, E.B. French and K.A. Wardle, eds., Bristol Classical Press 1988, pp. 229-234.

C.R. Floyd, *The Plateia Building at Pseira: Evidence for Regional Style, Social Ranking, and the LM IB Domestic Economy*, Ph.D. Dissertation, University of Pennsylvania 1996.

C.R. Floyd, *Pseira III: The Plateia Building*, University of Pennsylvania 1998.

J. Forsén, "The Early Helladic Period," in *The Berbati-Limnes Archaeological Survey 1988-1990*, B. Wells, ed., Paul Aströms Förlag, Stockholm 1996, pp. 75-120.

P.Y. Forsyth, *Thera in the Bronze Age*, New York 1999, pp. 81-83.

E. Foster, "An Administrative Department at Knossos Concerned with Perfumery and Offerings," *Minos* 16 (1977) 19-51.

E. Foster, "The Flax Impost at Pylos and Mycenaean Landholding," *Minos* 17 (1981) 67-121.

E. French, "Cult Places at Mycenae," in *Sanctuaries and Cults in the Aegean Bronze Age*, R. Hägg and N. Marinatos, eds., Stockholm 1981, pp. 41-48.

E. French, "Mycenaean Figures and Figurines, Their Typology and Function," in *Sanctuaries and Cults in the Aegean Bronze Age*, R. Hägg and N. Marinatos, eds., Stockholm 1981, pp. 173-178.

E. French, "Chapter VI: The Figures and Figurines," in C. Renfrew, *The Archaeology of Cult: The Sanctuary at Phylakopi*, British School at Athens Supplementary Volume No. 18, Thames and Hudson, 1985.

E. French, *Mycenae: Agamemnon's Capital - The Site in its Setting*, Tempus Publishing Co., 2002.

E. French and †W.D. Taylour, *The Service Areas of the Cult Centre, Well Built Mycenae: The Helleno-British Excavations within the Citadel of Mycenae 1959-1969,* fascicule 13, W.D. Taylour, E.B. French and K.A. Wardle, series eds., Oxbow Books, 2007.

A. Furumark, "Ägäische Texte in griechischer Sprache," *Eranos* 52 (1954) 18-60.

M.L. Galaty, *Nestor's Wine Cups*, British Archaeological Reports 1999a.

M.L. Galaty, "Wealth Ceramics, Staple Ceramics: Pots and the Mycenaean Palaces," in *Rethinking Mycenaean Palaces: New Interpretations of an Old Idea*, M.L. Galaty and W.A. Parkinson, eds., The Cotsen Institute of Archaeology at UCLA 1999b, pp. 49-59.

P. Garelli, "Le problème de la 'féodalité' assyrienne," *Semitica* 17 (1967) 5-21.

M. Gérard-Rousseau, *Les Mentions Religieuses dans les Tablettes Myceniennes*, Rome 1968.

G. Gesell, *Town, Palace, and House Cult in Minoan Crete*, Paul Aströms Förlag, Göteborg 1985.

L. Godart, "Les tablettes de la série Co de Cnossos," in *Acta Mycenaea II* (*Minos* 12), M. S. Ruipérez, ed., Salamanca 1972, pp. 418-424.

L. Godart, "Les collecteurs dans le monde égéen," in *Mykenaïka* (*BCH* Suppl. 25), J.-P. Olivier, ed., Athens 1992, pp. 257-283.

S. Hadjisavvas, "A Late Cypriot community at Alassa," in *Early Society in Cyprus*, E.J. Peltenburg, ed., Edinburgh 1989, pp. 32-42.

R. Hägg, "The House Sanctuary at Asine Revisited," in *Sanctuaries and Cults in the Aegean Bronze Age*, R. Hägg and N. Marinatos, eds., Stockholm 1981, pp. 91-94.

R. Hägg, "Mycenaean Religion: The Helladic and the Minoan Components" in *Linear B: A 1984 Survey* (*BCILL* 26), A. Morpurgo Davies and Y. Duhoux, eds., Louvain-la-Neuve 1985, pp. 203-225.

R. Hägg, "The Role of Libations in Mycenaean Ceremony and Cult," *in Celebrations of Death and Divinity in the Bronze Age Argolid*, R. Hägg and G.C. Nordquist, eds., Stockholm 1990, pp. 177-184.

R. Hägg, "Sanctuaries and Workshops in the Bronze Age Aegean," in *Economics of Cult in the Ancient Greek World*, T. Linders and B. Alroth, eds., Uppsala 1992, pp. 29-32.

R. Hägg and N. Marinatos, "Conclusions and Prospects," in *Sanctuaries and Cults in the Aegean Bronze Age*, R. Hägg and N. Marinatos, eds., Stockholm 1981, pp. 213-217.

R. Halleux, "Lapis-lazuli, azurite, ou pâte de verre? A propos de kuwano et kuwanowoko dans les tablettes mycéniennes," in *Studi Micenei ed Egeo-Anatolici* No. 9 (*Incunabula Graeca* 39), Rome 1969, pp. 47-66.

P. Halstead, "On Redistribution and the Origin of Minoan-Mycenaean Palatial Economies," in *Problems in Greek Prehistory*, E.B. French and K.A. Wardle, eds., Bristol Classical Press 1988, pp. 519-530.

P. Halstead, "Lost Sheep? On the Linear B Evidence for Breeding Flocks at Mycenaean Knossos and Pylos," *Minos* 25-26 (1990-1991) 343-365.

P. Halstead, "Agriculture in the Bronze Age Aegean: Towards a Model of Palatial Economy," in *Agriculture in Ancient Greece*, B. Wells, ed., Stockholm 1992, pp. 105-117.

P. Halstead, "The Mycenaean Palatial Economy: Making the Most of the Gaps in the Evidence," *Proceedings of the Cambridge Philological Society* 38 (1992) 57-86.

P. Halstead, "Plough and power: The economic and social significance of cultivation with the ox-drawn ard in the Mediterranean," *Bulletin on Sumerian Agriculture*, vol. 8, Cambridge 1995, pp. 11-22.

P. Halstead, "Towards a Model of Mycenaean Palatial Mobilization," in *Rethinking Mycenaean Palaces: New Interpretations of an Old Idea*, M.L. Galaty and W.A. Parkinson, eds., The Cotsen Institute of Archaeology at UCLA 1999, pp. 35-47.

J. Hazzidakis, "An Early Minoan Sacred Cave at Arkalochori in Crete," *BSA* 19 (1912-1913) 35-47.

M. Heltzer, *The Rural Community in Ancient Ugarit*, 1976.

M. Heltzer, "Royal Economy in Ancient Ugarit," in E. Lipinski, ed., *State and Temple Economy in the Ancient Near East*, vol. II, 1979, pp. 459-496.

Hemberg, *Die Kabiren*, Uppsala 1950.

R.A. Higgins, "The Terracotta Figurines," in *The Minoan Unexplored Mansion at Knossos, BSA* Supplement 17, Vols. I and II, Thames and Hudson 1984, p. 198.

S. Hiller, "*ka-ko na-wi-jo*, Notes on Interdependences of Temple and Bronze in the Aegean Bronze Age," in *Colloquium Mycenaeum*, E. Risch and H. Mühlestein, eds., Neuchâtel 1979, pp. 189-195.

S. Hiller, "Mykenische Heiligtümer: Das Zeugnis der Linear B-Texte," in *Sanctuaries and Cults in the Aegean Bronze Age*, R. Hägg and N. Marinatos, eds., Stockholm 1981, pp. 95-126.

S. Hiller, "Tempelwirtschaft im mykenischen Griechenland," *Archiv für Orientforschung* 19 (1982) 94-104.

S. Hiller, "Zu PY Tn 316," in *Palaeograeca et mycenaea Antonino Bartonek quinque et sexagenario oblata*, Brno 1991, p. 84.

L.A. Hitchcock, "Cult, Context, and Copper: A Cypriot Perspective on the Unexplored Mansion at Knossos," in *Proceedings of the 9th International Congress of Cretan Studies, 1-7 October 2001*, 2006, pp. 341-353.

L.A. Hitchcock and D. Preziosi, "The Knossos Unexplored Mansion and the 'Villa-Annex Complex'," in *The Function of the "Minoan Villa,"* R. Hägg, ed., Stockholm 1997, pp. 51-62.

H. Hodges, *Technology in the Ancient World*, Penguin Press 1970.

S. Hofstra, *Small Things Considered: The Finds from LH IIIB Pylos in Context*, Ph.D. Dissertation, University of Texas at Austin 2000.

J.T. Hooker, "The Language of the Thebes Tablets," *Minos* 16 (1977) 174-178.

J.T. Hooker, "The End of Pylos and the Linear B Evidence," *SMEA* 23 (1982) 209-217.

J.T. Hooker, "Titles and Functions in the Pylian State," in *Studies in Mycenaean and Classical Greek presented to J. Chadwick* (*Minos* 20-22), J. Killen, J. Melena and J.-P. Olivier, eds., Universidad de Salamanca 1987, pp. 257-267.

P. Ilievski, "A Re-examination of PY Cn Tablets," in *Atti e Memorie del 1° Congresso Internazionale de Micenologia*, Rome 1968, pp. 92-96.

P. Ilievski, "Some Observations on Mycenaean Epigraphy," *Klio* 50 (1968) 39-52.

P. Ilievski, "Observations on the Personal Names from the Knossos D Tablets," in *Mykenaïka* (*BCH* Suppl. 25), J.-P. Olivier, ed., 1992, pp. 321-349.

S.A. Immerwahr, *Aegean Painting in the Bronze Age*, Pennsylvania State University Press 1990.

V. Isaakidou, P. Halstead, J. Davis, and S. Stocker, "Burnt Animal Sacrifice at the Mycenaean 'Palace of Nestor', Pylos," *Antiquity* 76 (2002) 86-92.

N.B. Jankowska, "Communal Self-Government and the King of the State of Arrapha," *JESHO* 12 (1969) 233-282.

N.B. Jankowska, "Extended Family Commune and Civil Self-Government in Arrapha in the 15th-14th Century B.C.," in I.M. Diakonoff, ed., *Ancient Mesopotamia: Socio-Economic History, A Collection of Studies by Soviet Scholars*, 1969, 235-252.

D.M. Jones, "Land Tenure at Pakijane: Some Doubts and Questions," in *Proceedings of the Cambridge Colloquium on Mycenaean Studies*, L. Palmer and J. Chadwick, eds., Cambridge 1966, pp. 245-249.

V. Karageorghis, "Kition: Mycenaean and Phoenician," *Proceedings of the British Academy* 59 (1973) 259-281.

V. Karageorghis, *View from the Bronze Age: Mycenaean and Phoenician Discoveries at Kition*, E.P. Dutton Press 1976.

V. Karageorghis and M. Demas, *Excavations at Kition V: The Pre-Phoenician Levels*, Nicosia 1985.

N. Kardulias and C. Runnels, "The lithic artifacts: Flaked stone and other nonflaked lithics," in *Artifact and assemblage: The finds from a regional survey of the southern Argolid, Greece*, C. Runnels, D. Pullen and S. Langdon, eds., Stanford University Press 1995, pp. 74-139.

V. Kassianidou, "The Organisation of Copper Production in Late Bronze Age Cyprus: Thoughts from a Metallurgical Perspective," Paper Presented at the Seventeenth Annual Conference of the Theoretical Archaeology Group, University of Reading, 18-21 December 1995.

V. Kassianidou, "Small-scale mining and smelting in ancient Cyprus," in *Social Approaches to an Industrial Past: The Archaeology and Anthropology of Mining*, A. B. Knapp, V. Pigott and E.W. Herbert, eds., Routledge Press 1998, pp. 226-241.

P.S. Keswani, "Models of Local Exchange in Late Bronze Age Cyprus," *Bulletin of the American Schools of Oriental Research* 292 (1993) 73-83.

K. Kilian,"Ausgrabungen in Tiryns 1976," *AA* (1978) 449-470.

K. Kilian,"Ausgrabungen in Tiryns 1977," *AA* (1979) 379-411.

K. Kilian, "Zeugnisse Mykenisher Kultausubung in Tiryns," in *Sanctuaries and Cults in the Aegean Bronze Age*, R. Hägg and N. Marinatos, eds., Stockholm 1981, pp. 49-58.

K. Kilian, "The Emergence of Wanax Ideology in the Mycenaean Palaces," *Oxford Journal of Archaeology* 7 (1988) 291-302.

K. Kilian, "Patterns in the Cult Activity in the Mycenaean Argolid: Haghia Triada (Klenies), the Profitias Elias Cave (Haghios Hadrianos and the Citadel of Tiryns," in *Celebrations of Death and Divinity in the Bronze Age Argolid*, R. Hägg and Nordquist, eds., Stockholm 1990, pp. 193-196.

J.T. Killen, "The Wool Industry of Crete in the Late Bronze Age," *ABSA* 59 (1964) 1-15.

J.T. Killen, "The Knossos *o-pi* Tablets," in *Atti e Memorie del 1º Congresso Internazionale de Micenologia*, vol. II, Rome 1968, pp. 636-643.

J.T. Killen, "Two Notes on the Knossos Ak Tablets," in *Acta Mycenaea* II (*Minos* 12), M.S. Ruipérez, ed., Salamanca 1972, pp. 425-440.

J.T. Killen, "A Problem in the Knossos Lc(1) (Cloth) Tablets," *Hermathena* 118 (1974) 82-90.

J.T. Killen, "Linear B *a-ko-ra-ja/jo*," in *Studies in Greek, Italic and Indo-European Linguistics Offered to L.R. Palmer*, A. Morpurgo Davies and W. Meid, eds., Innsbruck 1976, pp. 117-125.

J.T. Killen, "The Knossos Ld(1) Tablets," in *Colloquium Mycenaeum*, E. Risch and H. Mühlestein, eds., Université de Neuchâtel 1979, pp. 151-179.

J.T. Killen, "Mycenaean Possessive Adjectives in *-e-jo*," *TPhS* (1983) 66-99.

J.T. Killen "The Textile Industries at Pylos and Knossos," in *Pylos Comes Alive*, C.W. Shelmerdine and T.G. Palaima, eds., New York 1984, pp. 49-63.

J.T. Killen, "The Linear B Tablets and the Mycenaean Economy," in *Linear B: A 1984 Survey* (*BCILL* 26), A. Morpurgo Davies and Y. Duhoux, eds., Louvain-la-Neuve 1985, pp. 241-305.

J.T. Killen, "Piety Begins at Home: Place-names on Knossos Records of Religious Offerings." in *Tractata Mycenaea, Proceedings of the Eighth International Colloquium on Mycenaean Studies*, P. Ilievski and L. Crepajac, eds., Skopje 1987, pp. 163-178.

J.T. Killen, "Epigraphy and Interpretation in Knossos WOMAN and CLOTH Records," in *Texts, Tablets and Scribes: Studies in Mycenaean Epigraphy and Economy Offered to E.L. Bennett* (*Minos* Suppl. 10), J.-P. Olivier and T.G. Palaima, eds., Salamanca 1988, pp. 167-183.

J.T. Killen, "Observations on the Thebes Sealings," in *Mykenaïka* (*BCH* Suppl. 25), J.-P. Olivier, ed., Athens 1992, pp. 365-380.

J.T. Killen, "*Ke-u-po-da e-sa-re-u* and the Exemptions on the Pylos Na Tablets," *Minos* 27-28 (1992-1993) 109-123.

J.T. Killen, "Records of Sheep and Goats at Mycenaean Knossos and Pylos," in *Domestic Animals of Mesopotamia* (*Bulletin on Sumerian Agriculture*, vol. 7), J.N. Postgate and M.A. Powell, eds., Cambridge 1993, pp. 209-218.

J.T. Killen, "Thebes Sealings, Knossos Tablets and Mycenaean State Banquets," *BICS* 39 (1994) 67-84.

J.T. Killen, "Some Further Thoughts on 'Collectors'," in *Politeia: Society and State in the Aegean Bronze Age* (*Aegaeum* 12), R. Laffineur and W.-D. Niemeier, eds., Liège and UT-PASP 1995, pp. 213-226.

J.T. Killen, "Thebes Sealings and Knossos Tablets," in *Atti e Memorie del Secondo Congresso Internazionale de Micenologia* (*Incunabula Graeca* 98), E. De Miro, L. Godart and A. Sacconi, eds., Rome 1996, pp. 71-82.

J.T. Killen, "The Role of the State in Wheat and Olive Production in Mycenaean Crete," *Aevum* 72 (1998) 19-23.

J.T. Killen, "Critique: A View from the Tablets," in *Rethinking Mycenaean Palaces: New Interpretations of an Old Idea*, M.L. Galaty and W.A. Parkinson, eds., The Cotsen Institute of Archaeology, UCLA 1999, pp. 87-90.

J.T. Killen, "Mycenaean *o-pa*," in *Floreant Studia Mycenaea*, S. Deger-Jalkotzy, S. Hiller, and O. Panagl, eds., Wien 1999, pp. 325-341.

J.T. Killen, "New Readings and Interpretations in the Pylos Tablets," in *Floreant Studia Mycenaea*, S. Deger-Jalkotzy, S. Hiller, O. Panagl, eds., Wien 1999, pp. 343-353.

J.T. Killen, "Religion at Pylos: The Evidence of the Fn Tablets," in *Potnia: Deities and Religion in the Aegean Bronze Age* (*Aegaeum* 22), R. Laffineur and R. Hägg, eds., Liège and UT-PASP 2001a, pp. 435-443.

J.T. Killen, "Some Thoughts on *ta-ra-si-ja*," in *Economy and Politics in the Mycenaean Palace States*, S. Voutsaki and J.T. Killen, eds., Cambridge Philological Society, Supplementary volume no. 27, 2001b, pp. 161-175.

J.T. Killen, "Conscription and Corvée at Mycenaean Pylos," in *Fiscality in Mycenaean and Near Eastern Economies*, M. Perna, ed., Napoli 2006, pp. 73-87.

J.T. Killen, "Thoughts on the functions of the new Thebes tablets," in *Die Neuen Linear B-Texte aus Theben: ihr Aufschlusswert für die Mykenische Sprache und Kultur*, S. Deger-Jalkotzy and O. Panagl, eds., Wien 2006, pp. 79-110.

J.T. Killen, "The Language of Religious Texts: Some Fresh Thoughts on Old Problems," in *Proceedings of the 11th International Colloquium on Mycenaean Studies*, T.G. Palaima and C.W. Shelmerdine, eds., forthcoming.

J.T. Killen and J.-P. Olivier, "155 Raccords de fragments dans les tablettes de Cnossos," *BCH* 92 (1968) 115-141.

A.B. Knapp, *Copper Production and Divine Protection: Archaeology, Ideology and Social Complexity on Bronze Age Cyprus*, Göteborg 1986.

A.B. Knapp, "Ideology, archaeology and polity," *Man* 23 (1988) 133-163.

A.B. Knapp, "Power and Ideology on Prehistoric Cyprus," in *Religion and Power in the Ancient Greek World: Proceedings of the Uppsala Symposium 1993* (*Boreas* 24), P. Hellström and B. Alroth, eds., Uppsala 1996, pp. 9-25.

A.B. Knapp, *The Archaeology of Late Bronze Age Cypriot Society: The Study of Settlement, Survey and Landscape*, University of Glasgow 1997.

A.B. Knapp, "Ideational and Industrial Landscape on Prehistoric Cyprus," in *Archaeologies of Landscape: Contemporary Perspectives*, W. Ashmore and A. B. Knapp, eds., Blackwell Publishers 1999, pp. 229-252.

C. Knappett, "Overseen or Overlooked? Ceramic Production in a Mycenaean Palatial System," in *Economy and Politics in the Mycenaean Palace States*, S. Voutsaki and J. Killen, eds., Cambridge Philological Society, Suppl. Vol. 27, 2007, pp. 80-95.

E. Konsolaki, "Methana, Agios Konstantinos," *B' Ephoreia Proistorikon kai Klassikon Archaioteton, Archaiologikon Deltion* 46 (1991) [1996], 71-74.

E. Konsolaki, "The Mycenaean Sanctuary on Methana," *BICS* 40 (1995) 242.

E. Konsolaki, "A Mycenaean Sanctuary on Methana," in *Peloponnesian Sanctuaries and Cults*, R. Hägg, ed., Stockholm 2002, pp. 25-36.

E. Konsolaki-Yannopoulou, "A Group of New Mycenaean Horseman from Methana," in *Meletemata: Studies in Aegean archaeology presented to Malcolm H. Weiner as he enters his 65th year*, vol. II (*Aegaeum* 20), P. Betancourt, V. Karageorghis, R. Laffineur and Niemeier, eds., Liège and UT-PASP 1999, pp. 427-433.

E. Konsolaki-Yannopoulou, "New Evidence for the Practice of Libations in the Aegean Bronze Age," in *Potnia: Deities and Religion in the Aegean Bronze Age, Aegaeum* 22, R. Laffineur and R. Hägg, eds., Liège and UT-PASP 2001, pp. 213-220.

E. Konsolaki-Yannopoulou, "Mycenaean Religious Architecture: The Archaeological Evidence from Ayios

Konstantinos, Methana," in *Celebrations: Selected papers and discussions from the tenth anniversary symposium of the Norwegian Institute at Athens, 12-16 May 1999*, M. Wedde, ed., Göteborg 2004.

F.R. Krauss, *Die staatliche Viehhaltung im altbabylonischen Larsa*, 1966, pp. 55-57.

O. Krzyszkowska, "Aegean Ivory Carving: Towards an Evaluation of Late Bronze Age Workshop Material," in *Ivory in Greece and the Eastern Mediterranean from the Bronze Age to the Hellenistic Period*, British Museum Occasional Paper 85, J. L. Fitton, ed., British Museum 1992.

O. Krzyszkowska, "Cult and Craft: Ivories from the Citadel House Area, Mycenae," in *TEXNH*: Craftsmen, Craftswomen and Craftsmanship in the Aegean Bronze Age (*Aegaeum* 16), Liège and UT-PASP 1997, pp. 145-149.

O. Krzyszkowska, *The Ivories, Well Built Mycenae: The Helleno-British Excavations within the Citadel of Mycenae 1959-1969,* fascicule 24, W.D. Taylour, E.B. French and K.A. Wardle, series eds., Oxbow Books 2007.

E. Kyriakidis, "The Economics of Potnia: Storage in 'Temples' of Prehistoric Greece, in *Potnia: Deities and Religion in the Aegean Bronze Age* (*Aegaeum* 22), R. Laffineur and R. Hägg, eds., Liège and UT-PASP 2001, pp. 123-129.

R. Laffineur, "Craftsmen and Craftsmanship in Mycenaean Greece: For a Multimedia Approach," in *Politeia, Society and State in the Aegean Bronze Age* (*Aegaeum* 12), R. Laffineur and W.-D. Niemeier, eds., Liège and UT-PASP 1995, pp. 189-199.

M.L. Lang, "Cn Flocks," in *Cambridge Colloquium on Mycenaean Studies*, L. Palmer and J. Chadwick, eds., Cambridge University Press 1966, pp. 250-259.

M.L. Lang, *The Palace of Nestor at Pylos in Western Messenia, Vol. II: The Frescoes*, Princeton University Press 1969.

R. Laurence, "Space and text," in *Domestic space in the Roman world: Pompeii and beyond*," R. Laurence and A. Wallace-Hadrill, eds., *Journal of Roman Archaeology*, Supplementary series no. 22, 1997, pp. 7-14.

M. Lejeune, "Mycénien *da-ma/du-ma* 'Intendant'," in *Mémoires de Philologie Mycénienne* I, CNRS 1958b, pp. 187-201.

M. Lejeune, "Sur les Signes Notant des Syllabes a Groupe Consonantique Initial," in *Mémoires de Philologie Mycénienne* I, CNRS 1958a, pp. 257-282.

M. Lejeune, "Sur le vocabulaire économique mycénien" in *Mycenaean Studies*, E. Bennett, ed., University of Wisconsin Press 1964, pp. 95-96.

M. Lejeune, "Les dérivés en –ter," in *Mémoires de Philologie Mycénienne*, Vol. II (*Incunabula Graeca* 42), Rome 1971c, pp. 199-224.

M. Lejeune, "Les forgerons de Pylos," in *Mémoires de Philologie Mycénienne* II (*Incunabula Graeca* 42), Rome 1971, pp. 169-195.

M. Lejeune, "Prêtres et prêtresses dans les documents mycéniens," in *Mémoires de Philologie Mycénienne* II (*Incunabula Graeca* 42), Rome 1971b, pp. 85-93.

M. Lejeune, "Textes mycéniens relatifs aux esclaves," in *Mémoires de Philologie Mycénienne* II (*Incunabula Graeca* 42), Rome 1971a, pp. 65-81.

M. Lejeune, "Le *damos* dans la société mycénienne," *in Mémoires de Philologie Mycénienne* III (*Incunabula Graeca* 43), Rome 1972, pp. 137-154.

M. Lejeune, "Le Dossier *sa-ra-pe-da* du Scribe 24 de Pylos," *Minos* 14 (1975) 60-76.

A. Leukart, "Autour de *ka-ko na-wi-jo*: Quelques Critères," in *Colloquium Mycenaeum*, E. Risch and H. Mühlestein, eds., Neuchâtel 1979, pp. 183-187.

Liddell and Scott, *Greek-English Lexicon*, Oxford 1968.

S. Lupack, "Palaces, Sanctuaries and Workshops: The Role of the Religious Sector in Mycenaean Economics," in *Rethinking Mycenaean Palaces: New Interpretations of an Old Idea*, M.L. Galaty and W.A. Parkinson, eds., The Cotsen Institute of Archaeology, UCLA 1999, pp. 25-34.

S. Lupack, "The Role of the Religious Sector in the Economy of Late Bronze Age Mycenaean Greece" Ph.D. Dissertation, University of Texas at Austin 2002.

S. Lupack, "Deities and Religious Personnel as Collectors", in *Fiscality in Mycenaean and Near Eastern Archives*, M. Perna, ed., Studi Egei e Vicinorientali vol. 3, Naples 2006, pp. 89-108.

S. Lupack, "The Northeast Building of Pylos and An 1281," in *The Proceedings of the 12th International Mycenological Colloquium*, A. Sacconi, L. Godart and M. Del Freo, eds., Biblioteca di Pasiphae series, Rome 2008, pp. 467-484.

S. Lupack, "*Pa-ki-ja-ne* and its Religious Landholders," in *The Proceedings of the 11th International Mycenological Colloquium*, T. Palaima, ed., *Hesperia* supplement, in press.

R. Maddin, J.D. Muhly and T. Stech Wheeler, "Metal Working," in *Excavations at Athienou, Cyprus 1971-1972*, T. Dothan and A. Ben-Tor, eds., Jerusalem 1983, pp. 136-138.

J.G. Manning and I. Morris, *The Ancient Economy: Evidence and Models*, Stanford University Press 2005.

J. Maran, "Das Megaron im Megaron," *AA* (2000) 1-16.

J. Maran, "Political and Religious Aspects of Architectural Change on the Upper Citadel of Tiryns. The Case of Building T," in *Potnia: Deities and Religion in the Aegean Bronze Age* (*Aegaeum* 22), R. Laffineur and R. Hägg, eds., Liège and UT-PASP 2001, pp. 113-122.

N. Marinatos,"The West House at Akrotiri as a Cult Center," *Ath. Mitt.* 98 (1983) 1-19.

N. Marinatos, "Minoan Threskeiocracy on Thera," in *Minoan Thalassocracy: Myth and Reality*, R. Hägg and N. Marinatos, eds., Stockholm 1984, pp. 167-178.

N. Marinatos, "The Fresco from Room 31 at Mycenae: Problems of Method and Interpretation," in *Problems in Greek Prehistory*, E.B. French and K.A. Wardle, eds., Bristol Classical Press 1988, pp. 245-251.

N. Marinatos, *Minoan Religion: Ritual, Image, and Symbol*, University of South Carolina Press 1993.

S. Marinatos, *AA* 49 (1934) 251-254.

S. Marinatos, "Ἀνασκαφαὶ εν Πύλῳ," *Praktika* (1956) 238-250.

S. Marinatos, "Zur Frage der Grotte von Arkalochori," *Kadmos* 1 (1962) 87-94.

S. Marinatos, *Excavations at Thera III* (*1969 Season*), Athens 1970.

S. Marinatos, *Excavations at Thera IV* (*1970 Season*), Athens 1971.

S. Marinatos, *Excavations at Thera V* (*1971 Season*), Athens 1972.

S. Marinatos, *Excavations at Thera VI* (*1972 Season*), Athens 1974.

S. Marinatos, *Excavations at Thera VII* (*1973 Season*), Athens 1976.

E. Masson, "Le Dieu Guerrier d'Enkomi: Est-il Debout sur un Lingot? in *Studies in Honour of Vassos Karageorghis*, G.C. Ioannides, ed., Kypriakai Soudai, Leukosia 1992, pp. 155-156.

O. Masson, "Deux petites lingots de cuivre inscrits d'Enkomi," in *Alasia I: Mission Archéologique d'Alasia* 4, C.F.A. Schaeffer, ed., Paris 1971, pp. 449-455.

N. Maurice, "Analogie et Flexion Nominale en Grec Mycénien: Le Datif-Locatif Pluriel des Thèmes en *-n-*," *Minos* 23 (1988) 117-146.

L.R. McCallum, *Decorative Program in the Mycenaean Palace of Pylos: The Megaron Frescoes*, Ph.D. Dissertation, University of Pennsylvania 1987.

C.B. Mee and W.G. Cavanagh, "Mycenaean Tombs as Evidence for Social and Political Organisation," *OJA* (1984) 45-64.

D. Meijer, "Polanyi, Markets and Ancient Mesopotamia and Syria," in *Fiscality in Mycenaean and Near Eastern Economies*, M. Perna, ed., Napoli 2006, pp. 123-131.

J.L. Melena, "Coriander on the Knossos Tablets," *Minos* 15 (1974) 133-163.

J.L. Melena, *Studies on Some Mycenaean Inscriptions from Knossos Dealing with Textiles* (*Minos* Suppl. 5), Salamanca 1975, p. 29.

J.L. Melena, "Further Thoughts on Mycenaean *o-pa*," in *Res Mycenaeae*, A. Heubeck and G. Neumann, eds., Gottingen 1983, pp. 258-286.

J.L. Melena, "Mycenaean Religious Texts: The Significance of New Joins and Readings," Talk presented at the University of Texas at Austin, October 1999.

J.L. Melena and J.-P. Olivier, *Tithemy: The Tablets and Nodules in Linear B from Tiryns, Thebes and Mycenae* (*Minos* Suppl. 12), Salamanca 1991.

A. Michailidou, "The Lead Weights from Akrotiri: The Archaeological Record," in *Thera and the Aegean World* III, Vol. I: *Archaeology*, D.A. Hardy, ed., The Thera Foundation, London 1990, pp. 407-418.

A.D. Moore and †W.D. Taylour, *The Temple Complex, Well Built Mycenae: The Helleno-British Excavations within the Citadel of Mycenae 1959-1969,* fascicule 10, W.D. Taylour, E.B. French and K.A. Wardle, series eds., Oxbow Books 1999.

A.D. Moore and †W.D. Taylour, *The Room with the Fresco Complex, Well Built Mycenae: The Helleno-British Excavations within the Citadel of Mycenae 1959-1969,* fascicule 11, W.D. Taylour, E.B. French and K.A. Wardle, series eds., Oxbow Books, forthcoming.

A. Morpurgo Davies, "Mycenaean and Greek Prepositions: *o-pi*, *e-pi*, etc.," in *Res Mycenaeae*, A. Heubeck and G. Neumann eds., Gottingen 1983, pp. 287-310.

H.J. Morris, *An Economic Model of the Late Mycenaean Kingdom of Pylos*, Ph.D. Dissertation, University of Minnesota 1986.

M.A. Morrison, "Evidence for Herdsmen and Animal Husbandry in the Nuzi Documents," in *Studies on the Civilization and Culture of Nuzi and the Hurrians in Honor of E.R. Lacheman*, M.A. Morrison and D.I. Owen, eds., Eisenbraums 1981, pp. 257-296.

H. Mühlestein, "Panzeus in Pylos," *Minos* 4 (1956) 79-89.

J.D. Muhly, "The Late Bronze Age in Cyprus: A 25 year retrospect," in *Archaeology in Cyprus 1960-1985*, V. Karageorghis, ed., Leventis Foundation, Nicosia 1985, pp. 20-45.

K. Müller, *Tiryns III: Die Architektur der Burg und des Palastes*, Augsburg 1930.

G. Mylonas, Τὸ Θρησκευτικὸν Κέντρον τῶν Μυκηνῶν, or *The Cult Center of Mycenae*, Athens 1972 (with English summary on pp. 36-40).

G. Mylonas, "Ἀνασκαφὴ Μυκηνῶν," *PAE* (1973) 101.

G. Mylonas, *Mycenae Rich in Gold*, Athens 1983.

G. Nagy, "A Mycenaean Reflex in Homer: ΦΟΡΗΝΑΙ," *Minos* 29-30 (1994-1995) 171-175.

D. Nakassis, *The Individual and the Mycenaean State: Agency and Prosopography in the Linear B Texts from Pylos*, Ph.D. Dissertation, University of Texas at Austin.

W.-D. Niemeier, "On the Function of the 'Throne Room' in the Palace at Knossos," in *The Function of Minoan Palaces*, R. Hägg and N. Marinatos, eds., Stockholm 1987, pp. 163-168.

M.P. Nilsson, *The Minoan-Mycenaean Religion and its Survival in Greek Religion*, Lund second edition, 1950 (first edition 1927).

M.-L. Nosch, "The Geography of the *ta-ra-si-ja* Obligation," in *Aegean Archaeology*, vol. 4, *Studies and Monographs in Mediterranean Archaeology and Civilization*, ser. II, vol. 5, 1997-2000, pp. 27-44.

M.-L. Nosch, "Schafherden unter dem Namenspatronat von Potnia und Hermes in Knossos," in *Wiener Forschungen zur Archäologie*, J. Borchhardt and F. Krinzinger, eds., Vienna 2000, pp. 211-215.

J.-P. Olivier, *A propos d'un 'liste' de desservants de sanctuaire dans les documents en linéaire B de Pylos*, Brussels 1960.

J.-P. Olivier, "La série Dn de Cnossos," in *SMEA* 2 (*Incunabula Graeca* 18), Rome 1967, pp. 71-93.

J.-P. Olivier, "En marge d'une nouvelle édition des tablettes de Mycènes," *Kadmos* 8 (1969) 46-53.

J.-P. Olivier, "La série Dn de Cnossos reconsidérée," *Minos* 13 (1972) 22-28.

J.-P. Olivier, "Les "collecteurs": Leur Distribution Spatiale et Temporelle," in *Economy and Politics in the Mycenaean Palace States*, S. Voutsaki and J.T. Killen, eds., Cambridge Philological Society, Supplementary volume no. 27, 2001, pp.139-159.

T.G. Palaima, *Scribes of Pylos* (*Incunabula Graeca* 87), Rome 1988.

T.G. Palaima, "Perspectives on the Pylos Oxen Tablets: Textual (and Archaeological) Evidence for the Use and Management of Oxen in Late Bronze Age Messenia (and Crete)," in *Studia Mycenaea 1988, Ziva Antika Monographs* No. 7, T.G. Palaima, C.W. Shelmerdine, and P. Ilievski, eds., Skopje 1989, pp. 85-119.

T.G. Palaima, "Maritime Matters in the Linear B Tablets," in *Thalassa: L'Egee Prehistorique et la Mer* (*Aegaeum* 7), R. Laffineur and L. Basch, eds., Liège and UT-PASP 1991, pp. 273-309.

T.G. Palaima, "The Last Days of the Pylos Polity" in *Politeia: Society and State in the Aegean Bronze Age* (*Aegaeum* 12), R. Laffineur and W.-D. Niemeier, eds., Liège and UT-PASP 1995a, pp. 623-634.

T.G. Palaima, "The Nature of the Mycenaean *Wanax*: Non-Indo-European Origins and Priestly Functions," in *The Role of the Ruler in the Prehistoric Aegean* (*Aegaeum* 11), P. Rehak, ed., Liège and UT-PASP 1995b, pp. 119-139.

T.G. Palaima, "*Po-re-na*: A Mycenaean Reflex in Homer? An I-E Figure in Mycenaean?" *Minos* 31-32 (1996-1997 [1998]) 303-312.

T.G. Palaima, "Potter and Fuller: The Royal Craftsmen," in *TEXNH: Craftsmen, Craftswomen, and Craftsmanship in the Aegean Bronze Age* (*Aegaeum* 16), R. Laffineur and P.P. Betancourt, eds., Liège and UT-PASP 1997, pp. 407-412.

T.G. Palaima, "Kn02 – Tn 316," in *Floreant Studia Mycenaea, Acts of the 10th International Mycenological Colloquium held at the University of Salzburg*, S. Deger-Jalkotzy, S. Hiller, and O. Panagl, eds., Wien 1999, pp. 437-461.

L.R. Palmer, "Review of *Documents in Mycenaean Greek* by Ventris and Chadwick," *Gnomon* 29 (1957) 561-581.

L.R. Palmer, "Review of Olivier's *Liste*," *Gnomon* 34 (1962) 707-711.

L.R. Palmer, *The Interpretation of Mycenaean Greek Texts*, Oxford University Press 1963.

L.R. Palmer, "Some Points for Discussion," in *Proceedings of the Cambridge Colloquium on Mycenaean Studies*, Palmer and Chadwick, eds., Cambridge 1966, pp. 275-284.

L.R. Palmer, "War and Society in a Mycenaean Kingdom," in *Armées et Fiscalité dans le Monde Antique*,

No. 936, *Colloques Nationaux du C.N.R.S.*, H. van Effenterre and C. Mosse, eds., Paris 1977, pp. 35-64.

L.R. Palmer, "Some New Functional Gods?" *Nestor* 6 (1979) 1338-1339.

R. Palmer, "Wheat and Barley in Mycenaean Society," in *Mykenaïka* (*BCH* Suppl. 25), J.-P. Olivier, ed., 1992, pp. 475-497.

R. Palmer, *Wine in the Mycenaean Palace Economy* (*Aegaeum* 10), Liège and UT-PASP 1994.

R. Palmer, "Perishable Goods in Mycenaean Texts," *Floreant Studia Mycenaea*, Acts of the 10th International Mycenological Colloquium held at the University of Salzburg, S. Deger-Jalkotzy, S. Hiller, and O. Panagl, eds., Wien 1999, pp. 463-485.

W.A. Parkinson, "Chipping Away at a Mycenaean Economy," *Bulletin of the Central States Anthropological Society* 32 (1997) 12-26.

W.A. Parkinson, "Chipping Away at a Mycenaean Economy: Obsidian Exchange, Linear B, and Palatial Control in Late Bronze Age Messenia," in *Rethinking Mycenaean Palaces: New Interpretations of an Old Idea*, M.L. Galaty and W.A. Parkinson, eds., The Cotsen Institute of Archaeology at UCLA 1999, pp. 73-85.

A.W. Persson and A. Akerström, "Zwei mykenische Hausaltäre in Berbati," *Arsberättelse* (1937-1938) 59-64.

C. Piteros, J.-P. Olivier, and J.L. Melena, "Les inscriptions en linéaire B des nodules de Thèbes (1982): la fouille, les documents, les possibilités d'interprétation," *BCH* 114 (1990) pp. 103-184.

N. Platon, *Zakros: The Discovery of a Lost Palace of Ancient Crete*, Charles Scribner's Sons, New York 1971.

M.R. Popham, "The Unexplored Mansion at Knossos: A Preliminary Report on the Excavations from 1967 to 1972: The Minoan Building and its Occupants," *AR* 19 (1973) 50-61.

M.R. Popham, *The Minoan Unexplored Mansion at Knossos, BSA* Supplement 17, Vols. I and II, Thames and Hudson 1984.

M.R. Popham, "Pylos: Reflections on the Date of its Destruction and on its Iron Age Reoccupation," *OJA* 10 (1991) 315-324.

N. Postgate, "Land Tenure in the Middle Assyrian Period: A Reconstruction," *BSOAS* 34 (1971) 496-520.

N. Postgate, "The Role of the Temple in the Mesopotamian Secular Community," in *Man, Settlement and Urbanism*, P. J. Ucko, R. Tringham and D. W. Dimbleby, eds., Duckworth and Co., 1972, pp. 811-825.

N. Postgate, "Royal Ideology and State Administration in Sumer and Akkad," in *Civilizations of the Near East, Vol. I*, J. M. Sasson, ed., Charles Scribner's Sons, New York 1995, pp. 395-411.

N. Postgate, "System and Style in Three Near Eastern Bureaucracies," in *Economy and Politics in the Mycenaean Palace States*, S. Voutsaki and J. Killen, eds., Cambridge 2001, pp. 181-194.

S.R.F. Price, *Rituals and power: the Roman imperial cult in Asia Minor*, Cambridge University Press 1984.

G. Pugliese Carratelli, "La decifrazione dei testi micenei," *La Parola del Passato* 35 (1954) 81-117.

Pugliese Carratelli, "Aspetti e Problemi della Monarchia Micenea," *La Parola del Passato* 14 (1959) 401-431.

P. Rehak, "New Observations on the Mycenaean 'War Goddess'," *AA* (1984) 535-545.

P. Rehak, "Tradition and Innovation in the Fresco from Room 31 in the 'Cult Center' at Mycenae," in: *Aegean Bronze Age Iconography: Shaping a Methodology* (*Aegaeum* 8), R. Laffineur and J.L. Crowley, eds., Liège and UT-PASP 1992, pp. 39-62.

P. Rehak, "Enthroned Figures and the Function of the Mycenaean Megaron," in *The Role of the Ruler in the Prehistoric Aegean* (*Aegaeum* 11), P. Rehak, ed., Liège 1995, pp. 95-118.

C. Renfrew, "Questions of Minoan and Mycenaean Cult," in *Sanctuaries and Cults in the Aegean Bronze Age*, R. Hägg and N. Marinatos, eds., Stockholm 1981, pp. 27-31.

C. Renfrew, "The Sanctuary at Phylakopi," in *Sanctuaries and Cults in the Aegean Bronze Age*, R. Hägg and N. Marinatos, eds., Stockholm 1981, pp. 67-80.

C. Renfrew, *The Archaeology of Cult: The Sanctuary at Phylakopi*, British School at Athens Supplementary Volume No. 18, Thames and Hudson, 1985.

C. Renfrew, "The archaeology of religion," in *The Ancient Mind: Elements of Cognitive Archaeology*, C. Renfrew and E.B.W. Zubrow, eds., Cambridge University Press 1994, pp. 47-54.

G. Rethemiotakis, "Τὸ νέο μινωικὸ ἀνάκτορο στὸν Γαλατὰ Πεδιάδας καὶ τὸ 'Ἱερὸ Σπήλαιο' Ἀρκαλοχωρίου," in Κρήτες Θαλλασσοδρόμοι, Κύκλος Διαλεξέων, Ἰανουάριος - Ἀπρίλος 1996, A. Karetsou, ed., Herakleion, Crete 1999, pp. 91-111 (with an English summary).

J.F. Robertson, "The Social and Economic Organization of Ancient Mesopotamian Temples," in *Civilizations of the Ancient Near East*, Vol. 1, Jack Sasson, ed., Charles Scribner's Sons, New York 1995, pp. 443-454.

F. Rougemont, "La hiérarchie des responsabilités dans les économies palatiales mycéniennes: l'exemple de la gestion des troupeaux d'ovins et de l'industrie textile," in *Responsabilité et antiquité*, Paris 2003, pp. 37-59.

F. Rougemont, "Quelques remarques sur les entrées *o-pe-ro* et les "collecteurs" dans les enregistrements de moutons, de laine et de tissues à Cnossos," in *The Proceedings of the 11th International Mycenological Colloquium*, T.G. Palaima, ed., *Hesperia* supplement, in press.

C.J. Ruijgh, *Etudes sur la grammaire et le vocabulaire du grec mycenien*, Amsterdam 1967.

C.J. Ruijgh, "A propos de Myc. *po-ti-ni-ja-we-jo*," in *SMEA* 4 (*Incunabula Graeca* 23), Rome 1967, pp. 40-52.

C. Ruijgh, "*da-ma/du-ma* δάμαρ/δύμαρ et l'abbréviation *DA*, notamment en PY En 609.1," in *Tractata Mycenaea, Proceedings of the Eighth International Colloquium on Mycenaean Studies*, P. Ilievski and L. Crepajac, eds., Skopje 1987, pp. 299-322.

B. Rutkowski, *Cult Places in the Aegean World*, Wroclaw 1972.

B. Rutkowski, *Cult Places of the Aegean*, Yale University Press 1986.

M.L. Ryder, *Sheep and Man*, Duckworth and Co. 1983.

A. Sacconi, "La tavoletta di Pilo Tn 316: Una registrazione di caraterre eccezionale?" in *Studies in Mycenaean and Classical Greek Presented to John Chadwick* (*Minos* 20-22), J.T. Killen, J.L. Melena and J.-P. Olivier, eds., Salamanca 1987, pp. 551-555.

G. Säflund, "Cretan and Theran Questions," in *Sanctuaries and Cults in the Aegean Bronze Age*, R. Hägg and N. Marinatos, eds., Stockholm 1981, pp. 189-208.

A.P. Sainer, "An Index of Place Names at Pylos," in *SMEA* 17 (*Incunabula Graeca* 63), Rome 1976, pp. 17-63.

B. Santillo Frizell, "The Tholos Tomb at Berbati," *Op. Ath.* 15 (1984) 25-44.

C.F.A. Schaeffer, "An Ingot God from Cyprus," *Antiquity* 39 (1965) 56-57.

A.-L. Schallin, "The Late Helladic Period," in *The Berbati-Limnes Archaeological Survey 1988-1990*, B. Wells, ed., Paul Aströms Förlag, Stockholm 1996, pp. 123-175.

A.-L. Schallin, "The Late Bronze Age Potter's Workshop at Mastos in the Berbati Valley," in *Trade and Production in Premonetary Greece: Production and the Craftsman, Proceedings of the 4th and 5th International Workshops, Athens 1994 and 1995*, C. Gillis, C. Risberg and B. Sjöberg, eds., Paul Aströms Förlag 1997, pp. 73-88.

A.-L. Schallin, "Metallurgy, a Divine Affair?" in *Trade and Production in Premonetary Greece: Production and the Craftsman, Proceedings of the 4th and 5th International Workshops, Athens 1994 and 1995,* C. Gillis, C. Risberg and B. Sjöberg, eds., Paul Aströms Förlag 1997, pp. 139-172.

H. Schliemann (with contributions by Dörpfeld), *Tiryns*, London 1886.

E. Schofield, "Evidence for Household Industries on Thera and Kea," in *Thera and the Aegean World* III, Vol. I: *Archaeology*, D.A. Hardy, ed., The Thera Foundation, London 1990, pp. 201-211.

R. Schon, *Pu-ro a-mo-te-jo-na-de: The Northeast Building at the Palace of Nestor*, M.A. Thesis, Bryn Mawr College 1994.

C.W. Shelmerdine, "The Pylos Ma Tablets Reconsidered," *AJA* (1973) 261-275.

C.W. Shelmerdine, *The Perfume Industry of Mycenaean Pylos*, *SIMA Pocketbook 34*, Åstroms, Göteborg 1985.

C.W. Shelmerdine, "Architectural Change and Economic Decline at Pylos" in *Studies in Mycenaean and Classical Greek Presented to John Chadwick* (*Minos* 20-22), J.T. Killen, J.L. Melena and J.-P. Olivier, eds., Salamanca 1987, pp. 557-568.

C.W. Shelmerdine, "Industrial Activity at Pylos," in *Tractata Mycenaea*, P. Ilievski and L. Crepajac, eds., Skopje 1987, pp. 333-342.

C.W. Shelmerdine, "Mycenaean Taxation," in *Studia Mycenaea 1988, Ziva Antika Monographs* 7, T.G. Palaima, C.W. Shelmerdine, and P. Ilievski, eds., Skopje 1989, pp. 125-148.

C.W. Shelmerdine, "Workshops and Record Keeping in the Mycenaean World," in *Mykenaïka* (*BCH* Suppl. 25), J.-P. Olivier, ed., 1992, pp. 387-396.

C.W. Shelmerdine, "Review of Aegean Prehistory VI: The Palatial Bronze Age of the Southern and Central Greek Mainland," *AJA* 101 (1997) 537-585.

C.W. Shelmerdine, "Workgroups and Record Keeping in the Mycenaean World," in *TEXNH: Craftsmen, Craftswomen, and Craftsmanship in the Aegean Bronze Age* (*Aegaeum* 16), R. Laffineur and P.P. Betancourt, eds., Liège and UT-PASP 1997, pp. 387-396.

C.W. Shelmerdine, "Administration in the Mycenaean Palaces: Where's the Chief?" in *Rethinking Mycenaean Palaces: New Interpretations of an Old Idea*, M.L.

Galaty and W.A. Parkinson, eds., The Cotsen Institute of Archaeology at UCLA 1999, pp. 19-24.

C.W. Shelmerdine, "The evolution of administration at Pylos," in *Economy and politics in Mycenaean palace states*, S. Voutsaki and J.T. Killen, eds., Cambridge 2001, pp. 113-128.

C.W. Shelmerdine, "The World According to Perimos: A Mycenaean Bureaucrat Talks Back," in *Autochthon: Papers presented to O.T.P.K. Dickinson on the occasion of his retirement*, eds., A. Dakouri-Hild and S. Sherratt, BAR International Series 1432, 2005, pp. 200-206.

M. Silver, *Economic Structures of the Ancient Near East*, Croom Helm 1985.

M. Silver, *Economic Structures of Antiquity*, Greenwood Press 1995.

B. L. Sjöberg, *Asine and the Argolid in the Late Helladic III Period: A Socio-economic Study*, BAR International Series 1225, 2004.

D.B. Small, "Mycenaean Polities: States or Estates?" in *Rethinking Mycenaean Palaces: New Interpretations of an Old Idea*, M.L. Galaty and W.A. Parkinson, eds., The Cotsen Institute of Archaeology at UCLA 1999, pp. 43-47.

J. Smith, "The Pylos Jn Series," *Minos* 27-28 (1992-1993) 167-259.

J. Soles, "A Community of Craft Specialists at Mochlos," in *TEXNH: Craftsmen, Craftswomen, and Craftsmanship in the Aegean Bronze Age* (*Aegaeum* 16), R. Laffineur and P.P. Betancourt, eds., Liège and UT-PASP 1997, pp. 425-430.

J. Soles and C. Davaras, "Excavations at Mochlos, 1990-1991," *Hesperia* 63 (1994) 391-436.

J. Soles and C. Davaras, "Excavations at Mochlos, 1992-1993," *Hesperia* 65 (1996) 175-230.

J. Soles and C. Davaras, *Mochlos Period III: Neopalatial Settlement on the Coast*, the Artisan's Quarter and the Farmhouse at Chalinomouri, INSTAP Academic Press 2004.

Th. Spyropoulos and J. Chadwick, *The Thebes Tablets II, Minos Suppl.* 4, 1975.

T. Stech, "Urban Metallurgy in Late Bronze Age Cyprus," in *Early Metallurgy in Cyprus 4000-500 B.C.*, J. Muhly, R. Maddin and V. Karageorghis, eds., 1982, pp. 105-116.

W.D. Taylour, "The Citadel House" in *The Mycenae Tablets III, Transactions of the American Philosophical Society*, Vol. 52, Part 7, Philadelphia 1963, pp. 35-46.

W.D. Taylour, "A Note on the Recent Excavations at Mycenae, and the Scheme Proposed for their Publication," *ABSA* 64 (1969) 259-260.

W.D. Taylour, "Mycenae, 1968," *Antiquity* 43 (1969) 91-97.

W.D. Taylour, "New Light on Mycenaean Religion," *Antiquity* 44 (1970) 270-280.

W.D. Taylour, *Well Built Mycenae: The Helleno-British Excavations within the Citadel of Mycenae 1959-1969*, fascicule 1, W.D. Taylour, E.B. French and K.A. Wardle, series eds., Aris and Phillips 1981.

W.D. Taylour, *The Mycenaeans*, Thames and Hudson 1983.

I. Tegyey, "The Northeast Workshop at Pylos," in *Pylos Comes Alive: Industry and Administration in a Mycenaean Palace*, T.G. Palaima and C.W. Shelmerdine, eds., Fordham University Press 1984, pp. 65-79.

I. Tegyey, "Scribes and Archives at Knossos and Pylos: A Comparison," in *Tractata Mycenaea*, P. Ilievski and L. Crepajac, eds., Skopje 1987, pp. 357-366.

R. Torrence, "The obsidian quarries and their use," in *An island polity: The archaeology of exploitation in Melos*, C. Renfrew and M. Wagstaff, eds., Cambridge University Press 1982, pp. 193-221.

R. Torrence, "Appendix C: The Chipped Stone," in C. Renfrew, *The Archaeology of Cult: The Sanctuary at Phylakopi*, British School at Athens Supplementary Volume No. 18, Thames and Hudson, 1985, pp. 469-478.

R. Torrence, *Production and Exchange of Stone Tools: Prehistoric Obsidian in the Aegean*, Cambridge University Press 1986.

I. Tournavitou, "Towards and Identification of a Workshop Space," in *Problems in Greek Prehistory*, E.B. French and K.A. Wardle, eds., Bristol Classical Press 1988, pp. 447-467.

I. Tournavitou, *The 'Ivory Houses' at Mycenae*, British School at Athens 1995.

C. Tsountas, "Ἀνασκαφαὶ Μυκηνῶν τοῦ 1886," *Praktika* (1888) 59-79.

L. Tyree, *Cretan Sacred Caves: Archaeological Evidence*, Ph.D. Dissertation, University of Missouri 1974.

L. Tyree, "Diachronic Changes in Minoan Cave Cult," in *Potnia: Deities and Religion in the Aegean Bronze Age* (*Aegaeum* 22), R. Laffineur and R. Hägg, eds., Liège and UT-PASP 2001, pp. 39-50.

L. Tyree, "Minoan Sacred Caves: The Natural and Political Landscape," in *Proceedings of the 9th International Congress of Cretan Studies, 1-7 October 2001*, 2006, pp. 329-342.

I. Tzachili, "All Important yet Elusive: Looking for Evidence of Cloth-making at Akrotiri," in *Thera and the Aegean World* III, Vol. I: *Archaeology*, D.A. Hardy, ed., The Thera Foundation, London 1990, pp. 380-389.

A. Uchitel, *Near Eastern and Mycenaean Archives Compared*, Ph.D. Dissertation, University College, London.

F. Vandenabeele and J.-P. Olivier, *Les idéogrammes archéologiques du lineair B*, Paris 1979.

J.C. van Leuven, "Mycenaean Goddesses Called *Potnia*," *Kadmos* 18 (1979) 122-129.

J.C. van Leuven, "Problems and Methods of Prehellenic Naology," in *Sanctuaries and Cults in the Aegean Bronze Age*, R. Hägg and N. Marinatos, eds., Stockholm 1981, pp. 11-26.

M. Ventris and J. Chadwick, *Documents in Mycenaean Greek*, Cambridge University Press 1956; second edition, 1973.

S. Voutsaki, "Economic Control, Power and Prestige in the Mycenaean World: The Archaeological Evidence," in *Economy and Politics in the Mycenaean Palace States*, S. Voutsaki and J. Killen, eds., Cambridge University Press 2001, pp. 195-213.

A.J.B. Wace, "Mycenae 1950," *JHS* 71 (1951) 254-257.

A.J.B. Wace, *ABSA* 50 (1955) 177-179.

D.A. Warburton, "The Egyptian Example and the Macroeconomic Implications," in *Fiscality in Mycenaean and Near Eastern Economies*, M. Perna, ed., Napoli 2006, pp. 255-266.

P. Warren, "A Stone Vase-Maker's Workshop in the Palace at Knossos," *BSA* 62 (1967) 195-201.

P. Warren, *Minoan Stone Vases*, Cambridge University Press 1969, pp. 157-158.

P. Warren, *Myrtos: An Early Bronze Age Settlement in Crete*, Thames and Hudson 1972.

P. Warren, "The Unfinished Red Marble Jar at Akrotiri, Thera," in *Thera and the Aegean World* I, C. Doumas and H.C. Puchelt, eds., London 1978, pp. 555-568.

W.C. Weir, "Management of Sheep and Other Fiber-Producing Animals," in *Animal Agriculture: The Biology, Husbandry, and Use of Domestic Animals*, 2nd edition, H.H. Cole and W.N. Garrett, eds., W.H. Freeman and Co. 1980, pp. 586-598.

K.D. White, *Greek and Roman Technology*, Thames and Hudson 1984.

T. Whitelaw, "Reading between the Tablets: Assessing Mycenaean Palatial Involvement in Ceramic Production and Consumption," in *Economy and Politics in the Mycenaean Palace States*, S. Voutsaki and J. Killen, eds., Cambridge 2001, pp. 50-79.

T. Whitelaw, P.M. Day, E. Kiriatzi, V. Kilikoglou and D.E. Wilson, "Ceramic Traditions at EM IIB Myrtos, Fournou Korifi," in *TEXNH: Craftsmen, Craftswomen and Craftsmanship in the Aegean Bronze Age* (*Aegaeum* 16), Liège and UT-PASP 1997, pp. 265-274.

H. Whittaker, *Mycenaean Cult Buildings: A Study of their Architecture and Function in the Context of the Aegean and the Eastern Mediterranean*, The Norwegian Institute at Athens 1997.

D.J. Wiseman, *The Alalakh Tablets*, London 1952.

J.C. Wright, "Changes in Form and Function of the Palace at Pylos," in *Pylos Comes Alive: Industry and Administration in a Mycenaean Palace*, T.G. Palaima and C.W. Shelmerdine, eds., Fordham University Press 1984, pp. 19-29.

J.C. Wright, "Death and Power at Mycenae: Changing Symbols in Mortuary Practice," *Thanatos: Les coutumes funeraires en Egee a l'age du bronze* (*Aegaeum* 1), Liège 1987, pp. 171-184.

J.C. Wright, "The Spatial Configuration of Belief: The Archaeology of Mycenaean Religion," in *Placing the Gods: Sanctuaries and Sacred Space in Ancient Greece*, S.E. Alcock and R. Osborne, eds., Oxford University Press 1994, pp. 37-78.

J.C. Wright, "Empty Cups and Empty Jugs: The Social Role of Wine in Minoan and Mycenaean Societies," in *The Origins and Ancient History of Wine*, P.E. McGovern, S.J. Fleming and S.H. Katz, eds., Gordon and Breach Publishers1995a, pp. 287-309.

J.C. Wright, "From Chief to King in Mycenaean Society," in *The Role of the Ruler in the Prehistoric Aegean* (*Aegaeum* 11), P. Rehak, ed., Liège and UT Austin 1995b, pp. 63-80.

W.F. Wyatt, Jr., "The Ma Tablets from Pylos," *AJA* 66 (1962) 21-41.

J. Younger, "Chapter VII: The Sealstones," in C. Renfrew, *The Archaeology of Cult: The Sanctuary at Phylakopi*, British School at Athens Supplementary Volume No. 18, Thames and Hudson, 1985, pp. 281-297.

J. Younger, "Aegean Seals of the Late Bronze Age: Stylistic Groups, VI. 14th Century Mainland and Later 14th-Century Cretan Workshops," *Kadmos* 26 (1987) 44-73.

www.ingramcontent.com/pod-product-compliance
Lightning Source LLC
LaVergne TN
LVHW071210210926
848482LV00015B/773